610 (County of Chester) Auxiliary Air Force Squadron, 1936–1940

610 (County of Chester) Auxiliary Air Force Squadron, 1936–1940

DAVID J. BAILEY

FONTHILL

Fonthill Media Language Policy

Fonthill Media publishes in the international English language market. One language edition is published worldwide. As there are minor differences in spelling and presentation, especially with regard to American English and British English, a policy is necessary to define which form of English to use. The Fonthill Policy is to use the form of English native to the author. David J. Bailey was born and educated in England, and still lives in Wirral in the north west of England, therefore British English has been adopted in this publication.

Fonthill Media Limited
Stroud House
Russell Street
Stroud GL5 3AN

Fonthill Media LLC
12 Sires Street
Charleston SC 29403

www.fonthillmedia.com
office@fonthillmedia.com

First published in the United Kingdom and the United States of America 2019

British Library Cataloguing in Publication Data:
A catalogue record for this book is available from the British Library

ISBN 978-1-78155-714-3

Typeset in Minion Pro
Printed and bound in England

Dedication

In memory of all the pilots and ground crew of 610 (County of Chester) Auxiliary Air Force Squadron, who so heroically defended our freedom in 1940, particularly those who made the ultimate sacrifice.

A rare example of one of the first Spitfires to be delivered to 610 Squadron. The pilot was F/O. E. B. B. Smith, one of the founding members of 610 Squadron and a huge inspiration for me when writing this book. (*Copyright Smith family*)

Preface

When referencing 610 Squadron's Operations Record Book (ORB), I have put '(ORB)' after the quotation for the reader's ease, unless I have mentioned the ORB in the preceding text and it is obviously the source. When using other squadron, airfield or Group ORBs, I have followed the same principle, but to differentiate, have included the Squadron number or airfield/Group name in brackets after the relevant quote '(32 ORB)' or '(Biggin Hill ORB)'. For the relevant source, see The National Archives (TNA) section of the Bibliography.

Each list of pilots is as it appears in the ORB: individual aircraft identification letter as painted on the Spitfire's fuselage, aircraft serial number and each pilot's details, although I have standardised the punctuation for consistency. As a point of interest, the officers were usually listed by rank, initials, surname, while the sergeants were listed by rank, surname, initials, although occasionally the clerk used the same style for both. I have added 'DW' to the aircraft column (610 Squadron's identification letters which were also painted on the fuselage) and where possible the pilot's position in the formation, for example, 'Blue 1' or 'Red 2'. In some cases this is from a combination of the ORB and combat reports, along with an understanding of which section or flight the pilots usually operated in. Where it is uncertain, I have left the position out.

As part of my research, I have listed the number of recorded patrols carried out by each pilot at the end of the row in the battle order of pilots on patrol, or in brackets next to their name if it is in the text. This number includes each recorded patrol in the ORB and in the case of Pilot Officer (P/O) Merrick, Sergeants (Sgts) Else and Bamberger, it has some additional patrols from their logbooks. As the ORB does not record every patrol carried out, it is not a definitive list. But it does serve as a guide to the experience of each pilot as the book progresses. I started counting these patrols from 10 May 1940, the day that Germany invaded Holland, Luxembourg, Belgium and France. From this point on, with 610 Squadron in 11 Group, the pilots were much more likely to meet the *Luftwaffe* than when they had been based at RAF Wittering and RAF Prestwick. The ORB was not maintained during April 1940, so any record of flights prior to that month would have been incomplete.

I have been very fortunate to be able to include the latest information about 610 Squadron's losses, which were made available by The National Archives. The 'Air Ministry: Casualty Branch P4(Cas): Enquiries into Missing Personnel, 1939–1945 War Case Files' have been released in two batches, the second batch on 30 June 2017, while I was completing my final draft. For brevity, I have abbreviated it to 'AMCB file'.

In their combat reports and the ORB, 610 Squadron's pilots always refer to the German fighters as 'Me 109' and 'Me 110', rather than the official designation of 'Bf 109' and 'Bf 110'. For consistency, I have used the terminology of the RAF's pilots in 1940. I have also applied this principle to the pilots' most commonly used ranks for consistency: sergeant (Sgt), pilot officer (P/O), flying officer (F/O), flight lieutenant (F/Lt) and squadron leader (S/Ldr).

Acknowledgements

I should like to thank numerous people for their assistance in writing my first book. Firstly, the 610 (County of Chester) Squadron Association and primarily the chairman, Michael Lewis, for all his time and support. It has been a privilege to have enjoyed access to the Squadron's remarkable archive and rare photographs, to bring the Squadron's early history to life. Michael, with his great knowledge of 610 Squadron's proud history, has been an invaluable source of assistance, from proofreading the book, to the time-consuming preparation of the Association's photos and establishing contact with veterans' relatives. The Association also permitted the reproduction of extracts from Raymond Ellis's engrossing memoirs *The Rigger's Tale*—a vital source of information when telling the often neglected story of the ground crew.

An important fount of information has been Dave Brocklehurst MBE, chairman and historian of the Kent Battle of Britain Museum, situated on the site of RAF Hawkinge, from where 610 Squadron repeatedly flew during the Battle of Britain. Dave, with his encyclopaedic knowledge of the Battle of Britain, was a great help in confirming the facts in several of the Squadron's losses, taking me to some of the crash sites and making available sources and photographs pertaining to 610 Squadron. The Kent Battle of Britain Museum is an extraordinary memorial to all those involved in the Battle of Britain. It should be the first port of call for anyone interested in the period.

Another expert on the Battle of Britain whose assistance has been so important is Geoffrey Simpson, the Battle of Britain Memorial Trust's historical consultant. He has generously provided his own information on 610 Squadron's pilots, including 'The Flight of the Few' and contacts for relevant sources. Most importantly for this book, he granted permission to use *Men of the Battle of Britain* by Kenneth G. Wynn, (Third edition, Frontline Books in association with Battle of Britain Memorial Trust, 2015)—Geoff brought this edition of the excellent biographical source on the Battle of Britain pilots to publication. Thanks also to Kenneth G. Wynn for the use of this essential source in providing background information about the pilots' lives.

I would also particularly like to thank Norman Ramsay, Editor-in-Chief of *The Battle of Britain Then and Now*, and Chris Gibson, Editor of *Aeromilitaria* and Air-Britain's highly informative series of magazines. Norman Ramsay granted permission to use information and photographs from this essential source on the Battle of Britain's daily events. Chris Gibson allowed me to reference the service record of Spitfires which operated with 610 Squadron, which was a huge help in filling in some of the gaps in the Squadron's records.

I owe much gratitude to Jay Slater and Alan Sutton of Fonthill Media for taking on this project. I have relied on their guidance and expertise in the book's production, and would especially like to thank Alan for editing the manuscript. Fonthill Media's design team also deserve a special mention, for their incredible work using the iconic images of 610 Squadron, to create the front cover I had always envisaged.

On 5 August 2011 I had the honour of meeting Wing Commander Brian Smith, one of 610 Squadron's founding pilots, who served with the unit from 1936 to 1940. It was fascinating to hear first-hand the Squadron's history and his own remarkable story, particularly his vivid accounts of life flying a Spitfire during the Dunkirk evacuation and the Battle of Britain. Meeting Wg Cdr Smith, extremely lucid and welcoming at the age of ninety-six, was a huge inspiration to turning my research into this book. I hope he would have found it to be a fitting tribute to all those with whom he served.

I have had the pleasure of making contact with a number of pilots' relatives, and reserve a big 'thank you' to them for their reminiscences, access to photographs and logbooks, which have brought my book to life: Janie Smith (Brian Smith); Pamela Ward and Ian Coates (Medcalf); Christopher Kerr (Kerr); Clive Arnold (Medway); David Driver and the Nicholson family (Raven); Susan Ogilvy (Ogilvy); Mark Bamberger (Bamberger); Richard Kerr-Wilson (Kerr Wilson); Joyce Gregson and Frances Duckers (Manton); Jo Keighley (Keighley) and Nigel Denchfield (Denchfield).

I should also like to thank the schools and their archivists for kindly providing background information and photographs on some of 610 Squadron's pilots in their formative years: Bedford Modern School (Richard Wildman and Jenny Ulph); Charterhouse (Catherine Smith); Chatham House School (Chris Freeman); Dover College (Colonel (Retd) Philip Barry); Leeds Grammar School (David Pritchard and John Davies); Malvern College (Ian Quickfall); Oundle School (Stephen Forge) and Yardley Court (Louize Brewer).

Enormous thanks to the following museums and archives, for allowing use of their sources and photographs: RAF Museum Hendon (Derek O'Brien); Imperial War Museum (Joseph Wilson and Sebastian Wainwright); Biggin Hill Memorial Museum Trust (Jemma Johnson-Davey); The Second World War Experience Centre and *Everyone's War* (Anne Wickes); Bamburgh Castle Aviation Museum (Lisa Waters) and the Hooton Park Trust (Bob Frost). The National Archives at Kew, London, has been hugely important in providing the various Squadron, Group and Station Record Books, the combat reports and Air Ministry Casualty Branch Packs, around which the book is based. Thanks to Hugh Alexander for his assistance in including my photographs of the documents in The National Archives. The Cheshire Record Office (Adam Shaw) and Wirral Archives Service (William Meredith), have both been very helpful for information from local newspapers of the period.

Many thanks to the following for their assistance in providing essential photographs and information: Getty Images (Tiago Carvalho); Royal Aero Club Trust (Andrew Dawrant); additional 610 Squadron photos from Diane Reid née Woodfine and Sandra Hemsworth née Blackburne and D. J. Stephens; Norman Franks; Fonthill Media authors for kindly supplying photographs of the *Luftwaffe*—Ron Mackay, Joe Bamford and Jan Forsgren; Mark Postlethwaite of ww2images.com; Peter Moore and Anne Holmes for permitting use of quotations and photographs from Ray Holmes's *Sky Spy*; Mirrorpix (Simon Flavin); *Swift*; Robert Dixon—'Northern Eagle' website; Anne Anderson and David McNay—Scottish Military Research Group; Martin Edwards—ADF-serials website; Mrs R. Q. Edmonds; the RAF Club (Charlotte Gray); Peter Blythe; John Morris and Leonard Woodgate for their unique eye-witness accounts of 1940.

The Battle of Britain Memorial Monument's website (bbm.org.uk/) and Edward McManus have been especially helpful in providing further biographical information and photographs about 610 Squadron's pilots. The memorial on the bank of the River Thames, opposite the London Eye, is a fitting tribute to all those involved in the Battle of Britain. I should like to thank the BBC (Vicky Mitchell) for granting permission to transcribe Charles Gardner's radio broadcast. Furthermore, I should like to thank the following newspapers and websites for allowing use of their information (see the Bibliography for web addresses): *The Times*; *The Cambridge Evening News*; The Dover War Memorial Project; Commonwealth War Graves Commission; House of Commons Hansard; RAF Halton; 'Hemel at War' (Professor Richard Grayson); *The London Gazette*; *Flight*; *Bexhill-on-Sea Observer*; *The Isle of Wight County Press* archive.

Thanks are due to the following authors and publishers for very generously allowing me to use extracts from their books: James Holland and *The Battle of Britain*; Chris R. Davies and *Almost Forgotten: The search for aviation accidents in Northumberland*; The History Press and *Last of the Ten Fighter Boys* by Jimmy Corbin; Erick Mombeek for his *Jagdwaffe* series; Stephen Bungay's *The Most Dangerous Enemy* by Aurum Press; Tony Holmes's *Spitfire vs Bf 109 Battle of Britain*, Osprey Publishing part of Bloomsbury; John Weal's *Bf 109D/E Aces 1939-41*, Osprey Publishing part of Bloomsbury; *Tally Ho! From the Battle of Britain to the Defence of Darwin* by Wing Commander R. W. Foster, *Air Battle Dunkirk* by Norman Franks, and *The JG 26 War Diary Volume One 1939–1942* by Donald Caldwell, each published by Grub Street Publishing; Henry Buckton's *Voices from the Battle of Britain: Surviving Veterans Tell Their Story*, David & Charles Limited F&W Media International; Dennis Knight's *Harvest of Messerschmitts*, with permission of Derek Boughton; Simon Parry and Mark Postlethwaite, *Battle of Britain Combat Archives, Volumes One–Three*. Thanks also to the following publishers for granting permission for the use of quotations: *Ten Fighter Boys*, reprinted by permission of HarperCollins Publishers Ltd, © 1942, Athol Forbes & Hubert Allen; ***Forgotten Voices of the Blitz and the Battle of Britain*** by **Joshua Levine**, published by **Ebury**, reprinted by permission of The Random House Group Limited © 2006; acknowledgements to *The Battle of Britain* and Patrick Bishop: © 2009, reproduced by permission of Quercus Editions Limited.

Thanks too, to the numerous friends and colleagues who have been such a great source of support once I undertook to turn my research into a book—I have really appreciated it!

Finally, and most importantly, I would like to thank my family for all their help in enabling me to research and write this book, which has been ongoing for the best part of fifteen years—they have unquestioningly supported me every step of the way. Richard, for all his encouragement, Rebecca for having carried out a time-consuming proofread, my father for his interest in the early stages of my research—sadly he did not get to see the finished article, and my mother, for proofreading the book, a mammoth task in itself and for all her unending encouragement, support and advice. Without you it simply would not have been possible—I am forever grateful.

Contents

1

1936: *Alifero Tollitur Axe Ceres*

The first entry in 610 (County of Chester) Auxiliary Air Force Squadron's ORB was on 10 February 1936. On this auspicious day, 610 Squadron was formed 'as one of the three Auxiliary Air Force Squadrons approved during the early part of the Expansion period of the Royal Air Force. It was situated in temporary hutments and a Wartime Hangar at Hooton Park' (ORB). This expansion was due to heightened British fears over the threatening size of the *Luftwaffe*. Sir Hugh Montague Trenchard, (made a viscount in 1936), had been the original driving force behind the growing Auxiliary Air Force (AAF). 610 Squadron's first commanding officer (CO) was Squadron Leader (S/Ldr) I. R. Parker and the first adjutant (Adj.) was Flight Lieutenant (F/Lt) J. A. C. Stratton, and these two men, particularly Ian Parker, were the cornerstones on which the Squadron was built. It was their leadership and guidance in the Squadron's formative years which enabled it to be an effective fighting force by the time 610 Squadron went to war.

Interestingly, there is an article in *The Chronicle* of 4 April 1936, advertising the Squadron's formation, stating where it would be based and the type of new recruit it was looking for. Some early references to the Squadron, name it as the 'County of Cheshire' Squadron, as in this article. This seems to have been a simple error, as Chester is the county town of Cheshire and the administrative city. The College of Heralds would soon officially name the new unit as the 'County of Chester' Squadron.

On 5 August 2011, such a memorable occasion for me, I met Wing Commander [Wg Cdr] Brian Smith, another founder member of the Auxiliary Squadron. We discussed his time with 'The Chesters' and he was quick from the outset to stress the important, underrated role, played by the first squadron commander. He remembered how:

> We owe immense gratitude to I. R. Parker, and I've very seldom seen it in print. Ian was a wonderful man. Came from Glasgow, they were sugar merchants in the West Indies, and he certainly wasn't without means. Very generous, lots of parties—well that's how you get to know people. And he formed the Squadron…

and, 'But 610 Squadron made a very good reputation for themselves, chiefly due to Ian Parker—they knew what the job was about'. Smith also recalled that Parker:

> lived in Bromborough, but his business, Sandbach Tinne was based in Glasgow. And he owned one of the two Cumbrae islands in the River Clyde. The major island was rather like Blackpool, it was a holiday place for the Glaswegians, and a little bit off it was a lighthouse, a dilapidated castle a very nice house and the farm. And that was the island. Eventually Ian died there. He'd done so much building the Squadron—this needs to be mentioned.

Bromborough is a small town on the Wirral Peninsula close to Hooton Park and the vital port of Liverpool, which may have had a bearing on how Parker came to be in command of the local AAF Squadron.

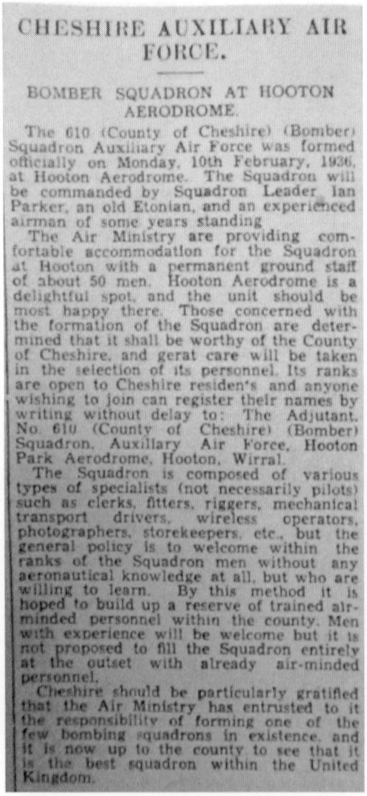

CHESHIRE AUXILIARY AIR FORCE.

BOMBER SQUADRON AT HOOTON AERODROME.

The 610 (County of Cheshire) (Bomber) Squadron Auxiliary Air Force was formed officially on Monday, 10th February, 1936, at Hooton Aerodrome. The Squadron will be commanded by Squadron Leader Ian Parker, an old Etonian, and an experienced airman of some years standing.

The Air Ministry are providing comfortable accommodation for the Squadron at Hooton with a permanent ground staff of about 50 men. Hooton Aerodrome is a delightful spot, and the unit should be most happy there. Those concerned with the formation of the Squadron are determined that it shall be worthy of the County of Cheshire, and gerat care will be taken in the selection of its personnel. Its ranks are open to Cheshire residen's and anyone wishing to join can register their names by writing without delay to: The Adjutant, No. 610 (County of Cheshire) (Bomber) Squadron, Auxiliary Air Force, Hooton Park Aerodrome, Hooton, Wirral.

The Squadron is composed of various types of specialists (not necessarily pilots) such as clerks, fitters, riggers, mechanical transport drivers, wireless operators, photographers, storekeepers, etc., but the general policy is to welcome within the ranks of the Squadron men without any aeronautical knowledge at all, but who are willing to learn. By this method it is hoped to build up a reserve of trained air-minded personnel within the county. Men with experience will be welcome but it is not proposed to fill the Squadron entirely at the outset with already air-minded personnel.

Cheshire should be particularly gratified that the Air Ministry has entrusted to it the responsibility of forming one of the few bombing squadrons in existence, and it is now up to the county to see that it is the best squadron within the United Kingdom.

Left: The Chronicle, 4 April 1936, p. 12. (*Copyright Mirrorpix/Cheshire Record Office*)

Above: S/Ldr I. R. Parker in 1937–38. (*Copyright 610 Squadron Association*)

Born on 27 October 1902 in Liverpool, Parker came from a fortunate background and having been educated at Eton, he became a sugar planter and merchant in the family business. Aged twenty-six, he gained his pilot's licence on 27 February 1929 at the Liverpool and District Aero Club,[1] which was originally based at Hooton Park. 'He was commissioned in Class 'AA' (section ii) of the RAFO [Reserve of Air Force Officers] in October 1931, transferred to Class 'C' on October 9 1932 and transferred back to Class 'AA' on May 19 1933… Parker relinquished his commission in the RAFO and was commissioned in the AAF'.[2] Parker's family had gained their elevated position in society from being partners in Sandbach, Tinne & Company, sugar merchants from the late 1700s onwards—hence the new squadron commander's affluent lifestyle. Parker's background also seems to fit in with the stereotypical portrayal of the AAF as an exclusive club, providing weekend flying for the very well off. There is no denying that the AAF was seen as 'a *corps d'élite*',[3] and Parker certainly did enrol budding pilots into the Squadron as officers. These were men who had enjoyed success in local businesses, or who had a university background, but they were not all from the aristocracy or millionaires, as shall be seen.

As the years went by, the officer class of pilots would quickly change. The 'élite' also referred primarily to the pilots, neglecting the air-gunners, who originally formed a vital part of the crew when airborne. The air-gunners were mainly from a less affluent background and were Auxiliary airmen with the rank of leading aircraftmen (LAC), along with the other ground trades referred to in the newspaper advertisement, all key to the Squadron's formation, such as fitters, riggers and photographers. The AAF appealed to a wide range of people who were fascinated by flying, which was a new and thrilling experience. Although some would never be in a position to fly themselves, they could still use their skills to work on the latest aircraft or carry out administrative tasks and play their part in a Squadron, while maintaining their civilian occupation.

A rare photo of some of 610 Squadron's earliest recruits, who originally joined as ground staff, posing in front of a Hawker Hart. The two men in overalls are unknown ground crew, but next to them are Horatio 'Ray' Chandler, Cyril 'Bam' Bamberger and John Walter Collingwood. Chandler and Bamberger would eventually go on to become pilots, whilst Collingwood was the first member of ground crew to sign up to 610 Squadron. The photograph is entitled 'Hooton Park 1936' in the Bamberger family collection, with the caption 'Early days not yet in uniform'. *(Copyright Bamberger family)*

Two other important members of the Squadron were the Adj. and assistant adjutant (Ass. Adj.). Brian Smith remembered them as follows:

> Oh they taught us to fly! The Adjutant was J. A. C. Stratton, and the Assistant Adjutant was J. W. A. Hunnard and he survived the war. I've never seen Stratton's name in print. I've often meant to get onto records and see, but I rather think he was posted to a Blenheim Squadron on the south coast, which was pretty tricky. I very much doubt if he survived that. What happened to them? They were both bachelors, Hunnard got married after the war, and lived in Scotland. Afraid I haven't made any contact, I should think his days are up. But he'd been in the RAF attached to the Fleet Air Arm [FAA] and he was a wonderful instructor.

When researching the career of John Arthur Charles Stratton, a Regular officer, *Flight* (7 June 1934) reported his promotion from flying officer (F/O) to flight lieutenant, and then on 27 February 1936: 'The following appointments in the Royal Air Force are notified:—*General Duties Branch Flight Lieutenants*:—J. A. C. Stratton, to No. 610 (Co. of Cheshire) (B) Squadron, Hooton Park, 10.2.36',[4] indicating he joined the unit just seventeen days after it was formed.

Similar research into John William Arthur Hunnard, revealed that he had been promoted to flight lieutenant following a course in flying instruction at the Central Flying School (CFS) from 27 April to 12 July 1936.[5] *Flight* (30 July 1936) shows that after this training he immediately joined 610 Squadron: 'The following appointments in the Royal Air Force are notified:—*General Duties Branch Flight Lieutenants*—J. W. A. Hunnard, to No. 610 (Co. Cheshire) (B) Squadron, Hooton Park, 13.7.36',[6] five months after the Squadron was formed.

Parker was to be in command of nine Auxiliary officers and forty-eight airmen, with the Squadron operating as a single flight at first, before later expanding to thirty-five officers and 164 airmen. By this time, there were three Flights, 'A' and 'B' equipped with Hawker Harts, while 'T' for 'Training' Flight was equipped with Avro Tutors, a Tiger Moth and a Hart Trainer. Additional support for training and administrative roles was provided by three Regular officers and forty-seven Regular airmen plus five civilians. All the new airmen took on a trade in which they were instructed by the Regular non-commissioned officers (NCOs). While the Squadron was formed on 10 February 1936, its new home at Hooton Park, Wirral, was not ready for the Squadron's pilots to start learning to fly until 16 April 1936. As a result, the early work for the formation of the Squadron was carried out

Adjutant, F/Lt J. A. C. Stratton, in 1937–38. (*Copyright 610 Squadron Association*)

at RAF Hendon, London (ORB). The new Squadron was part of No. 6 (Auxiliary) Group (Bomber Command). As a light bomber unit, the Squadron would operate the two-seat Hawker Hart, which had been designed by Sydney Camm, powered by a Rolls-Royce Kestrel 1B engine and with a steel tube fuselage. The Hart had first been flown in June 1928 and entered RAF service in February 1930, proving to be very successful in its role. The Hart was also a very adaptable aircraft, with a series of variants being produced based on its design, such as the Audax, Demon and Hind.

One of the new recruits hoping to become an Auxiliary airman was Raymond Ellis. He went on to record his unpublished memoires in 2009, entitled *The Rigger's Tale*, to which the 610 Squadron Association has given me access. When so much is written about the pilots in aviation books, it is of great interest to hear the first-hand account of a member of ground crew who served with 610 Squadron from 1939–1940. Ellis noted that, 'At first, the Squadron was manned entirely by Regular RAF officers, NCOs and airmen. As the Auxiliaries were trained and became qualified in all flying and ground duties, they gradually replaced most of the Regulars with the exception of the senior NCOs and flying instructors'.[7] He also reminisced about Hooton Park and his early training:

> Facing each other across the wide Tarmac (parade ground) were the giant sliding doors of two double-bay Belfast hangars—so called because the timber roof trusses had been designed in Belfast in the 14–18 War. The hangar on the left was occupied by 610 Squadron, whilst that on the right was used by the Liverpool and District Aero Club.
>
> At the weekend, the doors of these hangars would be opened spilling out the Squadron's shining and dignified bombers on the one side, and the cheerful but fragile looking Moths and other light aircraft of the Aero club on the other side. At the edge of the field, beyond the Tarmac, was the bright yellow windsock, and nearby would be parked a blue grey petrol bowser…
>
> As a young man, I was fascinated by the sight and sound of an aircraft starting-up, taxiing out to the south-eastern edge of the field, taking-off into the wind, climbing, circling, and disappearing into the blue. In the deep rear cockpit of the Hart or Hind would be an LAC air gunner sitting on a tip-up seat facing the tail. His harness would be attached to the aircraft by a slack cable—the 'monkey chain'; the latter allowed him to stand up to operate his Lewis gun. Occasionally we humbler members of the ground crew would be invited by a pilot to experience the joy of flight.

Excellent photo showing 610 Squadron's Hawker Harts. (*Copyright Medcalf family*)

> Without doubt, pilots were all splendid fellows. Happy by nature and easy of manner, they were never pretentious nor 'care-free'. At that time they were all officers, but they had an easy rapport with their ground crews upon whom they relied to provide them with aeroplanes that were fit to fly…
>
> The technical NCOs in the hangar, classrooms and workshops, were all professionals who seemed to enjoy passing on their knowledge and skills to the Auxiliaries. In order to pass the RAF exams and master a trade Auxiliaries needed to attend classes on Monday and Thursday evenings and all the weekend, staying in camp over the Saturday night…[8]

Brian Smith thought back to his point of view as a pilot, and how Hooton Park was, '…just green fields in my day, and there was a polo ground where you were asked not to land if you've got tail skids and to avoid frightening the horses! Oh, we learnt a lot. The airfield was situated right alongside the Manchester Ship Canal'. The importance of such a helpful source of navigation had understandably stayed with him from his days as a trainee pilot! Sadly, Hooton Park is now the site of the Vauxhall Motors plant at Ellesmere Port, but 610 Squadron's Association is based on the site of the airfield, where weekly meetings are held. The original First World War Belfast hangars are still in place, owned and cared for by The Hooton Park Trust. (During this book's publication, the Association began the process of moving to a more permanent home in Knutsford, Cheshire. Michael and Mark Oliver, have gone to great lengths to display the Squadron's artefacts at the site of their family business, to create a fitting and lasting tribute to honour 610 Squadron.)

For the next few months of 1936, the ORB was filled with entries such as on 28 April: 'Squadron visited by Brigadier General (Brig. Gen.) Sir W. Bromley-Davenport KCB, CMG, DSO, TD, Lord Lieutenant for the County of Cheshire and President of the Cheshire Territorial Army and Air Force Association. He was accompanied by Major (Maj.) S. D. Douglas-Jones DSO, MC'. The exclusive Grosvenor Hotel, still extant today on Eastgate Street, running through the centre of Chester, was where the officers' mess guest nights were held. On one such occasion on 12 June, the Squadron was presented with a silver cup by a Lt-Col. G. Rollo, CMG, DSO, and at a second event on 8 October, a silver cigarette lighter by Lieutenant (Lt) J. H. Lloyd Royal Navy Volunteer Reserve, which would have taken pride of place at Hooton Park.

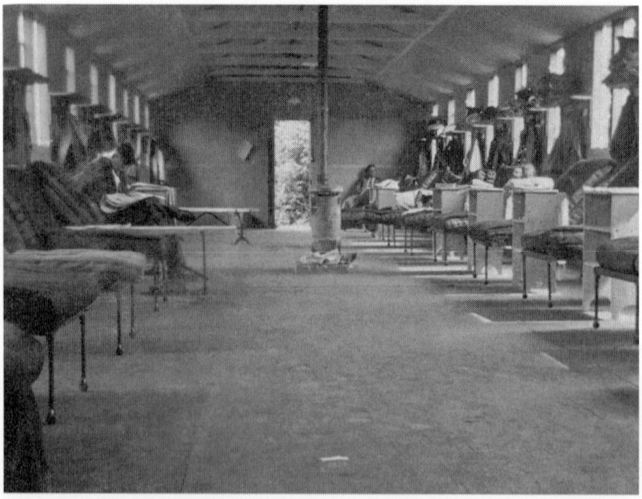

This photograph by Cyril Bamberger shows the basic furnishings of a barrack room at Hooton Park, where the men would have stayed during weekends. (*Copyright Bamberger family*)

While these entertainments were provided for the officers, dances were held for the airmen, one dance involving about 400 guests on 5 October 1936. The Squadron also carried out duties to the town and area to which it was linked, for example on 13 September 1936, 'A party of 25 Auxiliary airmen and one Regular NCO under the Command of P/O J. K. Wilson attended the Chester Church Parade and marched past the Saluting Bases of the Mayor and Council of Chester and the Lords Lieutenants of the Counties of Chester, Flint and Denbigh' (ORB). This would have brought the new unit to the attention of local people, who may well have been interested in joining.

On 29 October 1936, eight months into its existence, 610 Squadron received notification that the all-important Squadron Badge had met with the approval of King Edward VIII, (not long before his abdication). The formal description of the crest read:

> The Badge consists of the Standard Frame for R.A.F. Badges and placed in it is a Wheatsheaf divided into two parts and coloured red and blue. The motto at the foot is 'Alifero Tollitur Axe Ceres'. The reasons influencing the choice of the Badge were the fact that the Armorial Bearings of the City of Chester consists of a wheatsheaf one of which in their Arms is dimidiated. The colours of the Shield for the City of Chester are red and blue. The motto translated means 'Ceres (The Goddess of Corn) rises in a Winged Car' (ORB).

A lot of thought had gone into linking the new unit's badge with the city to which it was associated. Chester's link to the wheatsheaf is proudly shown in both the image of a wheatsheaf, along with the quotation from Ovid which cleverly connected corn to the Squadron's flying role. The Squadron's badge highlighted the military relevance of the Armorial Bearings of the City, even down to the red and blue coloured background. However, the badge was perhaps a little less martial than some of the Squadron's contemporaries, for example 74 'Tiger' Squadron had the fearsome head of a tiger with the motto 'Fear No Man', while even fellow Auxiliary 611 (West Lancashire) Squadron had a red rose with a trident behind it and the motto 'Beware! Beware!'

The ORB entry on the last day of the year for 1936 is very interesting in terms of how the Squadron evolved, as it records on the last day of the month, from February to December, the number of personnel and flying hours carried out:

The newly-approved Squadron badge, dated July 1936. (*Copyright 610 Squadron Association*)

	Officers	**Airmen**	**Flying Hours**
February	1	Nil	Nil
March	1	Nil	Nil
April	2	Nil	Nil
May	2	22	33
June	4	43	38
July	4	43	58
August	4	49	24
September	6	52	63
October	8	56	67
November	8	57	48
December	8	57	44
			375

Unfortunately, there is no record of who these men were at this stage, but in due course it is possible to establish their identity, with the help of other sources. However, it is safe to assume that the lone officer for February and March was S/Ldr Parker. Wynn's *Men of the Battle of Britain* makes reference to one of the earliest squadron pilots being James Anthony Leathart, (photo see page 27): 'Born in London on January 5 1915, Leathart was educated at St Edward's, Oxford and graduated from Liverpool University, as an electrical engineer. While there, he joined 610 Squadron, AAF on May 2 1936, as one of its founder members. He qualified to a wings and operational standard on Harts'.[9]

The only other pilot who received mention in the ORB to this point, was twenty-nine-year-old P/O J. Kerr Wilson who attended the Church Parade in Chester on 13 September 1936. John Kerr Wilson, 'Jack' as he was known, was born on 9 September 1907, in Little Sutton, near Hooton, Wirral. The eldest of four brothers and two sisters of Maj. Henry Kerr Wilson and his wife Gladys, he went on to live in Delavor House in Heswall, Wirral. He attended Charterhouse School in Surrey, where

John Kerr Wilson, known as 'Jack', at Pembroke College, Cambridge, in 1926. (*Copyright Kerr-Wilson family*)

he was a member of Lockites boarding house, from summer quarter 1921 to summer quarter 1925. Interestingly, the school records show that at some point the family name changed from Wilson to Kerr-Wilson, as his younger siblings Henry and Reginald, both of whom also attended Charterhouse, were recorded as Kerr-Wilson, while John was recorded as John Kerr Wilson. This explains some discrepancies in the records later on.[10] Wilson then enrolled at Pembroke College, Cambridge, on 21 October 1925, graduating with a BA in Engineering on 26 June 1928.[11] It is likely that he joined the Cambridge University Air Squadron (UAS). Following his graduation, he entered the family engineering firm, Henry Wilson & Co., in Liverpool in 1928, eventually becoming a director in 1939, having already gained his commission in the AAF as a pilot officer on 14 June 1936.[12]

Although the ORB failed to mention some of the other pilots who were prominent members of the Squadron in the early days, it has been possible to trace many of them through careful research, and restore them to their rightful place. One was P/O A. T. Smith, born on 21 September 1906 in Frodsham, Cheshire, the only son of Andrew Thomas and Marie Emily Gabrielle Smith. The family went on to live in a large house at 4 Croxteth Drive, Fulwood Park, Liverpool. The son, Thomas, attended Oundle School in January 1921. He entered New House and gained colours for rowing, and then in 1924, went up to St Catherine's College, Cambridge. After university, he joined the flour-milling company W. O. & J. Wilson Ltd., in Liverpool and the Grain Elevating and Automatic Weighing Company, of which he became a Director in due course.[13] He gained his pilot's licence on 7 August 1930 at the Liverpool and District Aero Club,[14] eighteen months after his new CO. While working as a corn miller, Tom, as he was known, became an Auxiliary officer with 610 Squadron when he joined the unit as a pilot officer on 9 April 1936.[15] As with the CO, it was men such as Smith on whom 610 Squadron was moulded.

Two more of the Squadron's pioneers who are not mentioned in the ORB until much later were Brian Smith, whom I had the good fortune to meet, and 'Tod' Medcalf. On 24 November 1936, *The London Gazette* noted in the AAF section under General Duties, '*No.* 610 *(COUNTY OF CHESTER) (BOMBER) SQUADRON*—The following are granted commissions as pilot officers:—E. B. B. Smith (September 22); A. R. J. Medcalf (September 23)',[16] indicating that they joined the Squadron very early on, as Brian Smith confirmed, with some additional information on their duties:

Andrew Thomas Smith as a flying officer, 1937–38.
(*Copyright 610 Squadron Association*)

> I obviously was one of the originals. It was up to Ian who was selected—you, you and you, yes! We were a day bomber squadron in Harts and Hinds, and our job was taking photographs of factories and tunnel entrances and things all over the country. And your biggest enemy in those days was weather, so we learnt a lot.

When asked what made him want to learn to fly, he replied:

> Seeing the trainers from Sealand, and seeing them drrrrrrrrrrrrr, [engine sound] you know, scarcely moving. They were Bristol Fighters, left over from the First World War. And our Harts and Hinds were only the modern equivalent of the first lot, redesigned and with better engines.

Edward Brian Bretherton Smith was born in Formby, Lancashire on 12 January 1915. He told me several interesting stories from his background, including how 'on my grandmother's side, they ran coaches, from Liverpool. Before the railways, they had 700 horses between here and London and then local ones too I suppose, and then the railways came and took all the business'. He also had strong links to the early running of the Grand National through his mother's side of the family, who had been landowners in West Lancashire. Brian Smith recalled how his:

> father was a civil engineer, building for petrol companies, building jetties for the ships to come, off-loading into these big tanks, and then he became supervisory. So in Ireland we never had a permanent house, they were rented houses. But I was sent to Boarding School at eight and a half. On the shores of Belfast Lough at Rockport School in Craigavad.

Smith then left Ireland to continue his secondary education: 'I went to the Isle of Man after that. Nice place to school, King William's. Well it's just on the edge of the aerodrome!' It is possible that this also sparked Brian Smith's early love of flying. He recalled how, 'I remember flying out of the field there before it was an aerodrome … oh a five bob trip, you know, in the Fokker. When the motor cycle races were on, they used to bring the daily newspapers into the field, which was all it was in those

Above left: P/O Brian Smith wearing his distinctive Squadron flying overalls, in the Watch Hut at RAF Hawkinge, Annual Camp 1937. (*Copyright 610 Squadron Association*)

Above right: P/O 'Tod' Medcalf, taken on 10 August 1937 at the Annual Camp, Hawkinge. (*Copyright 610 Squadron Association*)

days'. It must have been fascinating to be at school so close to such an exciting mode of transport which was still in its infancy.

Away from school, Smith spent some time on the Wirral, 'Father had a cottage at Parkgate … Before the war we used to meet at the swimming pools, that was the fashion. There was one at Parkgate. We went to North Wales, which was a Sunday routine really. All the family people …', and spent time in Hoylake, with a widowed aunt who lived on Stanley Road, which runs alongside the Royal Liverpool Golf Course. However, the family home was in Tattenhall, just south of Chester. Brian Smith went on to work in the brewing industry, starting as an apprentice, working for Threlfall's Brewery in Liverpool on Trueman Street, which was situated just by the Queensway Mersey Tunnel entrance. It was around this time that Smith came to join the ranks of the County of Chester Squadron, training at weekends to become a pilot.

Albert Rupert John Medcalf was born not far from Smith, in Crosby, Lancashire, just north of Liverpool, on 30 August 1913, to Rupert and Florence Medcalf. They later moved to a house called 'Framley' in Willaston, a small village on the Wirral. I've been fortunate to be in touch with his nephew Ian Coates and meet his two nieces, Pamela and Sue, who kindly supplied many of the details about his background, along with a fascinating collection of photos taken by Medcalf. Ian Coates recalls how Medcalf was called 'Tod' since childhood, 'It came from his favourite child's story book—"Budge and Toddie". Toddie was the "Just William" rascal of the time, although "Tod" was not! He was a gentle, caring individual who excelled at sport'.

Medcalf went to Bedford School from January 1928 to December 1931, and the school passed on several interesting pieces of information about him. As his nephew supposes, he was a keen sportsman, having gained school colours for the 1st XV, gym and cricket, and been in the House football team, while he went on to be a Senior Monitor. After school, he returned to the north-west and studied architecture at Liverpool University, graduating with a B.Arch in 1937. His relatives believe that he also learnt to fly at university, as part of the Liverpool UAS. This would explain why he eventually joined 610 Squadron as a pilot officer in September 1936. His niece Pamela also explained that, 'After university, he worked in the family architect's practice of Medcalf & Medcalf in Liverpool, founded by his grandfather J. A. Medcalf. "Tod's" father, Rupert Medcalf, was also an architect', while Pamela followed in their footsteps by becoming an architect too.

Another new member of the Squadron who joined shortly after Smith and Medcalf, was P/O Mark Christopher Topham, who arrived on 9 October 1936.[17] Little is known about him, the ORB failing to even mention his arrival. However, his family were presumably of some means, as he was a director of Topham's Limited in Liverpool, who managed Aintree Racecourse.[18] Another of the Auxiliary officers to join the Squadron in October was Douglas Strachan Wilson. He was born in Aberdeen on 9 August 1909, later learnt to fly at Newcastle-upon-Tyne Aero Club, while his occupation was a salesman. He received his pilot's licence on 25 October 1931.[19] By the time he joined 610 Squadron, Wilson was an experienced pilot, and *The London Gazette* of Christmas Day 1936 noted that: '*No.* 610 *(County of Chester) (Bomber) Squadron.* Douglas Strachan WILSON is granted a commission as pilot officer. 24th Oct. 1936',[20] when he was aged twenty-seven. By this time he was living in Dunsdale Cottage, Frodsham, Cheshire, with his wife May. On 9 July 1937, he was authorised to wear his pilot's flying badge (TNA, AIR 76/553/130). *The London Gazette*[21] mentioned his promotion to flying officer with effect from 24 April 1938, with 610 (County of Chester) Bomber Squadron, and Wilson's continuous stint with 610 meant that he would have been well trained by this time, like many of the early members of the Auxiliary Squadron, as noted by Wg Cdr Smith.

The ORB's account of the unit's first year closed with a description of S/Ldr Parker's initiative to keep the ground crew on their toes. He had introduced prizes for the men who kept their aircraft in the best condition—in this instance the fitter who won was Leading Aircraftman (LAC) MacLeod, with LAC Duffy (see photo p. 26) as runner-up and for the riggers there was a joint winner between LAC Lewis (probably in photo p. 46) and LAC Long. LAC Fairhurst came second.

Rare photo of Mark Topham on the far right, inspecting the 'Photo section'. Corporal (Cpl) Cooper is on the left, AC Blake on the right, whilst AC Bamberger is standing in the middle. (*Copyright Medcalf family*)

P/O. Douglas Strachan Wilson, smoking his pipe, photographed in the Watch Hut at Hawkinge in 1937. (*Copyright 610 Squadron Association*)

Aerial shot of Hawker Hart K.3054. Cyril 'Bam' Bamberger recalled how he flew a number of sorties as an aerial photographer. (*Copyright Bamberger family*)

2

1937: Development of 610 Squadron at Hooton Park

The ORB for 1937 is again sparsely notated. The first point of interest in the year was on 15 March, when the collection of silver in the officers' mess at Hooton Park was added to with a silver inkstand, blotter and blotting pad by a Lt-Col. I. R. T. Irvine. The following month on 23 April, the officers' mess guest night was held at the Bridge Inn in Port Sunlight, a small town near Hooton Park, where, 'Among the guests were Lieutenant Colonel G. Rollo CMG, DSO; Sir L. A. P. Warner and Major S. D. Douglas-Jones DSO, MC' (ORB). Sir Lionel Warner was the father of one of the Squadron's future pilots.

Just over a week later on 1 May, the Squadron's football team was awarded the McCall Clean Play Shield for the 1936–37 season. Out of all the different divisions of the Birkenhead and District Football League, they had recorded the least number of intentional fouls. The statement that, 'The football XI finished the season with the maximum number of points' (ORB), indicates that they had convincingly won their league and shows how important sport was in Squadron life before the War.

Another officer joined the Squadron on 1 March 1937, P/O Graham Lambert Chambers,[1] who almost certainly enjoyed the sporting aspect of squadron life (photograph see p. 122). Lambert Chambers was born on 8 April 1912 in Ealing, Middlesex to his parents Robert and Dorothea Katharine Lambert Chambers, his mother being a famous tennis player. Originally Dorothea Katharine Douglass, she won Wimbledon seven times between 1903 and 1914 (still a British female record today), being runner up twice and won a gold medal at the 1908 Olympics. She was also a top badminton and hockey player. I traced a distant relative of Lambert Chambers's father, from Alberta, Canada, who informed me that Graham Lambert Chambers's father had served with the 2/1st & 3rd City of London Volunteers, and commanded the anti-aircraft (AA) batteries in London in the Great War, having been a Cambridge University student. Lambert Chambers also went on to study at Cambridge, and like several of his comrades, possibly had his interest aroused in flying as a member of the Cambridge UAS.[2] At some stage he became a teacher at Mostyn House boarding school in Parkgate, Wirral, where he was remembered by a member of the 610 Squadron Association—it is likely he taught at the school while carrying out his training at Hooton Park.

A couple of months later, one of the youngest trainee pilots officially joined the ever-growing Squadron—William Henry Cromwell Warner was still at school at Malvern College, Worcestershire, when he became a pilot officer with the Squadron on 7 May. William Warner, known as Bill, was born on 21 October 1918 in New Brighton, Wirral, his father, Lionel Ashton Piers and mother, Nina Mary, having married in 1907. His father had been knighted in 1936, was the general manager and secretary of the Mersey Docks and Harbour Board, and had been mentioned earlier as a guest of the officers' mess.[3] Bill Warner grew up in a house called 'Yew Tree' on Poplar Road, Oxton, Wirral, another of the recruits who came from the area close to Hooton Park. That Warner was young enough to be attending Malvern College, is a clear sign of his early affinity for flying.[4] He was a member of School House between 1932 and 1937, where he was a good swimmer, winning his colours in 1935–37,

The Squadron's football team won the local league in the 1936–37 season, and this photo from the following season shows many of the players from that successful team. Back row: Price, unknown, Benson, unknown, unknown, Walker, Davies. Middle: Duffy, F/O A. T. Smith, S/Ldr Parker, F/Lt Stratton, unknown. Front: Halewood, unknown, Berry, unknown. (*Copyright 610 Squadron Association*)

while he also played second eleven football. Warner was clearly of an active disposition, and 'A very senior Old Malvernian … remembered him as an imposing school prefect, of which there were only ever about ten each year', so he was presumably seen as a responsible young man too.[5] Warner would enjoy a memorable week in November 1938, as on 3 November, aged just twenty, he was awarded his 'Wings', a most memorable day in any pilot's life, while on 7 November he was promoted to flying officer. This was a position of responsibility for someone so young; he was barely out of school, and Sir Lionel and Lady Warner must have been very proud of their high-flying son.

In order to function efficiently, the Squadron did not just need pilots, but men to carry out the administrative duties, and on 10 May 1937, John Harold Clayton Albrecht joined the unit for such tasks. Although little is known about Albrecht, an Auxiliary officer, he features in many of the early Squadron photos and 'Johnny' as he is named in the Squadron Association's archive, seems to have been a humorous character. While at this stage Albrecht filled an administrative role, he went on to an accountancy position.

On the same day, it appears that one of the first pilots to join the Squadron, James Leathart, transferred to the RAF, 'with a short service commission and was posted to 3 FTS [Flying Training School], Grantham, later moving with it to South Cerney'.[6] Leathart had an eventful career in the RAF, including rescuing his CO from a French aerodrome during the Dunkirk evacuation. He survived the war and died on 17 November 1988.

A special day for the country came on 12 May 1937, with the Coronation of King George VI and Queen Elizabeth, following Edward VIII's controversial abdication on 11 December 1936. The event provides an insight into some of the ceremonial tasks performed by the Squadron. A small party of ten Auxiliary airmen was honoured by lining the processional route in London, under the watchful eye of P/O Tom Smith. The men were accommodated in a camp at Kensington Gardens. At the same time, F/Lt

Right: William Henry Cromwell Warner at a Squadron event, probably at Hooton Park. The shield in the background was a trophy from the Squadron's annual camp at Hawkinge in 1937. (*Copyright 610 Squadron Association*)

Below: This photo of Albrecht at Hawkinge, 1937, bears the caption, 'I bow to my loyal subjects'. (*Copyright 610 Squadron Association*)

Rare evidence of Leathart's time with 610 Squadron. He is second from the left, alongside Jack Kerr Wilson (far left), the Adjutant Stratton (3), S/Ldr Parker (4), and Tom Smith (5). The photo was used as one of a collection of cigarette cards, produced by Ardath Tobacco Co., in 1936. (*Copyright 610 Squadron Association*)

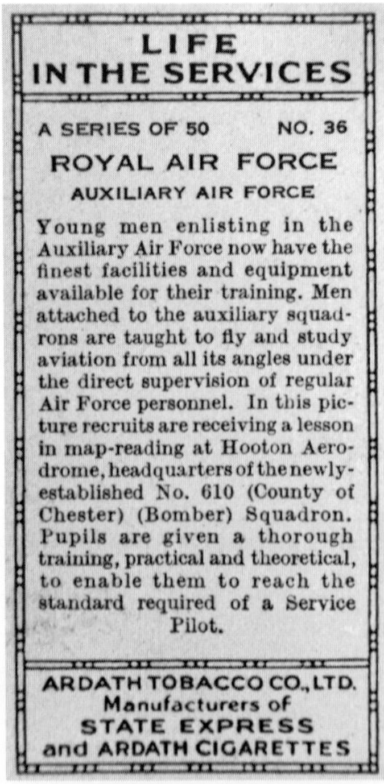
LIFE IN THE SERVICES

A SERIES OF 50 NO. 36

ROYAL AIR FORCE

AUXILIARY AIR FORCE

Young men enlisting in the Auxiliary Air Force now have the finest facilities and equipment available for their training. Men attached to the auxiliary squadrons are taught to fly and study aviation from all its angles under the direct supervision of regular Air Force personnel. In this picture recruits are receiving a lesson in map-reading at Hooton Aerodrome, headquarters of the newly-established No. 610 (County of Chester) (Bomber) Squadron. Pupils are given a thorough training, practical and theoretical, to enable them to reach the standard required of a Service Pilot.

ARDATH TOBACCO CO., LTD.
Manufacturers of
STATE EXPRESS
and ARDATH CIGARETTES

On the reverse of the previous photo, was the following description advocating life in the AAF. (*Author*)

Stratton participated in a military parade in Chester, at the head of eighty Regular and Auxiliary airmen to mark this auspicious day. To commemorate the event, the CO, S/Ldr Parker was awarded a Coronation Medal, along with Tom Smith, Sgt A. T. Knell and LAC G. D. Storry, for their efforts with the different parades.

Although their arrival was not recorded in the ORB, three more new pilots joined the Squadron in July 1937, the first of whom was P/O Paul John Davies-Cooke, born on 14 November 1916 (TNA, AIR 81/3448). He was another relatively local recruit, coming from North Wales and he also benefited from a comfortable background, his ancestral home being the Gwysaney Estate, Mold. 'Davies-Cooke was at Shrewsbury School from 1930 to 1935 and then at Trinity College, Cambridge',[7] another of the men recruited by S/Ldr Parker with a university background, the UAS having possibly fed his enthusiasm for flying. He was commissioned on 1 July when he joined the County of Chester Squadron. Davies-Cooke knuckled down to life in the AAF and eventually was awarded his 'Wings' on 16 December 1938 (ORB).

Two days after Davies-Cooke's arrival, the next pilot to join was Gerald Malcolm Theodore Kerr. Born on 11 November 1909 in Leeds, he too has an interesting family background, which Christopher Kerr, Malcolm's nephew, has been kind enough to help me with. Kerr's father was half German, called Frederick Althaus, and due to the First World War, Frederick and his wife Margaret changed their surname to Kerr. Malcolm Kerr, as he was known, went on to be another of the well-educated fraternity who helped form the Squadron's backbone, attending Leeds Grammar School. On joining the school in the third term of 1921, it seems their home address was 18 Lyddon Terrace, Leeds. He left Leeds Grammar in 1928. Having passed his Northern Board Higher School certificate in science with a distinction in chemistry,[8] Kerr attended Queen's College, Oxford, as a Hastings Scholar in Chemistry. He obtained second class honours in the School of Natural Sciences in 1932. He enjoyed swimming, skating and was a keen tennis player, being in the Tennis VI in his final year. Perhaps most pertinent to this book, he was also an active member of the Oxford UAS.

On leaving Oxford, Kerr spent a year on post-graduate work in chemical engineering at London University. He then joined ICI as a research chemist and was stationed at Billingham. In 1934 he moved to Runcorn where he stayed until 1939 as plant manager of the Castner Kellner site.[9] Throughout this time, Kerr had maintained his interest in flying, as in 1932, he joined the RAF Reserve and was, 'granted a commission in Class AA (ii) as a pilot officer, 8th Aug. 1932',[10] being promoted to flying officer on 8 February 1934.[11] His RAF special medical examinations show that he was five feet seven inches and had a history of illness, including pneumonia and empyema. In May 1935, he was hospitalised for four months. He did improve, but then relapsed for a further eight weeks. The report stated that, 'Since 13th February 1936 patient has led a normal life and feels quite fit. This officer appears to have made a good recovery from the effects of empyema and is considered as fit for full flying duties in the Reserve' (TNA, AIR 81/670). Having remained in the RAF Reserve for another three years, and by now a very competent pilot approaching his twenty-eighth birthday, he decided to relinquish his commission on the 3 July 1937, in order to become an Auxiliary, and was recorded as being a member of: '*No.* 610 *(County of Chester) (Bomber) Squadron.* Gerald Malcolm Theodore KERR is granted a commission as flying officer'.[12] His logbook records that by June 1937, he had amassed 250 hours and twenty minutes flying time, 152 hours and fifty minutes being solo.

Above: An interesting pair of photographs from the Association's archive, showing the Auxiliary airmen setting up camp in Kensington Gardens for the Coronation in 1937. (*Copyright 610 Squadron Association*)

Right: P/O Davies-Cooke, ready to bat in a Squadron cricket match, 28 July 1938, RAF Abbotsinch. (*Copyright 610 Squadron Association*)

Below: Malcom Kerr, second from left on the back row, with the Oxford University Air Squadron. This is probably taken at RAF Eastchurch on the Isle of Sheppey, during a summer training camp in 1932. Kerr had been flying an Armstrong Whitworth Atlas during the training camp, which is believed to be the type of aircraft in the background. (*Copyright Kerr family*)

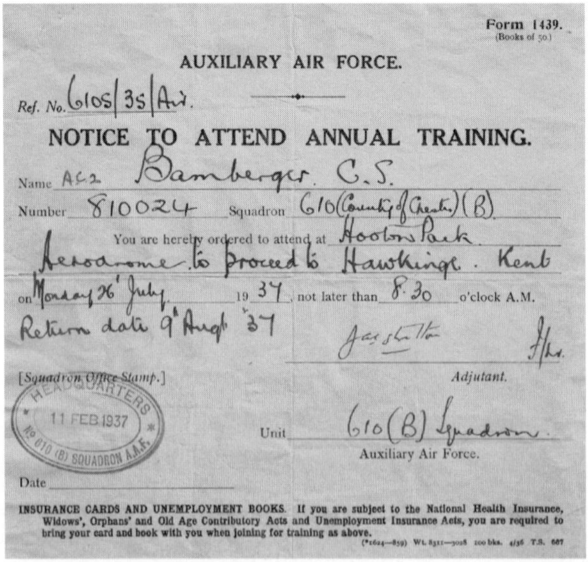

Form 1439.
(Books of 50.)

AUXILIARY AIR FORCE.

Ref. No. 610S/35/Air.

NOTICE TO ATTEND ANNUAL TRAINING.

Name AC2 Bamberger. C.S.
Number 810024 Squadron 610 (County of Chester) (B)
You are hereby ordered to attend at Hooton Park Aerodrome to proceed to Hawkinge. Kent
on Monday 26th July 1937 not later than 8.30 o'clock A.M.
Return date 9th Aug 37

F/Lt.
Adjutant.

[Squadron Office Stamp.]
HEADQUARTERS 11 FEB 1937 No 610 (B) SQUADRON A.A.F.

Unit 610 (B) Squadron.
Auxiliary Air Force.

Date

INSURANCE CARDS AND UNEMPLOYMENT BOOKS. If you are subject to the National Health Insurance, Widows', Orphans' and Old Age Contributory Acts and Unemployment Insurance Acts, you are required to bring your card and book with you when joining for training as above.

Left: The form AC2 Cyril Bamberger received calling him up for the Annual Camp, which took place at RAF Hawkinge during the summer of 1937. The form has been signed by J. A. C. Stratton and the dates involved differ slightly from those mentioned in the ORB. (*Copyright Bamberger family*)

Below: Hawkinge officers' mess. (*Copyright Medcalf family*)

This coincided with his time working in Runcorn and S/Ldr Parker would certainly have welcomed the arrival of such an experienced pilot. In January 1938, Kerr would marry Barbara Rudge.

The final pilot to join the Squadron in July was P/O C. R. Prichard, who arrived on 6 July 1937.[13] Although little is known about him, the ORB does state on 9 March 1938 that he was awarded his flying badge on 27 February 1938 (see photo p. 31).

Just over two months on from the Coronation celebrations, the Squadron went to RAF Hawkinge for its first annual camp, from 25 July to 8 August 1937. The purpose of the annual camp was to provide the Squadron with a more intensive period of training, to hone their skills as air or ground crew, while also bringing the men together to build up the Squadron's camaraderie. It was the highlight of the year for all those concerned with the Squadron. The full complement of thirteen Auxiliary officers and eighty-five out of eighty-eight Auxiliary airmen went to Hawkinge, situated on the south coast, just inland of Folkestone. Brian Smith well remembered the event when we met and this was an airfield that 610 Squadron was constantly being scrambled from in 1940.

Above left: Stratton and Prichard. (*Copyright 610 Squadron Association*)

Above right: P/Os Davies-Cooke, Warner and Brian Smith. (*Copyright Medcalf family*)

Although the ORB records little of this fortnight, there is a fascinating set of photos, mostly taken by P/O Medcalf, showing what life was like during these annual camps. I have been able to reproduce them thanks to the kindness of 'Tod' Medcalf's relatives and the 610 Squadron Association.

In the left hand photo (above), the Adj. J. A. C. Stratton, seems to be striking a pose with P/O Prichard. In the right hand photo (above), three of the Squadron's pilots have dressed up for a 'Guest Night', which would have been a lively evening.

The officers also enjoyed a trip to nearby Canterbury, where there was evidently a fun fair. Some Kentish memorabilia in the form of a shield with the County's emblem of a rampant white horse, was purloined as a memento of the Squadron's camp, shown in the following photo of Tom Smith and Johnny Albrecht (see p. 32). There was plenty of fun to be had in the AAF, it was not all about flying and military discipline!

However, the main reason for the Squadron's stay at Hawkinge was to improve its flying proficiency with a prolonged period of training. The next two photos (see p. 32) show some of the pilots at RAF Eastchurch, awaiting their training flight to the Leysdown Ranges for target practice.

The experience gained by the ground crew at the annual camps was just as important. The photo (on p. 34) shows a large group of 610 Squadron's ground crew enjoying a moment's respite at Hawkinge in the summer of 1937. On 5 August, the air officer commanding (AOC) of No. 6 Auxiliary Group, Air Commodore (Air Cdre) J. C. Quinnell, DFC, visited the Squadron at Hawkinge, to inspect and present the Squadron's badge. The ORB also made note of who won the CO's prizes for the best kept aircraft this year, the recipients being:

Above left: Albrecht and Tom Smith. (*Copyright Medcalf family*)

Above right: Brian Smith, Malcolm Kerr and Douglas Wilson. (*Copyright Medcalf family*)

Jack Kerr Wilson, Douglas Wilson, Malcolm Kerr and Brian Smith (*Copyright 610 Squadron Association*)

Fine example of a 610 Squadron Hawker Hart—P/O A. R. J. Medcalf at the controls at Hawkinge, 1937. (*Copyright 610 Squadron Association*)

561872 L.A.C. Pigdon, C.
335421 L.A.C. Halewood, E. V. (photo p. 26)
560352 L.A.C. Orford, J. E.
810029 A.C.2. Jackson, J. J.
810049 A.C.1. Huskisson, R. I.
810030 A.C.2. Alkin, A.
810010 A.C.2. Bellamy, L. H.

The Squadron left Hawkinge to return to Hooton Park on 8 August 1937.

Later in the year, the Squadron received two notable visits at its home station, from some of the RAF's hierarchy. On 21 October the annual inspection was carried out by the now familiar figure of Air Cdre Quinnell, DFC, while on Bonfire Night, the unit was visited by Air Chief Marshal Sir E. R. Ludlow-Hewitt KCB, CMG, DSO, MC, air officer commander-in-chief (AOC-in-C) Bomber Command, to see how 'The Chesters' were shaping up in their role as a light bomber squadron (ORB).

On a lighter note, during 1937, the Squadron played a football match against the AAF's other Squadron raised in the north-west, 611 (West Lancashire) Squadron, based across the River Mersey at Speke. There would certainly have been some rivalry between the two teams and the two photos (see p. 35) give an insight into the day. In the first, the two squadron commanders can be seen in conversation, S/Ldr Pilkington of 611 on the left, and S/Ldr Parker on the right, with an MG sports car in the foreground, reflecting the affluence of many of the Auxiliary officers. The second photo shows a group of the Squadrons' officers watching the game. The only person who is definitely recognisable is P/O Tom Smith, third from the right. Sport played an important role in the running of these Auxiliary squadrons. It was a good way of building team spirit with a competitive edge, highlighted by the numerous photographs and references to sporting events.

The final entry for 1937 in the ORB is another overview of the Squadron's strength and the number of hours flown each month, which worked out as follows:

Group shot entitled 'The troops', showing some of the ground crew at Hawkinge, with a hangar looming behind them. (*Copyright 610 Squadron Association*)

The type of line up the Squadron would have put on for a visit from one of the top brass, such as on 21 October 1937. This shows the Squadron's Hawker Harts, with some Avro Tutors at the far right, at RAF Hawkinge, probably at the annual camp of 1937. 'Bam' Bamberger noted in the caption to this photograph, that his first solo flight was in a Tutor. (*Copyright Bamberger family*)

The two AAF Squadron Leaders in discussion. (*Copyright 610 Squadron Association*)

A group of AAF officers watch the action. (*Copyright 610 Squadron Association*)

	Officers	Airmen	Flying Hours
January	8	57	50
February	8	77	47
March	9	77	58
April	9	78	77
May	10	78	98
June	11	90	134
July	13	88	133
August	13	88	87
September	13	88	52
October	13	88	91
November	13	88	79
December	13	87	40
			946

Undoubtedly, by the end of 1937, the Squadron had grown in size, with the arrival of five new officers and thirty new airmen. The increased number of pilots meant a drastic increase in the amount of time spent flying, with an additional 571 hours flying time having taken place over the same period in 1936, the two busiest months unsurprisingly being June and July. Slowly but surely, 610 (County of Chester) Squadron was becoming an effective bomber force.

Ian Parker is in the centre and Tom Smith on the left, both in the Squadron's dark flying kit, the air-gunners following on behind. The caption referred to Smith as a pilot officer, indicating it was taken prior to his promotion in 1938. (*Copyright 610 Squadron Association*)

3

1938: From Harts to Hinds

The first entries in the Squadron's ORB for 1938 relate to promotions for two of the older pilots. On 11 January, notification was received that thirty-one-year-old Andrew Thomas Smith had been promoted to flying officer, dating back to 4 December 1937, while on 3 February, John Kerr Wilson, aged thirty, received the same news with effect from 12 December 1937. Also on 3 February, Mr T. A. Mason, known as 'Alec', was 'granted a commission as pilot officer, Accountant Officer' (ORB), another cog in the wheel of a fully-functioning Squadron.

Three days later, on Sunday 6 February at 1530 hours, the newly promoted F/O Tom Smith crashed and overturned his Hawker Hart K.2424, while attempting a forced landing at Arley, near Nuneaton, as vividly shown in the photograph (see p. 38). The caption in the Association archive was suitably dark-humoured, seemingly annotated by Tom Smith himself, while a report of the crash appeared in *The Tribune* (see p. 39), a useful source, as surprisingly no mention of the accident is made in the ORB. Smith was flying the Hart from Maidenhead to Hooton Park, with an observer called Herbert Rushton on board, but finding themselves in awful weather, they had attempted to divert to Castle Bromwich. Smith was flung from the aircraft, while Rushton remained inside, both being fortunate to suffer nothing worse than shock; the Hart was taken away for repairs. While the airmen were very lucky to survive, it was a stark reminder of the hazardous nature of service life.

March was a busy month in the comings and goings of the Squadron, much of which revolved around the role of adjutant and assistant adjutant. F/Lt John Stratton had held the important position of adjutant since the Squadron's inception, but on 4 March 1938 F/Lt T. F. U. Lang arrived at Hooton Park. His role was described as 'supernumerary assistant adjutant, instructor duties' (ORB), which presumably meant Lang would be training the Squadron's pilots. Three days later, the reason for Lang's appearance became self-evident, as it was reported, 'F/Lt. J. A. C. Stratton posted to Air Ministry, Postings Dept.' (ORB). Lang was officially posted to 610 Squadron as assistant adjutant on 8 March, Stratton having helped to break him in gently. The Squadron would have missed its first adjutant, Stratton having been a key figure in the establishment of the unit: Thomas Frederick Umphelby Lang, 'Tommy', had some big shoes to fill. Despite Brian Smith's earlier fears for Stratton after leaving 610 Squadron, I found that he went on to take command of 59 Squadron flying Bristol Blenheims (as Smith remembered), on 12 August 1940, a role he survived. Stratton had a successful career in the RAF, being promoted to group captain (temporary) on 25 October 1942[1] and mentioned in despatches in June 1943,[2] finally retiring from the RAF on 24 August 1957 as Group Captain (Grp Capt.) Stratton, CBE.[3]

On 14 March, P/O Graham Lambert Chambers received his flying badge, which would have been a momentous occasion for him. F/Lt Tommy Lang became the fully fledged adjutant on 22 March 1938, while F/Lt B. J. Paul was another new arrival at Hooton, as the new assistant adjutant. It seems likely that Basil Jack Paul had previously been serving in Egypt, as *Flight* reported that a F/O B. J. Paul had been posted to RAF Depot Aboukir, Egypt on 5 May 1937.[4] The third event of note for this day was the departure of

Left: Alec Mason at Hooton Park, October 1938, when he was the Armament Officer. (*Copyright 610 Squadron Association*)

Below: (*Copyright 610 Squadron Association*)

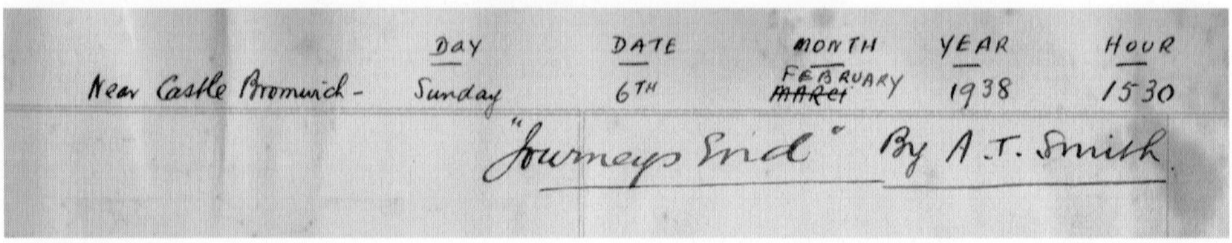

	DAY	DATE	MONTH	YEAR	HOUR
Near Castle Bromwich -	Sunday	6TH	~~MARCH~~ FEBRUARY	1938	1530

"Journeys End" By A.T. Smith

F/O A. T. Smith's dramatic crash-landing in Hart K.2424. (*Copyright Bamberger family*)

Pilot and Observer Escape Uninjured

The pilot and observer of a Hawker Hart bomber, attached to 610 Squadron, Hooton Park, Cheshire, had narrow escapes from being killed when the machine crashed at Slowly Green Farm, Arley, near Nuneaton, on Sunday afternoon.

The aeroplane was flying from Maidenhead to Hooton Park, but visibility became so bad that the pilot endeavoured to find the Castle Bromwich R.A.F. depot, which is about eight miles away from the spot, but lost his bearings. After circling round in the vicinity of Slowley Green Farm two or three times, the pilot officer, Andrew Thomas Smith attempted to land in a field, and in doing so hit the top of a tree. With its tail badly damaged, the aeroplane struck the field with force, and somersaulted. The pilot was thrown clear, but the observer, Herbert Rushton, was held fast in the cockpit when the crash occurred. The pilot went to his assistance, and when got out he was found to be uninjured, except for shock, as was the pilot also.

Slowly Green Farm is owned by Mr. Ralph Burton, and is situate on the main Coventry to Tamworth road, being about half a mile from the Nuneaton turn at Over Whitacre.

Eye-Witnesses Stories.

One of Mr. Burton's employees, Mr. Ernest Harness, a cowman, told the "Tribune" this morning that Mr. and Mrs. Burton, who were in the farmyard, Mr. James Goodwin, horseman, who was near the fowl-pens, and himself—he was in a field to the right of the farm, near the cow-pens—stood watching the 'plane circling about. The time was about 3.15 p.m. It was apparent that the occupants had lost their bearings, but he (Mr. Harness) had a shock when the machine nearly struck his home, a small cottage on the opposite side of the road to the farm. It then crossed the road and in flying over the farm the left wing span touched the top of a large chestnut tree in close proximity to the farmhouse. After this escape the 'plane banked to the right and made a circle in the opposite direction to that which it had come—from Fillongley. Crossing the road once more the engine shut off and the 'plane came down in a newly-ploughed field, finishing upside down Mr. Harness said that from his position he did not see the actual crash, but the noise was plainly heard. Both the pilot and the observer were on their feet when he ran across to them.

Terrific Noise.

Mr. James Goodwin said that the noise of the aeroplane—because it was so low—was terrific. It was so low he thought it would hit the fowl-pens. He saw the machine strike the ground and then bounce over on to its back. He at once ran to the scene. Pilot Officer Smith by that time had assisted the observer out of the cockpit, but only Mr. Rushton suffered from shock. Fortunately the 'plane did not catch fire.

Could Not See Depot For Fog.

After their alarming experience the two men went to Mr. Burton's farm and telephoned to the Castle Bromwich depot. They were entertained by Mr. and Mrs. Burton and left at 7 o'clock for Castle Bromwich. It appeared that at one time the airmen were actually over the Castle Bromwich racecourse and near the depot, but could not see it for the fog.

This morning a squad of mechanics from Castle Bromwich journeyed to the scene by lorry. They quickly righted the 'plane and towed it across the field to the entrance. They then dismantled the wings and the chassis was afterwards placed on the lorry and the whole taken to Castle Bromwich for repair.

Fortunate the Machine Did Not Fire.

A number of people visited the scene this morning, the machine having been guarded overnight by two pickets from Castle Bromwich. One of these said that about eighty gallons of petrol was spilled when the 'plane tipped upside down and the men were lucky it did not take fire. Apart from the tail, struts on the wings, and propeller, the machine was not badly damaged. Parts of the propellor were found 100 yards away. The holes in the ground, made when the crash occurred, were two feet deep.

Left: Account of Smith's emergency landing, 6 February 1938. It is unclear who added the annotations to the article, although they were possibly by A. T. Smith, given the overall caption in the Squadron's archive (see p. 38). (*Copyright 610 Squadron Association*)

Above: Tommy Lang (left), enjoys a joke with Tom Smith, wearing a wig and with cigarette in hand, on the day of the Officers v Men football match at Hooton Park, 15 April 1938. (*Copyright 610 Squadron Association*)

F/Lt J. W. A. Hunnard to 6 FTS at Netheravon, north of Salisbury. Although this is the only mention he received in the ORB, he had been the assistant adjutant since 13 July 1936. He assisted Ian Parker and John Stratton in getting the Squadron operational, and Wg Cdr Smith remembered him as a 'wonderful instructor'. After this, S/Ldr J. W. A. Hunnard commanded 266 Squadron, which was re-formed in October 1939. At first it operated Fairey Battles, before moving on to the Supermarine Spitfire. He claimed a Messerschmitt 109 unconfirmed during the Dunkirk evacuation, at 0700 hours on 2 June 1940.[5]

As is well documented, sport played a key part in the life of an AAF Squadron. On 15 April 1938, a football match took place between the officers and men. A series of photos exists in the Squadron Association's archive of this match, which seems to have been won 1–0 by the officers' team, the deciding goal being a penalty scored by Johnny Albrecht.

On 1 May 1938, 610 Squadron must have been preparing to take part in the Empire Air Day, as Air Cdre Quinnell, DFC paid another visit to the unit as it rehearsed its role in the event. Empire Air Days were organised by the RAF and the Air League of the British Empire, being designed to give a behind the scenes view of British aviation at aerodromes across the country. Empire Air Days

'Tod' Medcalf captures F/Lt Basil Jack Paul enjoying a moment's relaxation. (*Copyright Medcalf family*)

Peter Lamb, Basil Paul, Mrs Albrecht, Mark Topham and Johnny Albrecht look like they are on their way to the match, walking through Hooton Park. One of the hangars is just visible, rear left. (*Copyright 610 Squadron Association*)

Albrecht has been deposited on the ground, having been carried off the pitch after scoring the winner, whilst Basil Paul is in the foreground, with Brian Smith and Peter Lamb to the right of the photo. (*Copyright 610 Squadron Association*)

The two teams mingled for this photo, with many of those involved helpfully identified. (*Copyright 610 Squadron Association*)

Scene from the 1938 Empire Air Day at Speke, Liverpool, with the following caption in the archive: 'Glamour Girls—Jane Barnish, Kitty Tenison, Bill Warner, Sandy Stavert, Basil (Peach) Paul'. (*Copyright 610 Squadron Association*)

610 Squadron Hawker Hind Trainer, L.7227, at Abbotsinch annual camp, 1939. The aircraft was duped in yellow to indicate a training aircraft; the man was the aircraft's rigger, LAC Bob Clancy, a Regular airman of the Training Flight. The Hind's chocks are behind the wheels as its nose was parked into the wind. Before hand-cranking the engine, the chocks would be placed in front of the wheels. (*Copyright 610 Squadron Association*)

included military and civil aviation, thereby increasing attention on aviation and inspiring people to learn to fly. The first was held in 1934, and some of the RAF's budding new pilots undoubtedly joined up after being enthralled by the air displays at these annual events. Once the rehearsals had been completed, the air commodore finished his visit of Hooton Park by inspecting the airfield.

On 3 May, promotions were announced for two of the Squadron's pilots, with P/O Brian Smith promoted to flying officer with effect from 22 March 1938, while P/O 'Tod' Medcalf received the same promotion from 23 March, evidence that they were becoming two of the Squadron's more experienced members. The next day of interest proved to be 22 May. This was particularly memorable, as it saw an inspection of the Squadron by Honorary Air Cdre Brig. Gen. Sir William Bromley-Davenport and was also the day that the Squadron received its first Hawker Hind aircraft. The Hind had been introduced to the RAF to supersede the Hawker Hart, with a more powerful Rolls-Royce Kestrel V engine amongst its improvements. The Hind bridged the gap between the Hart and the new generation of monoplane bombers, such as the Bristol Blenheim and Fairey Battle which were already being developed. The Hind entered service quickly; following the prototype's flight on 12 September 1934, it went on to become operational in late 1935 and by early 1937 was considered an important bomber aircraft for the RAF. However, the Blenheims and Battles were soon being introduced to squadrons, and the Hart's brief interim role had been fulfilled. It went on to become a vital training aircraft during RAF expansion. From 610 Squadron's perspective, although the Hind was an improvement, it was already obsolete due to the arrival of the monoplane bombers.

Two of the men becoming accustomed to flying the Hind, were Mr A. D. Graham and Mr P. G. Lamb, who received news on 1 June 1938 that they had been gazetted on 23 and 25 April respectively (ORB). This is the only record of Del Graham in the ORB, although the Association's archive features him in a couple of photos (see team photo p. 41). However, much more is known about Peter Gilbert Lamb, another local recruit who was born in Liverpool on 16 June 1914. He was educated at Durham School, a public school situated in the centre of Durham, before gaining his commission in the AAF with 610 Squadron.

Above left: Peter Lamb, pictured as a fully-fledged pilot officer. (*Copyright 610 Squadron Association*)

Above right: 25 June 1938 and the opening of the new officers' mess at Hooton Park. From left to right, C. R. Prichard, Basil Paul, Lockett, A. T. Smith, Ian Parker, Alec Mason, Thomas Lang and Jack Kerr Wilson. (*Copyright 610 Squadron Association*)

During June 1938, the new officers' mess at Hooton Park was opened, which would have been a significant event at the Station. The month also saw the first real mention of the Squadron putting its training to use as a military force, as it carried out affiliation exercises with 64 Squadron flying Hawker Demon fighters, on 11–12 June and 26 June, as follows:

> In the above affiliation exercises various formations were tried out and nine appeared to be the ideal bomber formation, in Squadron Vic.
>
> Attacks and interceptions were carried out at varying heights between 3,000 and 6,000 feet. This was the maximum height allowed by the clouds. Much experience was gained by all concerned and it is considered that very valuable training was carried out, as invaluable experience was gained in working and wielding big formations compactly and quickly. Every person concerned did his best to work uniformly and effectively as a whole. (ORB)

Both squadrons were trying to establish the most effective means for the bomber squadron to defend itself in formation and for the fighter squadron to successfully attack the bombers. There is a sense from this report that the Squadron had pulled together and that the manoeuvres had been a success. Learning from this exercise, 610's bomber crews realised how important it was to keep their formation as tight as possible when facing 'enemy' fighters, in order to maximise their meagre defensive firepower. Being under 'attack' by fighters was also an excellent test of how good their formation flying actually was when it came to the crunch.

The following month the Squadron went for their second annual training camp, this time at RAF Abbotsinch, Scotland. It would last a fortnight from 17 July 1938, for a continuous spell of training as opposed to their usual, 'weekend flying'. Brian Smith recalled: 'Well we used to go to Annual camps

Left: July 1938 at Hooton Park—the caption in the Squadron archive is, 'Old man Kerr looks as tho' he had lumbago, whilst youthful Davies-Cooke smiles thro!' (*Copyright 610 Squadron Association*)

Middle: Hawker Hind L.7190. (*Copyright Medcalf family*)

Below: Men of 610 enjoy a picnic during Bombing Practice. From left to right, Tommy Lang, Ian Parker, Malcolm Kerr and Jack Kerr Wilson. (*Copyright 610 Squadron Association*)

'Tod' Medcalf's panoramic view of Donibristle airfield. (*Copyright Medcalf family*)

Photo by 'Tod' Medcalf showing the preparation for a practice bombing trip. Brian Smith is crouching in the centre, with Ray Chandler with his back to the camera in the white shirt. (*Copyright Medcalf family*)

together you see. Annual Camp Hawkinge, or Annual Camp Abbotsinch. That's right, we used to go to Camp on what is now Glasgow airport, on the edge of the Clyde River'. He also made it clear that there was more to these camps than the rigorous training, of which there was plenty:

> Because that was handy you see, we'd fly until lunchtime, then we used to go to the Island with Ian Parker. He was so generous, there were always parties, and you learnt to behave. And it's a good thing. Service life will teach most people to behave, because you've got to think how it affects other people—if you're all getting plastered, you all got plastered! But you did still behave.

The island Smith referred to was one of the Cumbrae Islands in the River Clyde, which S/Ldr Parker's family owned, and was used to provide welcome relief for the Squadron's aircrew. The ORB provides little detail on events carried out at Abbotsinch, but thanks to the photographic evidence from the Association's archive and the Medcalf family's collection, we know a few of the events that did occur, showing the full spectrum of what was involved in an annual camp. There are a couple of photos which show the pilots, including the CO, relaxing with a picnic, the caption in the archive stating that these were 'Refreshments during Bombing Practice at Donnibristle [Donibristle], Annual Camp 1938' (see p. 44). Donibristle was an airfield situated just over eight miles north-west of Edinburgh within sight of the Forth Bridge, a reasonable flight from Abbotsinch. It is likely the Squadron flew to Donibristle, from where they carried out their bombing practice on nearby Dalgety Bay, the local bombing range.

Training Flight at Abbotsinch, July 1938. From left to right: Basil Paul, instructor, with Paul Davies-Cooke, Del Graham and William Warner. Note the variety of flying gear, Davies-Cooke wearing one of the Squadron overalls, the Squadron badge partially hidden by his parachute straps. Behind them is Avro Tutor, K.3435, a long-serving training aircraft with the unit, '610' on the fuselage being just visible over Basil Paul's left shoulder. (*Copyright 610 Squadron Association*)

Bill Warner photographed by Medcalf, as he returns from a training flight guided by LAC Lewis. (*Copyright Medcalf family*)

While the experienced pilots practised this more challenging task, the less experienced formed part of Training Flight, or 'T' Flight. Under the watchful eyes of F/Lt Paul, they learnt the basics of flight in a more intensive fashion than at Hooton Park. Thanks to the fascinating photo of the Training Flight at Abbotsinch (see p. 46), we know this is what the inexperienced Paul Davies-Cook, Del Graham and Bill Warner were doing on this annual camp. The photo is very evocative of pre-war flying. It is interesting to note that Warner had not yet earned his precious 'Wings', his jacket yet to feature the distinctive badge, unsurprising given he was only nineteen and had barely left Malvern College.

Once again, sport played an important part of the annual camp, helping to bring the Squadron a greater feeling of unity and team spirit. A series of photos exists in the Association's archive of 'The Chesters' in the midst of a cricket match on 28 July 1938, against the Abbotsinch personnel (see p. 48). One photo has the caption, 'Lang loosens his muscles'. The Squadron does not seem to have fared too well against the Abbotsinch team, although Sgt Urquhart (see team photo p. 41) retrieved 610's good name with fifty not out!

The annual camp saw another inspection of the Squadron being carried out, this time by Grp Capt. C. W. Mackey. A photo very similar to the one on p. 49 is in the Association's archive, with the telling caption: 'Hawker Hinds of 'A' and 'B' Flights on Parade. 610 at Annual Camp Abbotsinch July 1938. (If only Adolph had known—perhaps he did!)'. The Squadron's aircraft do look impressive lined up in this fashion, but the caption seems to acknowledge that the *Luftwaffe* was a more advanced fighting force than the RAF in 1938.

The ORB is neglected for some months following the annual camp, until 1 November 1938, when at last the nineteen officers are named in the 'Nominal Roll of Officers'. For the first time, we are aware of who was serving with the Squadron, so can start to build a picture of the unit as a whole:

S/Ldr. I. R. Parker
F/Lt. T. F. U. Lang (adjutant)
F/Lt. B. J. Paul (assistant adjutant)
F/O. G. M. T. Kerr
F/O. A. T. Smith
F/O. J. K. Wilson
F/O. E. B. B. Smith
F/O. A. R. J. Medcalf
F/O. D. S. Wilson
P/O. M. C. Topham
P/O. G. L. Chambers
P/O. W. H. C. Warner
P/O. J. H. C. Albrecht (Admin).
P/O. P. J. Davies-Cooke
P/O. C. R. Prichard
P/O. A. D. Graham
P/O. P. G. Lamb
F/Lt. A. H. Graham (Equipment)
P/O. T. A. Mason (Accountant Officer).

All of these men have been mentioned already, apart from the equipment officer, F/Lt A. H. Graham, sadly little else being known about him.

Thanks to the Nominal Roll and having researched the backgrounds of the majority of these men, there is clearly a link to their recruitment to the Squadron. Most joined after attending university, frequently preceded by a public school education, although some had attended the local grammar school. University life may well have inspired the individual's interest in flying, as at least six of the pilots listed had been to university and then probably joined their UAS. However, this was an indication of the relatively élitist nature of an Auxiliary Squadron, as university places in the 1930s were hard won, and certainly were not as readily available as they are today. All had benefited from a sound education, enabling them to attend university, which in turn provided the stepping stone to joining their local Auxiliary Squadron, which aimed to recruit men from such backgrounds. The rest of the officers seem to have either been successful in business in a management role, such as Andrew Thomas Smith and the flour-milling business of which he was to become a director (he had also been to Oundle School and St Catherine's College, Cambridge), or those who were well connected, like William Warner, through his father Sir Lionel Warner.

View from the boundary. A group of the Squadron's officers either waiting to bat or looking on. 1. Johnny Albrecht, 2. Ian Parker, 3. Jack Kerr Wilson, 4. C. R. Prichard, 5. Alec Mason and 6. Tommy Lang. (*Copyright 610 Squadron Association*)

Tommy Lang prepares to go in to bat, with Alec Mason (left), the CO (on the floor) and Jack Kerr Wilson behind the bat. (*Copyright 610 Squadron Association*)

The Squadron's Hawker Hinds with their distinctive markings of '610' and the Wheatsheaf. (*Copyright Kerr family*)

The 'weekend fliers' of the Auxiliary Squadrons, had developed a reputation for being flashy millionaires, typified by 601 (County of London) Squadron, with their distinctive red silk-lined jackets. 601 was the first Auxiliary Squadron and had become known for 'wealth, high living, flouting of regulations of all kinds …'.[6] Although this certainly was not the same for the County of Chester Squadron, many of the pilots came from families with status and financial backing. The CO, Ian Parker, who had attended Eton and clearly had a lot of family wealth, had handpicked the pilots. It was little surprise that the somewhat less fortunate Cyril 'Bam' Bamberger had the following recollections about applying to join the Squadron:

> In 1936, an ad was put in the local press that an auxiliary squadron was being formed at Hooton Park and they wanted recruits. As soon as I was seventeen, I applied. At that time, all the pilots in the Auxiliary Air Force were officers—most of them were very affluent—so I did not aspire to be a pilot and when I was offered a choice of jobs, I chose to be trained as a photographer.… All of the officers in the squadron were very friendly. They were in a high financial category. They all ran cars and our commanding officer had a Rolls-Royce with a chauffeur.[7]

However, in a short time things would irrevocably change and 'Bam' would find himself flying alongside such affluent officers.

On 17 December 1938, the director of the AAF, Air Cdre Peake, paid Hooton Park a visit, with everyone keen to impress this important guest. As in the previous year, the ORB concluded with a résumé of the Squadron's strength and the number of hours flown. By May, the Squadron had gained three more officers, leaving them with a complement of sixteen which was maintained until the end of the year, although this does not tally with the nineteen listed on the Nominal Roll of 1 November. The sixteen probably only included pilots, excluding the three officers with other duties against their names, Albrecht (admin), Graham (equipment) and Mason (accountant officer). During 1938, the Squadron increased in terms of its number of airmen—by October, fifty new recruits had been added and the total of 154 airmen was maintained until the end of the year. Despite this increase in pilots, the total flying hours fell fractionally by five and three quarter hours to 940 hours and 25 minutes. The busiest month was easily July, when an impressive 224 hours and 40 minutes flying was carried out, due to the annual training camp in Abbotsinch. Once again, there is a sense of the Squadron's unmistakeable growth, however, nothing could have prepared them for their change of role which the new year was to bring.

An example of one of the officer's cars was 'Tod' Medcalf's much loved Rover Sport 'Miss Chief', complete with 'Wings' on the radiator. (*Copyright Medcalf family*)

From left to right: Peter Lamb, Del Graham (probably), Brian Smith and Malcolm Kerr relax at Hooton Park, along with Kerr's wife Barbara. (*Copyright 610 Squadron Association*)

4

1 January–9 October 1939: Fighter Command and, Finally, the Spitfire!

The first event of any significance for the Squadron, still based at Hooton Park, came on 6 January 1939 when P/O Prichard received news that he had been promoted to flying officer, which would have been warmly received by Prichard and his colleagues. Promotions were part of daily squadron life, but the next piece of news referred to in the ORB was anything but usual; in fact it could not have had a bigger impact on the Squadron, the fate of its personnel and the path the unit would take. On 19 January 1939, 610 (County of Chester) Squadron was transferred from Bomber Command to Fighter Command. This was due to the need to increase Fighter Command's strength, so that it was of a proportionate size to deal with any potential attack by the steadily growing *Luftwaffe*. It was part of a general plan for the Auxiliary units, as Hough and Richards noted, many Auxiliary squadrons which had originally been, 'equipped with bombers, were converted to fighters from 1934 onwards, and in 1940 made up nearly a quarter of Fighter Command's first-line strength'.[1]

This was a seismic shift for 610, which up until now had been preparing to go to an ever-increasingly likely war as a bomber squadron, to which all their training had been dedicated. Just over six months earlier, they had flown affiliation flights with 64 Fighter Squadron to evaluate their best formations as bombers. Now they would need to adapt to the tactics and formations employed by the likes of 64 Squadron, something which would not happen overnight. That 610 Squadron received a visit from two air commodores, a group captain, two wing commanders and a squadron leader on this day, along with the inspector general on 29 January, reflects the magnitude of the change!

The first day of February 1939 saw a return to the toing and froing of Squadron life, and it was now F/Lt Lang's turn to leave the Squadron. Since his arrival on 22 March 1938 he had been promoted to squadron leader, and he was posted to 11 Group's HQ for Air Staff AAF liaison duties. Lang had been with the Squadron just under a year, where his key role as assistant adjutant and adjutant seems to have been as a flying instructor to the Squadron's pilots.[2] The position of instructor now seemed to be filled, temporarily at least, by F/Lt Basil Jack 'Peach' Paul, who also became adjutant.

The third anniversary of the Squadron's formation was marked on 10 February, with a dance at the 'Bryne' (ORB) or most likely Byrne Avenue Assembly Hall, which would have been well attended. The venue was actually a public baths in Rock Ferry, Wirral, which could be converted into an assembly hall for such events.

The beginning of March 1939 saw the arrival of a man who would have a huge impact on the flying careers of several of the Squadron's pilots and latest recruits. The ORB reported that on 2 March 1939, 'P/O.I.B.WESTMACOT [WESTMACOTT] to this Unit for Flying (flying instructor) duties on completion of Flying Instructor's Course No. 57'. Innes Bentall Westmacott, aged twenty-five, hailed from Heybridge in Essex, and as Wynn records, 'was the son of a naval officer. His father was the first regular naval officer killed in action in the war, on HMS *Arethusa* on August 28 1914'.[3] Westmacott was another well-educated man, having been to Repton School followed by Jesus College, Cambridge, and his flying career effectively started when:

Innes Bentall Westmacott as a Squadron Leader. (*Copyright http://www.bbm.org.uk/airmen/Westmacott.htm*)

> In 1936 he began a course in aeronautical engineering at the De Havilland Aeronautical Technical School and whilst there, he learned to fly at the London Aeroplane Club.
>
> Westmacott joined the RAF on a short service commission and began his ab initio course on November 25 1937 at 4 E&RFTS [Elementary & Reserve Flying Training School], Brough. He was posted to 4 FTS, Abu Sueir on February 19 1938 and with the course completed, he joined 80 Squadron at Ismailia in September.
>
> He returned to the UK in December and on January 23 1939 he went to CFS, Upavon, for an instructor's course.[4]

His next posting was to 610 Squadron. Westmacott had enjoyed a varied career in the RAF, while he was also a reasonably experienced pilot and instructor, arriving at the Squadron with 223 hours and fifteen minutes flying time, as recorded in his logbook. It seems that there is a crossover period between the ORB and Westmacott's logbook in recording when he actually joined the Squadron: the ORB puts it as 2 March 1939, while Westmacott writes, 'Posted to No. 610 (F) Squadron A.A.F. 25.3.39',[5] just over three week's difference. Perhaps the Squadron ORB recorded when the posting was received, whereas Westmacott noted when he actually arrived.

Westmacott had been posted to the Squadron as a flying instructor, working alongside F/Lt Paul as his assistant adjutant, but also to help the pilots adapt to their new role as fighter pilots. It was not a straightforward transition, as Brian Smith vividly recalled, 'So we were old, because flying day bombers would have been just the job for older pilots. But, to suddenly turn us over to fighters …' When I asked if this was difficult, his response was an emphatic, 'Oh completely!'

Westmacott's logbook, preserved at the RAF Museum Hendon, provides a fascinating first-hand account of his role in the Squadron, the training he oversaw, the pilots he trained and the aircraft the Squadron flew as training machines from April–September 1939; the Tutor, Hind, Tiger Moth and for more advanced training, the Battle. The new instructor's first flight with a trainee 610 Squadron pilot was on 31 March 1939, flying an Avro Tutor, K.4818. His pupil was an airman from the Squadron who had now successfully applied to be trained as a pilot, LAC Cyril Bamberger.

'Bam' was nineteen and from Port Sunlight, Wirral, yet another local lad, who having won an electrical apprenticeship at Lever Brothers in 1934, joined the Squadron two years later as ground crew. Bamberger had jumped at the chance to train as a pilot and this flight was one of several he went on with Westmacott to assess his aptitude and ability to fly. This clearly was not 'Bam's' first flight, as in Westmacott's logbook it notes the numbers '5.6.15' under the column for what had been carried out, which stood for different types of flying activities, see page 53:

1. Air Experience.
1A. Familiarity with cockpit layout.
2. Effect of controls.
3. Taxying.
4. Straight and level flight.
5. Climbing, gliding and stalling.
6. Medium turns.
7. Taking off into wind.
8. Powered approach and landing.
9. Gliding approach and landing.
10. Spinning.
11. First solo.
12. Side slipping.
13. Precautionary landing.
14. Low flying (with instructor only).
15. Steep turns. (& steep gliding turns)
16. Climbing turns.
17. Forced landing.
18. Action in the event of fire (with instructor only).
18A. Abandoning an aircraft.
19. Instrument flying.
20. Taking off and landing out of wind.
21. Re-starting the engine in flight (with instructor only).
22. Acrobatics.

Bamberger recalled some of his memories of this time with the Squadron:

> The amount of training you did in the Auxiliary Air Force was somewhat up to yourself and how enthusiastic you were. There was Thursday evening ground training for everybody in their particular roles and then there was every Saturday and Sunday …
>
> … when it looked as if war was in the offing, we were told that we were to be turned from a bomber into a fighter squadron. At the same time the Air Ministry issued an order that the squadron could train four other rank pilots. I was the first to be chosen out of 600 men.… When I went solo, it went through my head that there I was, an electrical apprentice, on my own, flying an aircraft over the Wirral Peninsula. My thoughts about my life changed at that moment.[6]

While Innes Westmacott was bedding into the Squadron, two other noteworthy events took place in March 1939. The first was on 18 March, when P/O Davies-Cooke, who had only gained his 'Wings' with the Squadron three months earlier, relinquished 'his commission in 610 Squadron, on appointment to a permanent commission in the Royal Air Force' (ORB). Paul Davies-Cooke clearly wanted to make the most of his flying career and the opportunity of joining the Regular RAF was too good an opportunity to miss. He entered 'on a direct-entry Permanent Commission, as a University Entrant'.[7]

Cyril Bamberger (right) at Hooton Park. Before his flying training began with 610 Squadron, he was in the photographic section and his companion, named as Collingwood, appears to be carrying a camera. (*Copyright 610 Squadron Association*)

Paul Davies-Cooke captured by his friend 'Tod' Medcalf, preparing for another training flight. (*Copyright Medcalf family*)

The Squadron would doubtless have been sad to see the young Welshman go, as he had been part of the unit since early 1937; although this would not be the end of his association with the Squadron.

610 inevitably moved on, and as one pilot officer left, another, Geoffrey Keighley, received his commission in the Squadron on 21 March. Having contacted his son, Jo, who was very helpful, it has been possible to piece together some background information on this latest addition to the Squadron. Keighley was born on 2 July 1912 in Leeds, his father being a wholesale clothier. He went to Cross Flatts Council School, moving on to Leeds Grammar School in September 1921 to 25 July 1930, where he would probably have known Malcolm Kerr. His form teacher on his school record card commented: 'Thoroughly dependable, keen and efficient. A good organiser', while his headmaster added: 'A good lad—but a trifle self-satisfied. Bit of a young man about town—plenty of *savoir faire*'.[8]

Keighley then went up to Caius College, Cambridge, where he read modern languages. It is likely that his interest in flying was initiated during his time at Cambridge, through the UAS. Following his graduation in the mid-1930s, Keighley became the food hall manager at Harrods, a position which would help to boost morale in 1940, as shall be seen. It then seems Keighley, known as 'Peter' as he did not like the name Geoffrey, moved to the north-west, as he gained his pilot's licence while living in Bowdon, Cheshire. Like I. R. Parker and A. T. Smith, he learnt at the Liverpool and District Aero Club (possibly how he came to join 610), passing on 22 August 1938 on a Tiger Moth—Gipsy Major, (his profession is listed as merchandise manager[9]), before eventually joining the Squadron as an Auxiliary.

It is possible his link to Malcolm Kerr, now an established member of 610 Squadron, also helped lead him to join the Squadron. Keighley was one of Westmacott's first pupils—the instructor's logbook records one of Keighley's earliest flights, quite possibly his first with Westmacott given that it was entered as 'Air Experience' and that he was an 'Acting' pilot officer. It occurred on 8 April 1939 in Avro Tutor K.3311, although it was an inauspicious start to Keighley's AAF career, as after sixty-five minutes in the air, the Tutor crashed! Quite what happened is unclear, but K.3311 was never used again by Westmacott during his time with 610 Squadron, suggesting it may have been written off. Westmacott was not injured, as he took another two flights that day, but it would have been a sharp reminder both to the instructor and his pupil of the inherent dangers in what they were doing. Whether or not 'Peter' Keighley escaped unscathed is unclear, as he is not mentioned again in his instructor's logbook for another month, by which time he had progressed to more advanced flying.

Geoffrey Keighley's photograph from his pilot's licence.
(*Copyright Royal Aero Club Trust*)

Before the incident happened, Westmacott's logbook recorded a second entry for Cyril Bamberger, who had gained another thirty minutes flying time on similar exercises to his previous flight, while two other LACs, Corfe and Benson, were up with him on April Fool's Day and during the following week. Little is recorded about LAC Benson, other than that he seemed to have been an engineering student at Liverpool University, which probably explained how he came to be with the Squadron. (This is possibly the Benson in the team photograph, p. 26.) However, much more is known about his colleague.

Douglas Frederick Corfe was a twenty-year-old local boy, who lived with his parents Frederick and Charlotte Corfe in a house called 'Tara' on Park Road, Meols, Wirral.[10] He had been to school at Rock Ferry Higher Grade School before:

> he went to Park High School, Birkenhead in September 1929. He gained his School Certificate in 1934 and left on April 4 1935 to begin work as a clerk with the Mersey Docks and Harbour Board in Liverpool, where his father was employed in a similar capacity. In 1936 Corfe joined the AAF (810075) to serve on the ground staff of the newly-formed 610 Squadron at Hooton Park.'[11]

Like Bamberger—whom Corfe would have known well given their similar backgrounds—he was trying to become a pilot in the expanding AAF. He enjoyed a forty-minute flight with Westmacott on 1 April, on the following elements in his course of instruction: '4.5.6.7.8.10', indicating it was not his first experience of flying. Benson had a series of lessons starting with a thirty-five-minute flight on 1 April, forty minutes two days later and a fifteen-minute return flight to Speke aerodrome in Liverpool on 6 April, one of the last successful flights of Avro Tutor K.3311, before its crash two days later.

On 8 and 9 April, Corfe spent one hour thirty-five minutes focusing primarily on 'Medium turns', 'Taking off into the wind' and 'Powered approach and landing' with Westmacott, while Benson was occupied with 'Spinning' and 'Steep turns' during his eighty minutes in Tutor K.3387. Westmacott was not solely concerned with instructing these inexperienced Airmen-under-training, but also with the experienced officers. He went up in K.3387 for thirty-five minutes with F/O Brian Smith, to go through 're-starting the engine in flight', clearly a risky manoeuvre as this lesson had the bracketed rider '(with instructor only)'.

Following this flight with Smith, Westmacott did not take to the air again until 15 April, when he made the short hop from Hooton to Speke, seemingly to pick up P/O Mason, the Squadron's Accountant Officer, whom he brought back in K.3387. Westmacott carried out instructional flights with P/O Lloyd (about whom little is known), for thirty minutes, Benson for the same time period and Corfe for thirty-five minutes, 'Medium turns' and 'Taking off into the wind' being a focus for all of them. Once again, there is an interlude in Westmacott's flying and training, this time for twelve days, perhaps a period of leave, before giving an air experience flight to P/O Raven for thirty minutes.

Born on 31 December 1915 in Toronto, Ontario, Canada, to English parents, Arthur Lionel Boultbee Raven at some stage came to England, where he was schooled at Yardley Court in Somerhill, Tonbridge, Kent. He joined Yardley Court in June 1925, as a day boy, aged nine. Little further was found in the school's records but the following information was found in *The Yardley Courtier* editorial, December 1931: 'A. L. B. Raven wrote during the holidays and gave us news of himself. After leaving us, he was a chorister at Salisbury Cathedral School for three years. He is now at King's College, Taunton, and is hoping to pass the London Matric, next year'.[12] Thanks to David Driver, Arthur's great nephew, we know he was at Salisbury Cathedral between 1927 and 1930 and he, 'entered King's College as a member of King Alfred House in September, 1930, and left in July, 1932'. While he was at King's, 'Raven was a member of the 2nd XV and entered into many of the School's activities, notably debating, boxing and fives'.[13] On leaving school, Arthur, 'began a five year course in Architecture and Town Planning at Liverpool University School of Architecture, obtained his diploma there in 1938, and, in 1940, was elected an Associate of the Royal Institute of British Architects. On leaving the university, Raven was appointed an assistant in the City Architect's Department at Liverpool'.[14] As a student at Liverpool University, he joined 610 Squadron, like other members such as 'Tod' Medcalf, who had also studied architecture. Raven is first mentioned in the ORB on 22 September 1939, having been granted a commission in the AAF from 18 August 1939. This air experience flight may have been one of the first to test his aptitude for flying.

Westmacott spent a further forty minutes in the air with P/O Lloyd practising taking off, and half an hour with Bamberger, before carrying out a short ten-minute air test in Hind K.6654. On 28 April, Westmacott carried out a brief twenty-minute return flight from Hooton to nearby RAF Sealand, North Wales, with Sgt Knell, before carrying out four further training flights on 30 April. Having given Raven his 'Air Experience' course, he followed this up with the next three basic lessons—'Familiarity

Arthur Raven enjoying some sailing before the war, aged about twenty-two. (*Copyright Nicholson family*)

with cockpit layout', 'Effect of controls' and 'Taxying', in Tutor K.4818. Corfe and Benson both received thirty-five minutes on amongst other things, 'Medium turns' and 'Taking off', and Bamberger spent five minutes less than his colleagues on the same lesson. So Westmacott had carried out his first month of instructional duties, as the CO of the Squadron's Training Flight according to his logbook stamp. He had amassed thirteen hours and forty minutes on Tutors, plus the short ten-minute test flight on the Hind in April, taking his total flying hours to 238 hours and ten minutes.

Westmacott's logbook is a remarkable source of information into the daily, weekly and monthly training routine of 610 Squadron. As he put the airmen-under-training and officer pilots through their paces, the whole process also built up the twenty-five year old's own flying experience. May 1939 was a busy month of training flights for Westmacott, going on a fifty-five-minute flight with F/O Lambert Chambers in Tutor K.4818, the focus being 'Flying Practice and Aerobatics', this type of flying being reserved for the more experienced men.[15] P/O Lamb practised 'Forced landing' for thirty-five minutes during the course of two flights in May, which lasted a total of fifty-five minutes—a crucial skill for a single engine fighter pilot. On 4 May, Acting pilot officer (APO) Keighley returned to the skies with Westmacott in Tutor K.3435, the first time since their unfortunate crash. The twenty-five-minute flight concentrated on 'Medium turns', 'Taking off into the wind' and 'Powered approach and landing', which formed the basis of much of May's training.

They followed a steady progression, with Keighley carrying out a further fifty minutes on similar flight patterns on 6 and 7 May, before a week later Westmacott took him up to do twenty-five minutes on 'Steep turns' and then on 20 May, 'Side slipping'. A ten-minute Test completed Keighley's flying with his instructor for May, gaining two hours and fifteen minutes with him during the month. APO Raven's flying routine also picked up during May; on 4 May he had thirty minutes on the basics of 'Straight and level flight' and 'Climbing, gliding and stalling', which was repeated on 6 and 7 May for a further one hour and fifty minutes. His next flight came on 11 May, an hour in Tutor K.4818, repeating these basics, but with the addition of some 'Spinning', a nerve-wracking experience for the uninitiated. Two days later Raven went on a similar flight, but this time added 'Low flying (with instructor only)' to the fifty-minute flight. That Raven was the only pilot Westmacott took on any low flying during his first two months as an instructor; perhaps indicated that Raven was showing real promise with his flying, and was a quick learner. By the end of the month, Raven had carried out seven hours and twenty-five minutes with Westmacott. The pilots who were undergoing training flights, were also taken up by the Squadron's other instructor, F/Lt Paul, thereby increasing their flying hours.

During May, Innes Westmacott flew for thirty hours and fifty minutes, half of which was spent on the airmen-under-training, the key focus for them being to gain as much experience as possible of 'Medium turns', 'Taking off into the wind' and 'Powered approach and landing', which were basic but essential for these budding pilots. As a result, Bamberger gained five hours and twenty minutes practising these skills, (apart from a thirty-five-minute flight on the more dangerous 'Spinning'), while Corfe spent two hours and fifty minutes on the same instruction and Benson spent at least five hours and fifteen minutes on them (plus some additional time, from two flights which are obscured in the logbook).

Another member of the ground crew who had been accepted for pilot training, LAC Chandler, spent his first fifty minutes in the air with the Training Flight's CO, flying on 11 and 14 May. Born in 1917 in Bexhill-on-Sea, 'Horatio Herbert Chandler, known as 'Ray', was the younger son of Mr F. B. Chandler, the London Road printer, and brother of Len Chandler, a popular Bexhill sportsman. Ray was educated at the Country School and both boys were members of the Bexhill Rowing Club'.[16] Chandler joined 610 Squadron, 'on March 10 1936, as an Aircraft hand (810021). In April 1939 he went into a new NCO pilot-training scheme',[17] which he would have done alongside his work as a skilled compositor on a Wirral newspaper, the *Birkenhead News and Wirral General Advertiser*.[18] Now he was one of the fortunate applicants to have been chosen for pilot training, joining his colleagues Corfe, Bamberger and Benson under Westmacott's watchful eye.

Ray Chandler, (centre, back to camera), shown working as ground crew. Facing him is Brian Smith, whilst Tom Smith is in uniform (second from right), two men Chandler would serve with as fellow pilots. On the right is a member of 610's ground crew, AC 1, L. M. Fauré. (*Copyright Medcalf family*)

Training continued unabated during June, although Westmacott's logbook is less explicit about the type of training. The numbered system of 1 for Air Experience, 6 for Medium turns etc., is replaced with a generic 'Dual', the only exception being the occasional 'Test' or flight to another aerodrome. And so Bamberger gained another four hours and fifty-five minutes on dual control, Corfe four hours and thirty-five minutes (including a brief twenty-minute return flight to Speke), Benson three hours and thirty minutes, while Chandler gained the least time in the air with two hours and forty-five minutes. At the same time, Westmacott needed to act as an instructor to the junior officers. Thus, APO Arthur Raven amassed the most flying time during June, benefiting from eleven hours and ten minutes of Westmacott's tutelage, while APO Geoffrey Keighley gained three hours and forty-five minutes dual instruction. Westmacott had run up a combined total of forty hours and forty-five minutes flying time in June, nearly all of which served to bring on these less experienced officers and aircraftmen.

On 3 July, APO McQuillin arrived for accountancy duties, before he was graded as a pilot officer on 12 July 1939, these being the only entries in the ORB for July until the end of the month, when the Squadron moved to Abbotsinch. In the meantime, Westmacott continued training his newest recruits. Bamberger gained another three hours and fifteen minutes, Corfe two hours and thirty minutes, Chandler three hours and thirty-five minutes and Benson three hours and fifty minutes, a total in July of thirteen hours and ten minutes for the aircraftmen, slightly less than in June. The two least experienced officers each gained slightly more time; Raven picking up four hours and fifteen minutes and Keighley four hours and twenty minutes, including an eighty-minute cross country flight.

Westmacott again spent time in the air with some of the more experienced men, including on 11 July when he flew Brian Smith to Hatfield, taking one hour and five minutes, returning alone in two hours and fifteen minutes. On 13 July, F/O Lambert Chambers gained fifty-five minutes flying dual control in Fairey Battle N.2107 and on 16 July, F/O Kerr went up in the same Battle for fifty minutes dual control. These last two flights were probably to give the Squadron's more skilled pilots the experience of flying a monoplane, following the move to Fighter Command. As Raymond Ellis recalled, 'A few Fairey Battles were acquired to accustom the pilots and ground staff to the new features of a new generation of aircraft such as the monoplane with metal skin construction, retractable undercarriages etc. ...'[19]

On 30 July 1939, the Squadron moved *en masse* to Abbotsinch, Scotland, the home of another AAF unit, 602 (City of Glasgow) Squadron. These lucky pilots had the good fortune of operating the Supermarine Spitfire, almost certainly to the envy of their guests from Hooton Park. 610 moved in three groups for this annual camp, by air, road and rail. All fifteen of the Squadron's officers went, along with 185 airmen, representing 90.7 per cent of their total strength—quite a logistical challenge.

An interesting photo in the Squadron Association's archive, showing Training Flight's aircraft at the 1939 Annual Camp. The aircraft are a Hawker Trainer, two Avro Tutors and a De Havilland Tiger Moth. (*Copyright 610 Squadron Association*)

P/O Westmacott went via air and from his logbook it is possible to see that he flew with a Sgt Gentry as passenger (see team photo p. 41), flying from Hooton Park to Carlisle which took seventy-five minutes, then another hour to Abbotsinch.

By the end of July, Westmacott had flown thirty-five hours and ten minutes in total for the month. The Squadron stayed at Abbotsinch for the best part of a fortnight, returning to Hooton Park on 12 August. It is interesting to note how the ORB divides the time spent there into two main categories, the training of the pupil pilots referred to as 'Training: 1 AB. INITIO' and the second being that of 'Service', where the experienced pilots were put through their paces. For the *Ab Initio* group, the, 'Training of pupil pilots was carried out by "1" Flight. There were 3 officers and 4 airmen pilots under instruction and 90 hours, 30 minutes were flown. Good progress was made'. Thanks to P/O Westmacott's logbook, we know that two of the officers were Raven and Keighley, while the third appears to have been P/O T. A. Mason who had gained his commission in February 1938 as an accountancy officer. As expected, the four airmen-under-training were Bamberger, Corfe, Chandler and Benson, and these seven men operated as the Training Flight under Westmacott's command.

It is partly possible to ascertain which pilot did what to make up the ninety hours and thirty minutes carried out by 'T' Flight, by using Westmacott's logbook. Raven gained two hours and thirty-five minutes flying during seven flights, while Keighley amassed five hours and fifty-five minutes. Meanwhile, Alec Mason, the least experienced officer, enjoyed two flights on 3 and 11 August, undergoing 'Air Experience', which amounted to an hour in the air. These three officers gained a combined total of nine hours and thirty minutes of primarily dual control flying with Westmacott. Douglas Corfe gained the most recorded flying time of the airmen with Westmacott, flying three hours and twenty minutes, while Chandler carried out two hours and fifty minutes, Bamberger two hours and thirty-five minutes and Benson two hours and twenty minutes, of which the majority was 'dual' flight, a total of eleven hours and five minutes. This amounts to twenty hours and thirty-five minutes dual control flying for the two groups. Given that the 'Training Flight' flew ninety hours and thirty minutes, there are just under seventy hours flying time which are not accounted for in Westmacott's logbook, which is most certainly accurate for the dual flying time he carried out. It is logical to assume that the seventy hours of unaccounted flying time were probably spent on dual control with F/Lt Paul, the Squadron's other instructor, while some of the time may have been taken up on early solo flights by the men.

While Training Flight was striving to cram in as much flying time as possible, the seasoned pilots were working just as hard to adapt to their role as a fighter squadron:

> In view of the fact that the Squadron anticipated being re-armed with Defiants, practice—fighting tactics, concentrated rear-gun attacks, 6.50 hours night flying carried out by nine aircraft, 3rd August 1939. Total of 135 hours flown by "A" Flight and 125 hours 40 mins. by "B" Flight. Total flying times for Squadron 351 hours 10 minutes. 5 pilots, flights in Spitfires lent by 602 Sqdn. (ORB)

Avro Tutor, K.4818 of the Training Flight, with Raymond Ellis, whose memoires are included in this book. (*Copyright 610 Squadron Association*)

Some of the Squadron's Auxiliary Airmen at Abbotsinch, in front of the Fairey Battle, which the Squadron used as an advanced training aircraft. From back left to right, unknown, Eric Stephen, Pat Bannon, unknown; front (left) Arthur Rushton and (right) Joe Morris. (*Copyright 610 Squadron Association*)

The Squadron's Hawker Hinds were now camouflaged in brown and green instead of the usual aluminium finish, and 610's aircraft were painted in the Squadron's original identification letters of 'JE', as shown on K.5476. (*Copyright 610 Squadron Association*)

The extract provides an insight into the uncertainty that surrounded the Squadron's role within Fighter Command, the feeling being that they would soon be operating the Boulton Paul Defiant. This would have been a logical move for a squadron used to a pilot and gunner combination, the Defiant's gunner being positioned in its rear power-operated turret, armed with a battery of four Browning .303 machine guns. This new fighter was an exciting proposition at the time: 'The first prototype made its inaugural flight at Wolverhampton on August 11, 1937, and attained 302 mph on the power of its Merlin I engine. Its flying characteristics were pronounced excellent'.[20] Given that 'the first production Defiant flew on July 30, 1939',[21] 610's aircrew would have believed they would be operating one of the RAF's latest aircraft. However, they may equally have wondered if the Defiant would live up to its early promise, especially after five lucky pilots gained time flying the state-of-the-art Spitfire, loaned by 602 Squadron, which was so much quicker and more manoeuvrable than the Defiant. One of these pilots was probably F/O Tom Smith, aged thirty-two; he received news of his promotion to the 'Acting rank of Flight Lieutenant (unpaid)' (ORB), on 11 August, an indication of his growing seniority in the Squadron. During August 1939, he was also made a director of the Flour Milling Company W. & O. Wilson, so this was a particularly successful time in his life.

The camp at Abbotsinch also involved a musketry course which was completed by all ranks. However, the Squadron's time was not just spent training and flying—there was opportunity for recreational events and 610's sporting prowess was put to good use, too:

> Football Match was played against Station and 269 Squadron, 8th August. Resulted in a win for the Squadron 4 goals to 2. Officers Squash Rackets Tournament was also held, which was won by the Squadron 6 matches to nil. Tennis and Golf was also played by all ranks. Motor coach tours for airmen round Lochs arranged for week-end. (ORB)

610 entertained some top brass during their stay in Scotland. The AOC, Air Vice-Marshal (AVM) Trafford Leigh-Mallory, DSO (Distinguished Service Order), a Cheshire man himself having grown up in Mobberley, visited the Squadron on Friday 4 August, which involved a guest night in the mess, while on 9 August, Air Cdre Peake visited the Camp (ORB). The Squadron returned to Hooton Park on Saturday 12 August 1939, having completed another successful annual camp, which most importantly had involved the pilots clocking up plenty of flying hours with no major mishaps.[22]

Boulton Paul Defiants on patrol with 141 Squadron. (*ww2images.com*)

Some of the Squadron's Officers taking part in shooting practice. Second in line from the camera appears to be Jack Kerr Wilson, whilst fourth in line seems to be Bill Warner. (*Copyright Medcalf family*)

Once again, three groups set off for the journey by air, road and rail and Westmacott's logbook states he flew back in Tiger Moth N.6934, once again with Sgt Gentry. They flew from Abbotsinch to Carlisle for an hour and then Carlisle to Hooton Park which took one hour and twenty minutes—the journey would have been considerably longer for those going by road and rail!

On returning to Hooton Park, the Squadron would have been very busy settling back in and the next record in the ORB was that Peter Lamb had been awarded his flying badge on 22 August 1939. The following day, Innes Westmacott was posted to 6 FTS for flying instructor's duties, with effect from 8 September 1939, an inevitable move given the arrival of F/Lt K. J. Rampling on 7 August. Westmacott's spell of just under six months with 610 Squadron had provided excellent experience for him in his new role. He would continue to teach novice pilots, having spent 173 hours and fifty minutes in the air with such men at 610 Squadron. The men he had instructed from April to September 1939 had a lot to thank Westmacott for in the coming year and his departure would have been met with sorrow by those who had been under his watchful tutelage. Westmacott's logbook continued to record training flights with the Squadron up until 1 September 1939, including two flights noted as 'Flying Practice' with his replacement, perhaps to accustom Rampling to the surrounding countryside.

The whole Squadron during its annual camp at Abbotsinch in August 1939. (*Copyright Diane Reid née Woodfine*)

On 25 August 1939, as tensions heightened in Europe, particularly between Germany and Poland, the Agreement of Mutual Assistance was signed by Poland and Great Britain, whereby if Germany attacked either country, the other would come to its aid. As if to signify the importance of this fact, 25 August was also the day the Squadron was 'embodied' into the RAF, effectively making the Squadron the same as a regular RAF Squadron. The ORB records the Nominal Roll of the Squadron on mobilisation:

Commanding Officer	S/Leader I. R. Parker 90335.
Adjutant	S/Leader B. J. Paul (Handing over).
Adjutant	F/Lieut. K. J. Rampling (Taking over) 34242.

F/Lt. A. T. Smith 90337.	F/Off. J. K. Wilson 90338.
F/Off. G. M. T. Kerr 90336.	F/Off. D. S. Wilson.
F/Off. C. R. Pritchard.*	F/Off. A. R. J. Medcalf 90339.
F/Off. W. H. C. Warner 90344.	F/Off. J. H. C. Albrecht 90345 (Acct. Off.).
F/Off. E. B. B. Smith 90340.	F/Off. G. L. Chambers 90343.
P/Off. T. A. Mason 90380 (Arm. Off).	P/Off. P. G. Lamb 90349.
P/Off. V. O. McQuillin 21333 (Acc. Off).	A/P/Off. G. Keighley 90667.

*As ORB, but probably should be 'Prichard'.

This mobilisation would have brought home to the Squadron's personnel the stark reality of their situation: they were no longer learning to fly as 'weekend fliers' but could soon be engaged in a deadly encounter with Germany, against whom many of the Squadron's family members had fought just over twenty years earlier, although now in the much more sinister guise of the Nazis. It must have been almost impossible to believe that it could be happening again, when the Great War was supposed to have been the war to end all wars. However, the Squadron had to prepare for the worst and this sense of inevitability is echoed in the message the Squadron received on 28 August 1939 from Air Cdre Sir Bromley-Davenport: 'Best wishes to No. 610. I know that all ranks will do their best, and their best will be very good' (ORB). Bromley-Davenport was the lord lieutenant for the county of Cheshire and the president of the Cheshire Territorial Army and Air Force Association; it was his duty to rouse the spirits of the units under his remit with a statement of belief in their capabilities. Given the ominous events in Europe, the news that their Adj., S/Ldr B. J. Paul, was to be posted to RAF Andover as of 30 August 1939, would have been a blow (ORB). The loss of such an integral member of the Squadron would have been disappointing at any time, but even more so on the eve of war. However, F/Lt Rampling's arrival earlier in the month had heralded this change and after eighteen months with 610 Squadron, it was time for 'Peach' Paul to move to pastures new.[23]

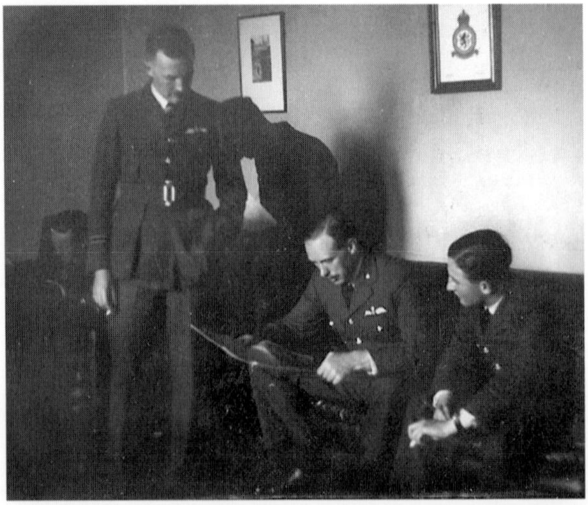

Basil Paul, standing, looks on as Jack Kerr Wilson and Bill Warner read a newspaper article. (*Copyright Medcalf family*)

In these final days of August 1939, with war looming, the last few hours of training which the pilots and airmen gained at the hands of Innes Westmacott, suddenly must have assumed a new importance. No-one could say if, or when, a state of war would exist, and then how quickly the RAF would be in action. Cyril Bamberger would later recall:

> As the war came closer, my friends and I were wishing for it. Let's have a war! It was a release from the boredom of going to work. In August 1939, I was on holiday near Caen in France when I was told that a telegram was waiting for me at the local Post Office. It was dated August 26 and it was recalling me to the squadron…
>
> On returning to the squadron, things became very intense. We were now regulars and the easy-going times had gone. Sergeants and corporals were roaring orders. The first job I was given was filling sandbags.[24]

Raymond Ellis also recalled this dramatic time:

> Eleven days after returning from Abbotsinch, the Squadron was mobilised on the 24th [25] August 1939. Ignorant of this order, the writer turned up as usual on that Thursday evening to be greeted by Fergie with, 'Where's your kit, lad? Go and get it quick. You're embodied in the RAF now'.[25]

At Hooton Park, the trainee pilots had their last few hours flying time with Westmacott; their total flying time for August comprised: Bamberger three hours and thirty-five minutes, Chandler four hours and forty-five minutes, Corfe seven hours and thirty minutes, Benson two hours and forty-five minutes, Raven four hours and forty-five minutes and Keighley eight hours and five minutes; a combined total of thirty hours and five minutes flying time. Westmacott had flown forty-seven hours and twenty minutes during August, easily his busiest month, proof of how much time he had spent training the least experienced men. Some other flights of note recorded in Westmacott's logbook for August, involved pilots who would feature more prominently with the Squadron in the coming months. The most significant came on 26 August when Westmacott returned from RAF Wittering in Battle N.2064 with F/O Ellis, almost certainly John Ellis, who would rise to fame with the Squadron. Additionally, LACs Manton and Baker enjoyed dual flights with Westmacott, both of whom went on to fly with the Squadron in 1940.

Westmacott's final day of instruction with 610 Squadron came on 1 September, when he took all his pupils up for one last flight. It would have been a sad moment for the men to lose their mentor at this stage in their training, as an understanding would have developed with their instructor, upon whom they would have been quite reliant. Westmacott flew for three hours and fifty minutes on this day, all bar fifteen minutes as an instructor and his final flight was with his latest recruit LAC Manton, in Tutor K.3435. He signed his logbook for the last time as 'Officer Commanding 'T' Flight No. 610 (F) Squadron A.A.F' on 8 September 1939, having had a massive impact on the whole Squadron, but particularly on the men who had been his immediate responsibility. The skills they put in to practice during 1940 may well have stemmed from their first few hours flying with Westmacott. He had amassed 173 hours and fifty minutes flying time while with 610 Squadron, the vast majority of which had been spent instructing these pilots. He now had a total of 297 hours and five minutes flying experience, which would stand him in good stead during the trials to come. Westmacott survived the War, leaving the RAF as a wing commander in 1958. He died on 21 November 1991.[26]

With Westmacott's departure, the main source of information on the Squadron now returns to the ORB. However, it makes no reference to the dire news that on 1 September 1939, German forces invaded Poland, an attack which meant Great Britain would almost certainly go to war with Germany. This was confirmed by the ORB on 3 September 1939, with perhaps the most significant note made in it: 'Signal received from Air Ministry. "War declared on Germany" T.O.O. 1115 hours'. Suddenly, everything had changed and war was a cold, hard fact which would have an irrevocable impact on everyone in the Squadron. Within thirty minutes of the declaration of War, the air raid sirens in London were tested, an ominous sign of what Britain could face in the near future, and what 610 Squadron would be expected to prevent. Raymond Ellis recalled of that day:

> On the morning of 3rd September, the whole Squadron paraded in the Belfast hangar. All our aircraft had been painted in camouflage colours and had been dispersed around the airfield ... the voice of the Prime Minister could be heard coming from a radio in one of the offices. Hitler had ignored our ultimatum to stop invading Poland so that Britain and France were now at war with Germany. The news was repeated by the officer in charge of the parade. We were then dismissed to think about it.[27]

From now on, everything the Squadron practised and trained for could decide the fate not just of the individual concerned and his colleagues, especially in the case of the pilots, but the whole nation.

Later that day, France declared war on Germany, as did Australia, as events took a seemingly inexorable course to the Second World War. The Squadron's move to a war footing meant a particularly busy September 1939, with a lot of comings and goings. On 4 September, with the increasing likelihood of the Squadron being on the move, P/O Lamb took over duties as the officer in charge of motorised transport (ORB). A key announcement in the history of the Squadron came on 5 September, as the 'Squadron commenced re-equipment with Hurricane aircraft' (ORB). This news would have been greeted with great excitement and possibly relief by all concerned with the unit. They were going to be operating one of the RAF's most high-performance aircraft in the Hurricane—an improvement on the Boulton Paul Defiant, which the Squadron seemed destined to fly just over a month earlier.

The Hurricane was the brainchild of Sydney Camm, chief designer of the Hawker Company, which had a proud history in building military aircraft such as the Hawker Hart and Fury. The new fighter was designed after the Air Ministry realised the RAF needed to establish an effective defensive force, due to the increased threat from Germany. As a result, 'In 1930 the Air Ministry decided to issue a challenge to the aircraft industry by formulating a new fighter specification called F7./30. It called for a machine capable of 250 mph and armed with four machine guns, and it was widely regarded as impossible to fulfil'.[28] When these proposals met with disappointing results, the Air Ministry followed it up with fresh ones, for a fighter which would eventually be armed with eight machine guns: 'These specifications were F.36/34 and F.37/34 (Experimental High Speed Single Seat Fighter) and had been issued to Hawker and Supermarine respectively as a result of their efforts on F7.30'.[29] Based on previous Hawker biplanes such as the Fury, Sydney Camm felt that:

> this gene pool was not yet exhausted… He submitted his design for the 'Fury Monoplane' to the Air Ministry in September 1934 and there was a conference on the mock-up in January 1935. On 21 February 1935 Camm received a contract for one experimental high-speed fighter, which was Dowding's specification F.36/34… The prototype which flew on 6 November 1935 was christened the Hurricane.[30]

When it was tested three months later, the original Hurricane reached, '315 mph at 16,200 feet, a service ceiling of 34,000 feet and a startling rate of climb of 8.4 minutes to 20,000 feet'.[31] An order for 600 Hurricanes soon followed. Two years later, in November 1937, 111 Squadron became the first Hurricane squadron, and eventually this exciting new aircraft filtered through to some AAF units, including 610 Squadron. It was only when the pilots came to fly one that they would really appreciate just how cutting-edge it was compared with their previous aircraft.

As the Hurricanes started arriving at Hooton Park and the more experienced pilots converted to them, new recruits were added to the Squadron's ranks with the arrival of POs Bowring and Marples on 8 September 1939. John Harvey Bowring was born in Charter-Oak, America, on 12 January 1913, but had British ancestry and later lived in Goudhurst, Kent. He was awarded his pilot's licence on 25 September 1930, aged just seventeen, at the Cinque Ports Flying Club, Kent.[32] By the time he joined 610 Squadron, he was twenty-six and an experienced pilot.

Marples was born in 1920 in Muswell Hill, London, but later he lived in Manchester:

Very rare photo of a 610 Squadron Hurricane, taken at Hooton Park, 1939. LAC Jones is in the foreground, whilst Tom Smith, right, leaning over the wing, is watching what the rest of the ground crew are doing, as is Alec Mason, on Smith's left. Mason was the armaments officer and the Hurricane's machine guns are the focus of all their attention. Also note the standard wartime camouflage paint. (*Copyright 610 Squadron Association*)

Above left: The photo from Bowring's pilot's licence. (*Copyright Royal Aero Club Trust*)

Above right: P/O Roy Marples. (*Copyright http://www.bbm.org.uk/airmen/Marples.htm*)

> He was educated at Stockport Grammar School and Manchester University. He joined the RAFO and began his ab initio course on January 17 1938, as a pupil pilot, at E&RFTS. He was commissioned in the RAFO on March 26 1938. Marples then went to 8 FTS, Montrose on April 9 and with the course completed, he joined 19 Squadron at Duxford on October 29 1938. He relinquished his RAFO commission when granted an RAF short service one on May 8 1939.[33]

Marples joined 'The Chesters' from 19 Squadron, so he probably had some experience of fast monoplanes, as 19 Squadron was the first RAF unit to be equipped with the Spitfire the previous year. For these men, the perfect chance to get to know their new Squadron may have arisen as a result of F/O Kerr Wilson's thirty-second birthday on 9 September, an event which would surely have seen some celebrations. Several of the Squadron's 'old hands' were now in their thirties and it would be interesting to see how they coped flying one of the RAF's latest fighters, where reaction times were suddenly that much shorter. They awoke the following morning to the momentous news that the British Expeditionary Force (BEF) had started arriving in Europe, while Britain gained another ally in Canada, who declared war on Germany on 10 September 1939.

On Monday 11 September, F/O C. R. Prichard departed to 12 Group's HQ, for staff duties,[34] as the Squadron's allocation of pilots continued to be adjusted. The following day saw the arrival of two more new recruits, Sgts Jenkins and Medway, notable in that they were the first sergeants to fly with the Squadron. Until then, the Squadron's pilots had all been officers, and so there would be quite a change in the social balance of the Squadron. Peter Douglas Jenkins, whose parents were Frederick Seymour and Dorothy Marian Jenkins, was born in Streatham, south London, on 19 September 1919 and went on to live in Breage, Cornwall (TNA, AIR 81/676). When the opportunity arose he joined the RAF Volunteer Reserve (RAFVR) and, after undergoing the necessary training, was finally posted to 610 Squadron.

Left: Jack Kerr Wilson in his 610 Squadron flying overalls, with the Squadron badge. (*Copyright Medcalf family*)

Below: A very rare photo of Sgt Medway on his wedding day. (*Copyright Clive Arnold*)

William Thomas Medway, known as 'Bill', was born in Bristol on 30 July 1915, in the midst of the First World War. From the fascinating information provided by Clive Arnold, the son of Medway's widow's second marriage, it seems that Medway: 'may have been an orphan, or was somehow separated from his parents, as I understand that he was living with an uncle at this time in the Sneyd Park area of Bristol. Apparently, he was working with W. D. & H. O. Wills…, the famous Bristol Tobacco firm'. At some stage he joined the VR and carried out his training in order to become an operational pilot, before joining 610 Squadron. This change in the Squadron's composition was inevitable once the group of 610's own aircraftmen began training to be pilots, and it was a sign of things to come. Gaps in the Squadron's ranks would steadily become filled with NCOs, who would come to form the Squadron's backbone.

F/O Lambert Chambers took over the duties of intelligence officer on 12 September, and the following day, the Squadron welcomed F/O Michael Courtney Franklin Mee into its ranks for flying duties. Born in Walton-on-Thames on 4 May 1917, he was only with the Squadron until 27 October 1939, so little is recorded about him (ORB). On 15 September, F/O Ellis was posted to the unit, and it seems his arrival on the Squadron had been expected, given his visit to Hooton Park on 26 August with Westmacott. 'John Ellis was born in Deal, Kent, in 1917, and educated at Sutton Valance School. He worked for a short time for the bankers Jardine Mathieson, but his passion was for flying and he joined the RAF in March 1936'.[35] Aged nineteen when he joined up:

John Ellis, in his 'Mae West' at Wittering. (*Copyright Kerr family*)

He went to No 1 RAF Depot, Uxbridge on May 18 for a short induction course, after which he was posted to 11 FTS, Wittering on June 2 1936 for intermediate and advanced training. With the course completed, he joined 66 Squadron at Duxford but he soon moved to 213 Squadron when it was reformed at Northolt on March 8 1937.[36]

'Then equipped with the Gloucester Gladiator… it re-equipped with Hurricanes early in 1939, giving Ellis experience of a decent modern interceptor before the war broke out. When it did he moved to 610…'[37] It was important to get an experienced fighter pilot into the ranks of 610 Squadron, as it adapted to flying the latest single-engined interceptors of the day.

Ellis joined the County of Chester Squadron as a flight commander, where it was hoped he could pass on some regular Air Force discipline along with his flying experience. The following day, news was received of his promotion to acting flight lieutenant. When I asked Brian Smith about his friend, he recalled:

> John Ellis, he was a super bloke! He was with 213 Squadron I think it was. He was at Wittering, and he was posted to look after 610 as the Air Fighting Instructor. 'Blind John' he was called! He came in through a tree one day… Say no more! John was a nice person, we were very fond of him and he knew us all. And that's the whole point, you know your people.

The sense of comradery amongst the Squadron still held strong…On the same day, 16 September, the ORB records the following re-allocation of pilots to 'A' and 'B' Flights:

'A' Flight	'B' Flight
F/Lieut. A. T. Smith 90337.	F/Lieut. J. Ellis 39001.
F/Off. E. B. B. Smith 90340.	F/Off. J. K. Wilson 90338.
F/Off. M. C. F. Mee 37414.	F/Off. G. M. T. Kerr 90336.
F/Off. W. H. C. Warner 90344.	F/Off. A. R. J. Medcalf 90339.
P/Off. P. G. Lamb 90349.	F/Off. G. L. Chambers 90343.
A/P/Off. G. Keighley 90667.	P/Off. R. Marples 70868.
Sgt. W. T. Medway 740320.	Sgt. M. F. Mills 590608.
Sgt. P. D. Jenkins 740830.	Sgt. S. J. Arnfield 564115.

P/O Raven, second from the right, in his uniform. The occasion was his elder sister Joyce's wedding to Edward Sealy Nicholson, in the autumn of 1939. (*Copyright Nicholson family*)

This confirms Ellis's promotion to acting flight lieutenant as 'B' flight commander, in place of F/O Jack Kerr Wilson, and it also mentions two more sergeants who would soon join 'B' Flight. To complete a busy day, Air Cdre Bromley-Davenport once again visited the Squadron.

As the Squadron's pilots became accustomed to the Hurricane, accidents were inevitable, and on 17 September F/O William Warner wrote off Hurricane L.2115 on his first solo on this aircraft. Warner was exonerated of blame (TNA, AIR 81/4758), the 'rough surface of aerodrome' (ORB), being the cause. The same day would have brought better memories for Geoffrey Keighley who was awarded his flying badge, thirteen months after he had gained his private licence, highlighting the training's rigorous nature. Over the coming days, further changes in personnel occurred. On 20 and 22 September, APO Michael George Pascalis, of whom little is recorded, and APO Arthur Lionel Boultbee Raven were granted their commissions respectively, Pascalis's dating back to 22 August and Raven's to 18 August.

In between these events, on 21 September, P/O Bowring's brief spell with the Squadron came to an end, with his posting to No. 1 Ferry Pilot's Pool (ORB).[38] On 21 September, Andrew Smith celebrated his thirty-third birthday, making him second oldest on the Squadron. The expected arrival of Sgt Stanley John Arnfield came on 24 September. He was born on 3 October 1913 in Bombay, India (TNA, AIR 81/2741), where he was educated before he went to:

> the Royal Masonic School at Bushey, Hertfordshire. He joined the RAF as an aircraft apprentice in January 1930, passing out as a Fitter of Aero Engines in December 1932. By 1933 he was based at Abingdon with the rank of Leading Aircraftman, he was then posted to Quetta in India in 1935 where he helped with the earthquake tragedy that struck Baluchistan at that time. (It is estimated that between 30–60,000 people died when a force of 7.7 Mw was recorded). During 1936–37 he was involved in assorted supply drops and minor bombing.

Sgt Johnny Arnfield. (*Copyright 610 Squadron Association*)

> LAC Arnfield returned to the UK in the summer of 1937 and applied for pilot training. He was accepted and commenced flight training at the Perth Flying Club, flying in Tiger Moths. By November 1937 Sgt. Arnfield had transferred to 7 FTS at Peterborough.
>
> In June 1938 he began flying Westland Wallace aircraft and carried out a variety of bombing exercises. He had his first flight in a Hurricane on 30th September 1938.[39]

Arnfield was posted to 610 Squadron for Flying Duties just under a year later.

On 25 September, Air Marshal (AM) Sir Charles Burnett, KCB, CBE, DSO, inspector general of the RAF, visited the Station by air (ORB). It is possible that this visit may have led to the departure of one of 610's stalwarts, as the following day, F/O Douglas Wilson was posted to the Air Ministry to the staff of the inspector general, although he would return to 'The Chesters' at a later date. On the same day, Sgt Maurice Francis Mills (of whom little is known), who had seemingly been expected for nine days, brought the steady rise in sergeant pilots to four.

However, the most important news the Squadron received since the outbreak of War, came on 28 September, when the order arrived for the Hurricanes to be transferred to 605 (County of Warwick) AAF Squadron, as 610 was now going to be operating the Supermarine Spitfire! On 30 September the unit began to re-equip with what was to become an icon of the Second World War. The fact that the County of Chester Squadron's pilots had been given the RAF's most advanced fighter to fly, would inevitably have far-reaching consequences for their role in the coming conflict.

The Spitfire was designed by Reginald Mitchell the chief designer of Supermarine, a small manufacturer of aircraft in Southampton. When the Air Ministry's Specification F7/30 was issued, as mentioned earlier in relation to the Hurricane, Mitchell and his team set to work on 1 October 1931 on a design which became known as Supermarine's Type 224. This aircraft:

> with its distinctive low-mounted cranked wing and fixed 'trousered' undercarriage, made its first flight in February 1934, and the combination of evaporative cooling and the low-wing monoplane design soon presented Supermarine with serious engine overheating problems. The aircraft's performance was also disappointing, with a top speed of just 238 mph due to its overly thick wing and fixed undercarriage.[40]

A photo taken from Medcalf's collection featuring Jack Kerr Wilson, Basil Paul, Malcolm Kerr, Douglas Wilson and two of the ground crew, LACs Fitzgerald and Rogers. Kerr and Wilson are both in their 610 Squadron flying overalls. *(Copyright Medcalf family)*

An early 610 Squadron Spitfire, probably L.1009, or possibly L.1003, photographed at Hooton Park on 10 October 1939, less than a fortnight after the Squadron was ordered to transfer from Hurricanes. *(Copyright 610 Squadron Association)*

Recognising the Type 224's problems, Mitchell, 'modified it, producing the improved Type 300, but the Air Ministry was unimpressed. In November 1934, the chairman of Vickers, Sir Robert McLean, authorised Mitchell to go ahead with further work on the Type 300',[41] and Mitchell devoted himself to making the design a reality.

> A month later, the Air Ministry issued a contract worth £10,000 and formalised it on 3 January 1935 with Dowding's F. 37/34 specification. So Mitchell went back to his drawing board and started again, going for speed above all. He wanted as thin a wing and as narrow a fuselage as possible, and a retractable undercarriage to reduce drag.[42]

The Type 224 had been seriously underpowered, so the aircraft's engine would be critical and Mitchell immediately turned to the world-renowned Rolls-Royce for the Type 300's power plant, whose V12 engines he had enjoyed earlier success with in the Schneider Trophy. Rolls-Royce, 'rated the engine at 790 hp when unveiled, but the manufacturer hoped to eventually get 1,000 hp from it'.[43] Thankfully, Rolls-Royce proved true to its word and the Merlin went on to be a synonymous success story with the aircraft it was most famous for powering.

After two years of designing, the Type 300 was built at Supermarine's Woolston factory and the first flight of prototype K.5054 was on 5 March 1936, flown by the experienced test pilot Joseph 'Mutt' Summers. Mitchell had achieved his goal and the Air Ministry soon ordered 310 Spitfires, however, the first Spitfires only arrived at 19 Squadron in August 1938. Tragically, Reginald Mitchell never saw his creation fly for an operational squadron, as he succumbed to his ongoing battle with bowel cancer on 11 June 1937, aged just forty-two. Few people can have left behind a machine of such national importance, which having served its country in its darkest hour and throughout the Second World War, is still, over eighty years on, a revered sight in the skies at air shows across the globe.

The Spitfires that 610 Squadron received, just after a year from the first operational examples 19 Squadron was given, had undergone further improvements, and these developments continued throughout the coming months. Problems with the eight Browning machine guns were overcome, the Merlin engine was upgraded and the angular cockpit canopy, evident in some early photos of 610's Spitfires, was replaced with the famous bulged canopy, which was more suitable for tall pilots and gave improved visibility. The pilots quickly started coming to terms with their new aircraft and Brian Smith recalled his admiration for the Spitfire, 'Oh it was a lovely thing, absolutely forgiving'. 'Bam' Bamberger was at this stage too inexperienced to be put in control of one, however his later memories of the basics of taking off and landing a Spitfire paint a vivid picture of what was involved:

> Taking off in the Spitfire; you taxied from side to side to see where you were going on the ground. You had to remember that you had an undercarriage to retract and you had to put your propeller into fine setting. You lined up the aircraft and eased the throttle forward—not too hard or the tail would lift up. You bounced along the grass airfield, keeping the Spitfire straight with the rudder. Then as you got faster, you eased the tail off the ground by pushing the stick forward just a little—but not too much because you didn't want your propeller to hit the ground. Then you opened the throttle wide open, you felt the Spitfire wanting to leave the ground and you eased the stick back. There you were, airborne in a Spitfire. The first task was to pump the undercarriage up. You roared off into the blue sky and when you got about a thousand feet, you put your pitch into 'coarse' and eased back on the throttle.
>
> When you were coming in to land at about a thousand feet, you'd let your undercarriage down. When you turned across wind, you went into fine pitch again and then you lowered your flaps. You came in on a curved approach because if you came in on a straight approach, you couldn't see anything because of the nose of the aircraft. You only straightened out, one or two hundred feet above the ground. You reduced your speed, keeping it above stalling speed. You might have to put a little extra power if it was dropping too fast. When the ground was whistling past, you eased the throttle back and brought the control column back and aimed for a three-point landing.[44]

There was clearly a lot to master in just getting airborne and landing this state-of-the-art machine, never mind the intricacies of flying the aeroplane effectively as a fighter in combat. Inevitably, this would have been an especially busy time as pilots and ground crew familiarised themselves with the Spitfire. As Raymond Ellis remembered, although his trade as an AC was 'Metal Rigger', once the Squadron re-equipped with monoplane Spitfires, 'The setting of angles of incidence, dihedral, sweepback and stagger were now confined to non-operational aircraft such as the DH Tiger Moth and other biplanes. I was now automatically re-mustered as a Fitter Airframe but unofficially still known

A rare photograph at Hooton Park, showing 610 Squadron's progression from Hawker Hurricanes to Supermarine Spitfires. On the extreme right is the distinctive outline of a Hurricane, whilst lined up are the new Spitfires. From the left is DW-D, L.1010, DW-G, L.1014, nearest to the camera is DW-Q, L.1016, and DW-E, L.1013 is the Spitfire furthest to the right. (*Copyright D. J. Stephens*)

as a 'Rigger'.[45] By the end of September, the pilots had been reallocated into the following Flights of eight men, under the command of S/Ldr Parker as listed in the ORB:

F/Lieut. A. T. Smith 90337.	F/Lieut. J. Ellis 39001.
F/Off. E. B. B. Smith 90340.	F/Off. J. K. Wilson.
F/Off. M. C. F. Mee 37414.	F/Off. G. M. T. Kerr 90336.
F/Off. W. H. C. Warner 90344.	F/Off. A. R. J. Medcalf 90339.
P/Off. P. G. Lamb 90349.	F/Off. G. L. Chambers 90343.
A/P/Off. G. Keighley 90667.	P/Off. R. Marples.
Sgt. W. T. Medway 740320.	Sgt. M. F. Mills.
Sgt. P. D. Jenkins 740830.	Sgt. S. J. Arnfield 564115.

Tom Smith was 'A' Flight's commander and John Ellis was 'B' Flight's commander and the rest of the Squadron appears to have been split between the two Flights in terms of experience, even down to having two sergeants in each Flight. It is interesting to note that APO Raven is not recorded here, and was not ready to serve as an operational pilot. Geoffrey Keighley with whom he had undergone training is listed in 'A' Flight, although Keighley had been at a more advanced stage in his flying career.

October began with the news that F/O Topham had resigned his commission in the AAF (ORB). As a result, 610 was losing one of its more experienced men, Topham having joined the Squadron on 9 October 1936. The following day more weighty news was recorded: 'Orders received from No.12 Group that Squadron was to move to WITTERING by 10th October 1939' (ORB). This signalled a move from Hooton Park, away from the homes of many of the Squadron's men, another step towards readying themselves for war.

RAF Wittering was in Northamptonshire, just outside Peterborough and represented another logistical challenge in transporting the Squadron to its new home, especially with the unit trying to re-equip to the Spitfire. On 4 October, the adjutant and equipment officer had been to Wittering to check the accommodation and administrative arrangements (Wittering ORB). By 6 October, the day that saw an end to the Polish forces' brave defence of their homeland, the Squadron had received all but one of its new aircraft, which was unserviceable at St Athan. This probably meant twenty Spitfires, as the ORB later stated it reached its full complement of twenty-one Spitfires on 4 December. However, only eighteen are listed as departing from Hooton Park on 10 October 1939. Raymond Ellis explained how this number of aircraft was used by the Squadron:

Mark Topham in the white shirt, enjoying some fun with his friend Johnny Albrecht, at a football match at Hooton Park, 15 April 1938. (*Copyright 610 Squadron Association*)

> The twelve Spitfires in the Flights were augmented by a further nine in the care of Servicing Flight. Of these, five were "Command Reserves", being cared for by us pending the availability of space in one of the new Maintenance Units [MUs] being built on isolated sites around the country. The remaining four aircraft were to replace unserviceable aircraft that had been passed to Servicing Flight for repair,[46]

to ensure the Squadron could always put up twelve Spitfires if required.

By 8 October, the Squadron's advance party set out for Wittering at 1000 hours, with P/O McQuillin in command, followed the next day by the main party led by Warrant Officer (WO) Bentall. Raymond Ellis recalled: 'Fully trained Auxiliary ground personnel travelled in Crosville coaches that had been liberally decorated externally with disrespectful comments about the Nazi leaders. Auxiliary airmen who had not yet qualified in a trade were sent to RAF technical training schools'.[47] Finally, on 10 October the rear and air parties made the Squadron's last departure from Hooton Park at 1100 hours. In total, sixteen officers and 144 airmen moved to Wittering. It would have been a sad day for all of them, as they left their family and friends behind and headed off to an uncertain future. They had spent the best part of three and a half years based at Hooton Park, which was regarded as 610 Squadron's home.

The full itinerary for the move to Wittering was detailed, listing every man involved in the move, leaving nothing to chance, even stating what each member of the Squadron should do with their Personal Kit. One gets a sense of the enormity of the task facing the recently appointed officer in command of motor transport, Peter Lamb! While the airmen had the most mundane journey to Wittering by road, in uncomfortable Crosville buses, the pilots would have made a grand departure taking off from Hooton Park in their Spitfires, most likely involving some sort of fly-past of their old home and the family and friends who had come to wave them off. They would have been just as keen to make a good impression as an Auxiliary Squadron on their arrival at Wittering in their new mounts, where they were joining the Hurricanes of 213 Squadron and Blenheims of 23 Squadron. Appendix "C" lists the Nominal Roll of aircraft and pilots as follows:

The scene at Hooton Park on the morning of 10 October 1939, as 610 Squadron prepares to move to Wittering. The Spitfires are arrayed for take-off at 1100 hours, whilst a Fairey Battle sits in the foreground, probably belonging to the Training Flight. (*Copyright 610 Squadron Association*)

A group photo of Squadron personnel and family as they wait to leave Hooton Park. Johnny Albrecht is third from left, whilst Bill Warner is fourth from left, talking to a lady called 'Joan'. On the far right is S/Ldr Parker, with his wife next to him. (*Copyright 610 Squadron Association*)

F/Lt John Ellis walks purposefully towards Johnny Albrecht, with Hooton's hangars and three Spitfires in the background. The lady walking behind Ellis could be 'Joan', seen talking to Warner in the previous photo. The nearest Spitfire appears to be DW-G, L.1014, which was flown from Hooton to Wittering by Sgt Bill Medway. (*Copyright 610 Squadron Association*)

Appendix "C".
NOMINAL ROLL OF A/C [Aircraft] AND PILOTS

"A" Flight.		"B" Flight.		
S/Ldr. I. R. Parker.	E.	F/Lt. J. Ellis.	M.	
F/O. W. H. C. Warner.	F.	F/O. C.* Lambert Chambers.	P.	
Sgt. Jenkins.	L.1044.	P/O. R. Marples.	O.	
F/Lt. A. T. Smith.	A.	F/O. J. K. Wilson.	K.	
F/O. M. C. F. Mee.	D.	Sgt. Arnfield.	L.	
P/O. G. Keighley.	L1074.	Sgt. Mills.	Q.	
F/O. E. B. B. Smith.	B.	F/O. G. M. T. Kerr.	R.	
P/O. P. G. Lamb.	H.	L1075.	]	To be Ferryed.[*sic*]
Sgt. Medway.	G.			
		L1045.		
F/Lt. K. Rampling.	]	Moth		
P/O. A. T. Mason.		N6934.		

*Typographical error in ORB, should be 'G' for Graham.

This is the first mention of individual Spitfires, and while most of them are just recorded with the Squadron single identification letter, some are distinguished by the aircraft's serial code, for example Sgt Jenkins's Spitfire, L.1044, and this indicates which particular aircraft the Squadron had received. 610's new identification code on the fuselage, 'DW', replaced the pre-war 'JE'. This method of recording flights undertaken by the Squadron would soon become the norm. Unsurprisingly, even this throws up some confusion, as L.1044 was later coded DW-H, but DW-H is a different aircraft at this point, flown by P/O Lamb! This is addressed in more detail below. By using a variety of sources, it is possible to ascertain the majority of the individual Spitfires the Squadron had been originally allocated, the eighteen which were taken to Wittering being as follows:[48]

On 10 October 1939, DW-F, L.1011, was piloted by F/O Warner, shown here ready to take off for Wittering. Once again, 'Joan' is in shot to see him off. The Spitfire has the small red and blue fuselage roundel at this stage and the original type of cockpit hood, without a 'bubble'. Also note the familiar wartime camouflage paint. (*Copyright 610 Squadron Association*)

1.	DW-K. L.1062:	Delivered to 27 MU, 22.7.39, then to 603 Squadron 16.9.39, then to 610 Squadron 30.9.39.
2.	DW-P. K.9960:	Delivered to 10 MU, 6.5.39, then to 610 Squadron 2.10.39.
3.	DW-M. L.1000:	Delivered to 10 MU, 5.6.39, then to 610 Squadron 2.10.39.
4.	DW-R. L.1006:	Delivered to 10 MU, 12.6.39, then to 610 Squadron 2.10.39.
5.	DW-O. L.1008:	Delivered to 10 MU, 14.6.39, then to 610 Squadron 2.10.39.
6.	DW-A. L.1001:	Delivered to 10 MU, 7.6.39, then to 610 Squadron 3.10.39.
7.	DW-B. L.1009:	Delivered to 10 MU, 14.6.39, then to 610 Squadron 3.10.39.
8.	DW-D. L.1010:	Delivered to 10 MU, 13.6.39, then to 610 Squadron 3.10.39.
9.	DW-E. L.1013:	Delivered to 5 MU, 14.6.39, then to 610 Squadron 3.10.39.
10.	L.1044:	Delivered to 19 MU, 7.7.39, then to 610 Squadron 3.10.39. DW-H soon, if not already.
11.	L.1045:	Delivered to 19 MU, 6.7.39, then to 610 Squadron 3.10.39.
12.	DW-F. L.1011:	Delivered to 10 MU, 12.6.39, then to 610 Squadron 4.10.39.
13.	DW-Q. L.1016:	Delivered to 5 MU, 16.6.39, then to 610 Squadron 4.10.39.
14.	DW-L. L.1017:	Delivered to 5 MU, 19.6.39, then to 610 Squadron 4.10.39.
15.	L.1074:	Delivered to 24 MU, 18.8.39, then to 610 Squadron 5.10.39.
16.	DW-N. L.1075:	Delivered to 24 MU, 14.8.39, then to 610 Squadron 5.10.39.
17.	DW-G. L.1014:	Delivered to 5 MU, 14.6.39, then to 610 Squadron 14.10.39.*

*(Must have been delivered earlier than this, in time to be flown to Wittering.)

18. DW-H. Unsure which aircraft this is. Later, Spitfire 'H' was L.1044, but in ORB on 10 October 'H' and L.1044 are listed separately, being flown by two different pilots. Following my research, this was probably a clerical error, with 'H' and L.1044 being the same aircraft, while the one noted as 'L.1044' should have been either L.1003, L.1015, or L.1076, which although not mentioned in the ORB, had joined the Squadron in early October according to *Air-Britain Aeromilitaria* volume 32, see below:[49]

DW-J. L.1003:	Delivered to 10 MU, 7.6.39, then to 610 Squadron 7.10.39.
L.1015:	Delivered to 5 MU, 16.6.39, then to 610 Squadron 4.10.39.
L.1076:	Delivered to 24 MU, 14.8.39, then to 610 Squadron 5.10.39. (Coded DW-V, although not 'V' in ORB.)

The Spitfire which brought the Squadron up to twenty-one was evidently the one which joined 610 on 4 December 1939; L.1043. It would later be coded DW-O, having previously been at 19 MU since 7.7.39.[50]

Another photo of the final moments at Hooton. F/O Brian Smith is possibly in the middle of the photo, with flying jacket and parachute on, standing behind the wing of the nearest Spitfire, in which the four machine gun ports are clearly visible. (*Copyright 610 Squadron Association*)

The pilot of this Spitfire is squeezing into his cockpit, its engine already fired up by the attendant ground crew. It appears from the letter behind the cockpit that this was DW-H—if so, the pilot was either P/O Lamb or Sgt Jenkins. (*Copyright 610 Squadron Association*)

Spitfire DW-M, L.1000 was flown to Wittering by F/Lt John Ellis. Here, it is being helped on its way with an 'erk' on either wingtip. Based on his attire in another photo, F/O Warner is the man watching proceedings in the foreground. Note the new Squadron code letters 'DW'. (*Copyright 610 Squadron Association*)

Tiger Moth N.6934, propeller-spinning and ready to go, was the mount of F/Lt Rampling and P/O Mason on their way to Wittering—three photos showed their departure. (*Copyright 610 Squadron Association*)

The Tiger Moth is waved on its way. (*Copyright 610 Squadron Association*)

Before becoming a speck on the horizon, perhaps symbolic of the huge change that faced all of 610 Squadron's personnel, as they moved to their ominously-named 'War Station'. (*Copyright 610 Squadron Association*)

5

10 October–31 December 1939: New Home at Wittering

Upon their arrival in Northamptonshire, the officers and NCOs took up accommodation in their respective quarters. The airmen drew the short straw in terms of housing, as they had to put up with being quartered in 'half-finished barrack blocks' (ORB). Unsurprisingly, given the upheaval of the move from the Wirral Peninsula, little is recorded in the ORB during the first week at Wittering. It does state that on 11 October, APO Keighley was posted to 2 FTS at Brize Norton for advanced flying training, to complete his transformation into a fully-fledged fighter pilot. The course would run, 'from October 11 to December 16 1939',[1] and all the tutelage from Westmacott and his fellow pilots on 610 Squadron would have stood Keighley in good stead, proven by his successful flight from Hooton to Wittering in a Spitfire. It would not be too long before he returned to 610 as an operational pilot. On 18 October, F/O Medcalf, who had been conspicuous by his absence from the rota of pilots flying to Wittering, rejoined the Squadron to bring it up to full strength, having been on his sick bed since 7 October. Brian Smith summarised all these events as follows:

> Just before '39, they said, 'It's been changed, you're now a fighter squadron'. Right! So, they gave us Hurricanes, we got them painted but they took 'em away. They went to the boys in the Birmingham Squadron [605 AAF Squadron], and they gave us the other one, the Spitfire. So what do we do then? Our war station was Wittering, near Stanford, you know Stanford on the Great North Road—it's still working as RAF Wittering. We did coastal patrols, yes, shipping, which was all learning and getting to know the Spitfire.

Another memorable day for the Squadron came on 21 October 1939, as it saw 610 Squadron's first reported patrol of the war in the ORB, as follows:

> Yellow Section 'A' Flight was ordered to patrol, orbiting the aerodrome at 20,000 ft. at 13.30 hours—No enemy observed. Weather—Clear 6/10ths. cloud at 15,000 ft

DW-D. L.1010	F/O. M. C. F. MEE.	1330–1510
DW-K. L.1062	F/O. E. B. B. SMITH.	
DW-F. L.1011	F/O. W. H. C. WARNER.	

Although uneventful, the patrol was a sign of things to come, the Spitfires circling their home base for one hour and forty minutes before being recalled, providing the pilots with additional flying time in their new aircraft. The following day, Sgt Peter Jenkins carried out a lone patrol for ninety minutes:

> Single aircraft was ordered to patrol SKEGNESS at 6,000 ft. at 11.00 hours—No enemy observed.—Weather, clear—4/10th cloud at 10,000ft.

DW-Q. L.1016	Sgt. P. D. JENKINS.	1100–1230

Left: This house was 610 Squadron's dispersal accommodation at Wittering. (*Copyright 610 Squadron Association*)

Below: F/O Warner (right) at Wittering in 1939, alongside the Spitfire he flew on 21 October 1939. He had also flown from Hooton Park to Wittering in DW-F, L.1011. Note the small blue and red roundel and the more regulation size letters either side of it. (*Copyright 610 Squadron Association*)

While the Squadron was carrying out these early patrols, the movement of personnel continued apace and on 23 October, P/Os H. C. Kennard and S. C. Norris arrived from 66 Squadron. Prior to his arrival, Hugh Charles Kennard had, 'Joined the RAF on a short service commission and began his *ab initio* course on October 25 1937 at 12 E&RFTS, Prestwick. He was posted to 11 FTS, Shawbury on January 9 1938 and with training completed, joined 66 Squadron at Duxford in August 1938'.[2] 66 Squadron had been equipped with Spitfires since late 1938, so it is likely that Kennard was reasonably experienced on them when he joined 610 Squadron.

Stanley Charles Norris was born in Tooting, London in 1919. According to Wynn, he:

> joined the RAF on a short service commission and began his ab initio course at 8 E&RFTS, Woodley, on November 29 1937. Norris moved on March 5 1938 to 9 FTS, Hullavington. He got his flying badge

Above left: P/O Kennard later in the war. (*Copyright Wynn, Men of the Battle, p. 287*)

Above right: P/O Norris. (*Copyright 610 Squadron Association*)

> on June 1. With his training completed, Norris joined 29 Squadron at Debden on September 17 1938. He was detached to 4 E&RFTS, Brough from October 9 1938 to January 10 1939, for a navigation course. Norris joined 66 Squadron at Duxford on September 19 1939…,[3]

before joining 610 Squadron, presumably to continue his development on Spitfires.

On 27 October, F/O Mee's brief stay with 610 came to an end when the twenty-two year old was posted to 46 Squadron, Digby. Tragically, he was Killed in Action on board the aircraft carrier HMS *Glorious* on 8 June 1940, along with the majority of 46 Squadron's pilots, when *Glorious* and her escorting destroyers, were sunk by the German battleships *Gneisenau* and *Scharnhorst*, on their return journey from operations in Norway (TNA, AIR 81/912). Mee's move seems to have been a straight swap for P/O R. A. McGowan, who was posted to 610 from 46 Squadron three days later, when he was also promoted to pilot officer. He perhaps had a couple of days leave, as he left Digby on 28 October at 1500 hours (Digby ORB). Before his posting to 'The Chesters', Roy Andrew McGowan had:

> joined the newly-formed RAFVR in March 1937, as an Airman u/t Pilot (740090). He began training at 2 E&RFTS, Filton and soloed in April. At the request of Air Ministry, McGowan's employers released him for six months from December 1938 for continuous training with the RAF. He joined 66 Squadron at Duxford, was commissioned in late March 1939 and posted to 46 Squadron at Digby.[4]

On 30 October, P/O Mason left 610 Squadron after about twenty months, for Operations Room duties in 12 Group (ORB).

While it might appear that this was the last noteworthy event during October, the ORB has an interesting caveat, recording what happened to the remaining trainee pilots and Airmen-under-training:

P/O McGowan. (*Copyright Wynn, Men of the Battle, p.337*)

The following pilots although on the strength of the Squadron remained at Hooton Park and were posted on the dates stated against their names:–

7.10.39	A/P/O. A.L.B. Raven	No. 2 Flying training school, Brize Norton.
7.10.39	810021 L.A.C. Chandler	
7.10.39	810075 L.A.C. Corfe	
21.10.39	A/P/O. Pascalis M.G.	No. 11 Elementary and Reserve Flying School, Reading.
21.10.39	810024 L.A.C. Bamberger.	
21.10.39	810145 A.C.2. Baker.	
21.10.39	810081 A.C.I. Manton	
20.10.39	810031 L.A.C. Benson.	Released from active service for an indefinite period in order to continue his Engineering studies at Liverpool University

All the hours invested in these men had paid off as they went to FTS to complete their training, and all of them, except Pascalis, would return to 610 Squadron during 1940 as fully-trained fighter pilots.[5] It seems a shame that Benson's time as a fighter pilot was cut short due to his studies, but it is likely that his engineering ability was important for the war effort. So the Squadron was now made up solely of operational pilots, in keeping with its operational status, as they were now carrying out regular patrols and gaining crucial experience on the Spitfire.[6] The Wittering ORB reported on the last day of October 1939, that 610 was still waiting for its dispersal points to be constructed, so was using 213 Squadron's dispersal while its flights were operating from West Raynham. It also noted that the Squadron had seventeen officers, fourteen of whom were pilots, four sergeant pilots and 145 airmen (Wittering ORB).

One of the key aspects of flying the Spitfire which the pilots had to learn quickly, was the art of air-to-air firing, a tricky skill to master. In their original role as bombers, 610's pilots did not worry about the intricacies of deflection shooting, but concentrated on flying and positioning the aircraft while the gunner did the shooting. In the Spitfire, the pilot now had eight Browning .303 machine guns available to him at the push of a button. However, bringing this firepower to bear on a target was difficult, particularly

An unusual photo of S/Ldr Parker showing a Spitfire's (probably DW-N, L.1075) cockpit and controls to former Adjutant J. A. C. Stratton. They had clearly kept in touch and Parker appears to have given Stratton the chance to fly the fighter. (*Copyright 610 Squadron Association*)

when chasing a highly manoeuvrable fighter like the Messerschmitt 109, the *Luftwaffe's* equivalent of the Spitfire. So unsurprisingly during November, several flights practising 'front-gun' firing were carried out. The first example came on Guy Fawkes day: 'Sixteen aircraft carried out front-gun practice at SUTTON BRIDGE' (ORB).[7] As 610 practised their shooting, they must have made an impressive sight and a deafening sound of roaring Merlin engines and staccato rattles of machine gun fire. But it would take plenty more of these flights before the pilots became accurate in hitting the targets.

Another problem they would find was establishing the range at which the machine guns were most effective, as at this stage they would have been harmonised to hit their target at a range of about 400 yards. However, Hurricane pilots reporting back from the early combats over France soon realised that this was not effective, and squadrons realised the need to harmonise to a range of 250 yards, to give the Browning machine guns a much better chance of bringing down an enemy aircraft. As Cyril Bamberger stated years after the War, 'I'll make a bold statement. Eighty per cent of pilots during the Battle of Britain were firing out of range—over 250 yards. But even when I was firing out of range, I was hoping that it would make the enemy weave and slow down'.[8] Work on the Squadron's aerial marksmanship continued: on 15 November, eight Spitfires 'carried out front-gun practice at SUTTON BRIDGE' (ORB), on 24 November, sixteen Spitfires again visited Sutton Bridge, followed on 27 November by a section of three aircraft, while on 18 November, three Spitfires had carried out practice attacks with bomber crews from 185 Squadron based at RAF Cottesmore. Clearly the hope was that practice would make perfect.

The pilots were on a steep learning curve, needing to get to grips with the Spitfire both as a flying machine, and as seen at Sutton Bridge, as a fighting machine. It was also imperative that they quickly learnt the RAF's tactics for single-seater fighters. With the dogfights of the First World War considered a thing of the past, due to the much higher speeds attained by contemporary fighters, these tactics mainly focused on bringing 'Vics' of three fighters into contact with unescorted bombers. Called Fighter Command Attacks 1–6, No. 1 was designed for a section of three to take on a lone bomber from astern in a follow-my-leader type attack, with an alternative means of the same attack if it was being carried out above cloud, while No. 6 was much more complex, involving a Squadron attacking a large formation of bombers. Having learnt the different attacks the Air Ministry thought would be effective and practical in 'modern' aerial warfare, the pilots would have been keen to put it in to practice. There was no better way of doing this than teaming up with some Bomber Command aircraft, just as they had done in their earlier bomber role. This gave both groups of airmen vital experience of what to expect when attacking, or being attacked by, an enemy formation.

Therefore, on 9 November 1939, while Wittering received the inspector general, AM Sir C. S. Burnett, and AVM Leigh-Mallory who inspected the Squadron, important practice fighter attacks were carried out by two sections of Spitfires with Wellington bombers, this time from RAF Marham. Leigh-Mallory would have been keen to find out how successful this training was and the effectiveness of the fighter attacks upon their return to Wittering. It seems he took a real interest in the safety of his men, as Brian Smith had cause to remember: 'Wittering was where Leigh-Mallory was our area commander, and he didn't let us out until we got armour plating behind us, which was very wise. I think it saved me in the end'. This addition of armour plating was another example of the alterations being made to the Spitfire, concerning safety and performance, which continued throughout the coming months.

On 10 November 1939, Sgt Maurice Mills's brief spell with the Squadron ended when he was posted to 22 MU in Silloth, Cumbria.[9] Then on 11 November, Sgt Bill Medway married Muriel Madge London, both aged twenty-four. Muriel was born in 1914 and her father was Henry London, on the board of the Bristol brewery, Georges & Company Ltd. Clive Arnold told me:

A photo from the Squadron's archive, showing a typical readiness scene at Wittering, late 1939. The pilots do not look very comfortable, whilst in the background groups of ground crew are ready to get the Spitfires airborne immediately. DW-A is L.1001, usually flown by F/Lt A. T. Smith. The pilots have not been named, however, I believe that the pilot lying down on the left is Warner, whilst the man sitting up in the Squadron's dark flying overalls is S/Ldr Parker. Next to him is the equally recognisable 'B' flight commander, John Ellis, whilst the pilot sitting up in the foreground is unknown. (*Copyright 610 Squadron Association*)

> They lived in Westbury on Trym, Bristol. Unknown to her father, Mum took flying lessons and was good at it. She entered a competition (in 1938) and won it equally with a man, but the prize was awarded to him under some controversy—better for the war effort coming up etc and women still not equal then! This event was published in the local press and her father went a bit crazy over her hiding this from him! Hence, her flying experiences gave her something in common with Bill. She met Bill at a dance class in Whiteladies Road, Clifton near the BBC, in spring 1939. They fell in love, and with the War starting in September 1939 and all the implications of that, got married in Stoke Bishop in November 1939.[10]

On 17 November, P/O R. W. C. H. le Fleming arrived (see photo p. 125), a VR officer who was to take over as vice-adjutant from P/O R. N. H. Hughman, who would be posted to 139 Squadron on 28 November.[11] The ORB noted that F/Lt Rampling would carry on as adjutant in order to instruct le Fleming in his duties, a role he seems to have maintained until at least the end of 1939. Monday 20 November 1939 saw the departure of F/O John Harold Clayton Albrecht, who had been with the Squadron for two and a half years as an administrative officer (he had gained a promotion during his time with the Squadron). He was not actually changing location, having been posted to RAF Wittering for accountancy duties, but sadly this terminated his association with the County of Chester Squadron.[12]

The final event of interest in the month came on 29 November, with AVM Leigh-Mallory again visiting Wittering to inspect the Squadron. 610 set out to impress him with a demonstration of a Battle Climb to 20,000 feet, then landing and a rapid re-arming practice which put both pilots and ground crew through their paces in roles which would prove vital in the months ahead. The full Squadron roaring off from Wittering must have been an impressive sight and the Squadron would have been keen to show Leigh-Mallory how well organised they were; that they were ready to answer the call to arms whenever it came. The ability to get airborne as a cohesive unit was crucial, as was the need to be turned around as quickly as possible having landed. Such skills would determine how the Squadron was viewed as a fighting force, where every second counted. 610 would have had a stopwatch out on every practice drill, to try and whittle down the time spent on each facet of the operation.

J. H. C. Albrecht practising his shooting at Abbotsinch in August 1939. Behind Albrecht is P/O 'Peter' Keighley. (*Copyright 610 Squadron Association*)

F/O Milson. (*Copyright 610 Squadron Association*)

Friday 1 December 1939 saw another new arrival, this time F/O Denis Edwin Milson, who had been posted in from 7 Air Observers' School in Porthcawl. Milson was a very experienced pilot but a complete novice on the Spitfire, which would provide a steep learning curve for him. Meanwhile, just after midday, there would have been a flurry of activity as Blue Section was scrambled to intercept an unidentified aircraft in the Sector, the following pilots and aircraft taking off at 1220 hours, in overcast conditions:

DW-M. L.1000	F/Lt. J. Ellis.
DW-O. L.1008	P/O. R. Marples.
DW-Q. L.1016	P/O. S. C. Norris.

Twenty-five minutes later, the Spitfires returned having encountered not one, but two aircraft. The first one was an Avro Anson, and they were then ordered to identify an aircraft over Peterborough, which turned out to be a Vickers Wellesley. The successful interceptions of these aircraft in such a short space of time, was an early example of the ability of Fighter Command's aerial defence system, still in its infancy, involving the early detection of hostile aircraft approaching the British coastline.

In late 1934, the Air Ministry had requested that any scientific ideas which might help improve the country's air defence should be investigated. Despite some fanciful concepts, one would prove vital to Britain in her hour of need, and the man behind it was Robert Watson-Watt. He was a Scottish scientist whose work as a meteorologist had confirmed to him that, 'radio waves were bounced back to earth not only by certain atmospheric conditions but also by the metal fuselages of aircraft overhead'.[13] Watson-Watt's reports and plans on the subject were met with enthusiasm by men in the Air Ministry such as Hugh Dowding, Fighter Command's commander-in-chief (C-in-C). Tests throughout 1935 proved the equipment's potential, and by the end of the year, 'the range of the equipment had been expanded to 50 miles, and plans had been drawn up to create a chain of twenty coastal "Chain Home" radar stations covering the approaches from Germany, and to make the new technology a cornerstone of air defence'.[14]

Throughout 1936, work continued on the project which became known as Radio Direction Finding (RDF), and over the next few years, strange looking masts started sprouting up along the English coastline, with an improved accuracy and range. To support these Chain Home stations which could detect high-level aircraft, a series of Chain Home Low stations (CHL) were used to detect low-level aircraft. The CHL programme of stations was only implemented in autumn 1939, and it was a remarkable achievement that thirty stations were operational by June 1940.

The RDF system provided Fighter Command with the range, bearing, height and number of aircraft approaching the country, and as such it would hopefully be the RAF's secret weapon in defence of Britain's air space. Without it, standing patrols would have been a prerequisite, exhausting on pilots and fuel supplies alike. The new system also meant there was a science to the interception, as opposed to the pilots looking for the proverbial needle in a haystack. The weakness was that RDF was unable to detect aircraft inland, once they had crossed the coast. To fill this void, the Observer Corps was set up, involving groups of volunteers, totalling around 30,000 across the country. They would spot aircraft using binoculars and sighting equipment, and then pass on the essential information to their command centre at Horsham, before it was sent to Fighter Command's HQ at Bentley Priory. (The role of the Observer Corps was to prove so valuable to the defence of the nation in the coming months, that the king bestowed the title of *Royal* Observer Corps to the unit in April 1941.) All this information was then used at the Filter Room to establish which aircraft were hostile and needed to be intercepted, before being sent to the Fighter Command Operations Room and Group and Sector Operations Rooms, such as at Biggin Hill. The group controller would then decide which sector would be detailed to intercept each raid, while the sector controller decided which Squadrons under his remit should carry out the interception, based on his knowledge of their availability. Once the Squadron had been scrambled, an experienced controller would direct the formation to the most advantageous position to attack, the leading pilot crying 'Tally Ho!' on sighting the enemy. That was how it would work in theory at least, and the theory would soon be tested to its limits.

A notable day for the Squadron came on 4 December 1939, as it saw 610 reach its full complement of twenty-one Spitfires, with the arrival of L.1043 from 10 MU, St Athan, South Wales. On 11 December 1939, P/O Litchfield joined the Squadron. Peter Litchfield was born on 30 April 1915 to Frederick George and Mildred M. Litchfield, in Croydon, London. He seemed to have been involved with the RAF since 1936, when he would have been about twenty-one. 'He joined the RAF VR about December 1937, as an Airman u/t Pilot (741035). Called up on September 1 1939, he completed his training at 11 FTS, Shawbury, on No 14 Course, which ran from September 27 to November 18 1939, for advanced training only'.[15] Litchfield joined 611 (West Lancashire) AAF Squadron at Digby in Lincolnshire on 20 November, before finally joining 'The Chesters'. (The RAF Digby ORB surprisingly states that Litchfield was joining 219 Squadron at Catterick on 11 December, not 610 Squadron.) Now aged twenty-four, he had recently been promoted from sergeant to pilot officer on probation with effect from 1 December 1939 and with seniority of 18 November 1939.[16]

On 16 December, the Squadron welcomed P/O Keighley back to the fold. Having completed his advanced flying training which had taken just over two months, his return would have been overshadowed by an unfortunate incident which took place at Wittering. F/O Milson and P/O Marples, were taxying their Spitfires across the airfield while practising a quick squadron scramble, when they were involved in a collision, Milson in L.1074 and Marples in L.1008. Marples was uninjured but Milson broke both collar bones and was therefore, 'struck off Squadron strength' (ORB). The Spitfire's long nose made it very hard for pilots to see where they were going when taxying, the pilot being effectively blind going forward, and so they fishtailed their aircraft from side to side in order to check for obstructions—it was easy for such a collision to occur. Two days later a court of inquiry was convened at Wittering to investigate the accident, with the officer commanding Sutton Bridge as its president, Wg Cdr Barwell, DFC. The outcome of the investigation is unclear, but it probably

A rare image of P/O Litchfield, in the centre of the photograph. (*Copyright 610 Squadron Association*)

was not a coincidence that P/O Marples was posted on 20 December, to 616 (South Yorkshire) AAF Squadron. With seventy-eight hours and fifty-five minutes on Spitfires, Marples had some experience of this machine, and perhaps he took a higher proportion of the blame for the incident, although this is conjecture. Despite Milson being a vastly more experienced pilot with 3,657 hours and twenty minutes on all types, he only had seven hours and fifty minutes on the Spitfire.

Marples went on to be a successful fighter pilot and by 1944 was leading a Wing. However, he was killed on 26 April 1944, when he collided with another aircraft and he is buried in Chichester Cemetery.[17] With Milson hospitalised, the Squadron had lost two pilots in a matter of days; twelve days after the collision, the two Spitfires were sent away for repairs, L.1074 to 43 Group and L.1008 back to the Supermarine Works, leaving the Squadron with nineteen Spitfires, disappointing given that they had only recently gained their full quota.[18] Also on 20 December, the Squadron again practised its fighter attacks, this time with 101 Squadron from Cottesmore, flying Bristol Blenheim IVs. But with Christmas fast approaching there was to be a big change for 610, when on 23 December a new CO arrived.

S/Ldr Alexander Lumsden Franks was a thirty-one-year-old Dubliner, born on 17 October 1908, his parents being James Gordon and Margaret—his mother died on 23 June 1938. Alexander Franks had been posted in from, 'No.5 F.T.S., to take over Command, Vice S/Ldr. I. R. PARKER (90335) w.e.f. 1-1-40' (ORB). Franks was basically given a week to be shown the ropes by Parker. Franks's RAF career was recorded in *The Times*:

> He entered the R.A.F. College in September, 1926, and graduated as pilot officer on July 28, when he was posted to a fighter squadron. From September, 1929, he served with a bomber squadron in Palestine, both on flying duties and as Adjutant, until seconded in October, 1931, for duty as A.D.C. to the High Commissioner in Iraq. On his return he qualified as a flying instructor, but in June, 1933, was seconded for duty with the newly formed Iraqi Air Force, where he served for five years. For a year before the war he was employed on administrative duties at a school of technical training. He was promoted flying officer in 1930, flight lieutenant in 1934, and squadron leader in 1938. The AFC [Air Force Cross] was awarded [to] him ... for good service in Iraq.[19]

S/Ldr Alexander Lumsden Franks, AFC. (*Copyright 610 Squadron Association*)

Franks was an experienced officer, with more than eleven years' service behind him, and an experienced pilot too. However, it is likely that he was inexperienced on Spitfires and would need plenty of practice on the RAF's latest fighter aircraft. As Norman Franks noted, Alexander Franks was, 'known affectionately as 'Bonzo'. He was a highly skilled pilot, ex-Cranwell, who had a marked effect on his auxiliary squadron'.[20] It must have been a very proud moment for the Irishman to be assuming command of a front-line Spitfire squadron, the crowning moment of a successful career. At the same time, it was a daunting task given the increasing likelihood that in the not too distant future, he would lead his new Squadron into battle.

As 1939 came to a close, a new plan for the Squadron's dispersal was introduced, with 610 and 213 Squadron, the latter flying Hurricanes, taking alternate weeks in sending a Flight of fighters to Wittering's forward aerodrome at West Raynham, situated to the east of King's Lynn. This gave the Squadrons more time to patrol the coastal convoys and meant they were better positioned to intercept any raiders over Norfolk. In the event, the Squadrons actually used an airfield at Bircham Newton, about ten miles north of West Raynham due to the latter being flooded. In a break from operational activity, Christmas Day was marked at Wittering by the aerodrome's CO and officers of each Squadron, serving the Christmas meal to the airmen who were not on Christmas leave (Wittering ORB).

On 29 December 1939, 'B' Flight's Spitfires headed to Bircham Newton for the first stint away from Wittering. This arrangement suited Brian Smith in particular, as his future wife, Pam, was stationed there: 'Bircham Newton—we were there once a fortnight when I was at Wittering. She was on ciphers, a cipher girl'. As it turned out, the first of these postings was highly inauspicious, when two Spitfires collided mid-flight to Bircham Newton. Sgt Jenkins, in Spitfire L.1043, (the Squadron's newest Spitfire), hit the tail wheel of F/O Kerr's DW-R, L.1006, with his propeller, which left the airscrew damaged and Kerr's tail wheel unserviceable. Both pilots must have been shaken, although fortunately they were uninjured. Nevertheless, the Flying Accidents and Forced Landings Log for December makes interesting reading, as it records that Malcolm Kerr had gained forty-four hours and twenty-five minutes flying time on the Spitfire, while he had 376 hours and forty minutes solo flying time on all types. On the other hand, Peter Jenkins had an impressive eighty-four hours and twenty-five minutes on Spitfires, making him much more experienced on this aircraft than Kerr, who was presumably his section leader, although Jenkins was less experienced overall, with 252 hours solo flying time. No investigation is recorded as having been carried out, but this incident, along with Milson and Marples's crash, is evidence of the pilots battling to come to terms with flying such a high-powered machine in operational conditions—the Squadron now had four aircraft off its strength.

The final day of 1939 was a sad day for 610 Squadron, as not only was the year being ushered out, but so, too, was the Squadron's founding father, S/Ldr I. R. Parker. The ORB noted that Parker, 'gave a farewell party on being promoted to acting wing commander w.e.f. 1-1-40, and being posted to command R.A.F. Station Digby'. Parker was looked on very fondly by his men, as can be seen by Brian Smith's reminiscences more than eighty years on, and this particular New Year's Eve/leaving party would have been a night to remember! Despite his pivotal role in forming and establishing the Squadron and its spirit, Smith stated that Parker never got the credit he deserved for it in print. Smith was insistent on ensuring that the first CO got his rightful place in history in this book. Hopefully this sets the record straight for a man who had given so much time and effort to the creation of 610 (County of Chester) Squadron.

After almost four years in command of the Squadron, leaving 'The Chesters' must have been an emotional strain for Ian Robertson Parker, but promotion to wing commander and command of a Fighter Station, acknowledged the excellent job he had done with 610. The Digby ORB recorded on 2 January 1940 that, 'Wing Commander I. R. Parker arrived from Wittering to take over Command RAF DIGBY', and that he assumed command of the Station on 8 January. Parker would fly one operation during the Battle of Britain, which meant that fittingly he was recognised as one of 'The Few'. He died on 23 December 1959 and is buried on the Isle of Wee Cumbrae, the island his family owned in the Clyde, where 610 Squadron's officers had enjoyed so many happy times in their formative years.[21] Now it was time for S/Ldr Franks to take over. The last day of 1939 also saw the arrival of another new pilot,

A fly-past by 610 Squadron of S/Ldr I. R. Parker's family home on the Isle of Wee Cumbrae. The house is just visible on the shore, directly opposite the small island with the little castle on it, between the two formations of Hawker Hinds. Parker was flying the aircraft from which 'Bam' Bamberger took this photograph, during an annual camp at RAF Abbotsinch. (*Copyright Bamberger family*)

F/O Riley. (*Copyright Wynn, Men of the Battle, p. 442*)

F/O Riley being posted to the Squadron from the Group Fighter Pool at Aston Down. William Riley was an experienced pilot, another Irishman, hailing from Manorhamilton, County Leitrim, who had:

> joined the RAF on a short service commission and began his ab initio course on August 26 1935, as a pupil pilot. He was posted to 11 FTS, Wittering on November 2 and with training completed, he joined 54 Squadron at Hornchurch on May 11 1936. Riley went to the Electrical and Wireless School, Cranwell on February 9 1937, as a staff pilot on the Signals Squadron. On December 16 1938 Riley was posted to HQ RAF Far East, Singapore, on the administrative staff, on organisation duties. Back in the UK, Riley was sent to 12 Group Pool, Aston Down on November 11 1939.[22]

Having converted to Spitfires, Riley was posted to 610 Squadron.

With the end of the year and the endless series of pilot arrivals and departures, the adjutant recorded the Squadron roll call again, a very useful source of information going into 1940:

COMMANDING OFFICER:	S/Ldr. A. L. FRANKS.
ADJUTANT:	F/Lt. K. J. RAMPLING (Handing over).
	P/O. R. C. W. H. le FLEMING (Taking over).
"A" Flight.	"B" Flight.
F/Lt. A. T. Smith.	F/Lt. J. Ellis.
F/O. E. B. B. Smith.	F/O. J. K. Wilson.
F/O. W. H. C. Warner.	F/O. G. M. T. Kerr.
F/O. W. Riley.	F/O. G. L. Chambers.
P/O. P. G. Lamb.	F/O. A. R. J. Medcalf.
P/O. G. Keighley.	P/O. S. C. Norris.
P/O. H. C. Kennard.	P/O. P. Litchfield.
P/O. R. A. McGowan.	Sgt. S. J. Arnfield.
Sgt. W. T. Medway.	Sgt. P. D. Jenkins.

The Squadron had nineteen fighter pilots at its disposal with Tom Smith still 'A' Flight commander and John Ellis still 'B' Flight commander. The men were listed in order of seniority again, all the flying officers with the exception of Riley, having been long-term Squadron members. The Squadron had a core of very experienced pilots, if a few too many of them were approaching thirty years old or more. That the Squadron now had three sergeant pilots, went to show how things had changed during 1939, as at the end of 1938 the Squadron had been the sole reserve of officer pilots.

The final event of the year recorded by F/Lt Rampling, was to report a crash which left another Spitfire in need of repair away from the Squadron. The guilty party this time was John Ellis. The Flying Accidents and Forced Landings logbook records that Ellis was unhurt, although it would have been a blow to his pride to have crash-landed his precious Spitfire L.1015, in full view of the Squadron. Ellis only had forty-two hours flying time on the Spitfire at this time, but with 680 hours and twenty minutes flying time solo, he was an experienced pilot. The fact that even Ellis could crash a Supermarine Spitfire highlighted that although it was evidently a joy to fly, you were never far away from potential disaster. In just fifteen days, five Spitfires had been struck off the serviceable list and were in need of repair due to accidents. This was a worrying trend for S/Ldr Franks to keep an eye on, although on the plus side, at least the Squadron had not suffered any fatalities as a result.

1939 had been an incredibly busy and memorable year for 610 Squadron, which had seen it undergo a massive transformation. The transition to Fighter Command was a mammoth change in itself for 'The Chesters', with much of the original training becoming irrelevant, as they adapted to flying the Spitfire. A fast, single-seat interceptor, could not have been a more different proposition from flying a two-seat bomber, although the pilots must have been thrilled by the switch. The year had also seen key changes in personnel, with the arrival of Innes Westmacott, who had a relatively brief stint

Another photo of pilots at Readiness at Wittering, again not looking particularly comfortable! Reading seems to be the main pastime of this group, although one of them, possibly Bill Warner (far right), seems to be enjoying a snooze. It is hard to make out which pilots are involved, but at least three of them are probably Auxiliaries, given their dark flying suits. Second from the left looks like Tom Smith. (*Copyright 610 Squadron Association*)

with the unit, but a huge impact on its pilots, and John Ellis, who would become a key figure in the Squadron, not to mention the departure of the unit's fulcrum, S/Ldr Parker.

The arrival of the first sergeant pilots in Peter Jenkins, Bill Medway and Johnny Arnfield, was another important shift in the Squadron's composition, signalling the beginning of the end of the image of the élitist AAF and its officer class of pilots. The departure of the Squadron's air-gunners was yet another change, but some of them would return, along with some of the ground crew, as pilots themselves. The most important event in the year was the declaration of war with Germany, which put a completely different complexion on their role as 'weekend fliers'. Now they would be relied upon equally to perform their duty with the RAF's regular squadrons, with the grim possibility of paying the ultimate sacrifice. After such a hectic 1939, 610 Squadron's personnel must have faced the new year with trepidation, but they could never have expected the weight of responsibility which would fall on their shoulders in 1940.

An atmospheric photograph of 610 Squadron's Spitfires, DW-E and DW-K, ready for action, probably at RAF Wittering. The Squadron's identification letters are larger on DW-E, whilst DW-K has the earlier, smaller style lettering. Both aircraft still have the small blue and red roundel. (*Copyright 610 Squadron Association*)

6

1 January–9 May 1940: Convoy Patrols from Bircham Newton and Prestwick

There is some confusion over the first entry in the Squadron's ORB for 1940, as on 1 January, the only record is that, 'At 1110 hours "B" Flight proceeded to Advanced Landing Ground [ALG] at Bircham Newton'. Yet it was assumed that 'B' Flight was already there, having flown there on 29 December ostensibly for a week, and there is no mention of their return in the interim period. The next day, 'A' Flight followed them to Bircham Newton at 0825 hours, but it was only Blue Section of 'B' Flight who had the opportunity of an interception, being scrambled at 0930 hours. John Ellis in Spitfire DW-M, L.1000 leading F/O Lambert Chambers (DW-P, K.9960) and Sgt Jenkins (DW-Q, L.1016), were ordered to patrol Cromer at 15,000 feet, but during the course of a forty-five-minute patrol no enemy aircraft were sighted. At 1600 hours, the whole Squadron returned to Wittering.

Throughout the course of January to March 1940, such activities would become the norm, either 'A' or 'B' Flight moving to the ALG at Bircham Newton to carry out a mundane patrol over the east coast convoys. Rather than recording each of these patrols, throughout the chapter I've provided a record of the number of patrols carried out each month, to give an idea of the scale of the task they were undertaking, along with any incidents which were out of the ordinary. These patrols must have been incredibly frustrating for the pilots, as well as being tiring and keeping the men constantly on edge, as there could potentially be contact with a German aircraft every time they went up. On the other hand, it provided vital experience for the pilots in operating under wartime conditions as sections and flights, being vectored around by the ground controllers using a system still in its infancy.[1] Also, it seemed that if they did encounter enemy aircraft, they were likely to be lone bombers which they had been thoroughly trained to intercept. Fighter Command's pilots had to become accustomed to such activities as a daily routine.

'A' Flight enjoyed a break from the monotony of patrols on 4 January, when they carried out further affiliation exercises with Bomber Command. This time it was with the Hampdens of 44 Squadron from RAF Waddington, involving a series of exercises at Wittering, probably more practice attacks on bomber formations. Although perhaps not the best tactics, at least the pilots were getting used to 'engaging' bombers, which gave them an inkling of what to expect. Some good news was received by twenty-five-year-old P/O Peter Lamb on 9 January, when 'A' Flight was at Bircham Newton, as he heard he had been promoted to flying officer with effect from 25 October 1939. On 12 January, F/O Brian Smith celebrated his twenty-fifth birthday, while on 15 January, work was completed on No. 6 Barrack Block, to provide better accommodation for the airmen. The new block had been under construction since 610 Squadron was posted to Wittering in October 1939.

Saturday 20 January proved to be quite an eventful day, 'A' Flight being based at Bircham, while 'B' Flight were at Wittering (12 Group's ORB Appendices). F/Lt Tom Smith in DW-A, L.1001, supported by F/O Warner (DW-F, L.1011) and the recently promoted F/O Lamb (DW-G, L.1014) carried out a patrol off Wells at 1335 hours, lasting twenty-five minutes. F/Lt Smith was ordered to lead his section to 5,000 feet to identify a lone aircraft and the Spitfire pilots must have been surprised to encounter a flight of six Wellington bombers! P/O 'Peter' Keighley wrote up the ORB during January, and he adds some interesting snippets of information to the descriptions of the flights. On this occasion, he recorded, 'Section left ground in 6 minutes from Operations telephone first ringing'. He also noted that the Radio Telephony (R/T) system which enabled communication between the ground controller and the pilots, and between the pilots themselves, had been good. This is further proof that the Squadron was constantly monitoring everything they did operationally in a bid to improve it.

The need to reduce the time taken to get the Spitfires airborne was critical, while the performance of the R/T was equally important in enabling the necessary communication channels for a successful interception. Red Section was back on the ground by 1400 hours but during the afternoon the Flight was struck by illness, two pilots having contracted measles. One of them was Peter Lamb, who had participated in the earlier patrol, while the other was P/O Hugh Kennard, who had now been with the Squadron for three months. To avoid further contamination amongst 'A' Flight's pilots, the two men were sent by ambulance back to Wittering for medical attention. Meanwhile, 'B' Flight was also having a busy time, carrying out affiliation exercises with the Blenheims of 101 Squadron, which probably involved further practice of the 'Fighter Attacks'. This was followed up with some air-to-ground firing at Sutton Bridge, the pilots expending 16,900 rounds of ammunition. It is likely that these two exercises were carried out in the morning, as, 'Snow fell heavily in the afternoon' (ORB).

During 23 January, two new pilots arrived, P/O Philip Stephen Baddesley Ensor and Sgt Barrowman from 12 Group's Pool, while P/O Antonio Simmons Dini, a New Zealander, departed for 66 Squadron at Duxford. Dini had only joined 610 Squadron four days earlier on 19 January, the only reference to him. Dini's life was cut short while with 605 Squadron on 31 May 1940. After taking off from Hawkinge in Hurricane L.2117, it is thought he was overcome by fumes from a glycol leak due to an overheating engine, which led to him stalling and crashing. Dini was killed instantly (TNA, AIR 81/2186). It was particularly sad, as he was about to get engaged. P/O Dini is buried in Hawkinge Cemetery.

In terms of the two new pilots, while little is recorded of George Barrowman, Philip Ensor:

> was born in Beckenham, Kent in 1920 and educated at Bradfield College. He joined the RAF on a short service commission and began his flying training on June 27 1938, as a pupil pilot.
>
> He completed his training and at the outbreak of war he was with 'D' Flight of No 2 AACU [Anti-Aircraft Co-operation Unit] at Eastchurch. Ensor joined 229 Squadron at Digby from Eastchurch on December 4 1939. Six days later he went to 12 Group Pool, Aston Down, for further training. He rejoined 229 on January 12 1940 at Digby.[2]

He then joined 610 Squadron.

On 25 January at 1050 hours, F/Lt Smith in DW-A, L.1001, took off on an interception with F/O Warner (DW-F, L. 1011) and F/O Riley (DW-O, L. 1043), as follows:

> … ordered to patrol SHERINGHAM at 6,000 feet. They were then given three successive courses to steer, and sighted 3 aircraft flying S.W. Control refused permission to investigate and section were sent to CROMER at 3,000 feet, and thence along the coast to WELLS. They were then ordered to land. No other aircraft sighted. R/T was good. Section left ground in 4.5 minutes. (ORB)

They landed at 1120 hours, and once again, the pilots' frustration is almost tangible. Having been refused permission to investigate the unknown aircraft, one can only assume that the Controller already knew that it was an RAF formation! It is interesting to note that the time taken for the section to get airborne was an improvement of a vital minute and a half on the previous time of four days earlier. The Squadron would continue to work on whittling this time down.

P/O Philip Stephen Baddesley Ensor. (*Copyright Wynn, Men of the Battle, p. 158*)

The following day was distinctly more eventful for Sgt Arnfield. The twenty-six year old had been flying a 'Dummy Run' in Spitfire DW-R, L.1006, but was experiencing difficulty in maintaining R/T communication. Presumably in bad weather, Arnfield lost his bearings and, short on fuel, was forced to land twelve miles north of Driffield, in the East Riding of Yorkshire! It is no surprise he had run out of fuel as he was just under 100 miles from his home airfield, but his embarrassment at getting so lost would have been slightly assuaged, by the fact that he had successfully got his machine down undamaged. Once his Spitfire had been refuelled, Arnfield was confident he could fly it out of the field and back home. But luck was not on his side. The bad weather struck again with another heavy snowfall and his Spitfire was snowed in. Johnny Arnfield was forced to make an ignominious return journey to Wittering by train, while 'L.1006 was dismantled and taken by road to RAF Station, Leconfield for re-assembly' (ORB).

Arnfield would doubtless have been the butt of jokes as a result of this incident, but he had actually managed to do remarkably well given his predicament. The fact that Arnfield and his Spitfire had survived unscathed was proof of his skill as a pilot, which would stand him in good stead for any future trials. The heavy snowfall which had struck in Driffield, also hit Wittering, making flying impossible on 28 and 29 January, although ashes and sand were sprinkled liberally on the runway to try and clear it and improve the surface (Wittering ORB).

A relative flurry of activity for 'A' Flight came on 30 January, despite the weather still being far from ideal for flying. According to Wittering's ORB, snow ploughs had been brought in to clear the runways, and 610's ORB describes the first patrol, including the difficulties in getting the three Spitfires airborne:

> Red section, "A" Flight, F/Lt. A. T. Smith (DW-D, L.1010), F/O. W. H. C. Warner (DW-N, L.1075) and P/O. R. A. McGowan (DW-G, L.1014) were ordered to patrol convoy. When order was given the aircraft were grounded and in the hangar undergoing a modification. The section taxied out 11 minutes after receiving the order. Owing to snow on the aerodrome and the necessity of removing snow from the intakes before taking off, a further 6 minutes were required before the section were airborne. The convoy was picked up South of HALESBOROUGH LIGHT. Patrol was maintained for one hour. Visibility 1,000 yards, cloud 10/10, 600 feet. Two climbs were made through the clouds at 4,000 feet in an endeavour to establish R/T communication with the ground. Time took off 1200 hours. Time landed 1335 hours.

Although the caption shows it was taken at the end of 1939, this photo gives a good idea of how heavy the snowfall was going into early 1940. It would certainly have made flying impossible. The ground crew faced an unenviable task trying to keep the Squadron operational, with little more than spades to help them. (*Copyright 610 Squadron Association*)

It is surprising that while the Spitfires were grounded for modification, they should be expected to go on patrol. The detailed description highlights the problems that the ground crew and pilots ran into on this patrol—despite their best efforts, they could not be expected to find any enemy aircraft given the extent of the cloud cover. Notwithstanding the trials involved in getting Red Section up, just under an hour later Yellow Section received instructions for a patrol, with F/Lt Smith leading in DW-A, L.1001, followed by F/O Riley (DW-N, L.1075) and F/O Smith (DW-G, L.1014). Tom Smith received instructions to lead his men on a:

> patrol 10 miles out to sea, CROMER to WIMBERTON. Patrol was carried out between HALESBOROUGH and NEWART LIGHT. Visibility was poor. One tanker and one drifter sighted. Time of take-off 1425 hours. Time landed 1550 hours. (ORB)

The poor visibility must have made these convoy patrols nerve-wracking experiences. The greatest danger probably came from a mid-air collision with another Spitfire, although the pilots would have opened up their usually tight 'Vic' formation to reduce this likelihood. The ORB does not record whether 'A' Flight was still operating out of Bircham Newton, as they had gone there on 18 January with no mention of returning to Wittering. The fact that Red Section's aircraft were being modified in a hanger perhaps indicates that they were back at Wittering, as it is unlikely that an ALG had the full facilities of an established Station like Wittering.

However, 'B' Flight was also in operation on this day, seemingly from its home station: 'Blue section, "B" Flight, were ordered to patrol 10 miles out to sea from CROMER, at 1330 HOURS. No E/A [enemy aircraft] sighted, and patrol returned to WITTERING at 1510 hours' (ORB). The uneventful patrol involved: F/O Kerr Wilson (DW-L, L.1017), F/O Medcalf (DW-H, L.1044) and P/O Norris in (DW-Q, L.1016), thus completing fourteen hours of patrol work by the Squadron in very trying circumstances. P/O Keighley's last comment in the ORB for January, was to note down the total flying hours for the month, which came in at 261 hours and twenty minutes and involved at least fifteen recorded patrols of varying strength. This was despite the bad weather, which had brought the aerodromes to a standstill for some days.

The arrival of February did not bring an immediate improvement in the weather, little work being carried out on the first two days of the month, the first mention of any flying only appearing on 3 February. F/Lt A. T. Smith was again sent up in very difficult conditions, flying DW-A, L.1001:

> Ordered to intercept E/A approaching WELLS from CROMER. Flew from WELLS to CROMER at 50 feet, penetrated cloud at 3,000 feet at CROMER to obtain R/T instructions. Told to return to WELLS to hunt E/A and if nothing seen, to land. At WELLS told E/A at HUNSTANTON. Went there and told E/A at CROMER. Continued chase at 50 feet. When East of OVERSTRAND saw people pointing East in direction E/A had gone. At HAPPISBURG climbed to 5,000 feet to obtain R/T instructions and was told E/A were 10 miles ahead. Came down and continued to GREAT YARMOUTH, lost R/T touch, later picked up order to land—Visibility at sea not more than 500 yards. Duration of flight 1.20 hours. (ORB)

Smith showed real determination in his pursuit of the enemy aircraft around the Norfolk coastline, in a flight which put his navigational skills to the test, along with his actual flying ability at such low altitudes in the cloud and fog. Amazingly, he was given assistance in his hunt for the elusive enemy aircraft by people pointing out its flight path, while on his return flight, he was so low that 'small boys threw stones at his aircraft without registering any hits' (ORB), an additional and unexpected threat to an already dangerous flight.

The actions of one of the Squadron's oldest and longest-serving members had not gone unnoticed however, and, 'his very fine performance' was 'highly praised' (ORB) by the AOC. The weather through which Tom Smith had ploughed on regardless clearly worsened, and from 4–8 February, flying was impossible for 610 Squadron, with Wittering and Bircham Newton being unserviceable due to the deep snow. On 4 February, 'A' Flight was based at Bircham, with 213's Red Section (12 Group's ORB).

By 9 February, the weather had improved and the airfields were operational again. Yellow Section, composed of F/O Warner (DW-F, L.1011), P/O Kennard (DW-D, L.1010) and Sgt Jenkins (DW-N, L.1075) took off at 0900 hours to patrol the Halesborough, Newark Knoll and Hammond's Knoll lightships, and returned to Bircham Newton two hours later. This patrol was slightly more eventful than usual as Hugh Kennard was forced to return after just ten minutes with an engine problem, leaving Warner and Jenkins to carry on. It is interesting to note that P/O Kennard, as well as Lamb, were back on duty, having recovered from the measles. They had been sent back to Wittering on 20 January, and it seems likely that they rejoined their Flight at Bircham Newton during the period when the two airfields were snow-bound. However, illness struck again. On 10 February, F/O Kerr was admitted to hospital at Wittering with, 'Pharyngitis, malaise and sore throat', being discharged when he had recovered, on Valentine's Day (TNA, AIR 81/670).

Photo taken by Medcalf at an earlier date, with Tom Smith flanked by Douglas Wilson, left, and Ian Parker, right, who had now both left the Squadron. (*Copyright Medcalf family*)

A remarkable photo of the aftermath of Sgt Barrowman's landing in DW-D, L.1010, in snowy conditions. *(Copyright 610 Squadron Association)*

On 15 February, 12 Group's AOC, Trafford Leigh-Mallory, visited Wittering once again. Before the inevitable dinner, 'he spoke to all Officers and operational pilots on the methods which are being employed by the Group' (ORB), the focus being on 'Air Defence Measures for this Group' (Wittering ORB). This presumably involved the flying training schedule, as the Squadron had some inexperienced pilots who still needed further training on Spitfires. One of these was Sgt George Barrowman, who just the day before the AOC's visit had come a cropper while landing DW-D, L.1010. His inexperience on the aircraft was put as the reason for the bad landing, causing his Spitfire to, 'skid on its nose, thereby buckling the airscrew' (ORB). Such incidents, although inevitable, needed to be kept to a minimum, as they were costly in terms of aircraft, but more importantly put an added risk on the pilots' lives. Leigh-Mallory left Wittering on 16 February, just in time to avoid the thaw which began on the 18th and made the aerodrome unserviceable for a short spell (Wittering ORB).

On the morning of 19 February, with 'A' Flight ready to head back to Wittering, the discovery of a case of infantile paralysis at Bircham meant that pilots who had flown there the previous day would now be forced to stay at the ALG for nine days, until the outbreak had been cleared. This would have been an unexpected and unpopular eventuality. However, infantile paralysis is a serious infectious disease and it was a necessary precaution to prevent further contagion.

On 22 February, at 1225 hours, Red Section set off on yet another convoy patrol which involved:

DW-H. L.1044	F/O. W. RILEY.
DW-F. L.1011	P/O. H. C. KENNARD.
DW-G. L.1014	P/O. G. KEIGHLEY.

While no aircraft were encountered, the pilots reported seeing two convoys beneath them. The patrol certainly ended in an eventful manner for Red 3, P/O Kennard, whose misfortune continued as he had managed to run short of petrol and made a, 'forced landing at 1410 hours one mile to the east of Stiffkey' (ORB), not far from the Norfolk coast. The patrol had lasted one hour and forty-five minutes for Kennard, so he should have been able to get back, as the rest of his section returned to their airfield just five minutes later. No real harm was done though, as Kennard's Spitfire was undamaged and as in other examples, getting his machine down safely in a tricky situation reflected very well on the pilot officer's flying skills.

It had been a busy day for the Squadron, flying twelve sorties which amounted to nineteen hours and fifty-five minutes flying time. This makes it clear how exhausting such convoy patrols were. Although it was proving unlikely that enemy aircraft were going to be encountered, the fighter pilots could never relax from the moment they took off until they were safely back down on their aerodrome again, and this constant strain was debilitating.

An example of this arose on 23 February, involving Yellow Section, when the final patrol took off at 1310 hours. They were off the ground for precisely an hour, being ordered to patrol Sheringham at 17,000 feet before being instructed to gain altitude and patrol at 25,000 feet. The three pilots were F/O Riley (DW-P, K.9960), F/O Kerr (DW-L, L.1017) and Sgt Arnfield (DW-K, L.1062), and nothing untoward happened during the flight. However, just when Sgt Arnfield thought he could relax, he had the misfortune of taxying over a hole in the ground which caused his Spitfire's airscrew to buckle and left him shaken. There is some confusion over whether Arnfield was flying DW-K, L.1062 as recorded in the 'Detail of work carried out' section of the ORB, or DW-J, L.1003, as noted in the 'Summary of Events' section. But on 26 February, P/O le Fleming added this correction: 'For Spitfire L.1003 in item of 23 February, read Spitfire L.1062, otherwise precisely the same narrative', so Arnfield had actually been flying DW-K, L.1062. This aircraft was not reported as flying again until 3 March, while DW-J, L.1003 is not listed as flying again until 7 March 1940.

After being on standby for three consecutive days, 610 Squadron seems to have enjoyed a few days without carrying out any of the tedious patrols which had become their bread and butter. 213 Squadron perhaps took the strain. On 28 February, there was cause for a celebration, as it was the twenty-third birthday of 'B' Flight's young commander, John Ellis. This opportunity to wind down would not have been missed and there would have been some drinks consumed either in the mess or the local pub. Although the ORB does not report it, the Squadron's pilots who had been at Bircham Newton since the outbreak of infantile paralysis, would have returned to Wittering on 28 February too. This was nine days on from when the outbreak was reported, although it is difficult to confirm who was patrolling from where given the lack of definite information.

On 29 February, 'A' Flight headed off from Wittering for Bircham, led by F/Lt Tom Smith. However, the visit to the ALG did not go smoothly, as another Spitfire ran into a pot hole, this time DW-H, L.1044, piloted by F/O Warner. In his report, P/O le Fleming stated that, 'On this occasion, however, only the pitot head was damaged' (ORB). It seems likely that this happened after the first patrol, as Warner flew DW-H as one of three Spitfires which took part in Red Section's patrol of a convoy of forty to fifty ships. By the time 610 Squadron carried out its final patrol of the month on 29 February, they had carried out at least twenty-two recorded patrols without any sign of the *Luftwaffe*, having spent at least ninety-two hours and fifty-five minutes recorded flying time largely on such patrols. However, all this time in their relatively unfamiliar fighter aircraft was very important in helping pilots come to terms with the Spitfire in wartime conditions.

March was to prove similar to February in the amount of convoy patrols performed by the Squadron and the comings and goings of personnel, with Saint David's Day setting the tone. The Squadron welcomed back F/O Milson from RAF Depot Uxbridge, following his recuperation from breaking both clavicles on 16 December 1939—the return of such an experienced pilot represented a real boost to its operational strength. The Squadron also received another pilot for flying duties with the arrival of P/O Victor Thomas Laurence Wood, who had been transferred from 23 Squadron, a man of whom little is recorded. His arrival seems to have been a direct swap of personnel, as P/O Ensor was posted to 23 Squadron after only a brief spell with 610 Squadron. Ensor went on to serve with distinction in 23 Squadron as a night fighter pilot, but lost his life on 8 September 1941, aged just twenty-one. He is buried in Kerfautras Cemetery, Brest.[3]

Meanwhile, the Squadron carried out nine section patrols throughout the day involving both of 'A' Flight's Sections and 'B' Flight's Blue Section, which ran from 0730 hours to the last one landing

610 Squadron's two Flight Commanders, John Ellis (left) of 'B' Flight and Tom Smith of 'A' Flight. They played a vital role in ensuring the Squadron functioned as an effective fighting force in their Spitfires. (*Copyright 610 Squadron Association*)

at 1845 hours. The whole Squadron was based at Bircham Newton on this day (12 Group ORB). The patrols passed uneventfully, but the pilots amassed thirty-seven flying hours, making it another exhausting day. The three sections had split the day's patrol work evenly, to avoid one section becoming over-worked and to share the flying time and experience between as many pilots as possible.

On the morning of 2 March, 'A' Flight was based at Bircham, while 'B' Flight returned to Wittering (12 Group ORB Appendices). Another full day of convoy patrols was carried out on 3 March, nine in total, the first one taking off at 0710 hours and the last one landing at 1845 hours. With all four sections being used, more pilots were inevitably called upon. Some sections used different pilots, so in actual fact fifteen different pilots flew operationally during the course of the day, eleven of them flying twice, with twenty-six sorties being flown. The landing strip at Bircham Newton again caused the drama of the day—this time it was F/O Riley who was the unfortunate pilot to taxi his Spitfire, L.1045, over ground which gave way, 'thus causing the wheel to fall into the hole thereby bending the airscrew on contact with ground' (ORB). This probably occurred upon arrival at the aerodrome or departure of Red Section for the first patrol, explaining why it only involved two aircraft. Although L.1045 seems to have been back flying operationally just eight days later, this was becoming an increasingly common occurrence, with three aircraft being damaged in this fashion in little more than a week. It must have been a concern for all the pilots, especially their CO.

Following a full day of convoy patrols totalling thirty-nine hours and five minutes, the Squadron seemed to have been given some respite from the arduous task, with other units taking up the duty. As a result, on 4 March, the only note made in the ORB was that the Squadron was losing its first Auxiliary airman, Cpl Clerk Williams who was being posted to RAF Upper Hayford. Williams's post was presumably filled by the promotion of LAC Davies to the temporary rank of corporal on 6 March. While Cpl Davies received this welcome news, the pilots of 'A' Flight were busy practising a battle climb to 25,000 feet, while F/O Brian Smith pushed on alone to 30,000 feet. The process took thirty minutes and the Squadron would now work on ways of reducing this time. On 7 March, the whole Squadron was operating from Bircham Newton, while 'A' Flight returned to Wittering the following day (12 Group ORB).

On 9 March, John Ellis led Blue Section at 0650 hours in DW-M, L.1000, along with F/O Lambert Chambers (DW-P, K.9960) and F/O Medcalf (DW-Q, L.1016). The patrol lasted ninety minutes, landing at 0820 hours, but the pilots could hear a German station interfering with the R/T transmissions. This must have been more than a little unnerving, increasing the perception that they could encounter

F/O A. R. J. Medcalf and one of the Squadron's new Spitfires. (*Copyright Medcalf family*)

a *Luftwaffe* machine at any moment. Green Section reported the same problem on the next patrol, but by the time S/Ldr Franks led Red Section at 0850 hours, the foreign voices had disappeared from their headsets. As a reminder that Squadron life continued in the background, despite the increased war footing of all the convoy patrols, 222 Squadron's CO, H. W. Mermagen arrived at Wittering at 1500 hours, to take 610's Miles Master back to his Squadron at Duxford.

On the next day, 610 Squadron received news that it was to lose one of its pilots to the same Cambridgeshire airfield, with P/O Kennard being posted to 66 Squadron. Hugh Kennard had been with the Squadron just under five months, and although it is likely he had mixed feelings about leaving this group of pilots, he was returning to his former unit. Kennard went on to have a distinguished career, leaving the RAF in 1946 as a wing commander. He passed away in 1995.[4] In the meantime, 'B' Flight returned to Wittering, while 'A' Flight headed to Bircham (12 Group ORB).

The patrols continued unabated on 11 March, with each section once again mounting a convoy patrol, six in total with three in the morning and three in the late afternoon. Some of the Squadron's newer members were now getting their first operational patrols with 610 under their belts, with P/O Litchfield, F/O Wood and Sgt Barrowman all part of these convoy patrols.[5] Once again, the pilots reported interference on their R/T from a German radio transmitter. By the end of the day, the Squadron had carried out eighteen sorties involving twenty-seven hours and forty-five minutes of flying time. On 13 March, Red and Blue Sections each carried out patrols between 0650 hours and 0920 hours. The patrols had passed off uneventfully totalling nine hours, but Bircham Newton witnessed another incident on the ground, when F/O Wood taxied his Spitfire, L.1076, into DW-B, L.1009, causing the following problems: 'Airscrew of L.1076 bent, and port main plane of L.1009 badly damaged' (ORB). Spitfire L.1076 seemed to be back in action ten days later, but L.1009 is not referred to in the ORB until 20 May 1940, so the damage was extensive. Whether Wood received any injuries is not mentioned, but there is no record of him flying another operational sortie, although he was on the Squadron's strength. He was originally from Australia, born in Geelong, Victoria, on 26 September 1916 (TNA, AIR 81/4914).

On 15 March, the Squadron was based at Bircham (12 Group ORB), and carried out three convoy patrols in the afternoon, but instead of flying in their usual sections of three, each patrol involved two aircraft, the reason for this being unclear. It could have been to trial a new formation or possibly to conserve the amount of fuel being used on such patrols, which although important, had not resulted in a single encounter with an enemy aircraft. On 16 March, it was more of the same for 'The Chesters', as they continued to operate in pairs. The Squadron had flown fourteen sorties, but this would have been twenty-one sorties if they had been at full section strength, thereby saving a lot of fuel. During the course of the day, another Spitfire was damaged 'on landing after patrol' (ORB), and, once again, the unfortunate pilot was Sgt Barrowman, a month on from his first crash. This time it may well have been another example of Bircham Newton's poor landing strip rather than his inexperience, as the undercarriage collapsed causing extensive damage to DW-K, L.1062. Remarkably, this was the Spitfire which had suffered the same fate on 23 February![6] Fortunately, Barrowman survived the crash, however, due to the vagaries of the ORB, this is the last mention of the sergeant who had joined the unit barely two months earlier.

On Saint Patrick's Day, 17 March, only 'A' Flight was at Bircham (12 Group ORB), while the Squadron received two new pilots straight from 7 FTS, Peterborough: P/Os Hubert Weatherby Cottam and Charles Edward English. Cottam, originally from Sunderland, had,

> joined 607 Squadron, AuxAF before the war as an Aircrafthand. He remustered as an Airman u/t Pilot about April 1939, when the opportunity for pilot training was first extended to non-commissioned members of the Auxiliary Air Force. Called up on August 24th 1939, Cottam completed his training, was commissioned in March 1940,[7]

before his first posting to an operational Squadron with 610.

English had followed a very similar path, being born in Cowsett, County Durham on 9 August 1912. He worked as a clerk and also joined 607 Squadron as an aircrafthand, but applied for pilot training successfully as an NCO, having already gained his pilot's licence on 24 September 1938 at Newcastle-upon-Tyne Aero Club.[8] 'Called up on August 24 1939, he was posted from 607 Squadron

Above left: P/O Hubert Weatherby Cottam. (*Copyright Robert Dixon*)

Above right: Charles Edward English, as pictured on his pilot's licence, aged twenty-six. (*Copyright Royal Aero Club Trust*)

to 7 FTS, Peterborough for No 12 Course, which began on October 7 1939. On completion of the course on March 6 1940, English was commissioned',[9] before joining 610 Squadron. It would seem the two new recruits were friends and they would both now be on a very steep learning curve, having joined a front-line fighter Squadron. On 18 March, another Airman left the Squadron, this time LAC Taylor. His posting was the first of a 610 Squadron Auxiliary Airman to duty overseas (ORB).

On 20 March, Sgt Johnny Arnfield was sent on an attachment to Farnborough after six months with the Squadron, for a course on the use of oxygen during flying. This was also the day when S/Ldr Leigh arrived at Wittering, to start giving instruction in night flying on the Squadron's Master aircraft (ORB). By this stage, the convoy patrols must have been a necessary evil for the fighter pilots. In fact, Wittering's ORB noted on 22 March that 'A' flight of 264 Squadron in Defiants had arrived from Martlesham Heath, to take over and assist 610 Squadron with such patrols. The senior commanders and indeed S/Ldr Franks, would have been aware of complacency slipping in as the patrols became 'routine'. A prime example of this arose during the course of 23 March, when 'A' Flight was at Wittering and 'B' Flight at Bircham Newton (12 Group ORB Appendices). One of 610's most experienced pilots, F/Lt Ellis, had a crash when landing, presumably after his patrol came to an end at 1450 hours. Ellis, 'piloting Spitfire L.1044, landing at BIRCHAM NEWTON failed to correctly and completely lower undercarriage, thus causing extensive damage to aircraft. Accident attributed to "staleness"' (ORB).[10] For such an experienced pilot to make this basic error, his second in less than three months, could only really be explained as a genuine mistake caused by the pilot's usually razor-sharp senses being dulled by the monotony of circling over convoys for hours at a time. If John Ellis could come unstuck in such a fashion, then comparatively novice pilots were even more likely to succumb to 'staleness'. Although such events are not recorded with any regularity, the CO would have found ways to spice up the day-to-day routines in a bid to prevent staleness creeping in, with regular practice events, like timed battle climbs, practice air-firing and dogfights, as a means to keep the men on their toes. The Squadron probably wanted to have a crack at the *Luftwaffe*, which had been operating small numbers of bombers against convoys and Royal Navy shipping around Scotland. Fellow Spitfire units had already encountered and shot down German aircraft. However, the saying one should be careful what you wish for could not have been more apt, as in due course, the RAF's pilots would be facing more *Luftwaffe* aircraft than they could cope with. At least while flying these convoy patrols the pilots were relatively safe.

The final two events of note for March both involved yet more crashes, the first by another of the experienced pilots, although this one did occur at night, probably following on from S/Ldr Leigh's night flying training on 20 March. F/O Riley, just like Ellis, forgot to lower his undercarriage while coming in to land at Wittering on 26 March, 'causing very extensive damage to Spitfire L.1014' (ORB). Although it may seem a basic error, it was probably more through inexperience in night flying than the staleness referred to in Ellis's crash. Nevertheless, another Spitfire had been put out of action and DW-G, L.1014 would not fly again with 610 Squadron, being sent away for repairs at a Civilian Repair Unit.[11] The following day, P/O English was at Digby, Lincolnshire, and when taxying to take off in the Squadron's Tiger Moth N.6934, he had the misfortune of being, 'caught in a strong gust of wind, thus causing damage to starboard wing and breaking the airscrew. Machine tipped up on its nose' (ORB). This would have been a blow to his pride, as there was little to be done about the vagaries of the weather.

Since the Squadron had received its first Spitfires on 30 September 1939, there had been sixteen 'incidents' reported in the ORB (plus English's on the Tiger Moth). This statistic highlights the dangers of operating a high performance military aircraft outside of combat, let alone with battle damage etc., and the Squadron was fortunate not to suffer any pilot deaths, the worst injury being F/O Milson's broken clavicles. This was P/O le Fleming's final entry in the Squadron's ORB for March. As with the previous month, although no enemy aircraft had been sighted during the countless convoy patrols, 610 Squadron had gained much experience over the course of 256 hours and thirty-three minutes flying time carried out in March.

Unfortunately, there is no written record of the Squadron's activities in April, either they were never written up or were lost. So there is clearly a large gap in the records as to pilot movements, the fate of their Spitfires and the Squadron as a whole. However, one can piece together some information for 610 Squadron during April 1940. Having studied the recorded comings and goings of pilots before the end of March and at the beginning of May, it is evident that F/O Riley, P/O McGowan and Sgt Barrowman left the Squadron during this period and they do not seem to have been replaced. At the end of March, the Squadron had a complement of twenty-three pilots plus the adjutant, as follows:

COMMANDING OFFICER: S/Ldr. A. L. Franks.
Adjutant P/O. R. C. W. H. le Fleming (Taking over).

F/Lt. A. T. Smith.	P/O. P. G. Lamb.
F/Lt. J. Ellis.	P/O. G. Keighley.
F/O. E. B. B. Smith.	P/O. S. C. Norris.
F/O. J. K. Wilson.	P/O. R. A. McGowan.
F/O. W. H. C. Warner.	P/O. P. Litchfield.
F/O. G. M. T. Kerr.	P/O. H. W. Cottam.
F/O. W. Riley.	P/O. C. E. English.
F/O. G. L. Chambers.	Sgt. W. T. Medway
F/O. A. R. J. Medcalf.	Sgt. S. J. Arnfield.
F/O. V. T. L. Wood.	Sgt. P. D. Jenkins.
F/O. D. E. Milson.	Sgt. G. Barrowman.

By the beginning of May, 610 Squadron was down to twenty pilots. On 3 May, William Riley, who had been promoted to flight lieutenant on 26 April, left 610 Squadron to join 263 Squadron which was destined for the ill-fated Norway campaign. Fortunately, he survived and went on to fight in the Battle of Britain. However, he was killed in a mid-air collision in 1942 as a wing commander, aged twenty-five, and is remembered on the Alamein Memorial.[12] Also, P/O Roy McGowan was destined for Norway, to serve with 46 Squadron, a posting which ended his six month period with 'The Chesters'. During this time he had become a key figure in the Squadron, carrying out many of the innumerable convoy patrols, so his departure would have been a blow. McGowan went on to fight in the Battle of Britain with 46 Squadron, but suffered burns on 15 September 1940 which required skin grafts and other treatment. He eventually returned to flying and survived the war. McGowan settled in New Zealand, but died in 2012.[13] While it is clear that Sgt Barrowman left the Squadron during this period, there is no record of where he went.[14]

In terms of the Squadron's movements, on 4 April, the pilots and some ground crew moved to RAF Prestwick on the west coast of Scotland north of Ayr, and when the ORB resumed on 3 May, the Squadron was still based at Prestwick in 13 Group. This may explain why 264 Squadron had recently arrived at Wittering to carry out the convoy patrols. Wittering's ORB makes the following statement about this move on 4 April:

> Signal from Headquarters, Fighter Command, for 610 Squadron to proceed to R.A.F. Station, Prestwick on 14 days attachment. 13 machines and pilots left at 1400 hours. Ensign troop carrier did not arrive to move operational personnel. These were despatched in two parties by road: the first party, the essential maintenance crew for the aircraft, going by Station bus, travelling through the night and arriving at Prestwick in the afternoon of the 5th April; the remainder of the convoy, consisting of 4 Bedfords, 5 Crossleys, 2 Humber Utility vans and 1 petrol tanker, left at 1830 hours, staying the night at Dishforth and arrived at Prestwick at 2300 hours on the 5th April.

13 Group's ORB, also noted that 'Squadrons 610 and 29 arrived in this Group at PRESTWICK and DREM respectively' (TNA, AIR 25/232).

The attachment was clearly extended, as they operated from here until 10 May, when they were sent south to 11 Group, flying straight from Prestwick. However, the ORB and Wittering's ORB noted that the rest of the Squadron's personnel moved south in six vehicles from Wittering, which must still have been their 'home' station. Wg Cdr Smith mentioned that during this period the Squadron: 'went up to the Clyde on the Norwegian campaign to provide cover for some of the shipping'. At this time, flotillas of warships from the British Home Fleet had sailed from naval bases in Scotland and British troop convoys were also sailing from the Clyde for Norway. This explains 610 Squadron's hurried posting to Prestwick and perhaps why only essential personnel had been sent there. This could also clarify why the ORB reports for April were missing. In the upheaval of the move, the records may have been misplaced or not been annotated.

The next entry in the ORB states that on 3 May 1940, the Squadron was still based at Prestwick, where they were visited during the afternoon by 13 Group's AOC, AVM Saul, who arrived by air. Richard Saul had flown during the First World War as an observer and having helped to organise the structure of Fighter Command in the 1930s, commanded 13 Group throughout the Battle of Britain, protecting the north of England and Scotland. The day also saw the departure of F/Lt Milson who had recently been promoted and was now attached to the intriguingly entitled 'Headquarters "X" (or possibly 'K') Force'.[15] With the threat of immediate action looming, the loss of such an experienced pilot would have been keenly felt, but his promotion created a superfluity of flight lieutenants.

On 8 May, the complement of pilots was further reduced to seventeen, with the postings of P/Os Cottam and English to 213 Squadron for flying duties. Their posting to a Hurricane squadron seems a little odd, having spent the last month and a half operating Spitfires. But from the entries in Wittering's Record Book, it appears that Cottam may have had links to 213 Squadron previously, as 610 and 213 Squadrons had shared Wittering as their home station. Tragically, both of them would be killed within seventeen months. English perished during the Battle of Britain on 7 October.[16] Hubert Cottam survived the trials of the Battle of Britain, only to be killed as a flying instructor in Zimbabwe on 5 December 1941.[17]

An image entitled '"B" Flight & others at Prestwick Spring 1940', showing members of 'B' Flight's ground crew. (*Copyright 610 Squadron Association*)

A photograph from the Squadron's archive entitled "'610' at Prestwick 4th April to 10th May 1940". The Spitfires are lined up ready for a 'scramble'. The fourth Spitfire along is DW-S, so is almost certainly N.3201, which joined the Squadron on 28 March 1940. Since the photos taken at Wittering, the Spitfires have adopted a larger roundel and larger letters, more like the size which are so distinctive of 610 Squadron later on in 1940. (*Copyright 610 Squadron Association*)

Another interesting photo from 610 Squadron's time at Prestwick, depicting four of the unit's key pilots in April 1940. From left to right, P/O Norris in his 'Mae West' life jacket, S/Ldr 'Bonzo' Franks, F/Lt Tom Smith with pipe in hand and F/O Bill Warner also in his flying gear. Facilities were evidently rudimentary, with an odd assortment of furnishings arrayed outside. (*Copyright 610 Squadron Association*)

7

10–25 May 1940: Arrival at Biggin Hill

Following the heavy fighting in Norway, the German assault on Holland, Luxembourg, Belgium and France was finally unleashed on 10 May 1940. While the Allied plans to stop the German advance swung into action, by the end of the day, Prime Minister Neville Chamberlain had resigned and been replaced by the pugnacious Winston Churchill, who quickly formed a new government. 610 Squadron's ORB noted the momentous events as follows: **'10th MAY, 1940.** HOLLAND and BELGIUM invaded. Signal received at approximately 1000 hours for Squadron to move at once to BIGGIN HILL'. This terse statement could not be more understated, but indicates the hurried nature of the Squadron's sudden departure south from Scotland. Whether the Squadron knew this posting was imminent is unclear, however the fact that 'B' Flight took off for Biggin Hill just two and three quarter hours after receiving the signal, showed the urgency of the posting. F/Lt Ellis led them off the ground with F/O Medcalf, Sgt Jenkins (Blue Section), F/O Kerr Wilson, F/O Kerr and F/O Lambert Chambers (Green Section) and they arrived at their new base at 1440 hours. Meanwhile, 'A' Flight led by S/Ldr Franks involved the following pilots: F/Lt A. T. Smith, F/O Lamb, F/O E. B. B. Smith, P/O Litchfield, F/O Warner, Sgt Medway and Sgt Arnfield. They left at 1305 hours and arrived at Biggin Hill at 1455 hours. These fourteen pilots were followed by P/O Keighley, who flew down on his own, taking off at 1315 hours and going via Shawbury and Harwell, arriving at their new home at 1510 hours.

The reason for the sudden move to Biggin Hill was to replace a former resident squadron which flew Hurricanes, 79 Squadron. It had moved to Merville in France to support the BEF, so 610, 'took over hangars, pilots' rooms etc., of 79 Squadron' (ORB). No Spitfire squadrons were sent to operate out of France, the duty of providing fighter cover falling to the Hurricane squadrons, which as Brian Smith recalled, was a very difficult posting: 'But the people who were based in France, flying Hurricanes, they had a rough time, very rough, but we weren't allowed to stay there. We did trips, but always came back to England'. The rest of 610 Squadron had to move south from Wittering, while those left at Prestwick moved under the watchful instruction of F/O Wood in charge of the road party and P/O Norris in charge of the rail party, to complete a complex logistical feat.

It was a memorable day for 610 Squadron, as they would now be based at the vital 11 Group Sector Station at Biggin Hill, arguably the most famous RAF station, at the hub of Fighter Command and the aerial defence of Great Britain. It was also an auspicious day in the history of the airfield, as 610 Squadron became the first Spitfire squadron to operate from Biggin Hill. They were joining 32 Squadron which flew Hurricanes, and these two Squadrons would form a strong partnership during the Battle of Britain, operating day after day from the airfield throughout July and August. Biggin Hill's Record Book confirmed this posting with the simple statement: '610 report for duty', although it took a few days more for the full complement to arrive.

610 Squadron would have seventeen pilots at Biggin Hill once they had all arrived, as follows:

This photo depicts 610 Squadron's engine fitter, Osbourne Jennings, struggling with a parachute pack. One of the Squadron's early Spitfires is in the background. It has the 'DW' code and an unusual fuselage roundel, with what appears to be a yellow ring inside a blue outer ring, instead of the other way round. (*Copyright 610 Squadron Association*)

S/Ldr. A. L. Franks.
F/Lt. A. T. Smith.
F/Lt. J. Ellis.
F/O. A. R. J. Medcalf.
F/O. J. K. Wilson.
F/O. G. M. T. Kerr.
F/O. G. L. Chambers.
F/O. P. G. Lamb.
F/O. E. B. B. Smith.
F/O. W. H. C. Warner.
F/O. V. T. L. Wood.
P/O. P. Litchfield.
P/O. G. Keighley.
P/O. S. C. Norris.
Sgt. P. D. Jenkins.
Sgt. W. T. Medway.
Sgt. S. J. Arnfield.

Each of them must have been all too aware of the daunting certainty of impending action, something for which all the training in the world could not prepare them. They would be depending on each other, while flying for their very lives: the stakes could not have been higher.

One real plus for 610 Squadron's pilots, was that they were lucky enough to be operating the Spitfire, the RAF's most modern aircraft. The Spitfire was constantly being developed, so that it was increasingly more powerful than the prototype K.5054 and, crucially for the pilots, being made safer to fly in combat. For example:

> In the spring of 1940, the RAF also introduced 100 octane fuel in place of the 87 octane it had previously used. The Spitfire I's Merlin engine had to be modified to use this petrol, and the higher octane allowed pilots to select double the supercharger boost for a maximum of five minutes (raising the top speed by up to 34 mph) without risk of damaging the Merlin III'.[1]

This would be crucial in the coming aerial combats. The greatest fear of many pilots was of their aircraft going down in flames with them trapped inside, a distinct possibility, as once a fuel tank was ruptured, a pilot could quickly be covered in fuel with disastrous consequences. So another potentially life-saving alteration was additional protection for some of the vulnerable fuel tanks, one of the improvements Raymond Ellis actually recalled carrying out upon their arrival in Kent:

> When the Germans invaded Holland and Belgium on the 10th May 1940 our squadron moved to 11 Group at Biggin Hill where, in the South Camp hangar, we in Servicing Flight were immediately occupied with fitting each of our Spitfires with a one inch thick glass windscreen and armour-plate in front of the top fuel tank… The top fuel tank was covered by a thick curved sheet of a light alloy.
>
> A rectangular rear-vision mirror was fitted above the windscreen and a Dural fairing made to streamline it. Our Engineering Officer, W/O Bentall, had managed to get the mirrors from local garages.[2]

Such changes could ultimately decide the pilot's fate, but also increase the chances of defeating the *Luftwaffe*, and modifications would continue to be made to give the pilots every confidence in their aircraft.

Being based in the 11 Group Sector, the Squadron was now under the control of 11 Group's commander, AVM Keith Park. He was a New Zealander who had fought courageously in the ANZAC Brigade at Gallipoli, in the British Army on the Western Front, before becoming a distinguished 'Ace' pilot with the Royal Flying Corps (RFC). After the First World War, Park joined the RAF, eventually becoming Dowding's senior air staff officer, with whom he forged a strong partnership at Fighter Command. Park's role as commander of Great Britain's main line of defence against aerial attack was an onerous task, but one that he felt more than capable of meeting, especially with the air defence system which his commanding officer, Hugh Dowding had put in place.

While Park's Group protected the south-east of England and London, by July the south-west of England would come under the remit of AVM Sir Quintin Brand, 10 Group's commander; the Midlands and Wales were under the command of AVM Trafford Leigh-Mallory and 12 Group; while AVM Saul was in command of 13 Group, as noted earlier. Park's demanding duties were only outweighed by the responsibility held by Dowding, Fighter Command's C-in-C. Born on 24 April 1882, he had flown as an RFC pilot and squadron commander in the First World War. He continued to serve in the RAF, becoming a highly experienced officer who had been at Fighter Command's head since 1936. Dowding was responsible for the introduction of the RAF's latest fast, monoplane, eight-gun fighters, along with the RDF system for Britain's aerial defence, which he had overseen as the air member for supply and research, to such an extent that it became known as 'The Dowding System'. As Brian Smith affectionately recalled, '"Stuffy" Dowding knew what he was doing, he'd organised it all himself'. Dowding would have had a much greater appreciation of 610 Squadron's operational efficiency now they were at the centre of likely operations.

With action imminent, there was little time for the pilots to become accustomed to their new surroundings, the first recorded patrol being undertaken on the very next day. This was carried out by F/O Brian Smith (DW-D, L.1010) when he took off at 1050 hours in order to investigate an 'X' raid, before being instructed to patrol base at 5,000 feet. No enemy aircraft were seen and he landed at 1130 hours. Smith had barely touched down before he was replaced on patrol by F/O William Warner (DW-F, L. 1011), who took off at 1135 hours with the following instructions: 'Ordered on patrol—vector 280° at 5,000 feet—and to look out for two aircraft. Ordered to orbit Gatwick & Kenley. Later ordered to orbit base at 20,000 feet. No a/c sighted' (ORB). This patrol ended at 1210 hours and Warner was replaced by Sgt Bill Medway who was airborne in L.1074 by 1216 hours and ordered to orbit Beachy Head on the south coast for fifteen minutes at 5,000 feet.[3] He was then instructed to return to Biggin and patrol the airfield at 10,000 feet and having sighted no enemy aircraft, told to 'Pancake' fifty-nine minutes later.[4]

On 12 May, the Squadron was not called on to patrol until 1645 hours when, 'Two aircraft of Yellow section ordered to patrol DUNGENESS at 5,000 feet. On arriving at coast were ordered to vector 90 degrees. R/T communication became impossible due to bad jamming. Aircraft returned to base. No

E/A sighted' (ORB). The two pilots were F/O Warner (DW-F, L.1011) and F/O Lamb (DW-G, L.1045), and their patrol ended at 1735 hours. While the skies over England remained relatively peaceful, even at this early stage there were ominous signs in the skies over Europe of the savage fighting which was to come. As 610 Squadron settled down for the night in the comfort of Biggin Hill, their Bomber Command colleagues were mourning heavy losses, following attacks on the Meuse bridges. The RAF's light bombers were being shown to be obsolete barely two days into the fight, an awful realisation for their brave crews. 610 Squadron's pilots must have realised their good fortune in being removed from their role as a bomber Squadron, given such heavy early casualties.

On 13 May, Yellow Section was again in operation, this time an early morning flight at 0630 hours to patrol RAF Manston near Ramsgate at 10,000 feet, before following the coast round to Dungeness, which jutted out towards France. With no aircraft sighted, the section was ordered home, landing at 0715 hours. The pilots involved were F/O Smith (DW-A, L.1001), F/O Lamb (DW-G, L.1045) and P/O Keighley (DW-E, L.1013). Next up at 1135 hours was Red Section, led by the squadron leader (DW-S, N.3201), flanked by P/O Norris (DW-F, L.1011) and Sgt Medway (L.1074), with orders to patrol the city of Canterbury at 5,000 feet. With no aircraft being sighted, they returned to base at 1205 hours. The final patrol of the day was flown by 'B' Flight's commander, John Ellis; he received orders at 1350 hours to shoot down a stray barrage balloon on the south coast. Ellis opened fire on it off Dymchurch and the balloon collapsed into the English Channel five miles south of Folkestone, while Ellis returned to base after an hour. Biggin Hill's Record Book noted that on 13 May, F/O Wood reported for duty, which meant he had successfully directed the road party in six vehicles, from Prestwick to Biggin Hill.

One member of Wood's party, Raymond Ellis of the Servicing Flight, provides a fascinating insight into their new home at Biggin Hill in his memoires, including a vivid description of the layout of the aerodrome and its key features:

> … the large triple-bay Belfast hangar, in which I worked as an airframe fitter, rarely contained more than one aeroplane, even though it was large enough to house a whole squadron of Spitfires. As much as possible of Servicing Flight's maintenance and repair work was done away from the hangar—usually out on our squadron's dispersal area. This had been so since we of 610 Squadron's Servicing Flight had arrived here from Wittering on 13th May 1940. On the 10th May, the Germans had outflanked the French and the B.E.F by invading neutral Belgium and Holland. On that day, our Squadron's Spitfires had left their temporary duties at Prestwick to fly to Biggin Hill, followed by 'A' and 'B' Flights ground staff.
>
> German photographs and my memory recall that the buildings were on the western side of the airfield, but were split into two groups that we knew as North Camp and South Camp. North Camp was the larger of the two, and it included the Sector H.Q.
>
> In South Camp, fronting the airfield, were a steel 'T' type hangar, and a canvas hangar from the 14–18 War. Behind these were the M.T Section and some barrack blocks. To the east and close to the edge of the airfield was the Officers' Mess in Koonowla House that had once been the home of the estate's owner. Further still were the Married Quarters.
>
> From South Camp, a perimeter track ran northward for about a quarter mile to the first buildings of North Camp. Prominent amongst these was our Servicing Flight's triple-bay Belfast hangar with brick walls, timber trussed roof and large steel sliding doors …
>
> Beyond North Camp, the perimeter track continued to the northern boundary along which was 610 Squadron's dispersal area with the Spitfires spread out to minimise damage from an air attack. Some of the planes were parked, in pairs, in double pens. These were open fronted with walls on three sides reinforced by earth banks on the outside. The bank along the back also served as cover for a shelter. 'A' Flight came first, and then, after quite a gap, came 'B' Flight. Offices and crew rooms for pilots and ground staff were in wooden huts and bell tents. I do not remember going beyond our

An example of the type of 'double pens' used for dispersing aircraft mentioned by Raymond Ellis, still extant at Biggin Hill today. (*Author*)

> dispersal, I believe that the perimeter track continued along the eastern boundary, past woodland, to the South Camp.[5]

With another day of fruitless patrolling successfully carried out, the pilots would have benefited from the opportunity to acclimatise to operating out of Biggin Hill. This unfamiliar environment had different features and landmarks, to which they needed to get accustomed when attempting to make it back home, low on fuel or in a damaged aircraft following combat. 610 Squadron's forward base was now Hawkinge, an airfield the Squadron's long-term pilots were familiar with following the summer camp spent there in the summer of 1937. Unfortunately, the ORB does not always stipulate when they were operating out of this airfield, situated on the coast, just inland from Folkestone. While 'The Chesters' adapted to life in 11 Group, Winston Churchill, did not mince his words in his first speech as prime minister to the House of Commons. Stating what lay ahead in the face of the German advance, he memorably warned:

> I have nothing to offer but blood, toil, tears and sweat. We have before us an ordeal of the most grievous kind. We have before us many, many long months of struggle and of suffering. You ask, what is our policy? I will say: It is to wage war, by sea, land and air, with all our might and with all the strength that God can give us; to wage war against a monstrous tyranny never surpassed in the dark, lamentable catalogue of human crime. That is our policy. You ask, what is our aim? I can answer in one word: It is victory, victory at all costs, victory in spite of all terror, victory, however long and hard the road may be ...[6]

Churchill eloquently underlined the magnitude of the task facing the Allies, but also, in what was to become typical of his broadcasts, the stirring hope of ultimate victory.

On 14 May, Yellow Section's pilots were up at the crack of dawn in order to take off at 0425 hours. S/Ldr Franks led the patrol (DW-S, N.3201), accompanied by F/Lt Tom Smith (DW-A, L.1001) and F/O Warner (DW-F, L.1011). They were instructed to patrol Manston, near Ramsgate, at 8,000 feet, 'to cover movements of aircraft. Maintained standing patrol until ordered to return. No E/A sighted' (ORB). This explains the need for the early start and their charges were probably aircraft being fuelled and armed before heading over to France—it was not until 0615 hours that the three pilots landed. At some stage they were probably joined by three more 610 Squadron aircraft, as F/O Kerr Wilson (DW-K, L.1062) led another early morning patrol at 0545 hours to patrol Manston, 'in connection with "X" raid' (ORB). Clearly the controller was taking no chances. Kerr Wilson was followed by F/O Medcalf (DW-Q, L.1016) and Sgt Jenkins (DW-M, L.1000), however the patrol passed off uneventfully and they returned at 0650 hours. Once again, 610 Squadron's pilots would have thanked their good fortune in being switched to a fighter squadron, as news filtered through of more unsustainable losses amongst the Blenheim and Battle bomber squadrons: 'Of the seventy-one aircraft that had set off for Sedan that afternoon, forty never returned. No RAF operation of similar size has ever suffered a higher rate of loss'.[7] The heroism of these bomber crews, knowing they were facing such terrifying odds, cannot be overstated…

On a non-operational note for 610 Squadron on 14 May, the Biggin Hill ORB noted that F/O le Fleming had reported for duty, so the Squadron was reunited with its adjutant, who had recently been promoted to flying officer. Two days later on 16 May, the Squadron received news that a P/O W. E. Lloyd was being posted to the unit from the Air Ministry for Intelligence duties, and it was recorded at Biggin Hill that he reported for duty the next day. The Squadron could now be certain of meeting enemy forces in the very near future. It was imperative that anything and everything could be gleaned about the enemy, from aircraft encountered and shot down, to the *Luftwaffe's* tactics. This was what Walter Lloyd was trained in and he would be of great assistance to le Fleming in managing these additional duties (see photo of Lloyd/Fleming p. 125).

On 18 May, the Squadron could have been forgiven for thinking they were going to be excused from any patrol work, but at 2125 hours Yellow Section was ordered to patrol Maidstone. The pilots were F/Lt A. T. Smith (DW-A, L.1001), F/O Lamb (DW-G, L.1045) and P/O Keighley (DW-F, L.1011). The flight passed off uneventfully, with the Spitfires returning to land at 2150 hours, totalling one hour and fifteen minutes flying. On 19 May, Yellow Section was called upon again, with a forty-minute patrol which took off at 1205 hours, and was 'ordered to vector 50° at 12,000 ft. Later ordered to vector 120° and to patrol MANSTON' (ORB). Tom Smith (DW-A, L.1001) was again Yellow 1, but this time he was flanked by F/O Warner in DW-F, L.1011, and F/O Lamb again in DW-G, L.1045. The pilots returned to base after a combined total of two hours flying.

The Squadron had another early start on 20 May. Red Section was covering the dawn readiness, and they took off at 0525 hours to patrol Manston at 10,000 feet, before being ordered to intercept an 'X' raid (ORB). F/Lt Tom Smith was Red 1 (DW-A, L.1001), operating with the same pilots as two days earlier, F/O Lamb (DW-G, L.1045) and P/O Keighley (DW-E, L.1013), however, this chase proved to be fruitless and they returned to base at 0620 hours, for a well-earned breakfast. Although the rest of the Squadron did not carry out another patrol that morning, the sense that they were gradually getting closer to the front line was inescapable.

At 1330 hours, 'A' Flight was ordered to cover a destroyer from Dunkirk on the French coast, across the Channel back to England. The formation involved the following pilots and aircraft, the squadron leader presumably leading Red Section, which patrolled the warship at just 500 feet to prevent any low-level attacks, while Yellow Section, led by Tom Smith, operated at 10,000 feet to prevent both the destroyer being attacked from high-level, and Red Section being bounced by prowling *Luftwaffe* fighters:

DW-S.	N.3201	S/Ldr. A. L. FRANKS.	3[8]
DW-B.	L.1009	F/O. E. B. B. SMITH.	3
DW-D.	L.1010	P/O. S. C. NORRIS.	2
DW-A.	L.1001	F/Lt. A. T. SMITH.	5
DW-E.	L.1013	F/O. W. H. C. WARNER.	5
DW-G.	L.1045	F/O. P. G. LAMB.	6

No enemy aircraft were sighted and the patrol ended two hours later at 1530 hours, the pilots all glad to get back on terra firma after a long flight. They were all too familiar with the tedium of convoy patrols from their days based at Wittering and Bircham Newton, but that had been child's play in comparison with these patrols. The likelihood of meeting enemy aircraft had increased immeasurably since their posting to 11 Group, along with the depressing news of the BEF and Allied armies unsuccessful attempts to stem the Nazi advance. The draining effect of such a patrol could not be underestimated, with the threat of their first action possible at any moment.

Despite the ground crew having barely had time to turn their Spitfires round, fifty minutes later Red Section took off again, at 1620 hours, the slightly different personnel being F/O Brian Smith as Red 1 (DW-B, L.1009), P/O Norris (DW-D, L.1010) and P/O Keighley (DW-E, L.1013). The section carried out, 'a standing patrol over a destroyer off DOVER' (ORB), quite possibly the one which 'A' Flight had covered across the Channel earlier on. At one point, Smith was instructed to break off the patrol and investigate an 'X' raid further up the Kent coast at Deal. As the Spitfire pilots readied themselves for action, they would have taken deep breaths of relief when the aircraft turned out to be a fellow Spitfire. Red Section's pilots returned to the defence of the destroyer, but again only saw more RAF aircraft in the shape of a Westland Lysander and a Bristol Blenheim. With no sign of any trouble, they returned to base two hours and ten minutes later at 1830 hours. It had been a very long day for the men, with a combined total of twelve sorties involving twenty-one hours and fifteen minutes flying time. Notably, Keighley, who had been on the early morning patrol, had carried out three hours and five minutes patrolling, while Brian Smith and Stan Norris had each amassed four hours ten minutes operational flying time. Such figures show just how tiring a fighter pilot's day was—it is likely that these patrols took place from Hawkinge rather than Biggin Hill, to conserve petrol. This would have entailed flights to and from the advance airfield at first light and dusk, adding to the length of the day.[9]

Tuesday 21 May 1940 saw 'A' Flight again on the earliest patrol which took off at 0410 hours, Red and Yellow Sections escorting another ship between Dover and this time Boulogne. The six Spitfires were led by F/Lt A. T. Smith in his favoured aircraft, DW-A, supported by the following pilots:

DW-A.	L.1001	F/Lt. A. T. SMITH.	6
DW-F.	L.1011	F/O. W. H. C. WARNER.	6
DW-G.	L.1045	F/O. P. G. LAMB.	7
DW-B.	L.1009	F/O. E. B. B. SMITH.	5
DW-D.	L.1010	P/O. S. C. NORRIS.	4
DW-S.	N.3201	Sgt. MEDWAY.	3

Nobody saw any sign of any enemy aircraft and the formation returned to base at 0620 hours, after a lengthy two hours and ten minutes in the air. By the time 'A' Flight's tired pilots had landed, their comrades in 'B' Flight had taken off, at 0525 hours—it seems they relieved them of their escort duty. 'B' Flight's orders were also to, 'patrol ship, Dover to Boulogne' (ORB), although it could easily have been another ship undertaking that increasingly perilous crossing. The following pilots participated on this patrol:

DW-T.	P.9452*	F/O. G. M. T. KERR.	1
DW-K.	L.1062	Sgt. ARNFIELD, S. J.	1
DW-O.	L.1043	Sgt. JENKINS, P. D.	2
	L.1074	F/Lt. J. ELLIS.	2
	N.3289**	F/O. J. K. WILSON.	2
DW-P.	K.9960	P/O. P. LITCHFIELD.	1

*As ORB, but should probably be DW-T, N.3177, which applies to all subsequent references until after 29 May, when P.9452 probably replaced it (see endnote 15, 8).

**Some sources state that this aircraft was coded DW-K. However, throughout N.3289's service with 610 Squadron, L.1062 was also serving with the unit and was definitely coded DW-K, as on this patrol. It is unlikely that two aircraft would have the same letters—as it is never referred to as DW-K in the ORB, there is no reason to suppose it should be. It was most likely a Command Reserve aircraft.

'A' Flight had done the majority of the recorded patrol work since arriving in 11 Group and this was the first recorded patrol for all of 'B' Flight except Ellis, Kerr Wilson and Jenkins. Ellis was probably leading the formation as Blue 1 with Kerr Wilson and Litchfield as his wingmen and Kerr was Green 1 with Sgts Arnfield and Jenkins supporting him. The patrol passed off without incident and they landed at 0700 hours, having amassed a further nine hours and thirty minutes flying time. 'B' Flight was again called upon at 0855 hours, once more to patrol Dover—Boulogne. Blue Section was led by Kerr Wilson and Green Section once again by Malcolm Kerr. Otherwise, the pilots were the same except for Medcalf, who completed Blue Section:

	N.3289	F/O. J. K. WILSON.	3
	L.1074	F/O. A. R. J. MEDCALF.	2
DW-P.	K.9960	P/O. P. LITCHFIELD.	2
DW-T.	P.9452	F/O. G. M. T. KERR.	2
DW-M.	L.1000	Sgt. ARNFIELD, S. J.	2
DW-O.	L.1043	Sgt. JENKINS, P. D.	3

After two hours and twenty minutes, Green Section landed following another uneventful patrol. Blue Section, having patrolled for slightly longer, returned to base at 1130 hours after an exhausting two hours and thirty-five minutes in the air; the pilots would have been glad of some lunch to sustain them.

The Squadron now enjoyed a brief respite, but it did not last long for 'B' Flight, as at 1405 hours the pilots were again taking to the sky.[10] The instructions were to patrol Calais at 15,000 feet to fend off any potential aerial threat to the beleaguered troops flooding into the port, as they retreated from the *Wehrmacht*. Blue and Green Sections remained largely unchanged, but F/O Lambert Chambers came in for his first recorded patrol since the Squadron's move south, to lead Blue Section in place of Kerr Wilson. With Ellis still not flying, it was most likely that F/O Kerr led Green Section and the whole Flight, as follows:

DW-P.	K.9960	F/O. G. L. CHAMBERS.	1
	L.1074	F/O. A. R. J. MEDCALF.	3
	N.3289	P/O. P. LITCHFIELD.	3
DW-K.	L.1062	F/O. G. M. T. KERR.	3
DW-O.	L.1043	Sgt. JENKINS, P. D.	4
DW-M.	L.1000	Sgt. ARNFIELD, S. J.	3

This patrol lasted one hour and thirty-five minutes with the Spitfires landing at 1540 hours, a collective effort of nine hours and thirty minutes, again without having seen the *Luftwaffe*. The pilots must have been increasingly frustrated, given that they knew the enemy was operating in their vicinity, but at least they had all returned safely. 'B' Flight had barely landed before the Squadron's busy day continued. Red Section was ordered up at 1550 hours, 'to investigate 3 "x" raids off Boulogne and Cap Gris-Nez at 15,000 feet' (ORB). This time the CO led the patrol (DW-S, N.3201), while his wingmen, Norris (DW-D, L.1010) and Medway (DW-J, L.1003), were on their second patrol of the day. The enemy was not encountered and the Spitfires returned to base at 1710 hours.

While these patrols had taken place, the BEF was attempting a counter-attack against the Germans to the south-east of Arras, where the garrison so far had stood firm. Around 2,000 troops reinforced by tanks, known as 'Frankforce', set out to relieve some pressure on Arras, but following initial success, 'Frankforce' was forced back by *Panzer* and *Wehrmacht* Infantry Divisions, supported by the *Luftwaffe*. They had caused the Germans relatively high casualties and the German commanders mistook the BEF force for a much larger one than it was. This battle was perhaps to have more far-reaching consequences than originally anticipated, as shall be seen.

610 Squadron's pilots, having clocked up five patrols between them, twenty-seven sorties totalling fifty-four hours flying time, must have thought that once Red Section returned, their operational activities had ended for the day. They could not have been more wrong. For the first time since moving to 11 Group, S/Ldr Franks received orders to take his whole Squadron up, 'to patrol Calais—Boulogne and to afford maximum protection for the coast and shipping against bombing attack' (ORB). Despite having seen no enemy aircraft during the previous five patrols over the Channel and French coast that day, the *Luftwaffe* was operating in the area. There was a high possibility that enemy bombers would take advantage of the gloaming to press home their attacks on the Army and Navy, something of which the following pilots would have been all too aware:

DW-S.	N.3201	S/Ldr. A. L. FRANKS.	Red 1**	5
DW-B.	L.1076*	F/O. E. B. B. SMITH.		6
DW-J.	L.1003	Sgt. MEDWAY, W. T.		5
DW-A.	L.1001	F/Lt. A. T. SMITH.	Yellow 1**	7
DW-G.	L.1045	F/O. W. H. C. WARNER.		7
DW-E.	L.1013	P/O. G. KEIGHLEY.		5
DW-P.	K.9960	F/O. G. L. CHAMBERS.	Blue 1**	2
	L.1074	F/O. A. R. J. MEDCALF.		4
	N.3289	P/O. P. LITCHFIELD.		4
DW-K.	L.1062	F/O. G. M. T. KERR.	Green 1**	4
DW-O.	L.1043	Sgt. JENKINS, P. D.		5
DW-M.	L.1000	Sgt. ARNFIELD, S. J.		4

*As ORB, but this Spitfire should probably be DW-B, L.1009.

**These section leaders are based on my reading of how the formation is listed and the pilot's usual role.

The formation took off at 1920 hours and the twelve Spitfires made an impressive sight as they crossed the Channel, a heart-warming one to any British ships ploughing through the waves beneath them. The twelve fighter pilots would have been concentrating on searching the sky for any hint of aircraft ahead of them. A fellow Spitfire pilot from 64 Squadron, James O'Meara, carrying out his first operational sortie on the same day, vividly described his feelings at the prospect of his first combat on 21 May:

> I wondered if I should see England again. There was a horrible sensation in the pit of my stomach: I felt empty and tight inside. I could feel myself shaking all over. I was afraid ... 'O Christ help me,' I whispered, 'let me get back safely.'[11]

These emotions would have been all too familiar for 610 Squadron's men as they approached the nearest point of France to England, the distinctive outcrop of Cap Gris-Nez. Suddenly, one of them spotted a large formation of twin-engined aircraft approaching from the East—this was it!

The ORB described the events:

> Sighted 14 twin-engined aircraft approaching from the East off Cap Gris-Nez. Squadron positioned for attack from astern, and Red section went in to attack. The leader opened fire and one aircraft was shot down. Yellow, Blue and Green sections did not follow up, as Yellow One considered the twin-engined aircraft were Blenheims, and broke off attack immediately. Red section leader decided that they were Blenheims, and also broke off attack immediately. Later it was confirmed that the aircraft were our own Blenheims on patrol. Visibility was extremely poor, owing to failing light and thick haze. The Squadron returned to Base.

Fate had struck in the cruellest fashion, with 610's first encounter with the 'enemy' actually being an early example of 'friendly fire'. Franks had positioned his men perfectly for attacking the bomber formation, which must have looked exactly like a squadron of Junkers Ju 88s, as the Ju 88 and Blenheim had very similar silhouettes. In the failing evening light, mixed up with haze and smoke spiralling up from the beaches, plus nervous pilots, inexperienced in combat, it was easy to see how the mistake had occurred. Franks's aim had been true, as from the report, only he had time to open fire before F/Lt Tom Smith, leading Yellow Section, yelled out his warning that these were not *Luftwaffe* aircraft. Smith's quick thinking had prevented what was a tragedy from becoming a disaster. However, the desperate call came too late for one hapless Blenheim crew, shot down in the most unfortunate circumstances.

610 Squadron had intercepted 18 Squadron's Blenheims, as recorded in Graham Warner's weighty tome, *The Bristol Blenheim, A complete history*, detailing all losses of this versatile aircraft. The Blenheim IV, P.9185 (TNA, AIR 81/467), failed to return, 'from bombing sortie to Boulogne, shot down by RAF Spitfires near there and crash-landed; P/O V. Rees, Sgt N. Pusey, and LAC K. Murray uninjured',[12] the pilot managing to crash-land his damaged aircraft near Wimereux. As if to underline the real dangers of incorrectly identifying potential enemy aircraft, another 18 Squadron crew had been less fortunate on an earlier patrol on 21 May, when one of their Blenheims was shot down by RAF Hurricanes—the three crewmen all perished.[13]

As 610's pilots broke off the engagement and Franks ordered them to head for home, he must have done so with a very heavy heart, devastated at the costly error. It must have been a difficult debriefing for him and his men once they had landed at 2115 hours, in the growing darkness. Although it was a terrible start for 610 Squadron, such errors were all too likely given the situation in which they were operating. Tiredness was another factor—four of 'B' Flight's pilots were carrying out their fourth patrol of the day, while 'A' Flight had been active since well before 0410 hours. It had almost been an eighteen hour day, involving thirty-nine recorded sorties and a combined sixty-five hours and thirty minutes flying time! They were exhausting conditions, especially when the pilots were complete novices in combat, something for which all the peacetime training could not prepare them. However, they were conditions they would have to adapt to very quickly indeed. The saying goes that one learns from ones mistakes, and this would have to apply to what had happened in the murky skies above Cap Gris-Nez.

Although the unfortunate Blenheim's crew survived this encounter and returned to their Squadron, the loss of an RAF aircraft due to 'friendly fire' must have required an investigation. As Franks was the only one to have opened fire, such an investigation would have centred on him, although it is likely that the other pilots would have been asked to provide evidence. This may explain why there is no record of 610 flying any patrols on 22 May, although they could simply have been stood down following a full day of intensive flying. Franks did not take part in any recorded operational flying for another six days, which possibly meant he was being given time to get over his error while it was investigated. Such accidents were far from uncommon, and sadly it was, and always will be, the nature of warfare that mistaken identity in the heat of battle can lead to self-inflicted losses.

After the events of 21 May, the Squadron received a boost two days later with P/O Raven's attachment to 6 Operational Training Unit (OTU) Sutton Bridge coming to an end, although it is unclear when this attachment began. He was last mentioned when being sent to 2 FTS Brize Norton in early October 1939. Having successfully completed this training, he would have gone on to the OTU before returning to 610 as his operational Squadron. Although his CO would have been wary to throw him in at the deep end, it was good that the Squadron now had another pilot in reserve, even if he was still undergoing further training, taking the number of pilots back up to eighteen. On 6 April 1940, Raven had received the welcome confirmation of his appointment as a P/O in the AAF.[14]

Patrols were resumed on 23 May, F/Lt Tom Smith leading the first one off in his trusty DW-A, L.1001 at 1010 hours, with F/O Brian Smith (DW-B, L.1009) and P/O Norris (DW-J, L.1003) on either wingtip. They were ordered to climb to 10,000 feet on a Vector of 130° and to intercept and identify an unknown aircraft. However, this course was changed by the Controller four times and without any sign of the mystery aircraft, they were finally told to patrol Ramsgate. They did not encounter any aircraft here either and landed after thirty-five minutes at 1045 hours (ORB). The afternoon patrol took off at 1825 hours and also seems to have been by 'A' Flight pilots, as follows:

DW-E.	L.1013	F/O. W. H. C. WARNER.	8
DW-D.	L.1010	P/O. S. C. NORRIS.	7
DW-G.	L.1045	Sgt. MEDWAY, W. T.	6

They patrolled their base (again, most likely a forward one, such as Manston) at 10,000 feet, but there was no sign of enemy aircraft and they landed after fifty minutes, at 1915 hours. The situation across the Channel was becoming very bleak indeed. With a concerted attack having started on Boulogne, the decision was made to start evacuating British troops from the port using destroyers. By the small hours of the morning of 24 May, some 4,360 men had been rescued by the warships. On 23 May, a siege of Calais had also begun, while the port of Dunkirk quickly became the centre of the gradually decreasing area of land defended by the BEF and other Allied troops.

Friday 24 May brought a return to operations for 'B' Flight, with Green Section ordered to investigate an 'X' raid over Manston, at 10,000 feet (ORB). F/O Kerr Wilson (N.3289) led this patrol which took off at 1020 hours, supported by F/O Medcalf (DW-N, L.1075) and P/O Litchfield (DW-O, L.1043), but it was another fruitless patrol and they landed at 1135 hours. In the early afternoon the whole Flight carried out the same patrol, taking off at 1310 hours, although the pilots involved did not see a thing and returned to base at 1400 hours (ORB):

	N.3274	F/Lt. J. ELLIS.	3
DW-T.	P.9452	F/O. G. M. T. KERR.	5
DW-P.	K.9960	F/O. G. L. CHAMBERS.	3
	N.3289	F/O. J. K. WILSON.	5
DW-N.	L.1075	F/O. A. R. J. MEDCALF.	6
DW-O.	L.1043	P/O. P. LITCHFIELD.	6

The final action of the day fell to 'A' Flight, a 'Navy Patrol' which must have been a nerve-wracking experience, recorded as follows:

> 'A' Flight ordered to proceed to MANSTON to cover Naval operations 'D' and 'E' against possible attack. Orders were to remain on ground at MANSTON at 'Super-Readiness', and to take off immediately

if required. Pilots remained in aircraft ready to take off, but were not called upon to do so. Returned from MANSTON at 2105—landed at base 2135 hours. (ORB)

It also states a flight time of 1740 to 1810 hours, for the flight from Biggin Hill to Manston, and from then onwards they were at 'Super-Readiness'. The pilots for this unusual activity were:

DW-A.	L.1001	F/Lt. A. T. SMITH.	9
	N.3284	F/O. P. G. LAMB.	8
DW-S.	N.3201	P/O. G. KEIGHLEY.	6
DW-B.	L.1009	F/O. E. B. B. SMITH.	8
DW-D.	L.1010	F/O. W. H. C. WARNER.	9
DW-J.	L.1003	Sgt. MEDWAY, W. T.	7

F/Lt Tom Smith was presumably leading the flight as Red 1 with F/O Brian Smith leading Yellow Section. Quite what the naval operations 'D' and 'E' were is unclear, possibly destroyers operating between the French and English coastlines.

On 24 May, the German commanders threw the BEF and their Allies a lifeline, with the controversial 'Halt Order', issued to the *Panzer* divisions which threatened to overrun the hub of Allied resistance at Dunkirk. The task for the destruction of these Allied forces was handed to Göring's *Luftwaffe*. Quite why this decision was taken is unclear, as it enabled the Allied forces to strengthen their defensive positions around Dunkirk. However, the stout defence of other ports like Boulogne and Calais, both holding out for four crucial days, along with the earlier surprise counter-attack from Arras, all probably contributed to Germany's more cautious approach. Now, the time was right for the Royal Navy to attempt to carry out a highly dangerous evacuation to save some of the BEF. One of the key aspects for its success would be the ability of Fighter Command's squadrons to prevent the *Luftwaffe's* bombers from wiping out both the Army on the beaches and the ships attempting to evacuate them.

Despite the late finish for 'A' Flight's pilots, they carried out the dawn readiness on 25 May. As early as 0540 hours, F/O Brian Smith was sent up in his favoured mount, DW-B, L.1009, to investigate yet another 'X' raid. However, he was immediately recalled and landed ten minutes later (ORB). After this early start, the Squadron had a day of nervously awaiting the order to get airborne, which did not come through until 1625 hours, when the Squadron was instructed to patrol Calais at 7,000 feet. Brian Smith seems to have been leading the five aircraft of 'A' Flight in the absence of both S/Ldr Franks and F/Lt Smith, while John Ellis was leading 'B' Flight's six Spitfires, and the patrol itself, which featured the following men:

DW-B.	L.1009	F/O. E. B. B. SMITH.	10
DW-J.	N.3284*	P/O. S. C. NORRIS.	8
DW-G.	L.1045	Sgt. MEDWAY, W. T.	8
DW-E.	L.1013	F/O. W. H. C. WARNER.	10
DW-A.	L.1001	F/O. P. G. LAMB.	9
DW-M.	L.1000	F/Lt. J. ELLIS.	4
DW-N.	L.1075	F/O. G. L. CHAMBERS.	4
DW-O.	L.1043	Sgt. JENKINS, P. D.	6
	N.3289	F/O. G. M. T. KERR.	6
DW-Q.	L.1016	P/O. P. LITCHFIELD.	7
DW-P.	K.9960	Sgt. ARNFIELD, S. J.	5

*Almost certainly a clerical error—probably DW-J, L.1003, or N.3284 as a Command Reserve (no 'DW' identification letter). Becomes 'DW-J' later on.

An evocative photograph of six of 610 Squadron's pilots just before the Dunkirk Evacuation: the newspaper's headline is 'First B.E.F. Heroes' Medals'. From left to right, P/O Norris, F/Lt Ellis, and F/O Kerr. The pilot holding the newspaper was originally believed to be F/O Kerr Wilson, but is now thought to be F/O Lambert Chambers. The next pilot is unknown—through a process of elimination, he could be Sgt Jenkins. On the right is F/O Medcalf. (*Copyright Kerr family*)

With the increasing deterioration of the situation in France, 610's patrol of Calais was to protect one of the few strongholds the Allies were still defending and could expect to escape from. Calais was effectively acting as an outer line of defence for Dunkirk from the west. However, during 24 May, Churchill and his commanders realised that unlike at Boulogne, an evacuation might not be possible—the Allied troops in Calais might have to stand and fight to the end, sacrificing themselves so that the maximum number of the BEF could reach Dunkirk for evacuation. So it was critical that air superiority was maintained over Calais. As a result, the pilots were highly likely to confront the *Luftwaffe* en masse for the first time. The strain and tension amongst them must have been palpable, especially after the incident with the Blenheims. However, once again, 'The Chesters' did not see any sign of enemy aircraft and they returned to base at 1745 hours after a flight which lasted one hour and twenty minutes. There was time for the Squadron to send up one more patrol, this time Red Section to cover Manston at Angels 10 (altitude 10,000 feet). The patrol took off at 2030 hours and lasted exactly an hour, with the pilots listed below seeing no sign of the enemy:

DW-G.	L.1045	F/O. W. H. C. WARNER.	11
	N.3289	P/O. S. C. NORRIS.	9
DW-Q.	L.1016	P/O. P. LITCHFIELD.	8

Since arriving in 11 Group, the Squadron had carried out twenty-eight recorded patrols, nine of which had been over the Channel or northern France. It was remarkable that there had been no sign of a dangerous enemy, who were proving a real threat to the RAF's inexperienced fighter pilots:

> Since the German offensive began on 10th May, an official figure of pilot losses in the Group (11) totalled fifty-four during 112 offensive patrols. Thirty of these losses had occurred in just six days—20th to 25th May. Park was also to be handicapped by a directive from Air Ministry to provide continuous weak fighter patrols throughout the eighteen hours of daylight. Park objected to this order, forecasting that this would undoubtedly incur heavy casualties.[15]

This inevitably meant long, exhausting days for Park's fighter pilots, which is what 610 Squadron was experiencing. The Squadron had been lucky not to encounter a foe which was far more experienced in modern aerial warfare than themselves. No matter how well the RAF's men were trained, there was nothing that could prepare them for the first encounters with the *Luftwaffe*. Life would also be getting harder for the ground crew, and Raymond Ellis recalled how 25 May brought about a big change in his daily life for the next few weeks:

> On the 25th May, together with engine fitters Cpl Arthur Holford and two LACs, I was detached to join members of 32, 79 and 242 Hurricane squadrons in forming a Station Maintenance Flight in the triple-bay Belfast hangar in North Camp where we were to repair aircraft that had been damaged in action…We had neither the equipment nor the time to repair the badly damaged fuselage of a Spitfire which had to be returned to the factory on a long 'Queen Mary' trailer. Damaged main planes, control surfaces, undercarriages, engines etc. could be dealt with by 610's own Servicing Flight in the South Camp hangar.[16]

As a result of this detachment, Ellis would soon find himself at a different airfield altogether from his own Squadron.

By now, the future of the BEF and the Allied armies was very bleak indeed, being pushed back by the rampant German armies to a small pocket on the coast, centred on Dunkirk. Boulogne's brave defence finally ended on 25 May. On that evening, Churchill decided to sacrifice his troops in Calais. Brigadier Claude Nicholson, the officer in charge of around 4,000 men defending the port, was left to fight a brave rearguard action, to delay the *Panzer* divisions and German infantry. The remainder of the Allied forces were flooding into Dunkirk in the seemingly vain hope of being rescued by the Royal Navy. The planning for this evacuation, code named 'Operation Dynamo', was going into overdrive. As a result, AVM Park needed to redeploy his forces and 610 Squadron's stint at Biggin Hill came to an end after sixteen days. The order came through on 26 May for it to move immediately to RAF Gravesend.[17]

8

26–31 May 1940: Move to Gravesend and 'Operation Dynamo'

The airport at Gravesend, Thong Lane, Chalk, which opened in 1932, had originally been for general aviation, aiming to serve as an alternative to Croydon, which at that time was London's main airport. In 1937, 20 E&RFTS was also established there for the RAF, as part of the rearmament programme.

> In September 1939 the aerodrome was requisitioned by the government and it became a satellite of Biggin Hill in No. 11 Group of Fighter Command.
>
> Pilots were accommodated in the control tower as well as at Cobham Hall, the nearby home of the Darnley family. The Laughing Waters roadhouse on the A2 road was also used to accommodate ground crews as well as local commandeered houses. Aircraft were dispersed around the aerodrome, together with hastily erected Nissen huts and machine gun emplacements.[1]

F/Lt Ellis had some interesting reminiscences about this time:

> We used the clubhouse as our officers' mess where the facilities were minimal so Flying Officer 'Peter' Keighley, who was a manager in Harrods before the war, arranged for them to run our Mess. A Harrods van arrived every morning with staff, food and drink for the day. So for those eight hectic days we lived well—fillet steak for lunch and lobster thermidor for dinner! It was well worth the cost as the novelty of the arrangement did quite a lot for morale ...[2]

The pilots would have missed the facilities which were standard at a Sector station like Biggin Hill, so any luxuries they could acquire for themselves were only too welcome—610 was lucky to have Keighley's contacts. It was, perhaps, one last hurrah for the image of the AAF! Jo Keighley, the pilot's son, told me his father also did regular runs in his sports car to Harrods for a food hamper, when the Squadron was based at Biggin Hill, which was equally popular.

It is likely that the Squadron moved to Gravesend during the afternoon of 26 May, as they carried out three patrols in the morning, although as they were all carried out by 'B' Flight, 'A' Flight may have moved in the morning. The first patrol took off at 0710 hours with orders to patrol Manston and '15 miles out to sea' (ORB). The pilots were F/O Kerr Wilson (N.3289), F/O Medcalf (N.3274) and Sgt Arnfield (DW-N, L.1075)—with no sign of the enemy they returned to base at 0830 hours. When an 'X' raid was plotted over Manston, another section was scrambled at 0950 hours to investigate it at 3,000 feet. This time, F/Lt Ellis led (DW-M, L.1000), with Sgt Jenkins (DW-O, L.1043), and Sgt Arnfield (DW-Q, L.1016) who was carrying out his second patrol of the day. Again, the search proved fruitless and they returned to base at 1030 hours. The third and final recorded patrol of the day was a short one—Green Section took off at 1135 hours to patrol Manston, but was recalled when it was over the airfield and returned to base fifteen minutes later (ORB). This patrol involved:

610 Squadron at RAF Gravesend. From left to right, the Adjutant F/O le Fleming, Brian Smith, P/O Lloyd the intelligence officer and Peter Lamb. The four men seem to be enjoying a joke. The pilot in the background, between the two pillars of the control tower, is probably P/O Norris. (*Copyright 610 Squadron Association*)

	N.3274	F/O. J. K. WILSON.	7
	N.3289	F/O. A. R. J. MEDCALF.	8
DW-T.	P.9452	P/O. P. LITCHFIELD.	9

Having completed this brief sortie, it is probable that 'B' Flight headed off to Gravesend to settle in as quickly as possible, before the onset of further operations. Action was imminent after the devastating news of the fall of Calais that evening. The fact that the Germans had lifted the 'Halt Order' on their land forces, enabling them to get within artillery range of Dunkirk, meant the decision was finally taken to start the BEF's evacuation from Dunkirk.

Vice-Admiral Bertram Ramsay received the order to begin 'Operation Dynamo' at 1857 hours on 26 May 1940. Ramsay, whose position in command of Dover saw him oversee the evacuation, for which he had been given less than a week to prepare, 'had assembled 15 passenger ferries at Dover and a further 20 at Southampton. These it was hoped, would be able to embark troops direct from the quays at Dunkirk'.[3] In time, their numbers would be greatly bolstered by the famous 'little ships', which are forever associated with the Dunkirk evacuation. Protection for these vessels was provided by a powerful force of Royal Navy destroyers, supported by corvettes, sloops, minesweepers and gunboats, which would also play a key role in attempting to evacuate British and Allied troops in the face of constant German attack. In reality, the Admiralty hoped to bring home about 45,000 troops before Dunkirk fell.

On the first morning of 'Operation Dynamo', Monday 27 May, F/O Brian Smith (DW-S, N.3201) was ordered on patrol at 0925 hours off Dungeness for just over an hour. Upon landing, he barely had time for his aircraft to be refuelled before he was up again, this time as part of an 'A' Flight patrol at 10,000 feet of their forward Base, (most likely Manston) at 1100 hours for forty-five minutes. The formation was led by the squadron leader:

DW-S.	N.3201	S/Ldr. A. L. FRANKS.	6
DW-G.	L.1045	F/O. P. G. LAMB.	10
DW-J.	K.3284*	Sgt. MEDWAY, W. T.	9
DW-E.	L.1013	F/O. E. B. B. SMITH.	12
DW-K.	L.1062	F/O. W. H. C. WARNER.	12
DW-D.	L.1010	P/O. S. C. NORRIS.	10

*Almost certainly a clerical error—probably DW-J, L.1003, or N.3284 as a Command Reserve (no 'DW' identification letter). Becomes 'DW-J' later on.

No contact was made with the *Luftwaffe*.

In the early evening, orders came through for a Squadron patrol of Dunkirk along with the Hurricanes of 56 Squadron, as follows:

DW-S.	N.3201	S/Ldr. A. L. FRANKS.	Red 1	7
DW-D.	L.1010	F/O. E. B. B. SMITH.	Red 2	13
DW-J.	N.3284*	Sgt. MEDWAY, W. T.	Red 3	10
DW-F.	L.1011	F/Lt. A. T. SMITH.	Yellow 1	10
DW-G.	L.1045	F/O. P. G. LAMB.	Yellow 3	11
DW-E.	L.1013	F/O. W. H. C. WARNER.	Yellow 2	13
DW-M.	L.1000	F/Lt. J. ELLIS.	Blue 1	6
	N.3289	F/O. G. M. T. KERR.	Blue 2	7
DW-K.	L.1062	F/O. G. L. CHAMBERS.	Blue 3	5
DW-L.	L.1017	F/O. J. KERR WILSON.	Green 1	8
DW-Q.	L.1016	F/O. A. R. J. MEDCALF.	Green 2	9
	N.3274	P/O. P. LITCHFIELD.	Green 3	10

*Almost certainly a clerical error—probably DW-J, L.1003, or N.3284 as a Command Reserve.

610 Squadron left Gravesend at 1810 hours and formed up at 3,000 feet with the Hurricanes over Manston. The two Squadrons then climbed to their patrol heights, 610 at 18,000 feet, 56 Squadron in support at 20,000, as pre-arranged by the two COs. Having crossed the Channel without incident, the Squadrons patrolled from Gravelines towards Furnes, when heavy anti-aircraft fire (AA) was encountered between Bergues and Furnes, but ceased on their arrival in the area. However, this was the calm before the storm, as S/Ldr Franks went on to report: '5 miles south of Dunkirk, 2 sections of 610 attacked a single E.A ME 111 [HE 111] at 15000' and shot it down. No. 1 attacks being used' (TNA, AIR 50/172/27). Franks himself concentrated solely on identifying the Heinkel He 111, an understandably cautious approach given the recent 'friendly fire' incident. The ORB described in some detail the Squadron's first success of the war:

> Red Section dived and carried out a No.1 attack from above. Red 1 (S/Ldr.FRANKS) did not open fire, but overtook it on the starboard side to make certain that it was an E/A. As soon as Red.1 saw that it was a Heinkel, he ordered Red.2 (F/O.E.B.B.SMITH) and Red.3 (Sgt. MEDWAY,W.T.) to attack. Red.2 fired all his ammunition at the fuselage and starboard engine, which when he broke off the attack was emitting flames and black smoke. Red 3 continued the attack, and fired a burst of about 5 seconds. Yellow section then attacked, and F/Lt. A.T.SMITH, F/O.WARNER & F/O.LAMB, all gave the E/A short bursts. Blue section then dived to attack, but Blue leader (F/Lt. J.ELLIS) broke his section away before opening fire, as the Heinkel III by this time was on fire and diving steeply.

This is the frightening view the Heinkel 111's dorsal gunner would have had as Red Section's Spitfires closed in to carry out a No. 1 attack on 27 May. The photo was actually taken later in the summer from an RAF aircraft, as part of a series of aerial shots of 610 Squadron on patrol. (*Copyright Imperial War Museum, CH 737*)

While 'A' Flight and Blue Section had intercepted the lone aircraft, it seems that Green Section had been left as a top cover, while 56 Squadron was presumably higher still. The first pilot to open fire on the unfortunate Heinkel was F/O Brian Smith. He reported the following about the combat which took place at 1905 hours, five miles south-east of Dunkirk at 15,000 feet:

> I was Red 2 and flying northwards along the coast south of Dunkirk when we sighted one a/c on our starboard. Red section approached to identify and I saw the enemy markings on the fuselage and crossed from the port to the starboard side of e/a to initiate my attack.
>
> On opening fire I saw pieces fly out of the starboard wing, smoke came out of the starboard engine and the wheels came down. I expended all my ammunition and broke away at 20 yards with oil and smoke pouring out of e/a which I identified as a HE 111. As I broke away a number of the crew baled out: previously the a/c had fixed [fired] a verey [Very] light. (TNA, AIR 50/172/68)

Smith's attack on the bomber had been devastating, primarily because he had flown into such close range. With one engine badly damaged and the undercarriage down, its German crew must have known their number was up, especially when they could see more Spitfires following in to attack, hence their decision to start to bale out. Brian Smith recalled when I met him how he was pleased that at least some of the crew had got out alive:

> And the big thing about the Heinkel, which I shot down with an engine on fire, was that they all jumped out! So I was delighted, because we weren't hunting people we were hunting aeroplanes, and if they jumped out so much the better. The odd one didn't think that way, but most of us did.

Sgt Bill Medway completed Red Section's attack with another burst of fire, adding to the damage, before Yellow Section followed in behind him, led by F/Lt Tom Smith:

> As leader of Yellow Section I saw Red Section identify and deliver a No. 1 attack on a Heinkel 111 Red one identifying and Red 2 and 3 engaging enemy. After Red 2's attack a parachute came out as No. 3 was attacking a 3 star red cartridge was fired. When my Section attacked smoke was coming out of the e/a and it was flying very slowly. I gave a burst of only 2 seconds and had to break away owing to overshooting, estimate the speed not more 120 m.p.h. When I broke away something fell off the e/a. (TNA, AIR 50/172/66)

The Heinkel was doomed. The biggest problem for the RAF pilots was the Heinkel's reduced speed, which meant they barely had time to sight their guns on the aircraft before they had passed it, a problem echoed by Yellow 2, F/O Warner: 'One He 111 was attacked by three aircraft and when I attacked it, it was pouring out smoke from both engines. I gave a short burst of about 2 seconds, and had to break away owing to the e/a going so slowly. He used no evasive tactics' (TNA, AIR 50/172/77).

F/O Lamb provides a similar picture of the attack:

> I was Yellow 3—I saw heavy A.A fire over Dunkirk as we approached from N.W. A HE 111 was seen flying east. Red 2 & 3 attack—Yellow 1 gave line astern. We followed with No 1 attack as we approach E/A (Fire 3 star) Red Very Light—Smoke was coming from Port Engine. I saw Yellow 1 & 2 break away very quickly. Also noted E/A had undercarriage down—I immediately closed throttle which enabled me to get 2 second burst in 300—50 yds. E/A speed about 100mph ... (TNA, AIR 50/172/45)

A Heinkel He 111H, the type of bomber which 610 Squadron encountered and claimed to have shot down on 27 May 1940. (*Ron Mackay*)

Lamb's forethought to reduce his speed enabled him to get in a short burst of fire, again at very close range, which sealed the aircraft's fate. As a result, F/Lt Ellis called off his section's attack:

> I ordered Blue Section to carry out a No1 attack also, but on approaching E.A I could see it was completely disabled flames appearing from the engine nacelles and its u/c lowered. I therefore ordered my section to break away before opening fire. The section reformed into Vic, and proceeded to climb towards Dunkirk. (TNA, AIR 50/172/20)

The Squadron was using the textbook style of attacks which they had practised against RAF bombers in pre-war training; a No. 1 attack on a single bomber, the pilots flying in a follow-my-leader line astern formation. The method was successful in this instance, but while it was one thing to train against RAF bombers over the English countryside, it was a totally different proposition to do so in the dangerous, smoke-filled skies over Dunkirk, where prowling *Luftwaffe* fighters lurked.

In the combat reports and the ORB, there is a common theme that the Heinkel fired a red very light or flare, either a signal for help from the bomber's crew in the face of impossible odds, or a signal to spring a trap, which was fired too late. Whichever it was, the flare was recognised by a large formation of twin-engined Messerschmitt 110 fighters stalking above this one-sided action, and they came screaming down on 610's Spitfires to avenge the loss of the hapless bomber. As Wg Cdr Smith aptly recalled about the Heinkel—'Yes, ah I remember that very well, 'cos I remember so clearly their chaps streaming down. I think the Heinkel was a decoy. Yes, I think it was, because all hell got loose afterwards'.

The pilots of Red and Yellow Sections seem to have been the most under threat of being bounced, as they had their attention very much focused on attacking the Heinkel. Their predicament is outlined in each of their combat reports, as they were suddenly beneath an enemy formation which greatly outnumbered them. S/Ldr Franks described events after the attack on the Heinkel as follows:

> 30—40 ME 110 then appeared above us and a general dog fight ensued. I engaged one ME 110 that dived on another Spitfire, I got on its tail and with a 7 sec. burst saw it turn on its back. I followed it down and saw it crash into the sea N.E of Dunkirk. I climbed up into the sun from 1000 to 15000 ft, the sky was full of ME 110s and Spitfires. I saw a ME.110 on the tail of a Spitfire and engaged it. I hit it and saw it break off its pursuit of the Spitfire. My ammunition ran out and I dived for Sea level and returned to Gravesend. (TNA, AIR 50/172/27)

Franks had done well to pick off one of the enemy fighters and damage another given the *Luftwaffe's* numerical and positional advantage. However, he was taking a real risk in following his first victim down to confirm that it crashed, as he lost altitude and was not concentrating on what might in turn have been trying to shoot him down. Such decisions could prove fatal.

Having done the lion's share of the damage to the Heinkel, F/O Smith now found himself in an even more dangerous situation, as he had used up all his ammunition. As a result, he was a sitting duck and had to rely on his flying and guile to get back home: 'On turning away I saw a very large number of Me 110 diving down to attack, 3 of which were on my tail and so having no ammunition left I made for the nearest smoke (coming from Dunkirk which had just been bombed). I then made my way back here to base. I observed no return fire' (TNA, AIR 50/172/68). Being unarmed with three enemy fighters on your tail in your first dogfight must have been daunting indeed, but Smith maintained his composure and was able to use the thick palls of smoke to evade them and make his way back to Gravesend. This trick came in handy for several of 610's outnumbered pilots.

Following Yellow Section's attack, F/Lt Tom Smith reformed his section before being engaged by the 110s:

> As I reformed my section I climbed up into the sun and heard an R/T call that the fighters were coming down on my port. A dog fight ensued in which, as when getting a M.E.110 off my tail, I gave another a burst of 5/6 seconds deflective, both diving and turning. The e/a finally went into a left hand spin at the same time I saw the fire entering the fuselage, the wings on top had yellow roundels and black crosses. On breaking away I climbed into the sun to 15000' and chased another ME.110 on his tail down to 2000' into the smoke of burning Calais. This one covered my wings and windscreen with oil. My ammunition was expended and I doubt if he could pull out of his dive. When I gave up the chase I was down to 2000 ft in thick smoke. (TNA, AIR 50/172/66)

There is a real sense of the chaos and confusion of the dogfight in this report, Smith realising the importance of altitude and climbing into the sun. Again, the thick smoke spiralling up from the ports gives an idea of the damage that was taking place on the ground from the aerial bombardment. Smith lost his foe in it, although it is likely the Me 110 was doomed.

While Smith had maintained the upper hand in this confrontation, his number 2, Bill Warner, was less fortunate and struggled to shake off the numerous 110s:

> After that we were attacked by Me 110s and we broke up and selected our own targets. I attacked one formation and then saw one on my own tail. I turned and got a deflection shot in at another and broke away. Another came on my tail and followed me down to about 15,000 feet when I got away in the smoke which was coming from Dunkerque and returned to base. My a/c was hit twice once at the root end of the airscrew and once through the tip of the port main-plane. (TNA, AIR 50/172/77)

Despite bravely pressing home his attacks, Warner had to escape using the smoke cover due to repeated attacks from the numerically superior force, and he was fortunate to make it back given that DW-E, L.1013 had been hit twice. The Messerschmitt 110, aptly named *Zerstörer* or 'Destroyer', was a formidably armed aircraft with two 20-mm cannon and four 7.9-mm MG 17 machine guns in the nose and one 7.9-mm MG 17 machine gun for defending the rear. Often, all it would take was one accurate cannon shell to bring down a Spitfire, but this time Warner's luck held and he lived to tell the tale.

The third member of Yellow Section, F/O Lamb, reported in fairly terse terms how the inexperienced Spitfire pilots were outnumbered by the Me 110s, once the attack on the Heinkel was complete:

> I then reformed with Yellow Section who were going towards a quantity of 110s—I noticed about 10 more 110s astern diving towards us—I picked out one ahead and to port, followed him in steep turn firing full deflection at about 300 yds for a burst of about 4 seconds—I had to break off attack as 110 was on my tail—Diving through smoke I evaded him—After short time in smoke I came out to see 2 Ju 88 going North. I was about to attack when I saw about 3 110s coming towards me. I went back into smoke cloud and came out again looking for rest of Squadron. Saw another 110 climbing gave short burst at about 400 yards decided E/A was outclimbing me and broke off attack. (TNA, AIR 50/172/45)

Like his fellow pilots, Lamb repeatedly tried to engage the enemy formations, but had to break off and hide in the great palls of smoke from the burning ships and oil refineries around the devastated ports. Although he did escape, being alone in such a swirling dogfight was about as dangerous as it could get for a novice fighter pilot and he was lucky to come away from his first combat unscathed. The Squadron would be fortunate indeed if all twelve of its pilots were so lucky.

Blue Section was in a slightly stronger position because F/Lt Ellis realised the need to break off their initial attack on the Heinkel. However, this did not last long as they were forced to escape from the massed ranks of attacking *Zerstörers*:

An atmospheric shot of a *Schwarm* of Messerschmitt 110s of 15. (*Zerstörer*)/*Lehrgeschwader* 1, on patrol over Paris in June 1940. This was the type of fighter which attacked 610 Squadron *en masse*, following the flare being fired from the doomed Heinkel. (*ww2images.com*)

> At about 18,000' one flight of 5 flights of 6 ME 110s which had been circling at about 5,000 above us dived down in line astern to attack us from behind. I ordered the section to break up and I climbed up straight in to the sun, turning round almost immediately to try and get on their tail but could see no sign of E.A. I tried unsuccessfully to collect my section at 20,000 over Dunkirk and so proceeded towards Furnes climbing to 25,000. Over Furnes I saw 4 ME 110s in vic formation 2,000 below me. I dived down on the outside right aircraft and got in a burst of about 7 seconds at 400-300x. When about to start my second burst I noticed 6 more Me 110s doing a quarter attack from above, the front machine firing green tracer bullets. I immediately broke away and climbed up again into the Sun, on turning round again all E/A had disappeared. This attack took place at 1925. My burst had no apparent effect of [on] the E/A but I feel certain I must have hit the aircraft.
>
> I continued the patrol at 20,000 until 1945 and then proceeded home. (TNA, AIR 50/172/20)

The frantic nature of this dogfight is plain to see. It is interesting to note how Ellis gained altitude by climbing up into the sun, as soon as his original break from the attacking 110s was complete, repeating the manoeuvre later on. This was a tactic which had been planned in advance, with height being so crucial in the battle for survival in a dogfight.

F/O Kerr also found himself in the thick of his first dogfight, having followed Ellis in the abortive attack on the Heinkel:

> I was flying No. 2 in Blue Section. Just before reaching the patrol area, the Sqdn. was ordered to form echelon port. As we approached the coast one E/A was observed flying N. Red & Yellow Sections carried out No. 1 attacks on this E.A and Blue Section were ordered to form line astern and follow it down. I overshot and broke off to starboard and joined up with Blue 1. We then climbed up to about 15000 as a section. I then observed 2 separate groups of a/c considerably about and on either side of us flying in circles. Shortly after this Blue 1 gave the order to break up and I turned sharply to starboard

> still climbing. I then became involved in a dog fight with a group of the 110s. I got in a short burst on one but observed no effect. I then broke off the engagement and gained height. After some time I observed a ME 110 much lower down and dived to attack him. Eventually I got on his tail and fired the rest of my ammunition at him at about 50—100 yds range while he was diving in a tight left hand turn. Return fire was experienced from his back gun (white tracer) and one bullet passed through the fin of my a/c. I did not observe any effects of my fire and after breaking off the attack, I was unable to observe the a/c again. Having no ammunition left I then returned to Gravesend where I landed. (TNA, AIR 50/172/44)

Kerr's phrase that the enemy aircraft were 'considerably about and on either side of us' sums up the predicament the Spitfire pilots found themselves in, Kerr, being forced to fight on his own against groups of enemy fighters who held all the aces. Despite this, it was Kerr who turned the tables on his foe and got a short burst of fire off, before he saw sense and broke away to gain altitude. Malcolm Kerr's inexperience showed during his second attack, in that such a long burst of fire from close range did not seem to do the Messerschmitt any damage. Overall though, this long-term member of the Squadron could be pleased with his efforts, despite slight damage to his Spitfire, N.3289.

Blue Section's third pilot was F/O Graham Lambert Chambers. He made the first real reference to the Heinkel having been a trap for the vastly superior force of 110s to take advantage of:

> I was Blue 3 and followed Blue section in the first attack on the decoy He 111. I then followed Blue 1 back up to 20,000 ft. but lost him in the sun. I patrolled Gravelines to Dunkirk at 20,000 for 15 minutes and did not sight any aircraft either friendly or enemy. I then saw about 6 aircraft dive bombing at a ship outside Dunkirk harbour and dived down on them. When I was about 5,000 ft 2 Ju 87 saw me and turned inland and went down to sea-level. I followed them inland but overshot them having a great deal of surplus speed and when I had done a turn, lost sight of them. I returned to the ship which was no longer being bombed, sighted Green 1 and returned to base with him. (TNA, AIR 50/172/46)

Lambert Chambers's report highlights one of the greatest anomalies of contemporary air combat, as while he did not see another aircraft for fifteen minutes, the rest of his section and most of his Squadron were fighting for their lives in the same area. With the high speeds at which aircraft now travelled, this was to become a familiar feature of the air battles: one minute the sky was full of twisting and turning aircraft, but the next there might be none. The length of time Lambert Chambers spent on his own with so many enemy aircraft in his vicinity, meant he was lucky not to be singled out for attack, although his decision to maintain a patrolling altitude of 20,000 feet was a wise one. In the combat report's synopsis, he stated that his engagement with the dive-bombers took place at 1915 hours, two miles inland from Dunkirk, but he overshot the slow *Stukas*, showing his lack of combat experience, before he headed home with Green 1.

Green Leader was F/O Kerr Wilson, the Squadron's second longest serving member and an experienced pilot, hence his position as a regular section leader. Green Section's part in this engagement differed greatly from the other three sections. As the pilots state, they had been left to act as a top cover while the other nine Spitfires engaged the lone bomber. This was a sensible tactic to employ, although with hindsight it might have been more effective to have let 'A' Flight take on the bomber and leave the whole of 'B' Flight as top cover. It seems hard to understand how Green Section did not see the massed formations of Me 110s which were circling over Red, Yellow and Blue Sections, but the two surviving combat reports from Green Section outline what happened. The first from Kerr Wilson:

> 12 A/C of 610 Sqdn left Gravesend Aerodrome at 1810 hours to patrol from Gravelines—Furnes at 18000 ft. I was leading Green Section and soon after arriving on Patrol, Red, Yellow and Blue Section

> dived down and attacked enemy a/c. I remained with my Section at 18000 ft as a Security patrol. At about 19.10 hours Green 3 reported a/c over Dunkirk and on investigation these proved to be JU88 and Me.110s. I ordered to Section to form line astern and carry out attacks. The E.A broke up their circle and Green 2 and I attacked a JU 88 which dived very steeply. Green 2 attacked first and I gave a deflection burst of about 2 seconds which failed to achieve any result and broke away. I climbed up to 18000 ft again and instructed Green 2 and 3 to join me and was shortly joined by Green 3. Green 2 did not answer my radio call. Green 3 and I patrolled until about 1925 when Green 3 reported an a/c low down, so I instructed him to investigate it. He dived down into a cloud of smoke and I remained above to intercept any a/c which might come out from the other side. However I saw nothing and Green 3 returned to base on his own. I continued to patrol at 18000' until about 1935 hrs when I decided to return to base, but just off Dunkirk I saw a vessel being attacked by 8 JU 87s. I dived down approaching from the sun and carried out attacks on 4 a/c in turn, but was unable to see if they had been shot down as in each case I broke away sharply at about 100 yds. I succeeded however in driving off the JU 87s as they quickly disappeared. I attacked from the rear in a number 1 attack in each case and opened fire at about 300 yds. Each a/c did a sharp climbing turn to left which gave a wonderful opportunity for a deflection shot, but forced me to break away before I could observe any definite results.
>
> When approaching the aerodrome, my engine stopped at a distance of about 1 mile away due to lack of petrol, although to [the] gauge showed 30 gallons, but as I was flying at a height of about 4000' I was able to land on the aerodrome. Unfortunately, however, my starboard wheel had been shot and as soon as I touched down, it fell off, so that the aircraft tipped up on its nose. (TNA, AIR 50/172/79)

From the timings, it is likely that Green Section saw the enemy formation they intercepted at roughly the same time as the other three sections had been engaged by the Me 110s. This explains why they had not been able to head off the Messerschmitts. Green 3, P/O Litchfield, spotted the initial enemy aircraft which Green Section attacked, forcing them to break from their defensive formation. It is interesting to see how the section interacted very well using their R/T to coordinate various attacks, but the sudden lack of response from Green 2, F/O Medcalf, must have been a worry after the joint attack on the Ju 88 bomber at 1915 hours.

Kerr Wilson's extended patrol helped save a ship from a dive-bombing attack at about 1935 hours, most likely the same one Lambert Chambers had assisted, but he was unable to make a claim. Fascinatingly, footage of this encounter survives from Kerr Wilson's gun camera, but it is only possible to make out a fleeting image of a gull-winged Ju 87.[4] Having bravely fended off this enemy formation, the thirty-two year old from Heswall, Wirral, made the return flight across the Channel in the company of Lambert Chambers. But the drama was not over, as a faulty fuel tank gauge left Kerr Wilson short of petrol, before battle damage caused his aircraft, DW-L, L.1017 to crash on landing at Gravesend! He could not really have had a more dramatic first encounter with the enemy, but at least he had survived it. Following repairs, L.1017 did not rejoin 610 Squadron.[5]

Peter Litchfield's combat report is the final one from this dogfight, and I have included a photo of his original typewritten report (see p. 134), including Sections A–M, the summary to each pilot's report.

Litchfield's account establishes that the enemy aircraft Green Section attacked were four miles south of Dunkirk, and over eight miles away from where the rest of the Squadron became entangled with the 110s. Therefore, it is no surprise that they had not intercepted the enemy aircraft which attacked the rest of the Squadron. It had been a successful patrol for the pilot officer, as Litchfield claimed a Messerschmitt 110 destroyed at about 1915 hours, which he had originally diverted from Kerr Wilson's tail. Litchfield was very sharp-sighted, as he had also spotted the low flying aircraft later on, identifying it as a Blenheim despite the difficult conditions. Additionally, he was an accomplished marksman, both critical attributes for a fighter pilot.

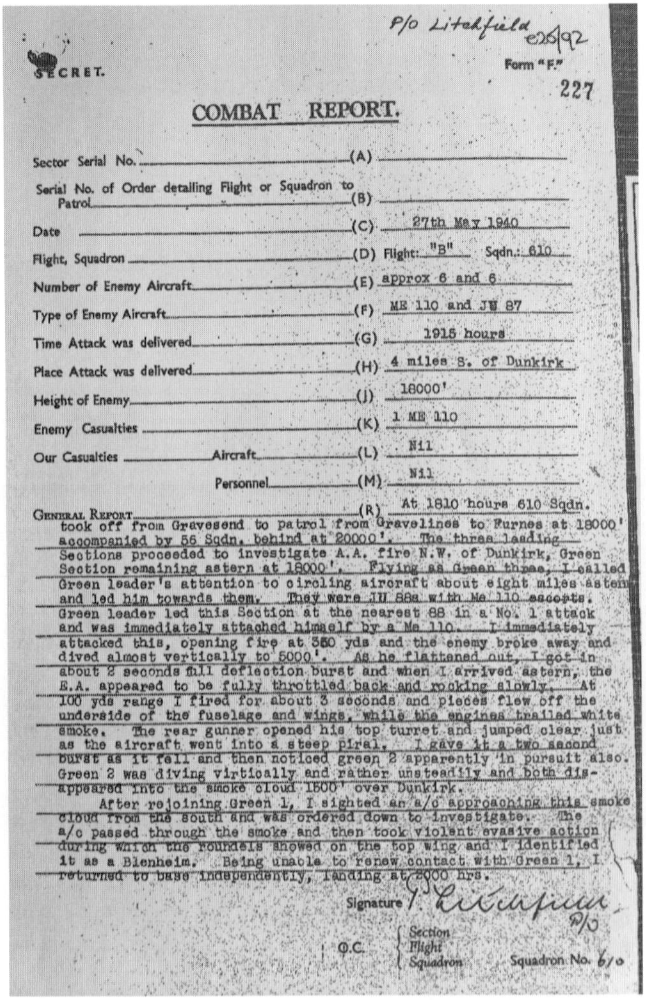

P/o Litchfield e26/92

SECRET. Form "F."

227

COMBAT REPORT.

Sector Serial No. (A)

Serial No. of Order detailing Flight or Squadron to Patrol (B)

Date (C) 27th May 1940

Flight, Squadron (D) Flight: "B" Sqdn.: 610

Number of Enemy Aircraft (E) approx 6 and 6

Type of Enemy Aircraft (F) ME 110 and JU 87

Time Attack was delivered (G) 1915 hours

Place Attack was delivered (H) 4 miles S. of Dunkirk

Height of Enemy (J) 18000'

Enemy Casualties (K) 1 ME 110

Our Casualties Aircraft (L) Nil

Personnel (M) Nil

General Report (R) At 1810 hours 610 Sqdn. took off from Gravesend to patrol from Gravelines to Furnes at 18000' accompanied by 56 Sqdn. behind at 20000'. The three leading Sections proceeded to investigate A.A. fire N.W. of Dunkirk, Green Section remaining astern at 18000'. Flying as Green three, I called Green leader's attention to circling aircraft about eight miles astern and led him towards them. They were JU 88s with Me 110 escorts. Green leader led this Section at the nearest 88 in a No. 1 attack and was immediately attached himself by a Me 110. I immediately attacked this, opening fire at 350 yds and the enemy broke away and dived almost vertically to 5000'. As he flattened out, I got in about 2 seconds full deflection burst and when I arrived astern, the E.A. appeared to be fully throttled back and rocking slowly. At 100 yds range I fired for about 3 seconds and pieces flew off the underside of the fuselage and wings, while the engines trailed white smoke. The rear gunner opened his top turret and jumped clear just as the aircraft went into a steep piral. I gave it a two second burst as it fell and then noticed green 2 apparently in pursuit also. Green 2 was diving virtically and rather unsteadily and both disappeared into the smoke cloud 1500' over Dunkirk.

After rejoining Green 1, I sighted an a/c approaching this smoke cloud from the south and was ordered down to investigate. The a/c passed through the smoke and then took violent evasive action during which the roundels showed on the top wing and I identified it as a Blenheim. Being unable to renew contact with Green 1, I returned to base independently, landing at 2000 hrs.

Signature P. Litchfield P/O

O.C. Section / Flight / Squadron Squadron No. 610

P/O Litchfield's detailed combat report, 27 May 1940. (*TNA, AIR 50/172/48*)

Litchfield was the only man to record his arrival back at Gravesend as 2000 hours. The ORB states that the patrol finished at 1945 hours, so it is fair to assume that all the pilots would have been returning around this time. Kerr Wilson made the most dramatic arrival in Spitfire DW-L, L.1017, while Kerr's N.3289 and Warner's DW-E, L.1013 had both picked up German bullets and F/Lt Smith's DW-F, L.1011 was besmirched with oil from a *Zerstörer*. To those awaiting their return at Gravesend, it would have been obvious they had been in a huge dogfight. However, as time passed, the biggest sign of their scrap was that two pilots had failed to return. S/Ldr Franks recalled in his combat report at two separate points, emphasising the enormity of the fact: '2 SPITFIRES OF MY SQDN. NOT RETURNED, 2 PILOTS MISSING' and '10 of my Squadron returned after individual combats. Two are not accounted for' (TNA, AIR 50/172/27). The two pilots were Sgt Medway, Red 3 in DW-J, L.1003 (not N.3284, as recorded in the battle order) and F/O Medcalf, Green 2, (DW-Q, L.1016). Both men were reported as, 'Missing as a result of operations against the enemy' (ORB) on 27 May 1940.

By piecing together the evidence available from the various combat reports, it is most likely that Sgt Bill Medway was shot down by the Me 110s which attacked Red Section following their successful attack on the Heinkel 111. The ORB records that 'Red 3 (Medway) continued the attack, and fired a burst of about 5 seconds'. When Red 2, Brian Smith, broke off his attack, he described seeing three

A moving photo of F/O A. R. J. Medcalf, in one of the Squadron's early Spitfires, DW-P, K.9960. Although the photo is posed, the pilot, one of the Squadron's longest-serving Officers, has a wistful expression. Medcalf was Killed in Action over the Dunkirk evacuation on 27 May 1940. (*Copyright Medcalf family*)

110s on his tail. It is probable that Medway found himself in a similar predicament, and that he was shot down by some of them, although none of 610 Squadron's pilots reported seeing Bill Medway going down. In S/Ldr Franks's report, he twice mentions attacking 110s which were already attacking a Spitfire, so perhaps one of these was Medway's aircraft, and Franks had arrived just too late. Medway was originally listed as 'missing', but further details would become available.

By looking at Green Section's combat reports, it is also possible to work out the likely fate of F/O Medcalf, aged twenty-six and from Willaston, Wirral, who had been with the Squadron since its early days. It was about 1910–1915 hours when Green Section attacked the Junkers 88s and Me 110s, as described by the section leader, Kerr Wilson concentrating on a Ju 88, which Medcalf, Green 2, had attacked first. The attack's outcome is unknown, as Kerr Wilson climbed back up to 18,000 feet, but P/O Litchfield, bringing up the rear, saw Kerr Wilson coming under attack from an escorting 110, which Litchfield immediately attacked. Litchfield continued his pursuit, successfully hitting the *Zerstörer*, before stating, 'I gave it a two second burst as it fell and then noticed green 2 apparently in pursuit also. Green 2 was diving vertically and rather unsteadily and both disappeared into the smoke cloud 1500' over Dunkirk' (TNA, AIR 50/172/48). This was the last sighting of Albert Rupert John Medcalf, as when Kerr Wilson called up his wingmen to reform at 18,000 feet, he did not receive a reply.

It is probable that Medcalf was either hit by return fire from the Junkers 88 he attacked in the first instance; was picked off by an Me 110 coming in to attack the Spitfires, like the one Litchfield had shot off Kerr Wilson's tail, which would explain why Litchfield saw him diving vertically and 'rather unsteadily'; or that he was indeed pursuing the 110 Litchfield had already hit and failed to pull out for some reason. The most likely reason is that he had been hit by an Me 110 following his attack on the Ju 88s and was going down out of control; whatever the cause, Medcalf went missing between 1915 hours and a few minutes before 1925 hours, when the remaining two Spitfires of Green Section broke off their patrol again. Tragically, it had taken little more than five minutes in direct combat for the flying officer to be killed.

Ian Coates, 'Tod's' nephew, recalled how 'Tod' was devoted to his Country 'but my father, who flew in the FAA, was of the strong opinion that he was just not suited to flying Spitfires'. Perhaps the drastic change from flying bombers to high-speed fighters had simply not been appropriate for Medcalf. Albert 'Tod' Medcalf had no known grave for his parents Rupert and Florence to visit, presumably having come down in the Channel. As a result, he is remembered on the Runnymede Memorial, Panel 6. There would be a lingering hope that Medcalf and Medway might have baled out and been picked up by one of the ships in the Channel, but, ultimately, they were to become the Squadron's first two losses of the Second World War.

Recently, The National Archives in Kew, London, started releasing the Air Ministry Casualty Branch (AMCB) files from the Second World War, which note all the vital details of any RAF pilot and aircraft involved in a crash. This information is available on numerous 610 Squadron pilots including Medway and Medcalf. The following photo shows Tom Smith's report to his station commander concerning their loss. It confirms most of the details that have been established. The files contain all communications about a pilot's loss, including letters sent to and from his next of kin, providing a fascinating insight into the awful range of emotions the parents and wives of missing pilots went through.

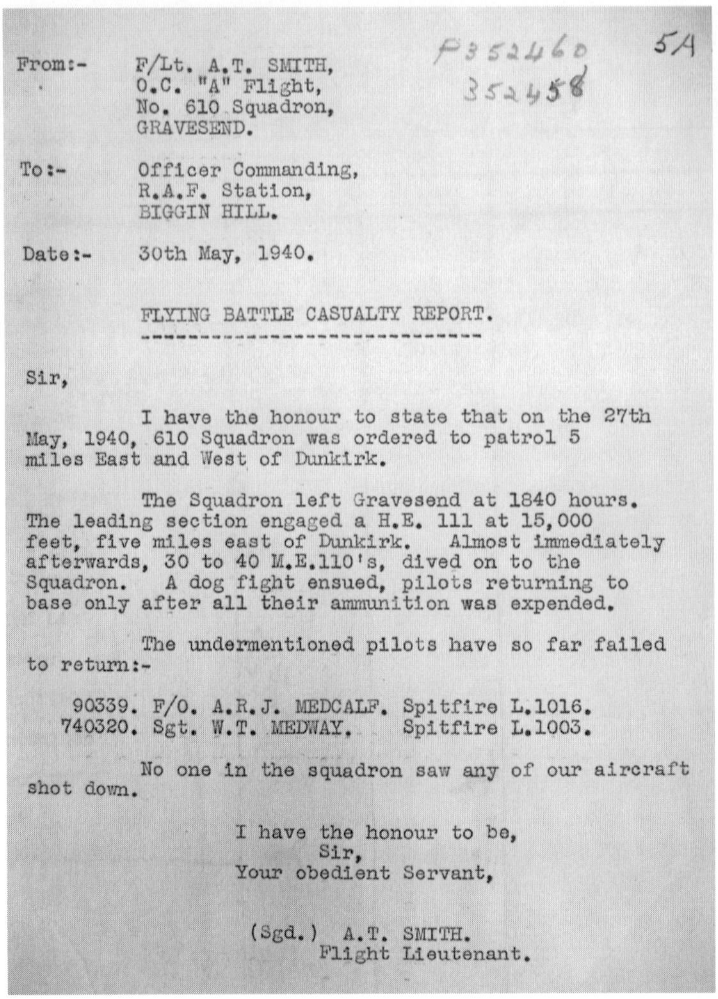

P352460 5A
352458

From:- F/Lt. A.T. SMITH,
O.C. "A" Flight,
No. 610 Squadron,
GRAVESEND.

To:- Officer Commanding,
R.A.F. Station,
BIGGIN HILL.

Date:- 30th May, 1940.

FLYING BATTLE CASUALTY REPORT.

Sir,

I have the honour to state that on the 27th May, 1940, 610 Squadron was ordered to patrol 5 miles East and West of Dunkirk.

The Squadron left Gravesend at 1840 hours. The leading section engaged a H.E. 111 at 15,000 feet, five miles east of Dunkirk. Almost immediately afterwards, 30 to 40 M.E.110's, dived on to the Squadron. A dog fight ensued, pilots returning to base only after all their ammunition was expended.

The undermentioned pilots have so far failed to return:-

90339. F/O. A.R.J. MEDCALF. Spitfire L.1016.
740320. Sgt. W.T. MEDWAY. Spitfire L.1003.

No one in the squadron saw any of our aircraft shot down.

I have the honour to be,
Sir,
Your obedient Servant,

(Sgd.) A.T. SMITH.
Flight Lieutenant.

The official Casualty Report written by Tom Smith, describing 610's losses on 27 May. The statement that Medcalf and Medway had 'so far failed to return', three days after they went missing, suggests the hope that they might still show up. (*TNA, AIR 81/615*)

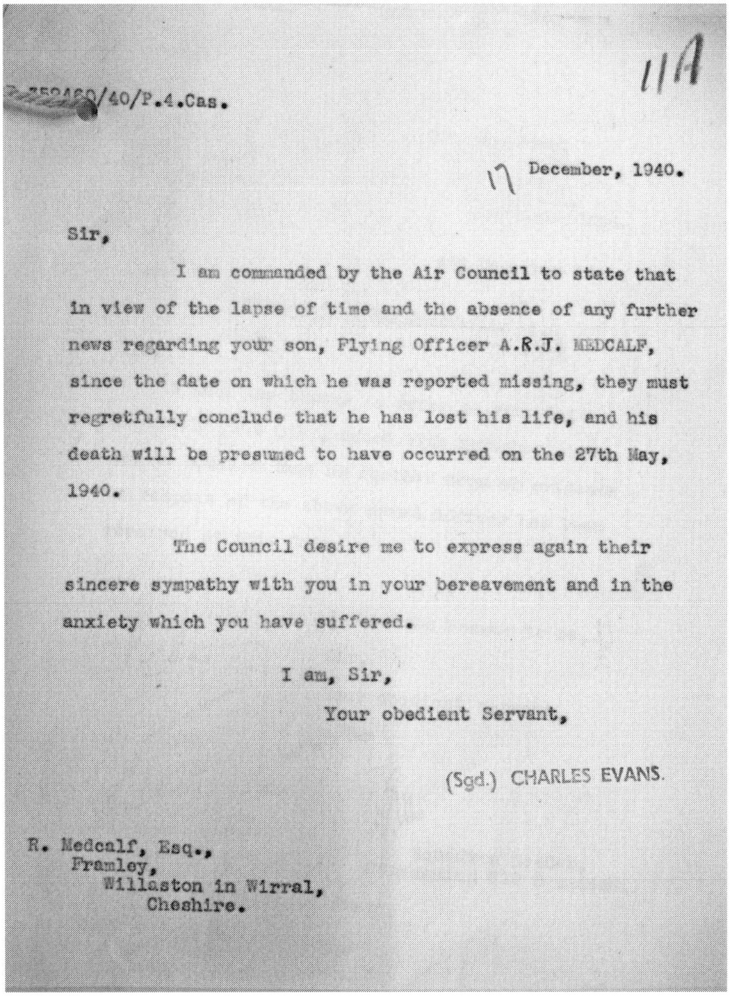

[illegible]/40/P.4.Cas.

114

17 December, 1940.

Sir,

I am commanded by the Air Council to state that in view of the lapse of time and the absence of any further news regarding your son, Flying Officer A.R.J. MEDCALF, since the date on which he was reported missing, they must regretfully conclude that he has lost his life, and his death will be presumed to have occurred on the 27th May, 1940.

The Council desire me to express again their sincere sympathy with you in your bereavement and in the anxiety which you have suffered.

I am, Sir,

Your obedient Servant,

(Sgd.) CHARLES EVANS.

R. Medcalf, Esq.,
Framley,
Willaston in Wirral,
Cheshire.

Letter from the Air Ministry confirming that F/O Medcalf died on 27 May 1940. (*TNA, AIR 81/615*)

In 'Tod' Medcalf's case, his father was contacted immediately after his failure to return was reported. This was followed up with a sympathetic letter from the Air Ministry on 30 May, explaining the next steps to be taken. Just over six months after Medcalf's parents received the first news that 'Tod' was 'Missing', they received a final letter, confirming their worst fears (see above). One can only imagine how his parents, Florence and Rupert, reacted to the news that they would never see their son again, nor have a grave at which to pay their final respects.

The series of events following the report that Sgt Medway was 'Missing' followed a much more convoluted path. Muriel, Medway's wife of just six months, would have been convinced she would hear no more about him from the Air Ministry once she received a letter dated 8 April 1941, stating he was presumed killed on 27 May 1940. Remarkably, it seems that a few days later, on 17 April 1941, the Belgian Red Cross sent news recording the death and burial of Medway in a cemetery near Ostend.

When Mrs Medway was first told this news is unclear, as in a subsequent notification she received from the Air Ministry, dated 8 August 1941, he is still reported as 'Missing'. Perhaps the reason for this delay was the Air Ministry awaiting definite information on the whereabouts of his grave. This arrived at the Air Ministry on 8 February 1942, with an extract from the Belgium official Death List (see photo p. 138), received by the American Embassy as early as 9 July 1941.

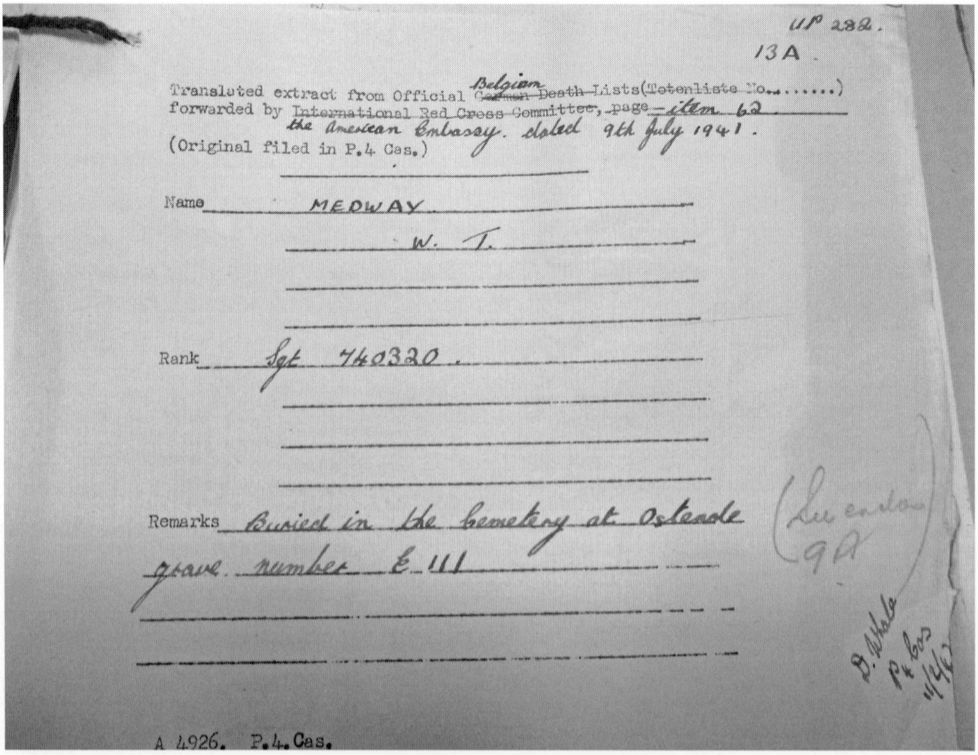

UP 282.
13A.

Translated extract from Official Belgian ~~German Death~~ Lists(~~Totenliste No.......~~)
forwarded by ~~International Red Cross Committee, page~~ – item 62
the American Embassy. dated 9th July 1941.
(Original filed in P.4 Cas.)

Name MEDWAY.
W. T.

Rank Sgt 740320.

Remarks Buried in the cemetery at Ostende
grave number E 111

(See enclos 9A)

A 4926. P.4.Cas.

Belgian Death List which records Medway's place of burial. (*TNA, AIR 81/613*)

From the records in The National Archives, it is unclear whether or not Mrs Medway was fully aware that her husband had a known final resting place until 4 May 1945, when she received formal confirmation. The Air Ministry may have been waiting to receive further official confirmation, which only came to light once Belgium had been liberated. Further confusion over Medway's death and burial arose during this time, as it seems he may have been buried in one grave prior to his final resting place, while the Belgian authorities thought the pilot was Canadian.

In January 1946, those searching into service personnel listed as Killed or 'Missing' had a final investigation into Medway's death. The report confirmed where his Spitfire crashed, (the AMCB file includes a piece of aluminium with a serial number on it from Pobjoy Airmotors & Aircraft Ltd), and where he was buried, with the confusion over his nationality still evident. The investigation was officially closed on 23 March 1946, almost six years after the twenty-four year old had been killed. It seems Sgt Medway was shot down and killed in the attack by the Messerschmitt 110s in the immediate aftermath of Red Section's attack on the Heinkel 111, and that his aircraft fell inland, just inside the Belgian border, the official Place of Crash being Oostduinkerke (2/H.49) (TNA, AIR 81/613). At least his widow, Muriel, who had since remarried, now had a grave to visit in order to remember him: Oostduinkerke Communal Cemetery, Belgium, Row E, Grave 111. Happily, Clive Arnold, Muriel's son from her second marriage, was able to meet Wg Cdr Smith in 2010. Smith had flown in the same section as Medway on the fateful patrol when he was killed, and they discussed Smith's memories of the sergeant whose life was so tragically cut short on his first contact with the enemy.

Returning to events in May 1940, while the survivors of this combat came to terms with the news of the two missing pilots, and filed their combat reports back at Gravesend, a clearer picture of the dogfight was established. With hindsight it seems that the *Zerstörer Gruppe* (Group) had used the

Sgt Medway's grave, Oostduinkerke communal cemetery, Belgium, Row E, Grave 111. (*Copyright Clive Arnold*)

He 111 as bait for 610 Squadron, indicated by the large number of circling Me 110s referred to by all the pilots. Despite the loss of two of their own, the Squadron's successes were recorded as follows:

S/Ldr. A. L. FRANKS	–	1 Me. 110—confirmed
		1 Me. 110—unconfirmed
F/Lt. A. T. SMITH	–	1 Me. 110—confirmed
		1 Me. 110—unconfirmed
P/O. P. LITCHFIELD	–	1 Me. 110—confirmed
F/O. G. M. T. KERR	–	1 Me. 110—unconfirmed
F/O. E. B. B. SMITH	–	1 Heinkel III. shot down

After this engagement, F/O.J.KERR WILSON sighted and attacked 8 Ju.87s. and some Ju.88s;- result uncertain. (ORB)

It seems likely that the Heinkel should go down as shared with Sgt Medway, F/Lt Smith, F/O Warner and F/O Lamb who all pressed home attacks on it, although F/O Smith certainly did most of the damage. In Medway's case, this may well have been the last thing he did, perhaps concentrating too much on the bomber, not enough on the vengeful Me 110s. Four enemy aircraft confirmed destroyed and three unconfirmed was no mean feat for 610 in their first combat situation (even though Kerr's report gives no real indication that his target had been hit). Despite these successes, their evening would have been muted by the loss of their first friends and fellow pilots, both being well-established in the Squadron. Although 610 Squadron's personnel could not possibly know it, their actions that day, and Medway and Medcalf's sacrifice, had helped the ships beneath them give safe passage out of the hell of Dunkirk to just over 7,000 men.

One other point worth investigating here is what had happened to 56 Squadron, supposedly flying as top cover for 610 Squadron, the two units operating as a pair. Unfortunately, they too, had been overrun by Me 110s, which had prevented them from offering any assistance. The RAF formation of twenty fighters had been vastly outnumbered by the twin-engined *Luftwaffe* fighters, and overall it is clear that 610 Squadron had acquitted itself admirably, especially as this was its first experience of aerial combat. They had certainly been lucky that their losses were not even more grievous.

As the evening closed at Dunkirk, it was apparent that a change in plan was required to increase the number of soldiers being evacuated. It was then decided that the beaches to the east of Dunkirk would have to be used to evacuate the troops, as it was not feasible to use the port's quays. This would prove time consuming, but the eastern mole, running 4,250 feet out of the harbour, would now be used as a potential berth for ships, to greatly speed up the boarding of troops. Once the mole was established as safe, the differences in loading speed between the beaches and the mole were vast; 'HMS *Sabre* took two hours to load 100 men from the beach, but alongside the mole 500 troops boarded in 35 minutes'.[6]

Having recovered as best they could from the previous day's tumultuous dogfight, the next day 610 Squadron flew two patrols, both nine Spitfires strong. F/Lt Tom Smith led the first one at 1415 hours, the following pilots being ordered to patrol Dunkirk:

DW-J.	N.3284	F/Lt. A. T. SMITH.	11
DW-S.	N.3201	F/O. P. G. LAMB.	12
DW-D.	L.1010	F/O. E. B. B. SMITH.	14
DW-F.	L.1011	F/O. W. H. C. WARNER.	14
DW-T.	P.9452	F/Lt. J. ELLIS.	7
DW-K.	P.9495*	Sgt. JENKINS, P. D.	8
	N.3289	F/O. G. M. T. KERR.	8
	N.3274	F/O. G. L. CHAMBERS.	6
DW-N.	L.1075	Sgt. ARNFIELD, S. J.	8

*As ORB, as are subsequent references, but should probably be DW-K, L.1062, as this was not shot down until 29 May 1940. P.9495 listed in *Aeromilitaria* as joining 610 on 2 June 1940, probably to replace L.1062.[7]

The pilots would have been on high alert for further action, but probably due to poor weather, the enemy were not encountered and they returned safely to Gravesend two hours later. The second patrol, also over Dunkirk, left the ground at 1820 hours this time led by S/Ldr Franks, and returned without mishap to Gravesend at 2035 hours, as follows:

DW-S.	N.3201	S/Ldr. A. L. FRANKS.	8
DW-F.	L.1011	P/O. S. C. NORRIS.	11
DW-D.	L.1010	F/O. E. B. B. SMITH.	15
DW-J.	N.3284	P/O. G. KEIGHLEY.	7
DW-M.	P.9451*	F/Lt. J. ELLIS.	8
DW-K.	P.9495	Sgt. JENKINS, P. D.	9
	N.3289	F/O. J. KERR WILSON.	9
	N.3274	P/O. P. LITCHFIELD.	11
DW-N.	L.1075	Sgt. ARNFIELD, S. J.	9

*DW-M seems to have switched from L.1000 to P.9451 from now on. L.1000 later becomes DW-D.

For both patrols, it is likely that the first six pilots listed operated in pairs and the final three as a rear guard section, given that of the pilots in the first patrol, Smith, Smith, Ellis and Kerr were usually section leaders, the same applying to the second patrol with Franks, Smith, Ellis and Kerr Wilson. This is confirmed by the ORB the following day.

John Ellis subsequently remembered that on,

> 28th May, we carried out two patrols but visibility was very poor and we saw no enemy aircraft. We flew low over the beaches from time to time to give the Army a bit of encouragement and show them we were about. We also saw the roads all along the coast packed with civilian evacuees riding in horse drawn carts, pushing prams and pulling hand carts.[8]

Such scenes would have given the pilots a good idea of the BEF's desperate situation, and the importance of providing air cover. However, despite the RAF's best efforts to protect their beleaguered comrades below them, the Army and Navy felt abandoned by the junior service. There are countless tales of soldiers and sailors treating downed RAF airman poorly, even trying to stop them getting on ships back to England to return immediately to the air battle, as feelings ran high at the constant bombardment the Army and Navy had to endure. The following quotes illustrate such feelings:

> Able Seaman Reginald Heron, *Telegraphist aboard HMS Keith*: 'The only British planes we saw were the Sunderland flying boats. They just steamed through very slow and majestic. We didn't see much of the RAF'...
>
> Sergeant Major Martin McLane, *2nd Battalion, Durham Light Infantry*: 'The RAF did a very poor job of defending us. The Germans were working in close co-operation with their aircraft. When they wanted support, they called in their dive-bombers and their fighters who strafed and bombed us to clear the way. And what support did we have? We had no damn thing at all. Not a bloody thing. We were just left to God and good neighbours'.[9]

Understandably, this was met by equally bad feeling from RAF personnel, who were losing friends like Medcalf and Medway, in desperate battles over the beaches, Channel and Allies' defensive positions. This misconception by the Army and Navy was partly due to the ever-changing tactics of aerial combat, which constantly evolved with the improving performance of contemporary aircraft. Height was key, and the ceiling at which the fighting took place gradually rose, as both sides increased the altitude at which they were operating at on a daily basis. As a result, the Army and Navy simply could not see the RAF fighters protecting them, as they were frequently operating out of sight. Despite the Squadron failing to encounter the *Luftwaffe* on this day, their presence had helped around 18,000 stranded troops reach the safety of England. On the next day, Wednesday 29 May 1940, there could be no questioning that 610 had more than given their all for the British Army and naval forces below them.

610 Squadron's first patrol on another cloudy day came relatively late on, with twelve Spitfires taking off at 1645 hours to patrol Dunkirk at 25,000 feet, the ORB stating that the Squadron was working in pairs. Presumably this was to try to improve their effectiveness in observing enemy aircraft and also make their formation more manoeuvrable, both when going on the attack or if there was a sudden need to break. This supports my supposition regarding the Squadron's composition during the previous two patrols—perhaps they had been trial runs. It was a drastic change in tactics, given they had only encountered the enemy once, but showed that the Squadron was flexible in learning from its combat experiences. The pilots were:

DW-T.	P.9452	S/Ldr. A. L. FRANKS.	Red 1	9
DW-D.	L.1010	P/O. S. C. NORRIS.	Red 2	12
DW-G.	L.1045	F/O. E. B. B. SMITH.		16
DW-F.	L.1011	F/O. W. H. C. WARNER.		15
DW-J.	N.3284	F/Lt. A. T. SMITH.		12
DW-E.	L.1013	P/O. G. KEIGHLEY.		8
DW-M.	P.9451	F/Lt. J. ELLIS.	Blue 1	9
DW-K.	L.1062	Sgt. JENKINS, P. D.	Blue 2	10

DW-R.	L.1000*	F/O. G. M. T. KERR.	9
	N.3274	F/O. G. L. CHAMBERS.	7
	N.3289	F/O. J. KERR WILSON.	10
DW-N.	L.1075	P/O. P. LITCHFIELD.	12

*As ORB, but definitely an error and should be DW-R, L.1006.

The leader of each pair of aircraft would have been Franks, Brian Smith, Tom Smith, Ellis, Kerr and Kerr Wilson, the Squadron's senior pilots, who were regularly section leaders. They were flying in a Wing with three other Squadrons, 64 also flying Spitfires at 25,000 feet, 229 and 242 both in Hurricanes at 10,000 feet, making an impressive sight. However, the Hurricanes seem to have been operating at a very vulnerable height, with the Spitfires almost too high to protect them. The RAF hoped this larger formation would counter the *Luftwaffe's* own large formations, like the one encountered by 610 on 27 May. As S/Ldr Franks led 610 Squadron towards Dunkirk, they suffered a blow when F/Lt Tom Smith experienced icing trouble, and was forced to leave the formation at 1755 hours, with his wingman P/O Keighley as an escort.[10] With the Wing now down to forty fighters, the RAF pilots were unwittingly approaching a much larger formation of Messerschmitt 109s, and were, 'bounced by two Gruppen of JG 26, plus III/JG 3. III/JG 26 struck the Hurricanes first, from out of the clouds. Before the Spitfires could intervene, they too were struck by a superior number of Messerschmitts, these from Hptm. Ebbighausen's Second Gruppe'.[11]

F/Lt Ellis was leading Sgt Jenkins, and he succinctly records a prolonged dogfight with the attacking 109s:

> I was the leader of Blue Section consisting of 2 aircraft on a high altitude patrol from Dunkirk to Furnes. The whole Squadron of 12 aircraft took part in the patrol aircraft flying in pairs. At 1735 hrs I sighted 6 Me 109s approaching head on from the N.E and about 100' above us. As soon as they had passed overhead I broke my section away and Blue 2 and myself engaged the leading pair. After a dog fight lasting roughly three minutes during which time I had fired four full deflection bursts, the engine of the 109 stopped suddenly in a tight turn, & the aircraft then stalled and spun violently. Black smoke was pouring out of a hole my bullets had made in his top engine cowling. The pilot baled out just as my ammunition ran out and I broke away and seeing no sign of friendly or enemy aircraft I returned home. (TNA, AIR 50/172/20)

Ellis's reference to the extra height enjoyed by the *Luftwaffe* fighters is proof that they had the upper hand, just 100 feet proving crucial in the opening stages of any dogfight. However, Ellis managed to extricate himself and Jenkins out of a tricky situation, and thanks to his sharp-shooting he made his first confirmed claim of the War. Ellis was not alone in his success, with fellow 'B' Flight pilot F/O Lambert Chambers filing the following report on the engagement (see photo p. 143), which he thought took place at 1745 hours at 20,000 feet, to the East of Dunkirk.

It is evident that Lambert Chambers was F/O Kerr's wingman and that they were formatted off S/Ldr Franks's section. It is good that Lambert Chambers's first instinct on hearing the 'Break!' order, was to climb into the sun in a turn; this was a lesson that needed to be learnt very quickly. That Lambert Chambers had singled out an Me 109 for such a concentrated attack, and yet he was only able to claim it as 'probable', would seem to be an early example of the sometimes ineffective armament of the Spitfire and Hurricane. It would become a recurring theme in combat reports, especially with the eight Browning machine guns set to converge at 300 yards. With experience, this range would be reduced.

Another pilot to file a combat report was Peter Litchfield, flying in the rear pair of aircraft which bore the brunt of the attack. His account reads as follows, taking place four miles north-east of Dunkirk at 20,000 feet:

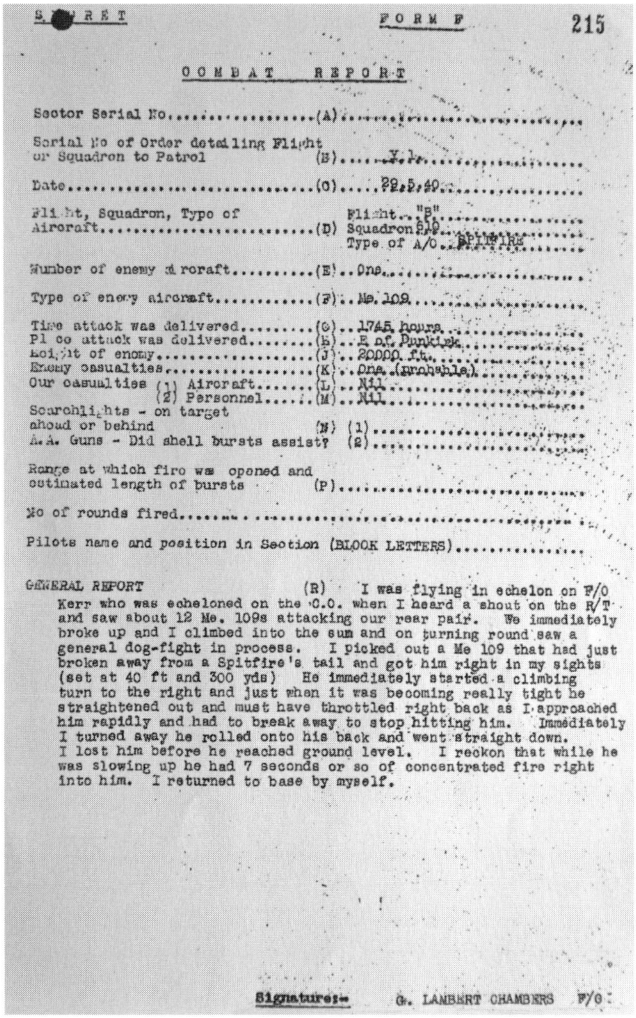

SECRET FORM F 215

COMBAT REPORT

Sector Serial No. ....(A) ....

Serial No of Order detailing Flight or Squadron to Patrol (B) ....Y.1.......................

Date ....(C) ....29.5.40..................

Flight, Squadron, Type of Aircraft ....(D) Flight .."B"..............
Squadron 610..............
Type of A/C ..SPITFIRE........

Number of enemy aircraft ....(E) ..One..........................

Type of enemy aircraft ....(F) ..Me. 109......................

Time attack was delivered ....(G) ..1745 hours....................
Place attack was delivered ....(H) ..E of Dunkirk..................
Height of enemy ....(J) ..20000 ft......................
Enemy casualties ....(K) ..One (probable)................
Our casualties (1) Aircraft ....(L) ..Nil...........................
(2) Personnel ....(M) ..Nil...........................
Searchlights - on target ahead or behind (N) (1) ....
A.A. Guns - Did shell bursts assist? (2) ....

Range at which fire was opened and estimated length of bursts (P) ....

No of rounds fired ....

Pilots name and position in Section (BLOCK LETTERS) ....

GENERAL REPORT (R) I was flying in echelon on F/O Kerr who was echeloned on the C.O. when I heard a shout on the R/T and saw about 12 Me. 109s attacking our rear pair. We immediately broke up and I climbed into the sun and on turning round saw a general dog-fight in process. I picked out a Me 109 that had just broken away from a Spitfire's tail and got him right in my sights (set at 40 ft and 300 yds) He immediately started a climbing turn to the right and just when it was becoming really tight he straightened out and must have throttled right back as I approached him rapidly and had to break away to stop hitting him. Immediately I turned away he rolled onto his back and went straight down. I lost him before he reached ground level. I reckon that while he was slowing up he had 7 seconds or so of concentrated fire right into him. I returned to base by myself.

Signature:- G. LAMBERT CHAMBERS F/O

Right: Lambert Chambers's combat report. (*TNA, AIR 50/172/46*)

Below: This photo of a Messerschmitt 109E of *Jägdgeschwader* 2, clearly shows the angular lines of the *Luftwaffe* aircraft the RAF pilots feared the most in 1940. The distinctive insignia of the 'Richthofen' *Geschwader* is visible underneath the cockpit. (*ww2images.com*)

> I was the second of two aircraft flying astern of the squadron formation on patrol near Dunkirk at 1730 hours, proceeding south eastwards when I noticed several aircraft approaching in line astern (probably) from our port side ahead. As they approached they turned parallel to us on the opposite course and immediately the white enemy crosses and angular lines of the Me.109 were clearly visible in the sun. They turned a complete half circle on to our tails and calling a warning of the R/T I broke [*sic, space left*] to engage the nearest. I gave him two bursts, full deflection, before he passed out of range and then attacked a second E.Z. [E.A.] immediately after another Spitfire had broken away from it. I exhausted my ammunition on this one in two long bursts, also with full deflection and a piece of airframe appeared to break off his stern and fly past me, but although I watched him for another half minute he still appeared to be under control. (TNA, AIR 50/172/48)

As in the previous combat, Litchfield was quick to spot and identify the 109s, keeping track of their progress and calling the Squadron to break when required. This was probably one of the reasons he was acting as rearguard for the Squadron, with F/O Kerr Wilson almost certainly his leader. One gets a sense of the swirling dogfight in which the Squadron had become embroiled from Litchfield's report, and one can sense his frustration that although he had hit the enemy fighter, it was still under control when he had to break off with no ammunition. He was clearly a promising fighter pilot, having extracted himself unscathed from the trickiest position on the Squadron, but was unable to file a claim, even for a damaged enemy aircraft.

'A' Flight was also heavily embroiled in the fighting, S/Ldr Franks being credited with an Me 109 destroyed, while Stanley Norris, almost certainly flying as his wingman, recorded his encounter with the enemy as follows:

> On 29/5/40 I was on patrol near Dunkirk at a height of 20,000'. We had been on patrol for about 25 minutes when my section leader, red leader, suddenly turned sharply & I saw two ME 109s crossing in front of me from port to starboard. I turned to attack & found myself in a dogfight with 10–15 ME109s. The E.A. got on my tail & fired shells from his canon [cannon]. I managed to get on his tail & fired three short bursts of about 1–2 secs each while he was in a climbing turn. E.A. went straight into a spin with engine going full out. No smoke could be seen. The E.A. went straight down until I lost sight of him. By this time the sky was clear so I made my way back to base. (TNA, AIR 50/172/53)

Norris was able to claim his first victory of the conflict, with the 109 seemingly in a terminal dive. However, his Spitfire had been damaged by a cannon shell, presumably in the initial attack by the 109s, so his safe return across the Channel was some achievement.

Another 'A' Flight pilot whose completed combat report survives belonged to F/O Warner. His engagement took place against ten Me 109s at 1730 hours at 23,000 feet:

> I attacked 1 ME. 109 near Dunkirk and gave it about an eight second burst. This aircraft seemed to dive very steeply and a plume of smoke came from it. The aircraft may possibly have been damaged. I broke off that engagement and attacked another and finished my remaining ammunition. I then set course for base. Half way over the channel an E.A. Me 109 attacked me twice and shot a hole in my petrol tank at the bottom and another in the radiator. I forced landed the aircraft N.E. of Dover.
>
> After the first attack on my return journey, I climbed into a cloud, and the E.A. must have followed me, as when I came out he delivered another attack and shot my glycol radiator. On landing I inspected the aircraft and found sixteen holes, three of which I presumed to be canon [cannon]. The control wires of the starboard aileron had also been cut in two. (TNA, AIR 50/172/77)

Warner was extremely fortunate to have made it back from this patrol as having used all his ammunition up, he was effectively defenceless when the opportunistic 109 tried to pick him off. He perhaps switched off after a draining dogfight, with the apparent safety of England's coastline moments away and been bounced by the 109. It was a prime example of the need to maintain vigilance at all times, until safely back on the ground at an aerodrome. Just like the bomber crews returning from raids on Germany later in the war, the false sense of safety as an operation drew to a close and the white cliffs drew nearer, could prove just as fatal as when in the maelstrom of a dogfight. Thankfully for Warner, his petrol tank did not become a fireball and despite heavy damage, he landed DW-F, L.1011 with great skill. Warner would only have realised how lucky he had been when noting the three cannon shells which had hit his aircraft, never mind the thirteen machine gun bullets he also counted. The Spitfire was sent away for repairs and did not rejoin the Squadron.[12]

As 610's Spitfires returned home, most of them landed at Gravesend. Others, like Warner, had to land nearer the south coast, before contacting Gravesend to inform the Squadron of their safety. Thus, the outcome of the frantic dogfight over Dunkirk, just ten minutes fighting between about 1735 and 1745 hours, would only gradually have become clear. As Franks describes in *Air Battle Dunkirk*, from the four squadrons involved, 'ten of their number—one quarter of their force—did not get back. It was to prove the blackest half hour of the Dunkirk battle in the air'.[13] When 610 Squadron's intelligence officer interviewed the pilots it emerged that Franks, Ellis, Lambert Chambers and Norris had each been able to claim an Me 109 shot down, plus Warner claiming a damaged 109. However, given the nature of the dogfight, it was highly unlikely that all of the Spitfire pilots would have made it home.

Echoing the Squadron's first run-in with the enemy two days earlier, two more of them had not yet returned, two of the experienced section leaders, F/O Kerr (DW-R, L.1006), and F/O Kerr Wilson (N.3289). Although fearful for what may have happened to them, the Squadron's personnel hoped they had escaped unscathed, either by parachute or making a forced landing and were attempting to return as best they could. But, 'Bonzo' Franks must have been deeply worried as he reorganised the Squadron in case of a further patrol. With two more experienced pilots, and friends, 'Missing', 610 was missing four pilots after two engagements, a heavy price to pay despite claiming eight destroyed, three unconfirmed and one damaged *Luftwaffe* aircraft in return. Given the unsuitable weather conditions, Franks would have hoped that his men were not required to head for the murky skies over Dunkirk until the morning, but as luck had it the order came through for another patrol.

Franks led them off from Gravesend at 1955 hours to patrol Dunkirk, in company with five aircraft of 64 Squadron (TNA, AIR 81/671). S/Ldr Franks had replaced F/Lt Smith and P/O Keighley with F/O Lamb and Sgt Arnfield, while Bill Warner was understandably left out of the patrol following the previous engagement. The nine-man formation operated as follows:

DW-T.	P.9452	S/Ldr. A. L. FRANKS.	Red 1	10
DW-E.	R.6629*	P/O. S. C. NORRIS.	Red	13
DW-J.	N.3284	F/O. P. G. LAMB.	Red	13
DW-M.	P.9451	F/Lt. J. ELLIS.	Blue 1	10
DW-K.	L.1062	Sgt. JENKINS, P. D.	Blue 2	11
DW-N.	L.1075	P/O. P. LITCHFIELD	Blue 3	13
DW-G.	L.1045	F/O. E. B. B. SMITH.	Green 1	17
	N.3274	F/O. G. L. CHAMBERS.	Green	8
DW-O.	L.1043	Sgt. ARNFIELD, S. J.	Green	10

*As ORB, but should probably be DW-E, L.1013, which R.6629 replaced.

From this battle order it seems likely that the Squadron had reverted back to flying in sections of three, each led by the most experienced pilots: Franks, Ellis leading Blue Section and Smith. However, as the fourteen Spitfires from the two squadrons crossed the Channel, 610 Squadron at 14,000 feet, Franks's formation of nine Spitfires dwindled down to seven. First, P/O Norris was forced to turn for home with engine trouble, and then F/O Lamb had to follow suit due to an oxygen leak in DW-J, N.3284, the same aircraft which Tom Smith had returned early in due to icing on the previous patrol. How Franks reshuffled his formation is unclear, as he seems to have lost both his wingmen. Presumably, one of the other sections became a pair, thereby providing Franks with a wingman. 610's seven remaining Spitfires roared on towards the French coast, their pilots apprehensive at what lay ahead. F/Lt Ellis recounted what happened in his combat report:

> I was the leader of Blue section 610 Sqdn. on a Sqdn. patrol over Dunkirk. At 2020 hrs at 14000' the Sqdn. encountered a small amount of accurate A.A. fire from Dunkirk. Very shortly after the A.A fire had started, Blue 2 called me up and said there were 2 aircraft on our tail. I immediately turned my section round to investigate and saw two Spitfires behind us and which I presumed belonged to 64 Sqdn. Having straightened up in our original direction I looked round to see where Blue 2 was. I saw him 100 (x) behind me and in flames going down in a vertical dive. I immediately did a steep turn round behind Blue 2 but could see no sign of E/A or of the 64 Sqdn. Spitfires or of A.A fire. Blue 2 burst into flames at 15,000'. I circled round Blue two for some minutes looking for E/A and saw him (Blue two) bale out at 5,000 and land in the sea about 10 miles north Dunkirk. I then saw what I thought were two enemy aircraft but when I approached them I saw they were the 2 wings of the crashed Spitfire floating down. On turning towards Dunkirk to try and get help for Blue 2, I saw a Me 109 at 1000' and delivered a No 1 attack on it, but on seeing me it immediately made for the clouds. I gave it a burst of about 8 secs from between 400 & 500 yds just before it disappeared. I lost sight of the E/A in the cloud before I had time to see the effect of my fire. I then continued to fly towards Dunkirk to get help for Blue 2. I approached 4 or 5 different destroyers and tried to attract their attention but was fired on by each one in turn despite the fact I was flashing the letter of the day. I continued for some ten minutes flying from the destroyers to Blue 2 but as they continued firing on me and did not alter course and as my petrol was getting low I returned home at 2110 hrs and immediately reported Blue 2's position to the Sector Controller. BLUE 2 is Sgt. Jenkins. (TNA, AIR 50/172/20)

From Ellis's somewhat confused report, it is unclear what actually happened to Sgt Jenkins—was he the victim of friendly fire from over-zealous Army or Royal Navy AA gunners, the Spitfires of 64 Squadron, or were these 'Spitfires' actually Me 109s, especially as Ellis tried to shoot one down moments later? It would have been useful to know what happened to 64 Squadron during this joint patrol. Sadly, the Squadron's adjutant appears to have forgotten to record it, making it difficult to verify 64 Squadron's movement (64 ORB).

Whatever the cause, Jenkins had to bale out into the Channel at 5,000 feet, and despite his flight commander's best efforts to alert the destroyers to his wingman's plight, the sailors' failure to recognise Ellis's aircraft as a Spitfire compounded the situation. With Ellis coming under fire from several destroyers, it suggests the Navy took a 'shoot first, ask questions later' policy regarding any approaching low-level aircraft. It is possible that it was these same gunners who had failed to recognise the original formation of Spitfires as they approached at 14,000 feet, and that an unlucky burst had brought Jenkins down. There is an understandable sense of frustration and worry in Ellis's combat report, and as he wrote, 'BLUE 2 is Sgt. Jenkins' in the present tense, he clearly felt his unfortunate wingman was still alive. However, as Ellis subsequently commented, Jenkins, 'was never seen again. As Jenkins was an outstanding pilot it was particularly tragic he should be lost in this way. At this stage of the war, the Army and Navy did not know the difference between a Spitfire and a Ju87!'[14] This also suggests that Ellis was convinced AA fire was to blame, as recorded in the ORB at the time 'Sgt. Jenkins was shot down in flames, believed by A.A. gunfire'.

Sgt Jenkins remembered on the Runnymede Memorial. (*Author*)

Given the sudden fate which befell his aircraft, Jenkins had done well to successfully bale out of DW-K, L.1062. But the cold waters of the English Channel were very unforgiving and the destroyers' failure to heed Ellis's attempts to guide them to the stranded pilot sealed his fate. Peter Douglas Jenkins was an experienced VR pilot, as he had eighty-four hours and twenty-five minutes on Spitfires by late 1939. One would think this should have stood him in good stead for the coming battles, however he only lasted three encounters with the enemy—there was no accounting for the chance of being hit by your own side's AA fire. Jenkins's death, aged just twenty, was down to tragic misfortune. He is remembered on the Runnymede Memorial, Panel 16.

With the release of certain AMCB files, it is now possible to establish further details regarding Sgt Jenkins's death. The Air Ministry received news from 610 Squadron almost twenty-four hours after the action, informing them that he was 'Missing', along with other basic information which had been established by this time.

Jenkins's mother was immediately contacted and although there must have been some hope that he had been picked up by a passing ship, weeks passed without further news. Finally, in January 1941, Jenkins's mother Dorothy, whose surname was now given as Bernau, received a letter from the Air Ministry, effectively stating that her son had been killed on 29 May 1940. One can only imagine how terrible this news must have been for her to receive, especially when there was no definite report of his death, just simply his disappearance, last seen after baling out into the English Channel.

As the years of the Second World War passed by, his mother understandably held a glimmer of hope that he may have become a prisoner of war (PoW). As a result, in August 1945, three months after Victory in Europe was celebrated on 8 May 1945, Dorothy Bernau wrote one last time to see if anything could be found out about her son. It is incredibly moving to read that Jenkins had written to his mother on the morning of his death—it must have been very hard for her to know that by the time she received his letter, her son had lost his life. The time of the incident was certainly against Jenkins, as it was growing dark, making rescue all the more difficult. This may also have explained the poor aircraft recognition of the sailors on board the destroyers, when Ellis tried to indicate Jenkins's position.

Ultimately, his mother received one final, sickening letter, advising her that in light of there being no news on Peter Jenkins for so long, the only conclusion to be made was that he had been 'lost at sea'. Her final response acknowledged that she accepted this to be the case, as difficult as it must have been, but it highlights the traumatic and lengthy struggle for those left behind, still trying to establish what happened to their relatives reported as 'Missing'.

Back with the patrol on 29 May, while John Ellis was trying to help rescue his wingman, the Squadron's remaining aircraft continued the patrol, more than a little distracted by the events surrounding Blue Section. But on their return to Gravesend, Sgt Jenkins was not the only pilot missing. S/Ldr Franks had been left with, at the most, four other pilots to lead, and it seems likely that they were attacked by Me 109s—enemy fighters were clearly in the vicinity as observed by F/Lt Ellis. Given the chaotic nature of this patrol, it is unsurprising that none of Franks's pilots saw him go down, as their formation must have been ragged by this stage. But the thirty-one-year-old squadron leader, flying Spitfire N.3177, who was reported as 'Missing' at about 2000 hours, had failed to return.[15] The surviving pilots did not land until after 2100 hours, so by the time they had been debriefed, there would have been little chance to investigate the whereabouts of their CO, especially as no one had seen him go down. However, late on the next day, with no further information, the Squadron informed the Air Ministry of the news.

There was a request for the next of kin only to be informed of the news on 1 June 1940. The reason for this was probably over the uncertainty as to what had happened to Franks, and the initial communication was sent to Franks's wife Kirsten, at Home Farm Cottages, Thornhaugh, Lincolnshire, albeit stating the incorrect date of 30 May for when he went missing. Following the standard process, this was promptly followed by a letter on 3 June, confirming the facts for Kirsten Franks, which had been established by F/Lt Tom Smith in his flying combat casualty report to Biggin Hill's CO. This report outlined the loss of Sgt Jenkins too (see photo p. 149).

Smith recorded events largely as they have already been established. From 610 Squadron's point of view it was a disordered patrol, with only nine Spitfires available in the first place. 'Bonzo' Franks was presumably leading Red Section, with Lamb and Norris his wingmen. When they both had to return early with aircraft problems, this represented a real blow, even before the disastrous events surrounding the loss of Jenkins. Smith's report highlights a further problem, that Green Section, probably led by Brian Smith and his two wingmen, lost contact with Franks, when they tried to establish what had happened to Jenkins. This would effectively have left Franks patrolling with perhaps one other Spitfire, that of Peter Litchfield, unless 64 Squadron's Spitfires were still in sight.

The fact that Franks was 'Missing' was confirmed by two further letters to his wife, one on 29 July 1940, while the other was sent in early October, which must have been very distressing for Kirsten to receive. However, a little over a month later, the Air Ministry received news from the International Red Cross which provided the first information that Franks had in fact been buried on a small island called Memmert, off the north German coast, part of the Frisian Islands. Quite how his body had been found there was unclear, as it was many miles to the east of where the patrol took place. Presumably he had either crashed or baled out into the Channel in the vicinity of Dunkirk and his body had drifted all the way round the Dutch coast to these islands. The cause of Franks's death will probably remain a mystery, but at least his wife and family would have some sort of closure and a grave to visit. A couple of days later, on 18 November 1940, news was sent to Kirsten Franks, informing her that it was now believed her husband had definitely lost his life, and would no longer be recorded as 'Missing'. A letter in response soon informed the Air Ministry that Mrs Franks had moved to America and that all mail should be sent to her solicitors. There were no new developments until after the war, when his brother, Air Cdre John Gerald Franks, of Esher, Surrey, requested that an enquiry should take place into his brother's death. He received the following response (see photo p. 150) on 13 August 1946.

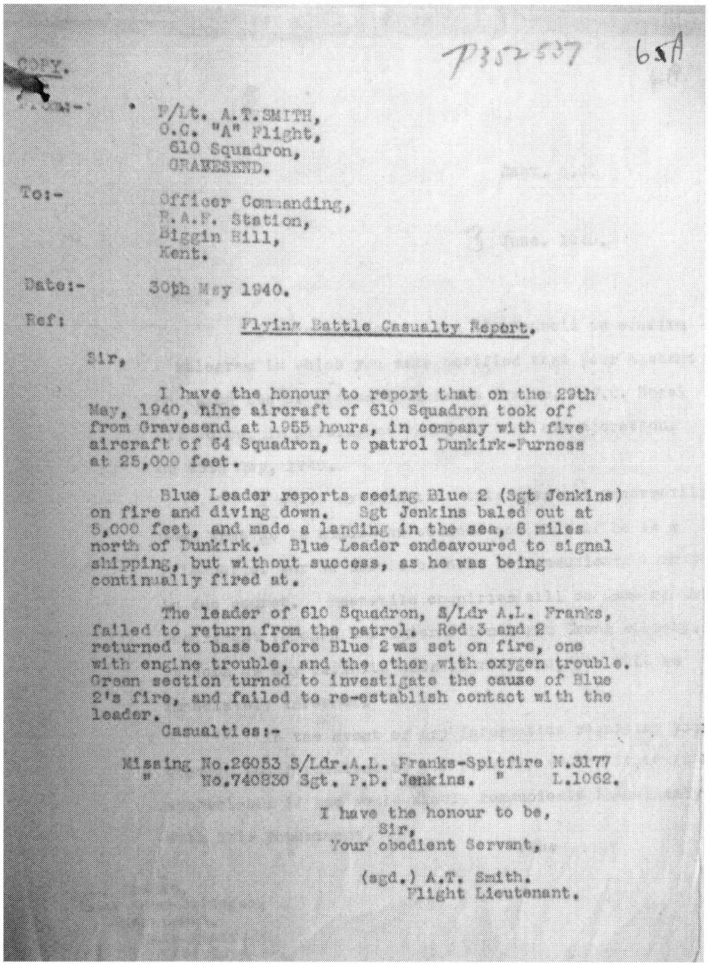

COPY.

From:- F/Lt. A.T.SMITH,
O.C. "A" Flight,
610 Squadron,
GRAVESEND.

To:- Officer Commanding,
R.A.F. Station,
Biggin Hill,
Kent.

Date:- 30th May 1940.

Ref: Flying Battle Casualty Report.

Sir,

I have the honour to report that on the 29th May, 1940, nine aircraft of 610 Squadron took off from Gravesend at 1955 hours, in company with five aircraft of 64 Squadron, to patrol Dunkirk-Furness at 25,000 feet.

Blue Leader reports seeing Blue 2 (Sgt Jenkins) on fire and diving down. Sgt Jenkins baled out at 5,000 feet, and made a landing in the sea, 8 miles north of Dunkirk. Blue Leader endeavoured to signal shipping, but without success, as he was being continually fired at.

The leader of 610 Squadron, S/Ldr A.L. Franks, failed to return from the patrol. Red 3 and 2 returned to base before Blue 2 was set on fire, one with engine trouble, and the other with oxygen trouble. Green section turned to investigate the cause of Blue 2's fire, and failed to re-establish contact with the leader.

Casualties:-

Missing No.26053 S/Ldr.A.L. Franks-Spitfire N.3177
" No.740830 Sgt. P.D. Jenkins. " L.1062.

I have the honour to be,
Sir,
Your obedient Servant,

(sgd.) A.T. Smith.
Flight Lieutenant.

Flying battle casualty report for events on 29 May. (*TNA, AIR 81/671*)

Three new pieces of information arise for the Franks family as a result of this communication, firstly, that he was buried in, 'Comrades grave No. 1/3' and secondly, that he had not been buried until 2 August 1940, just over two months after he went missing, the letter stating that his body had come ashore a long time after his death. This must have been sickening to discover and in other documents in the AMCB file, John Franks clearly wondered how it was possible for his brother to end up on the Frisian Islands. However, if Franks's body had been in the Channel for this period of time, it is quite possible that he had come down in the Channel near the engagement, and the tides had swept him round to the Frisian Islands. Thirdly, it was apparent that Franks's body may be moved to a cemetery in Germany. In the meantime, he would remain buried at the site on Memmert, confirmation of which was quickly established by information from captured German records.

Air Cdre Franks must have hoped that this would bring some sort of closure to his brother's death, some six years after his disappearance, except for the possible reburial. However, as the search into the dead and 'Missing' of the Second World War continued, on 20 June 1947, S/Ldr Franks's body was exhumed, ostensibly for the reburial. The report on the exhumation provided some interesting information on Franks, including that he was six feet two inches, of broad build and that his uniform and AFC were still identifiable. The most remarkable piece of information was that he had been buried in his 'Mae West' inflatable life jacket, which explained how he had remained afloat for so long in the Channel.

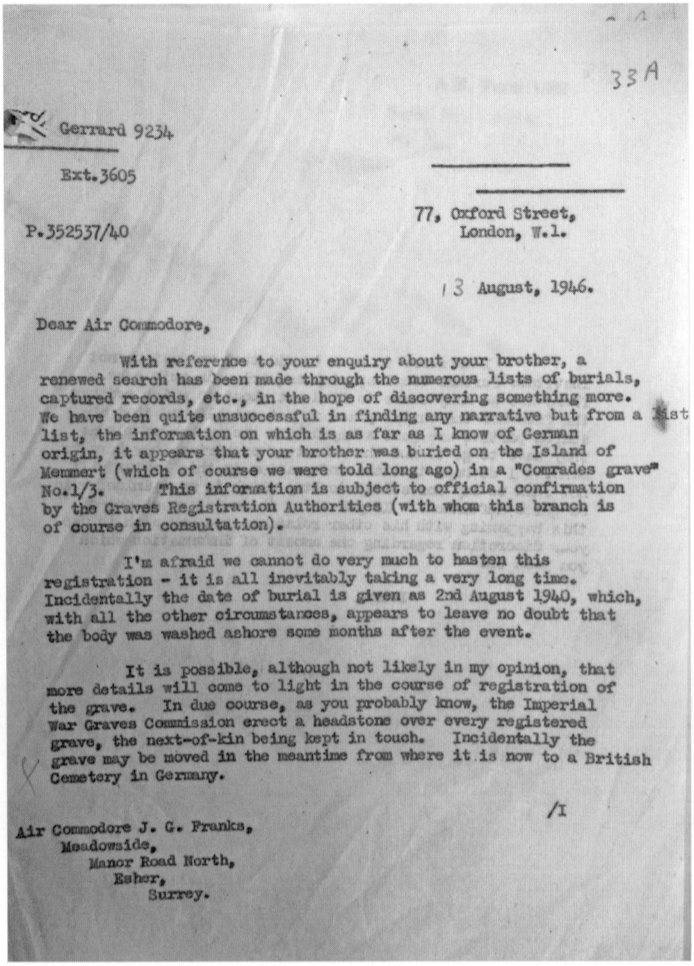

33A

Gerrard 9234

Ext.3605

P.352537/40

77, Oxford Street,
London, W.1.

13 August, 1946.

Dear Air Commodore,

With reference to your enquiry about your brother, a renewed search has been made through the numerous lists of burials, captured records, etc., in the hope of discovering something more. We have been quite unsuccessful in finding any narrative but from a [illegible]st list, the information on which is as far as I know of German origin, it appears that your brother was buried on the Island of Memmert (which of course we were told long ago) in a "Comrades grave" No.1/3. This information is subject to official confirmation by the Graves Registration Authorities (with whom this branch is of course in consultation).

I'm afraid we cannot do very much to hasten this registration - it is all inevitably taking a very long time. Incidentally the date of burial is given as 2nd August 1940, which, with all the other circumstances, appears to leave no doubt that the body was washed ashore some months after the event.

It is possible, although not likely in my opinion, that more details will come to light in the course of registration of the grave. In due course, as you probably know, the Imperial War Graves Commission erect a headstone over every registered grave, the next-of-kin being kept in touch. Incidentally the grave may be moved in the meantime from where it is now to a British Cemetery in Germany.

/I

Air Commodore J. G. Franks,
Meadowside,
Manor Road North,
Esher,
Surrey.

The date of S/Ldr Franks's burial is revealed as being 2 August 1940. (*TNA, AIR 81/671*)

The report also states that Franks would be reinterred at Oldenburg (Sage) British Military Cemetery, Plot VII, Row F, Grave 15—perhaps now the painful memory of his death could finally be put to rest. However, amazingly there was one more twist in the tale. In August 1949 there was some confusion over whether or not it was S/Ldr Franks who was buried in the Oldenburg Cemetery plot. The confusion revolved around Franks and another S/Ldr G. D. Franks, DFC, a Wellington bomber pilot, who went missing on 29 June 1942. His name had been allocated to the grave in which the 610 Squadron commander had actually been buried, in a letter dated 22 August 1949, the case now over nine years old.

Each new missive from the Air Ministry must have stirred up painful memories for the Franks family. The key to confirming who had been buried in this plot came from the exhumation, as the body's size, six feet two inches and broad, matched A. L. Franks, whereas G. D. Franks was five feet 9.5 inches and less well built. Only now, nine years after his death, did the family know of 'Bonzo' Franks's final place of rest. Tragically, their gain was another family's loss, as the family of S/Ldr G. D. Franks, DFC, now had no such grave to visit, his name being added to the Memorial of the 'Missing', at Runnymede. This case of Alexander Franks again highlights the ongoing ordeal that families with 'Missing' relatives had to endure. The painstaking work being carried out to trace those who were 'Missing' or confirmed buried, dragged out painful memories, in this case, for the best part of a

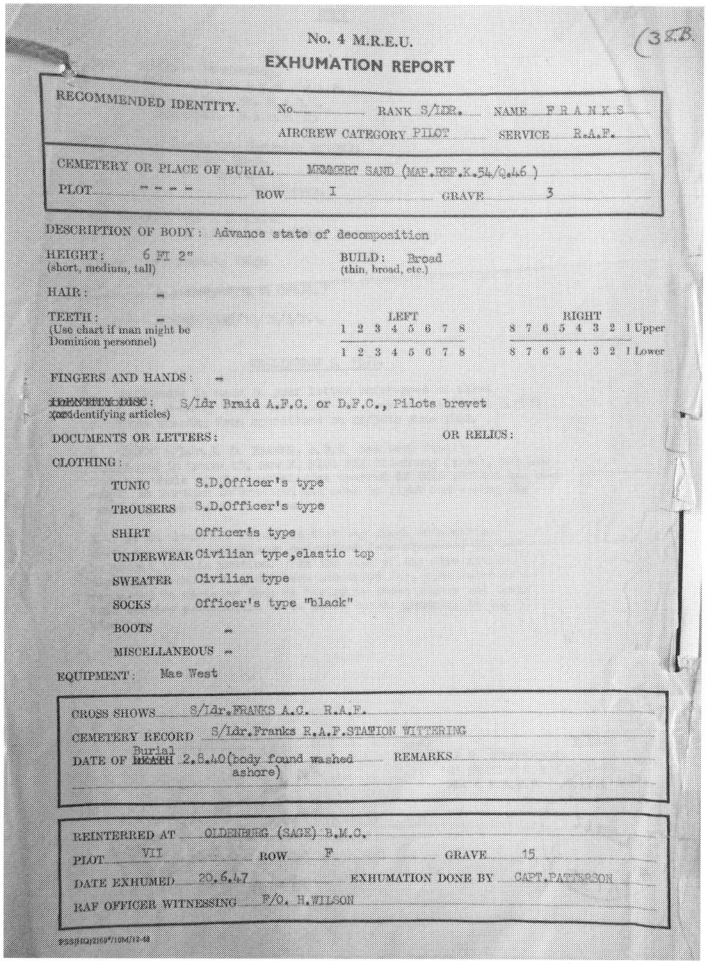
No. 4 M.R.E.U.
EXHUMATION REPORT

RECOMMENDED IDENTITY. No. RANK S/LDR. NAME F R A N K S
AIRCREW CATEGORY PILOT SERVICE R.A.F.

CEMETERY OR PLACE OF BURIAL MEMMERT SAND (MAP.REF.K.54/Q.46)
PLOT - - - - ROW I GRAVE 3

DESCRIPTION OF BODY: Advance state of decomposition
HEIGHT: 6 FT 2" (short, medium, tall) BUILD: Broad (thin, broad, etc.)
HAIR: -
TEETH: - (Use chart if man might be Dominion personnel)

	LEFT	RIGHT	
	1 2 3 4 5 6 7 8	8 7 6 5 4 3 2 1	Upper
	1 2 3 4 5 6 7 8	8 7 6 5 4 3 2 1	Lower

FINGERS AND HANDS: -
IDENTITY DISC: (or identifying articles) S/Ldr Braid A.F.C. or D.F.C., Pilots brevet
DOCUMENTS OR LETTERS: OR RELICS:
CLOTHING:
TUNIC S.D.Officer's type
TROUSERS S.D.Officer's type
SHIRT Officer's type
UNDERWEAR Civilian type,elastic top
SWEATER Civilian type
SOCKS Officer's type "black"
BOOTS -
MISCELLANEOUS -
EQUIPMENT: Mae West

CROSS SHOWS S/Ldr.FRANKS A.C. R.A.F.
CEMETERY RECORD S/Ldr.Franks R.A.F.STATION WITTERING
DATE OF Burial 2.8.40(body found washed ashore) REMARKS

REINTERRED AT OLDENBURG (SAGE) B.M.C.
PLOT VII ROW F GRAVE 15
DATE EXHUMED 20.6.47 EXHUMATION DONE BY CAPT.PATTERSON
RAF OFFICER WITNESSING F/O. H.WILSON

Exhumation report on S/Ldr Franks, on 20 June 1947. (*TNA, AIR 81/671*)

decade. It is impossible to imagine what an awful experience this must have been for so many relatives throughout the war years and for many years after 1945.

Franks had taken over command of the Squadron on 23 December 1939 with effect from New Year's Day 1940, and had a key role in shaping the Squadron for the coming conflict. His loss was devastating for his men, as recorded by his senior flight commander, John Ellis, whose description of his CO makes a fitting epitaph for Franks: '… a regular officer who ... was a large, cheerful Irishman—a great character with a fund of marvellous Irish stories. It was a great loss to the squadron and the RAF when he was shot down over Dunkirk'.[16] Although Franks went down unobserved, he had a great impact on the men under his command, and they would fight on to avenge his loss, and the other pilots who were missing in action.

By the end of the day there had still been no news about F/Os Kerr and Kerr Wilson and sadly, this was to remain the case—neither pilot was heard of again. Both of these pilots plus the squadron leader were in their thirties, quite old for a fighter pilot whose reactions and eyesight were not as sharp as they had once been, particularly when flying state-of-the-art fighters like the Spitfire. As Brian Smith recalled: 'Wilson, now he ran an engineering firm, I used to have one of his boilers in the kitchen. I'm afraid we lost him too, because age comes into it a bit, as your reflexes had to be pretty quick!' While no one saw either of them going down, it seems both men were shot down by Me 109s, quite

S/Ldr Alexander Lumsden Franks AFC, Killed in Action 29 May 1940, aged thirty-one. (*Copyright 610 Squadron Association*)

possibly in their initial attack. It is conceivable that the 109 which F/O Lambert Chambers attacked, which had just broken away from a Spitfire's tail, was responsible for the demise of one of the pilots.

Kerr Wilson, aged thirty-two, had been with 610 since its early days, first being mentioned in the ORB on 13 September 1936. He was an experienced pilot, a section leader and a brave man, indicated by his aggressive flying in the defence of a ship two days earlier, when he successfully warded off a dive-bombing attack. Jack was an integral member of 610, whose sudden loss must have been keenly felt by the Squadron, while he left behind his parents Henry and Lucy Kerr Wilson and his younger brothers and sisters. His name is remembered on my local war memorial in Heswall, Wirral, and having grown up in the same small town as this man whose sacrifice has largely gone unknown, like so many others who fought in both world wars, he has become one of the spurs behind my writing the early history of 610 Squadron and its courageous men. The Heswall war memorial overlooks a picturesque park, with beautiful views across the River Dee to the Welsh hills—Dawstone Park. It was opened on 1 July 1931, and Kerr Wilson's father, as chairman of the Heswall cum Oldfield Council, was a driving force behind its creation, his name being engraved on the boundary sandstone wall, just a short distance from where his son's name would be engraved and fittingly recalled forever. Kerr Wilson is also remembered on Panel 6 of the Memorial to the Missing, at Runnymede.

Further information is now available on the loss of Jack Kerr Wilson from the AMCB files, including 610 Squadron's original communication to the Air Ministry from Gravesend. While some of it was slightly inaccurate, including the spelling of his surname and the likely time of his loss, it does confirm that Kerr Wilson was flying Spitfire N.3289.

News was sent on the same day to Kerr Wilson's parents, providing them with the worrying news that he was, 'missing as the result of air operations on 29 May 1940' (TNA, AIR 81/672). This awful news was followed up with a letter on 4 June 1940, the contents of which are possible to decipher from the polite reply sent by Jack's father, Henry Kerr Wilson (see photo p. 154). As the time passed without any further news, it became increasingly likely that the missing airman would have to be recorded as presumed killed.

Above: Heswall war memorial, overlooking the River Dee. (*Author*)

Right: F/O Kerr Wilson's name, on the plaque on the left of the war memorial. (*Author*)

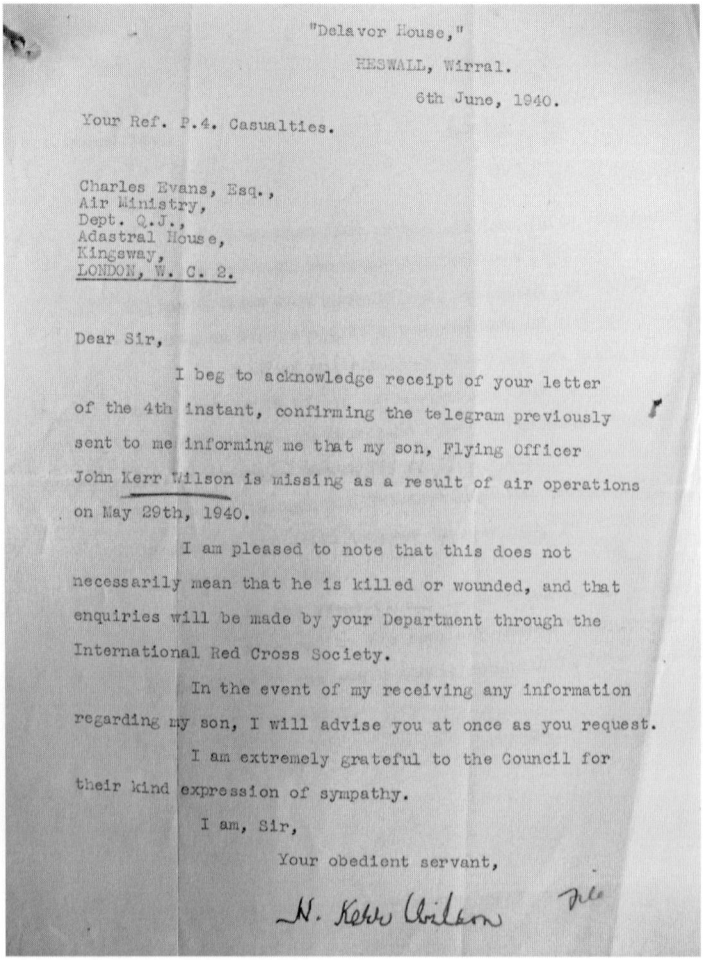

"Delavor House,"
HESWALL, Wirral.
6th June, 1940.

Your Ref. P.4. Casualties.

Charles Evans, Esq.,
Air Ministry,
Dept. Q.J.,
Adastral House,
Kingsway,
LONDON, W. C. 2.

Dear Sir,

I beg to acknowledge receipt of your letter of the 4th instant, confirming the telegram previously sent to me informing me that my son, Flying Officer John Kerr Wilson is missing as a result of air operations on May 29th, 1940.

I am pleased to note that this does not necessarily mean that he is killed or wounded, and that enquiries will be made by your Department through the International Red Cross Society.

In the event of my receiving any information regarding my son, I will advise you at once as you request.

I am extremely grateful to the Council for their kind expression of sympathy.

I am, Sir,
Your obedient servant,
H. Kerr Wilson

Response from Henry Kerr Wilson to the news that his son was 'Missing'. (*TNA, AIR 81/672*)

The Air Ministry sent three more letters to his family, each one receiving a response from his father, stating that they had heard nothing of their son. This was until 8 January 1941, when the family was finally informed that Jack Kerr Wilson was believed to have been killed in action on 29 May 1940. Again, the terrible burden of wondering what had happened to their beloved relative had haunted a family of a 610 Squadron pilot for more than seven months. Despite this letter's conclusive nature, the fact that there was no body to confirm the death, meant his family and friends continued to hold a glimmer of hope that Jack had somehow survived. Therefore, it is unsurprising that this AMCB file contains a letter to the Air Ministry, dated more than a year later, asking them to look into the possibility that Kerr Wilson had become a PoW, and that the family had not been informed due to a mispronunciation of his name. A F/O John Carson Wilson had been listed in *The Times*, and 'Kerr' and 'Carr' were similarly pronounced by some people. This letter came from the family's solicitors, without the knowledge of Mr Henry Kerr Wilson. It was a solicitor who picked up on this tenuous link to the family name, indicating how desperate those close to missing personnel were to clutch at a potential straw that offered hope. Just over a week later, the Air Ministry, as thorough as ever when dealing with such sensitive tasks, dashed any optimism by confirming that a F/O John Carson Wilson was being held captive. Sadly, another flicker of hope had been snuffed out for the family in Heswall, although in this instance at least, it is believed the family were not aware of it.

F/O John Kerr Wilson in 1940. (*Copyright Kerr-Wilson family*)

By looking at the combat reports, it is possible to piece together the likely events surrounding Kerr Wilson's death. We know from John Ellis's report that the Squadron was operating in pairs and that they ran into a formation of Messerschmitt 109s. From the ORB we know that Jack Kerr Wilson, usually a section leader, was almost certainly leading P/O Peter Litchfield, and Litchfield's combat report states that they were at the rear of the formation and were attacked from behind by 109s. The perilous situation in which Kerr Wilson and Litchfield found themselves is also clarified by F/O Lambert Chambers, who recalled seeing about twelve Me 109s attacking 610's rear pair. It is therefore highly likely that Kerr Wilson's Spitfire was shot down as a result of this first attack by the 109s, which had concentrated on the vulnerable rearmost section, explaining why nobody saw him go down. Some pilots were evidently more aware of the enemy formation than others—perhaps Litchfield's warning cry had come a second too late to save his section leader, the experienced Auxiliary officer failing to break in time, before his Spitfire, N.3289, was assailed by heavy fire from a *Luftwaffe* fighter. We will never know exactly what happened, but it is probable that this was the case, as 610 Squadron's casualty list continued to rise.

Equally, little is known about the loss of thirty-year-old F/O Malcolm Kerr, from Frodsham, Cheshire, another experienced Squadron member who frequently flew as a section leader. However, it is likely he was lost in similar circumstances to his old friend Jack Kerr Wilson. We know from Graham Lambert Chambers's combat report, that Lambert Chambers was flying as Kerr's wingman, probably making him the last person to see Kerr alive at about 1745 hours. If Kerr survived the first pass by the 109s, he was almost certainly shot down in the immediate aftermath, within minutes of Kerr Wilson and was reported 'Missing'. Once again, the AMCB files provide interesting background information on him. The flying battle casualty report for Kerr covers the loss of Kerr Wilson, and briefly outlines the events surrounding the patrol.

The lack of detail surrounding the loss of both pilots is very apparent in the terse description, although it states that Kerr was flying DW-R, L.1006, and that their formation had been intercepted by a sizeable formation of Messerschmitt 109s. The report had been filled in the day after the dog-fight, so while there was plenty of time for Kerr to have appeared after a dunking in the Channel, or crash-landing near the evacuation beaches, every passing hour must have made the likelihood of his safe return all the more remote. The pilot's wife, Mrs Barbara M. Kerr, of Turfhills, Beech Avenue, Frodsham, was contacted, but the Air Ministry was a little slow in realising she was his wife not his mother; the first communication warning Mrs Kerr that her husband was 'Missing', referred to her 'son'. Once again, the paper trail of letters between the Air Ministry and the next of kin is tragic reading, as hope that her husband may have survived and become a PoW gradually disappears. In Kerr's case, it is particularly saddening as his wife states she is expecting their child, due to be born in five months. It was just as hard for the pilot's mother, May, who searched every available source for information. Her phrase in one letter, that, 'the suspense and anxiety become increasingly hard to bear' (TNA, AIR 81/670), sums up the awful circumstances each family across Britain endured throughout the course of the War, when a relative or friend was reported as 'Missing'. No news was received and as the months continued to pass, the family's hopes must have all but faded. During that time, Kerr's baby was born, a daughter called Geraldine, but with no further news, it became inevitable that the Air Ministry would write to confirm that he was presumed to have lost his life on 29 May 1940. The letter arrived shortly after 9 January 1941.

Despite the conclusive nature of this letter, throughout the remainder of the Second World War, Malcolm Kerr's mother and his wife maintained a glimmer of hope. When Victory in Europe had finally been achieved, almost five long years later, May Kerr tried one last moving appeal for any news on her son, which might provide 'some comfort in a lasting & irreparable loss & grief' (TNA, AIR 81/670). However, she would never receive the news she longed for, and F/O Gerald Malcolm Theodore Kerr's fate remained as missing in action, 29 May 1940. He is remembered on the Runnymede Memorial, Panel 6.

A pipe-smoking F/O Malcom Kerr, Empire Air Day, Liverpool Airport, Speke, 1938. (*Copyright 610 Squadron Association*)

Notwithstanding the obvious experience of both Kerr and Kerr Wilson, nothing could have prepared them for the dangerous skies over Dunkirk. Survival of the early dogfights was the key, and this combat experience stood those who came through them in good stead for the future. For all their flying hours, Kerr Wilson and Kerr were novice dogfighters, just like Franks and Jenkins, and they tragically disappeared without trace on their second encounter with the enemy.

So ended a very difficult day for 610 Squadron, losing its squadron leader, two long standing members, and a highly competent sergeant pilot in the course of two patrols, which had lasted a total of just two hours and twenty-five minutes. Despite having claimed four Me 109s destroyed and one damaged in the first patrol, the Squadron was taking heavy losses, and the experience the surviving pilots gained was coming at a high price. Six pilots had now been lost or were 'Missing' in three engagements, and morale must have been hit hard. If such losses continued, the Squadron would soon be non-operational—the enforced early return of two Spitfires from the last patrol was proof that the aircraft were feeling the strain too. The man chosen as the new squadron leader was Andrew Thomas Smith, originally a pilot officer as one of 610's founder members. John Ellis later recalled: 'Flight Lieutenant Tom Smith, one of the original Auxiliary officers, was appointed the commanding officer. This was a mistake as although he was a very good officer, he had insufficient flying experience to lead his squadron in the air so I took over this responsibility for the next twelve months'.[17] If Smith lacked the experience to lead the Squadron in the air, he certainly seemed happy to delegate this to his capable deputy, F/Lt Ellis, who led the remaining patrols over Dunkirk.

It was perhaps 'Big Bill' Smith's ability to lead the Squadron in the face of adversity, to keep the remaining hard-pressed pilots' morale up after their heavy losses and to keep them motivated in the face of intense pressure which they had never experienced before, that the powers-that-be appointed Smith as CO. Having been with the Squadron from the early days, Smith embodied its spirit, and to some of the young pilots, the experienced thirty-three year old would have seemed a fatherly figure, who could be relied upon to weld the men into a nucleus of experienced pilots for the battles ahead. One of the new CO's first actions, despite all the additional pressure he now faced, was to commend William Warner for returning safely from the day's first patrol, an early indication of his concern for his men and readiness to give praise where it was due. At the end of Warner's combat report, Smith wrote the following addendum: 'P.S. I should like to draw special attention to this report as in my opinion F/O Warner displayed exceptional coolness and ability in bringing his machine back. Signed: A. T. Smith F/Lt. acting C.O. 610 Sqdn' (TNA, AIR 50/172/77). His men would have realised immediately that their new C.O, who they knew so well as a flight commander, had their best interests at heart, instead of trying to come to terms with an outside officer who had been 'parachuted in' to take command.

During that evening, it must have been difficult for everyone concerned with the Squadron to come to terms with the number of missing faces—the hard truth was that a third of the Squadron's pilots had been lost during the course of three dogfights with the enemy. If the exhausted pilots and ground crew had known that an amazing number of men had been rescued from the beaches during those twenty-four hours, just under 50,000 in total, it might have alleviated some of the pain they all felt. Although they were being hit hard, what they were doing really did matter.

On 30 May, F/Lt Ellis led not just eight Spitfires from 610, but a Wing of another three Squadrons on two patrols of Dunkirk. The first was from 1600 to 1805 hours and involved the following pilots from 'The Chesters':

DW-M.	P.9451	F/Lt. J. ELLIS.	11
DW-N.	L.1075	P/O. P. LITCHFIELD	14
DW-O.	L.1043	Sgt. ARNFIELD, S. J.	11
DW-J.	N.3284	F/O. W. H. C. WARNER.	16

	N.3274	P/O. G. KEIGHLEY.	9
DW-B.	L.1009	F/O. E. B. B. SMITH.	18
DW-S.	N.3201	P/O. S. C. NORRIS.	14
DW-G.	L.1045	F/O. P. G. LAMB.	14

Blue, Red and Yellow Sections were on a:

> medium height patrol of DUNKIRK. Weather very unfavourable. Much cloud from ground level to 6,000 feet, with poor visibility. Twin-engined aircraft sighted over NIEUPORT, proved to be Blenheims. No E/A sighted. (ORB)

Ellis was almost certainly Blue Leader, with Warner and Smith leading the other two sections (probably Yellow and Red respectively), Warner's presumably being just a two-man section. After this lengthy patrol, the Squadron had a short rest, before being sent up again between 1940 and 2125 hours when, 'Squadron ordered to patrol DUNKIRK at medium height. Six aircraft only serviceable. Both sections were narrowly missed by A.A fire. No E/A sighted' (ORB).

This time Ellis was leading the following three-man section, with Smith leading the other one:

DW-M.	P.9451	F/Lt. J. ELLIS.	12
DW-N.	L.1075	P/O. P. LITCHFIELD.	15
DW-J.	N.3284	F/O. W. H. C. WARNER.	17
DW-D.	L.1010	F/O. E. B. B. SMITH.	19
DW-S.	N.3201	P/O. S. C. NORRIS.	15
DW-G.	L.1045	F/O. P. G. LAMB.	15

Again, the Squadron encountered 'friendly' AA fire, and while the Army and Navy were understandably trigger-happy, 610 Squadron's pilots must have been particularly perturbed by this, especially with Sgt Jenkins's loss fresh in their minds. Brian Smith recounted the following story relating to the dangers of AA fire over Dunkirk:

> They were following me down the coast, the shore battery of some kind or other. They had a shoot at me, and they missed me. I was just ahead of their fire—I wasn't going quickly, I would have been saving petrol. But no I was coming down gently so they got me just about right, but just not quite right—so I got away with that one!

After the previous day's casualties, Ellis would have been glad to have carried out two uneventful operations, although the number of patrols was evidently having an effect on the aircraft as well as the pilots; only six Spitfires were available for the second patrol. It was a proud moment for Ellis as a young flight commander, to lead a Wing. This recognised his ability as a tactical fighter leader and 610 Squadron was fortunate to have him in its ranks. Although no enemy aircraft had been intercepted, Fighter Command was doing a good job, along with the inclement weather, in staving off the *Luftwaffe's* attacks, as nearly 54,000 soldiers had been evacuated during the day so far.

With the BEF's evacuation now in full swing, 610's pilots were again in action on 31 May, being ordered on patrol from Gravesend at 1555-1600 hours. The battle order was:

DW-M.	P.9451	F/Lt. J. ELLIS.	Blue 1	13
DW-N.	L.1075	P/O. P. LITCHFIELD.	Blue 2	16
DW-O.	L.1043	Sgt. ARNFIELD.	Blue 3	12

DW-B.	L.1009	F/O. E. B. B. SMITH.	Red 1	20
DW-G.	L.1045	F/O. P. G. LAMB.	Red	16
DW-D.	L.1010	P/O. S. C. NORRIS.	Red	16
DW-J.	N.3284	F/O. W. H. C. WARNER.	Yellow 1	18
	N.3274	F/O. G. L. CHAMBERS.	Yellow 2	9
DW-E.	R.6629*	P/O. G. KEIGHLEY.	Yellow 3	10

*As ORB, but should definitely be DW-E, L.1013.

The Squadron was operating as part of a Wing once more and, 'three sections … took off from Gravesend to carry out high altitude offensive patrol in company with Nos. 64 and 66 Squadrons, who were acting as the above guard' (TNA, AIR 81/735). F/Lt Ellis was leading 610's Spitfires at the head of Blue Section, followed by F/O Brian Smith's Red Section and F/O William Warner's Yellow Section. John Ellis described the ensuing action:

> I was leading 610 Sqdn. of 9 aircraft on a patrol of Dunkirk—Furnes at 20,000'. At 1715 I saw a dog fight going on below me, so put my section in to line astern and dived down to join in. Just as I reached the melée of aircraft below me I saw six Me 110s in line astern flying East. I broke away from the dog fight and gave chase and quickly caught them up. The rear gunner of the last Me 110 opened fire at about 700x but ceased immediately I opened fire at 300x. I carried out a No 1 attack from slightly above and gave the E/A two long bursts at each engine and the remainder of my ammunition at the front cockpit. White smoke belched out of each engine and soon after I had opened fire at the cockpit the machine did a bunt and I broke away and returned home. J. Ellis F/Lt. (TNA, AIR 50/172/20)

Ellis carried out a textbook No. 1 attack on the twin-engined enemy fighters, and quickly claimed his second victory of the war. His well-aimed bursts of fire disabled the Me 110, before he returned to Gravesend. Ellis's wingmen had differing levels of success, the outcome of the dogfight being unclear for P/O Litchfield, who had shot down an Me 110 on 27 May:

> On 31st May 1940, I was Blue two of a Squadron of 9 aircraft patrolling at 22000' over Dunkirk. At 1715 numerous aircraft, including engine types [*sic*], were observed about 5000' below. Blue Leader ordered line astern but my engine faltered and I had to lower the nose. I saw 6 (probably 7) ME 110s in Vic flying eastwards away from the sun and dived on the tail of the starboard end aircraft. Opening fire late, I continued firing for about four seconds and then broke away to avoid collision, without observing any decisive result. (TNA, AIR 50/172/48)

Litchfield only claimed this as 'One possible'. However, the ORB reports that 'F/Lt. J. ELLIS and P/O. P. LITCHFIELD each shot one down (confirmed)', so perhaps unbeknownst to Litchfield at the time, someone witnessed the demise of his target. This seems likely if his aim was accurate, as it was carried out at close range.[18]

Sgt Arnfield was the third pilot of the leading section, and he recorded his problematic patrol thus:

> While on patrol as Blue 3 of 610 Sqdn. over Dunkirk at 20000' my oxygen gave out. I remained with my section as long as I could but was forced to leave through oxygen shortage. Almost immediately after breaking away I saw my Sqdn. engaged in a dog fight with about 10 ME 110s and promptly joined in, firing a long burst at a 110 passing in front of my sights. Although I think many bullets went in the E.A managed to out turn me and get away. Seeing nothing more of either E.A or my own Sqdn. I returned home. No enemy fire observed. S.J.ARNFIELD Sgt. (TNA, AIR 50/172/5)

The demanding nature of this patrol is apparent, as Arnfield frantically juggled his oxygen supply while maintaining formation and keeping an eye out for marauding enemy aircraft. Not for the first time, an oxygen supply problem was causing difficulties for a pilot. Just like Peter Lamb two days earlier, Arnfield was lucky to realise his predicament in time to manage the situation, gamely remaining on patrol for as long as possible. Showing real bravery, he returned to the fray to aid his comrades in their attack on the Me 110s, and it was perhaps a combination of this 110 being flown by a very competent pilot and Arnfield's technical issue, that he was unable to out-turn a machine not renowned for its manoeuvrability. Again, the mediocre firepower of the .303 machine guns seems to have prevented a definite victory being claimed, with Arnfield noting 'Nil' against the enemy casualty column on his combat report.

While Blue Section had attacked the 110s below, it seems that Red and Yellow Sections had been left as a top cover for them, but they were attacked from above by six Me 109s. Yellow Section bore the brunt of the 'bounce', with both F/O Warner's wingmen being shot down. The CO's flying battle casualty report, written on 1 June 1940 is photographed below. F/O Graham Lambert Chambers was reported as 'Missing' on the Squadron's return to Gravesend. Lambert Chambers was another long-standing Squadron member, and had an Me 109 destroyed to his name. Alas, with no warning

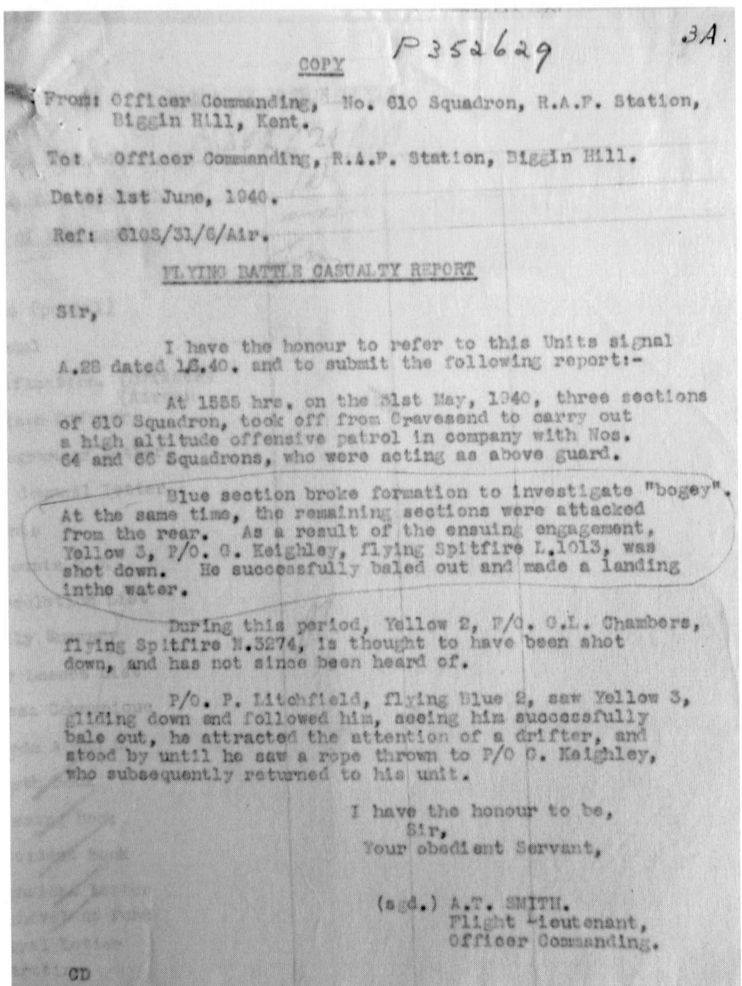
P352629 3A.

COPY

From: Officer Commanding, No. 610 Squadron, R.A.F. Station, Biggin Hill, Kent.

To: Officer Commanding, R.A.F. Station, Biggin Hill.

Date: 1st June, 1940.

Ref: 610S/31/6/Air.

FLYING BATTLE CASUALTY REPORT

Sir,

I have the honour to refer to this Units signal A.28 dated 1.6.40. and to submit the following report:-

At 1555 hrs. on the 31st May, 1940, three sections of 610 Squadron, took off from Gravesend to carry out a high altitude offensive patrol in company with Nos. 64 and 66 Squadrons, who were acting as above guard.

Blue section broke formation to investigate "bogey". At the same time, the remaining sections were attacked from the rear. As a result of the ensuing engagement, Yellow 3, P/O. G. Keighley, flying Spitfire L.1013, was shot down. He successfully baled out and made a landing inthe water.

During this period, Yellow 2, F/O. G.L. Chambers, flying Spitfire N.3274, is thought to have been shot down, and has not since been heard of.

P/O. P. Litchfield, flying Blue 2, saw Yellow 3, gliding down and followed him, seeing him successfully bale out, he attracted the attention of a drifter, and stood by until he saw a rope thrown to P/O G. Keighley, who subsequently returned to his unit.

I have the honour to be,
Sir,
Your obedient Servant,

(sgd.) A.T. SMITH.
Flight Lieutenant,
Officer Commanding.

CD

The flying battle casualty report from P/O Keighley's folder in The National Archives. (*TNA, AIR 81/2198*)

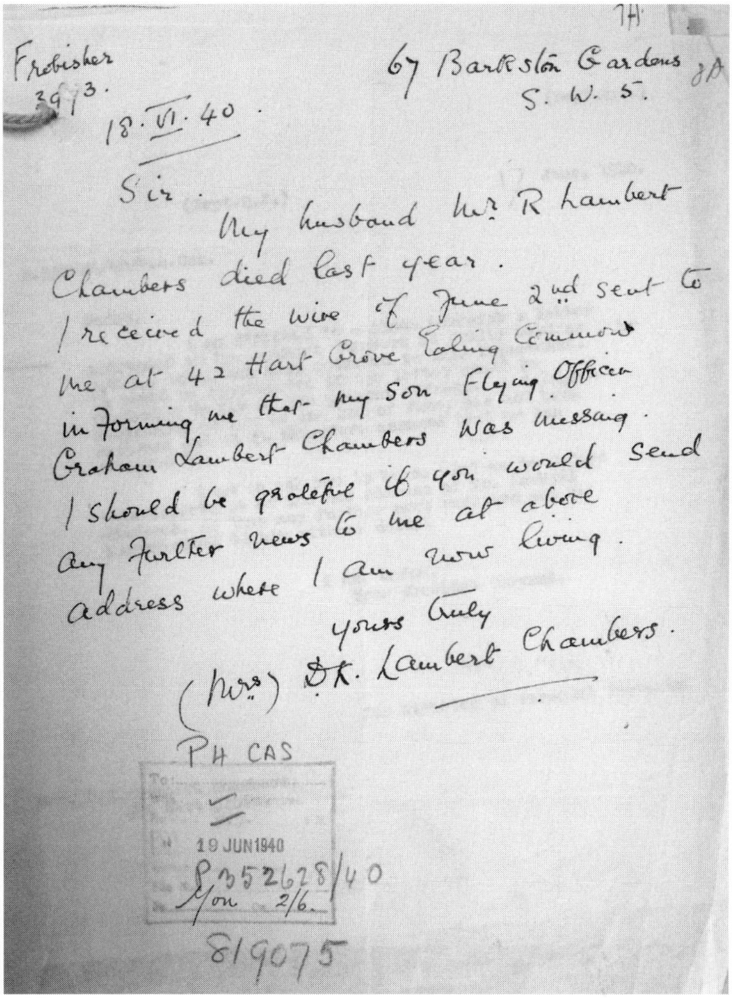

Frobisher 3973.

67 Barkston Gardens
S.W.5.

18.VI.40.

Sir.

My husband Mr R Lambert Chambers died last year. I received the wire of June 2nd sent to me at 42 Hart Grove Ealing Common informing me that my son Flying Officer Graham Lambert Chambers was missing. I should be grateful if you would send any further news to me at above address where I am now living.

yours truly

(Mrs) D.K. Lambert Chambers.

PH CAS

19 JUN 1940

819075

Letter from Lambert Chambers's mother acknowledging receipt of the wire. (*TNA, AIR 81/735*)

of the sudden attack from above and behind, Lambert Chambers was helpless, and nobody saw him go down in N.3274.

Sadly, little is recorded of him, especially when he had been with the Squadron over two years. 610 Squadron could not afford the loss of another of its more experienced pilots and his disappearance would have been sorely felt by all concerned. The dreaded news was sent to his next of kin, supposedly his father. However, as the correspondence flowed between the Air Ministry and Lambert Chambers's family, it became apparent that his father had died in 1939, so his mother was now next of kin (see photo above). Some two months later, Lambert Chambers's mother, the famous Wimbledon Champion, received an account of what had happened, and even after this interval, little was known about F/O Lambert Chambers's disappearance. This information could actually have been given to the family much earlier, as it was known in the dogfight's immediate aftermath, the ORB stating, 'Meanwhile Red and Yellow sections were attacked from above by 6 Me.109s, and Yellow 2 (F/O. G. L. CHAMBERS) was shot down'. Although Mrs Lambert Chambers almost certainly never gave up hope of receiving news about her son, the months continued to pass without any new facts arising at all.

Finally in early January 1941, Mrs Lambert Chambers, who had been evacuated from London to Idmiston, Wiltshire due to the bombing, received a letter which gave her the news she had been

This very rare photo is believed to show F/O Lambert Chambers in the cockpit of Spitfire DW-P, K.9960. (*Copyright Kerr family*)

dreading. Officially, all hope had been given up of her son being alive, and there was to be no fairy tale ending—Lambert Chambers was lost forever while defending Europe's freedom. F/O Graham Lambert Chambers is remembered on Panel 5 of the Runnymede Memorial.

P/O Geoffrey 'Peter' Keighley had been very fortunate to survive his encounter with the *Luftwaffe*, owing a great deal to Peter Litchfield for his rescue from the dangerous waters of the English Channel. It is remarkable that Litchfield made no mention of this in his own combat report. Keighley, in DW-E, L.1013, had almost certainly fallen foul of the same Messerschmitt 109s which had shot down Lambert Chambers,[19] the Squadron's ORB recording that:

> Red and Yellow sections were attacked from above by 6 Me.109s, and…Yellow 3 (P/O.G.KEIGHLEY) had his aircraft severely damaged by cannon and machine gun fire, but [he] managed to fly two-thirds of the way back across the Channel. The engine then began to fail, and he baled out at 3,000 feet. He was picked up by a trawler, transferred to a naval pinnace and landed at RAMSGATE.

He had landed in the sea about fifteen miles south-east of Ramsgate, at approximately 1740 hours, with a head injury (TNA, AIR 81/2198). Upon his return to Gravesend he would have been quick to thank Litchfield, and been glad of the food he had arranged to be supplied through his old links as a Harrods manager! Keighley was another pre-war Squadron member and his safe return after a parachute descent was presumably well celebrated. There are some blurry photos of Keighley just after his return, presenting a ghostly record of some of his injuries. The caption in the Association's archive reads, 'P/O G. Keighley's first parachute descent. (On his return.) Photograph taken at night by Tom Smith in O Mess Gravesend'.

To continue with events over Dunkirk, as Red Section's, Brian Smith, Peter Lamb and Stanley Norris realised they were under attack, they, along with Yellow Section's Bill Warner, became, 'engaged in a dogfight with the Me.109s, but none were confirmed as having been shot down' (ORB). Once again, 610 had endured a mixed day, losing yet another of its stalwart pre-war pilots in F/O Lambert Chambers, while P/O Keighley became the first Squadron member to survive a parachute descent and join the Caterpillar Club.[20] On the plus side, while the unit claimed two Me 110s destroyed, their efforts helped the Navy and the flotilla of little ships evacuate the highest number of troops in a single day of the evacuation—over 64,000 on the last day of May. Perhaps F/Lt Ellis and S/Ldr Smith were thankful that the Squadron's losses had not been worse, as other squadrons had lost whole sections of aircraft when bounced by the battle-hardened *Luftwaffe* pilots. Brian Smith recalled how well versed the enemy fighter pilots were in surprise attacks:

> Ah yes, that's right, Dunkirk: we were up high, the top lot, we weren't down below. We were there for an hour, once we'd mixed it up. And when the hour was up, you'd see a flash of light behind, and then you would break—we were being followed by the *Luftwaffe*. They'd got it worked out. Then it was time for 'Home boys!'

610's men might have expected 64 Squadron's Spitfires, some 2,000 feet higher, to have intervened or given a warning shout, but their ORB states that they were probably too busy to help, losing one pilot, with two other Spitfires returning damaged, while claiming to have shot down four *Luftwaffe* aircraft (64 ORB). The Dunkirk evacuation was a testing time for them all.

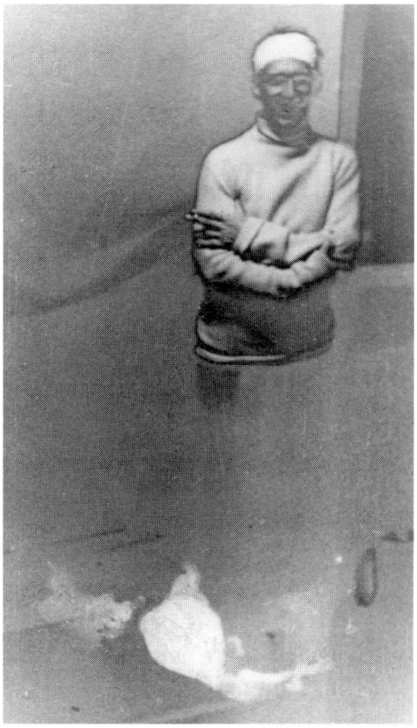

A rare photo of Geoffrey Keighley in the officers' mess, having returned to Gravesend after his parachute descent. One can clearly see the bandaging across Keighley's forehead from the head injury he suffered, whilst the young pilot enjoys a cigarette, thankful to have survived. (*Copyright 610 Squadron Association*)

9

June 1940: Rest, Recuperation and Replacements at Acklington and Gravesend

With the arrival of June, plans were set in motion for 610 Squadron's withdrawal from the front line and the battle to protect the Dunkirk evacuation. 72 Squadron, earmarked as their replacements, 'received orders to move to Gravesend, No.11 Group for temporary duty' (72 Squadron ORB), at 0130 hours on 1 June. It is probable that 610 Squadron was informed that it would be moving out of Gravesend at a similar time, however, there was still time for another patrol in the mid-afternoon. At 1545 hours, F/Lt Ellis led 'B' Flight on a high altitude patrol of Dunkirk. The pilots involved, all aware that this was the last patrol they would have to survive before a welcome rest, were as follows:

DW-M.	P.9451	F/Lt. J. ELLIS.	14
DW-N.	L.1075	P/O. P. LITCHFIELD.	17
DW-O.	R.6595*	SGT. ARNFIELD, S. J.	13
DW-B.	L.1009	F/O. E. B. B. SMITH.	21
DW-S.	N.3201	F/O. W. H. C. WARNER.	19
DW-G.	L.1045	P/O. S. C. NORRIS.	17

*DW-O suddenly changes from L.1043 to R.6595. L.1043 reportedly moved to 266 Squadron 18 June 1940.[1]

The ORB noted, 'Weather conditions difficult. 9/10ths. 10/10ths. cloud, 8,000 feet thick. Sighted 3 E/A, which were thought to be Heinkel 113. Enemy dived into cloud on being chased and our patrol became separated. Aircraft continued patrol individually. No other aircraft sighted'. Given the outcome of the other recent patrols in equally tricky conditions, Ellis would have been delighted to get home at about 1730 hours with the Flight still intact. It would be 610's last patrol of the Dunkirk evacuation.

In the meantime, 72 Squadron's Spitfires had arrived to replace 'The Chesters'. 72 Squadron's ORB notes how at 1510 hours, 'Fifteen aircraft left ACKLINGTON for GRAVESEND', arriving at 1645 hours:

> The Squadron arrived at GRAVESEND Airport where S/Ldr. LEES took over command of the Station from the O.C. No.610 Squadron which then left for ACKLINGTON. A.V.M. KEITH PARK A.O.C. No 11. Group who had just returned from a solo flight in a Hurricane over DUNKIRK, was on the aerodrome to welcome the squadron on its arrival at GRAVESEND. Immediately on arrival the squadron came to readiness.

So 610 Squadron left Gravesend almost as soon as Ellis's six Spitfires had been refuelled, in the early evening of 1 June. The extract from 72 Squadron's ORB is interesting, as it shows the hands-on nature of AVM Keith Park. He carried out flights over the evacuation to gain a first-hand understanding of the situation his men faced, a highly dangerous activity for such a senior RAF officer. Park welcomed the new incumbents of Gravesend in person, but he would equally have been keen to bid 610 Squadron a well-earned rest, after a harrowing few days over Dunkirk's beaches.

Although 72 Squadron believed that 610 was going directly to Acklington, 610 Squadron's ORB stated that there would be a slight diversion for the pilots and some ground crew:

GRAVESEND, 1st JUNE, 1940.

Following pilots proceeded by air to ACKLINGTON, stayed night at DIGBY as guests of WING COMMANDER I. R. PARKER, and returned on 6th June, 1940.

F/LT. A. T. SMITH	(90337)	F/LT. J. ELLIS	(37850)
F/O. E. B. B. SMITH	(90340)	F/O. W. H. C. WARNER	(90344)
F/O. P. G. LAMB.	(90349)	P/O. S. C. NORRIS	(40361)
P/O. P. LITCHFIELD	(76461)	P/O. W. E. LLOYD	(79271)
P/O. A. L. B. RAVEN	(91089)	Sgt. ARNFIELD, S. J	(564115) and 25 airmen.

The pilots must have been exhausted, eight of them having flown under the constant threat of action since their posting to Biggin Hill on 10 May, and this was intensified during the hectic week spent at Gravesend. 'Peter' Keighley would have been given time to recover from his wounds and possibly spend some time at home, as he is not listed here. Lloyd was the intelligence officer, not an operational pilot, however, while Raven had not yet flown an operational patrol with 610, it seems that he may have had an equally eventful time. A report, probably from his school, stated that on completing his training, he had been sent to France, 'with an emergency unit but his train was bombed near Amiens, and he escaped back to this country',[2] before rejoining 610 Squadron.

The overnight stay at Digby, Lincolnshire, was a welcome escape from the front line, and a chance to see their former CO, Wg Cdr I. R. Parker, the original fulcrum of the Squadron. He must have been keen to hear how his former charges had fared, and been deeply saddened by their losses, involving pilots whom he had handpicked and helped mould into the Squadron during peacetime. Brian Smith remembered this visit to Digby and I. R. Parker, 'No, just wondering if we passed through, we might have landed at Digby at some point. That's right, I think we may well have done. Oh yes, he was a wonderful man'. From Raymond Ellis's memories he recalled that, 'The personnel of 'A' and 'B' Flights were flown (to Acklington) in RAF transport aircraft and they all returned to Gravesend on 6th June 1940'.[3] This accurately confirms the duration of 610 Squadron's stay at Gravesend during the Dunkirk evacuation, as different books have stated inaccuracies on the matter.

Saturday 1 June 1940 was also an important day for Brian Smith, as he was promoted to acting flight lieutenant, a position he held unpaid for twenty-one days, before being granted the rank of a paid acting flight lieutenant (ORB). With the twenty-five-year-old pilot being one of the Squadron's stalwarts, it would have been hoped that this promotion from within the Squadron's ranks would have a stabilising effect on the unit. Both Brian Smith as a flight commander and fellow long-serving Auxiliary Tom Smith as CO, understood how the Squadron ticked, while John Ellis brought his tactical nous as the Regular flight commander.

After spending the night of 1 June at Digby, on, '2/6/40 No 610 Squadron arrived at Acklington to replace No 72 Squadron'. (Acklington ORB) The pilots and ground crew enjoyed a brief period of relaxation in Northumberland, the best part of four days, which they richly deserved as did all those in Fighter Command who had fought so bravely over the evacuation. 610's sacrifice, seven pilots 'Missing' or Killed and one wounded, was very heavy, and stands testament to the extremely difficult conditions faced by RAF pilots, and their heroic efforts to protect the vulnerable men on the beaches and ships. On a larger scale, Fighter Command had suffered heavy losses too: '55 pilots killed, six Defiant air-gunners killed, eight pilots taken prisoner (of whom one later died), eleven pilots and one air-gunner wounded, and one pilot killed in a flying accident'.[4] The so called 'Miracle of Deliverance'

Brian Smith in his uniform at Hooton Park, in more peaceful times. (*Copyright 610 Squadron Association*)

This photograph shows two others who would be the Squadron's key figures following 610 Squadron's heavy losses over Dunkirk. John Ellis, left, was the 'B' flight commander, an experienced Regular Officer, whilst on the far right is the face of Tom Smith, the new CO. (*Copyright 610 Squadron Association*)

at Dunkirk could not have taken place at all, without the RAF's selfless efforts in keeping the *Luftwaffe* at bay. The awful losses sustained by units such as 610 Squadron were only made bearable by the fact that a staggering total of 338,226 men had been evacuated. This was a remarkable achievement, made possible in equal measure thanks to the bravery of the Navy's sailors and the civilians manning the 'little ships'; it had been a truly combined effort.

Even Prime Minister Churchill, in his famous, 'we shall fight on the beaches' speech delivered to the House of Commons on 4 June 1940, while 610 Squadron was recovering at Acklington, was quick to point out Fighter Command's magnificent effort in defending the troops and ships. He referred to them in glowing terms. This was a direct response to the impression in certain quarters that the RAF's fighter pilots had not done their job:

> We must be very careful not to assign to this deliverance the attributes of a victory. Wars are not won by evacuations. But there was a victory inside this deliverance, which should be noted. It was gained by the Air Force. Many of our soldiers coming back have not seen the Air Force at work; they saw only the bombers which escaped its protective attack. They underrate its achievements. I have heard much talk of this; that is why I go out of my way to say this. I will tell you about it.
>
> This was a great trial of strength between the British and German Air Forces. Can you conceive a greater objective for the Germans in the air than to make evacuation from these beaches impossible, and to sink all these ships which were displayed, almost to the extent of thousands? Could there have been an objective of greater military importance and significance for the whole purpose of the war than this? They tried hard, and they were beaten back; they were frustrated in their task. We got the Army away; and they have paid fourfold for any losses which they have inflicted. Very large formations of German aeroplanes—and we know that they are a very brave race—have turned on several occasions from the attack of one-quarter of their number of the Royal Air Force, and have dispersed in different directions. Twelve aeroplanes have been hunted by two. One aeroplane was driven into the water and cast away, by the mere charge of a British aeroplane, which had no more ammunition. All of our types—the Hurricane, the Spitfire and the new Defiant—and all our pilots have been vindicated as superior to what they have at present to face.
>
> When we consider how much greater would be our advantage in defending the air above this island against an overseas attack, I must say that I find in these facts a sure basis upon which practical and reassuring thoughts may rest. I will pay my tribute to these young airmen. The great French Army was very largely, for the time being, cast back and disturbed by the onrush of a few thousands of armoured vehicles. May it not also be that the cause of civilisation itself will be defended by the skill and devotion of a few thousand airmen? There never had been, I suppose, in all the world, in all the history of war, such an opportunity for youth. The Knights of the Round Table, the Crusaders, all fall back into a prosaic past: not only distant but prosaic; but these young men, going forth every morn to guard their native land and all that we stand for, holding in their hands these instruments of colossal and shattering power, of whom it may be said that 'When every morning brought a noble chance,' 'And every chance brought out a noble knight,' deserve our gratitude, as do all of the brave men who, in so many ways and on so many occasions, are ready, and continue ready, to give life and all for their native land.[5]

Churchill's fine piece of oration could not have been more complimentary about Fighter Command's efforts, although it was not until well after the war that the general public became aware of this memorable speech, as it was only given in Parliament. His reference to the Knights of the Round Table in Tennyson's *Morte D'Arthur*, adds to the heroic impression of the fighter pilots' efforts in the skies over Dunkirk. Everything they did in those difficult days was a learning curve, particularly for the Spitfire pilots who had not fought over France. Pilots found themselves dealing with technical problems with their aircraft in combat and trying to survive against a battle-tested foe, who had learnt the tricks of their trade over Poland and France, some even during the Spanish Civil War.

In comparison, much of what had been drilled into the RAF's pilots pre-war, such as flying in neat 'Vics' of three and the 'Orders of Attack', had proven terribly obsolete for the rigours of contemporary air fighting. It had been a case of learning what worked in the thick of battle. For many, including the brave pilots of 610 Squadron, it was learning what did not work too late, which cost them so dearly. Brian Smith recalled how the pilots knew they needed to adapt their tactics following on from the Dunkirk operations:

> This business of staying in threes—I think we learnt about operating in pairs from the Germans, otherwise you were spending all your time not running into the bloke next door! It was after the Dunkirk time, we thought there was something wrong here. Because we just stayed up for our hour until we were jumped from behind, and of course all you could do then was break, and hope to come round.

This process of having to learn what worked and what did not, when fighting for your life, was key for Smith, as he brought it up again:

> But we soon learnt to get away from the squadron formation, because it was proving to be fatal. That must have been after the Dunkirk business, and I think we picked it up from the Germans. Because we did do line astern, and that was a much safer formation, because you could see what was going on in front. It was up to either their discretion or yours to break. Oh you learn, you learn.

Although 'Operation Dynamo' officially started on the night of 26 May 1940—the day before 610 was ordered to Gravesend—the Squadron's first real patrol in the combat area came on 20 May from Biggin Hill. During the course of their time in 11 Group, 10 May to 1 June 1940, 610 Squadron amassed forty-two recorded patrols, varying from single aircraft up to Squadron strength. Only four patrols involved combat with enemy aircraft. However, the loss of seven pilots 'Missing' or killed, one wounded, plus various other Spitfires damaged, for ten enemy aircraft claimed destroyed, three unconfirmed and one damaged, shows how brutal the dogfights were. Perhaps the starkest way of looking at 'The Chesters' losses is by studying the original list of aircrew who arrived at Biggin Hill with such high expectations on 10 May. The Squadron had seventeen pilots, boosted to eighteen by P/O

This photo of the Squadron's Hinds taken in August 1938, shows the basic close 'Vic' formation which was still being used by the RAF well into 1940, despite the casualties suffered as a result of adhering to such obsolete tactics. (*Copyright Medcalf family*)

Raven's return on 23 May, although neither Raven nor F/O Wood flew a recorded operational patrol during this period. 'B' Flight had been annihilated—of the six pilots who flew down from Prestwick to Biggin Hill, only John Ellis had survived with F/Os Medcalf, Kerr Wilson, Kerr, Lambert Chambers and Sgt Jenkins all having been lost. 'A' Flight had flown down that morning with eight pilots, and they were now down to six having lost S/Ldr Franks and Sgt Medway, while P/O Keighley was wounded. Obviously the pilots had been shuffled around the two flights as was necessary, but it shows how the Squadron boasting eighteen pilots, had been hit hard and by 1 June was down to just ten pilots, with only eight operational. However, vital experience had been gained by the survivors, and the cadre of those with the most flying time in this period was led by Brian Smith who had flown twenty-one recorded patrols, along with F/O William Warner, nineteen patrols, and then P/Os Peter Litchfield and Stanley Norris who had both carried out seventeen patrols. The number of victory claims made by each pilot by 1 June 1940 is as follows, along with the totals and type of enemy aircraft shot down:

S/Ldr Franks	109 destroyed 29 May, 110 destroyed, 110 unconfirmed 27 May.
P/O Litchfield	110 destroyed 27 May, 110 destroyed 31 May.
F/Lt Ellis	109 destroyed 29 May, 110 destroyed 31 May.
F/Lt A. T. Smith	110 destroyed, 111 shared destroyed, 110 unconfirmed 27 May.
P/O Norris	109 destroyed 29 May.
F/O Lambert Chambers	109 destroyed 29 May.
F/O Warner	111 shared destroyed 27 May, 109 damaged 29 May.
F/O E. B. B. Smith	111 shared destroyed 27 May.
F/O Lamb	111 shared destroyed 27 May.
Sgt Medway	111 shared destroyed 27 May.
F/O Kerr	110 unconfirmed 27 May.
F/O Kerr Wilson	No claims.
F/O Medcalf	No claims.
P/O Keighley	No claims.
Sgt Jenkins	No claims.
Sgt Arnfield	No claims.
F/O Wood	No patrols recorded.
P/O Raven	No patrols recorded.

	Destroyed/Confirmed	Probable	Unconfirmed	Damaged	Total Claims
Me 109	4	N/A	N/A	1	5
Me 110	5	N/A	3	N/A	8
He 111	1	N/A	N/A	N/A	1
Total	10	N/A	3	1	14

Following on from their brief respite at Acklington, the Squadron returned to Gravesend on 6 June with Tom Smith promoted to squadron leader. Although Acklington's ORB failed to mention 610's departure, full details of it are supplied by 72 Squadron's ORB:

6/6/40

GRAVESEND	**1400**	No.610 Squadron arrived at Gravesend and S/Ldr.Lees handed over the Station to S/Ldr.Smith.
	1615	Squadron left GRAVESEND for ACKLINGTON.
ACKLINGTON	**1755**	Squadron arrived ACKLINGTON and immediately came to readiness.

Given 72 Squadron's flight time to get from Gravesend to Acklington, it is safe to assume that 'The Chesters' left Acklington at around 1220 hours to arrive at Gravesend for 1400 hours. It is interesting that the CO of the incumbent Squadron at Gravesend, also had command of the Station itself, presumably as the senior officer at the aerodrome.

With 610's recent heavy losses, it was essential that the Squadron received replacement pilots swiftly to swell its ranks. During the course of June, fourteen new pilots are recorded as being sent to the Squadron to help fill the gaps made by the *Luftwaffe*. Although some pilots left during June too, the Squadron quickly had a full operational quota of pilots, men who would benefit from the experience of the pilots who had survived Dunkirk's tumultuous skies. Several of the Squadron's Spitfires were replaced too, as can be seen in the aircraft lists.

The first two new additions joined on 6 June, the day 610 Squadron returned to Gravesend, with Sgts R. F. Hamlyn and P. Else both arriving from 72 Squadron. Ronald Hamlyn was:

> Born in Harrogate on February 26 1914, Hamlyn was educated at Clifton House and Pockling School, near York. He joined the RAF as a direct-entry Airman u/t Pilot in 1936 (580244). He began his ab initio training at 11 E&RFTS, Perth on June 29 1936, as a pupil pilot. On the satisfactory completion of the course, he formally enlisted in the RAF on August 24 1936. He carried out his intermediate and advanced training at 8 FTS, Montrose and passed out as a Sergeant-Pilot. Hamlyn was with 72 Squadron at Church Fenton at the outbreak of war. After Dunkirk, Hamlyn was attached to 610 Squadron at Gravesend on June 6 1940 and this attachment later became a posting.[6]

Peter Else was born three years later, on 28 February 1917 at Newmarket in Suffolk:

> He joined the RAFVR on February 23 1938, as an Airman u/t Pilot. He began his flying training at 22 E&RFTS, Cambridge. At that time Else was working there, as an engineer at Marshall's Flying School, the operators. Called up on September 1 1939, Else went to 6 FTS, Little Rissington on October 7 1939 for advanced training. At the end of the course he was posted direct to 72 Squadron at Church Fenton on December 16 1939,[7]

Peter Else's pilot's licence photo in 1938, aged twenty-one. (*Copyright Royal Aero Club Trust*)

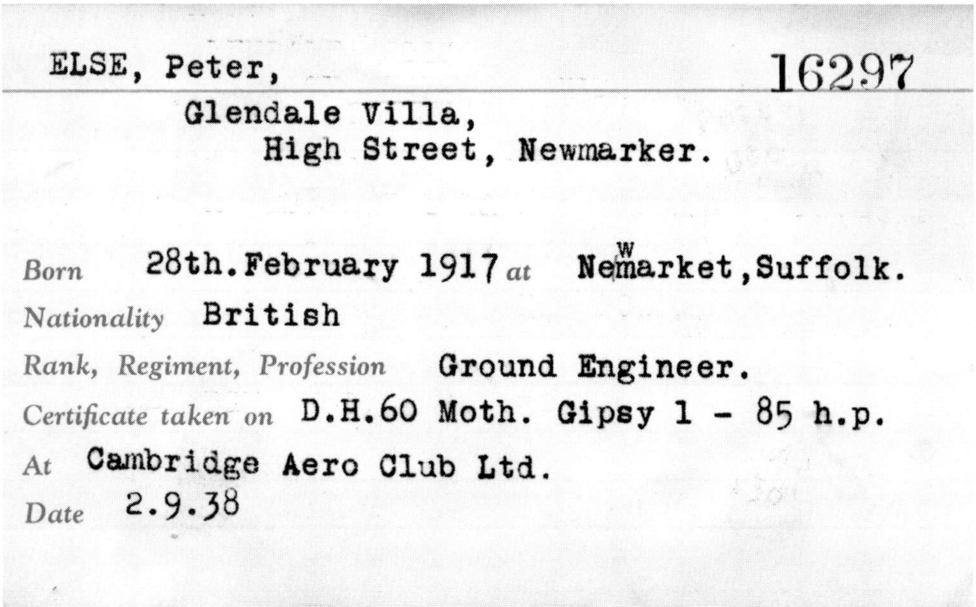

ELSE, Peter, 16297

Glendale Villa,
High Street, Newmarker.

Born 28th.February 1917 *at* Newmarket,Suffolk.

Nationality British

Rank, Regiment, Profession Ground Engineer.

Certificate taken on D.H.60 Moth. Gipsy 1 - 85 h.p.

At Cambridge Aero Club Ltd.

Date 2.9.38

Peter Else's flying licence, which he seems to have passed whilst being a member of the RAFVR. (*Copyright Royal Aero Club Trust*)

before being posted to 610 Squadron due to their pilot shortage.

Interestingly, both men had received mentions, albeit slightly ignominious ones, in 72 Squadron's ORB. On 2 June, the day after the bulk of 72 Squadron arrived at Gravesend:

> 1840 P/O. ELLIOTT arrived at GRAVESEND from ACKLINGTON. He and SGT. ELSE had left together at 1510 hours and P/O. Elliott had found it necessary to land at HALTON owing to lack of fuel. Sgt. Else also landed there where he crashed. (72 ORB)

This was a disastrous start for Else, crashing his aircraft before he had even reached his destination. Hamlyn suffered an equally unfortunate incident on 5 June: '**2053** The squadron (12 aircraft) took off to intercept a raid over DUNGENESS at 20,000 feet. **2152** Nothing was seen however, and the squadron returned to base. Sgt. Hamlyn crashed on landing' (72 ORB). Such accidents would have been looked on very dimly, (Hamlyn's may well have been the cause of a future fine which will come to light), although it is unclear where the error lay. 72 Squadron flew some patrols from Gravesend, including operations over Dunkirk, but there was no record of Hamlyn or Else filing a claim against the *Luftwaffe*, while 72 Squadron's ORB does not mention them leaving for 610. It seems likely they remained at Gravesend when 610 Squadron arrived on 6 June, bidding their former 72 Squadron colleagues farewell as they returned to Acklington.

On the evening of their arrival at Gravesend, once the Squadron had settled into what would once more be home, there was still time for a dusk patrol. F/O Brian Smith led Red Section over Canterbury at 5,000 feet. Smith (22) was flying DW-H, L.1044, with F/O Bill Warner (20) (DW-J, N.3284) and F/O Peter Lamb (17) in the reserve Spitfire CR, R.6630. They took off at 2055 hours, but returned fifty minutes later without incident. On the next day, the same patrol was repeated in the morning, this time a full Flight led by John Ellis patrolling the cathedral city of Kent for an hour, having taken off at 0750 hours. The pilots involved were:

DW-M.	P.9451	F/Lt. J. ELLIS.	15
DW-L.	P.9496	Sgt. HAMLYN.	1
DW-P.	R.9495*	Sgt. ELSE.	1
DW-J.	N.3284	F/O. E. B. B. SMITH.	23
DW-H.	L.1044	F/O. P. G. LAMB.	18
DW-E.	R.6629	P/O. G. KEIGHLEY.	11

*Probably DW-K. P.9495.

The patrol passed uneventfully and no other aircraft were spotted. This was the first recorded patrol undertaken by the Squadron's two new sergeant pilots, Else and Hamlyn, both flying on either wingtip of the flight commander—Ellis would have been trying to establish how competent they were.

The only other event of note on 7 June was that the Australian F/O Victor Thomas Lawrence Wood, aged twenty-three, was posted away from 610 Squadron to 4 Ferry Pilot's Pool, Filton (ORB). He had flown a handful of convoy patrols on Spitfires with the Squadron in March, but following his accident on 13 March, had not recorded any flying again, most noticeably during the Dunkirk operations. Although there's no photographic evidence of Wood in the Squadron Association's archive, Wood's drawing of Tom Smith survives, however, Smith may not have thanked him for his somewhat unflattering efforts! Wood was still operating as a ferry pilot in January 1941 (TNA, AIR 81/4914).

During the course of the next few days, 610 Squadron continued to carry out patrols from Gravesend across Kent. On 8 June at 1415 hours, one section was ordered to patrol Manston at 5,000 feet, as follows:

DW-J.	N.3284	F/O. W. H. C. WARNER.	21
DW-B.	L.1009	Sgt. HAMLYN.	2
DW-L.	P.9496	Sgt. ARNFIELD, S. J.	14

They landed at 1510 hours, without having seen anything of note. On 9 June, the Squadron was either stood down or there was no need for them to be called on, as no activity is recorded; it is likely that S/Ldr Smith had at least some of his men carrying out training. On 10 June, Bill Warner led

Victor Wood's sketch of Tom Smith. (*Copyright 610 Squadron Association*)

another section patrol, this time of Dover at 10,000 feet. The three pilots of Green Section, Warner (22) (DW-O, R.6595), P/O Keighley (12) (DW-T, P.9452) and Sgt Else (2) (DW-L, P.9496) took off at 1502 hours and returned at 1530 hours—no enemy aircraft sighted.

There was an increase in the Squadron's activity on 11 June, as at 1215 hours, Blue Section (usually in 'B' Flight), was ordered to patrol Canterbury—Binwash—Ashford, which was uneventful. The pilots were:

DW-H.	L.1044	P/O. S. C. NORRIS.	18
DW-J.	N.3284	F/O. W. H. C. WARNER.	23
DW-K.	P.9495	Sgt. ARNFIELD, S. J.	15

They returned to Gravesend at 1305 hours. A little later, F/Lt Brian Smith (24) was ordered to patrol Maidstone at 20,000 feet. He took off in DW-B, L.1009 at 1455 hours, returning thirty minutes later without seeing anything. This was the first time that Smith was given the title of flight lieutenant following his promotion to the 'acting' rank on 1 June. Shortly afterwards, he was ordered to lead 'A' Flight on a patrol at 1555 hours. The following pilots took off in two sections, Smith leading one and Warner the second composed of a pair:

DW-B.	L.1009	F/Lt. E. B. B. SMITH.	25
DW-E.	R.6629	P/O. G. KEIGHLEY.	13
DW-G.	L.1045	Sgt. HAMLYN.	3
DW-J.	N.3284	F/O. W. H. C. WARNER.	24
DW-H.	L.1044	P/O. S. C. NORRIS.	19

However, the Flight was immediately recalled, and landed just ten minutes later. This concluded the day's flying, the Squadron having carried out a total of three hours and fifty minutes patrolling the skies.

Despite the day's mundane patrols, further recruits had been arriving, this time in the shape of P/O Iain Hunter Stewart and Sergeant Norman Hugh Donald Ramsay, both from 92 Squadron, Hornchurch. The 92 Squadron ORB records on 10 June: 'In the evening a signal was received posting two non-operational Pilots to 610 SQUADRON at GRAVESEND. P/O. STEWART and SGT. RAMSAY were instructed to report in the morning' (92 ORB). On 31 May, Stewart, who had been, 'granted leave to go to the AIR MINISTRY returned, and has gone to report for flying duties with the SQUADRON AT DUXFORD' (92 ORB). P/O Stewart endured an unfortunate time with the County of Chester Squadron, as the only further reference to him comes on 7 September 1940, the day his short service commission was terminated on account of ill health.

However, the same cannot be said for Sgt Ramsay, who was born on 29 July 1919 in Hull. He later worked as an apprentice at Vickers Supermarine in Southampton, while he joined the RAFVR in March 1939, as an Airman u/t Pilot.

> Ramsay began his elementary flying training at 3 E&RFTS, Hamble and had soloed on the Avro Cadet before he was called to full-time service at the outbreak of war. After 3 ITW [Initial Training Wing], Hastings, Ramsay was posted to 10 FTS, Tern Hill for No 16 Course, which ran from November 6 1939 to May 11 1940. With training completed, Ramsay joined 92 Squadron at Northolt on May 14.[8]

His first duty with 92 Squadron was recorded on 15 May—'W/Cdr HAMILTON arrived to inspect the MASTER this morning and then took off for PRESTWICK with SGT. RAMSAY who returns to 92 SQN tomorrow' (92 ORB)—quite what he was doing is unclear. On 30 May, Ramsay carried out air fighting practice between 1120 and 1210 hours, in Spitfire P.9368, his first recorded such flight

Two of the new Sgt Pilots who arrived in early June 1940, Ronnie Hamlyn (left) and Norman Ramsay. Whilst Hamlyn, aged twenty-six, had participated in operations over Dunkirk with 72 Squadron, Ramsay aged twenty, had joined from 92 Squadron as a non-operational pilot. This photo was probably taken not long after their arrival at RAF Gravesend, and certainly between 11 June and 2 July 1940. (*Copyright 610 Squadron Association*)

indicating that he was at least gaining some experience. On 31 May, Ramsay carried out two further exercises, the first from 1015–1045 hours in Spitfire N.3250, classed as 'Local flying'; the second was a 'Sector Recce' in N.3167, from 1510 to 1615 hours, both of which would have been to familiarise him with his new fighter and the surrounding countryside. On 1 June, Ramsay carried out formation flying with a P/O Hargreaves for fifty-five minutes from 1500 hours, in Spitfire P.9367. On 4 June, an incident took place between 0830–0850 hours involving Ramsay, which he was fortunate to survive unscathed. 92 Squadron was flying to RAF Northolt in bad weather when 'P/O. WADE crashed the MASTER at HEMEL HEMPSTEAD owing to bad visibility and lack of good airmanship. The MASTER was badly damaged but P/O. WADE and his passenger SGT. PILOT RAMSAY were unhurt' (92 ORB). Ramsay had little time to dwell on this scare though, as he carried out two more 'Local flying' flights, at 1110–1210 hours in N.3248 and between 1945 and 2000 hours in N.3285.

The following morning he repeated the exercise in the same Spitfire, from 0950–1100 hours, his longest recorded flight thus far with 92 Squadron. On 6 June, he performed, 'Practice attacks' in Spitfire N.3193, from 1455–1555 hours. On 7 June he carried out a Battle Climb for an hour from 0900 hours, in Spitfire R.6616, repeating the exercise at 1040 hours in Spitfire N.3192, returning at 1125 hours. Later in the day, more local flying was performed in P.9371, from 1620–1700 hours and 1825–1920 hours, to round off a busy day. On 9 June he flew with the Squadron to Hornchurch, again in P.9371 taking off at 1155 hours and landing twenty minutes later, his last flight with the Squadron. After just under a month with 92 Squadron, still not aged twenty-one, and non-operational, he joined 610 Squadron. He had gained ten hours and twenty-five minutes extra flying time on Spitfires, during the course of thirteen flights.

Wednesday 12 June was the Squadron's busiest and most eventful day since returning to Gravesend, with Blue Section involved in the interception of a single Heinkel He 111. F/Lt John Ellis (16) (DW-M, P.9451) was leading Sgt Johnny Arnfield (16) (DW-K, P.9495) and the flight commander's description is as illuminating as ever:

An early example of aircraft camouflage on an airfield. 610 Squadron went to great lengths to protect their aircraft on the ground at Gravesend from attack or being observed from the air. A small 'hut' has been erected over the engine and cockpit of the Spitfire, along with camouflage sheeting, to try and disguise the aircraft. (*Copyright 610 Squadron Association*)

> I was the leader of Blue section 610 Sqdn. which was ordered to take off at 0745 hrs on 12/6/40. There were two aircraft only in the section as Blue 3 had trouble starting and when he did take off he failed to contact us. Immediately we were airborne we were ordered to 'vector 120' and 'gate'. When in the vicinity of Canterbury we vectored 45 and three minutes later 40. By this time we were about 5 miles out to sea at 1500 off Birchington. I then sighted an aircraft flying due East at about 400'. I put the section into line astern and gave chase. I could see the aircraft was diving steeply for the sea and at about 800x I recognised it as a Heinkel 111. I ordered the section to carry out a No1. attack but at about 400x range I noticed another Spitfire below and in front and obviously carrying out an attack. I therefore turned away slightly and so started the attack again when the first Spitfire had broken away. I was diving down from above on the E/A and fired a burst of 4 secs (approx) from 300x closing to 50x. My overtaking speed was considerable. I estimated the speed of the E/A to be 200 mph. and my speed 250 mph. After No 2 of the Section had broken away the Heinkel still appeared to be flying normally so I started another No1. attack from above opening fire at 300x. After a short burst of 2 secs. at the nose, the E/A. crashed into the sea five miles N. of Margate. The machine floated well but I saw no sign of the crew when circling it so I climbed up to get into R/T touch again and on doing so I was vectored again out into the Channel and so saw no more of the Heinkel. There were a number of small boats in the vicinity of the E/A when it crashed. J. Ellis No fire encountered from rear gunners. (TNA, AIR 50/172/20)

The description of this dramatic incident is interesting due to the swift interception of the enemy aircraft, which took about twenty minutes from take-off. This was thanks to a combination of RDF, a competent ground controller, and the fact that the Heinkel had been in a running cat and mouse chase with two 64 Squadron Spitfires. It seemed to show how effective a No. 1 attack from the 'Fighter Attacks' could be against an unescorted single bomber, with both fighter pilots familiar with the plan. Ellis had all the time he needed to line up his attacks, and it must have seemed like another practice attack against an RAF Wellington or Battle, with no return fire being encountered. But reliance on such rigid lines of attack would prove much more risky with prowling enemy fighters in the vicinity, which was why RAF pilots learnt quickly to adapt or forget such methods when facing large, escorted formations of bombers. These methods did provide a comparatively safe line of attack against the bomber's defensive armament and allowed pilots the opportunity to bring their guns to bear in an effective manner. It is likely that this unfortunate Heinkel 111 belonged to *Wettererkundungsstaffel* 51, a weather reconnaissance unit; only two of the crew survived.

John Ellis having just stepped out of his cockpit after his combat with the Heinkel 111 on 12 June. It is interesting to note the full sized roundel which became so symbolic of 610 Squadron's Spitfires, although the 'DW' letters are not yet of a similar size, both of which would aid recognition. (*Copyright 610 Squadron Association*)

Having studied the combat reports of 64 Squadron's pilots, the order of events soon become apparent: the Heinkel was first encountered near Gatwick at 0743 hours, moments before 610's Blue Section was scrambled. The first pilot to intercept the bomber was Flight Sergeant (F/Sgt) Gilbert who reported:

> I as Green 1 was ordered to scramble and climb to 15000 ft. Just after leaving ground I tested my contactor and found it U/S so I was told to patrol Horsham. At approx. 0743 when at 12000ft I noticed another a/c about 500ft below me about 1 mile to port. I dived underneath and established his identity as a Heinkel 111. I broke away and carried out a No1 attack getting in a short burst of approx 2 seconds at 150 yds range. E/A evasive action was to throttle right back to a very slow speed and then turn quickly either port or starboard. Enemy fire appeared to come from blister guns and possibly top gun as well, but it was inaccurate. After this after about 3 minutes again saw E/A about 6000ft to 4000ft below and about 1 mile to port. I carried out a further No.1 attack at between 100 and 150 yds range using up the remainder of my ammunition. I observed a large amount of black smoke coming from port engine and E/A finally was lost in cloud at 600 ft approx. 12 miles E by S of Chatham … (TNA, AIR 50/24/234)

The German pilot had fled east towards the River Medway, before trying to follow the north Kent coast towards North Foreland and the open sea, however, Sgt Laws soon took up the chase:

> As Green 2 I was ordered off alone (after it had been discovered that Green 1 which had left 10 minutes earlier had a faulty R T) at 0735 hrs on a course 150 degrees—further order followed to alter course to 100 deg: at height of 2,500 ft. I lost R/T touch until crossing coast approx: West of Herne Bay. Control then ordered course of 030 degrees later to 040 degrees and warned me that E/A was flying out to sea ay [*sic*] zero altitude. My height when crossing coast had been 5000 ft in order to avoid clouds but weather was clear over sea and I lost height gradually. I sighted E/A at 0807 hrs heading East at approximately 600 ft (my height was then 3,000 ft) I flew ahead of enemy toward sun, losing height

> and turned for a beam attack. I carried out two beam attacks from either side, opening fire at 250 yds. The E/A when first seen and during the action, was travelling slowly (about 160 mph) as though one engine was damaged. E/A dived to sea level and made gentle turns each way, the tail unit occasionally touching the sea. At this moment two other Spitfires joined in, carrying out attacks from astern and above. I joined in with similar attack until remainder of my ammunition was expended. E/A had then settled on water and crew was inflating dinghy. I circled for a short period before being last to leave the scene ...I believe that this was the E/A attacked earlier by F/S Gilbert (Green 1) who left Kenley about 10 minutes before me … (TNA, AIR 50/24/280)

There are slight discrepancies in the timings of the final attacks on the Heinkel, but it seems likely that Ellis spotted the bomber, diving for sea level, just as Laws was about to carry out his first attack and it was already badly damaged by the time Ellis opened fire on it; the reason that he experienced no return fire was evidently a result of the efforts of the two 64 Squadron pilots. By the time the Heinkel crashed in the sea, the two 64 Squadron pilots had used up all their ammunition on it, Ellis had fired half his ammunition and Arnfield presumably slightly less during his single pass (there is no record of his combat report). This was further evidence of how ineffective the Browning .303 bullets could be in bringing down enemy aircraft, particularly the larger bombers which took more punishment. It had taken a huge amount of ammunition to finally down the bomber, in near perfect conditions. It also highlights that the Fighter Command style of attack was perhaps not as successful as it first seemed, although the target had finally been brought down.

Ultimately, it was Ellis's final two second burst at the vulnerable cockpit, the main weakness of the German bomber fleet, which forced the bomber down. The Heinkel 111, Junkers 88 and Dornier twin-engined bombers all had their crew in a glass-house cockpit, which provided good visibility, but was a perfect target for enemy pilots to aim at, with little protective armour plating. As the Battle of Britain progressed, the dangerous but highly effective head-on pass would prove a devastating means of stopping German bomber waves. Ellis and Arnfield returned to Gravesend at 0845 hours and were able to claim the shared destruction of the Heinkel, although this should certainly have been classed as shared with the two 64 Squadron pilots, too.

The air of excitement at Gravesend when Ellis and Arnfield returned from the sortie is palpable in one of the photos taken of Ellis immediately after they landed (see p. 178). Everyone on the ground would have been keen to hear about their combat. However, P/O Litchfield (18), ordered to patrol Maidstone on his own at 0855 hours, had to wait a little longer. He was flying DW-T, P.9452 and was instructed to patrol at 10,000 feet, but was immediately recalled and landed at 0911 hours, before finding out how Blue Section had fared with their earlier interception.

After the successful first patrol, expectations of further action would have increased. It was not long before another patrol was sent off, this time of Manston at 10,000 feet. Litchfield (19) was leading Green Section in DW-T, P.9452, having had its fuel topped up following the earlier short operation, and his wingmen were Sgt Else (3) (DW-L, P.9496), and P/O Raven (1) (DW-Q, P.9502). This was Lionel Raven's long-awaited first recorded patrol, the twenty-four year old originally from Ontario, Canada; it is easy to imagine his nervous excitement. In the end, no other aircraft were observed and they returned to Gravesend at 1100 hours, after a combined one hour and forty-five minutes flying.

The next couple of hours passed without incident, but at 1310 hours Red Section was ordered to patrol Hawkinge, as follows:

DW-J.	N.3284	F/O. W. H. C. WARNER.	25
DW-H.	L.1044	P/O. S. C. NORRIS.	20
DW-A.	R.6693	Sgt. HAMLYN.	4

Another photo of John Ellis in the immediate aftermath of having shot down the Heinkel 111. A mixture of satisfaction and relief is on his face. It must have been surreal to be photographed on his return to Gravesend and hailed as a hero, when minutes earlier he had been in such a life-threatening situation. (*Copyright 610 Squadron Association*)

It was carried out at 6,000 feet, above 9/10th cloud cover and no enemy aircraft were sighted. They returned to Gravesend at 1340 hours. After a fairly active morning and early afternoon, it is likely the Squadron was put on a less advanced state of readiness for a few hours, as their next recorded activity did not come until the evening and it marked an important event.

Since the Dunkirk operations, the Squadron had not carried out any full strength patrols—at first they simply did not have enough operational pilots. Although they would have practised operating in four sections of three Spitfires, it was another matter when it came to an operational patrol. So, when the order came through for a Squadron patrol at 1855 hours, it was probably quite an event at Gravesend. S/Ldr Smith was going to lead his first recorded operational flight of the month, the eleven Spitfires taking off behind him making a breath-taking sight as they moved into formation. The pilots were as follows, with the first six under Tom Smith's command in 'A' Flight, and the second six of 'B' Flight logically being led by John Ellis:

DW-A.	R.6693	S/Ldr. A. T. SMITH.	13
DW-J.	N.3284	F/O. W. H. C. WARNER.	26
DW-H.	L.1044	P/O. S. C. NORRIS.	21
DW-B.	L.1009	F/Lt. E. B. B. SMITH.	26
DW-G.	L.1045	F/O. P. G. LAMB.	19
DW-E.	R.6629	P/O. G. KEIGHLEY.	14
DW-T.	P.9452	P/O. P. LITCHFIELD.	20
DW-Q.	P.9502	P/O. A. L. B. RAVEN.	2
DW-L.	P.9496	Sgt. ELSE, P.	4
DW-M.	P.9451	F/Lt. J. ELLIS.	17
DW-K.	P.9495	Sgt. ARNFIELD, S. J.	17
DW-F.	P.6694*	Sgt. HAMLYN.	5

*Should be R.6694.

The patrol line was Dover to Folkestone at 7,000 feet—perhaps an enemy formation had been detected over the English Channel. For Raven, Else and Hamlyn, it was their first recorded full Squadron patrol with their new unit, and they would have been keen to prove their ability. No enemy aircraft were sighted however and the Squadron returned to Gravesend at 2000 hours. It had at least been good practice of getting airborne together and the sight of twelve Spitfires patrolling the south-east coast would have warmed the hearts of any natives who spotted them.

Although 610's pilots would have hoped to be stood down for the evening after this patrol, the Spitfires would once more have been refuelled and as another long day drew to a close, the two men who had been the first on duty early in the morning were called upon again, this time for a dusk patrol. At 2140 hours, one section was ordered to patrol Deal, as follows:

DW-M.	P.9451	F/Lt. J. ELLIS.	18
DW-J.	N.3284	Sgt. HAMLYN.	6
DW-K.	P.9495	Sgt. ARNFIELD, S. J.	18

Unlike the first patrol of the day, no aircraft were sighted, and with the night sky almost concealing them, the Spitfires returned to Gravesend at 2215 hours. Finally, the men could relax after a draining day of regular patrols and waiting at readiness for orders to come through, something to which Fighter Command's pilots were more than becoming accustomed. It had been a busy day for the unit, carrying out a combined total of twenty hours and one minute flying time, with just one contact with the enemy to show for it, although this successful encounter with the Heinkel would have boosted morale.

The Squadron seemed to enjoy a couple of days with reduced activity, perhaps concentrating on training while other 11 Group Squadrons were given the operational duties. It was not until 14 June that an operational flight was carried out. At 1540 hours, Yellow Section patrolled Manston at 5,000 feet, as some unidentified aircraft were in the vicinity. Brian Smith (27) led his section off in DW-B, L.1009, flanked by P/O Norris (22) (DW-H, L.1044) and Sgt Hamlyn (7) (DW-F, R.6694). As it transpired, the unknown aircraft were a section of Blenheims, and after a half-second of fear that they were about to encounter three Junkers Ju 88s, with their worryingly similar silhouette, Yellow Section returned without incident to Gravesend at 1625 hours. Back on the ground, it had been an important day for Geoffrey Keighley, as his appointment as pilot officer in the AAF had been confirmed and graded with effect from 16 December 1939.[9]

On the morning of 15 June, two section patrols took place, the first one at 0820 hours, as follows:

DW-J.	N.3824	F/O. W. H. C. WARNER.	27
DW-H.	L.1044	P/O. S. C. NORRIS.	23
DW-F.	R.6694	Sgt. HAMLYN.	8

Warner and his wingmen had been ordered to investigate an 'X' raid, or unidentified aircraft and were first vectored on to 135°, then 145°, before a final vector of 190°. After this wild goose chase, they were instructed to orbit Dungeness at 7,000 feet, and then 'pancake' at Gravesend at 0855 hours. At 1140 hours, Yellow Section was scrambled to intercept another 'X' raid, and this time the three pilots were:

DW-F.	R.6694	F/Lt. E. B. B. SMITH.	28
DW-A.	R.6693	F/O. P. G. LAMB.	20
DW-E.	R.6629	P/O. G. KEIGHLEY.	15

The section had been ordered straight to Dungeness, but shortly after becoming airborne, the Spitfires were recalled and landed at 1155 hours. It was another frustrating false alarm, which still amounted to a combined sortie time of forty-five minutes.

As June marched on, so too did the steady flow of new recruits. Two more sergeant pilots were posted to the Squadron on 15 June 1940. F/Sgt Pilot J. H. Tanner had been posted to 610 Squadron from HQME (probably Headquarters Middle East) and Sgt C. A. Parsons arrived from 6 OTU. John

Henry Tanner was born on 29 March 1915 in Gravesend, the son of John William and Eva Eleanor Tanner, of Ivy Cottage, Clay Hill, Enfield, Middlesex, and educated at Enfield Grammar School.[10] In January 1931 Tanner joined RAF Halton, where he trained as a fitter, aero engines in class 23 F2. From his record card at Halton, Form 1074, his strength academically was clearly in mathematics ahead of English, science and drawing. He, 'passed out in December 1933… He later applied for pilot training and was selected. It would seem that Tanner had completed his training before the outbreak of war and he was in Egypt until the spring of 1940'.[11] He went on to achieve his goal of joining a front-line unit on arriving at 610 Squadron, a very similar path to the one Sgt Arnfield had taken.

Claude Arthur Parsons originated from, 'Halterworth, Romsey, Hampshire, [and] worked in the Vickers-Armstrong Supermarine factory at Eastleigh. He joined the RAFVR about April 1939 as an Airman u/t Pilot. Called up on September 1, he completed his training and arrived at 6 OTU, Sutton Bridge on May 27 1940'.[12] Parsons seemed to have done his initial training with Bob Foster, who survived the war to be a wing commander, and wrote of his experiences in *Tally Ho! From the Battle of Britain to the Defence of Darwin*. Parsons went on to record his own early memoirs of his flying days as part of a book published during the war called *Ten Fighter Boys*, the experiences of ten pilots from 66 Squadron. There is no better way of getting an idea of Parsons than this description of him, written by S/Ldr Allen, DFC, his CO in 66 Squadron, who edited the book along with Wg Cdr Forbes, DFC:

> Claude was of medium height, well built and inclined to tubbiness. He was always well turned out. He had one of those cheerful smiles and happy dispositions which are a joy to meet, and I can't recall a single occasion on which his cheerfulness deserted him.
>
> He knew more about Spitfires than any of the other peelows [*sic*], as he had been with Supermarines before he joined the R.A.F. This knowledge of his machine and his keenness as a pilot often came out in discussions, as he was able to answer most queries, which he did invariably with the aid of model machines.[13]

The book is a fascinating insight to the lives of RAF fighter pilots in the early stages of the Second World War. In the following extract, it is possible to hear Parsons's own thoughts on his pre-operational flying days, his determination to fly the aircraft he knew so well and his excitement at being posted to 610 Squadron:

> It was just after the wonderful evacuation of our army from Dunkirk that I joined my first fighter squadron. I was particularly thrilled, because I had applied from the very first interview with my commanding officer at Initial Training Wing and throughout my training to be allowed to fly Spitfire fighters. Here I will just say that before the war I built and serviced Spitfires as a representative of Messrs. Vickers Armstrong, Ltd., hence my desire to become a pilot of one of the aircraft I really loved.
>
> After my training I was posted to a Hurricane Operational Training Unit; this meant usually that I would never see a Spitfire squadron, or, I would like to add, that's what I thought! When I was posted it was to a Spitfire squadron. I felt on top of the world: rather like a school boy who had just received his first prize at the annual sports day.
>
> I did quite a lot of flying as soon as I joined my squadron, practising attacks and generally getting the handling of the Spitfire taped.[14]

Parsons was fortunate to be granted his wish of flying Spitfires with 610 Squadron, and one can sense his appreciation of the machine he had worked on and now flew. S/Ldr Smith needed to familiarise his new recruits with the Spitfire as quickly as possible, which was evidently met with enthusiasm by Parsons. It was also noted on this day that one of the Squadron's airmen, AC 2 W. R. Williams, was discharged from the AAF, classed as medically unfit.

Claude Parsons, second from right, back row, probably at Anstey, near Coventry. (*Tally Ho! From the Battle of Britain to the Defence of Darwin by Wing Commander RW Foster, published by Grub Street Publishing*)

On 16 June, three more pilots arrived from 6 OTU. P/Os Rees, confirmed in his appointment as a pilot officer on 16 August 1939, Gardiner (despite being referred to here and in his first few entries in the ORB as a pilot officer, he had been promoted to flying officer as of 16 February 1940, something which was not reported in *The London Gazette* until 25 June 1940)[15] and Pegge. Brian Victor Rees, known as 'Taffy', prior to his posting to 610 Squadron, had:

> joined the RAF on a short service commission and began his ab initio course on May 16 1938. With training completed, he joined 'Y' Flight, No 1AACU at Manorbier on December 18 1939. He was detached to RAF Locking on December 30, for a parachute course. Rees arrived at 6 OTU, Sutton Bridge from No 1 AACU on May 28 1940…after converting to Spitfires.[16]

Frederick Thomas Gardiner was twenty-two. Born on 24 September 1917 in Belfast, he attended Stowe School and then read mechanical sciences at Trinity College, Cambridge. Around this time, Gardiner was already learning to fly, as he gained his pilot's licence when he was still a Student, aged just seventeen. It is therefore unsurprising that when he studied at Cambridge:

> He was a member of the University Air Squadron from 1935 to 1937 and also a member of the University Gliding Club. He was commissioned in the RAFVR in February 1938. Gardiner was a contestant in the National Gliding Championships in 1939.
>
> Called to full-time service on September 25 1939, Gardiner completed his training at RAF College FTS, Cranwell on No 6 Course, which ran from November 6 1939 to May 9 1940. Gardiner was with the Advanced Training Squadron of RAF College FTS, when it arrived at 10 B&GS [Bombing and Gunnery School], Warmwell on April 26 1940, for the final part of No 6 Course. He arrived at 6 OTU, Sutton Bridge on June 1 1940, where he converted to Spitfires…,[17]

before joining 610 Squadron.

Far left: P/O Brian Victor Rees. (*Copyright 610 Squadron Association*)

Left and below: A very youthful looking Gardiner and his pilot's licence. (*Copyright Royal Aero Club Trust*)

GARDINER, Frederick Thomas 12843

Thornhill, 117, Malone Road,
Belfast, N.Ireland.

Born 24th Sept. 1917 *at* Belfast, Ireland.

Nationality British

Rank, Regiment, Profession Student

Certificate taken on Avro Club Cadet. Genet Maj. 140

At Airwork School of Flying, Newtownards.

Date 26.4.35.

The third of the new arrivals was Constantine Oliver Joseph Pegge, known as Joe, born in 1914 in Slough, Middlesex. Before joining 610 Squadron:

> He joined the RAF on a short service commission and began his ab initio course on August 29 1938, as a pupil pilot. With training completed, he was on 'B' Flight of No 1 AACU, Carew Cheriton by November 1939. He crashed Hawker Henley L3283 at Farnborough on November 24, on a ferry flight.
>
> Pegge moved from 'B' Flight to 'J' Flight No 1 AACU, when it was formed at Farnborough on December 1 1939. It moved to Penrhos on February 16 1940. Pegge was posted to 6 OTU, Sutton Bridge on May 27 1940.[18]

That evening the three latest recruits would probably have met the rest of the Squadron, as F/O Lamb had turned twenty-six, doubtless the cause of some celebrations!

The next flying activity for the Squadron came on 17 June, when Red Section patrolled Canterbury at 6,000 feet. The following aircraft took off at 1800 hours:

P/O Pegge enjoys some relaxation in the summer sunshine outside the Control Tower at Gravesend, one of a series of photos from the second half of June, whilst 610 was stationed there. (*Copyright 610 Squadron Association*)

DW-A.	R.6693	F/Lt. E. B. B. SMITH.	29
DW-F.	R.6694	Sgt. HAMLYN.	9
DW-D.	L.1000*	Sgt. RAMSAY.	1

*This aircraft formerly coded DW-M, seems to have been recoded DW-D. DW-M now P.9451.

However, they were only airborne for a total of twenty minutes, having been swiftly recalled, bringing an abrupt end to Sgt Ramsay's first recorded operational patrol with the Squadron. Shortly after Red Section returned to Gravesend, 'B' Flight, under John Ellis's leadership, was ordered to patrol Manston, taking off at 1830 hours:

DW-M.	P.9451	F/Lt. J. ELLIS.	19
DW-O.	R.6595	P/O. A. L. B. RAVEN.	3
DW-K.	P.9495	Sgt. ARNFIELD, S. J.	19
DW-Q.	P.9502	P/O. P. LITCHFIELD.	21
DW-T.	P.9452	F/O. W. H. C. WARNER.	28
DW-L.	P.9496	Sgt. ELSE, P.	5

It was a fruitless vigil and no enemy aircraft were sighted. The pilots were back on the ground by 1935 hours after a combined flying time of six hours and thirty minutes, all valuable flying experience, particularly for P/O Raven.

Red Section was on morning readiness again on 18 June, and at 0830 hours they scrambled to investigate another 'X' raid. This time S/Ldr Smith (14) was leading the formation, just his second recorded operational trip of the month, flying in DW-A, R.6693, with F/O Lamb (21) (DW-F, R.6694), and P/O Keighley (16) (DW- E, R.6629) as his wingmen. The ground controller gave Smith various vectors and told them to orbit Rye, but they returned to base at 0935 hours after another wild goose chase. Red Section's pilots rested when the next patrol took off at 1010 hours, involving nine Spitfires patrolling Canterbury on a twenty-five-minute flight. Ellis was leading the formation, probably as Blue Leader, with Warner leading Green Section and Brian Smith leading Yellow Section, as follows:

DW-M.	P.9451	F/Lt. J. ELLIS.	20
DW-N.	L.1075	P/O. A. L. B. RAVEN.	4
DW-K.	P.9495	Sgt. ARNFIELD, S. J.	20
DW-Q.	P.9502	F/O. W. H. C. WARNER.	29
DW-P.	R.6695	P/O. P. LITCHFIELD.	22
DW-L.	P.9496	Sgt. ELSE, P.	6
DW-B.	L.1009	F/Lt. E. B. B. SMITH.	30
DW-J.	N.3284	P/O. S. C. NORRIS.	24
DW-D.	L.1000	Sgt. HAMLYN.	10

Once again no enemy aircraft were seen, and the Spitfires were back on the ground at 1035 hours. This draining routine of endless patrols, chasing an invisible enemy, must have taken its toll on the nerves of each pilot. Once in the air, there was always the possibility of meeting the *Luftwaffe*, perhaps a formation of fearsome Me 109s, so they had to constantly be on their guard. Fighter Command's men realised that the *Luftwaffe* was rebuilding its strength after its successful yet costly campaign against France, with operations still ongoing. This was probably the calm before the expected storm.

On 19 June, 'The Chesters' enjoyed a day free from operational flying, perhaps being stood down for a day's rest, to ensure the pilots were kept fresh. This rotation would prove an essential part of their weekly routine. Two more pilots joined the unit, Sgt Pilot Sydney Ireland, born on 25 May 1918 in Belfast, Ireland, and Sgt Pilot Ronald William Haines, born 22 March 1920, in Gillingham, Kent, both coming fresh from 5 FTS Sealand, with a lot still to learn. Raymond Ellis recalled that, 'they missed going on to an Operational Training Unit before being posted to 610 Squadron. It was then up to the Squadron to complete their training when not otherwise engaged in its front-line duties such as interceptions and escorting convoys through the Channel'.[19] The following day the pair were sent on a course of instruction in 11 Group on R/T procedure and elementary attacks (ORB). The two new sergeants had both been on the same FTS course as Ray Holmes, who interestingly enough hailed from West Kirby, Wirral, not far from Hooton Park. In his fascinating memoirs, *Sky Spy—From Six Miles High to Hitler's Bunker*, Holmes records the exhilaration of flying over his home:

> Then to my joy I was briefed to fly solo to Liverpool, across the Wirral to the Dee, up to Chester and back to Barton. This took me over my home at West Kirby, and it was an experience I shall never forget exploring from the air my own neighbourhood, Calday School and its playing fields, the open air swimming baths in West Kirby lake, and Hilbre Island in the Dee.[20]

This experience was enjoyed by many of 610 Squadron's pilots who came from this locality.

Holmes's path to a front-line fighter squadron was basically the same as Ireland and Haines. Having originally attended 4 ITW, Bexhill-on-Sea, Sussex, on 29 October 1939 as a VR sergeant, they went on to be posted to Sealand, as he recalled:

> Then, suddenly, our postings to FTS came through. The postings worked down an alphabetical list. G to M, which included all the Hs, went to Sealand, a First World War flying training school …
>
> Next morning Wing Commander Morrison told us we would all be going home on 48 hours' leave from Bexhill, and that we were to report to our FTS on 12 December. The flying course there would be three months of intermediate training, and three months advanced. From there we would be posted to an operational squadron, the ultimate pinnacle of every pupil pilot's ambition.[21]

Holmes and his comrades belonged to 'D' Flight and found themselves suddenly operating a more powerful machine than anything they had previously flown, the Miles Master. This experience would have resonated with all new fighter pilots, none more so than 610 Squadron's original pilots, who must have had the same misgivings having operated slow bombers for so long. Holmes also recalled some snippets of information about his colleagues, particularly Sid Ireland, with whom he seemed to have formed a close friendship. Ireland had an ear for music, was a keen sportsman, and yet had a fiery temper, as Holmes noted during his training:

> Many an evening Sid Ireland rode the fifteen miles home with me on the pillion of my BSA. Pre-war, a broken ankle had put an end to my rugger career when playing fly-half to Danny Evans, a Welsh international scrum-half. But when I learned that Sid was an Irish international scrum-half, I knew I must play out-side half to him, and took up the game again at Sealand. We enjoyed several games together for the station against local clubs until my ankle broke again. Sid cracked his nose in the same game, so during a few days in sick quarters we decided to concentrate on flying.
>
> Sid was a man of moods. One moment he was starry-eyed strumming his guitar and crooning about leaving the Emerald Isle. But in his next breath he could be blasting some fellow's soul to eternity…[22]

Having shared so many experiences together for such a long time, it was with mixed feelings that the group went their separate ways, especially given the uncertainty they faced from the continuing German onslaught. Holmes joined 504 (County of Nottingham) Squadron at Wick, Scotland, while Ireland joined 610 Squadron. It was a whirlwind experience for these sergeants and all the new pilots across the country, who found themselves with such little experience, suddenly part of an operational fighter squadron responsible for defending the nation.

While the two young sergeants were being taught the ins-and-outs of radio procedure and the RAF's flying formations, another replacement arrived from 6 FTS on 20 June, South African P/O Thomas Young Wallace, who, '… was born in Johannesburg on October 5 1916. He joined the RAF on a short service commission and did his *ab initio* course at 7 E&RFTS, Desford in August 1939 (42919). He went on to 6 FTS, Little Rissington for No 16 Course, which ran from November 6 1939 to June 20 1940',[23] prior to joining 'The Chesters'. Wallace followed Ireland and Haines on the course of instruction on 23 June, for some much needed training. In the meantime, the rest of the Squadron was still carrying out daily patrols, intensive flying training, practising dogfights, squadron scrambles, formation flying and gunnery flights. There could be no let-up for even the more experienced pilots, as constant training and flying was necessary to maintain sharpness.

Sgt Ireland playing his guitar, one of his favoured pastimes. (*Copyright Holmes, Sky Spy, p. 52*)

P/O Wallace. (*Copyright Wynn, Men of the Battle, p. 606*)

Against this backdrop to Squadron life, operational flying resumed on 20 June, with Red Section once more being called on to carry out the early morning patrol of Manston. Brian Smith was the leader of the following formation:

DW-B.	L.1009	F/Lt. E. B. B. SMITH.	31
DW-A.	R.6693	F/O. P. G. LAMB.	22
DW-E.	R.6629	P/O. G. KEIGHLEY.	17

No enemy aircraft were spotted during the one hour and twenty-five-minute patrol, and the Spitfires landed at 0900 hours. The next operational activity took place at 1730 hours, when 'B' Flight took to the skies. The six men on patrol were as follows:

DW-M.	P.9451	F/Lt. J. ELLIS.	21
DW-K.	P.9495	Sgt. ARNFIELD, S. J.	21
DW-P.	R.6695	P/O. A. L. B. RAVEN.	5
DW-Q.	P.9502	F/O. W. H. C. WARNER.	30
DW-T.	P.9452	P/O. P. LITCHFIELD.	23
DW-L.	P.9496	Sgt. ELSE, P.	7

The ground controller instructed Ellis to Vector 130° and later 100°, before finally ordering him to patrol the key port of Dover. Yet again, the Spitfire pilots were chasing shadows and failed to make contact, landing at 1815 hours. While this was being carried out by the pilots, Raymond Ellis, who had been based at Biggin Hill with his comrades in the station maintenance flight, was about to be reunited with his 'own' Squadron, as he recalled: 'With outstanding work on Hurricanes completed, our Station Maintenance Flight was disbanded on the 20 June when I accompanied the rest of Servicing Flight by road to Gravesend. For the next fortnight I was attached to 'B' Flight'.[24]

With the recent influx of pilots came the necessity for some pilots to move on. Thus, on 22 June, F/Lt Milson who had been on attachment to HQ 'X' or (possibly 'K') Force since 3 May 1940, was posted to RAF Church Fenton on operational duties; this vastly experienced pilot would later attain the rank of at least wing commander. After a two-day break from recorded operational activity, 'A' Flight's pilots were in demand, with Red Section carrying out the day's first patrol. The men involved were:

DW-B.	L.1009	F/Lt. E. B. B. SMITH.	32
DW-A.	R.6693	F/O. P. G. LAMB.	23
DW-E.	R.6629	P/O. G. KEIGHLEY.	18

They took off at 1320 hours to patrol Hawkinge—no enemy aircraft were sighted and Brian Smith led his wingmen back to base at 1350 hours. Later in the afternoon, the same pilots were off on another patrol, this time with Yellow Section, as 'A' Flight was ordered to patrol Manston at 11,000 feet. They took off at 1540 hours, F/Lt Smith leading the following men:

DW-B.	L.1009	F/Lt. E. B. B. SMITH.	33
DW-D.	L.1000	F/O. P. G. LAMB.	24
DW-E.	R.6629	P/O. G. KEIGHLEY.	19
DW-S.	N.3201	P/O. S. C. NORRIS.	25
DW-J.	N.3284	Sgt. HAMLYN.	11
DW-A.	R.6693	Sgt. TANNER.	1

Sgt Tanner was on his first recorded operational sortie, and the experienced Stan Norris would have been keeping an observant eye out for his novice wingman. Once more, nothing was spotted, and they returned to Gravesend at 1620 hours.

On 23 June, S/Ldr Tom Smith (15) took off at 0430 hours to carry out a weather check over the Channel. He returned just under an hour later to report dense low cloud, which perhaps prevented any further operational flying until the evening, when 610 Squadron was planning a reconnaissance over enemy territory. It was to be a full Squadron operation led by F/Lt Ellis commanding 'B' Flight, with F/Lt Smith leading 'A' Flight and some of the least experienced pilots such as Ramsay and Tanner would be included. The reconnaissance would be Gardiner's first recorded patrol, so it represented a particularly daunting task for him. The men involved were:

DW-M.	P.9451	F/Lt. J. ELLIS.	22
DW-K.	P.9495	Sgt. ARNFIELD, S. J.	22
DW-N.	L.1075	P/O. A. L. B. RAVEN.	6
DW-T.	P.9452	P/O. P. LITCHFIELD.	24
DW-L.	P.9496	Sgt. ELSE, P.	8
DW-D.	L.1000*	P/O. F. T. GARDINER.	1
DW-B.	L.1009	F/Lt. E. B. B. SMITH.	34
DW-E.	R.6629	P/O. G. KEIGHLEY.	20
DW-A.	R.6693	Sgt. RAMSAY, N. H. D.	2
DW-J.	N.3284	P/O. S. C. NORRIS.	26
DW-S.	N.3201	Sgt. TANNER.	2
DW-D.	L.1000*	Sgt. HAMLYN.	12

*One of these aircraft is incorrectly recorded in ORB.

They took off from Gravesend at 1805 hours and landed at Hawkinge at 1825 hours to refuel. The Squadron left the advance airfield at 1915 hours, before crossing the Channel and making landfall at Dieppe, heading inland in a horseshoe shape to Aumale, then Poix (most likely Poix-de-Picardie), Flexicourt and finally Abbeville before heading home. Each of these towns probably had an airfield nearby which the Squadron was observing. Sgt Hamlyn had been forced to stay at Hawkinge as his Spitfire had become unserviceable, so eleven Spitfires went on the sortie and they all returned safely at 2105 hours—possibly to Gravesend, although it may have been Hawkinge. On being debriefed by the intelligence officer, it transpired that, 'At POIX 10 Me.110s were seen, not dispersed, and one three-engined aircraft. At ABBEVILLE, 6 unidentified aircraft were outside a hangar' (ORB).

Overall, the patrol had been successful in ascertaining some information about the *Luftwaffe's* dispositions, but no enemy aircraft had been engaged. The fact that no enemy fighters had attempted to intercept the Squadron, showed that the *Luftwaffe's* defences were not as robust as those put in place by the RAF. It is likely that this sortie was carried out to provide information for Bomber Command, to enable attacks on the airfields at a later date. After this lengthy flight and late return, the pilots must have felt that they deserved a rest the following day and it seems that this is just what they got, as there is no mention of operational flying that day.

While the Squadron was stationed at Gravesend during June, they naturally enjoyed some rest time to keep them fresh and break up the monotony of training flights and patrols. In the airfield's vicinity was a boating lake called 'Laughing Waters'. This spot was used by the pilots and airmen, as a means of relaxation and the restaurant/inn which adjoined the lake provided accommodation for the ground crew. (This hotel is now called the 'Inn on the Lake Hotel', situated just off the A2, in Shorne, Kent.) 610 Squadron's Association is fortunate to own some photos of the pilots enjoying themselves at the lake. Given the personnel involved, the photos were taken between 19 June and 2 July 1940, and show a different side to Squadron life from the usual images of the men in their uniform. The sight of these fighter pilots enjoying a swim and messing around in boats is a little incongruous, given that the *Luftwaffe* was gearing up for an all-out assault on Britain at any moment. However, a few hours of relaxation would have done the pilots the world of good, and helped form a bond between them. The tragedy is that some of those photographed would be killed in a matter of days, if not weeks.

Above left: In the background is P/O Arthur Raven, aged twenty-four, who had begun his training with the Squadron at Hooton Park in April 1939. In the middle, holding a towel to his face, is Frederick Gardiner, who only arrived on 16 June. In the foreground, looking very serious, is Sydney Ireland who had arrived on 19 June. (*Copyright 610 Squadron Association*)

Above right: Three different pilots enjoying the sunshine and swimming at 'Laughing Waters'. On the left is Peter Keighley, who has recovered from his parachute descent into the Channel in late May, whilst Bill Warner is in the middle, hands on his head. Nearest the camera, holding a towel is one of the Squadron's more recent incumbents, Joe Pegge. (*Copyright 610 Squadron Association*)

After a day of non-operational flying, all concerned with 610 Squadron would have been expecting a return to carrying out patrols the following day and it was Blue Section's turn first on 25 June, this time to patrol Tenterden, Kent, at 10,000 feet. The patrol was led by John Ellis, flying a recently delivered Spitfire P.9498,[25] which had yet to be assigned an identification letter, and he led the following formation off at 1040 hours:

	P.9498	F/Lt. J. ELLIS.	23
DW-T.	P.9452	P/O. P. LITCHFIELD.	25
DW-Q.	P.9502	P/O. A. L. B. RAVEN.	7

No enemy aircraft were seen, and they returned to Gravesend at 1110 hours. The rest of the day was uneventful until the evening, when the Squadron had been assigned another reconnaissance over enemy territory. The plan was similar to the previous reconnaissance operation, Ellis leading a full Squadron patrol, while Brian Smith led 'A' Flight. This time it was the turn of P/O Joe Pegge to carry out his first recorded operational patrol, and he seems to have been flying as one of Smith's wingmen. The twelve men involved were:

DW-P.	R.6695	F/Lt. J. ELLIS.	24
DW-K.	P.9495	Sgt. ARNFIELD, S. J.	23
DW-Q.	P.9502	P/O. A. L. B. RAVEN.	8
DW-T.	P.9452	P/O. P. LITCHFIELD.	26
DW-O.	R.6595	F/O. W. H. C. WARNER.	31
DW-L.	P.9495*	Sgt. ELSE, P.	9
DW-B.	L.1009	F/Lt. E. B. B. SMITH.	35
DW-F.	R.6694	F/O. P. G. LAMB.	25
DW-J.	N.3284	P/O. C. O. J. PEGGE.	1
DW-S.	N.3201	P/O. S. C. NORRIS.	27
DW-E.	R.6629	Sgt. HAMLYN.	13
DW-D.	P.9503**	Sgt. TANNER.	3

*Probably should be DW-L. P.9496.

**P.9503 did not join Squadron until 11 July 1940, so should probably be DW-D, L.1000 each time it appears, until after 10 July 1940. Left ORB as original.[26]

Ellis led his men off from Gravesend at 1905 hours, refuelling at Hawkinge at 1925 hours. Just twenty-five minutes later, the Squadron took off on a heading for Dieppe, and the Spitfire formation, 'Carried out inspection of aerodromes at DIEPPE—ROUEN—POIX—ABBEVILLE—BERCK SUR MERE [MER]' (ORB). This operation took them much deeper over France. It was a lengthy journey, fraught with potential danger—Ellis's navigation would have needed to be spot on. Thankfully it was, and the Squadron returned to base after two hours on patrol, at 2125 hours, possibly to Hawkinge given the length of the flight. A report was made that twelve aircraft were seen lined up at Abbeville, but no other aircraft had been seen (ORB). Once again, it seems likely that this information would be passed on to Bomber Command for them to act on.

On 26 June 1940, a series of photos was taken of a formation of nine 610 (County of Chester) Squadron Spitfires on patrol, some of which became iconic images of the Battle of Britain.[27] The exact date of when they were taken had been unclear, but Dave Brocklehurst, MBE, chairman of the Kent Battle of Britain Museum, believes he saw the event recorded on 26 June in John Ellis's logbook, who was flying DW-O, R.6595. Raymond Ellis also confirms that DW-O, so prominent in the photos, was being flown by John Ellis.[28] The Squadron was not required to fly operationally until the evening, so the photos would have been taken in the morning or perhaps early afternoon.

One of the most iconic images of the summer of 1940, with F/Lt Ellis pictured at the head of his section in DW-O, Sgt Arnfield in DW-K and F/O Warner in DW-Q. (*Copyright Imperial War Museum, CH 739*)

The section of Spitfires which is the focus of the photos depicts the aircraft coded DW-O, DW-Q and DW-K. Given that it was late June, we know DW-O was R.6595, DW-Q was P.9502, while DW-K was P.9495. All three Spitfires had joined the Squadron earlier that month.[29] Thanks to F/Lt Ellis's testament, we know he was flying DW-O, while Warner was flying DW-Q and Arnfield was at the controls of DW-K, so the section belonged to 'B' Flight. In this photo (see above), the Spitfires are in a tight 'Vic' formation which had been practised constantly before the War, but in reality proved to be hazardous, as the wingmen had to focus all their attention on maintaining formation instead of scanning the skies for possible threats.

Another photo shows all nine Spitfires closing in on the photographer's aircraft, showing just how tight the formations could be—it highlights the need for concentration by the two wingmen on keeping formation. The fighters then proceed to dive away, the photographer capturing the striking moment that the six Spitfires follow the first section down in a dive to port. As the photographer continued his work, 610 Squadron changed formation from 'Vics' of three to the same three in line astern, which gave the whole section more time to scan for the enemy. This formation was regularly used by 610 Squadron in the coming months, the pilots having realised very quickly over Dunkirk that flying in tight 'Vics' of three was an obsolete and extremely dangerous tactic, as noted by Wg Cdr Smith.

In another renowned image of the Battle of Britain period (see p. 192), the Spitfires of Ellis, Warner and Arnfield continued in line astern, with another section visible in the background. It seems to show the RAF enjoying mastery of the skies over England, the County of Chester Squadron's sleek, highly-advanced fighters defending the realm, while the cotton wool clouds in the background offer a deceptive air of calm and tranquillity. The reality was that the Spitfires were patrolling in a lethal environment. The fact that all three Spitfires of Ellis's section would be lost within two months of the photo stands testament to this: DW-O, R.6595 was in the thick of the fighting during the Battle of Britain, being damaged twice, before being shot down on 26 August; DW-Q, P.9502 was lost soon after these photos were taken, crashing on 12 July during a training flight; DW-K, P.9495 survived the early stages of the Battle, but succumbed to battle damage during a dogfight on 12 August.

Nine Spitfires of 610 Squadron, showing off their close-formation flying skills. Having zoomed in on the first section, it is likely that the leading Spitfire is DW-D, with DW-J nearest to the camera and DW-H furthest away. (*Copyright Imperial War Museum, CH 735*)

The focus turns to the second and third sections, before they follow the leading section, which has already dived away. (*Copyright Imperial War Museum, CH 733*)

The second and third sections start to dive away in formation. (*Copyright Imperial War Museum, CH 734*)

A famous image which has come to represent Fighter Command's role in the Battle of Britain, as 610 Squadron majestically patrols the skies over Kent. (*Copyright Imperial War Museum, CH 741*)

Another interesting pair of photos from this series of images shows all nine Spitfires flying in sections line astern. Although they are less celebrated, they are certainly very evocative. One can identify the likely aircraft involved from the Spitfires' individual squadron letter, just visible in some cases by zooming in on it. The lead aircraft is DW-D, as that is leading the other two aircraft in other photos. This Spitfire was probably L.1000, one of the Squadron's original Spitfires and a veteran of Dunkirk, having earlier been coded DW-M. DW-H was L.1044, another of the Squadron's original aircraft, which had been damaged a couple of times earlier in the year, most notably when John Ellis failed to lower his undercarriage correctly while landing at Bircham Newton. This section's third Spitfire was DW-J, N.3284, which had replaced the aircraft Sgt Medway was shot down in over Dunkirk, DW-J, L.1003. The middle section of aircraft are DW-O, 'Q' and 'K', but the three Spitfires in the background are coded 'B', 'X' and 'T'. DW-B, L.1009 was another of the Squadron's originals and a veteran of Dunkirk—it led a charmed life until probably being damaged in combat on 14 August 1940. DW-X, R.6630 joined the Squadron just as they were about to leave Gravesend on 31 May,[30] being mainly operational in July, before being lost in combat on 11 August 1940. The ninth Spitfire, apparently lagging behind slightly, was DW-T, P.9452, which carried out its first recorded patrol in the ORB on 21 May 1940, and flew regularly until it was lost without trace within little more than a fortnight of this photograph.

'The Chesters' were instructed to carry out another Squadron patrol in the evening, this time over Calais at 14,000 feet. The CO himself led the patrol and 'B' Flight, with Brian Smith leading 'A' Flight again—unusually F/Lt Ellis was not involved. They took off at 2130 hours, as follows:

DW-N.	P.9512*	S/Ldr. A. T. SMITH.	16
DW-O.	R.6595	P/O. F. T. GARDINER.	2
DW-T.	P.9452	P/O. P. LITCHFIELD.	27
DW-Q.	P.9502	F/O. W. H. C. WARNER.	32
DW-K.	P.9495	Sgt. ARNFIELD, S. J.	24

A less well-known photo of 610's Spitfires on patrol. (*Copyright Imperial War Museum, CH 744*)

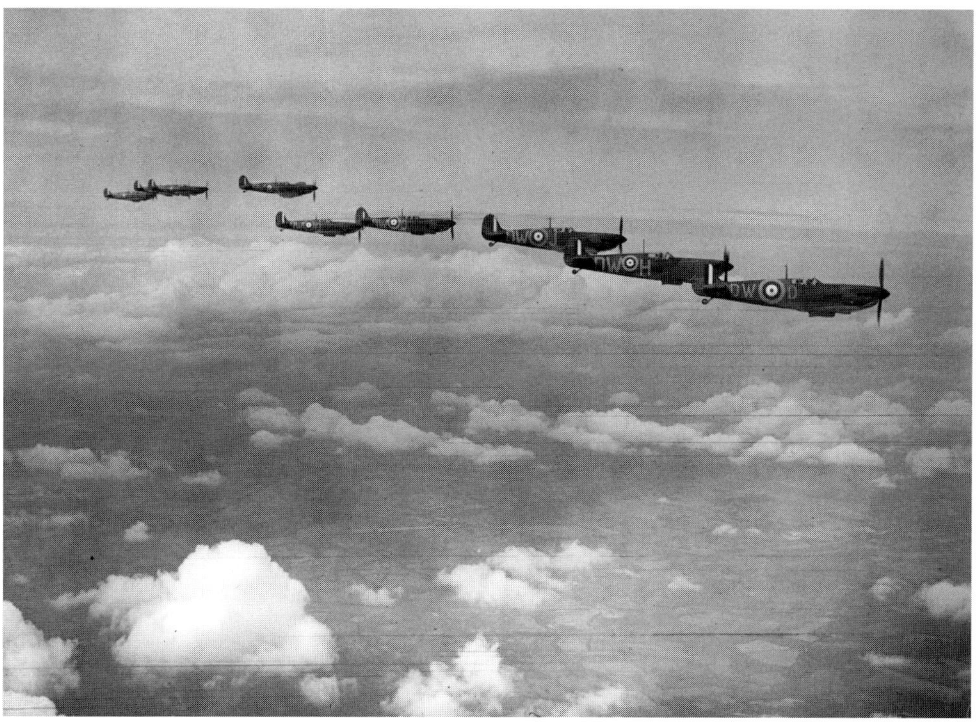

The same nine Spitfires, in the same order, travelling in the opposite direction. (*ww2images.com*)

DW-P.	R.6695	Sgt. ELSE, P.	10
DW-B.	L.1009	F/Lt. E. B. B. SMITH.	36
DW-A.	R.6693	F/O. P. G. LAMB.	26
DW-J.	N.3284	P/O. C. O. J. PEGGE.	2
DW-S.	N.3201	P/O. S. C. NORRIS.	28
DW-E.	R.6629	Sgt. HAMLYN.	14
DW-G.	L.1045	Sgt. TANNER.	4

*As ORB but probably an error. DW-N should probably be L.1075 until 8 July 1940, when it was shot down. P.9512 only joined 610 on 7 July 1940.[31] Adhered to ORB listing until then.

The Squadron, 'Ran into violent storm over CALAIS. Compelled to return. No E/A sighted' (ORB), and they all landed at 2220 hours. Despite their late return home, the following morning on 27 June, five of the six pilots of 'B' Flight were again on patrol, this time over Dungeness at 10,000 feet. It seems that P/O Litchfield was leading the patrol, with F/O Warner leading the second section. Litchfield had proven himself to be one of the Squadron's more accomplished fighter pilots during the engagements with the *Luftwaffe* over Dunkirk and he now regularly flew as a section leader. This patrol took off at 0850 hours:

DW-T.	P.9452	P/O. P. LITCHFIELD.	28
DW-O.	R.6595	P/O. F. T. GARDINER.	3
DW-P.	R.6695	Sgt. ELSE, P.	11
DW-Q.	P.9502	F/O. W. H. C. WARNER.	33
DW-N.	P.9512	P/O. A. L. B. RAVEN.	9
DW-K.	P.9495	Sgt. ARNFIELD, S. J.	25

Unsurprisingly, no enemy aircraft were sighted and the Spitfires returned to Gravesend at 0950 hours. The Squadron did not carry out any further patrols until after lunch, when 'A' Flight repeated the morning patrol. Brian Smith led his men off at 1330 hours, with F/O Peter Lamb probably leading the second section:

DW-B.	L.1009	F/Lt. E. B. B. SMITH.	37
DW-D.	L.1000	P/O. G. KEIGHLEY.	21
DW-F.	R.6694	P/O. C. O. J. PEGGE.	3
DW-A.	R.6693	F/O. P. G. LAMB.	27
DW-S.	N.3201	P/O. S. C. NORRIS.	29
DW-V.	L.1076	Sgt. TANNER.	5

This patrol was slightly longer, however the outcome was the same and they were all back on *terra firma* by 1440 hours.

Once 'A' Flight had returned, the Squadron prepared for an escort operation for twelve Bristol Blenheims carrying out a photographic reconnaissance of enemy occupied territory. This was another new role for the Squadron and would have required detailed planning, as they were to provide escort along with 64 Squadron's Spitfires. While preparations were underway, S/Ldr Smith was at Biggin Hill, to participate in a medal ceremony which was due to take place that afternoon. His Majesty King George VI was presenting medals to members of 79 and 32 Squadrons for their actions over France and Dunkirk. Smith can be seen in a photo of the occasion (see p. 195), standing in the background behind the pilots who were about to be invested. Smith would have been there as the CO of one of Biggin Hill's squadrons, but would have had to leave almost immediately after the ceremony to return to Gravesend.

King George VI is about to decorate 32 Squadron's P/O Daw, whilst P/O Grice of 32 Squadron, and P/O Stones, Sgts Whitby and Cartwright of 79 Squadron are next in line. S/Ldr Tom Smith is standing behind Cartwright as part of the parade. (*Crown Copyright*)

Tom Smith was leading his Squadron on the escort operation, with Bill Warner probably leading 'B' Flight's second section, while Brian Smith, as was now customary, was leading 'A' Flight, with Stan Norris leading the other section, probably Yellow Section:

DW-K.	P.9495	S/Ldr. A. T. SMITH.	17
DW-P.	R.6695	Sgt. ARNFIELD, S. J.	26
DW-O.	R.6595	P/O. F. T. GARDINER.	4
DW-Q.	P.9502	F/O. W. H. C. WARNER.	34
DW-N.	P.9512	P/O. A. L. B. RAVEN.	10
DW-T.	P.9452	P/O. P. LITCHFIELD.	29
DW-B.	L.1009	F/Lt. E. B. B. SMITH.	38
DW-D.	P.9503	P/O. G. KEIGHLEY.	22
DW-F.	R.6694	P/O. C. O. J. PEGGE.	4
DW-S.	N.3201	P/O. S. C. NORRIS.	30
DW-H.	L.1044	F/O. P. G. LAMB.	28
DW-J.	N.3284	Sgt. TANNER.	6

610 Squadron left Gravesend at 1700 hours, landing at Hawkinge twenty minutes later to refuel. At 1815 hours the Squadron was getting airborne again—a longer time period on the ground this time, probably because they needed to rendezvous with 64 Squadron, which had left Kenley at 1810 hours (64 ORB). The Blenheims' first port of call was the Belgian port of Ostend and then the formation of about thirty-six aircraft worked its way down the coast to Dunkirk. For the veterans of the evacuation, seeing the landmarks they had valiantly fought over would have brought back painful memories of lost friends, but there was no time for that, as at any point the formation could be ambushed by *Luftwaffe* fighters. The Blenheims' next target was to head inland to St Omer to view its aerodrome, before turning almost due west and photographing the port at Boulogne. From here, the lumbering formation headed further south along the coast, to Berck-sur-Mer. Once the Blenheims had finished with this port, the formation turned for England. The Squadron landed at 1950 hours—another lengthy and dangerous patrol successfully completed.

The Blenheims were photographing the number and type of aircraft on the aerodromes they visited and in the case of the ports, trying to observe any sign of an invasion force building up. The British knew that Hitler would soon be turning his full attention to the land that lay just across the English Channel, and if the Nazis were to attempt an invasion, there would soon be a build-up of vessels to transport the invaders. The most surprising aspect of this operation was that a sizeable RAF formation could fly around the coast and over German occupied territory, including several airfields, and yet they were not intercepted by *Luftwaffe* fighters. It was to be hoped that the RAF's defences would stand up better to any snooping or bombing raids by *Luftwaffe* forces.

In the early hours of 28 June, enemy activity caused two separate night flights to be carried out, a very dangerous task in a Spitfire which was not really suited to night fighter operations. At 0140 hours, P/O Peter Litchfield (30) was ordered to patrol Gravesend aerodrome at 10,000 feet. He carried out the patrol in his favoured Spitfire, DW-T, P.9452, but when he landed at 0220 hours, he reported that the searchlight defences had been unable to catch an enemy aircraft in their cone of light, making it very difficult for Litchfield to engage the lone bombers (ORB). A little later, F/O Bill Warner (35) was ordered to take off at 0340 hours and head to Tonbridge. Warner was flying DW-Q, P.9502, and he returned home after 30 minutes without sighting an enemy aircraft. Such night operations were good experience for the two pilots involved, and they had thankfully returned unscathed—it was testament to their flying ability that they had accomplished the operations without mishap. During the course of daylight hours on 28 June, F/O Douglas Strachan Wilson rejoined the Squadron at Gravesend, following his posting to the Air Ministry on 25 September 1939. The return of an old head and familiar face would have been only too welcome by the Squadron, although he would have been shocked that so many friends had been lost at Dunkirk.

F/O Douglas Wilson, seated right, smoking his pipe and relaxing with Squadron members at Gravesend. The photo was probably taken between 28 June and 2 July. Standing on the left is the Adjutant, F/O le Fleming, with P/O Walter Lloyd the intelligence officer next to him, smoking a cigarette. John Ellis is seated on the left of the photo. (*Copyright 610 Squadron Association*)

While 610 Squadron's pilots were carrying out constant patrols, not to mention the regular training required to gel the new faces and the more experienced pilots into an effective fighting force, it was of paramount importance that the aircraft were maintained to as high a standard as possible. Despite the advancements made with the introduction of the RAF's latest fighter aircraft, the early Spitfires and Hurricanes still had fixed pitch propellers, which necessitated the pilot changing the pitch control. The vital step in converting 610's Spitfires to constant speed propellers was taken at the end of June, as Raymond Ellis recalled: 'By the time that the squadron had returned to Biggin Hill on 2nd July, our fitters had installed constant speed propellers and control systems in our Spitfires thereby increasing their rate of climb to out-climb the Me 109….'[32] Another of the ground crew, Corporal Bert Lunt, was one of those heavily involved in this improvement. He had been sent, 'on a very thorough and interesting course on propellers and the constant speed unit (CSU) that controlled the pitch of the propeller to maintain engine speed set by the pilot',[33] prior to implementing the CSU on 610's Spitfires.

Given the lack of flying carried out by 610 on 28 June, it is highly possible the improvements got underway then. The modifications required familiarisation for the pilots and yet more practice. However, this was a small price to pay for an upgrade which would give them a real edge in the coming dogfights, and S/Ldr Smith and his pilots would have been delighted to have their Spitfires' performance radically improved. Another way in which the Spitfire and other RAF aircraft had been enhanced was linked to the RDF system. Although RDF stations could pick up different raids coming in, it was very hard to distinguish friend from foe. This could have disastrous consequences. The need to eradicate this problem was vital, and so the installation of Identification Friend or Foe (IFF) equipment was critical. It was fitted to all of Fighter Command's aircraft in the aftermath of Dunkirk, and would prove to be a key improvement in the coming months.

On 29 June, with the training of pilots in full swing, P/O Rees was sent to 4 Air Navigation School for a course of instruction, thirteen days after joining the Squadron. On his return he would find that one of the pilots to whom even he was senior, had been killed in a flying accident, which coincidentally related to the two-speed variable pitch propeller. Sgt Ronald Haines was taking off to practise formation flying at about 1045 hours, when disaster struck. Raymond Ellis was a witness to the tragic events as they unfolded and the description of them is best left to his moving first-hand testimony:

> On the 29th June, Sgt Haines and Sgt Ireland were briefed to fly in formation with their flight commander on a training exercise. At the far end of 'B' Flight's line of aircraft, my fitter mate and I (the 'rigger') were squatting beside our charge—Spitfire P9498. About a hundred yards beyond us was the boundary hedge of the airfield where we could see a party of the Pioneer Corps working. It was a fine day, and our 'kite' was ready for action.
>
> The squadron was on '30 Minutes Availability' so we did not start up the engine at the sight of a pilot walking towards us with parachute and flying helmet. I did not know his name. He was a sergeant and new to the Squadron. Sgt Haines climbed into the cockpit. He would have seen from the Form 700 in our Flight Sergeant's office that the 'plane was signed up by all trades as serviceable, re-fuelled, re-armed and ready to fly. We had ground tested the engine earlier that morning. The fitter stood by the battery trolley on the starboard side, whilst I, standing on the port wing root, helped the pilot with his straps, and then I closed the side flap door. We went through the normal start-up procedure including a run-up with us crouched on the tail plane. At the usual signal from the pilot, we pulled away the chocks and gave him the 'thumbs-up' that it was all clear ahead. He taxied away to join his flying companions at the other end of the field.
>
> At the sound of the Merlin engines opening up, Cpl Bert Lunt stepped out of the hangar to see them gathering speed on their take-off run along the grass runway. One of the Spitfires did not sound right. It failed to lift more than a few feet off the ground, whilst the others soared away. It was obvious to Bert that, instead of being in 'fine pitch', its propeller was in 'coarse pitch' so that the engine could not attain the

'revs' and torque needed for take-off. From where we were we could not see the take-off, and so we did not know that our Spitfire was in trouble. We heard afterwards that, failing to get airborne, it had hit and killed the driver of a tractor that was cutting the grass. The plane then swung off its course to port towards us.

The first we knew about it was when, to our astonishment, our Spitfire appeared less than twenty feet above our heads. The engine was 'labouring' like a car struggling up a steep hill in top gear. It was losing height and heading for the Pioneers. It seemed to turn slightly to starboard as though to avoid them before it hit a low-lying concrete 'pillbox' with a sickening 'crump' and burst into flames. We were already running as we had never run before. By the time we got there, the flames were coming out of the cockpit. It was a sight that I have never forgotten. The heat was intense from the 100 gallons of burning petrol. We could not get nearer than the tip of the port wing. Never before had I seen aluminium burning. There was a loud bang—the oxygen bottle or the compressed air cylinders behind the pilot. A couple of rounds went off across the field ahead. We remembered the hundreds of rounds in the ammunition boxes and moved further away. Never had I felt so helpless.

One of the Pioneers told me that he had managed to get alongside the cockpit before we arrived. He could not see how to release the safety harness, and so he tried to cut through the straps behind the pilot's head using his spade. I was sure that Sgt Haines was already dead—killed instantly by the impact. The fire tender and ambulance arrived, followed by men from the flights. We could do nothing—just watch in silence. It was the first fatal accident experienced by the Squadron since its formation in 1936.

The following day, an Accident Inquiry was held in an office off the hangar. I remember being questioned by F/Sgt 'Tug' Wilson, but I never learned the findings of the Inquiry. It was obvious to us that the prop was in coarse pitch. Poor Haines. I felt depressed for some time afterwards. (I wish to express my thanks to C. H. Lunt for his evidence as a witness of the take-off of Sgt Haines with the airscrew in coarse pitch. It is ironic that, at that time, Cpl Lunt and other engine fitters were engaged in fitting constant-speed airscrews to our Spitfires in the hangar).[34]

This poignant description of events which led to the death of Sgt Haines, who after months of training was so tragically killed just before he finally became an 'operational' pilot, shows how fragile life was in a front-line fighter squadron. It also demonstrates the dangers involved for those on the ground at an RAF station, as the tractor driver had been killed in terrible circumstances. A simple aberration had cost them both their lives. Indeed, if the modification to constant speed airscrews had started a few days earlier, the tragedy would almost certainly have been averted. When recalling the number of accidents the experienced pilots had back in late 1939 when trying to master their new aircraft, five Spitfires written off in fifteen days with one pilot badly injured, it is hardly surprising that eventually a very new recruit paid the ultimate sacrifice, with so much less knowledge at his disposal. Spitfire P.9498 was one of the Squadron's newest machines, having joined the Squadron at the start of the month[35] and been on one recorded patrol with John Ellis at the controls.

The AMCB file relating to Haines's death was released by the National Archives on 30 June 2017, just in time for this publication. It confirms the details in Raymond Ellis's account. Failure to select 'Fine' pitch had indeed been the main cause of the fatal crash, the secondary factor being the lawn mower and tractor crossing the aerodrome, as recorded in the report into the accident (TNA, AIR 81/2325). I have included a photograph of S/Ldr Smith's detailed report on the accident (see p. 199). It highlights the sheer bad luck involved in the collision with the tractor, Haines's desperate attempt to recover from the crash and avoid an AA gun's crew before the horrific crash. It also praises the brave rescue attempts. This was twenty-year-old Sgt Haines's only recorded training flight in the ORB, although he doubtless carried out several other such flights during his ten days with 610 Squadron. He left behind his parents, Ernest and Alice Haines of Gillingham, who mourned at his burial on 3 July at Woodlands Cemetery, Gillingham, Kent, Section B, Grave 431. P/O Pegge, Sgts Parsons and Ireland, WO Merrin and four of 610's airmen attended the funeral (TNA, AIR 81/2325).

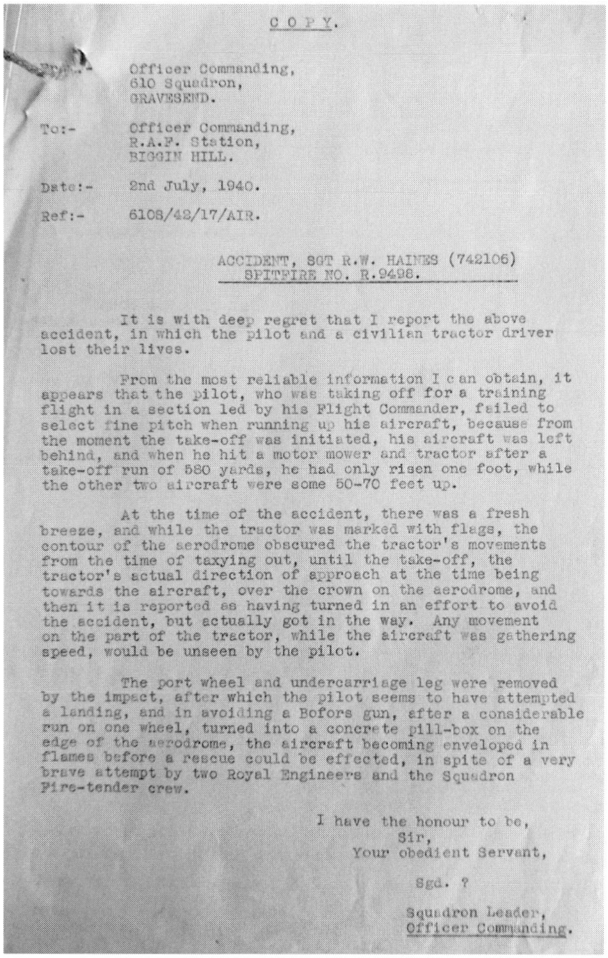

C O P Y.

From:- Officer Commanding,
610 Squadron,
GRAVESEND.

To:- Officer Commanding,
R.A.F. Station,
BIGGIN HILL.

Date:- 2nd July, 1940.

Ref:- 610S/42/17/AIR.

ACCIDENT, SGT R.W. HAINES (742106)
SPITFIRE NO. R.9498.

It is with deep regret that I report the above accident, in which the pilot and a civilian tractor driver lost their lives.

From the most reliable information I can obtain, it appears that the pilot, who was taking off for a training flight in a section led by his Flight Commander, failed to select fine pitch when running up his aircraft, because from the moment the take-off was initiated, his aircraft was left behind, and when he hit a motor mower and tractor after a take-off run of 580 yards, he had only risen one foot, while the other two aircraft were some 50-70 feet up.

At the time of the accident, there was a fresh breeze, and while the tractor was marked with flags, the contour of the aerodrome obscured the tractor's movements from the time of taxying out, until the take-off, the tractor's actual direction of approach at the time being towards the aircraft, over the crown on the aerodrome, and then it is reported as having turned in an effort to avoid the accident, but actually got in the way. Any movement on the part of the tractor, while the aircraft was gathering speed, would be unseen by the pilot.

The port wheel and undercarriage leg were removed by the impact, after which the pilot seems to have attempted a landing, and in avoiding a Bofors gun, after a considerable run on one wheel, turned into a concrete pill-box on the edge of the aerodrome, the aircraft becoming enveloped in flames before a rescue could be effected, in spite of a very brave attempt by two Royal Engineers and the Squadron Fire-tender crew.

I have the honour to be,
Sir,
Your obedient Servant,

Sgd. ?

Squadron Leader,
Officer Commanding.

The details of Sgt Haines's death recorded in his CO's report. (*TNA, AIR 81/2325*)

Although the Squadron's personnel were severely shaken and upset by the death of Haines, which happened so publicly and suddenly, the Squadron had to carry on with its usual operations. Plans were underway for what was termed an 'offensive patrol' (ORB). Nine aircraft had been ordered to patrol from Deal to Calais and then down the French coast to Boulogne at 20,000 feet, attempting to draw up enemy fighters. John Ellis was leading the Squadron and he had the least experienced pilot with him, Sgt Ramsay, while Bill Warner and Brian Smith were the other section leaders. The Spitfires left Gravesend at 1840 hours:

DW-M.	P.9451	F/Lt. J. ELLIS.	25
DW-N.	L.1075	P/O. A. L. B. RAVEN.	11
DW-P.	R.6695	Sgt. RAMSAY.	3
DW-K.	P.9495	F/O. W. H. C. WARNER.	36
DW-O.	R.6595	P/O. P. LITCHFIELD.	31
DW-L.	P.9496	Sgt. ELSE, P.	12
DW-B.	L.1009	F/Lt. E. B. B. SMITH.	39
DW-S.	N.3201	P/O. S. C. NORRIS.	31
DW-E.	R.6629	P/O. G. KEIGHLEY.	23

The peaceful backdrop to Sgt Haines's grave, front, centre, in the aptly named Woodlands Cemetery. (*Author*)

This time the Squadron was unencumbered with Blenheims to protect and the pilots must have hoped to have the advantage over any unsuspecting *Luftwaffe* formations operating in the area. However, once again no enemy aircraft were encountered and Ellis led his men back to Gravesend, landing at 1935 hours after a combined flying time of eight hours and five minutes. Even after all the years had passed, Brian Smith still recalled these nerve-wracking patrols: 'Oh yes coming down from Dunkirk we had sorties to Boulogne and Calais … we did circuits round there. Other odd sweeps I remember, were going to Rouen and back'.

The following day, 30 June, a new sergeant pilot arrived, Horatio 'Ray' Chandler, posted in from 501 Squadron, probably an immediate replacement for the unfortunate Ronald Haines. Chandler was a familiar figure, having originally belonged to 610 Squadron as ground crew and a trainee pilot, before he had left on 7 October 1939 to go to 2 FTS, Brize Norton:

> on No 42 Course, which ended on March 23 1940. On leaving 2 FTS, he probably rejoined 610 for a short spell before going to 6 OTU, Sutton Bridge on April 28. After he had converted to Hurricanes, he went to PDC [Personnel Despatch Centre], Uxbridge on May 15 for allocation to a squadron in France. It would seem that Chandler joined 501 Squadron at Anglure. The squadron was withdrawn from France on June 18 1940, operated from Jersey on the 19th, covering the withdrawal of the BEF, and then re-assembled at Croydon on the 21st.[36]

Chandler then returned to 'The Chesters'. The arrival of another face from Hooton Park would have been a welcome boost, especially given the death of Haines. At some stage, Chandler would have needed further training to convert to the Spitfire.

In the late morning, 610 Squadron carried out another offensive patrol following the same route as the day before. Ellis was leading the aircraft again, with Warner as one section leader while Norris seems to have been the other section leader, probably leading Red Section. The patrol took off at 1140 hours and flew to Calais, before turning south to Boulogne and back. Once again it was a fruitless sortie with no enemy aircraft sighted. The formation landed at Gravesend at 1245 hours, the following pilots with another patrol under their belts:

DW-M.	P.9451	F/Lt. J. ELLIS.	26
DW-O.	R.6595	P/O. A. L. B. RAVEN.	12
DW-P.	R.6695	P/O. F. T. GARDINER.	5
DW-K.	P.9495	F/O. W. H. C. WARNER.	37
DW-L.	P.9496	P/O. P. LITCHFIELD.	32
DW-V.	L.1076	Sgt. RAMSAY.	4
DW-S.	N.3201	P/O. S. C. NORRIS.	32
DW-D.	P.9503	P/O. C. O. J. PEGGE.	5
DW-F.	R.6694	Sgt. HAMLYN.	15

By the time they landed, Yellow Section had been sent to patrol Hawkinge at 5,000 feet. There seems to have been some confusion over which patrol P/O Litchfield was on, as assuming the times recorded in the ORB are accurate (perhaps the second patrol took off later), he could not have been on both. It is more likely that he was on the first patrol, as the second patrol was by 'A' Flight, and Litchfield was consistently with 'B' Flight. It is likely the second patrol was led by another of the more experienced pilots, the battle order being:

DW-A.	R.6693	P/O. P. LITCHFIELD.*	
DW-E.	R.6629	P/O. G. KEIGHLEY.	24
DW-B.	L.1009	Sgt. TANNER.	7

*See text above.

No enemy aircraft were observed and Yellow Section landed at Gravesend at 1315 hours.

This was the Squadron's last recorded patrol in June, a month which had seen the pilots carry out a total of 156 hours and fifty minutes of recorded patrols, an amazing amount of flying time to show for one encounter with the enemy. Although this was frustrating for the men putting in such long days, not just in the air but also awaiting the call to scramble at readiness for hours on end, along with the attendant ground crews, it was good practice for the days ahead, when the *Luftwaffe* would surely turn its full attention to Britain. Deep down, they must have been equally relieved not to be in combat. F/Lt Brian Smith had now amassed the most recorded patrols, with thirty-nine, closely followed by F/O Warner, thirty-seven, while P/Os Norris and Litchfield had both recorded thirty-two since 10 May 1940. This period provided these Dunkirk veterans time to pass on their knowledge and experience to the numerous novice pilots who had joined the Squadron's ranks throughout June. The ORB repeatedly stated, 'No enemy aircraft sighted' after the endless patrols. This was most remarkable, when the Squadron had carried out sweeps or escort operations over German occupied France, when some sort of response must surely have been expected. Perhaps this shows that the *Luftwaffe's* priority during this period was completing the defeat of France, which finally happened on 22 June 1940. Once this had been achieved, the *Luftwaffe* reorganised itself, established new bases for its *Gruppen* in France, before turning its full attention to attacking Britain. For all the *Luftwaffe's* undoubted successes, it had suffered heavy losses during the campaign against Poland and then the attacks in the West. The German units desperately needed new men and machines, plus time to rest and recuperate, just like the RAF. But with the coming of July, Hitler and Göring knew that a return to the offensive was required if they were to invade Britain before the weather made any attempt to cross the Channel too dangerous. Therefore, the summer months of July and August would prove critical for their invasion plans, which needed to be carried out by the middle of September 1940.

A rare shot of two of the Squadron's more experienced pilot officers at Gravesend, who had both survived the Dunkirk operations: Stan Norris, left, and Peter Litchfield facing the camera on the right. On Norris's left is Samual, the Squadron's medical officer and on Litchfield's right is P/O Joe Pegge. This was taken in late June/early July 1940. (*Copyright 610 Squadron Association*)

10

1–13 July 1940: Return to Biggin Hill for the Start of The Battle of Britain

Monday 1 July saw 610 carry out two Squadron strength patrols, escorting six Blenheims on photo reconnaissance sorties from Calais to Boulogne. The first took off from Gravesend at 0931 hours and returned at 1245 hours—these times may be inaccurate due to the improbable length of the patrol. The second took off at 1432 hours and returned at 1547 hours. No enemy aircraft were spotted on either patrol, which involved the same twelve pilots and aircraft:

DW-S.	N.3201	P/O. S. C. NORRIS.	Red Section	33 & 34
DW-D.	P.9503	P/O. C. O. J. PEGGE.		6 & 7
DW-F.	R.6694	Sgt. HAMLYN.		16 & 17
DW-A.	R.6693	F/O. P. G. LAMB.	Yellow Section	29 & 30
DW-E.	R.6629	P/O. G. KEIGHLEY.		25 & 26
DW-J.	N.3284	Sgt. TANNER.		8 & 9
DW-M.	P.9451	F/Lt. J. ELLIS.	Blue Section	27 & 28
DW-O.	R.6595	P/O. A. L. B. RAVEN.		13 & 14
DW-K.	P.9495	Sgt. ARNFIELD S. J.		27 & 28
DW-Q.	P.9502	F/O. W. H. C. WARNER.	Green Section	38 & 39
DW-L.	P.9496	P/O. P. LITCHFIELD.		33 & 34
DW-P.	R.6695	Sgt. RAMSAY.		5 & 6

The sections were probably divided as shown above, each section being led by an experienced pilot who had fought at Dunkirk. Ellis would have been leading 'B' Flight and the whole formation, while Norris probably led 'A' Flight. It was hoped that by following the veteran pilots, the less experienced men would learn more quickly the necessary habits required to survive the vital first few engagements with the enemy.

On the same day, P/O Thomas Wallace was court-martialled and had his short service commission terminated. The South African had gone on a course of instruction on 23 June. As his court martial was for being absent without leave for two days in June, it is likely that it was during or immediately after this course that he went walkabout. Whatever Wallace did, it was a costly decision which he must surely have come to rue; all those months of training to get on a front-line Spitfire squadron seemingly squandered. However, all was not lost; the RAF was desperately short of trained pilots, and Wallace was accepted as a sergeant-pilot (1256954), perhaps the fall in rank being deemed punishment enough. It was not long before he joined 111 Squadron and claimed numerous enemy aircraft during the Battle of Britain, being awarded the Distinguished Flying Medal (DFM) in October. Sadly he did not survive the War, being killed in action on 11 November 1944.[1]

On Tuesday 2 July, 610 Squadron returned to the 11 Group sector station at Biggin Hill, from Gravesend. From here, the Squadron's role in dealing with *Luftwaffe* raids against the south coast

Here is the evidence of Brian Smith snoozing at dispersal in his flying jacket, probably at Wittering, in late 1939. The pilot on his left can just be made out to be reading. (*Copyright 610 Squadron Association*)

of England and the approaches to London would be critical. It must have been with a great sense of pride, mixed with more than a little apprehension that the County of Chester Squadron returned to 'The Bump'. The Squadron had been away from Biggin Hill since 26 May and much had changed since those pre-Dunkirk days. For half the Squadron, this was their first experience of such a key airfield, while for the 'old hands' it evoked memories of friends no longer with them after the Dunkirk battles. Brian Smith remembered the following of his time at Biggin Hill,

> We had the dirty end of the stick. There weren't many of us, and it meant that you were on call all the time virtually. We used to get to bed about midnight and be up again at three in the morning—down to the Flights. But, you did a lot of sleeping in your Irvine jacket or what have you. Well one or two people played bridge or something like that, but I was no card player. I was a snoozer waiting to go! But we'd do several trips a day.

Such memories give a great insight into the trials that lay ahead for 610 Squadron's men.

With the upheaval caused by the move from Gravesend to their new home, 2 July was one occasion when 610 did not fly any recorded patrols. The pilots and ground crew were now reunited with the personnel of 32 Squadron, still based at Biggin Hill. Raymond Ellis recalled how:

> The whole Squadron returned to Biggin Hill on the 2nd July. At sunrise on the following morning (my 23rd birthday), I was on 'B' Flight dispersal sniffing the pungent smell of the early air that always reminded me of the smell of hot steel produced by the hard braking of an express train. My thoughts were interrupted by the sergeant with the welcome news that Servicing Flight was being reformed. Much of the Flight's work would continue to be done on the dispersal in the open air.
>
> However some of the work needed to be done in a hangar which provided not only protection against the weather but also enabled work to continue after sundown. For this work Servicing Flight had been allocated the Belfast triple-bay hangar.[2]

On its return to the sector station, 610 Squadron had twenty-two pilots: S/Ldr A. T. Smith, F/Lt Ellis, F/Lt E. B. B. Smith, F/Os Lamb, Warner, Wilson and Gardiner, P/Os Norris, Keighley, Litchfield,

Raven, Pegge, Rees and Stewart, and Sgts Parsons, Arnfield, Else, Ramsay, Tanner, Ireland, Chandler and Hamlyn. Those going on operations at first would be the more experienced pilots, while the novice pilots would be sprinkled throughout sections on sorties to gain vital experience. With twelve Spitfires the usual maximum number sent on patrol, the luxury of twenty-two pilots meant that at least ten of them would be training, resting or on a short spell of leave. One slightly confusing caveat to this move to Biggin Hill is thrown up by Biggin's own ORB which states: '2/7/40 610 Move from Gravesend to Hawkinge', with no return date. Because the Squadron ORB clearly states the move to Biggin Hill, it is likely that this was the beginning of 610 using Hawkinge as an advance airfield which it could fly to, refuel and carry out any necessary patrols, before returning to Biggin Hill for the evening. The problem is sometimes trying to work out where the Squadron was operating from on any given patrol! Brian Smith recalled more than once that using the advance airfield at Hawkinge was an important means of saving petrol, 'Well, sometimes we went straight away to Hawkinge, but that was to save petrol. And the other boys, 32 Squadron, they were based at one end we were at the other', and 'Hawkinge, which is just behind Folkestone, was one of the forward airfields, which helped us to save petrol when we were operating from Biggin. We used to land there on our homeward flight or sometimes waiting to go out'. Incidentally, the first event the Squadron would have celebrated back at Biggin Hill, was probably Geoffrey Keighley's twenty-eighth birthday, on 2 July.

On Wednesday 3 July, 610 Squadron came to readiness in the afternoon. At 1516 hours the first patrol was sent off. Red Section led by F/Lt Brian Smith (40) (DW-B, L.1009), with F/O Lamb (31) (DW-J, N.3284) and Sgt Hamlyn (18) (DW-F, R.6694), was ordered to patrol from Margate to Hawkinge. Just twelve minutes later at 1528 hours, Blue Section was then scrambled to support Red Section on the same patrol line. This second 'Vic' of Spitfires was led by F/Lt Ellis (29) (DW-M, P.9451), followed by his wingmen Sgt Else (13) (DW-L, P.9496) and Sgt Ramsay (7) (DW-V, L.1076). Ellis strove to join Red Section as quickly as possible. Once the two sections formed up together, John Ellis described the ensuing action as follows:

> I was leading Blue section 610 Sqdn. with Red Section in line astern on a patrol between Margate and Dungeness. Both Sections had been patrolling for 1hr. 5 mins. when we were ordered to intercept 1 bandit [enemy aircraft, author] over Hawkinge below cloud. I saw the bandit a [Dornier] Do. 17 approaching from the North at rt. angles to our course. I wheeled the flight round in line astern and gave orders for a No1. attack. I attacked first and opened fire over the coast nr [near] Folkestone at 400yds. After a burst of roughly five seconds the top rear gunner baled out but I still received constant M.G. fire from the bottom gunner. I continued firing until my ammunition was exhausted and I noticed before breaking away large pieces of cowling presumably engine cowlings flying off and a small amount of black smoke from the starboard engine; a fire had also started in the top rear gunner's cockpit but I noticed the flames were extinguished just as I broke away. I turned to follow the aircraft and to watch the remainder of the flight attack but soon smelt burning oil and noticed the oil pressure was zero and the temperature 100° so immediately set course for Hawkinge. I switched off over the coast and forced landed on Hawkinge where I discovered I had been hit in the oil cooler and in two other places in the wing. (TNA, AIR 50/172/21)

Having opened fire at long range, Ellis had closed the distance while firing. Although this would have improved the effectiveness of his ammunition, it also gave the bomber's gunners a better chance to pick him off. Many of the German aircrew were very experienced, and armed with up to eight 7.9-mm MG 15 guns, a bomber's return fire could prove alarmingly accurate to any attacking RAF pilots. The dorsal gunner was forced to take to his parachute, but the ventral gunner bravely remained at his post, his fire presumably forcing the flight commander into an emergency landing at Hawkinge. P.9451 was sent away for repairs, but would return to 610 Squadron.[3] Ellis was fortunate that he was not too far out over the Channel with a damaged oil cooler. While he left the action, Blue 2, Sgt Else, began his attack on the Dornier, which was now at 2-3,000 feet and two to four miles off Dover:

> As the leader broke off his attack the Do.17 went into a dive in which I followed him down in my attack. At about 1000ft he gradually levelled out. I fired one burst of 4 secs on the way down in the dive but as he levelled out I overtook him too quickly and had to break away. I saw no return fire.
>
> At the start of the attack I saw one member of his crew descending by parachute over the sea. Two aircraft had made attacks before me. Other machines were attacking after I broke away and the Do.17 was still descending very gradually. (TNA, AIR 50/172/23)

It is unclear from this description whether Else's fire had caused further damage to the German bomber, but by now there was no return fire and the Dornier was in trouble. With the rest of the return trip across the Channel to come and being harried by a flight of Spitfires, its remaining crew was in an unenviable situation. One of the problems of engaging bombers in a fast aircraft like the Spitfire was overshooting, which Else experienced here; he still managed to get off four seconds of ammunition before he broke off his attack. Else also knew that Red Section was still to come in behind him, to follow up his attack. The order in which the aircraft attacked is slightly unclear, but Sgt Ramsay was probably the second pilot to attack (his combat report does not seem to have survived), as Else was the third. Next came Red Section, as recorded by F/Lt Smith:

> Blue & Red Sections 610 Sqdn on PATROL in the vicinity of Folkestone at Angels Seven were vectored onto a Do17. I was leading Red Section in Search formation 200-300 yds astern of Blue Section when I saw Blue Section doing a climbing turn to S'TBD Aircraft astern. I then put my section astern & sighted EA between myself & Blue Section. I then made a climbing turn STBD which brought me out slightly above & behind the E.A. I then opened fire and closed to 50 yds & then broke away to STBD. I did not observe any signs of distress from E.A. But saw whisps [wisps] of blue smoke which were I imagine the Tracer in return fire.
>
> After breaking away I headed off the EA which was diving down to sea level with Blue Section in pursuit. I then carried out a Beam attack & finished my ammunition. I last saw EA disappear out to sea with Two Spitfires in pursuit. (TNA, AIR 50/172/71)

Smith used all his ammunition during the course of these two passes, the first starting at 250 yards and closing to just fifty yards, with the second beam attack from 200 yards. For all his modesty concerning his marksmanship, it is likely that Smith damaged the unfortunate Dornier during the course of these two close-range attacks. Smith was evidently a skilful leader of his men in the air, giving his own section the best opportunity to attack the bomber, before helping Blue Section to engage the lone raider.

Another Red Section pilot to engage the bomber was Sgt Ronnie Hamlyn who attacked at 1645 hours:

> I followed up attack after four other aircraft had attacked a Do.17 whose height at this time was at sea level and about 10–12 miles out to sea. After my last burst and all my ammunition having gone, I noticed while breaking away a very big splash, after completing the break away I saw there was no aircraft in sight, but the sea appeared to look dark where the aircraft hit the water.
>
> I noticed one man bale out over the sea about 2 miles off the coast, before I made the attack and after the first a/c had made his attack. (TNA, AIR 50/172/34)

Hamlyn also used all his ammunition, firing four bursts, before the Dornier finally gave up the fight and crashed without trace into the English Channel. The engagement had been a success with six pilots all claiming a share in the bomber's destruction. It stood as testament to the RAF pilots' teamwork, with the No. 1 method of attack once again working against a lone bomber. What must have struck the pilots when they returned to Biggin Hill, was that it had taken six of them more than ten minutes to bring their foe down, using a tremendous amount of ammunition, in an engagement which started at 7,000 feet above Hawkinge and ended twelve miles out to sea off Dover. The ineffectiveness of the Browning .303 ammunition could plainly be seen, while the brave determination of the German pilot to get his aircraft and crew back to base in the face of impossible odds should also be recognised. It proved the scale of the task ahead of the RAF if they were to defeat the *Luftwaffe*. Brian Smith would later bemoan the inadequacy of the Browning machine guns, possibly recalling this very incident: 'Oh, we weren't terribly good shooters ... I think it was the .303 wasn't doing the job, the rate of them wasn't good enough. I remember shooting at things, single aeroplanes that had been on recce, and these gulls went on bloody well flying'.

At about 1650 hours, the five remaining Spitfires of Blue and Red Sections returned presumably to Hawkinge, where John Ellis had earlier made a forced landing, leaving everyone in no doubt that the Squadron had seen action. The airfield must have been a hive of activity, as almost simultaneously, Green Section was preparing to take off on a convoy patrol. This formation was led by F/O Warner (40) (DW-Q, P.9502), with his wingmen as P/O Litchfield (35) (DW-T, P.9452) and F/O Gardiner (6) (DW-O, R.6595). During this patrol the Spitfires encountered a lone enemy aircraft, this time a Dornier 215, and chased it back across the Channel to Cap Gris-Nez. The ORB indicates that Litchfield was the pilot who took the lead in this engagement. His fire silenced, 'the rear gunner and caused the enemy aircraft to wobble. Its nose went up and it stalled at 100 feet after his third burst. Heavy A.A. fire encountered over CAP GRIS-NEZ'. P/O Litchfield gave a much more detailed account of his adrenalin-filled chase across the Channel and French countryside:

> I was Green 2 of a Section led by F/O Warner, patrolling a convoy off falkestone [Folkestone] in fine weather. We were returning after being sent to Hawkinge, to the east end of the convoy and were in process of changing formation when A.A. fire from the ships was observed and an aircraft, identified as a Dornier 215, was seen heading for the French coast. We gave chase, going into line astern and I joined in in the rearmost position. We were still well out of range, and diving fast, when the enemy crossed the French coast at Cap Gris-Nez and dived into low thin 9/10th cloud at about 300'. Heavy anti-aircraft fire was encountered as we approached and crossed the coast, and the leader appeared to lose sight of the enemy, and turned to the east. I followed the enemy through the cloud, and he then led me at high speed as low as possible over the fields. After about two minutes of this, I observed fire from the rear gunner and gave him a three second burst at about 350x.
>
> He ceased firing and on getting closer, I gave another burst of three seconds and the aircraft rocked from side to side. As I fired for the last time, the enemy appeared to stand on his tail, and I broke to avoid collision and went over the top of him, as there was no room below. I did not see him again, although I looked both above and below the cloud. The anti-aircraft opened up again as I recrossed the coast, but no damage was done and I rejoined Green Section over the convoy. (TNA, AIR 50/172/48)

The Dornier 215 was sighted at about 1755 hours and involved a lengthy chase for Green Section, Litchfield especially, as according to the preamble to his report, he went about fifteen miles south-east of Cap Gris-Nez. He also stated that he fired two bursts of three seconds and one burst of two seconds, from 350 to 100 yards, firing approximately 1,200 rounds. It was an eventful pursuit and the bomber must have been flying at full throttle for the nimble fighters to take so long to close the range. Litchfield's sharp eyesight came to the fore again, as he was the rearmost Spitfire, yet managed to follow the Dornier when Warner and Gardiner lost it in cloud. His determination to hunt the bomber down is striking, the tree top chase being about as dramatic as it got given the thick cloud. It must have been galling after such a lengthy chase to be uncertain of the bomber's fate, but it provides further evidence of the difficulty involved in bringing down the *Luftwaffe's* twin-engined bombers with the Spitfire and Hurricane's armament. Litchfield was able to claim the Dornier as an unconfirmed.

During the pursuit, Gardiner's Spitfire DW-O, R.6595, was caught by AA fire over the French coast, but it only punctured the right wing, and all the pilots made it back to base at 1820 hours. Given that they had strayed so far over enemy territory, Green Section's pilots could count themselves lucky for failing to attract the attention of any *Luftwaffe* fighters. The day ended with one *Luftwaffe* bomber claimed as destroyed and another unconfirmed destroyed, for two damaged Spitfires, the two patrols having lasted a combined total of three hours and four minutes. Undoubtedly, the greatest importance of these patrols was the invaluable combat experience gained by the pilots.

It is interesting to note here that 610 Squadron had been operating in tandem with their sister squadron from Biggin Hill, 32 Squadron. The Hurricane squadron's ORB has the following entry for the afternoon of 3 July:

> 1555–1715 Red and Blue Sections of No.32 Squadron ordered Patrol Tenterden at 5,000' or below clouds. 1604 hrs ordered to intercept Enemy Raid (21). Dornier Do 17. 1615 hrs Red and Blue Sections ordered to intercept Enemy Raid (21). Raid cancelled but Dornier shot down by 610 Squadron.

It is evident that John Ellis's patrol had intercepted 'Raid 21', which 32 Squadron was also being vectored on to and that information about such victories was passed between the Squadrons. Shortly afterwards, 32 Squadron shot another Dornier down. The Dorniers operating over south-eastern England had certainly been up against it.

On Thursday 4 July, the pilots were awoken early for breakfast, before the following men were ordered to take-off at 0512 hours and fly down to Hawkinge for refuelling:

DW-X.	R.6630	S/Ldr. A. T. SMITH.	Red Section	18
DW-A.	R.6693	F/O. P. G. LAMB.		32
DW-F.	R.6694	Sgt. HAMLYN.		19
DW-B.	L.1009	F/Lt. E. B. B. SMITH.	Yellow Section	41
DW-J.	N.3284	P/O. C. O. J. PEGGE.		8
DW-S.	N.3201	Sgt. PARSONS.		1
DW-H.	L.1044	F/Lt. J. ELLIS.	Blue Section	30
DW-K.	P.9495	Sgt. ARNFIELD, S. J.		29
DW-E.	R.6629	F/O. F. T. GARDINER.		7
DW-Q.	P.9545*	F/O. W. H. C. WARNER.	Green Section	41
DW-T.	R.6765**	P/O. P. LITCHFIELD.		36
DW-L.	P.9496	Sgt. ELSE, P.		14

*DW-Q should probably be P.9502, until it was lost on 12 July, being replaced by P.9545. Error repeated in ORB until 12 July 1940. I have adhered to ORB listing until then. P.9545 only joined Squadron on 11 July 1940.[4]

**DW-T should be P.9452 until 18 July, when it was shot down and replaced by R.6765. Error repeated in ORB until 18 July 1940. I have adhered to ORB listing until then. R.6765 only joined Squadron on 13 July 1940.[5]

They took off again at 0600 hours, on a reconnaissance patrol of the *Luftwaffe's* new homes at Rouen–Boos and Abbeville aerodromes, flying at a minimum height of 5,000 feet. The Squadron encountered dreadful weather over Dieppe and nine of them returned home at 0645 hours. Whether or not Blue Section had become separated from the rest of the Squadron is unclear, but John Ellis's section pressed on, seeing nothing at Rouen–Boos or Dieppe. They carried on to Beauvais aerodrome where they observed twenty bombers, before returning to land at Biggin Hill at 0753 hours.

Despite the early morning's inclement weather over northern France, another reconnaissance was planned for the evening, this time in section strength, involving three different pilots. This ensured as many pilots as possible were involved in the operations, which in this instance would test to the limit their flying and navigation skills in murky conditions. Red Section took off from Hawkinge at 2030 hours, P/O Norris (35) leading (DW- J, N.3284), with P/O Keighley (27) (DW-E, R.6629) and Sgt Ramsay (8) (DW-L, P.9496) accompanying him, with orders to trace the same patrol line the Squadron had followed in the early morning. The ORB bluntly states, 'Saw one very large aircraft at Rouen Boos. Nothing at Abbeville. Big storm over Rouen'. After a ninety-minute patrol in stormy weather, the three tired pilots would have been relieved to touch down at 2200 hours.

The next recorded operation was not until Sunday 7 July. Either the bad weather had limited operations over England for a couple of days, the Squadron had spent their time cramming in training for the new pilots, or the ORB had not been updated. Whatever the reason, on 7 July, two sections were sent to Dungeness to intercept three Me 109s reportedly in the area, involving the following pilots:

DW-K.	P.9495	P/O. P. LITCHFIELD.	Blue Section	37
DW-N.	R.6806*	P/O. A. L. B. RAVEN.		15
DW-L.	P.9496	Sgt. ELSE, P.		15
DW-A.	R.6976**	F/Lt. E. B. B. SMITH.	Yellow Section	42
DW-F.	R.6694	Sgt. HAMLYN.		20
DW-H.	L.1044	Sgt. TANNER.		10

*As ORB but probably an error. DW-N should probably be L.1075 until 8 July 1940, when it was shot down (TNA, AIR 81/1046).

**As ORB but DW-A should probably be R.6693 until 25 July 1940. This error is repeated in the ORB until after 25 July, when DW-A becomes R.6976. R.6976 only joined Squadron on 24 July 1940.[6] I have adhered to ORB listing until then.

The Spitfires scrambled at 1730 hours and were vectored around after the 109s for ninety minutes, but the German fighters proved elusive. The flight of Spitfires returned at 1900 hours without seeing any other aircraft, something which the Squadron would not report at the end of the following day.

The morning of Monday 8 July proved uneventful enough, but the cloudy weather was perfect for the *Luftwaffe* to mount some raids on the shipping passing through the English Channel. As a result, at 1345 hours, Blue Section was ordered on a convoy patrol off Dover. The section leader was F/O Warner (42) (reportedly in DW-Q, P.9545, although it was probably P.9502) with two wingmen both on their sixteenth recorded operational patrols, Blue 2, P/O Raven (16) in DW-N, (ORB recorded it as R.6806, it was actually L.1075) and Blue 3, Sgt Else (16), in DW-L, P.9496. Convoy patrols were no longer the mundane task they had been for fighter pilots during the so-called Phoney War, as convoys passing through the Channel were now a tempting target for the *Luftwaffe*. Göring realised that by attacking the shipping, he forced Fighter Command's aircraft to come to their aid. Then if things went to plan, the *Luftwaffe* would shoot them down *en masse* to establish air supremacy over the Channel and southern coast, the first requirement for an invasion attempt. As a result, the skies above Kentish coastal towns and harbours such as Margate, Dover, Deal and Folkestone, and the shipping passing between them, had become extremely dangerous.

Blue Section's pilots would have spent a testing time maintaining formation above the convoy, while constantly swivelling their heads to search for enemy aircraft for over two hours. As will be seen, another formation from 610 Squadron was scrambled later, and while the ORB suggests they operated apart at two different places, a flying battle casualty report states they eventually operated together. The three Spitfires of Blue Section were eventually vectored on to an incoming raid, which was picked up by the pilots as nine small dots on the horizon. These dots quickly grew into nine Dornier Do 215s which were intercepted ten miles off Dover. A brisk action took place, details of which are sparse.

Peter Else reported having silenced the rear gunner of one of the bombers and was able to claim a Do 215 damaged, but the bad news was that he had seen a Spitfire burning in the sea. One of his fellow pilots had ditched, presumably having been hit by the German gunners' crossfire. Else would have ascertained very quickly over the R/T that it was twenty-four-year-old Arthur Raven who had been forced into the English Channel's treacherous waters, but the sergeant saw Raven leave DW-N and swim away. Landing a Spitfire on water was a very tricky manoeuvre, even more so in one which was on fire. Raven had done extremely well to ditch his aircraft and escape from it. Due to the length of the patrol and subsequent engagement, Else was unable to stay long over Raven, but although anxious for his comrade, would have felt reasonably sure he would be rescued and returned to the Squadron. These hopes ultimately proved futile, and Raven drowned before he could be found. Although most sources state that Raven was flying DW-N, R.6806, probably thanks to the ORB error, he was actually flying DW-N, L.1075, as confirmed in the AMCB file.

Raymond Ellis recalled having carried out repairs on DW-N, L.1074 (actually L.1075), after it had suffered a heavy landing, noting how it was Raven who then carried out the Spitfire's test flight:

> On the afternoon of 7th July the work was entered into the Form 700 and signed by me and by our only airframe NCO, Cpl Hodges who had come over from dispersal. We wheeled the 'plane out onto the apron where the engine fitter started and ran up the engine with two of us on the tail plane. When members of all trades had signed for their Daily Inspection, a pilot arrived carrying his parachute. I was pleased to see that it was Pilot Officer Raven, our youngest [Warner, at least, was younger] Auxiliary officer who had joined us 12 months earlier and had learned to fly whilst with our squadron. I still remember helping him with his safety harness and seeing him off on the test flight. On his return he taxied back to dispersal so we knew that he was satisfied with our work.
>
> On the following morning P/O Raven flew DW-N with the squadron to Hawkinge to intercept enemy 'planes attacking our shipping and ports. Whilst attacking a formation of Do 17 [Do 215] bombers, Raven was caught in their crossfire and crashed into the Channel close to Dover.[7]

This was clearly a haunting image of the young pilot that stayed with Raymond Ellis throughout his life.

While the ORB describes events surrounding Raven's death as the Squadron being involved in two distinct engagements over different parts of the south-east coast, the flying battle casualty report written by the squadron commander, Tom Smith, makes it sound like one engagement over the same convoy, see photo p. 212. Perhaps Red and Green Sections had added some much needed reinforcements to Blue Section. This report also throws up the possibility that Raven had been picked off by fighters escorting the bombers. This had not been considered by earlier evaluations of the encounters, as the bombers were said to be unescorted. However, as the report was not sent until 13 July, five days after the incident, the two patrols may have merged into one in the memory of the CO, particularly during this hectic time. Smith's report also provides further details about Raven's final moments, as he managed to climb on to the tail of his aircraft, which remained afloat for four minutes, before attempting to swim to safety. The incident took place six miles out to sea from Dover, three ships were sent to try and recover Raven, but he was never found.

The usual series of letters attempting to establish if any news had been heard of Raven passed back and forth between the Air Ministry and his father, Oscar, who lived in Maytree Cottage, Shrivenham, Swindon, Wiltshire. However, in early January 1941, with no news of him for six months, the Air Ministry confirmed that he must have lost his life at sea on 8 July 1940. Raven's great nephew, David Driver, informed me that the family believed that Arthur Raven had not been wearing his inflatable 'Mae West' jacket, because of its bulk in the cockpit, which restricted his movement.

A particularly tragic photo, depicting a cheerful P/O Arthur Raven, enjoying some time relaxing with his Squadron friends at 'Laughing Waters', where they had been for a swim. Less than three weeks later, Raven was battling in vain to stay afloat in the much more menacing and unforgiving waters of the English Channel. (*Copyright 610 Squadron Association*)

This was a very sad story to hear, particularly when the Squadron had lost so many men to the English Channel's dangerous waters during the Dunkirk evacuation. Had Raven worn this vital piece of equipment, it might have made all the difference.

Arthur Raven had been with 610 for some time before the war, having been granted an AAF commission on 18 August 1939 as an acting pilot officer, before going to 2 FTS, Brize Norton on 7 October 1939. He finally returned to 610 Squadron on 23 May 1940, after a brief mission to France as part of an emergency unit. Raven carried out his first twelve recorded patrols in June, including several over enemy-occupied territory, albeit ones which did not come in contact with the *Luftwaffe*, plus a further three in July. On his sixteenth recorded patrol, tragically his final one, he was being led by the experienced F/O Warner, who was a good friend of Raven, as recalled by Brian Smith, 'Raven, he and Billy Warner were a pair.' The difference on this patrol was that Raven encountered the enemy for the first time. His inexperience undoubtedly stood against him, perhaps causing him to leave himself vulnerable to the return fire from the Dorniers, or their escorts if they were present. However, even F/Lt Ellis had been forced into an emergency landing five days earlier by a bomber's return fire, and the successful pilots all had their share of luck. Raven's inexperience was telling, but he was very unfortunate not to be rescued from the Channel and on another day he would have lived to fight on. P/O Arthur Raven is remembered on Panel 9 of the Runnymede Memorial and also on his former school's roll of honour at Yardley Court, Tunbridge Wells, where a memorial service is carried out each Remembrance Day.

Sadly for Raven and his family, because he had been killed outside of the recognised period of the Battle of Britain, 10 July–31 October 1940, he was not remembered as one of 'The Few'. There had to be a specific time period for the Battle of Britain, but it is particularly harsh given that he died doing exactly what 'The Few' would do, defending the country from enemy raiders, albeit less than two

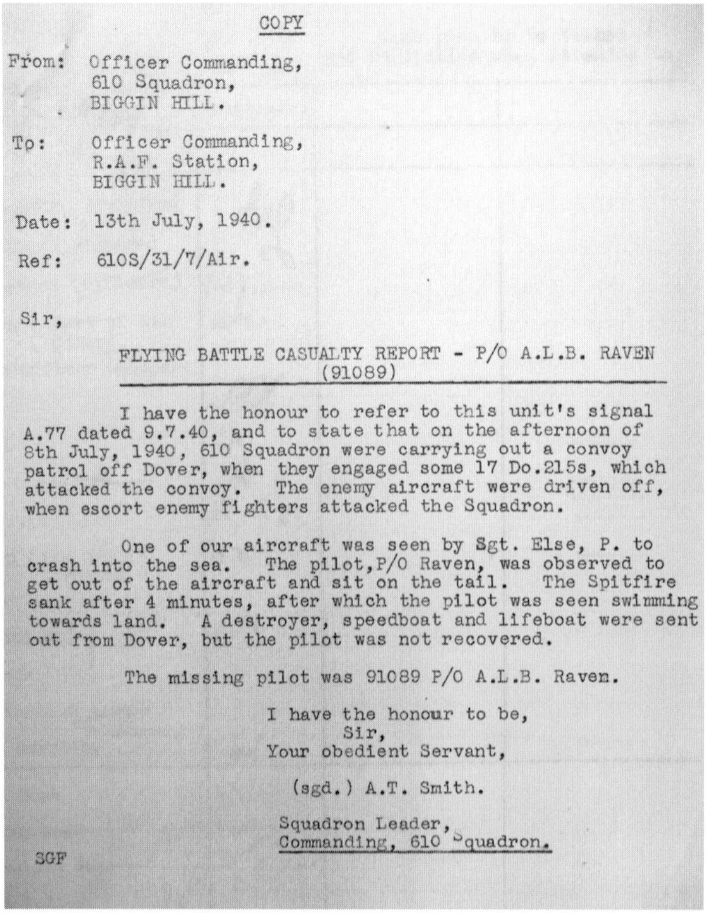

COPY

From: Officer Commanding,
610 Squadron,
BIGGIN HILL.

To: Officer Commanding,
R.A.F. Station,
BIGGIN HILL.

Date: 13th July, 1940.

Ref: 610S/31/7/Air.

Sir,

FLYING BATTLE CASUALTY REPORT - P/O A.L.B. RAVEN (91089)

I have the honour to refer to this unit's signal A.77 dated 9.7.40, and to state that on the afternoon of 8th July, 1940, 610 Squadron were carrying out a convoy patrol off Dover, when they engaged some 17 Do.215s, which attacked the convoy. The enemy aircraft were driven off, when escort enemy fighters attacked the Squadron.

One of our aircraft was seen by Sgt. Else, P. to crash into the sea. The pilot, P/O Raven, was observed to get out of the aircraft and sit on the tail. The Spitfire sank after 4 minutes, after which the pilot was seen swimming towards land. A destroyer, speedboat and lifeboat were sent out from Dover, but the pilot was not recovered.

The missing pilot was 91089 P/O A.L.B. Raven.

I have the honour to be,
Sir,
Your obedient Servant,

(sgd.) A.T. Smith.

Squadron Leader,
Commanding, 610 Squadron.

SGF

Squadron leader's report on the death of Raven. (*TNA AIR 81/1046*)

days before the 'official' start point. For anyone associated with Raven, whether family or through association with the Squadron, he would surely have been remembered as one of 'The Few'. Arthur Raven's CO clearly thought very highly of him, writing: 'Our loss is very great; not only was he a pilot above the average, but he had a personality that was liked by all and made a good officer in the example he set … he met the enemy in the right way'.[8]

As earlier mentioned, this was not the Squadron's only operation that afternoon. While Blue Section was on convoy patrol off Dover, two more sections of 610 were sent up on patrol at 1456 hours. P/O Norris (36) led the patrol as Red leader (DW-B, L.1009), with P/O Pegge (9) (DW-H, L.1044) and Sgt Parsons (2) (DW-F, R.6694) as his wingmen. P/O Litchfield (38) was Green 1 (DW-T, R.6765), with Sgt Arnfield (30) (DW-K, P.9495) and Sgt Ramsay (9) (DW-P, R.6695) forming the remainder of Green Section. The Squadron was again trying to build up the experience of the new recruits such as Parsons, with those who were combat experienced, like Arnfield, Litchfield and Norris. The ground controller ordered another successful interception, (by all accounts apart from S/Ldr Smith's report, this was in addition to Blue Section's encounter with the Dorniers) and five miles south of Hythe the six Spitfires engaged seven Dornier 215s and their escort of twelve Me 109s. The Squadron ORB described how the initial attacks had no apparent result, but that, 'P/O. Pegge after breaking away encountered 3 Me.109s'. Fortunately, Pegge's combat report survives to recount this engagement, which he recorded took place at 1515 hours, 'Over Channel near France' at 5,000 feet:

Arthur Lionel Boultbee Raven, Killed in Action, 8 July 1940. (*Copyright Nicholson family*)

> I was No. 2. of Red Section of A Flight 610 Squadron. We took off from Biggin Hill at 14.56 & contacted enemy bombers, Do 215s, about 7, who were attacking a convoy off Dungeness. Red section at 5,000' prepared to attack 3 enemy bombers in Vic formation. They broke up & we split up. I attacked 3 215s in succession. The first two I gave 2 2 sec' bursts & the last one a 3 sec' burst. The last one had smoke coming from its starboard engine from a previous attack. When it entered a cloud I broke away & saw 3 Me 109s after a Spitfire slightly above me. One of the 109s went into a cloud & I went after the second 109. From a range of about 100-150 yds I gave it a 3 second burst & it dived towards the sea with black smoke coming from it. When I last saw it it was over the vertical. I was then attacked from behind so I climbed to the right into a cloud.
>
> Confirmed by Sgt Ramsay. (TNA, AIR 50/172/58)

This Flight was operating from Biggin Hill, so it took them longer to reach Dungeness, although it gave them time to be fully prepared to attack the bombers, which Norris successfully did, breaking up the enemy formation. (These two patrols show the confusion over where 610 was operating from on a daily basis, about which the ORB is not always very clear. We know from Pegge's combat report that the second patrol took off from Biggin Hill, but there is no such information on the first patrol, so a certain amount of guess work has to be employed). Pegge reports that a bomber he engaged was already damaged, although the ORB does not mention anyone else filing a claim and no other combat reports are available.

After the initial attack on the Dorniers, twelve Me 109s intervened, preventing any bombers from being shot down and from Pegge's description, at least one Spitfire was fortunate to make it back (although perhaps this was Raven). However, Pegge picked off one 109 from 100–150 yards with a three second burst, and as Sgt Ramsay confirmed it, Pegge could claim his first victory of the War. Pegge survived further attacks by 109s and returned unscathed to Biggin Hill. The intelligence officer credited him with the Squadron's only victory of the encounter, possibly belonging to III./JG 51 if it was shot down or II./JG 51 if it had made it back across the Channel: 'An aircraft from III./JG 51 was also lost in action on this date with a fourth from II./JG 51 being damaged in combat with 610 Sqn'.[9]

This would not have helped alleviate the sense of loss the Squadron felt knowing that P/O Raven was 'Missing'—another of the old familiar pre-war faces gone forever, another claimed by the cold, unforgiving English Channel.

Tuesday 9 July proved to be another busy day for 610 Squadron, the first patrol coming at 0940 hours, with Red, Blue and Green Sections ordered to patrol Dungeness, led by F/Lt Brian Smith. The following pilots were under his command:

DW-G.	L.1045	F/Lt. E. B. B. SMITH.	Red 1	43
DW-A.	R.6976	F/O. P. G. LAMB.		33
DW-H.	L.1044	P/O. C. O. J. PEGGE.		10
DW-O.	R.6595	F/O. W. H. C. WARNER.	Blue 1	43
DW-K.	P.9495	Sgt. ARNFIELD, S. J.		31
DW-L.	P.9496	Sgt. ELSE, P.		17
DW-T.	R.6765	P/O. P. LITCHFIELD.	Green 1	39
DW-E.	R.6629	Sgt. TANNER.		11
DW-P.	R.6695	Sgt. RAMSAY.		10

The nine Spitfires carried out a sweep along the Channel coast and eventually encountered the enemy: 'Five pilots of the Squadron engaged 4 Me.109s at 15,000 feet but with no observed casualties to the enemy' (ORB). No combat reports exist to say who these five were, but with no losses to either side, nine Spitfires returned to base one hour and twenty-four minutes after taking off. There was a lull in activity until 1345 hours, when 'A' Flight was ordered on patrol, Red and Yellow Sections being given various vectors between Dungeness and Cap Gris-Nez—S/Ldr Smith must have wondered if they were on a wild goose chase. The pilots were:

DW-A.	R.6976	S/Ldr. A. T. SMITH.	Red 1	19
DW-E.	R.6629	P/O. G. KEIGHLEY.		28
DW-H.	L.1044	P/O. C. O. J. PEGGE.		11
DW-D.	P.9503	F/Lt. E. B. B. SMITH.	Yellow 1	44
DW-F.	R.6694	P/O. S. C. NORRIS.		37
	R.6630*	Sgt. PARSONS.		3

*As ORB, but almost certainly DW-X, or would become DW-X. Adhered to ORB listing.

However, the ever-increasing worth of the RDF system soon became apparent, as the ground controller's vectoring finally bore fruit. 'A' Flight caught sight of a lone Dornier 215 at 1420 hours. S/Ldr Smith's combat report reads as follows:

> While leading "A" Flight 610 Squadron after a Patrol from Dungeness to Dover and Cape Gris Nez [Cap Gris-Nez] we were directed each to Hawkinge when flying at 14000 feet a Do 215 was sighted above and to Port just below cloud.
>
> No 1 Attack was delivered at 16000 feet for about 8 secs. Smoke observed coming from Starboard Motor. No return fire from Bomber on break away. Second attack delivered at 2000 feet off Cape Griz Nez [Cap Gris-Nez] for 3 or 4 Secs. when Enemy Aircraft was flying right-wing low with starboard wing enveloped in black smoke and losing height rapidly. When breaking away saw some black objects pass my aircraft.
>
> Yellow 3 did a final attack while Enemy Aircraft was diving for the ground over land, but after breaking away could not see him anywhere. (TNA, AIR 50/172/69)

Smith certainly pressed his attacks home with real determination, his first lasting eight seconds from 250 to fifty yards, while his second was three to four seconds, from the same range. The German pilot tried to evade the Spitfires by diving, as Smith's first attack took place at 16,000 feet and his second at 2,000 feet, (this may equally have been a result of damage suffered during the attacks). By the time 'Yellow 3', most likely Sgt Parsons, carried out his second attack, the bomber was down to just 1,000 feet. Unfortunately there is no record of Claude Parsons's combat report. All but one of the pilots attacked the luckless bomber, again following the textbook No. 1 method of fighter command attacks, with 'the S/Ldr. and Sgt. PARSONS making a second attack when the E/A was just over the French coast' (ORB).

The bomber was in a bad way, as might be expected having been given a rough ride by five Spitfires. Tom Smith ordered his men to re-form, confident that the Dornier was doomed, and not wanting to risk continuing the pursuit over occupied territory, or incurring the wrath of any patrolling enemy fighters. On returning to the airfield, most likely Hawkinge, at 1450 hours, S/Ldr Smith and Claude Parsons were able to claim the Do 215 as shared destroyed, although at least three other pilots should also presumably have been able to claim a share in the victory. Not for the first time, and certainly not the last, the vagaries of combat claims are hard to follow.

Parsons's combat report does not exist in The National Archives. However, his description of a combat with a Do 17 in *Ten Fighter Boys*, (actually it was a Do 215), is almost certainly what he remembered of this encounter on 9 July, despite some discrepancies, given the context of the engagement and especially that his squadron leader also experienced objects being thrown at him by the German crew:

> I was No. 3 in the front section of six aircraft or, as we called it, a "flight". We stooged around for about half an hour on various courses given us by the controller. Suddenly a large form loomed up in front of us. We had caught our prey. The Hun immediately put his nose down and dived for the sea about 5,000 feet below, at the same time releasing his bombs, no doubt by the jettison button, for they went down in a large mass, hitting the sea in almost the same form as they left the aircraft. In the meantime we had been ordered into "line astern" for the attack. This attack was the only perfect attack, as per written instructions, made by a section in which I have been flying. The section-leader went in, attacked and broke away, No. 2 likewise and then myself. I got in a good burst, with considerable opposition from the rear gunner and all manner of objects thrown from the enemy, such as pieces of wire, rather like old netting from chicken-runs and small missiles of varying shapes and sizes. Having dodged the objects thrown I found myself going much too fast, and almost collided with the tail of the enemy aircraft, which I recognised as a DO. 17. I did a very split break away, terrified the front gunner would get me as I overshot. Next I knew there was something wrong with my aeroplane, but owing to the thick mist I could see nothing below or above. I took command of myself and stuck my head in the cockpit to sort things out on the blind flying panel. After what seemed minutes to me I suddenly realised that my aeroplane was upside down. I pulled the stick hard back and completed the bottom half of my loop. As I got nearly round to my correct position I saw the water very close. It's a job to describe my feelings at that moment. The nearest I can get is to say that I was dumbfounded. Instinctively I rammed the throttle full open and pulled back harder on the stick. Fortunately I missed the water. I climbed up again and very carefully flew back to my base, feeling completely lacking in physical strength.[10]

This is much more descriptive than any combat report, providing a vivid picture of his encounter with the Dornier. The textbook style of attack paid dividends against the lone bomber, but despite having hit it with 'a good burst', it was the unexpected missiles from the Dornier which put Parsons off, causing him to overshoot and at low altitude, nearly crash. Suddenly, the model attack unravelled, with almost fatal consequences. Every aerial combat could throw up an unexpected eventuality which had to be dealt with. In the heat of the moment, a split-second decision, like failing to roll his aircraft the right way up, could have killed him. Parsons writes in a very evocative style and one can almost sense his fatigue as he flew his Spitfire back to Hawkinge. This feeling would become the norm for those involved in the coming struggle, after each and every encounter.

As 'A' Flight's victorious pilots landed, Green Section was ordered off on a reconnaissance of four airfields in France: Dieppe, Abbeville, Berck and Le Touquet, much the same as had taken place five days earlier. F/O Warner (44) was leading this patrol, his second of the day, this time in DW-Q, P.9545, with Sgt Arnfield (32) again in DW-K, P.9495 and Sgt Chandler (1) (DW-J, N.3284) on his first recorded operation. The three pilots were to be disappointed however, as cloud at 2,000 feet obscured their view, and they returned home one hour and fifty minutes later, at precisely 1600 hours. So ended another day with the three patrols flown involving fourteen pilots, three of whom flew twice. Once more, this indicates how each pilot was given as much opportunity to gain experience against the *Luftwaffe*, and also to prevent individuals doing too many patrols and becoming tired.

On Wednesday 10 July, a large convoy code-named 'Bread' was passing through the English Channel, which had inevitably been noticed by the *Luftwaffe*. German bombers were readied to attack the convoy, and a formation of Me 109s was sent over the Channel to escort them. As the enemy aircraft approached England, 610 Squadron received a phone call at their dispersal and Red, Yellow and Blue Sections were scrambled at 1031 hours, led by F/Lt Brian Smith, the nine Spitfire pilots being:

DW-D.	P.9503	F/Lt. E. B. B. SMITH.	Red 1	45
DW-E.	R.6629	P/O. G. KEIGHLEY.		29
	R.6630	Sgt. PARSONS.		4
DW-F.	R.6694	P/O. S. C. NORRIS.	Yellow 1	38
DW-R.	K.9931	P/O. C. O. J. PEGGE.		12
DW-J.	N.3284	Sgt. TANNER.		12
DW-Q.	P.9545	F/O. W. H. C. WARNER.	Blue 1	45
DW-T.	R.6765	Sgt. ELSE, P.		18
DW-P.	R.6695	Sgt. RAMSAY.		11

F/Lt Smith would have ordered the men of 'Dog Rose' Squadron, to climb with their throttles 'through the gate', to gain maximum altitude in the short time available before being vectored into visual contact with the prowling Messerschmitts, which were spotted just after 1100 hours at 10,000 feet. ('Dog Rose' was 610 Squadron's call sign on the R/T, so on this patrol, Smith would have been 'Dog Rose Red Leader'.) The Spitfires were slightly outnumbered by the twelve German fighters over Dover, but on this occasion, 610 Squadron was not alone, being accompanied by 74 Squadron, also flying Supermarine Spitfires (TNA, AIR 25/197). 74 Squadron then tried to engage the bombers closer to Margate, while Brian Smith led his formation straight at the enemy fighters and during the brisk skirmish Red Leader was hit by cannon shells in his port wing. Falling out of the engagement, Smith headed for Hawkinge, which he managed to reach safely, before crash-landing his damaged Spitfire—fortunately, he was unhurt. On the credit side, Bill Warner, Blue Leader, singled out one of the 109s and caught it with three short bursts of machine gun fire which converged on the fighter's tail section. He claimed it as possibly destroyed, being eventually described as destroyed 'doubtful', or unconfirmed in the ORB. Interestingly, '11 Group Intelligence Bulletin No. 1' credited 610 Squadron with one Me 109 confirmed, although no mention is made of Smith's crash-landing and the timings are slightly different from 610 Squadron's record (TNA, AIR 25/197).

Overall, the engagement had been inconclusive with honours even. 610's flight commander was relieved to have survived his emergency landing and come out of the dogfight physically unscathed. Over the years, it has been repeatedly reported in books that the patrol was led by 610 Squadron's CO, A. T. Smith, perhaps because of slightly unclear notation in the ORB and it has been established as 'fact' that it was also S/Ldr Tom Smith who crash-landed his damaged Spitfire at Hawkinge, even in a famous painting portraying The Battle of Britain. In reality, it was F/Lt E. B. B. Smith who survived this encounter, as he recalled when I had the privilege of meeting him, an incident which also reminded him of his pre-war flying days:

> That's what made me think of Hunnard. He said, 'If you're going to hit a hedge, hit the far hedge and not the near one'. Well on one of our mixings, I had my oil cooler blown out, a hole in the wing about that size. But it took all my hydraulics and it took my airspeed indicator. So not to fly in too slowly, I came in well over the first fence and just managed to land on my nose at the next one. So all they had to do to that one was put a new wing on it! That was Hawkinge, that's right.

And on seeing the Squadron ORB notes, he said:

> 10,000 feet Red Leader hit by enemy cannon, crashed at Hawkinge on landing, that's right, that's what I told you, hit the far hedge and not the near one! Oh, there's a lot to learn! I got out quickly in case it caught fire! But it was quite intact, apart from my oil cooler, the hydraulics and air speed indicator—I hadn't got any of them.

Brian Smith had paid careful attention to his old Flying Instructor Hunnard's advice, which on this occasion helped to save his life. There is some confusion over which Spitfire Smith was flying: the ORB states DW-D, P.9503, however it seems that this machine joined the Squadron the following day, 11 July 1940,[11] and was still flying at the end of the month. Many sources state that it was DW-M, L.1000, however, it is probable that it was actually L.1000 with the Squadron identifying letters of DW-D (see photo p. 193), although we will probably never know for certain. It is possible that Smith's aircraft was damaged by one of the *Luftwaffe's* up-and-coming pilots, Oblt. Josef Priller of 6./JG 51 who damaged a Spitfire over Dover at 1115 hours. If so, it would have been the first of several encounters the County of Chester Squadron had with this crack *Jägdgeschwader* [JG] during the Battle of Britain.

Although it was not apparent at the time, this skirmish occurred on what became known in Britain as the opening day of the Battle of Britain, with the first phase of the Battle being attacks on the convoys. In addition to the *Luftwaffe's* hopes of drawing up RAF fighters to defend their shipping lanes and generally test the RAF's defensive system, the *Luftwaffe* hoped to force the Royal Navy and Merchant Navy to abandon using the Channel, assisting Nazi plans for invasion. Despite the losses suffered at Dunkirk, the Navy's destroyer force was still a real menace to any invasion fleet, and it was imperative for Germany to either eliminate this naval threat, or at least force them to ports further afield from those in the Channel, so that any potential invasion could take place. However, the Home Fleet, with its numerous battleships, cruisers and attendant destroyers, remained intact at Scapa Flow, if the worst case scenario arose.

There were no reported operations on Thursday 11 July, the Squadron using the time to practise, something which could prove as fatal as flying against the enemy. Dogfighting practice was an essential element of any Spitfire pilot's training, and on Friday 12 July, Sgts Chandler and Ireland took off from Biggin Hill for some much needed training. As they alternated their attempts to try and surprise one another and get a bead on their 'opponent', something went wrong for Ireland when he was diving through clouds and he lost control. The Spitfire could be lethal for an inexperienced pilot due to its phenomenal power, especially in comparison with training aircraft. Ireland, who had only been with the Squadron for twenty-three days, did not pull out of the dive. At about 1130 hours, he crashed into the grounds of Titsey Park, a country house situated four miles south of Biggin Hill.[12] Sydney Ireland had not flown a recorded operational patrol. But the dangers of being on a front-line Squadron were self-evident, as he was all too aware having seen Sgt Haines meet a similar fate just under a fortnight earlier. As Raymond Ellis later recalled about these two young pilots, 'Although they died without

Photo from Ray Holmes's book showing his fellow trainee pilots. Holmes is in the middle row, third from left. On his left, in the middle, is Sgt Ireland. Second from the left on the back row is Sgt Haines. The crosses marked on their chests macabrely indicate the fate that awaited them. (*Copyright Holmes, Sky Spy, p. 44*)

having the chance to fire a single shot at the enemy, they gave their all in the defence of Britain. They were victims of the desperate situation of that summer of 1940, when we were in need of pilots to replace those whom we had lost'.[13]

The AMCB file on Sgt Ireland, released on 30 June 2017, provides additional information, highlighting Ireland's inexperience on Spitfires, with just over seventeen hours solo, while he had 117 hours and twenty minutes on all types (TNA, AIR 81/2386). In the, 'Report on flying accident … not attributable to enemy action' form, S/Ldr Smith confirms that Ireland's Spitfire was completely wrecked in the crash and that although the cause was unknown, the 'pilot appears to have dived steeply and lost consciousness' (TNA, AIR 81/2386). Smith's report to his CO (see photo p. 219), explains what had happened, using testimony from Sgt Chandler, and an eyewitness on the ground. Chandler must have found the event terribly traumatic, having probably frantically talked to Ireland over the R/T to try and establish where he was, before spotting the plume of smoke spiralling up from the countryside, which confirmed his worst fears. Sgt Sydney Ireland, aged twenty-two, was buried on 18 July at Knockbreda Church of Ireland Churchyard, County Down, Sec. E. Grave 78, in the same grave in which his parents, Robert and Sarah, were later laid to rest.

Ireland's Spitfire, DW-Q, P.9502, had only been with the Squadron since 2 June, a replacement for the Dunkirk losses.[14] It was later excavated, as recorded in *Then and Now*: '*Site excavated by the London Air Museum which recovered a complete Rolls-Royce Merlin engine, propeller boss with two blades still attached, .303in Browning machine-gun with "P9502" stencilled on the ammunition feed mechanism, blind-flying panel and one complete undercarriage leg*'.[15] The propeller of P.9502 is now on display at the Shoreham Museum. In August 2009, I contacted Titsey Place, and they confirmed that two Spitfires had crashed on the Estate; one in the plantation and one nearer to Pitchfont Farm, that a dig had taken place, but they had no further records of what was found. On visiting the estate,

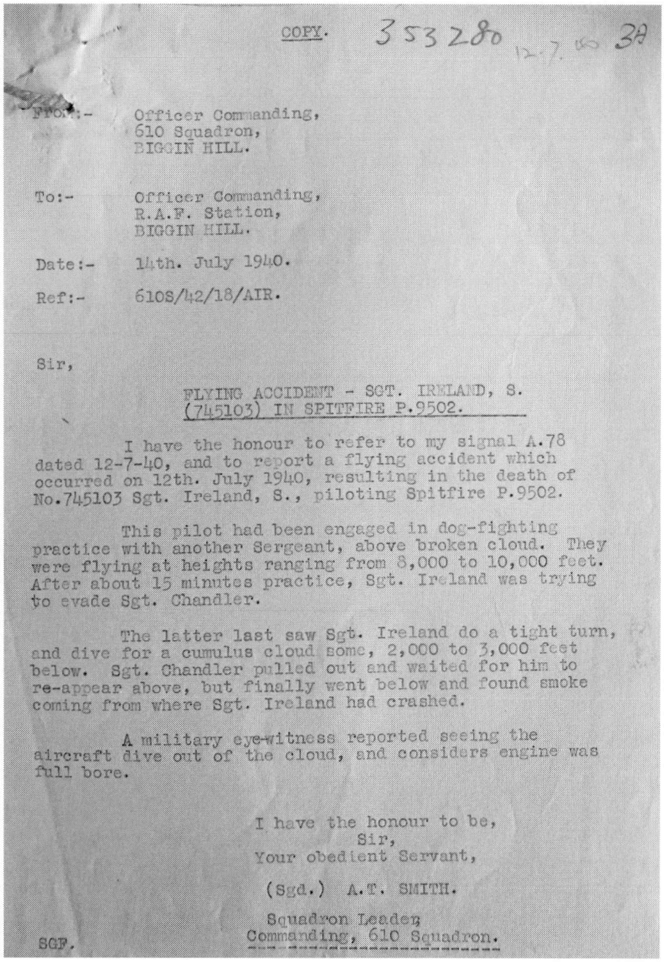

COPY. 353280 12.7.40 3A

From:- Officer Commanding,
610 Squadron,
BIGGIN HILL.

To:- Officer Commanding,
R.A.F. Station,
BIGGIN HILL.

Date:- 14th. July 1940.

Ref:- 610S/42/18/AIR.

Sir,

FLYING ACCIDENT - SGT. IRELAND, S. (745103) IN SPITFIRE P.9502.

I have the honour to refer to my signal A.78 dated 12-7-40, and to report a flying accident which occurred on 12th. July 1940, resulting in the death of No.745103 Sgt. Ireland, S., piloting Spitfire P.9502.

This pilot had been engaged in dog-fighting practice with another Sergeant, above broken cloud. They were flying at heights ranging from 8,000 to 10,000 feet. After about 15 minutes practice, Sgt. Ireland was trying to evade Sgt. Chandler.

The latter last saw Sgt. Ireland do a tight turn, and dive for a cumulus cloud some, 2,000 to 3,000 feet below. Sgt. Chandler pulled out and waited for him to re-appear above, but finally went below and found smoke coming from where Sgt. Ireland had crashed.

A military eye-witness reported seeing the aircraft dive out of the cloud, and considers engine was full bore.

I have the honour to be,
Sir,
Your obedient Servant,

(Sgd.) A.T. SMITH.

Squadron Leader
Commanding, 610 Squadron.

SGF.

S/Ldr Smith's report to his CO at Biggin Hill, on the tragic events surrounding Ireland's death. It had been a particularly ghastly experience for Sgt Chandler. (*TNA, AIR 81/2386*)

the impressive country house is set in the rolling countryside of the North Downs, typical of Surrey, with herds of cows, water features and a walled kitchen garden. The beauty of the place belied the fact that the Irishman tragically met his death on the estate. It is hard to imagine that the Spitfire with the letters 'DW-Q' emblazoned on its fuselage in the famous photos of 610 Squadron on patrol (see p. 192), had ultimately taken young Sydney Ireland to his death.

While the less experienced pilots were undergoing these training flights, the operational pilots were busy carrying out patrols. On 12 July, the first took off at 0800 hours. Another convoy was steaming through the Channel off Dover and Blue, Green and Red Sections were ordered to provide cover for it, led by F/Lt Ellis as Blue Leader. The rest of the formation was as follows, Litchfield and Brian Smith being the other probable section leaders:

DW-O.	R.6595	F/Lt. J. ELLIS.	Blue 1	31
DW-Q.	P.9545*	Sgt. ARNFIELD, S. J.		33
DW-J.	N.3284	Sgt. RAMSAY, N. H. D.		12
DW-T.	R.6765	P/O. P. LITCHFIELD.	Green 1	40
DW-P.	R.6695	F/O. F. T. GARDINER.		8
DW-H.	L.1044	F/Lt. E. B. B. SMITH.	Red 1	46

Above left: The excavation of Sgt Ireland's Spitfire. (*Copyright After the Battle*)

Above right: Sgt Ireland sowing his precious 'Wings' on to his uniform, having achieved his goal of becoming a pilot. (*Copyright Holmes, Sky Spy, p. 52*)

DW-A.	R.6976	F/O. P. G. LAMB.	34
DW-F.	R.6694	Sgt. HAMLYN, R.	21

*Arnfield was almost certainly flying DW-Q, P.9502, with Ireland's crash coming later in the day. P.9545 had only joined 610 Squadron on 11 July, so it is likely this aircraft became DW-Q, following the loss of P.9502.

The Spitfires patrolled at 10,000 feet for about thirty minutes, before landing safely. At 1530 hours, the same three sections took off to patrol Dover again at 10,000 feet, the pilots and probable section leaders being:

DW-T.	R.6765	P/O. P. LITCHFIELD.	Green 1	41
DW-L.	P.9496	Sgt. ELSE, P.		19
DW-P.	R.6695	F/O. F. T. GARDINER.		9
DW-O.	R.6595	F/O. P. G. LAMB.	Blue 1	35
DW-N.	R.6806*	Sgt. ARNFIELD, S. J.		34
DW-M.	P.9540	Sgt. RAMSAY, N. H. D.		13
DW-H.	L.1044	F/Lt. E. B. B. SMITH.	Red 1	47
DW-J.	N.3284	Sgt. TANNER, J. H.		13
DW-A.	R.6976	Sgt. PARSONS, C. A.		5

*DW-N which replaced L.1075 should possibly be P.9512, at least until 14 July, when it was possibly damaged.[16] Adhered to ORB listing until then.

The three sections returned to base without incident at 1635 hours. It had been a frustrating day for the pilots. They had lost a colleague without encountering the enemy, something which would have rammed home just how dangerous their daily lives were—a moment's aberration and you could kill yourself, regardless of the *Luftwaffe's* activity.

The following day, 13 July, was strikingly similar, with a fruitless patrol of the Dover Straits between 1210 and 1320 hours. Blue and Green Sections were ordered off to investigate an 'X' raid which failed to materialise. F/Lt Ellis led the patrol with the following pilots:

DW-O.	R.6595	F/Lt. J. ELLIS.	Blue 1	32
DW-J.	N.3284	Sgt. RAMSAY, N. H. D.		14
DW-M.	P.9540	Sgt. ARNFIELD, S. J.		35
DW-T.	R.6765	P/O. P. LITCHFIELD.	Green 1	42
DW-L.	P.9496	Sgt. ELSE, P.		20
DW-P.	R.6695	F/O. F. T. GARDINER.		10

What these patrols made clear, is that the pilots had been split into their two flights, some regularly flying in the same section, to ensure familiarity with each other and to make the Squadron a cohesive fighting unit. F/Lt Ellis, F/O Warner and P/O Litchfield were regularly Blue and Green Section leaders, with, as occurred here, Sgts Ramsay and Arnfield making up Blue Section and Sgt Else and F/O Gardiner forming the remainder of Green Section and the regular members of 'B' Flight. The same can be said for Red and Yellow Sections of 'A' Flight, whose pilots usually involved S/Ldr Smith, F/Lt Smith, P/O Norris and F/O Lamb as section leaders, supported by P/Os Pegge and Keighley, and Sgts Parsons, Tanner and Hamlyn. These pilots were the core of the Squadron, and although there were inevitably exceptions, the remainder spent most of their time training and preparing to fill-in when needed. Unfortunately, the uneventful patrol was not the only similarity with the previous day, as another fatality occurred in relation to the Squadron.

After this patrol had landed, a Sgt Patrick Ian Watson-Parker, flying Spitfire R.6807, was killed in a crash at Skid Hill, Tatsfield near Biggin Hill, at approximately 1505 hours. Over the ensuing decades, Watson-Parker came to be associated as a 610 Squadron casualty in numerous publications, the CWGC listing him as a 610 Squadron pilot adding even more credence to this belief. However, some equally formidable sources do not believe that Watson-Parker belonged to 610 Squadron. For example, he is not listed under 610's fallen while operating from the aerodrome on the Biggin Hill Chapel memorial, or the Battle of Britain Memorial at Capel-le-Ferne. Equally, there is no mention in 610's ORB of Watson-Parker having joined 610 Squadron, or his Spitfire, R.6807—despite the irregularities in the ORB, it is unlikely that they would both have been omitted. There was clearly some debate as to which unit Watson-Parker belonged to and what he was doing flying a Spitfire at Biggin Hill. This is a story I wanted to resolve.

Watson-Parker was educated at King's Mead School, Seaford and then at Dover College, The Dover War Memorial Project's website stating that, 'Patrick Watson-Parker died delivering a Spitfire to 610 Squadron at Biggin Hill on 15 July 1940, six months after his brother Derek. Patrick is no longer credited as one of "The Few" as he had not flown operationally'.[17] Despite some factual inaccuracies, the interesting theory that he may have been operating as a ferry pilot, delivering new Spitfires to 610 Squadron, arises as a distinct possibility, being loaned for this duty from his own unit, 263 Squadron. A family tragedy also comes to the fore, given that he had lost his brother just under six months earlier. The founder of The Dover War Memorial Project, Marilyn Stephenson-Knight, confirmed that the Watson-Parker brothers were 'Old Dovorians', being remembered on the Dover College Memorial. Maggie helpfully put me in touch with Dover College's Colonel (Retd) Philip Barry, who was equally informative, providing some interesting background snippets about Patrick Watson-Parker and his family, collated in 1971 for the Dover College Centenary Register.

Patrick's father, George, born on 26 July 1891, attended The School House between 1906 and 1907, fought in the Great War as a captain, married in 1917, and survived the two sons who followed him through Dover College. He died on 2 November 1966. Patrick Ian Watson-Parker was born on 28

January 1918, and after attending King's Mead School, he joined Priory House at Dover College between 1931 and 1934. He was athletic, playing for the first XV, was in the running team, and was even Junior Victor Ludorum. The register note for Patrick ends with him as a sergeant in the RAFVR, being killed on active service in July 1940. The actual date is unspecified as there was no record of his unit or how he was killed. His younger brother, Derek, was born on 19 September 1919, and after King's Mead School, followed his father through The School House at Dover College between 1933 and 1936, before he too become a sergeant in the RAF. He was killed on active service on 31 January 1940, an unimaginable blow for their parents to come to terms with.[18]

Patrick Watson-Parker joined up with the VR as an AC 2 on 4 April 1938, four years after leaving school, being promoted to sergeant the following day, aged twenty. He carried out his flying training during the ensuing sixteen months, before brief spells with 111 and 605 Squadrons on Hurricanes, between 1 August 1939 and 11 October 1939, when he joined 263 Squadron along with five other 605 Squadron pilots. 263 Squadron had formed on 2 October 1939, was equipped with the obsolete Gloster Gladiator and was based at Filton, Bristol (TNA, AIR 27/1547/1). Just eight days after joining 263, Watson-Parker suffered a severe accident:

> 21 Oct.—Sergeant Pilot WATSON-PARKER (741433) met with flying accident in Gladiator aircraft K.6145, whilst flying in the very near vicinity of the Severn Bridge, Nr. Lydney, Glos. The aircraft wing-tip struck the surface of the water whilst carrying out a turn. Pilot swam ashore and admitted to Lydney Hospital with facial injuries and exhaustion. Aircraft exploded and sunk in 30ft. of water. (TNA, AIR 27/1547/1)

This was a terrifying experience for Watson-Parker, his recovery period of four months being indicative of how serious the crash had been and how fortunate he was to have survived. He finally returned to 263 Squadron in late February 1940. The Squadron was sent to Norway operating Gladiators in April 1940, to provide air cover to Allied forces, but was eventually withdrawn. Its aircraft and many personnel were lost in the sinking of HMS *Glorious* on 8 June. 263 Squadron then reformed in late June at Drem, being intended to operate the Westland Whirlwind (TNA, AIR 27/1547/1).

There is no mention of Watson-Parker during the first operation to Norway in April. However, 263 Squadron's ORB does mention him travelling from Glasgow on 12 May, arriving in Skole, Norway, on 18 May. Interestingly, he was part of the main party under the command of a former 610 Squadron pilot, F/O William Riley, on the SS *Sobiesti* (TNA, AIR 27/1547/1). There is no mention of Watson-Parker during the Norwegian operations, but he made it back to Britain safely, 263 Squadron ending up at Grangemouth near Edinburgh. Barely two months later, the young sergeant was dead and there is a certain mystery surrounding his death, given it took place in a Spitfire, a few miles from Biggin Hill. There is a belief that at some stage between his return from Norway and his death, he had been detached to 5 OTU, before being loaned to 6 MU, to deliver new Spitfires from Brize Norton to operational squadrons such as 610 Squadron. He had remained a member of 263 Squadron though, as 263's ORB indicates in the following report, highlighting its role at Grangemouth and Watson-Parker's sudden death: 'During the month of July considerable progress was made in the task of reforming and re-equipping the Squadron after its return from Norway. The task was no light one. Many changes were made in personnel and the Squadron was unfortunate in losing three of its pilots (Pilot Officers Bell and Downer and Sgt. Watson-Parker) as the result of flying accidents' (TNA, AIR 27/1547/1). The note for 13 July confirmed the accident took place near Biggin Hill. Another source which suggests Watson-Parker was flying the Spitfire as a ferrying trip, is Spitfire R.6807's service history, the Spitfire having arrived at 6 MU on 25 June 1940: 'On delivery to 610 Sqn, stalled in Biggin Hill circuit and spun into ground, Skid Hill House, Tatsfield, Kent, Cat 3', on 13 July.[19] All this evidence points to the likelihood that Watson-Parker was indeed ferrying a new Spitfire to 610 Squadron, and that he was still a 263 Squadron member, not a 610 Squadron pilot.

Fortunately, one of the AMCB files which was released at the end of June 2017, just in time for this publication, was that of Patrick Watson-Parker. Numerous documents indisputably confirm that he was not a 610 Squadron pilot, as shall be seen, while they shed some more light on a very sad story. The most remarkable piece of information revealed in the file, is that this fatal flight was Watson-Parker's first experience in a Spitfire. In one document, it is listed as his 'first flight' and in another that he had just one hour's flying time on the Spitfire, as opposed to 205 hours solo on all types. It seems inconceivable that this should be the case, given the obvious risks involved. S/Ldr Smith's Flying Accident report provides an excellent description of each aspect of this tragic story (see photo below).

In paragraph two, it is clear that Watson-Parker was attached to 5 OTU, Aston Down, Gloucestershire, where he was on a twin-engined conversion course, presumably in preparation for flying the Westland Whirlwind with 263 Squadron. It confirms that he had been loaned to 6 MU, to deliver the Spitfire, while paragraph three provides the details surrounding the crash. Smith's concluding paragraph, about another pilot delivering a Spitfire at the same time, who was unable to stop the engine upon landing, is also astonishing. That precious Spitfires were being risked in this way is one thing, but that irreplaceable pilots were expected to risk their lives while uncertain even of the basic controls, is hard

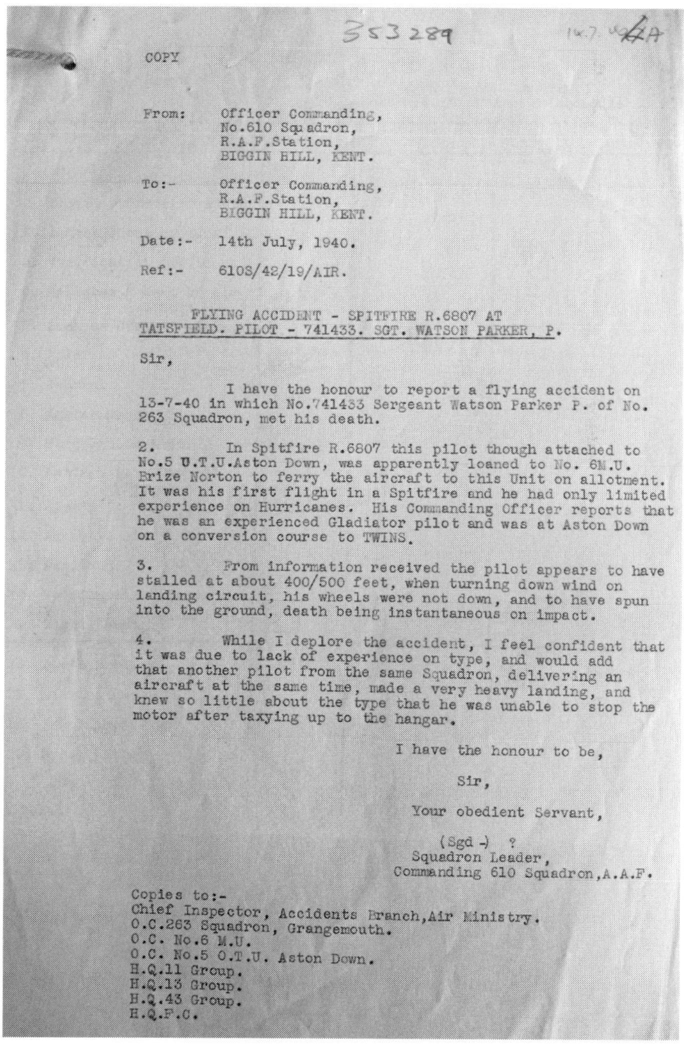

COPY

From: Officer Commanding,
No.610 Squadron,
R.A.F.Station,
BIGGIN HILL, KENT.

To:- Officer Commanding,
R.A.F.Station,
BIGGIN HILL, KENT.

Date:- 14th July, 1940.

Ref:- 610S/42/19/AIR.

FLYING ACCIDENT - SPITFIRE R.6807 AT TATSFIELD. PILOT - 741433. SGT. WATSON PARKER, P.

Sir,

I have the honour to report a flying accident on 13-7-40 in which No.741433 Sergeant Watson Parker P. of No. 263 Squadron, met his death.

2. In Spitfire R.6807 this pilot though attached to No.5 O.T.U.Aston Down, was apparently loaned to No. 6M.U. Brize Norton to ferry the aircraft to this Unit on allotment. It was his first flight in a Spitfire and he had only limited experience on Hurricanes. His Commanding Officer reports that he was an experienced Gladiator pilot and was at Aston Down on a conversion course to TWINS.

3. From information received the pilot appears to have stalled at about 400/500 feet, when turning down wind on landing circuit, his wheels were not down, and to have spun into the ground, death being instantaneous on impact.

4. While I deplore the accident, I feel confident that it was due to lack of experience on type, and would add that another pilot from the same Squadron, delivering an aircraft at the same time, made a very heavy landing, and knew so little about the type that he was unable to stop the motor after taxying up to the hangar.

I have the honour to be,

Sir,

Your obedient Servant,

(Sgd -) ?
Squadron Leader,
Commanding 610 Squadron,A.A.F.

Copies to:-
Chief Inspector, Accidents Branch,Air Ministry.
O.C.263 Squadron, Grangemouth.
O.C. No.6 M.U.
O.C. No.5 O.T.U. Aston Down.
H.Q.11 Group.
H.Q.13 Group.
H.Q.43 Group.
H.Q.F.C.

S/Ldr Smith's illuminating account of the sad death of Sgt Watson-Parker. (*TNA, AIR 81/2389*) to comprehend. The decision to allow Watson-Parker to carry out this flight seems reckless, but also highlights the shortage of trained pilots at the time. A valuable Spitfire would not have been risked in such a manner, if more suitable pilots had been available to carry out the relatively short flight. 263's squadron leader added the cause of the crash diagnosis as, 'Error of judgment owing to inexperience on new type' (TNA, AIR 81/2389). His statement that the crash had, 'occurred in circumstances in which I had no knowledge or control', being detached from 263 Squadron (TNA, AIR 81/2389), possibly hints that he had no idea his pilot would be involved in such activity, as he lacked the necessary experience. Above all, the incident reflects the press-on attitude of Watson-Parker, in accepting the task of supplying 610 Squadron with a vital Spitfire, given his lack of experience on the aircraft.

Watson-Parker was buried on 18 July 1940, in a tranquil grave at St Peter and St Paul's Churchyard in Cudham, Orpington, Kent, Section N, Grave 24. Fittingly, amongst the burial party, were one officer and two sergeants from 263 Squadron. Although Watson-Parker may not have gained the coveted recognition of being one of 'The Few', his sacrifice, like so many others, was part of the bigger picture which enabled the Battle of Britain to be won.

Patrick Ian Watson-Parker's headstone in St Peter and St Paul's churchyard, Cudham, Kent. (*Author*)

11

14–25 July 1940: Channel Duels

On the next day, Sunday 14 July, 610 was sent on dawn patrol at 0400 hours, for ninety minutes. Blue and Red Sections had been ordered to cover a convoy off Eastbourne, with the squadron leader seemingly operating as Blue Leader for once. No enemy aircraft were sighted by the following pilots:

DW-M.	P.9540	S/Ldr. A. T. SMITH.	Blue 1	20
DW-L.	P.9496	P/O. P. LITCHFIELD.		43
DW-K.	P.9495	Sgt. ARNFIELD, S. J.		36
DW-H.	L.1044	F/Lt. E. B. B. SMITH.	Red 1	48
DW-S.	R.6621*	P/O. C. O. J. PEGGE.		13
DW-G.	L.1045	Sgt. PARSONS, C. A.		6

* As ORB, but DW-S should be N.3201 until 20 July when it was shot down, to be replaced by R.6621, which only joined Squadron on 24 July 1940.[1] I have adhered to ORB listing until then.

These patrols were extremely wearing, and Claude Parsons once again provides some general observations on carrying out this vital duty:

> Aerial attacks on convoys were becoming the rule, consequently we had the job of patrolling convoys fairly regularly. It's a binding job while there is nothing doing, just stooging up and down and getting more fed-up each run…The telephone rings: Would the Senior Officer speak to the Controller. He would be told there was convoy off Beachy Head and we had to supply one section to fly over it until 9 a.m., when the Hurricane squadron from the same aerodrome would take over from us. Off went the first section of three aircraft. I usually was in the first section and stooged along as economically as possible once we reached the convoy. We would fly over it first to let them see who we were, then proceed to introduce ourselves to each ship in turn. We would fly very low over and round the ships as they went on their zigzag courses. The crews would wave all manner of queer things to us. I remember on one particular occasion, from a deckhouse of a small ship emerged a very fat man in a pair of trousers and vest only. He put the bucket he was carrying on the end of a broom and started juggling. Others waved caps, shirts and any old thing they could get hold of. I used to think, "Poor devils down there, they must have a rotten life, what with torpedoes and bombs it can't be pleasant." Apparently they enjoyed the security, for each convoy would greet us in a similar way.[2]

Two items of interest from this description are the need for the pilots to carefully control the amount of fuel they consumed on such patrols, conserving it for any possible dogfight which may arise. Also, the shared responsibilities with the Hurricane squadron, usually 32 Squadron, which was a feature throughout the Battle—it was quite a partnership.

The quiet start to 14 July in no way reflected what was to come in the afternoon, when a Squadron scramble was ordered at 1450 hours, to patrol Hawkinge at 10,000 feet. A convoy, perhaps the one S/Ldr Smith and his men had been patrolling at first light, was being attacked by Ju 87 dive-bombers escorted by Me 109s. Twenty minutes later, 610 Squadron joined Hurricanes from 151 and 615 Squadron in combat with the enemy. S/Ldr Smith was at the head of the Spitfires with his experienced section leaders of Ellis, Lamb and Litchfield in the following formation:

DW-G.	L.1045	S/Ldr. A. T. SMITH.	Red 1	21
DW-S.	R.6621	P/O. C. O. J. PEGGE.		14
DW-J.	N.3284	Sgt. TANNER, J. H.		14
DW-K.	P.9495	F/Lt. J. ELLIS.	Blue 1	33
DW-Q.	P.9545	F/O. W. H. C. WARNER.		46
DW-N.	R.6806	Sgt. RAMSAY, N. H. D.		15
DW-A.	R.6976	F/O. P. G. LAMB.	Yellow 1	36
DW-D.	P.9503	P/O. G. KEIGHLEY.		30
DW-F.	R.6694	Sgt. HAMLYN, R.		22
DW-T.	R.6765	P/O. P. LITCHFIELD.	Green 1	44
DW-M.	P.9540	Sgt. ELSE, P.		21
DW-P.	R.6695	F/O. F. T. GARDINER.		11

The ORB noted how 'P/O. LITCHFIELD encountered 3.M.E.109s at 10,000 feet off DOVER. The E/A dived to 3,000 feet', while Litchfield himself described the encounter in detail:

> At 15.15 hours, 610 Squadron, in Vic formation, with Green Section on the left, was approaching the north of Dover, when the leader's attention was drawn to three or more aircraft diving very steeply in line astern from approximately 18000' and passing to the right rear of the squadron which was then at 15000'. Section leaders put their sections into aircraft astern and wheeled to starboard. As I turned, I saw at least two and perhaps more Messerschmidt [Messerschmitt] 109s over the land below proceeding east and then turning south, at a height of perhaps 8000'. I told my section that they were 109s and dived steeply on to their tails, almost blacking out as I pulled out. Nos. 2 and 3 did black-out and lost the target. I attacked one Me 109 as he crossed the coast; his evasive tactics consisted of diving and climbing, but after the third burst he dived steadily and at the fourth there was a burst of flame and then smoke covered the target, leaving only the wing tips visible. At this, a second 109 came to his assistance, and received two good bursts and was last seen climbing away to France with smoke coming from his tail (although this may have been normal exhaust gases). I then set off back to my base. (TNA, AIR 50/172/48)

Litchfield provides a fascinating overall picture of the engagement, including the Squadron's tactics of patrolling in 'Vics' at 15,000 feet and adopting the more flexible line astern formation on spotting the Me 109s, plus his section's attack on the 109s. There is a real sense of the chase over Dover in his description as he went all-out to catch the fast 109s. While his wingmen, Else and Gardiner, blacked out, he closed in on a 109, hitting it decisively from 200 yards, which sent the fighter down. He claimed the second 109 as damaged, honestly stating that the smoke might have just been exhaust gases, having fired a total of 2,400 rounds. The ORB also states that, 'Blue section sighted E/A which were dive bombing but no signs of any bursts were observed from 20,000 feet. E/A were lost to sight before being attacked. E/A destroyed:– 1. M.E.109', seeming to neglect Litchfield's second claim.

It appears that John Ellis's Blue Section had been left as top cover at 20,000 feet, and perhaps as a result of this could not engage the *Stukas*, while Litchfield's Green Section, some 5,000 feet lower, had been able to engage the enemy escort. The lack of information makes it hard to establish what happened, where the different Spitfires were stationed, and who was actually engaged in the dogfight. This reflects the confusing nature of all aerial combat, where the action was a flurry of swirling aircraft, before the sky cleared and individuals tried to return home, relieved at having survived. However, on this occasion, witnesses to the events were watching thousands of feet below on the cliffs of Dover, among them by chance the BBC radio reporter Charles Gardner, whose report survives to this day:

> Well now the Germans are dive-bombing a convoy out at sea. There are one, two, three, four, five, six, seven German dive-bombers, Junkers 87s. There's one going down on its target now. Bomb! No! He missed the ships, he hasn't hit a single ship. There are about ten ships in the convoy, but he hasn't hit a single one … There, you can hear our anti-aircraft going at them now … They come in absolute steep dives, and you can see their bombs actually leave the machines and come into the water. You can hear our own guns going like anything now … I can hear machine gunfire, but I can't see our Spitfires. They must be somewhere there. Oh! Here's one coming down now. There's one coming down in flames! Somebody's hit a German and he's coming down with a long streak! He's coming down completely out of control … a long streak of smoke … The pilot's baled out by parachute! He's a Junkers 87, and he's going slap into the sea and there he goes! Smash! Terrific column of water and there was a Junkers 87. There was only one man got out by parachute, so presumably there was only a crew of one in it.
>
> Now, then, oh, there's a terrific mix-up now over the Channel! It's impossible to tell which are our machines and which are the Germans … There's a fight going on, you can hear the little rattles of machine gun bullets! Crump! That was a bomb, as you may imagine! Here comes, there's one Spitfire. There's a little burst. There's another bomb dropping … Oh, and it missed the convoy! You know, they haven't hit the convoy in all this! The sky is absolutely patterned now with bursts of anti-aircraft fire, and the sea is covered with smoke where the bombs have burst. But as far as I can see there is not one single ship hit, and there is definitely one German machine down … Well, that was a very unsuccessful attack on the convoy, I must say …
>
> You can't watch these fights very coherently for long. You just see about four twirling machines and you hear little bursts of machine-gun and by the time you've picked up the machines … they've gone … oh whoops, there's a dogfight going on up there … Now, hark at the machine guns going! Hark! One, two, three, four, five, six—now there's something coming right down on the tail of another … Yes, they are being chased home! And how they are being chased home! There are three Spitfires chasing three Messerschmitts now. Oh, boy! Look at them going … Oh, that is really grand! And there's a Spitfire just behind the first two. He'll get them. Oh, yes! Oh, boy! I've never seen anything so good as this! The RAF fighters have really got these boys taped. Our machine is catching up the Messerschmitt now. It's catching it up! It's got the legs of it, you know. Now right in the sights. Now, go on, George! You've got him! Boom, boom! No, no, the distance is a bit deceptive from here. You can't tell. But I think something definitely is going to happen to that first Messerschmitt!
>
> Erh … yes … just a moment, I think I wouldn't like to be in that first Messerschmitt. I think he's got him. Yes? Machine guns are going like anything. Oh, there's another fight going on .. .Yes, they've got him down, too. I can't see … Yes, I think that first Messerschmitt has been crashed on the coast of France all right.[3]

Given the life and death struggle being described, Gardner's report can make for uncomfortable listening (and reading), as the style of reporting is more suited to a football fixture, clearly inappropriate when describing an aircraft being shot down. Reporting on a dogfight which was taking place thousands of feet overhead, made it very difficult to identify friend from foe. Far from the aircraft being a Ju 87 which had smashed into the English Channel, it was actually a 615 Squadron Hurricane and it was this aircraft's unfortunate pilot who landed in the Channel. Tragically, P/O Mudie had been shot down by the escorting Me 109s and despite being rescued, died the following day having been badly burned. It gives Gardner's account of the 'German' aircraft's demise a very sobering reality.

Remarkably from 'Dog Rose' Squadron's point of view, the latter stages of the report were basically a running commentary on Green Section's three Spitfires chasing the 109s, then P/O Litchfield's final pursuit. Again, Gardner's description has the feel of a commentary on a sporting event, Litchfield's Spitfire having 'the legs' of the ill-fated 109, before Gardner imagined himself in the Spitfire's cockpit, willing on its pilot—'Now right in the sights. Now, go on, George! You've got him! Boom, boom!'[4] Despite the report's style (and countless people wrote in condemning its delivery), it is a remarkable first-hand account of Litchfield's victory, with the radio crew visualising the sights and even the sound of the machine guns which the Messerschmitt succumbed to, before it crashed on the French coast. When listening to the report, it is hard not to get caught up in the excitement of the chase and forget about the lives at stake. Many people approved of Gardner's style as it boosted morale, listeners believing they were German machines going down, with many of the public glad to hear it in the contemporary situation. This is reflected by north Londoner A. C. Fisher: 'to me it was inspiring, for I felt that I was sharing in it, and I rejoiced unfeignedly that so many of the enemy were shot down, and that the rest were put to ignominious flight. My uplift of heart was due to a better understanding, which the BBC enabled me to get, of the courage and daring of our pilots….'[5] While 615 Squadron had engaged the *Stukas*, preventing any ships from being hit and P/O Mudie had paid the ultimate sacrifice, 610 Squadron took on the escort and chased them off, Litchfield bravely pressing home his attack all the way across the Channel. Various sources agree that Litchfield's victims belonged to 8 *Staffel* (equivalent of a Squadron) of JG 3, as highlighted in *Then and Now*:

8/JG3

Messerschmitt Bf 109E-1. Crashed near Boulogne after engagement with No. 610 Squadron off Dover 3.20 p.m. Severely damaged by P/O. Litchfield. Pilot baled out wounded. Aircraft a write-off.

Messerschmitt Bf 109E-1. Damaged in attack by P/O. Litchfield of No. 610 Squadron during combat over the Channel off Dover 3.20 p.m. Returned to Wissant. Pilot unhurt. Aircraft 40% damaged.[6]

Despite twelve Spitfires of 610 Squadron being involved in this patrol, it is unusual that only Peter Litchfield registered any claims, but he was clearly establishing himself as a very competent pilot on the Squadron. With two confirmed victories over Dunkirk and an unconfirmed bomber to his name already, he could now add to his tally with a 109 destroyed and another damaged from today's patrol. On their return to Biggin Hill around 1615 hours, the Squadron would undoubtedly have been elated at Litchfield's success, but most of all, they would have been relieved that all twelve Spitfires had returned unscathed.

The following day, Biggin Hill's ORB reported that the, 'PM visits station'. Churchill would have been fascinated to hear the latest exploits of the sector station's home squadrons and it is likely Churchill met the pilots of 32 and 610 Squadrons and probably chatted to 'The Chesters' about their recent dogfight. There is no record of operational flying taking place on 15 July, due to another spell of bad weather which limited *Luftwaffe* operations. Indeed, 610 Squadron's next recorded operation came on Thursday 18 July, when the inclement weather had slightly improved, although there was still considerable cloud and showery spells in the south-east. As a result of this improvement, 610 Squadron, operating from Hawkinge, was visited by another dignitary, His Royal Highness the Duke of Kent who inspected the airfield's defences (Hawkinge ORB). Hawkinge was a dangerous place for anyone to arrive at by air, let alone a member of the Royal family, its close proximity to the coast making it a popular target for German fighters and bombers to raid with the reasonable expectation of catching RAF aircraft unawares. The air-fighting raged around the south-eastern corner of Kent, causing it to gain the unenviable nickname of 'Hellfire Corner'. Thursday 18 July was no exception to the rule, and the Royal visitor possibly witnessed a Squadron scramble by 610, with F/Lt Brian Smith leading twelve Spitfires off at 0937 hours to investigate and intercept, 'E/A reported to be approaching RAMSGATE from between CALAIS & DUNKIRK' (ORB), involving the following pilots:

DW-F	R.6694	F/Lt. E. B. B. SMITH.	Red 1	49
DW-J.	N.3284	Sgt. TANNER, J. H.		15
DW-A.	R.6976	Sgt. CHANDLER, H. H.		2
DW-O.	R.6595	F/O. W. H. C. WARNER.	Blue 1	47
DW-P.	R.6695	F/O. GARDINER.		12
DW-V.	P.9330	Sgt. RAMSAY.		16
DW-S.	R.6621	P/O. S. C. NORRIS.	Yellow 1	39
DW-D.	P.9503	P/O. C. O. J. PEGGE.		15
DW-G.	L.1045	Sgt. PARSONS.		7
DW-T.	R.6765	P/O. P. LITCHFIELD.	Green 1	45
DW-K.	P.9495	Sgt. ARNFIELD, S. J.		37
DW-L.	P.9496	Sgt. ELSE, P.		22

Brian Smith had a rare opportunity to lead the whole Squadron with both S/Ldr Tom Smith, and John Ellis from 'B' Flight perhaps entertaining the Duke of Kent. Brian must have been proud as eleven Spitfires followed him in a steep climb inland to gain height, before heading out to intercept the enemy. The Spitfires made a very impressive sight, engines snarling as they climbed in formation, the pilots anxiously juggling their throttles while trying to maintain a good lookout. However, Smith would have been concerned about the weather conditions which he led his men into: 'Cloud in three layers at 3,000, 6,000 and 10,000 feet' (ORB). This could provide perfect cover for any stalking Messerschmitt fighters waiting to pounce, which unsurprisingly there were, in the form of nine to twelve Me 109s of 5/JG 51.

The Spitfires encountered the enemy fighters at, '6,000 feet over Channel about 10 miles from French coast at 1000 hours. Very little fighting took place owing to abundance of cloud cover, and only two pilots fired, both without visible effect. One aircraft was seen to go straight down into the sea' (ORB). Which two RAF pilots opened fire remains unclear due to the lack of combat reports, however, one of the German pilots who opened fire that day was an ace with a growing reputation, 'Hauptmann [Hptm.] Horst 'Jakob' Tietzen, the Staffelführer of 5/JG 51 and a contemporary and disciple of Werner Molders'.[7] His aim had again proven deadly, his victim this time being the young pilot officer who had been doing so well, Peter Litchfield, ambushed in the clouds by the highly-experienced German. It seems that at least one of Litchfield's comrades saw his Spitfire fall into the Channel without him baling out, at about 1000 hours, off St Margaret's Bay, ten miles from the French coast (TNA, AIR 81/1140).

Various sources report that Litchfield was flying Spitfire DW-T, P.9452, proving that the ORB was erroneous when it reported he was flying DW-T, R.6765. This is confirmed in Litchfield's AMCB file, which states definitively that he was flying P.9452 (TNA, AIR 81/1140). The ORB's inaccuracy in terms of recording the aircraft involved on each patrol, is quite a problem. But as Raymond Ellis noted, it is easy to see how such inaccuracies arose: 'The squadron was in action several times a day from either Biggin Hill or Hawkinge. Often the 'rest' between landing and take-off was only that required for re-arming and re-fuelling. Sometimes the 'turn-around' was so hectic that the clerk later admitted that the accuracy of the record of pilots and 'planes taking part in an operation could not be guaranteed'.[8] The flying battle casualty report confirms the details of the combat, particularly the heavy cloud cover which enabled Litchfield to be bounced. Litchfield was in the process of leading Green Section against one small group of enemy fighters, when he came under attack from another group of 109s. Given the conditions, he possibly did not even realise he was under attack, but the aircraft that Green 3, either Arnfield or Else, saw crash into the Channel, must have been DW-T, P.9452. Tom Smith's report (see photo p. 230), written two days after the event, offered no hope of Peter Litchfield having survived.

The now all too familiar process of contacting the next of kin swung into action, but it was far from straightforward to pass on the tragic news. Litchfield's mother, Mrs Mildred Mary Howard Brown,

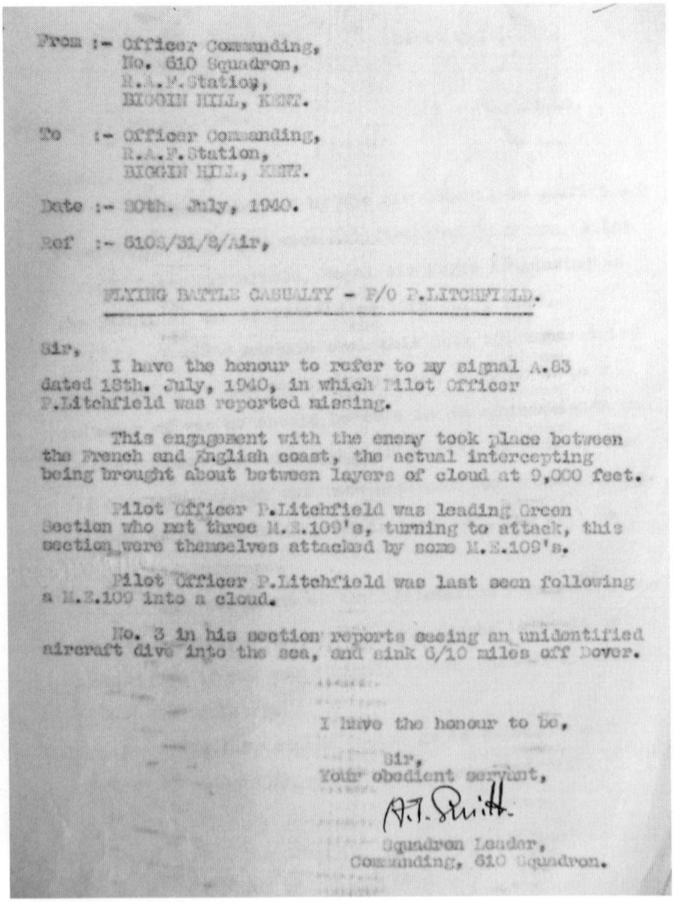

From :- Officer Commanding,
No. 610 Squadron,
R.A.F. Station,
BIGGIN HILL, KENT.

To :- Officer Commanding,
R.A.F. Station,
BIGGIN HILL, KENT.

Date :- 30th. July, 1940.

Ref :- 610S/31/8/Air,

FLYING BATTLE CASUALTY - P/O P.LITCHFIELD.

Sir,

I have the honour to refer to my signal A.83 dated 18th. July, 1940, in which Pilot Officer P.Litchfield was reported missing.

This engagement with the enemy took place between the French and English coast, the actual intercepting being brought about between layers of cloud at 9,000 feet.

Pilot Officer P.Litchfield was leading Green Section who met three M.E.109's, turning to attack, this section were themselves attacked by some M.E.109's.

Pilot Officer P.Litchfield was last seen following a M.E.109 into a cloud.

No. 3 in his section reports seeing an unidentified aircraft dive into the sea, and sink 6/10 miles off Dover.

I have the honour to be,
Sir,
Your obedient servant,
A.T. Smith.
Squadron Leader,
Commanding, 610 Squadron.

S/Ldr Smith's report on the loss of Litchfield. (*TNA, AIR 81/1140*)

was believed to live in southern France, in apartment K. Villa Ophelia, 13 Avenue Shakespeare, Nice, but given the situation in France since the German invasion, this was clearly far from certain. After attempts to reach his mother proved fruitless, on 7 August 1940 the Air Ministry tried to contact his older brother, Mr H. Litchfield (possibly a flight lieutenant), of Belmont Cottage, West Glen Road, Kilmacolm, Renfrewshire; thankfully they were more successful. Five days later, the missing pilot's brother responded that he was unsure of his mother's whereabouts, but to keep him informed of any developments. Then on 19 September 1940, Litchfield's mother contacted the Air Ministry, requesting further information, as she was now in Lisbon having taken refuge there, although nothing new could be sent to her.

As the months passed, no news came to light about Litchfield. Six months after Litchfield went missing, his mother sent another sad response from Portugal to the Air Ministry, confirming that she had not heard any news of him, since a letter from him in mid-June, when the Squadron was based at Gravesend (TNA, AIR 81/1140). She must now have feared the worst. 610 Squadron's adjutant and Litchfield's brother both agreed that there was no news of him, and his brother appears to have been the unfortunate family member who had to collect Peter's belongings, something which was usually done when, 'death has been presumed for official purposes' (TNA, AIR 81/1140). Finally on 17 February 1941, seven long months after the news was first received by his family, the Air Ministry sent out another letter, confirming that it had now concluded that P/O Peter Litchfield had lost his life on 18 July 1940.

The twenty-five year old from Croydon, who had been with the unit just over seven months, is remembered on the Runnymede Memorial, Panel 9. Litchfield's sacrifice is also recalled just across the

This plaque is placed above the front door of a house on a development near Biggin Hill. (*Author*)

road from his former aerodrome at Biggin Hill, where roads and some housing on a new development have been named after pilots from the Sector Station. Peter Litchfield is remembered by '1–4 Litchfield Lodge', and a commemorative plaque to his sacrifice, on Curchin Close (see photo above). It is a fitting and lasting memorial to Litchfield and so many others like him, who paid the ultimate sacrifice.

Peter Litchfield's loss would have been felt acutely amongst the Squadron, as he was one of the more gifted pilots in terms of being a good *fighter* pilot. He had survived the initial dangers over Dunkirk, was frequently the first to sight the enemy and was on his forty-fifth recorded patrol since 10 May. Also, he had 610's highest number of claims against the enemy so far, three aircraft destroyed, one unconfirmed and one damaged. The Squadron had lost one of its most promising members and another experienced section leader needed to be replaced. This was evidence of the fighter pilots' vulnerability, how even those with more of a fighter pilot's instinct and seemingly a knack of always coming back, could fall victim to the preying *Luftwaffe* fighters. The German pilots were frequently much more battle-hardened, and given the opportunity, would pick off RAF fighters at will when they operated on their 'free-hunts', with altitude and surprise on their side.

At Hawkinge, if it coincided with the timing of his visit, the Duke of Kent would have noticed that only eleven Spitfires returned, landing at 1108 hours, another brave pilot having died in the Channel. Litchfield had fallen to a very experienced *Luftwaffe* pilot in Hptm. Horst Tietzen, who had claimed several victories in the Spanish Civil War, Litchfield probably being his tenth victim of the Second World War. Remarkably, the two pilots had possibly been within range of each other's guns during the combat on which the BBC radio reporter Gardner had reported. The Hurricane which was shot down and led to the death of 615 Squadron's P/O Mudie, has been attributed as a partial claim of Tietzen. This would not be the last time that the German locked horns with 'The Chesters' either, in his Me 109 marked with the *Gruppe's* famous crying bird image and the belligerent 'Gott strafe England' slogan.

The following day, Friday 19 July, the Squadron's first recorded patrol came at 1255 hours. Blue and Green Sections were ordered to patrol Hawkinge with Blue Leader, S/Ldr Smith, at the head of 'B' Flight:

DW-O.	R.6595	S/Ldr. A. T. SMITH.	Blue 1	22
DW-K.	P.9495	Sgt. ARNFIELD, S. J.		38
DW-L.	P.9496	Sgt. ELSE, P.		23
DW-Q.	P.9545	F/O. W. H. C. WARNER.	Green 1	48
DW-P.	R.6695	F/O. F. T. GARDINER.		13
DW-V.	P.9330	Sgt. RAMSAY, N. H. D.		17

During the one hour and twenty-five-minute patrol which included a Channel sweep off Dymchurch, no enemy aircraft were encountered and the Spitfires returned to base at 1420 hours. 610 was not ordered up again until early evening, this time nine Spitfires led by F/Lt Ellis:

DW-O.	R.6595	F/Lt. J. ELLIS.	Blue 1	34
DW-K.	P.9495	Sgt. ARNFIELD, S. J.		39
DW-E.	R.6629	Sgt. PARSONS.		8
DW-N.	R.6806	F/O. W. H. C. WARNER.	Green 1	49
DW-P.	R.6695	F/O. F. T. GARDINER.		14
DW-V.	P.9330	Sgt. RAMSAY, N. H. D.		18
DW-F.	R.6694	F/Lt. E. B. B. SMITH.	Red 1	50
DW-H.	L.1044	Sgt. HAMLYN, R.		23
DW-A.	R.6976	Sgt. CHANDLER, H. H.		3

They patrolled Beachy Head as instructed, but after 40 minutes returned to base at 1940 hours, once again without having encountered any enemy aircraft.

On Saturday 20 July, 610 Squadron at some stage carried out the twenty-minute trip to their forward base at Hawkinge, a flight also carried out by 32 Squadron, at 1245 hours (32 Squadron ORB). However, 610 Squadron was not called to action until 1745 hours, when nine Spitfires of Red, Blue and Green Sections (only nine recorded, although 11 Group's ORB appendices states there were ten Spitfires), were ordered on patrol under the command of John Ellis. The Squadron's disposition was as follows:

DW-H.	L.1044	F/O. P. G. LAMB.	Red 1	37
DW-S.	R.6621	P/O. G. KEIGHLEY.		31
DW-A.	R.6976	Sgt. CHANDLER, H. H.		4
DW-O.	R.6595	F/Lt. J. ELLIS.	Blue 1	35
DW-K.	P.9495	Sgt. ARNFIELD, S. J.		40
DW-L.	P.9496	Sgt. TANNER, J. H.		16
DW-N.	R.6806	F/O. W. H. C. WARNER.	Green 1	50
DW-P.	R.6695	F/O. F. T. GARDINER.		15
DW-V.	P.9330	Sgt. RAMSAY, N. H. D.		19

The Squadron was operating in tandem with 32 Squadron, to cover a convoy in the Dover Straits, as 32 Squadron's ORB noted: 'Area 10 miles E. of Dover. At 1752 hours with 610 Squadron, intercepted a raid on convoy, consisting of 30 109s, Ju.87s and ME Jaguars. About 50 in all', the 109s belonging to JG 51. Due to the Spitfire's higher performance capabilities, the powers-that-be at Fighter Command HQ realised that it made tactical sense to pit the Spitfire against the dangerous *Luftwaffe* fighters, the Me 109s more so than the Me 110s. The German bomber formations would then be left to the slower, but equally effective Hurricane, which was a much better gun platform and could take a lot more punishment than its more glamorous fighting partner. While the bombers remained a prime target for Spitfires, and the Hurricanes were more than a match for the 109 in an experienced pilot's hands, the leaders in each squadron understood the key role they were required to play if the situation arose. Wg Cdr Brian Smith still recalled fondly the Hurricane squadron they frequently operated with: '32 Squadron, they flew Hurricanes at Biggin Hill with us, or we were with them, they were a regular squadron. They were very good to us, their attitude was we were to draw off the fighters, you know, and the Hurricane boys went in as they could'. With this edict fresh in the pilots' minds, it is clear from 610 Squadron's ORB that 610 was primarily operating against the escorting Messerschmitts:

> At 1800 hours, 4 pilots saw an attack taking place on a convoy off FOLKESTONE. Green 2 attacked a Me.109 and saw smoke coming from it. Red section saw 6 Me.109s, near FOLKESTONE, and climbed inland towards ASHFORD to attack out of the sun. Turned and attacked 3 Me.109s, which had followed, but did not appear to damage any E/A.

It seems that Blue and Green Sections had attacked the first group of enemy fighters, and in this engagement Green 2, possibly F/O Gardiner, was able to damage a 109. Meanwhile, Red Section, unusually led by F/O Lamb, probably left as cover to 'B' Flight, noticed a different formation of 109s, which Lamb tried to get into a position to attack. In the hectic dogfight, he was forced to lead his wingmen against three other 109s which had followed them. Red Section did not make any claims, but did lose an aircraft.

One of Lamb's wingmen, P/O Keighley, was attacked by the 109s, he was hit by a bullet in the leg and shrapnel in the shoulder and his aircraft was left out of control. Keighley, aged twenty-eight, had to bale out and landed at Lydden, less than five miles inland of Dover, while his Spitfire crashed at Wootton, just over three and a half miles away (TNA, AIR 81/1164). Keighley had already experienced the hazards of baling out of a Spitfire during the Dunkirk evacuation, and would have been glad at least to be landing on *terra firma* instead of the English Channel, as he had on 31 May. It must have been a terrifying experience as the Messerschmitt's fire devastated his aircraft's tail, shooting away the controls to such an extent that it is believed it removed the Spitfire's tail section, although this may have been after it went into a terminal spin. Either way, he was very fortunate to escape. His son, Jo Keighley, believes his father immediately realised his dire situation and got out very quickly, as it would have been too difficult to parachute from a spinning Spitfire. The usual report filed by the

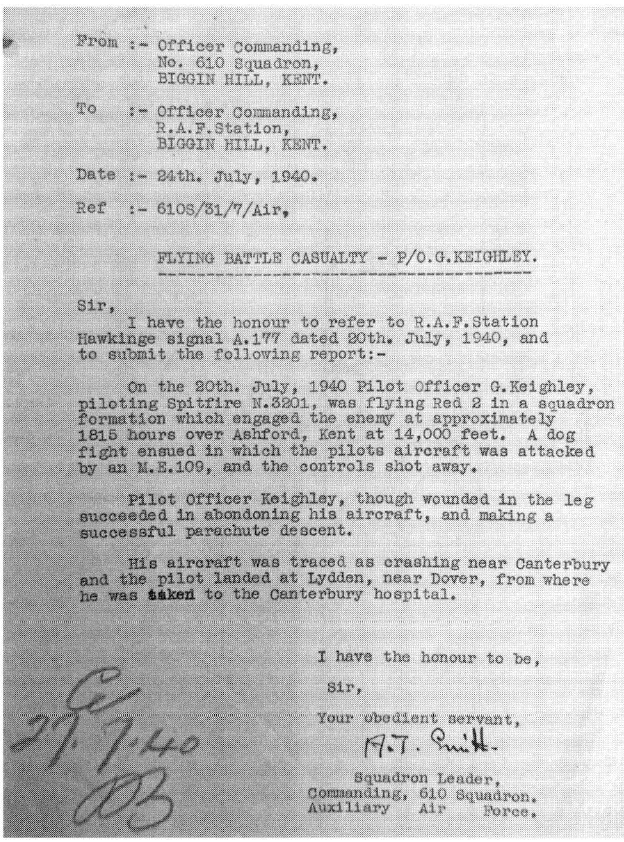
From :- Officer Commanding,
No. 610 Squadron,
BIGGIN HILL, KENT.

To :- Officer Commanding,
R.A.F.Station,
BIGGIN HILL, KENT.

Date :- 24th. July, 1940.

Ref :- 610S/31/7/Air,

FLYING BATTLE CASUALTY - P/O.G.KEIGHLEY.

Sir,

I have the honour to refer to R.A.F.Station Hawkinge signal A.177 dated 20th. July, 1940, and to submit the following report:-

On the 20th. July, 1940 Pilot Officer G.Keighley, piloting Spitfire N.3201, was flying Red 2 in a squadron formation which engaged the enemy at approximately 1815 hours over Ashford, Kent at 14,000 feet. A dog fight ensued in which the pilots aircraft was attacked by an M.E.109, and the controls shot away.

Pilot Officer Keighley, though wounded in the leg succeeded in abondoning his aircraft, and making a successful parachute descent.

His aircraft was traced as crashing near Canterbury and the pilot landed at Lydden, near Dover, from where he was taken to the Canterbury hospital.

I have the honour to be,
Sir,
Your obedient servant,
A.T. Smith.
Squadron Leader,
Commanding, 610 Squadron.
Auxiliary Air Force.

27.7.40

P/O Keighley was flying as Red 2, at 14,000 feet, when he was forced to bale out. (*TNA, AIR 81/1164*)

P/O Geoffrey Keighley. (*Copyright http://www.bbm.org.uk/Keighley.htm*)

Squadron's CO explains what happened officially (see photo p. 233). Once again, it is clear that the ORB had recorded Keighley's aircraft incorrectly; it was DW-S, N.3201 not R.6621.

It is likely that Keighley fell victim to the accurate shooting of *Oberfeldwebel* Schmid of 1/JG 51,[9] in the Squadron's latest run-in with this *Luftwaffe* unit, which had killed P/O Litchfield two days earlier. This was Schmid's seventh victory, although the twenty-seven year old had little more than two weeks to live, being lost in the English Channel on 5 August, having claimed two more RAF aircraft.[10] By chance, Keighley's plight was probably witnessed by Mary Smith, the daughter of the postmaster in Elham, who kept a diary of events of that fateful summer—this forms the basis for *Harvest of Messerschmitts*, still one of the most interesting books written on the Battle of Britain. Her entry for this day reads, 'Swoop of machine-gun fire almost overhead at 6.30 p.m. The plane crashed at Denton. Saw pilot descend by parachute over Adam & Eve'.[11] Although at least ten aircraft seem to have been damaged or destroyed in the engagement, and it could have been another pilot, it is very likely that she had seen the descent of Geoffrey 'Peter' Keighley, as this happened at 1830 hours too, while Denton and Wootton are very close. In a remarkable coincidence, Jo Keighley recalled the following incident, when he visited his father's crash site with Dave Brocklehurst from the Kent Battle of Britain Museum, who had dug the site in about 1985: 'Arriving there at dusk with my youngest son, we met a gamekeeper by chance and he had seen my father shot down when aged about six and led him back to his mother's house!'

Keighley had flown his last flight as a fighter pilot and Jo Keighley told me his father went to recover from his leg and shoulder injuries in hospital in Devon. It seems that when he came out of hospital he was classed as non-effective sick at Biggin Hill, until rejoining 610 again on 7 October 1940 (ORB). This was Keighley's seventh recorded patrol in July, four of which had involved combat with the *Luftwaffe*. He had also taken part in seven patrols over Dunkirk, two of which involved combat with the enemy, along with a dunking in the Channel, so he was an increasingly combat-experienced pilot. He had served with 610 since early 1939, and was another face which would be missed around the dispersal area.

Apart from Keighley, the remaining pilots all returned home safely, the only claim they made being the possible enemy fighter damaged by 'Green 2'. 32 Squadron's Hurricanes landed at the same time,

The ground crew became attached to 'their' Spitfire, just as much as the pilots. Here, Alf Bridson, poses next to one of 610's Spitfires with its very distinctive fuselage markings. Given these markings, there is a possibility this was the Spitfire from which P/O Keighley baled out on 20 July 1940. (*Copyright 610 Squadron Association*)

having had a more eventful time of it, with numerous claims filed against Me 109s and Me 110 'Jaguars'; five unconfirmed, four damaged along with one Ju 87 confirmed. 32 Squadron left Hawkinge between 1910 to 1940 hours (32 ORB), making the twenty-minute flight back to Biggin Hill. It is most likely that 610's men returned to Biggin Hill at a similar time. 'Jaguar' was a name used by RAF pilots for bomb-carrying Me 110s. A small number of prototype Messerschmitt Bf 162 light bombers with a glazed nose for a bomb aimer, called 'Jaguars', had been made for the *Luftwaffe*, although German propaganda exaggerated their numbers. As a result, RAF pilots frequently mentioned in combat reports that 110s carrying bombs were 'Jaguars', when they were really standard Me 110s. It is interesting to note how easily the best laid plans went out of the window in the heat of battle, as most of 32 Squadron's claims were against fighters as opposed to the bombers it was hoped the Hurricanes would have taken on.

No recorded operational patrols were flown on Sunday 21 July and just one patrol by Red Section took off at 0930 hours on Monday 22 July, the three pilots being:

DW-H.	L.1044	F/O. P. G. LAMB.	Red 1	38
DW-E.	R.6629	P/O. S. C. NORRIS.		40
DW-G.	L.1045	Sgt. PARSONS, C. A.		9

They escorted a Blenheim which was testing the effectiveness of the RDF system at varying heights and ranges from RDF stations on the south-east coast. Although the Blenheim would have been a tempting target for any German fighters in the area, none were encountered during the course of an hour and forty-five minutes. F/O Lamb led his section back to base without incident. While the patrol was uneventful, it was an important job, due to the critical nature of RDF in the defence of Britain's airspace. Any gaps or technical issues needed to be spotted and fixed as quickly as possible.

On the following day, the Squadron flew no recorded patrols, but things got much busier on Wednesday 24 July, when the Squadron had two engagements with the *Luftwaffe*, which have subsequently caused much confusion. It seems that 610 Squadron flew down to Hawkinge in the early morning to replace 32 Squadron. The Hurricane squadron had been at the forward airfield since dawn and had already carried out two convoy patrols, returning to Biggin at 0840 hours (32 ORB). At 1112 hours, nine Spitfires led by 'B' Flight's commander John Ellis, were ordered to patrol Dover at 12,000 feet, as follows:

DW-O.	R.6595	F/Lt. J. ELLIS.	Blue 1	36
DW-M.	P.9540	Sgt. ARNFIELD, S. J.		41
DW-N.	R.6806	F/O. D. S. WILSON.		1
DW-Q.	P.9545	F/O. W. H. C. WARNER.	Green 1	51
DW-L.	P.9496	Sgt. ELSE, P.		24
DW-R.	K.9931	Sgt. RAMSAY, N. H. D.		20
DW-A.	R.6976	F/Lt. E. B. B. SMITH.	Red 1	51
DW-D.	P.9503	Sgt. CHANDLER, H. H.	Red 2	5
DW-X.	R.6630	Sgt. PARSONS, C. A.	Red 3	10

Thanks to the RDF system, F/Lt Ellis and his men ran into an enemy fighter formation ten miles south of Dover, as Ellis stated in his combat report:

> I was leading three Sections of 610 Squadron on a patrol at 12,000' off Dover on 24/7/40. We took off at about 1115. At 1130 I sighted three Me 109s three thousand feet above us and flying West in the opposite direction to us. As I had to use full throttle to catch the e/a the remaining two Sections got left behind. The formation of 109s broke up on being attacked and I singled out one of them. I opened fire at 200yds on the first burst and he immediately rolled on to his back and dived vertically, he then pulled out and proceeded to climb practically vertically. He carried out this manoeuvre four times and each time I got in a good burst while he was climbing. Throughout these evolutions bluish—white smoke was coming from a point about a foot from each wing tip. On his final climb I got in a good burst of roughly 5 seconds from dead astern, the Me. 109 suddenly belched forth clouds of black and white smoke, turned on its back and spiralled down in a vertical dive. It looked to be completely out of control. I followed the burning a/c down until it entered a cloud at 3000' still going down almost vertically. F/O Wilson & Sgt. Arnfield saw this e/a go down. (TNA, AIR 50/172/21)

Ellis had used 2,650 rounds of ammunition, with the German pilot desperately flying to save his life, but Ellis's experience enabled him to stay with the 109 despite the violent series of dives and climbs executed by its pilot. Ellis could claim this 109 as destroyed (his third confirmed victory, along with two shared destroyed), because his wingmen, Arnfield and Wilson, witnessed its demise. This possibly meant they managed to stay with their leader throughout the dogfight, enabling the flight commander to concentrate on bringing the enemy fighter down, knowing his tail was protected. If so, Arnfield and particularly Wilson, who despite his flying experience was on his first reported combat patrol, had done well to stay with their leader, who had suddenly put his throttle 'through the gate' in order to engage the Me 109s. This action caused Green and Red Sections to become separated from Blue Section, either due to a breakdown in communication, or perhaps they just could not catch up due to Ellis's head start.

Red Leader, Brian Smith made no mention of losing Blue Section, despite his action taking place five minutes later at 1135 hours:

> I was leading Red Section in Squadron Vic being on the port of the leading section, on a patrol S. of Dover at about 14,000 feet, when I sighted 9—12 Me 109 approaching head on slightly beneath in a wide open formation almost line abreast. I turned about and selected one a/c. A general dog fight then ensued in which I fired several short bursts into a Me 109 from astern.
>
> The e/a began to smoke heavily and dived vertically into a cloud out of control with blueish and black smoke pouring from it. I then broke away and picked an unidentified a/c latter [later] thought to be a Chance-Vought, into which I finished my ammunition without any apparent result. I then returned for a rearm and refuel. (TNA, AIR 50/172/71)

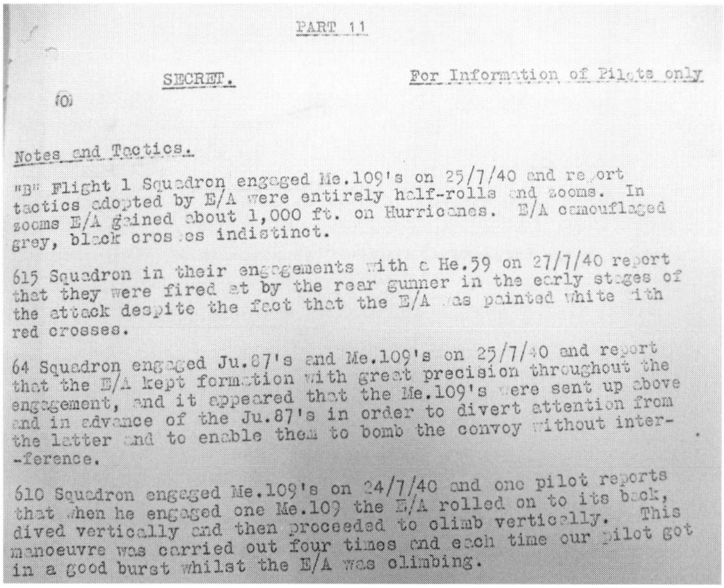

PART 11

SECRET.   For Information of Pilots only

Notes and Tactics.

"B" Flight 1 Squadron engaged Me.109's on 25/7/40 and report
tactics adopted by E/A were entirely half-rolls and zooms. In
zooms E/A gained about 1,000 ft. on Hurricanes. E/A camouflaged
grey, black crosses indistinct.

615 Squadron in their engagements with a He.59 on 27/7/40 report
that they were fired at by the rear gunner in the early stages of
the attack despite the fact that the E/A was painted white with
red crosses.

64 Squadron engaged Ju.87's and Me.109's on 25/7/40 and report
that the E/A kept formation with great precision throughout the
engagement, and it appeared that the Me.109's were sent up above
and in advance of the Ju.87's in order to divert attention from
the latter and to enable them to bomb the convoy without inter-
-ference.

610 Squadron engaged Me.109's on 24/7/40 and one pilot reports
that when he engaged one Me.109 the E/A rolled on to its back,
dived vertically and then proceeded to climb vertically. This
manoeuvre was carried out four times and each time our pilot got
in a good burst whilst the E/A was climbing.

A good example of how the pilots' combat reports would be used to inform HQ Staff about different *Luftwaffe* tactics and the RAF pilots' tactics employed to shoot them down. This reference to a 610 pilot is clearly John Ellis, from the description of the dogfight. (*TNA, AIR 25/197*)

Smith's aggressive flying paid off and he was able to claim the Me 109 as confirmed destroyed, because Red 2, Ray Chandler, saw the action, as noted in the ORB. The German fighter's fate had probably been decided by the fact that the flight lieutenant had carried out four or five short bursts of fire from 200 to just fifty yards range. This was his first confirmed victory along with two shared victories. The second aircraft he engaged, on which he used up his remaining ammunition, must have caused some confusion on his return, (he was still unsure about its identity when I met him): 'Possibly, I'm afraid I'm out on that, I don't remember a Chance-Vought'. At some stage, this mystery aircraft was at the centre of discussion with the intelligence officer, along with two other pilots who had encountered them. Smith's wingmen, Sgts Chandler and Parsons, also saw them, Chandler filing the following combat report against an aircraft he called a 'Dive Bomber. Possibly Chance Vought' in the pre-report description:

> Combat 10—15 miles South of Dover
> Enemy was sighted advancing head-on about 2000' feet below. I turned left 180° and dived below and attacked from underneath, allowing deflection. As range decreased, effect of fire became apparent, damage to enemy proved by pieces of aircraft falling off, and could see effect of fire. No return fire was noticed. I stalled and spun down through cloud. (TNA, AIR 50/172/11)

If this was a dive-bomber, perhaps the fighters that Smith intercepted were providing escort for them. Claude Parsons had witnessed the effect of Chandler's fire, and following their conversations on the ground, Chandler could claim a Chance-Vought as confirmed destroyed, his first confirmed victory. The ORB describes how Chandler:

> met 3 unidentified A/C below, wheeled round, and delivered a No. 2 attack and saw pieces falling away from E/A after closing to 30 yards. There was no return fire from E/A & Red 2 was convinced that E/A was out of control, his attack having been delivered against centre of E/A. Red 3 (Sgt. Parsons), confirms this, and says E/A was destroyed. This E/A was subsequently identified as a Chance Vought.

Three confirmed victories for no loss to the Squadron meant the patrol had been a great success, and the nine pilots must have returned to Hawkinge elated after the trials of the combat.

However, there is genuine confusion about the actual identity of the aircraft Red Section engaged, thought to be Chance-Voughts. Although Parsons's combat report is no longer available, the following extract from *Ten Fighter Boys* clearly refers to this engagement:

> A nice juicy bomber about to attack an isolated ship, down I go after him. I'm not the only one to have noticed it, another Spit. follows me down. We both hesitate before attacking. Never seen a German bomber like that before, better make sure it is a Hun. I break away to have a look at the markings. Sure enough, the black crosses were there. I recognise the machine as a French Chance-Vaught [Vought] bomber. We shoot it down into the sea between us. The other pilot turned out to be my Flight Commander [Brian Smith, author]. Another bit of information for the Intelligence Officer. The Huns are using French machines they have captured. Suddenly all is quiet. The battle is over…I am last back and getting quite a reputation for being the last home. My crew want to know what has happened. I delay a few moments and give them a brief outline. They appreciate that and set to work to get my plane ready in the shortest possible time. I join the other pilots and we have our customary excited chat about our last battle. The Flight Commander is talking to the Intelligence Officer about his attack on the French machine. I am able to assist him and make it known that I was with him when he attacked. We retire to the Dispersal Hut for refreshment. Our Intelligence Officer has ordered coffee to be sent up for us on our return. 'Good old Wallie' [almost certainly Walter Lloyd, author] comes simultaneously from all the pilots.[12]

It seems unusual for the *Luftwaffe* to have used captured French Chance-Voughts. Yet, if it was a dive-bomber, surely the three pilots could not have mistaken the all-too-familiar outline of the Ju 87, the *Luftwaffe's* dive-bomber? Parsons clearly states that care was taken to definitely identify it as an enemy machine, so it seems unlikely to have been an incident of 'friendly fire'. Nevertheless, some sources claim that this was the case, and that the aircraft engaged were actually, 'Blackburn Skua(s) of the Fleet Air Arm, attacked in error'.[13] Brian Cull, in his fascinating account of the seemingly endless number of 'friendly fire' incidents between 1939–1940, also believes the evidence from the combat reports and Parsons's writing point to another case of 'blue on blue', concluding that, 'The 'Voughts' were, in fact, Skuas of 808 Squadron up from RNAS Worthy Down on a training flight and one flown by Sub-Lt (A) Stuart Devonald … survived the subsequent crash-landing back at base, though suffering a leg injury. Possibly a second Skua was damaged in the incident'.[14] Adding further weight to this argument is Simon W. Parry, who notes in his excellent recent series on the daily action of the Battle of Britain:

> One of the most bizarre victory claims of the Battle of Britain was that made by Sergeant Chandler of 610 Squadron on 24th July for a 'Chance Vought 156'. It was assumed by RAF Intelligence that some of the 40 Chance Vought 156s supplied to the French Air Force had been pressed into service by the Germans due to a shortage of dive-bombers…In reality it seems that the 610 Squadron pilots may have run into a flight of Royal Navy Skuas, an aircraft which bore a strong resemblance to the American type.[15]

Nevertheless, in Ray Sturtivant's highly respected *Fleet Air Arm Aircraft 1939 to 1945*, there is no mention in the daily losses of a Blackburn Skua or Blackburn Roc having been shot down by Spitfires on 24 July, supporting the argument that the Squadron had not intercepted FAA aircraft.[16] Perhaps the fact that the 610 pilots noted black crosses on the aircraft indicates they had attacked German machines of some type, rather than friendly aircraft. Another examination of this incident will follow shortly, but it reflects the chaotic nature of dogfights, especially when large numbers of aircraft were involved.

While 610 Squadron had engaged the enemy over Dover, a convoy in the Thames Estuary attracted the attention of several large *Luftwaffe* fighter and bomber formations. 54 Squadron's Spitfires from Rochford and 'A' Flight of 65 Squadron from Manston, were ordered to intercept the raiders (54 and 65 ORBs). 54 Squadron's adjutant described the odds they faced, thus:

1125 For over an hour the whole Squadron took part in the "Battle of the Thames Estuary". 18 D.O. 215s escorted by at least two Squadrons of ME 109s and an unknown number of HE113s attacked a convoy in the Estuary. In this their biggest fight since the second day of DUNKIRK and in the face of these considerable odds, the casualties inflicted on the enemy by the Squadron (including three new pilots) can be considered eminently satisfactory and most encouraging. The ME109s engaged—at great cost to themselves—our fighters in an effort to enable the bombers to get at the convoy. 16 ME109s were disposed of in summary fashion. (54 ORB)

With hindsight, over-claiming was a real problem of aerial combat, due to the high speed at which the aircraft flew and the number of machines involved in the action. This meant that while one pilot felt he had shot down an enemy aircraft, there was nothing to stop somebody else moments later latching on to it to deliver what they thought was the *coup de grâce*, which could be repeated again, leaving three pilots to claim the aircraft which had actually been brought down, as happened with the claim of sixteen Messerschmitt 109s. 65 Squadron had also been in the thick of it, but they waded in slightly after 54 Squadron if the timings are accurate. 65 Squadron took off at 1200 hours, thirty-five minutes after 54 Squadron scrambled, while claiming one unconfirmed destroyed and seven damaged enemy aircraft (65 ORB). These reports certainly reflect the scale of the dogfight, and while this raged over the Thames Estuary, it was felt that these two squadrons needed further support.

Although there is no mention of a second patrol in 610's ORB, there are two more combat reports from 24 July, by the Squadron's ever-reliable flight commanders John Ellis (37) and Brian Smith (52), which record a patrol over Margate. It seems the Squadron adjutant or clerk must have failed to record who had flown on this patrol, as it occurred almost immediately after the first patrol had finished. The nine Spitfires had landed back at Hawkinge at around 1210 hours according to the ORB, the pilots flushed with their success. Thanks to 11 Group's ORB appendices, we know that 610 Squadron carried out a very quick turnaround between operations, and nine Spitfires of 'Dog Rose' Squadron, probably the same pilots in the same formation, were scrambled again less than fifteen minutes later, between 1230 and 1234 hours, to assist 54 and 65 Squadrons.

Ellis was leading the formation and the photograph of his handwritten account, gives an atmospheric description of the action, see p. 240.

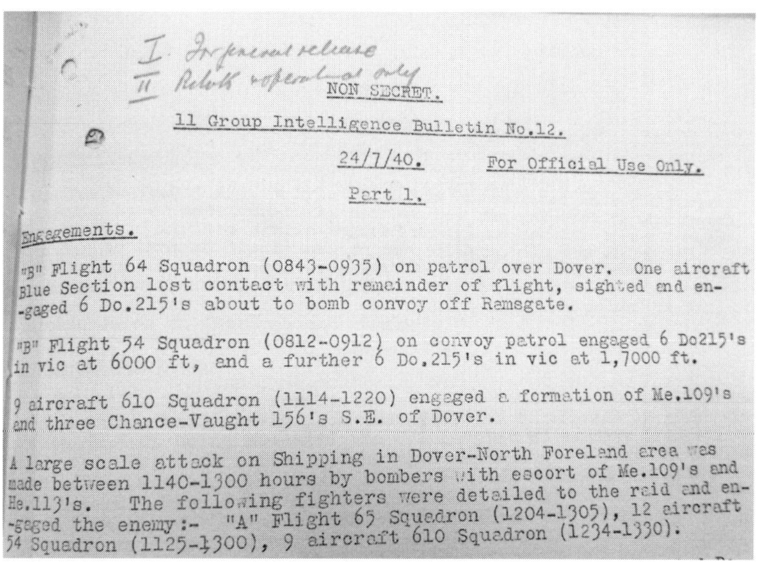

NON SECRET.

11 Group Intelligence Bulletin No.12.

24/7/40. For Official Use Only.

Part 1.

Engagements.

"B" Flight 64 Squadron (0843-0935) on patrol over Dover. One aircraft Blue Section lost contact with remainder of flight, sighted and en--gaged 6 Do.215's about to bomb convoy off Ramsgate.

"B" Flight 54 Squadron (0812-0912) on convoy patrol engaged 6 Do215's in vic at 6000 ft, and a further 6 Do.215's in vic at 1,7000 ft.

9 aircraft 610 Squadron (1114-1220) engaged a formation of Me.109's and three Chance-Vaught 156's S.E. of Dover.

A large scale attack on Shipping in Dover-North Foreland area was made between 1140-1300 hours by bombers with escort of Me.109's and He.113's. The following fighters were detailed to the raid and en--gaged the enemy:- "A" Flight 65 Squadron (1204-1305), 12 aircraft 54 Squadron (1125-1300), 9 aircraft 610 Squadron (1234-1330).

Whilst recording the times of the second engagement 610 Squadron took part in on 24 July, this extract adds weight to the belief that a small formation of 'Chance-Vaught 156's' had been intercepted earlier too. (*TNA, AIR 25/197*)

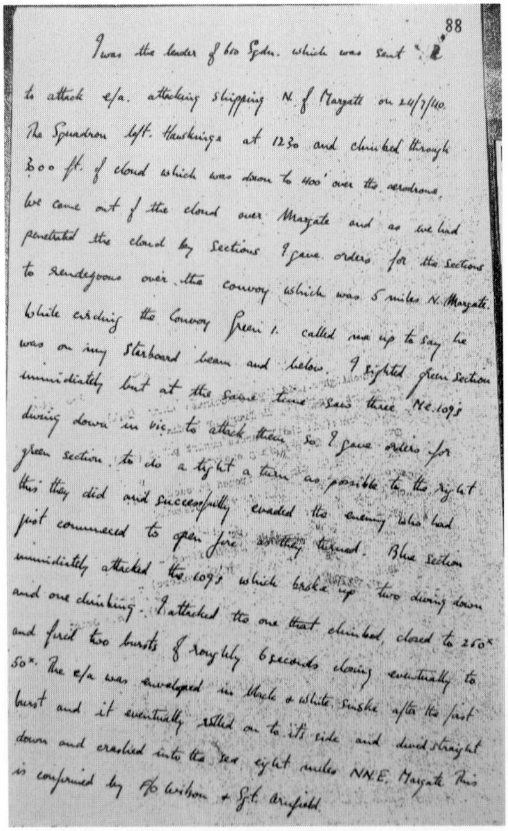

88

I was the leader of 610 Sqdn. which was sent to attack e/a. attacking shipping N. of Margate on 24/7/40.
The Squadron left Hawkinge at 1230 and climbed through 300 ft. of cloud which was down to 400' over the aerodrome.
We came out of the cloud over Margate and as we had penetrated the cloud by Sections I gave orders for the Sections to rendezvous over the convoy which was 5 miles N. Margate.
While circling the Convoy Green 1. called me up to say he was on my Starboard beam and below. I sighted Green Section immediately but at the same time saw three Me.109's diving down in vic. to attack them so I gave orders for Green section to do a tight a turn as possible to the right this they did and successfully evaded the enemy who had just commenced to open fire as they turned. Blue Section immediately attacked the 109's which broke up two diving down and one climbing. I attacked the one that climbed, closed to 250x and fired two bursts of roughly 6 seconds closing eventually to 50x. The e/a was enveloped in black & white smoke after the first burst and it eventually rolled on to it's side and dived straight down and crashed into the sea eight miles N.N.E. Margate. This is confirmed by P/O Wilson + Sgt. Arifield.

S/Ldr John Ellis's combat report from his second engagement on 24 July. (*TNA, AIR 50/172/21*)

This patrol highlights the efficient work of the ground crew, who had rearmed and refuelled the nine Spitfires in time to return to the fray—the work these men, like Raymond Ellis, performed should never be forgotten. Brian Smith fondly recalled how skilful and devoted the Squadron's ground crew were when I met him in 2011:

> The blokes who looked after the aeroplanes, they warmed up the engines, so that they were ready to go. You just went out and (whistle) off! But they were very good because, they all did a damned good job. They were from Lever Brothers, Shell, Prices' Candles, where they worked before the war. Proud men …

LAC Joseph Heaps, one of 610's engine fitters, would later reflect on the relationship between ground crew and pilot:

> Relations between pilots and ground crews were good, without too much formality, resulting in standards, which stood the test of combat well. In 1940 there was a tremendous sense of belonging to one's 'own' Fighter Squadron. Even ground-bound Fitters, Riggers, Armourers etc. worked with great enthusiasm, to allow 'their' pilots and aircraft to operate as effectively as possible.[17]

This patrol also shows the importance of the advance airfields on the coast; if the Squadron had needed to fly back to Biggin Hill, then they would have been too late to engage the enemy. Green Section, presumably led by F/O Warner as in the morning, were lucky to survive being bounced—they had Ellis's sharp eyesight and quick thinking to thank for their escape. Ellis was becoming a very efficient fighter pilot and leader, able to guide his men to safety, while simultaneously taking advantage of the situation to turn the tables on the attacking 109s. He closed in from 250 yards to fifty yards, expending 2,400 rounds of ammunition in two six second bursts, a hail of lead which hit the Messerschmitt 109 hard. Ellis's wingmen, Wilson and Arnfield, once again witnessed his foe crash into the sea and F/Lt Ellis had another Me 109E confirmed—now four confirmed enemy aircraft in total, plus two shared destroyed.

The second combat report on this sortie backs up Ellis, Brian Smith making the following comments:

> I was Red one astern of blue section on patrol over shipping N.E. of Margate. Red 2 and 3 had become detached whilst in cloud, I was therefore on my own. On looking round I saw a fourth section of 3 a/c which I knew to be e/a as they were diving on Green section. I immediately turned round and attacked one Me 109 into which I fired 4—5 short bursts when e/a disappeared to sight downwards apparently out of control. I then sighted another e/a painted light blue with black crosses with a hood over the fuselage similar to a Blackburn Skua. I approached from astern opening fire at 200 yds and extensively damaged his port wing seeing large pieces fall off but no fire. I then ran out of ammunition and returned for a rearm and refuel.
>
> E.B.B. SMITH. F/Lt.
>
> A/C thought to be a Chance—Vought Dive Bomber. (TNA, AIR 50/172/71)

Smith stated that this engagement took place ten miles north-east of Margate at about 1240 hours, and from 11 Group's ORB Appendices, he claimed an Me 109 probably destroyed and a Chance-Vought probably destroyed, expending all his ammunition in the two attacks which he started at 200 yards range. The Chance-Vought is again a surprise, although in the fraught circumstances of a dogfight, he may just have failed to recognise a Junkers 87, as he stated that the machine had black crosses on it, which would rule out any FAA aircraft. Once the pilots landed, and with no further patrols reportedly carried out on 24 July, they had the chance to discuss the 'mystery' aircraft, and probably

Results of Air Combats.

Squadron.	Time.	Enemy Aircraft Shot Down.	Own Casualties.
64 (1 aircraft)	0843-0935	1 Do.215 destroyed confirmed.	Nil.
610	1115-1218	2 Me.109 destroyed confirmed. 1 Chance-Vaught 156 destroyed confirmed.	Nil.
54	1125-1300	5 Me.109 destroyed unconfirmed. 9 Me.109 " probable	P/O Allen killed. Sgt.Collett wounded.
65	1204-1305	1 Me.109 destroyed probable 1 Me.109 damaged. 3 Do.215 damaged.	Nil.
610	1234-1330	1 Me.109 destroyed confirmed. 1 Me.109 " probable. 1 Chance-Vaught 156 destroyed probable.	Nil.
74	1721-1800	1 Do.215 damaged.	Nil.
	Totals =	5 destroyed confirmed 5 " unconfirmed. 12 " probable. 5 damaged.	

In addition Light A.A. guns at Dover Shot down one Do.215 at 1120 hrs.

Official claims by 610 Squadron during the two operations on 24 July 1940, making it a successful day. The scale of the dogfighting is self-evident, as is the over-claiming, which was inevitable in the heat of battle, the prime example being 54 Squadron claiming five Me 109s destroyed and a further nine probably destroyed! (*TNA, AIR 25/197*) decided amongst themselves that they had been facing Chance-Voughts. It is odd that several pilots saw them, particularly Smith who encountered them in two different raids.

Given the nature of these dogfights, where pilots had split seconds to recognise the aircraft around them while doing a multitude of other tasks, it is understandable that there was uncertainty over what they were facing. The news that 610 Squadron had encountered some unusual aircraft quickly filtered back to 11 Group HQ, as the following report on the Chance-Voughts can be found in 11 Group's ORB appendices:

> Chance-Vaught
>
> The Chance-Vaught 156, a type which was encountered on two separate patrols, is an American-built dive-bomber and was used by the French Air Force. It is a single-engined monoplane and its appearance is similar to that of the Blackburn Roc or Skua. It has one fixed machine gun in the wing firing forward, and one free machine gun firing from the observer's position. Those sighted by 610 Squadron are reported as being silver colour underneath, a darker colour on top, with black crosses on fuselage and wings. (TNA, AIR 25/197)

This document marked, 'Secret. For use of pilots only', shows how seriously the RAF took the report made by 610 Squadron's pilots. The detailed description was used to inform all pilots in Fighter Command of the potential of confronting them, preventing further confusion. If the Air Ministry suspected that 610 had mistakenly attacked friendly Skuas (which the Ministry would clearly have known about), it is unlikely that the RAF would have gone to such lengths to provide further details on a phantom machine. 'Friendly fire' incidents were a worryingly common feature of aerial combat in 1940 and the RAF carried out a court of inquiry into each occurrence. The pilot who had opened fire faced three options: a court martial, posting to another command or exoneration if the situation meant no blame could be placed on the pilot.[18] This would surely have been the case if 610 had fired on FAA aircraft, on two separate occasions. The evidence suggests that 610 Squadron had indeed encountered some Chance-Vought 156s or other German aircraft, rather than friendly aircraft.

There seems to have been real confusion over the years as to which German formations 610 Squadron had encountered, and where the fighting took place during these two patrols. Some sources believe 610 had intercepted JG 26's Me 109s, but the general weight of consensus agrees it was a formation of Me 109s of III/JG 52 on a patrol covering a formation of fighters and bombers, although they have been said to have been encountered both over **Dover**, in the **first** patrol, and over **Margate** in the **second** patrol. As Dennis Knight noted:

> Another battle developed over Dover, when III/JG 52 on a *Freie Jagd* (free hunt), grappled with 610 'City of Chester' Sqdn. up from Hawkinge. The fact that the Germans hadn't heeded 'Daddy' Molders' advice was reflected in their casualties. Hptm. Von Houswald, the Gruppen Kommandeur, Oblt. Fermer, Oblt. Ehrlich and Gefr. Frank were all sent into the Channel. When 'Big Bill' Smith's Spitfires returned to Hawkinge, there was wild excitement. F/Lt John Ellis had got three and F/Lt. Edward (Brian, author) Smith another.[19]

This is presumably in relation to the first patrol, although there is no mention here of Red Section's engagement with the mystery aircraft. Perhaps they had not intentionally shot down a Chance Vought or mistakenly a Skua, but another Me 109, one of the ones attributed to F/Lt Ellis, who certainly had not claimed three 109s. However, the fact that Chandler experienced 'no return fire' suggests it was a bomber-type aircraft he had engaged. It would make sense that 610's pilots were claiming three 109s as Oblt. Ehrlich was possibly shot down by 54 Squadron's Colin Gray, as shall be seen. This would leave the other three 109s as being one a piece for Ellis, Smith and Chandler, and a very successful engagement.

In James Holland's book on the Battle of Britain, he vividly brings to life the action from the point of view of the unfortunate JG 52 pilots, again over Dover, particularly Günther Rall, (although once again there is some confusion over the timings), as follows:

> A little after one o'clock, the Me 109s of 8/JG 52 took off from Coquelles airfield for their first operational flight to England …
>
> They met up with the Stukas and even at 160 mph they were nearing Dover in no time. Suddenly, without any warning at all, Spitfires of 610 and 54 Squadrons pounced upon them as the Stukas began bombing Dover and the shipping below. Günther saw Lothar Ehrlich, their *Staffel* commander, turn in towards the enemy, but then as aircraft and bullets filled the sky, it was all he could do to save his own skin …
>
> Somehow, Günther managed to extricate himself and make it back to Coquelles. Climbing down on to the ground, he joined some of the others who were already puffing on cigarettes and gesticulating wildly as they discussed the action. 'The Tommies caught us just as we had feared,' noted Günther, 'like proverbial clay pigeons.' None of them could understand how the Spitfires managed to find their formation in such poor weather and attack from such an advantageous position … As the minutes ticked by, hope began to fade. By evening the 7th Staffel commander, Herbert Fermer, and one of his pilots, Erich Frank, had been declared missing. So too had Wolf-Dietrich von Houwald, the *Gruppe* commander. Both von Houwald and Frank were washed up near Dunkirk a few days later. For Günther's 8th Staffel, there was a massive blow: their CO, Lothar Ehrlich, was also missing.[20]

This highlights RDF's role in enabling RAF fighters to find enemy formations. It also indicates that on their first patrol over the English coast, the 109s were for once at a disadvantage when facing the now battle-hardened men of units such as 610 Squadron.

Other accounts of the *Luftwaffe's* activity during this raid confirm the heavy casualties the escorting fighters suffered. John Weal's book on the Messerschmitt 109, supports the theory 610 had encountered III./JG 52, as follows: 'III./JG52 lost their Kommandeur equally quickly—on 24 July, only 48 hours after arriving at Calais–Coquelles from Berlin, *Hauptmann* Wolf Dietrich von Houwald and two of his *Staffelkapitäne* were all killed in a disastrous clash with No 610 Squadron Spitfires over Kent'.[21] *Then and Now* actually goes one step further by possibly crediting John Ellis with shooting down JG 52's third *Gruppe* Commander:

> **Stab III/JG52** Messerschmitt Bf 109E. Believed shot down into the sea by Flight Lieutenant Ellis of No. 610 Squadron during combat off Margate 11.35 a.m. Hptmn. Von Houwald (Gruppen Kommandeur) killed. Aircraft lost.
>
> **7/JG52** Messerschmitt Bf 109E. Failed to return to base following combat with fighters over Margate. Crashed in the sea. Oblt. Fermer killed. Aircraft lost.
>
> Messerschmitt Bf 109E. Shot down in combat over Margate and believed crashed in the Channel. Gefr. Frank killed. Aircraft lost.
>
> **8/JG52** Messerschmitt Bf 109E. Shot down by Pilot Officer Gray of No. 54 Squadron in combat off Margate 12.35 p.m and crashed in sea eight miles off-shore. Oblt. Ehrlich (Staffel Kapitan) baled out but missing. Aircraft lost.[22]

These same *Luftwaffe* casualties were suffered well to the north of Dover, being off Margate, and would have had to have been during the second patrol by 610 Squadron. Here, the loss of Oblt. Ehrlich is linked to Gray of 54 Squadron, but this would also tally with F/Lt Ellis's claim for an Me 109 in his second patrol, which he states took place 'eight miles NNE Margate', at a similar time. Simon Parry has JG 52 and JG 26's losses happening further to the north, by Margate, than 610's combat over Dover, and some fifty minutes later,[23] which coincides with 610's second patrol.

'The Chesters' did not carry out another recorded patrol during the rest of the day. During the two patrols, the pilots had made the following claims: Ellis with two Me 109s destroyed, Smith a 109 destroyed, one probably destroyed and an unknown/'Chance-Vought' probably destroyed, while Chandler could claim a fourth aircraft destroyed, most likely another 'Chance-Vought', with no losses to themselves which made for a very successful day's fighting. One thing that is certain is just how confusing aerial combat and recording the action that took place could be. Interestingly, the famous *Luftwaffe* pilot, Adolf Galland, flew his first combat patrol over the English Channel with III./JG 26 on 24 July 1940, and after the heavy fighting and losses suffered by the *Jägdwaffe*, he recalled: 'We were no longer in doubt that the RAF would prove to be a formidable opponent'.[24] The scale of these operations is also acknowledged in a message from AVM Park, recorded in the 54 Squadron ORB: 'Air Officer Commanding has read with great interest the combat report of No. 54 Squadron and congratulates the leaders and pilots on their magnificent fight against superior enemy numbers. He wishes 54 Squadron to know that No. 65 and No. 610 Squadron were also despatched to intercept the same raid and were also engaged with enemy fighters and bombers' (54 ORB). This congratulatory message served to assure 54 Squadron that although they may not have seen other RAF fighters and were outnumbered, they were certainly not on their own. Park's policy of attacking *Luftwaffe* raids with manoeuvrable single squadrons, instead of wings of three or four squadrons, was paying off.

The following day, Thursday 25 July 1940, threatened to be busy, due to a combination of fine, if hazy weather and another convoy, CW8 (Channel Westbound 8), bravely running the risk of passing through the English Channel's highly dangerous waters. Inevitably, CW8's twenty-one ships had already been observed by the Germans, and a huge dogfight developed before a massive formation of *Stukas* took a heavy toll on the convoy. 54 Squadron was scrambled at 1432 hours to engage the enemy between Deal and Dover, claiming an Me 109 destroyed, one probably destroyed and a third damaged, but lost an experienced pilot, P/O Allen DFC, in the process. 64 Squadron had also scrambled eleven Spitfires between 1445–1450 hours (54 and 64 ORBs).

While this battle was raging, 610 Squadron's pilots were sitting at dispersal, helplessly waiting to defend the convoy, which they could see was under heavy assault from their vantage point at Hawkinge. This indicates just how much of a forward base Hawkinge was. Today, one can see the coastal waters from the road which skirts the former aerodrome, now home to the excellent Kent Battle of Britain Museum, a lasting memorial to the dramatic events of the summer of 1940. In his combat report, John Ellis hinted that they could have been sent off to assist earlier, as, 'We could see the convoy being bombed before we were ordered to take off' (TNA, AIR 50/172/21)—it must have been highly frustrating. 610 Squadron was finally ordered up at 1458 hours, a critical eight minutes later than 64 Squadron.

Although S/Ldr 'Big Bill' Smith was flying one of the nine Spitfires which desperately sought altitude while closing with the enemy raiders, it was the more experienced fighter leader, John Ellis, who led 610 Squadron into the chaotic skies over convoy CW8. While Smith was a highly experienced pilot, Ellis's earlier comments about leading the Squadron in the air are true and it was testament to Tom Smith's character that he was open to admitting that his flight commander was better suited to leading his men in the air. Lesser men would have been too proud to acknowledge the fact and carried on regardless, but seeing Ellis's prowess, Smith put his trust in him not just to be more effective against the enemy, but to improve his own pilots' chances of survival. The following pilots were involved:

DW-N.	R.6806	F/Lt. J. ELLIS.	Blue 1	38
DW-L.	P.9496	Sgt. ELSE, P.	Blue 2	25
DW-O.	R.6595	F/O. F. T. GARDINER.	Blue 3	16
DW-A.	R.6976	S/L. A. T. SMITH.	Red 1	23
DW-J.	N.3284	P/O. S. C. NORRIS.	Red 2	41

DW-F.	R.6694	Sgt. PARSONS, C. A.		11
DW-B.	L.1009	F/Lt. E. B. B. SMITH.	Yellow 1	53
DW-G.	L.1045	Sgt. TANNER, J. H.		17
DW-X.	R.6630	Sgt. CHANDLER, H. H.		6

Ellis would have been Blue Leader, S/Ldr Smith probably Red 1 and F/Lt Smith probably Yellow 1. Each section leader had the usual two wingmen, although Norris in Red Section became separated from the formation during the scramble. On being ordered to defend the beleaguered convoy, Ellis would have instructed his men to push their throttles 'through the gate' in an attempt to engage the enemy aircraft as soon as possible. He described the ensuing action as follows:

> I was leading 610 Squadron which was sent off from Hawkinge at 1458 on 25/7/40 to intercept a raid on a convoy off Folkestone. We could see the convoy being bombed before we were ordered to take off and by the time we got to the convoy this particular raid had finished but it was followed immediately by another raid which consisted roughly of 20 Ju 87s and escorted by 15 Me.109. As 64 Squadron were below us I gave orders for 610 Sqdn. to attack the escorting fighters. We met the 109s head on and everybody broke up and a dog fight ensued. I attacked the leading Me.109 and in a fight lasting about 5 minutes I got in 4 or 5 short bursts at very close range. When I had finished my ammunition the e/a was definitely on fire, smoke and flames coming from the engine. I last saw the e/a doing a spiral towards the sea and obviously out of action. I was forced to stop following it down as I discovered 2 other Me. 109s on my tail. Blue three F/O Gardiner confirms that he saw this a/c burning & diving towards the sea. J. Ellis F/Lt. (TNA, AIR 50/172/21)

The raid's scale is self-evident, and although 610 Squadron was too late to attack the first enemy formation, as a result of Ellis's fast, direct approach to the convoy, they were in position to engage the subsequent wave of attackers just seven minutes after being scrambled. Ellis and his men had reached 'Angels 10' when the second raid came in and he was clearly aware of 64 Squadron below them in a position to attack the dive-bombers. This left 610 free to take on the escorts and give their comrades in 64 Squadron the best chance possible of preventing the bombers from hitting the shipping. It appears Ellis had singled out an experienced pilot, as it was unusual for a combat to last so long; the fact that this was the leading 109 would also suggest the German was a veteran. Ellis expended all his ammunition, having fired short bursts from 200 to fifty yards, despite being a good deflection shooter. The desperate evasive action of the 109 pilot suggests he was a very competent flyer but, in the end, Ellis's dogged pursuit and marksmanship took their toll. He claimed the 109 as destroyed, due to the smoke and flames coming from the engine, which both of his wingmen verified. While John Ellis clung to the tail of his wily opponent, he came under attack himself from the German pilot's vengeful comrades, evidence of the frantic nature of this dogfight, and he broke off his pursuit. It was a precarious situation to be in without any ammunition, but Ellis was wise enough, despite his drained senses, not to follow his opponent right down, which probably saved his life. He landed back at Hawkinge elated, but exhausted.

Two more of the surviving combat reports from this engagement come from the other pilots in Blue Section, one already mentioned as having witnessed the destruction of their leader's target; Sgt Else, Blue 2, and F/O Gardiner, Blue 3. The twenty-three-year-old Peter Else was flying directly behind his flight commander:

> I was flying No. 2 position in Blue section when we sighted about 20 or more ME109s above about 12 JU 87. We climbed in line astern to attack the ME and fired at one with considerable deflection with no result. I then had to shake off one ME 109 off my tail which I did with comparative ease with

> a tight diving turn. I then found myself on the edge of the melee and slightly on the starboard rear beam of two ME 109s flying in line astern.
>
> I attacked the rear machine from the quarter closing to astern opening fire at 200 yds and closing at [to] about 25 yds. I could see the explosive bullets from my guns hitting him in the rear of the fuselage and the tail unit.
>
> As I broke off the attack owing to the danger of hitting him he fell on one side evidently from the attitude the machine had adopted, out of control. Both ME109s took no evasive action at all, as I caught them both by surprise. The ME109s were definitely working in pairs.
>
> I also saw one ME 109 shot down by F/Lt Ellis. (TNA, AIR 50/172/23)

Despite the height advantage enjoyed by the German fighters, Ellis's direct approach had worked and Else got off a sharp burst of fire which failed to have an effect, before being forced to concentrate on saving himself due to the inevitable attention of another Me 109. It is interesting to note that by entering a tight diving turn, Else lost the enemy fighter with relative ease, something which would have given him (along with his fellow pilots whom he would have been quick to inform), confidence in his aircraft over that of his opponent. Else turned the tables once again on the enemy by surprising a *Rotte* (tactical section of two aircraft) of 109s—he closed in to just twenty-five yards range, to increase the effectiveness of his bullets, hitting the fighter with four seconds of fire, approximately 200 rounds from each machine gun. Despite the superior visual awareness enjoyed by the *Luftwaffe's* fighter pilots due to their flying formations, they were still vulnerable to the bounce if approached carefully. Peter Else did well to bravely press home his attack, being able to claim an Me 109 destroyed unconfirmed. Also, despite his own trials, he noticed the demise of Ellis's 109, which must have happened sometime after the initial pass.

In the meantime, Frederick Gardiner described how, five miles south of Dover:

> Six ME 109s were encountered at about the same height as ourselves (10,000 ft) flying in two sections of three in vic. Blue section was in line astern but was ordered to break up on nearing E/A. I turned left and in an attempt to get a target did one or two high speed stalls, before a ME 109 placed itself directly in front of me at about 150 yds. After two bursts of about five seconds each, the fuselage of the E/A was obscured by smoke. I then had to break away because of an E/A on my tail. I did not see the damaged A/C crash. My A/C was hit in several places, one or two rounds passing through the cockpit, from bottom to top, grazing my left arm. The A/C was flown back to Biggin Hill but was unserviceable operationally. (TNA, AIR 50/172/28)

This account gives a slightly different impression of the enemy formation, describing six 109s flying in two 'Vics' of three, as opposed to the pairs referred to by Else. Also, being ordered to break, possibly by members of the Squadron following on behind who saw the counter-attack coming from other 109s, was not mentioned by Ellis or Else. These subtle differences are interesting, as they demonstrate how frenzied the dogfights were. Different things stood out for different pilots in the sudden rush of adrenaline and activity, as aircraft became embroiled in lethal combat. Gardiner threw his Spitfire around violently to escape the attentions of the attacking 109, and also to bring his guns to bear on the 109s that Blue Section had initially engaged. Luck was with Fred Gardiner, as an enemy aircraft presented itself at almost point blank range, and his ten seconds of fire split between two bursts, apparently caused enough damage to allow him to claim the Me 109 as an unconfirmed destroyed. He could not confirm the claim because in the cut and thrust of combat, as he tried to apply the *coup de grâce*, another Messerschmitt pilot had him in his sights. An accurate burst of cannon and machine gun fire forced Gardiner to break off his attack, and he was injured by a couple of bullets grazing his arm, which must have been a terrifying experience. The shells passed from the bottom to the top of his cockpit and would have felt like unexpected hammer blows through his aircraft and body. Just as his concentration was focused on the 109 in front of him, his first claim of the war, he suddenly shifted focus to try and save his own life. The dangers of aerial combat are shown all too vividly in this combat report, where the tables were turned so quickly from being the hunter to the hunted. It was a thoroughly chastening experience for Gardiner, who did extremely well to return to Biggin Hill despite being wounded, in a Spitfire which was so damaged as to be classed as unserviceable upon landing. His Spitfire, DW-O, R.6595, had featured prominently in the famous series of photos from 26 June (see p. 190) and was now out of action for some time.

Blue Section's pilots were not the only ones to engage the enemy. P/O Norris reported on the battle as follows:

> I was Red 2. when the Sqdn was sent off to intercept E.A. attacking a convoy off Folkestone. During the take off I became separated from my section & arrived on the scene alone. I saw that another Sqdn was attacking the Ju 87s which were attacking the convoy. At this moment I saw some ME 109s, about 12, circling above so I climbed to attack. When I was at 17000' I saw 4 or 5 formations of ME 109s in vic formation about 9 or 12 in a formation.
>
> I attacked one formation of nine ME 109s & shot down one who was straggling behind he appeared to use no evasive action probably because he was unaware I was on his tail. He went over on his back after I had expended some ammunition, with clouds of black & white smoke pouring out & every indication of being out of control.
>
> By this time I had used practically all my ammunition so I returned to base. (TNA, AIR 50/172/53)

When Norris became separated from the rest of the formation, it left both the formation and himself more vulnerable to attack from the Me 109s. Norris, one of the Squadron's most experienced pilots, quickly weighed up the situation, and seeing 64 Squadron was ready to deal with the bombers, bravely elected to take on the escorting fighters high above them. He engaged these about 5,000 feet above the other Messerschmitts which Ellis and company attacked. Showing no caution, Norris took on a much larger formation single-handedly, although crucially he had surprise on his side. The 109 pilot he singled out for 1,500 rounds of ammunition from fifty yards, probably never knew what hit him. Norris returned to base to claim an unconfirmed destroyed victory, to add to the 109 he had shot down over Dunkirk.

As the enemy aircraft broke off their attack, the Spitfires of 610 and 64 Squadrons[25] were able to head for home themselves, the County of Chester Squadron's pilots well pleased with their efforts, returning to Hawkinge just under an hour after being scrambled. The Squadron claimed one Me 109 confirmed destroyed and three 109s unconfirmed destroyed, while F/O Gardiner was slightly wounded in his left arm and his Spitfire, DW-O, R.6595 was unserviceable.[26] However, in the midst of these claims initially being taken and the returning Spitfires being rearmed and refuelled, one Spitfire, DW-A, R.6693 (ORB provided the wrong serial number—R.6976; it was actually R.6693, which had joined the Squadron on 7 June),[27] appeared on the horizon with S/Ldr A. T. Smith at the controls. He was bravely attempting to get his battle-damaged Spitfire back to Hawkinge.

The circumstances leading up to Smith's predicament are unclear, but the ORB does state that, 'During a general dog-fight with Me 109s, the Commanding Officer was seen by his section attacking an enemy plane. He was next seen some 30 minutes later, circuiting HAWKINGE aerodrome'. It is likely the squadron leader was flying as Red 1, but with Norris having become separated from Red Section on taking off, it seems that the pilot who witnessed Smith attacking the enemy was probably Sgt Parsons, who appears to have been Red Section's third pilot. If S/Ldr Smith's section was composed of two Spitfires instead of three, it certainly left Smith more vulnerable. It is most likely that during the dogfight with the countless 109s, Tom Smith's Spitfire received heavy damage, forcing him out of the combat and in desperate need to land. Hawkinge's close proximity to the coast meant that even in his damaged aircraft, Smith's best bet was to try to get back to this airfield, with its wide expanses of unobstructed grass to make a forced landing on in a worst case scenario.

As the Spitfire appeared in the circuit to land, a trail of smoke could be seen emitting from the straining engine, the bold grey/white letters on the fuselage, DW-A, confirming it was 610's squadron leader in need of an emergency landing. Those on the ground would have realised as they heard the Spitfire approach that the Merlin engine was not making the usual resonant sounds, and that something was wrong. As everybody at Hawkinge aerodrome became transfixed by Smith's Spitfire, the pilots of 610 who had already returned would have had their hearts in their mouths, willing their leader home, believing that with all his experience—dating back to the very first days of the Squadron—he could coax his damaged aircraft in to land safely. But as Smith made his final approach, it now became apparent that it was not just the Spitfire which was damaged, but the pilot himself was in 'obvious difficulty' (ORB). Coming in over the airfield boundary, smoke billowing from the aircraft, onlookers watched in horror as S/Ldr Smith lost his battle with the struggling Spitfire—seconds from safety the engine stalled, choked and at 1518 hours DW-A, 'crashed into a disused engine testing shed. The aircraft caught fire and was burned out' (ORB). As ground personnel and quite possibly some of his pilots rushed to the scene, 'on the edge of the aerodrome' (ORB), accompanied by fire tenders, it was quickly apparent that it was to no avail. 610 Squadron had lost its gallant CO in harrowing circumstances. This brave man's death must have been a demoralising blow to both the Squadron and the whole Station.

Brian Smith was one of the pilots who had already returned from the combat, and witnessed his CO and friend's final approach. This awful moment was etched firmly in his memory, as it surfaced a couple of times during the course of our meeting: 'We lost a CO there, Tom Smith, who was one of Ian Parker's boys. He landed, oh, it wasn't Biggin … It must have been Hawkinge ... he came in between the hangars, obviously not himself and burnt up', and, 'I remember seeing him coming in through the hangars, quite out of the wind, and you know, obviously in trouble … But, you don't have to dwell on these things, you just accept them. I can dwell on it now, but in those days it was just one less …' As noted during the Dunkirk air battles, the age of some of the pilots probably went against them, especially those over thirty, and the same may well have applied to S/Ldr Smith, as his old friend Brian Smith pointed out, 'Oh we were lucky you see, we'd been about for two or three or four years ... Well we were experienced blokes, but the trouble was we were a bit too old ... Tom Smith, that's right, he ran a flour mill in Liverpool'. Tom Smith's willingness to enter combat, despite being 'old' for flying the latest fighter aircraft, may well have contributed to his death.

Once again, the chance of battle was all too apparent—Gardiner, also wounded and in a badly damaged aircraft, managed to return to fight another day, while his CO perished in similar circumstances, a fact which would not have been lost on the surviving pilots, none more so than Gardiner himself. The fate of the CO was also strikingly similar to that of 54 Squadron's ace P/O Allen DFC, whose aircraft stalled into the ground moments from safety on the previous day. It is conceivable they would both have been better off forsaking their Spitfires and baling out. There seems to have been an element of wanting to get their aircraft back home if possible, perhaps when the damage received was worse than they realised. But if Smith was injured, baling out may not have been an option, and a combination of a wound and heavy battle damage to his Spitfire caused him to crash.

Since taking over as squadron leader, Tom Smith had led his men successfully. He had managed to keep up morale after the unit's heavy losses over Dunkirk, helped bring new pilots into the Squadron and develop them as fighter pilots. Recognising John Ellis's superiority as a better leader and tactician in the air, he was happy to allow Ellis to lead the Squadron on patrol, knowing that his men were better off, and that they had a better chance of inflicting losses on the *Luftwaffe*. The fact that Tom Smith had been a Squadron member since its earliest days made his loss an even greater blow, having joined on 9 April 1936, before he progressed through the ranks from lowly pilot officer to squadron leader as a result of combat losses. It meant he embodied the Squadron's spirit, especially as one of the older pilots, and he undoubtedly had the total respect of his men. Remarkably, the day he was killed was three years to the day since he had arrived at Hawkinge for the Squadron's first annual camp, back in the

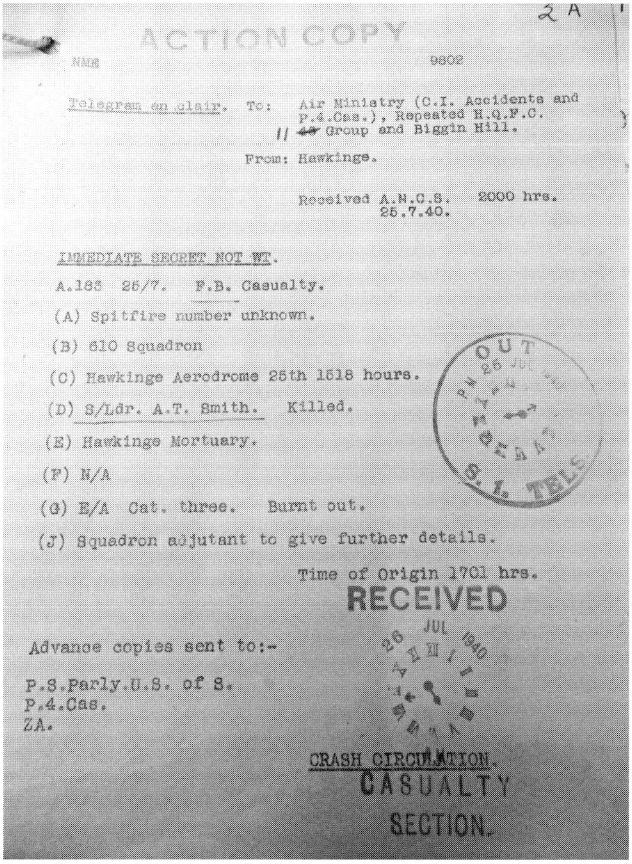

2A

ACTION COPY

NMB 9802

Telegram en clair. To: Air Ministry (C.I. Accidents and P.4.Cas.), Repeated H.Q.F.C. 11 ~~40~~ Group and Biggin Hill.

From: Hawkinge.

Received A.M.C.S. 2000 hrs. 25.7.40.

IMMEDIATE SECRET NOT WT.

A.183 25/7. F.B. Casualty.

(A) Spitfire number unknown.

(B) 610 Squadron

(C) Hawkinge Aerodrome 25th 1518 hours.

(D) S/Ldr. A.T. Smith. Killed.

(E) Hawkinge Mortuary.

(F) N/A

(G) E/A Cat. three. Burnt out.

(J) Squadron adjutant to give further details.

Time of Origin 1701 hrs.

OUT 25 JUL 1940 S.1. TELS.

RECEIVED 26 JUL 1940

Advance copies sent to:-

P.S.Parly.U.S. of S.
P.4.Cas.
ZA.

CRASH CIRCULATION.
CASUALTY SECTION.

A copy of the crash circulation, sent to the Air Ministry from Hawkinge hours after the incident, noting the key details of Smith's demise, including the time of the crash. The aircraft's serial number was officially confirmed on 28 July as R.6693. (*TNA, AIR 81/1198*)

peaceful days of 1937—Smith could never have imagined what fate had in store for him. Tragically, he left behind his wife Dorothy and a daughter, along with his mother, Marie Emily Gabrielle Smith.

I discovered several newspaper reports about Smith's death, as he was clearly a well-known figure in the Liverpool, Chester and Wirral area. One obituary appeared in the contemporary local Wirral newspaper, *The Birkenhead Advertiser and Wallasey Guardian* on Wednesday 31 July 1940, while a week later, another more detailed article appeared in *The Chronicle*, giving full details of the military funeral held at Delamere Parish Church. It provides a moving tribute to the fallen squadron leader:

SQUADRON-LEADER A. T. SMITH KILLED
HOOTON A.A.F. PIONEER
THREE-TO-ONE SUCCESS AGAINST ENEMY

> Mrs. Smith, New Pale Lodge, Manley, received news last Friday that her husband, Acting Squadron-Leader Andrew Thomas Smith, had been killed. The sympathy of her many friends in the Frodsham, Helsby, and Liverpool districts, where her husband was well-known, has been extended to her.
>
> Squadron-Leader Smith had been flying for four years, and was a pioneer member of the Auxiliary Air Force Squadron which, before the war, was organised and stationed at Hooton. When war broke out he joined a new squadron of the R.A.F becoming one of its first flight commanders. He took part in the operations of the R.A.F. which covered the evacuation of Dunkirk, and had since been in the thick of the fighting off the South East Coast.

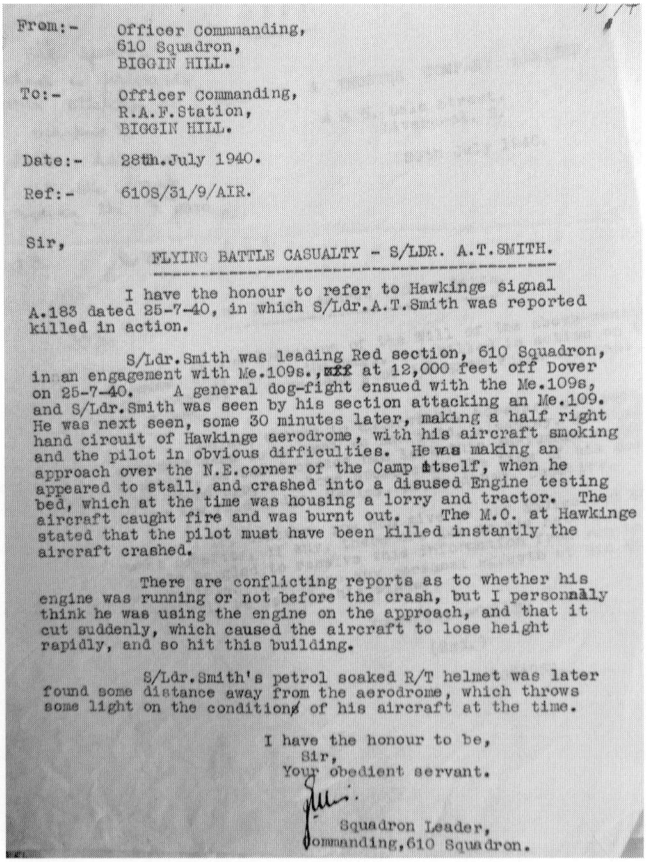

From:- Officer Commanding,
610 Squadron,
BIGGIN HILL.

To:- Officer Commanding,
R.A.F.Station,
BIGGIN HILL.

Date:- 28th.July 1940.

Ref:- 610S/31/9/AIR.

Sir,

FLYING BATTLE CASUALTY - S/LDR. A.T.SMITH.

I have the honour to refer to Hawkinge signal A.183 dated 25-7-40, in which S/Ldr.A.T.Smith was reported killed in action.

S/Ldr.Smith was leading Red section, 610 Squadron, in an engagement with Me.109s., at 12,000 feet off Dover on 25-7-40. A general dog-fight ensued with the Me.109s, and S/Ldr.Smith was seen by his section attacking an Me.109. He was next seen, some 30 minutes later, making a half right hand circuit of Hawkinge aerodrome, with his aircraft smoking and the pilot in obvious difficulties. He was making an approach over the N.E.corner of the Camp itself, when he appeared to stall, and crashed into a disused Engine testing bed, which at the time was housing a lorry and tractor. The aircraft caught fire and was burnt out. The M.O. at Hawkinge stated that the pilot must have been killed instantly the aircraft crashed.

There are conflicting reports as to whether his engine was running or not before the crash, but I personally think he was using the engine on the approach, and that it cut suddenly, which caused the aircraft to lose height rapidly, and so hit this building.

S/Ldr.Smith's petrol soaked R/T helmet was later found some distance away from the aerodrome, which throws some light on the condition of his aircraft at the time.

I have the honour to be,
Sir,
Your obedient servant.

Squadron Leader,
Commanding,610 Squadron.

John Ellis's report on the death of his former squadron leader Tom Smith. Ellis opined that Smith's engine was running when he crashed, but that it cut out on him. He also stressed the damage DW-A had received, and that Smith's 'petrol soaked R/T helmet was later found some distance away from the aerodrome'. Smith had presumably flung it clear in case of catching fire when attempting to land. (*TNA, AIR 81/1198*)

As the war progressed he rose to command the squadron, and led them in many engagements against the enemy, the record of his achievements being in the ratio of three enemy 'planes lost to one of his own. Squadron-Leader Smith was a director of Messers. W. and O. Wilson, flour millers, Liverpool and the Grain Elevating and Automatic Weighing Co., Ltd., Liverpool. He had been associated with the firm of Messers. W. and O. Wilson for 12 years, and was appointed a director last year.

He was the only son of the late Mr A. T. Smith, whose name was a household word in Runcorn and Northwich, where for many years he was manager of the Castner Kellner Works, and a director Messers Brunner, Mond and Co., Limited. He did great work during the last war, and being co-opted on to the Runcorn Urban Council became its chairman. He lived at Solna, Sefton Park, Liverpool.

Deep sympathy is felt for Mrs. Smith and her young daughter in their loss. Mrs. Smith has been an active worker in connection with A.R.P. in the district.

SQUADRON'S LOSS

A correspondent writes to "The Times": "In the death of Squadron-Leader Tom Smith, killed in action against enemy raiders, the nation has lost one of the finest examples of the Auxiliary Air Force officer. In private life a business man and happily married, he was sacrificing his week-end leisure and home comforts to the exigencies of training at a time when most of his countrymen and their leaders were only too blind to the menace that threatened us. Tom had those qualities which all real men look up to and admire, and in addition, a sense of humour which made him the best of good company at all times. His squadron and the rest of his friends will miss him sorely. Our only consolation is that but for him and those like him the enemy might even now be within our gates."

MILITARY FUNERAL
RECTOR'S TRIBUTE TO GALLANT LEADER

Delamere had its first military funeral on Tuesday, when the remains of Squadron Leader Andrew Thomas Smith were laid to rest in St. Peter's Churchyard. The casket was brought from the South of England on Monday and the remains, covered by the Union Jack, lay in state in Delamere Parish Church throughout the night. The service on Tuesday was conducted by the Rev. G. S. Payne (Rector), assisted by the Rev. F. H. Cooke (Vicar of Hooton). Mr. H. Pixton was organist, and he played Mendelssohn's "Oh for the wings of a dove" and Handel's "Largo." The hymns were "The King of love" and "Peace, perfect peace". Before the Nunc Dimittis was sung as a recessional, the organist played "O rest in the Lord" and the Dead March in Saul…

Relatives and friends present included Mrs. A. P. Smith, sen., Miss Marie Smith, Mr. and Mrs. S. Gaskell, Mr. and Mrs. F. Smith, Mr. and Mrs. Dumbell, Major and Mrs. Dodd, Mr. and Mrs. Thornton, Mrs. Campbell Wilson, Mdlle. Guyetant, Mr. N. Jackaman, Flying Officer Lamb, Wing Commander and Mrs. I. R. Parker…

Squadron Leader G. F. Mulholland was in command of a detachment of the R.A.F which formed a guard of honour and presented arms as the remains were committed to the grave. The grave was lined with evergreens, red rambler roses, and blue delphiniums. R.A.F. men and members of the staff at the mills formed the bearer party.[28]

The article ends with a lengthy list of all those who gave wreaths. It is interesting to note that F/O Peter Lamb had been sent to represent the Squadron, as one of its veterans, while other figures easily recognisable from their strong connections to the Squadron were Wg Cdr I. R. Parker and his wife, and Mrs. C. M. C. Smith (Tattenhall), the mother of F/Lt Brian Smith, who had known the deceased squadron leader through thick and thin for several years.

Andrew Thomas Smith
Killed in Action
July 25th, 1940
St. Peter's Church
Delamere
July 30th, 1940

The Order of Service for S/Ldr Smith's funeral, which took place on 30 July 1940. (*Copyright 610 Squadron Association*)

Above left: The grave of 610 Squadron's gallant S/Ldr A. T. Smith. (*Author*)

Above right: S/Ldr A. T. Smith, Killed in Action, 25 July 1940. (*Copyright Oundle School*)

I visited St Peter's Churchyard in Delamere, and after a lengthy search for a traditional CWGC headstone, I noticed a grave with an RAF eagle at its foot. Situated near the cemetery wall, underneath a lime tree, S/Ldr Smith's final resting place is in a very tranquil setting, in a low, white stone tomb with a sword down its centre, very much like that of a knight's tomb which might be found in a cathedral. The inscription on either side reads, 'Squadron Leader Andrew Thomas Smith, Killed In Action 25th July 1940 Aged 33', a simple, yet fitting memorial to such a brave man. In recent years, he has also been remembered at his former school, Oundle, as a reminder of his sacrifice for following generations of pupils to acknowledge.

On 25 July, Hptm. Horst Tietzen and Lt. Otto-Hans Lessing of 5/JG 51 filed claims for having shot down Spitfires, which may have belonged to 610 Squadron. Remarkably, it seems possible that Tietzen, who had killed P/O Litchfield seven days earlier, had cost 610 Squadron dear again, by causing the death of the CO. *Then and Now* records how an Me 109 from Tietzen's unit was damaged so badly it made a forced landing back in France, and this could have been one of the 109s claimed by 610's pilots: '**5/JG51** Messerschmitt Bf 109E-1. Forced landed at St Inveser (probably St Inglevert) with damage sustained in combat over the Channel. Uffz. Obst wounded. Aircraft a write-off'.[29] The damage done to Convoy CW8 itself was further proof of the battle which had raged throughout the afternoon, as despite the valiant efforts of the RAF's fighter pilots, five ships had been sunk and five more damaged.

It had been a gruelling fight for 610 Squadron's men, and as the surviving pilots at Hawkinge came to terms with the loss of their leader in such graphic circumstances, they must have been a disconsolate bunch. Any initial feelings of success the pilots had after the dogfight would have evaporated after witnessing their squadron leader's death. For the longer serving Squadron pilots like Brian Smith, they had lost a friend, while the newer recruits such as Sgt Tanner, had lost their inspiration—if a pilot with all Tom Smith's experience could be killed, what hope must they have had for themselves? The loss of any pilot was a serious blow, but the death of the CO was felt more harshly than any other, as he was the unit's figurehead. The emotions felt by 610's pilots would certainly have involved a need to avenge their fallen leader, and with the convoys coming under increasing attack, there was every likelihood that the men would get an opportunity to do so.

As the senior flight commander, John Ellis had to rouse the spirits of the men, and drill home the fact that although they had lost a well-liked man and leader, they had to rally themselves and press on if the call to scramble came again that day, and in the coming days ahead. For the sacrifice of Smith and their other fallen colleagues to be worthwhile, they needed to channel their emotions into helping defeat the *Luftwaffe*.

As the remaining operational Spitfires were given a quick turnaround, the pilots would have discussed the earlier violent dogfight and what exactly had happened to their squadron leader, whose burnt out Spitfire created a pall of pungent smoke which lingered over the airfield. However, further developments in the Channel meant that 610 Squadron had not finished for the day. As the convoy slowly edged its way to the west of Folkestone, 54 Squadron's ORB later reported: '**1621** "A" Flight patrolling over DOVER saw a number of enemy M.T.B.s [Motor Torpedo Boats] off CALAIS; this report led to the despatch of two destroyers to deal with them and resulted in the second big battle of the day when nearly 100 enemy fighters and bombers descended on the Destroyers'. 54 Squadron encountered Ju 88s, Ju 87s and Me 109s, but lost another pilot defending the destroyers. The crews of the destroyers HMS *Brilliant* and *Boreas* must have wished 54 Squadron had not spotted the German E-boats lurking off Calais, as they knew the welcome they would get from the *Luftwaffe*, given CW8's recent treatment. But they bravely pressed on in the true tradition of the Navy, and having thwarted the E-boats' efforts to intercept CW8, the destroyers were then forced to withdraw in the face of an overwhelming bombing raid, both being hit.

Although 610 Squadron had just seven Spitfires available for action, being stationed at Hawkinge made them an obvious choice to be sent to the destroyers' aid. At 1827 hours, the telephone at 610's dispersal hut rang and the order was given for a 'Squadron Scramble'. The following pilots raced to their aircraft:

DW-N.	R.6806	F/Lt. J. ELLIS.	Blue 1	39
DW-L.	P.9496	Sgt. ELSE, P.	Blue 2	26
DW-P.	R.6695	F/O. D. S. WILSON.	Blue 3	2
DW-J.	N.3284	P/O. S. C. NORRIS.	Red 2	42
DW-F.	R.6694	Sgt. PARSONS, C. A.	Red 3	12
DW-B.	L.1009	F/Lt. E. B. B. SMITH.	Red 1	54
DW-X.	R.6630	Sgt. CHANDLER, H. H.	Red 4	7

John Ellis was again in the lead, for the first time as the *de facto* leader. Although the ORB stated that 'Red, Blue and Yellow sections ordered to patrol', it is quickly apparent from the various combat reports that the Squadron had been divided into two sections, Ellis leading a three-man Blue Section, while F/Lt Brian Smith led a four-man Red Section. Ellis described the combat, which took place at 1840 hours, only thirteen minutes after being scrambled, as follows:

> I was leading 610 Squadron consisting of 7 a/c which was ordered to take off from Hawkinge at 1827 on 25/7/40. While patrolling Dover we saw a destroyer being bombed two miles out to sea. I personally did not see the bombers but saw about 20 Me 109s at 7000' so I gave orders for the Squadron to attack them. The e/a that I saw were flying in fours in line astern and the last a/c presented a very easy target. I attacked the last a/c of one of these sections and fired about half my ammunition into him at between 100 and 10x range. I must have taken the section by surprise as they did not break up or adopt any evasive action except gentle turns. This e/a rolled over and plunged towards the sea out of control. As I climbed up into the clouds after the attack I saw a 109 hit the sea and believe this was the one I attacked. After this I cruised around just in the cloud where it was possible to see quite clearly vertically downwards. While doing this I sighted another section of four Me. 109s in line astern. I dived down below the section and carried out a climbing attack again on the last a/c. I emptied the remainder of my ammunition into him at practically point blank range and he fell out of the sky burning furiously and hit the sea. Sgt ELSE Blue 2. confirms that he saw these two a/c crash. (TNA, AIR 50/172/21)

It is immediately apparent that Ellis had led his men into the perfect bounce of the German fighters who had been caught completely unawares, while Ellis's own ability as a fighter pilot is evident. He found the best position to attack from, and then picked off the rearmost Me 109 from very close range, before climbing away to safety, certain of his victory. Then he stalked the enemy again, before successfully repeating the process. The key to modern fighter tactics was to get in hard, fire from close range, and then climb or dive away out of trouble. Ellis was quick to implement such ideas. The fact that Sgt Else could confirm both claims shows he did his duty as a wingman very ably, covering Ellis from any possible counter-attack; it highlighted the value of working as a team. Amazingly, Ellis had shot down five of the dangerous 109s in the space of two days, an indication both of his expertise as a fighter pilot and how heavy the air fighting had become.

Despite F/O Douglas Wilson, aged thirty-three, being an experienced pre-war officer, he was only flying his second recorded combat patrol since re-joining the Squadron. He provided some additional information from his first successful encounter with the *Luftwaffe* in this copy of his report from The National Archives, see photo below.

In the report's preamble, Wilson thought they encountered approximately fifteen Me 109s at 1840 hours (1125 in the below report should be 1825 hours), between 6–8,000 feet, stating that he used about six seconds ammunition to destroy the 109 he finally attacked. The value of the R/T for transferring information between the fighter controller and the pilots is apparent here, while also highlighting the importance of RDF in predicting from where and what altitude the *Luftwaffe* was coming. As it was, Ellis and his men were perfectly positioned to attack the fighters providing escort to the dive-bombers, which were attacking the destroyers. Although Wilson was briefly involved in a swirling dogfight, he was quickly able to find an unsuspecting 'quarry', which he sent into the Channel. The fate of this unfortunate German pilot certainly seems sealed, and the two witnesses enabled Wilson to claim his first enemy aircraft destroyed when he returned to Hawkinge.

While Blue Section's pilots had enjoyed success, Red Section's pilots, who appear to have been providing cover for Blue Section at a slightly higher altitude, were quick to follow suit. Brian Smith described encountering twenty to thirty Me 109s at 10,000 feet south-east of Dover, see overleaf:

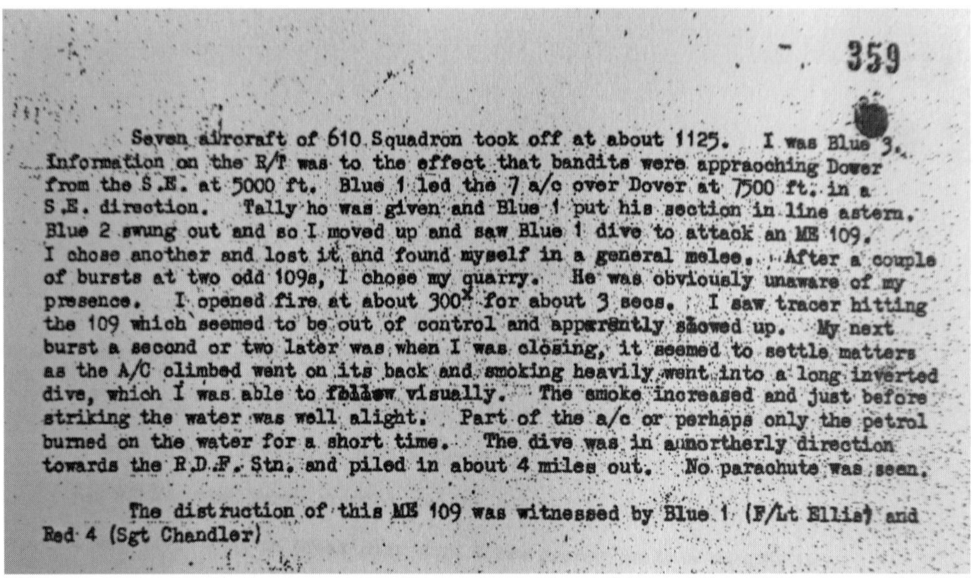

359

Seven aircraft of 610 Squadron took off at about 1125. I was Blue 3. Information on the R/T was to the effect that bandits were appraoching Dover from the S.E. at 5000 ft. Blue 1 led the 7 a/c over Dover at 7500 ft. in a S.E. direction. Tally ho was given and Blue 1 put his section in line astern. Blue 2 swung out and so I moved up and saw Blue 1 dive to attack an ME 109. I chose another and lost it and found myself in a general melee. After a couple of bursts at two odd 109s, I chose my quarry. He was obviously unaware of my presence. I opened fire at about 300x for about 3 secs. I saw tracer hitting the 109 which seemed to be out of control and apparently slowed up. My next burst a second or two later was when I was closing, it seemed to settle matters as the A/C climbed went on its back and smoking heavily went into a long inverted dive, which I was able to follow visually. The smoke increased and just before striking the water was well alight. Part of the a/c or perhaps only the petrol burned on the water for a short time. The dive was in a northerly direction towards the R.D.F. Stn. and piled in about 4 miles out. No parachute was seen.

The distruction of this ME 109 was witnessed by Blue 1 (F/Lt Ellis) and Red 4 (Sgt Chandler)

F/O Wilson's combat report, 25 July 1940. (*TNA, AIR 50/172/78*)

> Whilst flying as Red 1, astern of Blue Section, over Dover at 10000. I saw Bombs dropping around a destroyer and at the same time a large number of E/A. Blue leader put his A/c astern and I put Red Section astern. We then approached the E/A, Aircraft astern, when a general dog fight occurred just beneath a thin cloud layer. There were 3 or 4 formations of 5 each, ME 109s, aircraft astern.
>
> I turned about and carried out a quarter attack on the last of 5 ME 109, a/c astern, who were turning round into me. Finishing up slightly above and behind E/A. I gave him 3 or 4 short bursts and saw him break downwards emitting Bluish smoke.
>
> I then dodged into the cloud as the leading a/c was turning into me. I then met an unidentified E/A between the clouds and gave it a short burst into the underside as it was in a vertical turn away from me. No effect was seen, as it disappeared into a cloud. (TNA, AIR 50/172/72)

When Red Section engaged the enemy, more of a dogfight was taking place, with Smith turning on to the rearmost 109 in a formation, which was simultaneously trying to get on his tail. The unidentified aircraft was probably one of the Ju 87s which had attacked the destroyers. Smith had used up approximately 1,200 rounds of ammunition, and the experienced pilot was able to claim an Me 109 unconfirmed once he filed his combat report.

As Red Section followed Brian Smith into the dogfight, Messerschmitts continued to fall. Smith had the luxury of P/O Stan Norris as his wingman on this operation, and this veteran of Dunkirk was quickly in amongst the *Luftwaffe* formation:

> I was RED 2. when the Sqdn was sent off to intercept E.A attacking two destroyers off Dover. I saw several bombs dropping in the sea & some machines diving on the destroyers which I think were Ju. 87s. As the Sqdn came into position to attack 15–20 ME 109s appeared & a dog fight ensued. The 109s split up into pairs. I attacked one and in a short time white smoke poured from the machine followed by flames from the rear of the cockpit—or so it seemed. The machine did a steep spiral dive and quickly became enveloped in flames. I saw it hit the sea, and the burning petrol spread for some distance burning fiercely on the sea. The second ME 109 made no attempt to attack me while I was on the tail of his partner. It merely formated alongside. Sgt Parsons Red 3 confirms this. (TNA, AIR 50/172/53)

Norris, in DW-J, N.3284 (see photo p. 193) was the only pilot who mentioned that there were *two* destroyers bravely running the gauntlet of the *Luftwaffe's* dive-bombers. He states in the preamble (like a couple of the others), that their attention was drawn to the enemy aircraft by AA fire, presumably from the destroyers. Norris also gives the impression that they were originally going to attack the dive-bombers, before breaking off to attack the 109s which had appeared. Although the 109s split up into their usually effective defensive *Rotte* of two aircraft, this time the move did not pay off as the experienced pilot officer was able to hit one of them hard, firing about 2,000 rounds of ammunition from 100 yards to as close as twenty yards. Norris's aim was true and his rounds had a shattering effect on the Messerschmitt, which fell out of the sky. Claude Parsons was a witness, so Norris could add a confirmed 109 destroyed to his claim earlier in the afternoon of a 109 unconfirmed.

Sgt Parsons was one of a group of pilots gaining experience very quickly during July. His second sortie of the day was his twelfth recorded patrol and he also waded into the fray:

> I was Red 3 in Vic formation when at 8–10000 ft 15 ME 109s were encountered. They immediately split up into pairs. I turned sharply to the right and placed myself on the tail of one of the ME 109s at about 300 yds. This E/A turned to the left slightly diving. I opened fire for about 2 secs, my target appeared to fall out of the sky and went down vertically, smoking and apparently out of control. (TNA, AIR 50/172/57)

In the preamble to his report, Parsons fired only 200 rounds, but in closing to just seventy-five yards, his accurate burst of fire had a devastating impact on the small enemy fighter. As nobody else witnessed the demise of this 109, he could only claim it as an unconfirmed victory, adding to his shared destroyed bomber.

Another surviving combat report from this intense dogfight, filled in the following day, belonged to Sgt Chandler, flying at the rear of the formation. He stated that he encountered Me 109s and Ju 87s as follows:

> My position was Red 4, enemy aircraft (fighters) were intercepted head-on at same altitude, just below cloud layer. We went into long line astern and picked our targets. My target realised he was being chased but carried out no violent manoeuvres. I fired occasional bursts. After a few minutes he went into a dive for France, I managed to close to about 150–200 yds and fired a long burst, which resulted in black smoke immediately followed by fire. I immediately returned to the fight but saw no further targets.
>
> At one time during the encounter I was able to count 2 aircraft on fire, and going straight down emitting black smoke, and another on the water burning. These are additional to the one I disabled and destroyed. (TNA, AIR 50/172/11)

Although Chandler said that the 109s were 'intercepted head-on', 610's men had quickly turned the tables on them, attacking them from behind—the line astern formation allowed each Spitfire pilot to pick his target more easily. Ray Chandler understood the importance of firing from close range. Following on from his success the previous day, he closed to 150–200 yards, before delivering a fatal burst of fire into the fleeing Messerschmitt, which started to smoke and burn. Chandler, like Claude Parsons, was quickly learning from his initial experience of aerial combat during July, putting it to good use in this, just his seventh recorded patrol. The second paragraph in his report shows what a lethal dogfight 610 was involved in, with four aircraft having almost simultaneously met their fate in one way or another, further proof of which comes from the résumé in the ORB:

> They saw about 15 E/A bombing Destroyers in mid-channel & then about 24 M.E.109s appeared & a battle took place at 10,000 feet. P/O. Norris shot down a M.E.109 in flames, and saw it hit the sea. Sgt. Chandler chased a M.E.109 for 5 minutes & saw it go down burning ... Sgt. Parsons placed himself on the tail of a M.E.109 at about 300 yds, opened fire for about 2 seconds, E/A went down vertically, apparently out of control. F/O. Wilson engaged a M.E.109, after 2 bursts the E/A caught fire. Our pilot seeing it crash into the sea. F/Lt Ellis and Sgt. Chandler confirm this. F/Lt. Ellis attacked the rearmost of a section of four M.E.109s line astern causing it to spin down out of control. He then attacked another M.E.109 from below, which gave out clouds of smoke, and fell away burning furiously. Sgt. Else confirms both these victories. F/Lt. Smith attacked a M.E.109 which broke away emitting black smoke. He also attacked another single engined E/A, larger than a fighter without visible effect.

There was still one more claim to be made though, and it was by Sgt Peter Else. Having survived the dogfight unscathed, the increasingly experienced pilot was returning home when:

> At approximately 1900 hrs, I was circling Hawkinge preparing to land and was on the hangar side approaching towards the sea. I saw two machines approaching the aerodrome from the East which I took to be Hurricanes. A closer look revealed the fact that the rear machine was a Hurricane and the other a 109 who flew across the aerodrome at 500 ft towards the sea.
>
> I chased after them and delivered an attack from the quarter astern whilst the Hurricane was firing from astern. The Hurricane then broke away and I continued with an astern attack. My guns ceased firing very quickly and I broke away. When I looked for the E/A he had disappeared and I assumed he had gone into the sea as towards the end he was descending rapidly.

> This a/c made very gradual attempts at turns of about ½ rate at first but whether owing to the fact that we held our fire he soon gave even that up. My impression was that he was either an inexperienced pilot or a bad one.
>
> On returning to the aerodrome, I learned that two soldiers had actually seen the 109 go into the sea, one soldier through field glasses.
>
> One 109 in the big battle over the destroyer was painted almost Royal blue on the underside.
>
> One of my guns did not fire at all and I had three other stoppages. Previously I saw two E/A shot down by F/Lt. Ellis. (TNA, AIR 50/172/23)

The surprisingly short time span of the aerial combats over Britain during the summer of 1940 is no more apparent than here. The men of 610 had scrambled at 1827 hours, made contact with the enemy a little over twelve minutes later and a further twenty minutes after that, despite the size of the dogfight, the Spitfires were returning, as Else was in the circuit about thirty minutes after taking off. Pilots had to remain vigilant at all times when in the air, and Else was quick to spot his chance of engaging the 109, already being chased by P/O Wicks in a Hurricane of 56 Squadron.[30] Else opened fire from 250 yards and under, with two, three second bursts and then one long burst totalling 1,450 rounds, despite one Browning not working and suffering other stoppages. The 109's pilot must have realised in his final moments his misfortune in flying directly over Hawkinge, thereby attracting a seconder attacker, especially at such low altitude. Else applied the *coup de grâce* half a mile off Folkestone. As the Messerschmitt's demise was witnessed by soldiers at the airfield, Else claimed the enemy aircraft destroyed, Wicks not making a claim. Peter Else now had claims for one destroyed, one shared destroyed, an unconfirmed and a damaged to his name, all in twenty-six recorded patrols. The sergeant's action must have been a great boost to the embattled ground crew and personnel of Hawkinge aerodrome, on the front line in Britain's defence.

That each pilot made at least one claim shows how completely the Spitfires had surprised the German fighter pilots, highlighting the importance of catching the enemy off guard, a rare occurrence for Fighter Command's pilots thus far in the conflict. As the RAF men returned home, bathed in sweat and exhausted, yet proud at having dealt such a severe blow to a numerically superior enemy formation, the full extent of their success would have become clear. It seems that the seven pilots of 610 had set out to avenge the loss of their leader, and their brave efforts would certainly have made S/Ldr Tom Smith proud. Once they had returned, and their combat reports been completed, they were credited with '5 M.E.109s confirmed, 3 M.E.109s unconfirmed' (ORB). It seems that the five claimed as confirmed were the two shot down by Ellis, plus those claimed by Wilson, Norris and Else, while the unconfirmed went to Brian Smith, Parsons and Chandler, on the basis that those claimed by the first four pilots were all supported by witnesses. It had been the perfect 'bounce', just what was required to restore the Squadron's morale immediately after the loss of their leader.

Various texts describe the dogfight in defence of the destroyers, with James Holland describing how 610 Squadron seem to have run straight into III/JG 52, which was reeling from the previous day's losses:

> And, once again, there were Spitfires waiting for them, this time from 610 Squadron. By the time they landed back at Coquelles, just after 8 p.m., four more pilots had been lost, including Oberleutnant Keidal; the 7th Staffel had lost its second commander in just over twenty-four hours. The Gruppe's adjutant had also been lost, as had one of Günther Rall's men. All had been good, highly experienced pilots—the more senior men from the Gruppe—and yet they were being mauled. Günther was in no doubt as to why. 'As a fighter pilot,' he says, 'it should be up to you to make a plan how best to protect the bombers. It was stupid to escort Stukas at their slow speed. We should have been higher and had the freedom to manoeuvre.[31]

This explains why 610 Squadron's pilots had such an advantage over their *Luftwaffe* counterparts, with even experienced German pilots unable to utilise their ability when flying at the disadvantage of escorting the slow dive-bombers. Holland is supported by *Then and Now*, which lists JG 52's losses thus:

> **Thursday, July 25th**
>
> **III/JG52**, Messerschmitt Bf 109E. Shot down into the sea off Dover 6.40 p.m. during combat with No. 610 Squadron Spitfires. Lt. Schmidt missing. Aircraft lost.
>
> **7/JG52**
>
> Messerschmitt Bf 109E. Shot down in combat with Spitfires of No. 610 Squadron 6.45 p.m. Crashed into the Channel off Dover. Oblt. Keidel (Staffel Kapitan) missing. Aircraft lost.
>
> Messerschmitt Bf 109E. Crashed into the sea off Dover 6.40 p.m. during combat with No. 610 Squadron Spitfires. Oblt. Bielefeld (Staffel fuhrer) killed. Aircraft lost.
>
> **8/JG52**
>
> Messerschmitt Bf 109E. Brought down at Elvington Court near Deal following combat with No. 610 Squadron Spitfires 6.40 p.m. Uffz. Reiss captured. Aircraft 6+ a write-off.[32]

Ascertaining which Messerschmitt fell to an individual pilot from 610 Squadron is nigh on impossible, but it provides a clear indication of the one-sided nature of this ferocious dogfight over the English Channel.

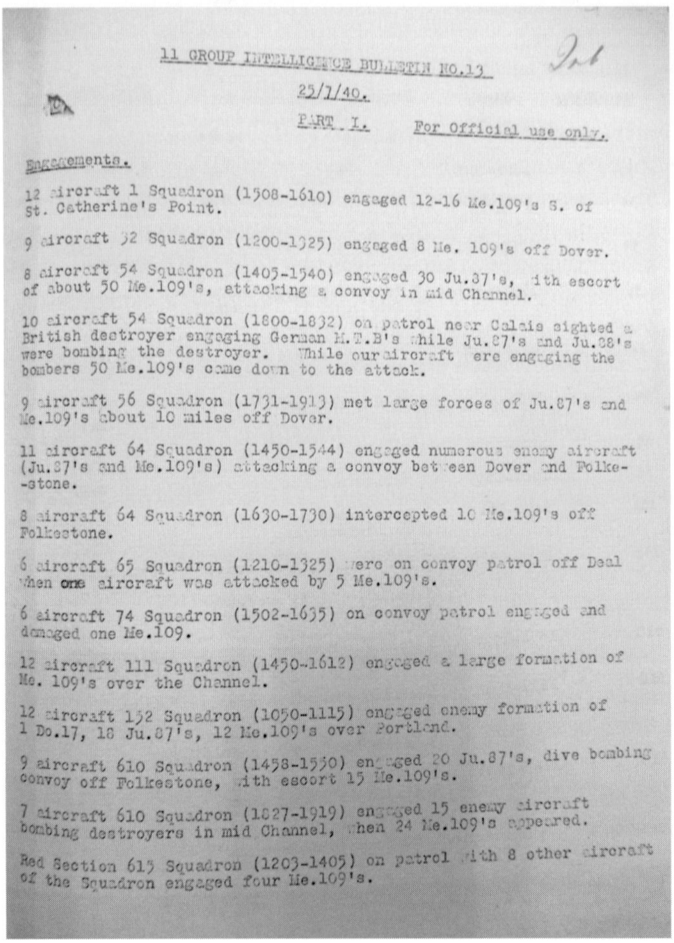

11 GROUP INTELLIGENCE BULLETIN NO.13

25/7/40.

PART I. For Official use only.

Engagements.

12 aircraft 1 Squadron (1508-1610) engaged 12-16 Me.109's S. of St. Catherine's Point.

9 aircraft 32 Squadron (1200-1325) engaged 8 Me. 109's off Dover.

8 aircraft 54 Squadron (1405-1540) engaged 30 Ju.87's, with escort of about 50 Me.109's, attacking a convoy in mid Channel.

10 aircraft 54 Squadron (1800-1832) on patrol near Calais sighted a British destroyer engaging German M.T.B's while Ju.87's and Ju.88's were bombing the destroyer. While our aircraft were engaging the bombers 50 Me.109's came down to the attack.

9 aircraft 56 Squadron (1731-1913) met large forces of Ju.87's and Me.109's about 10 miles off Dover.

11 aircraft 64 Squadron (1450-1544) engaged numerous enemy aircraft (Ju.87's and Me.109's) attacking a convoy between Dover and Folke--stone.

8 aircraft 64 Squadron (1630-1730) intercepted 10 Me.109's off Folkestone.

6 aircraft 65 Squadron (1210-1325) were on convoy patrol off Deal when one aircraft was attacked by 5 Me.109's.

6 aircraft 74 Squadron (1502-1635) on convoy patrol engaged and damaged one Me.109.

12 aircraft 111 Squadron (1450-1612) engaged a large formation of Me. 109's over the Channel.

12 aircraft 152 Squadron (1050-1115) engaged enemy formation of 1 Do.17, 18 Ju.87's, 12 Me.109's over Portland.

9 aircraft 610 Squadron (1458-1550) engaged 20 Ju.87's, dive bombing convoy off Folkestone, with escort 15 Me.109's.

7 aircraft 610 Squadron (1827-1919) engaged 15 enemy aircraft bombing destroyers in mid Channel, when 24 Me.109's appeared.

Red Section 615 Squadron (1203-1405) on patrol with 8 other aircraft of the Squadron engaged four Me.109's.

An indication of the scale of the aerial combats on 25 July is evident from this extract from '11 Group's Intelligence Bulletin', listing the Squadrons which had engaged the *Luftwaffe*. 610 Squadron's operations are second and third from the bottom. (*TNA, AIR 25/197*)

Douglas Corfe later in the war, proudly wearing his coveted 'Wings', something he had started to train for with his local AAF Squadron in 1939. (*Hoylake and West Kirby Advertiser, Friday, 22 May 1942, copyright Mirrorpix/Wirral Archives Service*)

Once the surviving pilots had returned to Biggin Hill for the night and met up with the pilots who had not been on operations, drinks would have been consumed in memory of their fallen leader and friend, but also to acknowledge their own success, further proof that they could take on the Germans at their own game. During the course of the two patrols, and obviously at the heavy cost of the death of S/Ldr Smith and the wounded F/O Gardiner, the Squadron claimed six Me 109s destroyed and six 109s unconfirmed,[33] with half of those claimed as destroyed falling to the guns of F/Lt Ellis, a remarkable feat in itself. P/O Norris and Sgt Else both finished the day with a 109 destroyed and one unconfirmed, F/O Wilson the other confirmed destroyed, while F/O Gardiner would have been able to console himself with an unconfirmed enemy fighter to his name despite his wounded arm, along with Brian Smith and Sgts Parsons and Chandler. 610 had given the much vaunted German fighter pilots a torrid time. It would have done the Spitfire pilots the power of good to know that they were more than a match for their battle-hardened opposite numbers.

But the loss of another of the original pilots meant the number of founder members was dwindling; the men must secretly have been wondering how much longer they would survive, who would be next. Of the eighteen pilots who had been with the Squadron during the Dunkirk evacuation, ten had been killed and one wounded twice, leaving only seven of the original pilots operational, plus the surviving replacements who had arrived in June.

To increase the number of pilots, Douglas Corfe, now a sergeant, was welcomed back from 73 Squadron, Church Fenton, at some stage during the day. Corfe was one of the ground crew being trained to be a pilot in the months before the war, under the instruction of Innes Westmacott. He had left the Squadron on 7 October 1939, joining 2 FTS, Brize Norton:

> on No 42 Course, which ran from October 9 1939 to March 23 1940. Corfe completed his training and rejoined 610 Squadron, then at Wittering, as a Sergeant-Pilot.
>
> He was posted to 6 OTU, Sutton Bridge, on April 28 1940. After converting to Hurricanes, he went to PDC, Uxbridge on May 15, for allocation to a squadron in France. He joined 73 Squadron at Gaye.[34]

Corfe started flying operational patrols with 73 Squadron's 'A' Flight on 17 June. He carried out four patrols, primarily of Saint-Nazaire, Brittany, to protect shipping which was evacuating from the port. On 18 June, he carried out three more patrols of the port, between 0430 hours to 1225 hours. At 1400 hours, he flew back to Tangmere on the south coast of England in Hurricane L.2047, before continuing on to Church Fenton, Yorkshire—the relief must have been unimaginable (73 ORB). He would have gained some invaluable experience from this brief stint of operational activity, during the chaotic evacuation of Allied forces from France.

Corfe continued to operate with 73 Squadron after a period of rest, but received his posting to 610 while he was at Prestwick, for night flying training with 'A' Flight, on 21 July. 73 Squadron's detailed ORB recorded the following: 'Sgt Pilot Corfe, who attached himself to us in France is posted to No. 610 Sqdn. and we thus lose a very promising and useful pilot'. Corfe had clearly made a good impression during his brief spell with 73 Squadron. (The wording of this statement suggests that Corfe had joined 73 Squadron of his own accord, rather than being posted to the squadron. Perhaps he had become separated from his original unit during the chaos of the retreat through France, and helped out with 73 Squadron, although there is nothing to substantiate this possibility. It would seem likely that he would then have returned to his original unit on arriving back in England).

Corfe must have been glad to meet up with so many old familiar faces at 610, such as Ray Chandler, with whom he had left for Brize Norton nine months earlier. He would have been very aware of the numerous faces from the 'old' crowd who were no longer with them, perhaps most notably P/O Raven, who had also accompanied him to Brize Norton. Douglas Corfe would have undergone training on flying the Spitfire, after his time on Hurricanes and he would very soon be flying his first operational patrol with 610 Squadron. He brought the Squadron up to seventeen pilots, with two wounded, and his arrival was a sign of things to come over the next few days.

12

26–31 July 1940: New Pilots, Training and Fox Film Company at Hawkinge

After the hectic nature of Thursday 25 July, no recorded operations were flown by the Squadron on 26 July. They would have needed the time to get the operational number of Spitfires back up to Squadron strength from the previous day's action. Following the loss of S/Ldr Smith, the vital role of leading the Squadron was, unsurprisingly, immediately handed over to the highly experienced F/Lt John Ellis, who had already proven himself a very capable leader and fighter pilot. His remarkable feat of downing three Me 109s the day before brought his tally of claims to seven destroyed (six 109s plus one 110), one half destroyed He 111 and one third destroyed Do 17, making him the Squadron's leading pilot in terms of successful claims so far. Raymond Ellis noted from the ground crews' perspective that John Ellis's promotion was good, as he, 'was a popular officer'.[1]

A new 'B' Flight commander was now required to replace Ellis, and F/O William Warner was granted the rank of acting flight lieutenant. Again, it was seen as a wise policy to promote from within and maintain the sense of Squadron spirit. Warner, a member of the Squadron since its early days, would have helped uphold its sense of identity and provide a feeling of continuity, particularly with the loss of so many of the original pilots. Although he had not made many claims for victories, (one He 111 shared destroyed and a 109 unconfirmed destroyed), Warner was one of the Squadron's most experienced pilots, having flown a recorded fifty-one patrols since 10 May, alongside the countless hours of convoy patrols before that momentous date. He had also been mentioned in dispatches for flying his badly damaged Spitfire back to England from Dunkirk. This promotion was clearly well deserved by the young twenty-one-year-old pilot. No doubt such promotions would have been cause for celebration that evening.

The following day, 610 Squadron was not required to do any operational flying until relatively late. In fact, Saturday 27 July was most noticeable for the arrival of numerous new recruits to fill the gaps left in the Squadron's ranks following the heavy fighting of July, with eleven pilots joining the unit. The Squadron ORB detailed it as follows:

> P/O. E. S. ALDOUS (42274) posted to Squadron for flying duties, from No. 9 F.T.S. P/O. H. K. COX[2] (?) posted to Squadron from No. 5 O.T.U Aston Down for flying duties. P/O. C. MERRICK (?) and P/O. D. M. GRAY (?) posted from No. 15 S.F.T.S. Chipping Norton for flying duties, also 741411 SGT. BEARDSLEY R. A. 810145 SGT. BAKER, C - 810024 SGT. BAMBERGER, C. S., and 810081 SGT. MANTON, E. posted to unit from No. 9 F.T.S for flying duties.
>
> 740601 SGT. GARDNER. B. G. D., 742644 SGT. WILLCOCKS, P. H., and 741783 SGT. NEVILLE. W. J. posted to Squadron for flying duties from No. 5 O.T.U. ASTON DOWN.

The bulk of these reinforcements came from two training schools, 9 FTS based at Hullavington, Wiltshire and 5 OTU, Aston Down, in neighbouring Gloucestershire, between Stroud and Cirencester. Eric Stanley Aldous, aged twenty-two, hailed from Sanderstead, Surrey, having been born on 1 January

P/O Aldous. (*Copyright Wynn, Men of the Battle, p. 6*)

1918 in Wandsworth. His father, Stanley George, had died in 1939, leaving him with his mother, Winifrede Mary Reade and two sisters. He had attended Dulwich College from 1931 to 1935, where he was a 'boarder in Ivyholme and in the Second XI in 1935'.[3] After school he:

> went to work for Charrington's, the coal merchants. Aldous joined the RAFVR in September 1938 (745796). He was called up on September 1 1939.
>
> After completing his elementary flying training, he went to 9FTS, Hullavington, on April 11 1940, on No 18 Course.[4]

As if the move to a front-line fighter station and 610 Squadron was not enough for Aldous, he also received news of his promotion to 'pilot officer on probation' on 27 July, making it a real red letter day for the VR pilot![5]

Aldous was joined by four sergeants, three of whom were returning to their old unit, as Douglas Corfe had done two days earlier. Sgts Baker, Bamberger and Manton had all undergone training with Innes Westmacott, as Airmen at Hooton Park. They had been on pilot training since 21 October 1939, and they would have been as surprised as Corfe at the unit's losses and the small number of former pilots they still knew. However, they would still have remembered the majority of the ground personnel. Aubrey Cyril Baker would have been quick to realise just how much progress he had made since he arrived on the Squadron, four years earlier as an aircrafthand. After attending flying school in Reading, 'Baker was posted … to 8 EFTS [Elementary Flying Training School], Woodley on October 29, as an AC2. He moved to 9 FTS, Hullavington, on No 18 Course, on April 18 1940 and on completion',[6] returned to his former Squadron.

I had the pleasure of speaking to Edward Manton's nieces Frances and Joyce, though sadly neither got to meet him. 'Ted' or 'Teddy' as he was known, was born on 26 July 1915 in Rock Ferry, Wirral, and is believed to have attended Wirral Grammar School. Manton's nieces put me in touch with Peter Blythe, who had carried out extensive research into Manton in 2005. Thanks to a letter written to Peter by Mr P. Fraser, a former Post Office colleague of Ted Manton, we know that Ted joined the

Cyril Baker with a carefree smile, (right), at annual camp Abbotsinch, August 1939. Eleven months later, Baker had been through pilot training and returned to 610 Squadron as a fully-fledged Sgt Pilot. Baker has his arm round Maurice Houseman, whilst next to him sits Jack Williamson. (*Copyright 610 Squadron Association*)

Post Office aged fourteen as a boy telegraph messenger, becoming a postman and finally a sorting clerk by the time he joined 610 Squadron.

Fraser explained that one of their colleagues joined the RAFVR (presumably actually the Auxiliary Squadron) and persuaded several others to try and join it. Fraser was unsuccessful, failing his fitness test, but later becoming a paratrooper in the Special Boat Service! Ted, who had grown up in Oakley Grove, Bebington, Wirral, a village very close to Hooton Park, passed. His AAF papers confirm he joined 610 Squadron on 3 June 1937, aged twenty-one years and 334 days, as an aircrafthand.

In a letter to Peter Blythe, 'Bam' Bamberger confirmed that he had not known Ted prior to them both joining 610 Squadron. Their paths rarely crossed during the weekend or evening training, apart from on parades etc., as 'Bam' was a photographer and Ted, probably, an engine fitter (Manton's papers suggest he was an 'equipment assistant' later on). While 'Bam' had experience of flying photographic exercises and knew the pilots as a result, which helped his selection for pilot training, Ted did not have this advantage, so 'Bam' believed he must have been very determined to be selected for pilot training. 'Bam' was surprised to find Manton on the same training course at Woodley in October 1939, but they then spent a lot of time on the same training courses, until re-joining 610 Squadron as pilots. Manton was called up on 24 August 1939, being 'posted to 11 EFTS, Perth on October 21. He moved on to 9 FTS Hullavington for No 18 Course, which ran from April 11 to July 27 1940',[7] before returning to his former unit, having turned twenty-five the day before.

Sgt Cyril 'Bam' Bamberger, aged twenty-one, had gained the most experience with Westmacott the previous year, and like Manton was another of the Squadron's local recruits from Wirral. He had last been with the Squadron in October 1939, when he was posted to 11 E&RFTS in Reading, before going on to 8 and 9 FTS, prior to returning to 610 Squadron.

9 FTS, Hullavington, 1940: front row, fourth and fifth from left is Manton and Bamberger; fourth row, far right is Aldous; and back row, far right is Baker. (*Copyright Bamberger family*)

Above left: Sgt Pilot Bamberger, Malta, 1941. (*Copyright Bamberger family*)

Above right: Bob Beardsley, photographed later in the war. (*Copyright 610 Squadron Association*)

The only completely new recruit to the squadron from the Hullavington group of sergeants, was Robert Arthur Beardsley, aged twenty, from Old Charlton, London, who 'was educated at the Roan School, Blackheath. He joined the RAFVR (741411) on April 2 1938 and carried out his elementary flying training at 20 E&RFTS, Gravesend. Called up on September 1 1939, he was sent to 3 ITW, Hastings, after which he was posted to 15 FTS, Lossiemouth moving later to Middle Wallop and Chipping Norton',[8] all of which was before his time at Hullavington, according to 610's ORB.

From Aston Down came Kenneth Henry Cox. He was born in 1916 to Henry and Beatrice M. Cox originally from King's Heath, Birmingham, who had married in April 1912 and with whom he was living in 1939 in Kings Norton, Birmingham. Cox had joined the VR in December 1937: 'as an Airman u/t Pilot (741176). He was called up on September 1 1939, completed his training on No 18 Course at 11 FTS, Shawbury, which ran from January 31 to June 29 1940. He was commissioned on July 6 and posted to 5 OTU, Aston Down',[9] where he converted to Spitfires prior to joining 610 Squadron. Cox was joined by Sgts Gardner, Willcocks and Neville, each of whom had converted to Spitfires at Aston Down. They had followed the same training path to 610 Squadron as Cox, after being called up on 1 September 1939.

Bernard George Derry Gardner was born on 25 July 1916 in Reading, the only child of Bernard and Lillian Gardner, who went on to live at 209 Hill Lane, Bassett, Southampton, Hampshire, before he, 'joined the RAFVR in September 1937 as an Airman u/t Pilot'.[10] He finally joined 610 Squadron two days after his twenty-fourth birthday. Peter Hamilton Willcocks, 'of South Croydon, was educated at Selhurst Grammar School. He worked for the County of London Electricity Supply Co. and began with the Iraq Petrol Co. one week before the war started. Willcocks joined the RAFVR in September 1938, as an Airman u/t Pilot'.[11] 610 Squadron was his first operational posting after his training had been completed.

William John Neville was born on 7 January 1914 in Chertsey, to William James and Julia Kathleen Neville of Shepperton, Middlesex. He joined, 'the RAFVR about July 1938, as an Airman u/t Pilot',[12] and after completing his training was posted to 610 Squadron. All four pilots from Aston Down would have found comfort and assurance from joining their first operational unit with some familiar faces.

610 Squadron's complement increased further with two more pilot officers, Merrick (83256) and Gray (83255), both of whom were granted their commission as pilot officers on probation on the same day as their posting, later recorded in *The London Gazette*.[13] Thanks to the records at The RAF Museum,

Peter Hamilton Willcocks. (*Copyright Wynn, Men of the Battle, p. 565*)

Hendon, Claude Merrick's logbook has survived and is a fascinating source for charting the progress of a trainee Battle of Britain fighter pilot.[14] By studying Merrick's logbook, we can trace his steps from first flight, to first solo flight, to finally his first flight in a Spitfire, but it also provides a blueprint for the training regime followed by each of the new recruits who joined the Squadron after Dunkirk. Merrick joined the RAF in October 1938 as a sergeant pilot, 742194, and was at 16 E&RFTS, Shoreham from 5 October to 16 November 1938. His first flight came on 8 October 1938, for twenty-five minutes as a passenger in a De Havilland 82, K.4258, better known as a Tiger Moth, piloted by a F/O Wintour. He was shown the 'Effect of the controls', 'Taxying' and 'Handling of the engine', plus 'Straight and level' flying. Merrick moved to 22 E&RFTS in Cambridge on 17 November 1938, by which time he had been in the air four times. While in Cambridge, his training focused on 'Medium turns', 'Taking off' and 'Powered approach and landing'.

On 6 January 1939, he returned to No. 16 Course at Shoreham for a month but did not carry out any flying, before returning to Cambridge and No. 22 Course on 10 February. He continued with basic flights as a passenger in a Tiger Moth, until 2 April, when he took the controls for the first time after a total of ten hours and forty-five minutes as a passenger, carrying out his momentous first take-off and landing. Having achieved this milestone, the flights became more regular, with an increasing number as the pilot, until on 14 May 1939, Merrick went solo in Tiger Moth K.4269, a forty-five-minute flight which must have made the past six month's work worthwhile. It was quite an achievement, having only spent nine hours and ten minutes as the pilot when his instructors thought he was ready to go solo. Merrick continued to amass flying time on the Tiger Moth, including some longer solo flights, such as a cross-country test to Stapleford to test his air navigation for one hour and thirty minutes on 7 June, and to Ipswich and back on 10 June, which took one hour and fifty minutes.

On 12 June, Merrick progressed from the Tiger Moth to the more powerful Hawker Hart, Hind and Audax, much like the trainee pilots such as Corfe and Bamberger had when learning to fly with 610 Squadron at Hooton Park. Merrick's first solo flight on an Audax came on 14 June 1939. He continued to operate these three aircraft throughout June, before joining 45 E&RFTS in Ipswich on 4 July 1939, although he did not carry out any flying until August. On 10 August, his proficiency as a pilot was rated as, 'Above Average', with thirty-five hours solo flying time. During August, he carried out plenty of flying, as by the end of the month he had attained fifty-three hours solo.

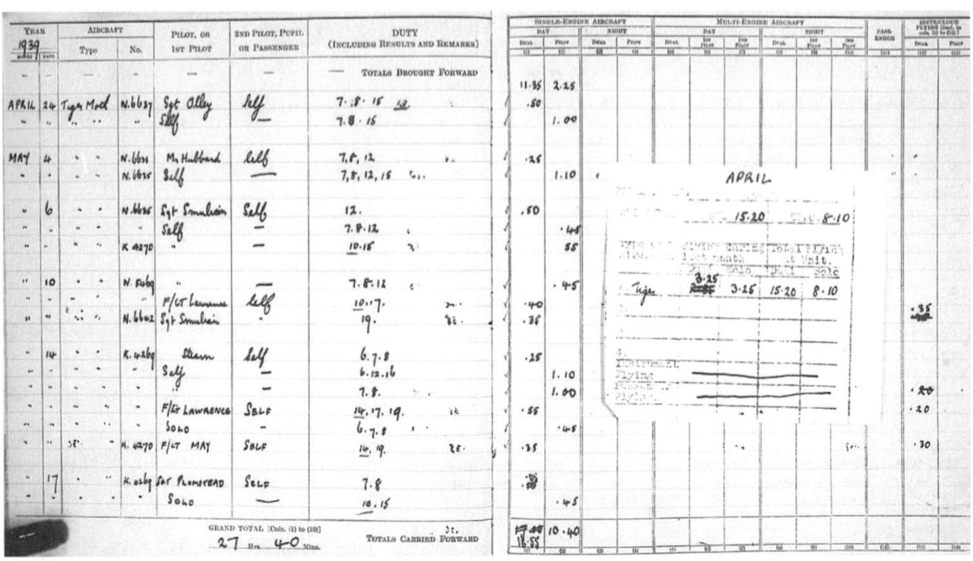

A page from Merrick's logbook, showing his first solo flight in a Tiger Moth, on 14 May 1939. (*Crown Copyright RAF Museum*)

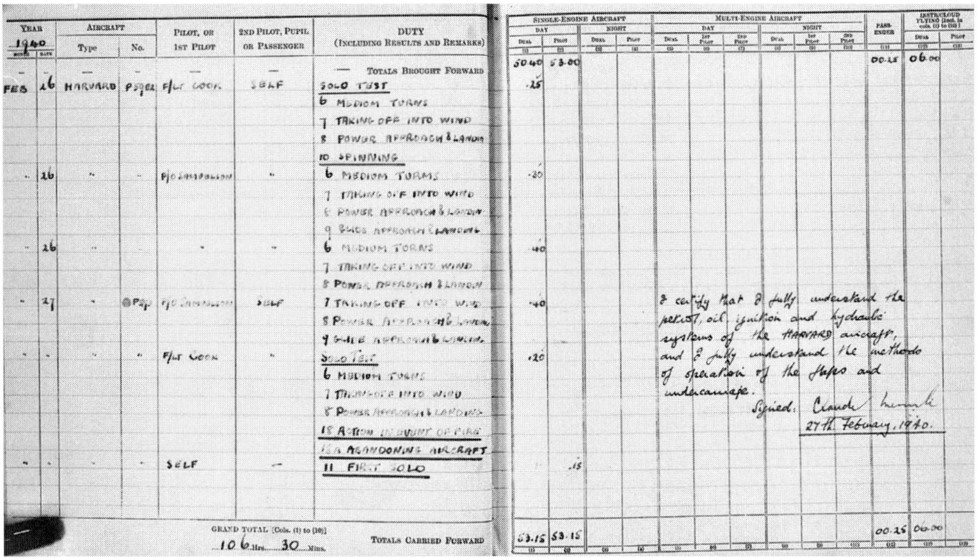

The last line on this page of the logbook shows Merrick's first Solo flight on a Harvard, the main aircraft he trained on to prepare for flying single-engined fighters. On the right is Merrick's declaration that he understood the basics of how to fly the machine. (*Crown Copyright RAF Museum*)

Merrick's logbook does not record any flying time at all between the end of August 1939 and 18 February 1940. This appears to be because he joined 3 ITW at St Leonards, near Hastings, on 2 October 1939 until 16 February 1940. The ITW was a way of introducing all and sundry who had joined the RAF to service life, with physical training, drilling and marching being key components of the daily routine, along with lectures on subjects such as mathematics and the principles of flight.

Having completed this course, Merrick continued his flying training with 15 Service FTS, at Lossiemouth, Scotland. On 17 February 1940, he moved on to the more advanced and powerful North American Harvard trainer, carrying out an air experience flight in one for the first time on 19 February, for thirty-five minutes with a P/O Samuelson. Merrick had just over six hours flying time as a passenger over the next eight days as part of 'C' Flight, getting used to the aircraft, before on 27 February he carried out his first solo on the Harvard for fifteen minutes—another landmark achieved, after fifty-three hours and fifteen minutes as a pilot. From now until mid-July, Merrick would almost exclusively train on the Harvard; the flights increasing in difficulty as he became more proficient.

In early March he was carrying out basic taking off and landing, but by the end of the month he had gone solo at night, a sure indication of his progress. In mid-April he carried out cross-country flights, testing his navigation skills, before his Service Flying Training School (SFTS) moved to Middle Wallop on 20 April until 11 June. By 9 May, Merrick had thirty hours on Harvards and the notes in his logbook on the type of flying he was doing become more martial in nature—on 14 May he carried out a 'war load climb' for an hour; on 20 May he practised high dive-bombing and low-level bombing for just over two hours; formation take-offs were focused on at the end of May, along with air-to-air and air-to-ground firing. Merrick was rated as 'average' on Harvards on 25 May 1940, being 'inclined to be inconsistent'. On 12 June, the course moved to Chipping Norton, and towards the end of the month the training concentrated on the vital use of R/T communication between pilots, another two sessions practised quarter attacks, before finishing the month with seventy minutes on advanced formation flying. This would be key once Merrick joined a squadron.

As the aerial fighting intensified over Britain in July, Merrick's training continued apace. Seven sessions focused on landing at night under floodlights and 'Glimlamps' while his final hour of training at 15 SFTS was spent on quarter attacks on 15 July, reflecting his imminent posting to a fighter squadron. By the end of the course on 26 July 1940, Merrick would have been pleased to be rated as, 'Above the Average'. It reflected very well on his endeavour during five months at the more advanced FTS, and was acknowledged in his promotion to pilot officer. He was now deemed ready to be posted to a fighter squadron, however, none of his 120 hours and fifteen minutes flying time had been on an operational aircraft. His logbook records that from 27–28 July he was posted to 610 Squadron at Prestwick, which seems hard to comprehend given that 610 had left that airfield back in May and that he carried out his final Harvard flight on 29 July. Equally surprising is that on 29 July, Merrick notes that he went to 610 Squadron at Gravesend, again odd as the Squadron had been based at Biggin Hill for the best part of a month. However, we know that at some point, probably on 29 July, he joined up with 610 Squadron.[15]

The other officer to arrive from Chipping Norton was P/O Donald McIntosh Gray, born on 26 June 1919 to his Scottish parents, Mary Jane Fraser and John Gray. They moved to London, where Donald was born, growing up in Palmers Green. Donald Gray clearly had an affinity for flying, passing his pilot's licence on 18 July 1939 at 21 E&RFTS, Stapleford, Essex, while working for De Havilland as a rigger. This was while he was a member of the VR, which he joined, 'about April 1938 as an Airman u/t Pilot (741463). Called up on September 1 1939, he completed his intermediate training and advanced training at 15 FTS, Lossiemouth on Course No 7, which ran from April 28 to July 26 1940',[16] before being commissioned and joining 610 Squadron at Biggin Hill, having followed a very similar course of instruction to Merrick. Gray had recently turned twenty-one.

Naturally, the new pilots' CO would have been keen to meet his new recruits and one of the first questions John Ellis would have wanted an answer to was how much flying experience the new pilots had, and more importantly how many hours they had spent flying Spitfires. From his point of view, none of them would have had enough experience on this state-of-the-art aircraft, especially when they were being sent straight into battle against a very experienced enemy. P/O Cox and Sgt Neville had already done a conversion course to Spitfires and would soon be flying operationally, as had Sgts Gardner and Willcocks, who probably received further training with 'The Chesters', before being declared operational. However, Ellis was shocked to discover that some of the replacements had never flown a Spitfire before! Bamberger described this incident many years later:

GRAY, Donald McIntosh, 19117

51 Avondale Road,
Palmers Green, N.13.

Born 26th.June 1919 at London
Nationality British
Rank, Regiment, Profession Rigger. De Havilland Co.
Certificate taken on D.H.82, Gypsy Major.
At No.21 E. & R. F.T.S. Stapleford.
Date 18.7.39

A very rare photo of Donald McIntosh Gray, from his pilot's licence. (*Copyright Royal Aero Club Trust*)

Donald Gray's pilot's licence. (*Copyright Royal Aero Club Trust*)

I got my wings on June 8, 1940 and I became sergeant and I was sent to rejoin my squadron at Biggin Hill. The squadron leader asked me what I'd last flown, which was a Hawker Hart and he said, 'Well, what bloody use are you to me?" So, twenty-four hours after joining the squadron, I was sent on again to 7 Operational Training Unit, RAF Hawarden, to convert to Spitfires. The switch to a Spitfire was dramatic … I had always been conceited and I thought that I would turn out to be a wonderful fighter ace but when I rejoined 610 Squadron at Biggin Hill at the height of the Battle of Britain, I immediately realised that I knew nothing about air fighting.[17]

Although this would undoubtedly have been a blow for 'Bam', he must have realised what a good service S/Ldr Ellis had done for him. Even if he had been given time on the Squadron to be shown the ropes, he would have been an easy target for any prowling Me 109s. While Ellis was doing the young sergeant a potentially life-saving favour, he would also have been doing it for the Squadron's sake, as he could not risk the lives of his experienced pilots in the hands of such novices. Bamberger was not the only one of the group to be sent away for Spitfire training, as Wynn records that Sgts Manton, Beardsley, Baker, and P/Os Aldous and Gray were also sent to 7 OTU at Hawarden, near Chester, for a conversion course which they seemed to complete between 12–16 August.

Claude Merrick had not carried out any training time on Spitfires either, so he also found himself sent to Hawarden, arriving there by 30 July. The logic of the powers-that-be in having sent such inexperienced men to a front-line Squadron is hard to comprehend but, interestingly, 32 Squadron's CO, S/Ldr Worrall, had the same problem, which he resolved in the same way. Biggin Hill's two COs were operating in tandem. But it also indicates just how desperate the situation was, with very inexperienced pilots filling the ranks of the casualties and what a baptism of fire they were given, where it would literally be 'do or die' in the skies over southern England. Brian Smith recalled the difference between the original pilots with their years of training, and the new recruits:

But we did miles at our training. We trained weekends and one night a week I think it was. And we'd have been round Scotland, down the south, we were well trained. Yet, these other poor blokes, the replacements, they'd come straight from Flying School. Oh, you couldn't help them an awful lot …

When I asked him if they tried to pass on their experience, his response was, 'Well as best we could. We didn't give them the tricky jobs, but …' It was obviously a highly dangerous time for the novice pilots.

As the new recruits acclimatised to life on a front-line fighter station at Biggin Hill on 27 July, the 'old' hands were sent off on an evening patrol of Dover, ten Spitfires led by 'A' Flight's commander Brian Smith. He was at the head of the following formation, which took off at 2015 hours:

DW-A.	R.6976	F/Lt. E. B. B. SMITH.	55
DW-F.	R.6694	Sgt. HAMLYN, R.	24
DW-J.	N.3284	Sgt. TANNER, J. H.	18
DW-S.	R.6621	P/O. S. C. NORRIS.	43
DW-D.	P.9503	Sgt. PARSONS, C. A.	13
DW-Q.	P.9545	F/O. W. H. C. WARNER.*	52
DW-L.	P.9496	F/O. F. T. GARDINER.	17
DW-R.	K.9931	Sgt. RAMSAY, N. H. D.	21
DW-K.	P.9495	Sgt. ARNFIELD, S. J.	42
DW-T.	R.6765	P/O. C. O. J. PEGGE.	16

*As ORB, Warner's recent promotion not mentioned here, or in the next few battle orders.

A slightly stern looking Frank Webster from his school days. (*Reproduced with permission of Bedford Modern School Archive*)

The pilots fruitlessly searched for enemy aircraft, and returned to base after fifty-five minutes. Such an uneventful day was probably a welcome relief to the pilots, following the constant fighting for survival endured earlier in the week. The remainder of the weekend passed peacefully, while another new pilot joined, this time P/O Frank Kinnersley Webster from 5 FTS, Sealand, Chester.

Webster, born on 17 December 1917 to Elizabeth and Jasper Kinnersley Webster, whose father had been a captain in the Royal Warwickshire Regiment, came from Lake on the Isle of Wight, where the family ran The Stag Hotel. Webster was educated at Bedford Modern School, which at the time, 'provided education not only for the locality but also for many colonial and military personnel seeking good education for their young families',[18] which would explain how Frank came to be a pupil there. School archivists Richard Wildman and Jenny Ulph, were able to provide the following synopsis on Webster: 'F K Webster attended Bedford Modern School, then situated in Harpur Street, Bedford, from May 1924 until Easter 1932. He was a boarder at Stamford House … first under the housemaster Mr A W Allen and then … under Mr G H Mason'.[19] In addition, the following is recorded about his sporting prowess: 'At School he was in the VIth Science, a member of the 1st XV in 1929 and 1930, and Captain in 1931. His other athletic accomplishments included running (Public Schools' Steeplechase), boxing, swimming and diving (he won many events at Sandown regattas)'.[20] The Christmas 1931 term was Webster's final one at the school, and the headmaster reported that, 'He has turned out very well indeed and has done good service for the school. A very satisfactory Monitor'.[21] These rounded attributes, shown here on the activities page (see photo p. 271), reflect his contribution to school life.

The school's archives confirm that, 'After leaving school he played for the Wasps R.F.C. In civil life he was buyer of travel goods for the firm of Messrs. Bourne and Hollingsworth, London'.[22] But Webster maintained a strong affiliation with Bedford Modern School, such that five years later, aged twenty-three, he was still in contact by letter. Two years later, in 1939, Webster wrote another letter, to request a reference to assist his application to join the RAFVR, including his reason for wanting

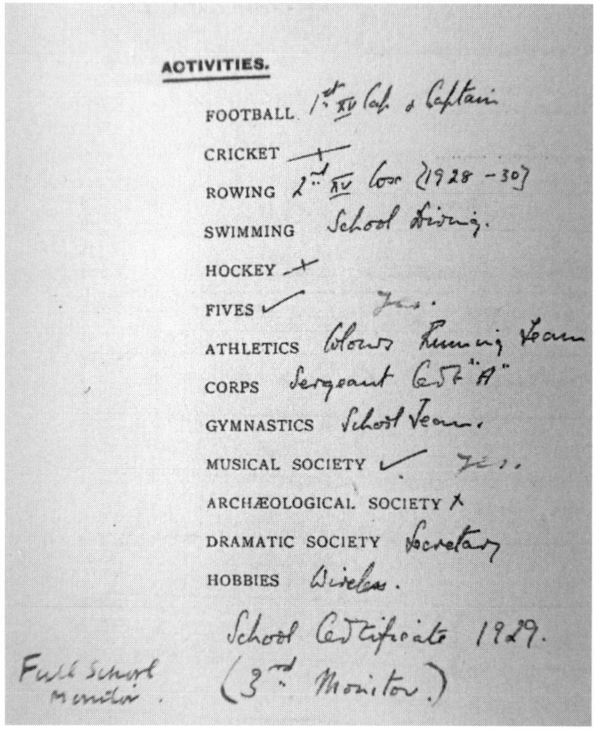

ACTIVITIES.

FOOTBALL 1st XV Cap. & Captain

CRICKET ✗

ROWING 2nd XV Cox (1928–30)

SWIMMING School Diving.

HOCKEY ✗

FIVES ✓ Yes.

ATHLETICS Colours Running team

CORPS Sergeant Cert "A"

GYMNASTICS School Team.

MUSICAL SOCIETY ✓ Yes.

ARCHÆOLOGICAL SOCIETY ✗

DRAMATIC SOCIETY Secretary

HOBBIES Wireless.

School Certificate 1929. (3rd Monitor)

Full School Monitor.

Webster's report. (*Reproduced with permission of Bedford Modern School Archive*)

to sign up and a very interesting description of what joining this service would involve. The other source of interest in the letter, is the mention of 'the crisis before Christmas', which was referring to the Munich agreement of September 1938 (see photos pp. 272–3). Mr Liddle's reply indicates that he thinks Webster would 'enjoy' life in the RAFVR, believing it to be 'a good plan'. Liddle was interested in what was going on in Germany, in fact he was planning a trip up the Rhine to see the 'political situation' for himself, which gives a sense of the contemporary feeling of foreboding in Britain.

It is amazing that just eight months before war was declared on Germany, Webster was still travelling to the country on business and Headmaster Liddle was planning an excursion there. Given what had gone on in the intervening years since Hitler's rise to power, such trips to the Fatherland seem hard to imagine. Frank Webster's determination to join the VR did not diminish. He joined it shortly after these letters, in: 'about April 1939, as an Airman u/t Pilot (745588). Called up on September 1, he completed his elementary training at 15 EFTS, Redhill. He moved on to 5 FTS, Sealand for No 47 Course, which ran from April 29 to July 25 1940. Webster was commissioned on the 27th',[23] before joining his first squadron. Webster also needed additional training on Spitfires, as, 'He was detached to 7 OTU, Hawarden on the 29th and after converting to Spitfires, he rejoined 610 on August 12',[24] along with the other pilots who had been sent to Hawarden.

On Monday 29 July, the Squadron flew down to Hawkinge from Biggin Hill, and would have found the aerodrome busy with a Fox Film Company camera crew. On a fine day, Hawkinge's ORB described the visit as follows, 'S/Ldr GILMAN F.C. accompanied the Fox Film representatives making instructional film at Hawkinge'. It was this footage which would become so symbolic of the Battle of Britain. Whether by design or otherwise, the arrival of the twelve Spitfire pilots must have been the film company's dream. It was not long until they were down at the Squadron's dispersal area at Gibraltar Lane, photographing the 610 Squadron pilots as they awaited the scramble, along with shots of their Spitfires, the squadron identification letters 'DW' instantly recognisable on the fuselage.

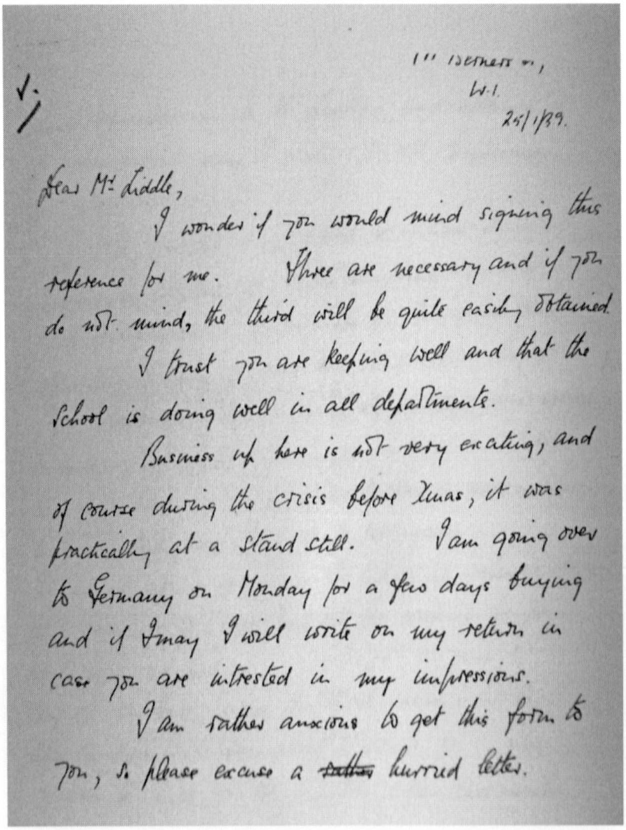

1 Berners St.,
W.1.
25/1/39.

Dear Mr Liddle,

I wonder if you would mind signing this reference for me. Three are necessary and if you do not mind, the third will be quite easily obtained.

I trust you are keeping well and that the School is doing well in all departments.

Business up here is not very exciting, and of course during the crisis before Xmas, it was practically at a stand still. I am going over to Germany on Monday for a few days buying and if I may I will write on my return in case you are interested in my impressions.

I am rather anxious to get this form to you, so please excuse a ~~rather~~ hurried letter.

Webster's letter, pages 1 and 3. (*Reproduced with permission of Bedford Modern School Archive*)

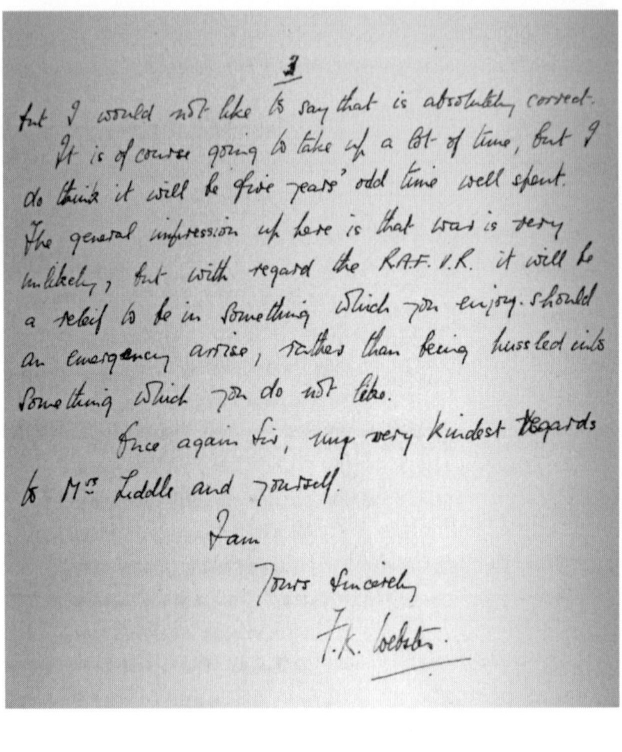

3

but I would not like to say that is absolutely correct.

It is of course going to take up a lot of time, but I do think it will be five years' odd time well spent. The general impression up here is that war is very unlikely, but with regard the R.A.F. V.R. it will be a relief to be in something which you enjoy should an emergency arise, rather than being hussled into something which you do not like.

Once again Sir, my very kindest regards to Mrs Liddle and yourself.

I am

Yours Sincerely

F.K. Webster.

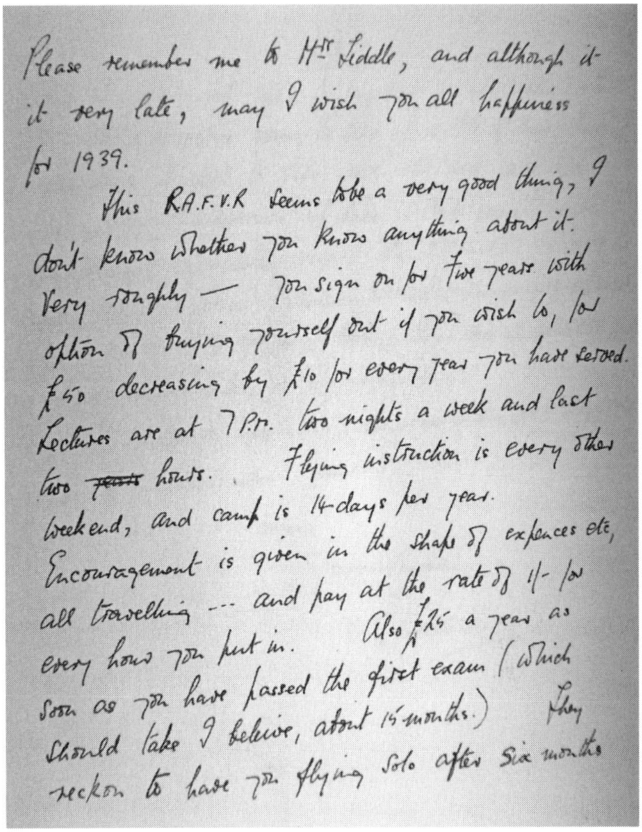
Please remember me to Mr Liddle, and although it it very late, may I wish you all happiness for 1939.

This R.A.F.V.R seems to be a very good thing, I don't know whether you know anything about it. Very roughly — you sign on for five years with option of buying yourself out if you wish to, for £50 decreasing by £10 for every year you have served. Lectures are at 7 P.M. two nights a week and last two ~~years~~ hours. Flying instruction is every other weekend, and camp is 14-days per year. Encouragement is given in the shape of expences etc, all travelling ... and pay at the rate of 1/- for every hour you put in. Also £25 a year as soon as you have passed the first exam (which should take I believe, about 15 months.) They reckon to have you flying solo after six months

Webster's letter, page 2. (*Reproduced with permission of Bedford Modern School Archive*)

Although this collection of photographs is very atmospheric, there is one in particular, of the pilots 'relaxing' between operations, which has since become an iconic image of the Battle of Britain, see p. 274 and the front cover. In the foreground there are eleven pilots probably 'talking shop', wearing their 'Mae West' life jackets, seven standing while four others sit or lie on the floor. Behind them the ground crew can also be seen chatting in a group, while a couple of Spitfires are ready for the scramble, the sun glinting on their fuselages. No. 1 hangar on the right can be used to establish exactly where the photo was taken. It seems to encapsulate that summer of 1940, the pilots and ground crew ready at an instant to get the Spitfires up and away to intercept the *Luftwaffe*—and it is particularly interesting to look at the pilots and their different demeanours. Standing from left to right are P/O Norris, Sgt Chandler with his back to the camera, recently promoted S/Ldr Ellis just visible, facing the camera, Sgt Ramsay, F/Lt Warner, Sgt Hamlyn and F/O Gardiner on the far right, while sitting from left to right are F/Lt Smith, P/O Pegge, Sgt Parsons and Sgt Corfe, the latter about to carry out his first recorded operational patrol with 610 Squadron. The missing pilot from the twelve who had flown down to Hawkinge, is F/O Wilson, who can be seen in conversation with the engineering officer in another photograph from the set. John Ellis is at the centre of the group partially obscured, as you would perhaps expect from the CO, possibly addressing the fairly thoughtful-looking pilots. In fact, in comparison with some other photos from the period, they make a very sober looking group—Warner and Norris appear to be having a relaxing cigarette, while the young Sgt Ramsay looks on in the background like a schoolboy listening to his peers, and Gardiner understandably looks tired and quite strained.

In the foreground, the pilots lying and sitting on the ground also paint an interesting picture. Brian Smith on the far left appears very thoughtful, perhaps addressing the two sergeants opposite him,

One of a series of iconic photos taken of 610 Squadron's pilots, ready for the call to 'Scramble' on 29 July 1940, at Hawkinge. (*Copyright Imperial War Museum, HU 1062*)

while Joe Pegge is flat on his back apparently without a care in the world, arms outstretched with the sun beating down on him. The pilots seem at ease with each other, officers and sergeants mingling, perhaps discussing tactics while they wait to be scrambled. They also come across as a very ordinary bunch of young men, certainly not a group on whom the fate of the nation depended, especially not from Pegge's appearance! The picture does symbolise the undaunted nature of Fighter Command's pilots, who one minute were 'relaxing' in the sun at their airfield, while minutes later they could be involved in a life and death struggle high above the fields of the Home Counties.

The film crew also took photos of 32 Squadron and its Hurricanes, 610's usual partner at Hawkinge, giving a rounded view of the key aircraft being used by Fighter Command in defence of the country. Brian Smith recalled: 'When we were at Hawkinge, they took photographs of us on the ground and 32 Squadron. Yes, one was at one end of Hawkinge and one was at the other … That's right, at the same time, they were at one end, one lot took off and then we followed or they followed—it was a bit hairy!' He even pointed himself out on the photo, 'That's me and that's DW [pointing at a DW- coded Spitfire]. That's Bill [William Warner]. Yes, and these were the boys'. It must have been a very poignant photo for the wing commander, looking back at his former friends who had all passed away before him, either during the war or over the ensuing decades.

As these photos show, the pilots were at readiness to be scrambled, and at 1245 hours the Squadron was ordered off on an interception. S/Ldr Ellis led as Blue Leader, Brian Smith was Red 1, Stan Norris was Yellow 1 and Bill Warner would almost certainly have been Green 1. As a best guess from the available information, the formation would have been composed as follows:

The other famous group photo, involving all twelve pilots. From the left standing, Norris, Chandler (back to camera), Ellis, Ramsay, Gardiner, Warner, Hamlyn and on far right the tall figure of Douglas Wilson talking to the station engineer (not 610), called F/Lt Jackson. On the ground, Brian Smith is lying on his front, Pegge on his back, Parsons facing the camera and Corfe. (*Fox Photos/Hulton Archive/Getty Images*)

DW-W.	R.6993	F/Lt. J. ELLIS.*	Blue 1	40
DW-T.	R.6765	F/O. F. T. GARDINER.	Blue 2	18
DW-K.	P.9495	Sgt. CORFE, D.	Blue 3	1
DW-Q.	P.9545	F/O. D. S. WILSON.	Green 2	3
DW-N.	R.6806	F/O. W. H. C. WARNER.	Green 1	53
DW-L.	P.9496	Sgt. RAMSAY, N. H. D.	Green 3	22
DW-A.	R.6976	F/Lt. E. B. B. SMITH.	Red 1	56
DW-D.	P.9503**	Sgt. PARSONS, C. A.	Red 2	14
DW-E.	R.6629	Sgt. CHANDLER, H. H.	Red 3	8
DW-X.	R.6630	P/O. C. O. J. PEGGE.	Yellow 3	17
DW-H.	L.1044***	P/O. S. C. NORRIS.	Yellow 1	44
DW-J.	N.3284	Sgt. HAMLYN, R.	Yellow 2	25

*As ORB, Ellis's recent promotion not mentioned here, or in the next few battle orders.
**This Spitfire was actually being flown by Norris, see ensuing explanation.
***This Spitfire may have been flown by Parsons instead.

There is some confusion over the events of this patrol, as while 'A' Flight carried out an interception at 1300 hours, the ORB recorded that 'B' Flight landed back at Hawkinge at 1316 hours. Either this suggests the two flights were operating completely independently, or perhaps as 'B' Flight came into the circuit to land, 'A' Flight, also over Hawkinge, was ordered to give chase to 'Raid 49' which had resurfaced on the RDF screens. Whatever happened will never be known precisely, but 'A' Flight, led by Smith, was ordered to intercept an enemy aircraft off Dungeness at 6,000 feet, as recorded in the experienced flight commander's combat report:

> I was Red one leading 'A' Flight and when over Hawkinge was ordered to intercept E/A off Dungeness. I sighted one E/A off Dungeness on my Starboard Beam. I then gave A/C astern No.1 attack go. I started a Beam attack on E/A which turned and compelled me to do an astern attack from slightly above. I fired two or three bursts, and then broke away. I was followed by Red 2 and 3, and yellow Section. I was then in a position for another attack. I followed yellow 2 trying to do a No.2 attack simultaneously, but E/A dived to sea level. I saw yellow 2's bullets hitting the port wing of E/A and small pieces coming off, also a certain amount of smoke from its engines which cleared away. I then followed up and saw my bullets hitting the wing of E/A and expended my ammunition. The E/A continued to fly on. Its camouflage was dark green and it had a small upper turret, from which an Air Gunner was firing. (TNA, AIR 50/172/72)

Smith led a textbook attack on the Dornier 215. From the detailed report it is possible to imagine him issuing his terse instructions over the R/T, 'Aircraft astern, Number 1 attack. Go!' before the well-drilled pilots followed his lead. After his first attack of two or three bursts of fire from 200 yards, Smith attempted to carry out a No. 2 attack alongside Sgt Hamlyn, to split the gunners' fire. The German pilot reacted to this by diving to sea level, having originally been at 6,000 feet, thereby reducing the chance of attacking him from below. Yet again, the Spitfire's firepower proved to be inadequate when attempting to bring down a bomber.

As the Dornier fled for France, by the time Yellow Section attacked they were ten miles south of Dungeness, at just twenty feet. With the waves of the English Channel so close to them, this left no margin of error for the onrushing RAF pilots or the German pilot taking evasive action. P/O Norris, described the encounter as follows:

> I was Yellow 1 in "A" Flt 610 Sqdn when "A" Flt was ordered to intercept an E.A. When at 7000' Red 1. sighted E.A flying on a Northerly course just approaching Dungeness.
>
> Red section attacked E.A. followed by Yellow section—No.1 attack being used. I followed E.A. nearly to the French coast at a height of about 20'. I fired all my rounds & he still appeared to be in perfect control turning from side to side as an evasive action. The rear gunner was still firing & hit me in the port leading edge which penetrated my port wheel & puncturing the tyre. (TNA, AIR 50/172/53)

Despite Norris's persistence, firing from 200 yards to just fifty yards and using all his ammunition, the bomber continued on its flight to safety. To make matters worse, Norris would have heard the sickening sound of bullets hitting his Spitfire, leaving him with a nerve-wracking return flight to Hawkinge. Thankfully the damage was not serious enough to bring his aircraft down. Norris returned physically unscathed although, it must have been a tricky landing given that the port tyre had been punctured. Despite the uneven odds of this engagement, the Spitfires were vulnerable to the return fire of German bombers, especially when pressing attacks home to such close range, as seen earlier in the month when P/O Raven was shot down in similar circumstances.

There is some confusion over the Spitfire involved in this incident, as the ORB noted it as DW-H, L.1044, while P.9503 was recorded as being been flown by Sgt Parsons on this patrol. In addition, the ORB noted that Norris later flew another patrol that day in L.1044, which given the damage sustained, seems unlikely. This would indicate it was P.9503 which had been damaged, although it must have been quickly repaired, as it was back flying two days later.[25] *Then and Now* recorded, '**P9503.** Damaged by return fire from Do 17 of Stab KG2 engaged over Channel off Dungeness 1.15 p.m. Landed at base on

A Do 17Z of KG2, believed to be the unit encountered by 610 Squadron on 29 July 1940. (*Ron Mackay*)

punctured tyre. P/O S. C. Norris unhurt. **DW-D** damaged but repairable'.[26] Having investigated the different possibilities, this seems to be the most likely Spitfire.

A third combat report survived from this battle, that of Sgt Hamlyn, Yellow 2:

> One Dornier 215 sighted 5 miles South of Dungeness. On being intercepted it dropped all its bombs into the sea and turned 180° and dived to sea level. Red section then attacked and I stayed at 7,000 feet with Yellow section until Red 3 had finished his attack. I then made my approach and at 300 yards range the rear gunner opened fire: I held my fire until I was 200 yards away, I then opened fire on the port engine and I could see my ammunition entering the engine, after my third burst I noticed large pieces falling off the bomber and a burst of white smoke started, but this stopped again soon afterwards and the engine was still working. The rear gunner was still firing when I broke off the attack. I noticed a small gun turret on the upper side of the fuselage. The camouflage was a dark olive green.
>
> (sgd) R. F. Hamlyn. Sgt.
>
> 4 bursts of 4 sec. each. Total no of rounds—2380. Sgt. Hamlyn. (TNA, AIR 50/172/34)

Hamlyn gives a real sense of the bomber's crew immediately realising their predicament, making an about turn and running for home, frantically ditching bombs to make the Dornier as light and fast as possible. Yellow Section had maintained their altitude at 7,000 feet while Red Section attacked, as a precaution against any escorting fighters. It also enabled the second section to build up speed in a dive, before they attacked the bomber. Hamlyn closed in to 200 yards before firing through to 100 yards, focusing on one of the aircraft's weak points, the engine, with four bursts of four seconds each. But despite hitting the bomber, as Smith had witnessed, he failed to do any fatal damage, and the dark green-camouflaged Dornier 215 (subsequently thought to be a Dornier Do 17 by *Then and Now*), made its escape at twenty feet, the gunner still stubbornly firing.

As the 'Dog Rose' Spitfires returned to Hawkinge at about 1330 hours, and filed their reports to 610's intelligence officer, Walter Lloyd, it would immediately have become apparent that despite the accuracy of their fire and pressing home their attacks to close range, the bomber could only be claimed as damaged. This was primarily as a result of the inadequacy of the .303 machine gun bullets against the bomber's armour, which was by no means particularly thick. In 2011, Brian Smith still wished his

A section of 610 Squadron landing at Hawkinge, believed to be part of the Fox Film Company's series of photographs taken on 29 July 1940. The leading Spitfire is DW-W, probably R.6993 flown by S/Ldr John Ellis. The second Spitfire is DW-T, probably R.6765 flown by F/O Gardiner. The third Spitfire, just visible over the perimeter fence, is likely to be DW-K, P.9495 flown by Sgt Corfe, the third member of Ellis's Section on 29 July. (*ww2images.com*)

fighter had more powerful armament: 'We used to hit some enemy aircraft, and they used to go on flying! And what we wanted was these cannon, because the cannon if they're on—pssst!' (indicating a destroyed German aircraft). The ORB summarised the engagement as follows:

> Spitfires attacked in succession, 4 using all their ammunition, and 1 about 800 rounds. E/A was considerably damaged, pieces falling off, and smoke pouring from port engine. Pilots comment on speed of E/A necessitating opening the gate wide to engage. Tactics adopted were evasive turns—when action broken off, E/A was last seen in mid-channel flying steadily at 50 feet. Enemy casualties:– 1 DO215 damaged.

Interestingly, one thing that was picked up on in a later '11 Group Intelligence Bulletin', was that the Dornier 215 had a small turret for the rear gunner, noted by both Smith and Hamlyn. It is fascinating to see such information being passed on to all units on a regular basis, to ensure all fighter pilots were aware of any enemy equipment or tactics, which could help them in any way. One would have expected the six fighters to have brought the enemy aircraft down, but to the bomber crew's credit they escaped—indeed the rear gunner put up a valiant defence, and it was probably this gunner who damaged Stanley Norris's Spitfire. *RAF Fighter Command Victory Claims of World War II Part One 1939–1940* refers to the following pilots as being awarded a share in the damage, a Do 17 not a 215 as the pilots originally claimed:

Sgt R. F. Hamlyn	Do 17 damaged	Near Sangatte 1300
F/L E. B. B. Smith	- shared -	
P/O S. C. Norris	- shared -	
Sgt C. A. Parsons	- shared -.[27]	

It is a little strange that Parsons is included in this list but Pegge and Chandler are not, when they also made up 'A' Flight, and there are only surviving combat reports for Smith, Norris and Hamlyn. The ORB states that five Spitfires had attacked in succession, so presumably either Pegge or Chandler were unsuccessful in their attack—it is impossible to say for certain.

Brian Smith, lying on his front, his Flight Lieutenant's stripes standing out, talks to Joe Pegge, still lying on his back, whilst Claude Parsons props himself up. Behind them, Stanley Norris, left and Ronnie Hamlyn, right, enjoy a cigarette, either side of John Ellis, who is slightly more visible from this angle, whilst the other pilots have drifted away. The distinctive Squadron markings are clear to see on the Mark I Spitfire in the background. (*Fox Photos/Hulton Archive/Getty Images*)

Although the men of 'A' Flight must have been disappointed not to have been more successful, they had caused extensive damage to the unfortunate Dornier Do 17Z (again, a Do 17 here), which apparently belonged to Stab KG2: 'Landed back at St Inglevert severely damaged in attacks from 'A' Flight No. 610 Squadron over the Channel off Dungeness 1.00 p.m. Lt. Hunger wounded. Aircraft 60 per cent damaged',[28] making it all the more impressive that the German crew got their machine back.

After the drama of the interception, the rest of the day passed without incident, until P/O Norris (45) was ordered up on his own at 2140 hours, 'to patrol Patrol line No. 3' (ORB), for fifteen minutes before returning to Hawkinge at 2155 hours. He was in DW-H, L.1044 and did not see any aircraft, either friend or foe. It shows what a long day the fighter pilots had to endure, up at the crack of dawn, and still flying patrols as late as 2155 hours—it was exhausting. On this occasion, it is more than likely that Norris would have hurried off to a local pub once the Squadron had returned to Biggin Hill, to join the rest of the Squadron in a birthday celebration. 29 July 1940 was Sgt Ramsay's twenty-first birthday, which underlines the age of these pilots. They were by and large very young, Ramsay being the age of a final year student at university, and yet so much responsibility lay on their shoulders. Perhaps the greatest gift that Ramsay received was returning from another operational patrol unscathed. In the photographs taken that day, Ramsay barely looks his age, although few people could have had such iconic pictures taken on their birthday!

One other interesting piece of news that arose on 29 July, was that John Ellis had been awarded the Distinguished Flying Cross (DFC), the first such award for a member of 610 (County of Chester) Squadron. It is recorded in 11 Group's ORB appendices and a citation would be released in due course, when the inevitable celebrations would take place.

Another view of some of 610 Squadron's pilots on 29 July, probably discussing the encounter with the Dornier. From left to right, F/O Gardiner, P/O Pegge, Sgt Parsons, Sgt Hamlyn and Sgt Chandler in deep conversation. The tall member of ground crew behind Chandler is AC Goff. A Mark I Spitfire is hurriedly being readied for action in the background. (*Fox Photos/Hulton Archive/Getty Images*)

The Squadron ORB for the last couple of days of July is a little confusing, as the notes are recorded as being in August, however the pilots mentioned include men who could not possibly have been flying at the end of August. So it is safe to assume the patrols carried out below are not 30 and 31 August but 30 and 31 July 1940. The two days did not involve anything particularly momentous, but included a full Squadron patrol early on the morning of 30 July. Given that this patrol had some different pilots from the previous day, it is most likely that the Squadron had returned to Biggin Hill on the evening of 29 July. Either the Squadron had flown to Hawkinge early the following morning and taken off from there at 0831 hours, or the patrol started from Biggin Hill at 0831 hours, with orders to patrol Hawkinge at 'Angels 10' in overcast conditions. F/Lt Smith's formation was:

DW-B.	L.1009	F/Lt. E. B. B. SMITH.	57
DW-F.	R.6694	Sgt. HAMLYN, R.	26
DW-G.	L.1045	Sgt. PARSONS, C. A.	15
DW-Q.	P.9545	F/O. W. H. C. WARNER.	54
DW-R.	K.9931	Sgt. RAMSAY, N. H. D.	23
DW-P.	R.6695	Sgt. CORFE, D.	2
DW-S.	R.6621	P/O. S. C. NORRIS.	46
DW-J.	N.3284	P/O. C. O. J. PEGGE.	18
DW-E.	R.6629	Sgt. CHANDLER, H. H.	9
DW-T.	R.6765	F/O. F. T. GARDINER.	19
DW-N.	R.6806	F/O. D. S. WILSON.	4
DW-V.	P.9330	P/O. H. K. COX.*	1

*As ORB, but should be 'K. H. Cox'. I have adhered to the ORB, but it applies throughout August too.

As soon as the Spitfires had landed, the ground crew swarmed over them, checking for damage, plus refuelling and rearming the fighters. Here, the vital work of preparing four of the Spitfire's eight .303 Browning machine guns is being carried out. This is almost certainly one of the Spitfires of 'A' Flight, which had fired its guns at the Dornier, as the red doped fabric which covered the muzzles has been blasted off when the pilot opened fire. (*Fox Photos/Hulton Archive/Getty Images*)

Another team of armourers at work on a 610 Squadron Spitfire. The danger of the constant aerial threat at Hawkinge is highlighted by the prominence of the man's tin hat. (*Copyright Imperial War Museum, HU 54520*)

A tired looking Sgt Ramsay, centre, on his twenty-first birthday flanked by Sgt Hamlyn, (left), possibly eating a piece of chocolate to keep his energy up, and P/O Pegge, looking more thoughtful than in the rest of the photos. They are in conversation, probably about the attack on the Dornier. (*Fox Photos/Hulton Archive/ Getty Images*)

The layout of the Squadron is uncertain, but it is most likely that Brian Smith was leading Red Section, with Norris leading Yellow Section to make up 'A' Flight, while Bill Warner led Blue Section and Gardiner led Green Section, these six Spitfires composing 'B' Flight. At 0910 hours, 'B' Flight was ordered to land, but 'A' Flight, in a repeat of the previous day's operation, was subsequently ordered to intercept 'Bandits' between Cap Gris-Nez and Dungeness. No enemy aircraft were sighted (ORB). The rest of 610 returned to Hawkinge at 0930 hours. It was an important day in the flying career of P/O Cox, who notched up his first recorded operational patrol just three days after joining the Squadron. He was clearly at a more advanced stage than the likes of Sgt Bamberger, who had been sent away to convert to Spitfires, and it showed the urgency with which these new pilots were being thrust into the battle. No other flying was recorded for the remainder of 30 July.

There was little to be done by the men of 610 on the last day of the month, save for Red Section's five-minute patrol of Dungeness in the morning, following an early flight to Hawkinge given the timescales involved. The pilots who took off in fine weather at 0620 hours were:

DW-X.	R.6630	F/Lt. E. B. B. SMITH.	Red 1	58
DW-F.	R.6694	Sgt. HAMLYN, R.		27
DW-G.	L.1045	Sgt. PARSONS, C. A.		16

Red Section was almost immediately recalled and landed at 0625 hours.

July ended with a whimper for the Squadron, although it had been a very busy month overall, with much more contact with the *Luftwaffe* than in June. The Squadron had carried out thirty-three recorded patrols during July, fifteen of which had resulted in action with the enemy, however this does only reflect the recorded patrols. The Squadron almost certainly carried out quite a few more sorties, which the ORB did not record as there was no contact with the enemy. The Squadron had lost another four pilots, three of them killed in action and one while training, along with two wounded, one of whom would take no further part in the Battle. During July 1940, 610 Squadron had filed claims for fourteen enemy aircraft destroyed, two probable, eight unconfirmed and four damaged, see below:

	Destroyed	Probable	Unconfirmed	Damaged	Total Claims
Me 109	11	1	7	2	21
Do 17	1	N/A	N/A	N/A	1
Do 215	1	N/A	1	2	4
Chance Vought	1	1	N/A	N/A	2
Total	14	2	8	4	28

The pilots who had made the claims in July are as follows:

F/Lt. E. B. B. Smith	17 shared destroyed 3/7, 109 destroyed 24/7, 109 probable 24/7, Chance Vought probable 24/7, 109 unconfirmed 25/7, 215 shared damaged 29/7
Sgt. Ramsay	17 shared destroyed 3/7
F/Lt. Warner	109 unconfirmed 10/7
Sgt. Parsons	215 shared destroyed 9/7, 109 unconfirmed 25/7
Sgt. Arnfield	No claims.

A deceptively calm looking scene at Hawkinge on 29 July 1940, with 610 Squadron's Mark I Spitfires lined up ready for a scramble from the Gibraltar Lane dispersal area. It appears that the group of pilots are standing in the far distance, above the engine of DW-K. At the ring of a telephone, this scene would have transformed into a noisy drama, as 610 Squadron rushed to get airborne. DW-K was P.9495, flown by Sgt Corfe on this day, whilst DW-T was R.6765, the mount of F/O Gardiner, which replaced DW-T, P.9452 in which Peter Litchfield had been killed. DW-A, probably R.6976, was piloted by Brian Smith. It had replaced R.6693, the aircraft in which S/Ldr Tom Smith had recently been killed. Behind DW-A, is DW-L, P.9496, which was being flown by Norman Ramsay on his birthday. (*Fox Photos/Hulton Archive/Getty Images*)

P/O. Norris	109 unconfirmed 25/7, 109 destroyed 25/7, 215 shared damaged 29/7
S/Ldr. Ellis	17 shared destroyed 3/7, 109 destroyed 24/7, 109 destroyed 24/7, 109 destroyed 25/7, 109 destroyed 25/7, 109 destroyed 25/7
Sgt. Else	17 shared destroyed 3/7, 215 damaged 8/7, 109 unconfirmed 25/7, 109 destroyed 25/7
F/O. Gardiner	109 damaged? 20/7, 109 unconfirmed 25/7
P/O. Litchfield	215 unconfirmed 3/7, 109 destroyed 14/7, 109 damaged 14/7
P/O. Pegge	109 destroyed 8/7, 215 shared damaged 29/7
Sgt. Hamlyn	17 shared destroyed 3/7, 215 shared damaged 29/7
Sgt. Tanner	No claims.
Sgt. Chandler	Chance Vought destroyed 24/7, 109 unconfirmed 25/7, 215 shared damaged 29/7
F/O. Lamb	17 shared destroyed 3/7
P/O. Keighley	No claims.
S/Ldr. A. T. Smith	215 shared destroyed 9/7
F/O. Wilson	109 destroyed 25/7
P/O. Raven	No claims.
Sgt. Corfe	No claims.
P/O. Cox	No claims.

This brought the total claims to twenty-five destroyed, two probable, eleven unconfirmed and five damaged, forty-three claims altogether, which showed how successfully the Squadron had been operating in such highly dangerous skies. The dreadful proof of the danger lay in the fact that since hostilities began, 610 had lost twelve pilots killed and three wounded, heavy losses indeed. The pilots who had carried out the most recorded patrols in July were F/Lt Brian Smith and Sgt Norman Ramsay, who had amassed nineteen patrols each. F/O Warner had carried out seventeen sorties, while Sgts Parsons and Arnfield had both done sixteen.

By the end of July, the Squadron was fortunate to have a group of veterans who had survived Dunkirk and the ensuing months, while it had a core of replacement pilots who had now gained much experience too. 610 Squadron was very well placed to continue the fight against the *Luftwaffe* from Biggin Hill, although all concerned must have feared that the worst was still to come.

13

1–13 August 1940: Beware of the Hun in the Sun

The next record in the Squadron's ORB is not until Sunday 11 August, although the Squadron was operational during this period, being based at the key sector station of Biggin Hill. Evidently, despite a reduction in activity in the first week of August in the south-east, the task of compiling the ORB was neglected, as the Squadron would still have carried out patrols. But poor weather limited the *Luftwaffe's* operations, and although there were a couple of skirmishes, they did not involve 'The Chesters'. In fact, there were no engagements at all on 6–7 August in 11 Group, as shown on the photo on p. 287. While bad weather partially explains the lack of activity, another reason was that Göring was busy preparing his *Luftwaffe* for the continuation of the battle. Although it had achieved remarkable success during the *Blitzkrieg*, the *Luftwaffe* had not had it all its own way, suffering heavy losses, particularly in the Battle for France and over Dunkirk. So this lull served as an opportunity to prepare to renew the offensive against Britain.

Fighter Command and its squadrons were also busy organising themselves for the battle ahead, and 610 Squadron was no exception. Training and practice flights were the order of the day, to give the new pilots as much experience as possible, such exercises being led by the 'old hands', trying to impart their hard won knowledge to the latest recruits. Very little has been recorded from other sources during this period, even regarding the comings and goings of new pilots, however it is likely that the influx of pilots at the end of July had brought the Squadron up to its full complement. At the start of August, the list of pilots would have read as follows:

1	S/Ldr. J. Ellis.	12	Sgt. S. J. Arnfield.
2	F/Lt. E. B. B. Smith.	13	Sgt. P. Else.
3	F/Lt. W. H. C. Warner.	14	Sgt. N. H. D. Ramsay.
4	F/O. P. G. Lamb.	15	Sgt. J. H. Tanner.
5	F/O. D. S. Wilson.	16	Sgt. H. H. Chandler.
6	F/O. F. T. Gardiner.	17	Sgt. R. F. Hamlyn.
7	P/O. S. C. Norris.	18	Sgt. D. F. Corfe.
8	P/O. C. O. J. Pegge.	19	P/O. K. H. Cox.
9	P/O. B. V. Rees.	20	Sgt. B. G. D. Gardner.
10	P/O. I. H. Stewart.	21	Sgt. P. H. Willcocks.
11	Sgt. C. A. Parsons.	22	Sgt. W. J. Neville.

In addition to these twenty-two operational pilots, the following eight men belonged to 610 Squadron, but were converting to the Spitfire:

23	P/O. E. S. Aldous.	25	P/O. D. McI. Gray.
24	P/O. C. Merrick.	26	Sgt. R. A. Beardsley.

27	Sgt. A. C. Baker.	29	Sgt E. Manton.
28	Sgt. C. S. Bamberger.	30	P/O F. K. Webster.

The Squadron was in a healthy state for the coming trials, with a strong nucleus of pilots with numerous combat patrols under their belts. Nevertheless, the dangerous skies over south-eastern England were no training ground for the novice pilots, and the Messerschmitt 109s and 110s would prove merciless to any of the 'new boys' who were caught unawares, which is all too evident once the ORB resumes.

The first event of any import in August for the men of 610 Squadron, was that F/Lt Brian Smith was about to get married to his fiancée, assistant Section Officer Pamela Smith of the Women's Auxiliary Air Force (WAAF). Their wedding was due to take place on Saturday 3 August in Upton, Wirral, not far from the Squadron's old home at Hooton Park, so Smith would have been granted leave for this special event. News of the nuptials was announced in *The Chronicle*, tragically, in the very same edition which reported S/Ldr A. T. Smith's funeral, someone who would have been sorely missed by the groom. This was a memorable day for Brian Smith, and the newly-weds spent their honeymoon at Beaumaris, Anglesey.

While Brian Smith was on honeymoon, nothing was recorded as having taken place in the ORB. But an incident which occurred in this void in the Squadron's history, is noted in an '11 Group Intelligence Bulletin' for Thursday 8 August (see photo p. 287), helpfully recording what happened and which squadrons were involved. The *Luftwaffe's* probing of Fighter Command defences and the attacks on the convoys had gradually been ratcheted up, and the cause of the engagements was Convoy CW9 'Peewit', a large westbound convoy, which had set sail from Southend-on-Sea at 0700 hours on Wednesday 7 August. It was observed by the Germans and came under repeated attack on 8 August as it crept past Beachy Head and the Isle of Wight. The Spitfires of 610, 41 and 64 Squadrons all became entangled with groups of Me 109s, probably from III/JG 51, in the late morning and early afternoon.

Given the heavy fighting on 8 August which involved 610 Squadron, it is surprising that the ORB does not mention it. There are no surviving combat reports either, which also suggests 'The Chesters' were not responsible for the demise of any *Luftwaffe* aircraft. However, the 'Intelligence Bulletin' shows exactly when each unit was on patrol; 610 Squadron's 12 Spitfires took off at 1020 hours and carried out a patrol, before returning to base at 1150 hours. Thanks to the AMCB files, we now know that Sgt Ramsay was shot down during this patrol, which took place at about 20,000 feet over Dungeness.

The wedding of F/Lt Brian Smith and Assistant Section Officer Pamela Smith. (*Copyright Smith family*)

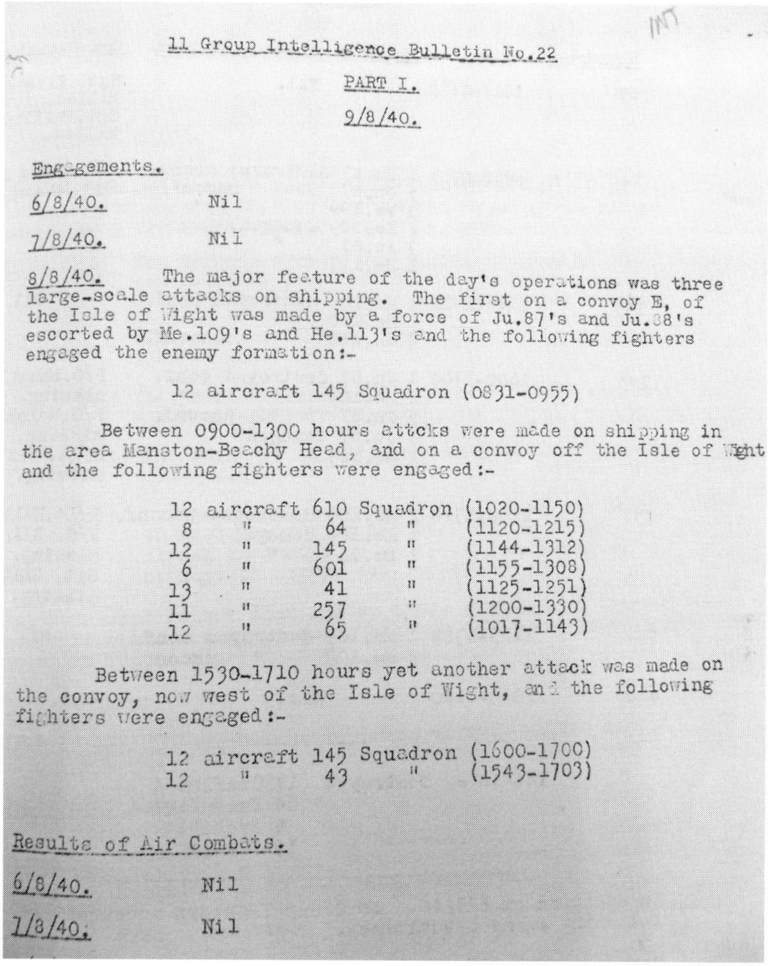

11 Group Intelligence Bulletin No.22

PART I.

9/8/40.

Engagements.

6/8/40. Nil

7/8/40. Nil

8/8/40. The major feature of the day's operations was three large-scale attacks on shipping. The first on a convoy E, of the Isle of Wight was made by a force of Ju.87's and Ju.88's escorted by Me.109's and He.113's and the following fighters engaged the enemy formation:-

12 aircraft 145 Squadron (0831-0955)

Between 0900-1300 hours attcks were made on shipping in the area Manston-Beachy Head, and on a convoy off the Isle of Wight and the following fighters were engaged:-

12	aircraft	610	Squadron	(1020-1150)
8	"	64	"	(1120-1215)
12	"	145	"	(1144-1312)
6	"	601	"	(1155-1308)
13	"	41	"	(1125-1251)
11	"	257	"	(1200-1330)
12	"	65	"	(1017-1143)

Between 1530-1710 hours yet another attack was made on the convoy, now west of the Isle of Wight, and the following fighters were engaged:-

12	aircraft	145	Squadron	(1600-1700)
12	"	43	"	(1543-1703)

Results of Air Combats.

6/8/40. Nil

7/8/40. Nil

Record of 11 Group's operations on 8 August 1940. (*TNA, AIR 25/197*)

Ramsay (24) was in Green Section at the Squadron's rear, acting as a 'weaver', along with Green 2, the most dangerous position to be in. While keeping a look out for everyone else in front of them, the two 'weavers' became the most vulnerable targets. It is interesting to see that 610 had adopted this tactic too. While the Squadron climbed to investigate a report of enemy fighters above them, one Me 109 decided to take advantage of this situation and pick off a 'weaver', Ramsay as it turned out. The 109 escaped, despite Green 2's best efforts. Ramsay's Spitfire had been hit quite badly, while in addition, the cooling system had been damaged (AIR 81/1272). Ramsay needed all his skill and training to get DW-T, R.6765, down safely, successfully landing at Hawkinge despite the damage and being wounded in the leg.

The whole experience must have been terrifying for the twenty-one year old, and this explains why he did not fly another recorded operation until six days later. Ramsay is confirmed as 'slightly wounded' in 11 Group's ORB Appendices, along with the fact that 610 Squadron did not make any claims. However, it seems another Spitfire also came into difficulties during this patrol, whether through enemy activity or technical problems is unclear, as there is no mention of it in either 610's or 11 Group's ORB Appendices.

Then and Now, has the following information about 8 August in relation to 610 Squadron:

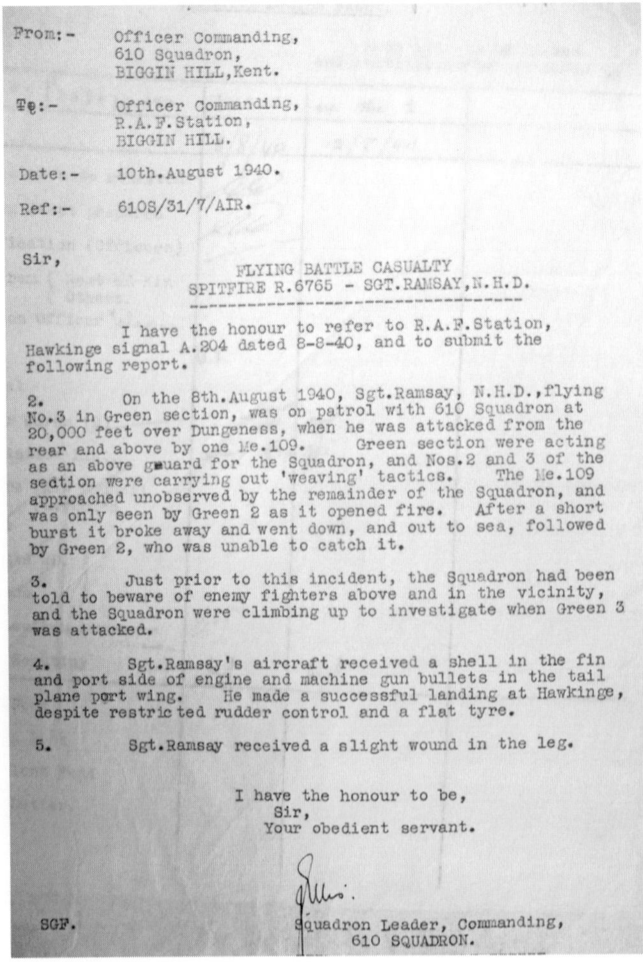

From:- Officer Commanding,
610 Squadron,
BIGGIN HILL,Kent.

To:- Officer Commanding,
R.A.F.Station,
BIGGIN HILL.

Date:- 10th.August 1940.

Ref:- 610S/31/7/AIR.

Sir,

FLYING BATTLE CASUALTY
SPITFIRE R.6765 - SGT.RAMSAY,N.H.D.

I have the honour to refer to R.A.F.Station, Hawkinge signal A.204 dated 8-8-40, and to submit the following report.

2. On the 8th.August 1940, Sgt.Ramsay, N.H.D.,flying No.3 in Green section, was on patrol with 610 Squadron at 20,000 feet over Dungeness, when he was attacked from the rear and above by one Me.109. Green section were acting as an above guard for the Squadron, and Nos.2 and 3 of the section were carrying out 'weaving' tactics. The Me.109 approached unobserved by the remainder of the Squadron, and was only seen by Green 2 as it opened fire. After a short burst it broke away and went down, and out to sea, followed by Green 2, who was unable to catch it.

3. Just prior to this incident, the Squadron had been told to beware of enemy fighters above and in the vicinity, and the Squadron were climbing up to investigate when Green 3 was attacked.

4. Sgt.Ramsay's aircraft received a shell in the fin and port side of engine and machine gun bullets in the tail plane port wing. He made a successful landing at Hawkinge, despite restricted rudder control and a flat tyre.

5. Sgt.Ramsay received a slight wound in the leg.

I have the honour to be,
Sir,
Your obedient servant.

Ellis.

SGF. Squadron Leader, Commanding,
610 SQUADRON.

S/Ldr Ellis's detailed account of the interception, which led to Ramsay's emergency landing at Hawkinge. (*TNA AIR 81/1272*)

Thursday 8 August, Hawkinge.

R6765. Severely damaged in combat with Bf 109s of JG 51 over base 11.30 a.m. Pilot unhurt. **DW-T** damaged but repairable.

L1045. Forced-landed near Wittersham following combat with Bf 109s of JG 51 over base 11.20 a.m. Pilot believed unhurt. Aircraft damaged but repairable.[1]

While we now know the pilot of R.6765 was Ramsay, the latter appears to be a mystery, but thanks to Wynn's research, it is apparent that the pilot of DW-G, L.1045 was Sgt William Neville (1), who had crash-landed, 'at Potmans Heath Marsh, Wittersham … in Spitfire L 1045. The aircraft overturned but Neville was unhurt'.[2] Neville had only been with the Squadron for thirteen days, and given his inexperience, had done well to get his Spitfire down in an emergency, in one of the many flat fields surrounding Wittersham. Surviving such an incident unscathed must have been a boost to his confidence, despite having to escape from an upturned aircraft. But the young VR pilot had experienced a frightening lesson in just how perilous the skies were over the south-east coast, especially when coming into contact with a roving group of Me 109s. He would have been all too aware that one of his first patrols with 610 Squadron, could so easily have been his last … Neither of the two Spitfires seems to have flown with the Squadron again, being sent away for repairs.[3]

It is likely that JG 51 was the cause of Ramsay's downfall in DW-T, R.6765, and possibly Neville in DW-G, L.1045. Simon Parry believes that JG 51 had actually engaged 64 and 41 Squadrons later in the morning, although he does list a claim for a Spitfire by Hptm. Johannes Trautloft of III/JG 51 over Dungeness,[4] the precise area where Ramsay had been shot down. Andy Saunders, in his interesting book on the attacks on this convoy, states of III/JG 51, that, 'at least three of that unit's aircraft returned home with varying degrees of damage although with the pilots unharmed'.[5] 11 Group's ORB Appendices only mentions the injury of Ramsay, and as there is no AMCB file for Neville, it is probable Neville was not injured and that his predicament may not have been the result of enemy activity.

This seems to have been 610 Squadron's only action for over a week, and so during such periods of inactivity, those waiting at readiness had to while away hours at dispersal. Claude Parsons gave a very interesting account of what went on at such times:

> During our waiting periods on the ground the pilots use a room in the Dispersal. There we all talk, play games, write letters to our relatives, read new orders and discuss generally our tactics against the crafty Hun. By this method we sort out the best way to attack various types of Hun aircraft. The Intelligence Officer is often present and picks up lots of useful information, which the pilots have omitted to tell him in the excited statement given him on landing …
>
> I frequently used to go out and talk to the crew of my aeroplane. This I found to be a very good policy, for by doing so one gets to know the capabilities of the men and it also gives them an interest and something to work for. A little talk with the fitter about the engine and its performance helps him quite a lot to locate little troubles without putting the aircraft unserviceable. The rigger also likes to know how the aeroplane flies and if he can improve its qualities. Every pilot likes his flying kit in a certain position inside the cockpit, so if you go along and tell the crew just how you like your helmet positioned and gloves in a definite place, parachute either in the pilot's seat with the straps in easily-get-at-able places, or on the tail plane so that the fitter can be starting the engine whilst the pilot is getting his parachute on. Attention to small details is a very considerable help to the pilot in getting off the ground quickly. If we were more than four minutes getting the whole squadron into the air the C.O. wanted to know what was wrong. One thing that would have been very impressive, if the public could have seen it, I'll endeavour to describe. The squadron is at readiness, the crews are by the aircraft and pilots in the Dispersal Hut. The telephone rings, every pilot springs to his feet, ready to dash to his aeroplane. Betty, the driver of our Humber brake, starts the engine, ready to take pilots who have a long way to go round to their aircraft. 'It's a lady to speak to Pilot-Officer Hotstuff about a date he didn't keep.' Everybody relaxes again and Pilot-Officer 'Peg-leg' puts on another Bing Crosby record, to everybody's delight. Again the phone rings. Up we all get again and I pop a piece of chewing-gum into my mouth. Chewing-gum is a great help when flying, I think; it keeps the saliva up and prevents a dry feeling in the back of one's throat. This time it's the waiter from the sergeant's mess, who wants to know how many late dinners to save. Betty… again switches off her engine as the pilots relax. We start to play table tennis … Amidst the ping-pong of the table tennis and the gramophone, with an officer and sergeant jittering on the floor, the phone rings again. 'Squadron take off, patrol Dover-Dungeness 20,000 feet.' The telephone operator yells to the nearest crew through the window, 'Start up.' In a few seconds every engine bursts into life. Betty had departed with her load of pilots. She's a good driver and knows where to stop for each pilot. We are all in our cockpits and straps done up. The fitter's last words as we taxi out are, 'The oxygen is on, Sarge, and best o' luck.' We are on the aerodrome, sorting ourselves out into prearranged sections of three. We take off six at a time right across the aerodrome. No sooner have the first flight got half-way across the aerodrome than the second flight opens up.[6]

Douglas Wilson celebrated his thirty-fourth birthday on 9 August, making him the Squadron's oldest pilot by several years. 610's other pilots of a similar age had all lost their lives, most recently Tom Smith, and there was a theory that flying fighter aircraft was more of a young man's occupation, given the high speeds and forces involved on the body, but Wilson was bravely carrying on regardless and the Squadron would certainly have been glad of his experience. The first time the ORB provides some concrete information in August comes two days later, when the more detailed accounts of operations resume. Again, because of bad weather, it seems sorties had been scarce throughout Fighter Command between 9–10 August.

On Sunday 11 August, 610 Squadron was operating from its forward base of Hawkinge, where the pilots were at readiness to scramble, twelve Spitfires led by S/Ldr Ellis having flown down from Biggin Hill early in the morning. Since the influx of new pilots a fortnight earlier, the CO had used the interim period to ascertain which of the new faces were the most advanced, and could be filtered into patrols immediately, with the inherent danger of contact with the enemy. As a result, three of the 'new' pilots were involved today—Sgt Neville back on patrol following his fortunate escape three days earlier, P/O Cox also on his second recorded day of operations and Sgt Gardner on his first day. Ellis interspersed these fresh faces amongst the sections, each of them being led by an experienced pilot. At 1045 hours, the dreaded call came through for all 'Dog Rose' aircraft to patrol the Channel, and the twelve Spitfire pilots would have leapt up and enacted the sudden departure so vividly portrayed by Claude Parsons earlier. John Ellis was at the head of the following men:

DW-W.	R.6993	S/Ldr. J. ELLIS.	Blue 1	41
DW-K.	X.4067*	SGT. ARNFIELD, S. J.		43
DW-O.	X.4011**	P/O. H. K. COX.		2
DW-B.	X.4166***	F/LT. E. B. B. SMITH.	Red 1	59
DW-D.	L.1037†	SGT. TANNER, R.§	Red 2	19
DW-X.††		SGT. NEVILLE, W.	Red 3	2
DW-R.	X.4239†††	F/O. F. T. GARDINER.	Green 1	20
DW-M.	K.9947‡	F/O. D. S. WILSON.		5
DW-P.	P.9451	SGT. GARDNER, G.§		1
DW-A.	R.6976	F/O. P. G. LAMB.	Yellow 1	39
DW-E.	P.9453‡‡	P/O. C. O. J. PEGGE.		19
DW-F.	X.4028‡‡‡	SGT. HAMLYN, R. F.		28

*As ORB, but DW-K was probably P.9495 until 12 August when it was damaged and probably replaced by X.4102, applies to entry on 12 August too.

**As ORB, but DW-O was probably R.6595 up to 26 August when it was destroyed, although X.4011 may have replaced R.6595 while it was being repaired after earlier damage on 25 July.

***As ORB, but most likely to be DW-B, L.1009, until 14 August 1940.[7] The next DW-B was probably X.4166, which arrived with 610 Squadron on 15 August 1940.[8] Applies to subsequent references.

†As ORB, but actually DW-D, R.6918.

††As ORB, but actually DW-X, R.6630.

†††As ORB, but DW-R was probably still K.9931, until 25 August.[9]

‡As ORB, but actually DW-M, P.9540 on this patrol, K.9947 probably replaced it after 14 August 1940. Applies to subsequent references to K.9947 until after 14 August.

‡‡This is probably a typographical error and is meant to be P.9433. However, DW-E had been R.6629 up to this point, and thanks to Merrick's logbook we know it was still flying on 18 August 1940, so some confusion exists over which aircraft DW-E was throughout August 1940. Should probably be R.6629 here at least and until 18 August.[10] Applies to subsequent references to P.9433 until 18 August.

‡‡‡As ORB, but DW-F was probably still R.6694, until after 18 August, when X.4028 may have replaced it.[11]

§As ORB, but Tanner's initials are 'J. H' and Gardner's are 'B. G. D'. There are several occurrences of this in August—each time I've just highlighted what it should be once for each pilot, leaving the ORB record as it was originally.

The ORB describes F/Lt Smith as Red Leader, and John Ellis would almost certainly have been Blue Leader. F/O Gardiner was probably leading Green Section and F/O Lamb Yellow Section, as the more experienced pilots. About half an hour into the patrol, Ellis ordered Smith to take his section down and, 'investigate E/A on the water in mid-Channel, remainder of Squadron acting as above guard' (ORB). F/Lt Brian Smith's combat report survives:

> I was Red Leader in Squadron Formation over Dover at 26000 ft. when I was ordered to investigate E/A seaplane on the Water in midchannel exercising caution. I lost height down channel and flew along the French coast flying N.E. at Sealevel. I sighted an enemy seaplane, a ME.59 [He 59] flying low over the water. I then put the section astern and approached to a attack from the landward side. I fired 2 or 3 short bursts and saw tracers appear to hit it. I then had to break away owing to large difference in speed. I assume Red 2 and 3 attacked also as they were in line astern of me when I set course homewards. I sighted 3 or 4 enemy Fighters 1500 ft above and warned Red 2 and 3.
>
> I then sighted astern enemy aircraft circling a speed boat at which I fired several bursts and when breaking away, saw it had Red crosses and civil markings on it. It was painted cream colour with a single tail, tapering fuselage and twin engines and retractable undercarriage. This I did not identify. After breaking away, I fired the remainder of my ammunition (one short burst) into what I took to be a ME. 109 without apparent result. I saw one of my Section behind me and not engaged. This is the last I saw of Red 2 and 3 as they did not reply when I called them up in the R/T. There was a naval coastal motor boat in the immediate vicinity. I then returned to rearm and refuel. (TNA, AIR 50/172/72)

This report holds a lot of key information about the patrol. It is interesting to note that the Squadron was patrolling at 26,000 feet, while in the preamble to his report Smith noted that he attacked the He 59 seaplane at sea level just three miles off Calais at 1115 hours, the second attack being about ten miles south of Dover. He seemed to damage the He 59, firing two or three short bursts from 200 yards to just fifty yards. Smith had positioned Red Section carefully to surprise the seaplane, losing height down Channel, and approaching it from the French coast, from where an attack would have been least expected, with his wingmen in line astern—another textbook attack. Spotting enemy fighters, Smith sensibly elected to head for home rather than carry out a further attack.

Then he spotted an unidentified Red Cross machine, which he also attacked in line with recent British Government orders about Red Cross aircraft, before finishing off his ammunition on an Me 109. It may seem surprising that Smith attacked a machine with Red Cross markings, but these aircraft were frequently armed and thought to be using their aforementioned markings to disguise their reconnaissance of British convoys for the *Luftwaffe*, something which the Government could not tolerate. A communiqué of 14 July stated that any aircraft with Red Cross markings which flew within range of British or Allied military operations or territory, risked being shot down. Brian Smith still recalled the reasons for attacking such Red Cross aircraft when I met him: '11 August, Yes. A float plane, with a red cross on it? We were told to attack it. It was a biplane, a twin engine biplane, off the coast of France, and yes ... we were told to put them down, because they were spying on us, or that was the theory'. A few days after this incident, on 15 August, further advice on engaging Red Cross aircraft was given, possibly in light of this action. The instruction from Operations Branch to controllers bluntly stated, 'Attempts should be made whenever possible to destroy enemy Red Cross aircraft which approach our shores to pick up German pilots from the sea. Patrols should only be despatched for this purpose when there are forces in hand and they should not be permitted to sweep too far out to sea' (TNA, AIR 25/197). Smith's engagement with the He 59 was inconclusive, as was the brief engagement with the 109, but Smith was able to claim an He 59 as damaged.

Flying high above this action, F/O Wilson probably saw the same formation of machines as Smith, when he reported having seen, '3 motor boats off CAP GRIS NEZ pointing toward DOVER' (ORB),

A Heinkel He 59, similar to the one Brian Smith attacked on 11 August, which was dark green and brown in camouflage. (*ww2images.com*)

while more interestingly F/O Gardiner, 'saw a large splash which he attributes to an A/C crashing in mid Channel but was unable to identify it' (ORB), probably as a result of their operating height. At this point, Smith was aware of one of his wingmen with him. However, as the ominous silence suggested when Brian Smith called up his wingmen later, tragically neither William Neville nor John Tanner were seen again. The large splash witnessed by Gardiner probably meant that he had unwittingly observed the final moments of one of his Squadron. That Tanner and Neville were 'Missing' would only have become clear upon the return of the ten surviving Spitfires to Hawkinge at about 1145 hours, Brian Smith presumably arriving on his own, while the others would have returned in formation. There was a possibility that one or both of them had ditched successfully and were in need of rescue, had been picked up and returned to a port such as Dover, become a PoW, or had crash-landed somewhere on the south coast. 610 Squadron may well have launched its own patrols back over the scene of Smith's encounter, to see if there was any trace of their missing colleagues, but sadly they were out of luck. Sgts Tanner and Neville had to be added to the growing list of casualties. The ORB confirmed the news, with the following statement about the patrol, 'Sgt. Tanner & Sgt. Neville are reported missing. The colouring of the H.E.59 was dark green & brown. Enemy casualties:– 1.H.E.59 damaged. Our casualties:– 2 pilots & A/C missing'.

With the release of the AMCB files, one can now ascertain a much clearer picture of what happened than was possible previously. The Squadron's CO wrote his reports on the combat three days later, the reports being identical apart from changing the two names and aircraft details. It states that the pilots were under orders to shoot down the German rescue plane if possible, while Tanner and Neville were still astern of Smith immediately after the first attack. It is most likely that they were hit during or after the second attack, being picked off by the Me 109s that Smith had warned his wingmen about, particularly as Smith saw one of his wingmen just after his run-in with the 109. Tanner and Neville possibly focused their attention on the unusual seaplane, lulled into a false sense of security by the friendly aircraft flying as top cover, watching their tails. Ellis reports that at least one section was patrolling above Red Section to give them protection, so it is surprising that an attack on Red Section went unseen by their comrades. It is also strange that neither pilot was able to call for help on their R/T, possibly a result of being surprised and hit at low altitude with no room to manoeuvre. The only thing that is certain, is that the County of Chester Squadron had paid a heavy price for this patrol, the loss of two pilots and their aircraft in exchange for a damaged He 59.

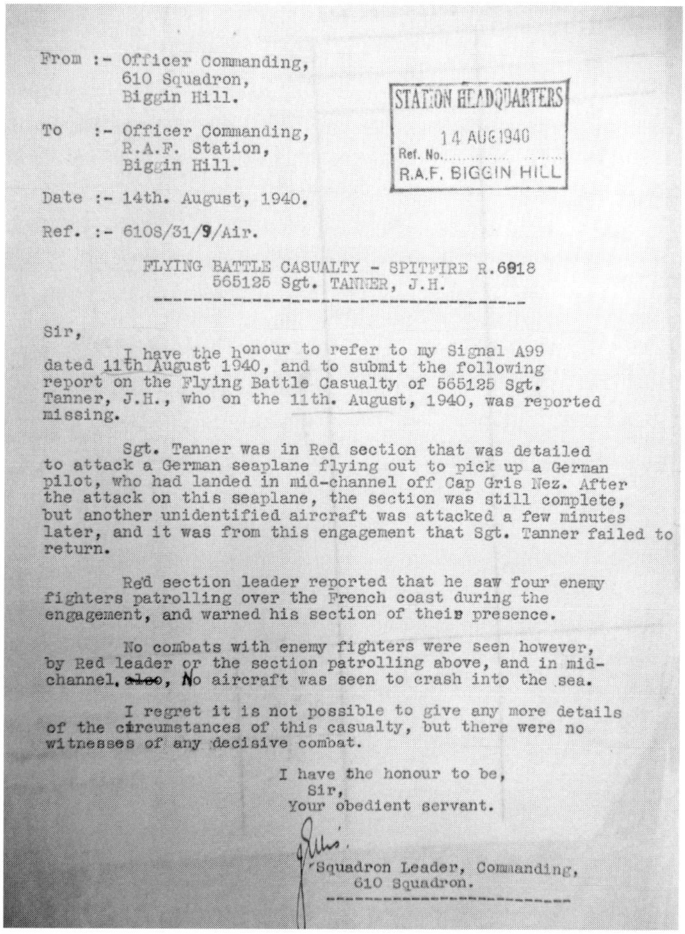

From :- Officer Commanding,
610 Squadron,
Biggin Hill.

STATION HEADQUARTERS
14 AUG 1940
Ref. No.........
R.A.F. BIGGIN HILL

To :- Officer Commanding,
R.A.F. Station,
Biggin Hill.

Date :- 14th. August, 1940.

Ref. :- 610S/31/9/Air.

FLYING BATTLE CASUALTY - SPITFIRE R.6918
565125 Sgt. TANNER, J.H.

Sir,

I have the honour to refer to my Signal A99 dated 11th August 1940, and to submit the following report on the Flying Battle Casualty of 565125 Sgt. Tanner, J.H., who on the 11th. August, 1940, was reported missing.

Sgt. Tanner was in Red section that was detailed to attack a German seaplane flying out to pick up a German pilot, who had landed in mid-channel off Cap Gris Nez. After the attack on this seaplane, the section was still complete, but another unidentified aircraft was attacked a few minutes later, and it was from this engagement that Sgt. Tanner failed to return.

Red section leader reported that he saw four enemy fighters patrolling over the French coast during the engagement, and warned his section of their presence.

No combats with enemy fighters were seen however, by Red leader or the section patrolling above, and in mid-channel, ~~also~~, No aircraft was seen to crash into the sea.

I regret it is not possible to give any more details of the circumstances of this casualty, but there were no witnesses of any decisive combat.

I have the honour to be,
Sir,
Your obedient servant.

Ellis.
Squadron Leader, Commanding,
610 Squadron.

S/Ldr Ellis's report about the loss of Tanner—Neville's report was virtually identical. (*TNA, AIR 81/1304*)

The ORB gives some incorrect information on the aircraft being flown by the two pilots, as it recorded that Tanner was flying DW-D, L.1037 and Neville a DW-X, with no serial number. The AMCB files officially confirm that Tanner was flying DW-D, but R.6918 and Neville was indeed in an aircraft with the letter X, but its serial was R.6630. Spitfire R.6918 had only joined 610 Squadron on 28 July 1940 from 6 MU, while R.6630 had been with the Squadron since the end of May.[12]

It is possible that the fighters which attacked 610 Squadron once again belonged to JG 51, as that unit made claims against Spitfires in the Calais area. This supports the theory that the Spitfires fell to the guns of escorting Messerschmitt 109s. It is likely that the two sergeants never knew what hit them, given they made no contact on the R/T. 'Beware of the Hun in the sun' was an old adage from the First World War, which the RFC had learnt the hard way; it was a truism which was just as applicable to the RAF pilots fighting in the Second World War, as seen here. Another *Luftwaffe* unit which made claims of shooting down Spitfires at about this time, was JG 52, with *Feldwebel* Herbert Bischoff recording, 'I had just half a kill to my name—a Spitfire together with Uffz Ignatz Schinabeck between Calais and Dover on 11 August 1940'.[13] Oblt. Carl Lommel and Ltn. Günther Büsgen were possibly the other two 109s which Smith had seen, as they also made claims for having shot down Spitfires in this area.[14] Although this is obviously conjecture, Simon Parry has also posited the possibility.[15] *Then and Now* mentions two He 59s which were intercepted (the other one by aircraft of 604 and 152 Squadrons), and it was most likely the second which was engaged by Brian Smith:

Sunday, August 11th Seenotzentrale Cherbourg

Heinkel He 59. Shot down by RAF Spitfires during rescue of three crew from RAF Blenheim brought down by Hptmn. Wiggers of I/JG51. One NCO wounded. Aircraft lost.

Heinkel He 59. Failed to return from search and rescue mission over the Channel. Believed crashed in the sea. Crew missing. Aircraft lost.[16]

From this, it seems that Smith had in fact destroyed the He 59, as both of the floatplanes are recorded as 'lost'.

Various details have come to light in the AMCB files about 610's casualties, one which arose in 1947 being that although Tanner's rank was given as sergeant in the ORB, he was actually a flight sergeant. He had been promoted with effect from 15 May 1940, however 610 Squadron had not been informed of this at the time of his death (TNA, AIR 81/1304). The twenty-five-year-old F/Sgt John Henry Tanner, who had been with 610 Squadron since mid-June, had amassed nineteen recorded patrols by the time of his final flight, and there is no record of Tanner having made a claim against the *Luftwaffe*. In the immediate aftermath of the patrol, Tanner was reported as 'Missing' and his wife, Helen, who it appears he married in Cairo, Egypt in 1939, would have received the dreaded telegram at her address in Bromley, Kent. Although this state of affairs lasted for some time, eventually the family received news that John Tanner had actually been buried in Calais. The French Red Cross got news to the British via the American Embassy, that he had been killed in action at Calais on 11 August, being buried in a civilian cemetery; Calais Nord Cemetery, Section 4, Row 2, Grave R. Further details came to light after the War, when it was established that Tanner had been found by a German Gendarme at 1500 hours, just under four hours after the combat had taken place, see photo below.

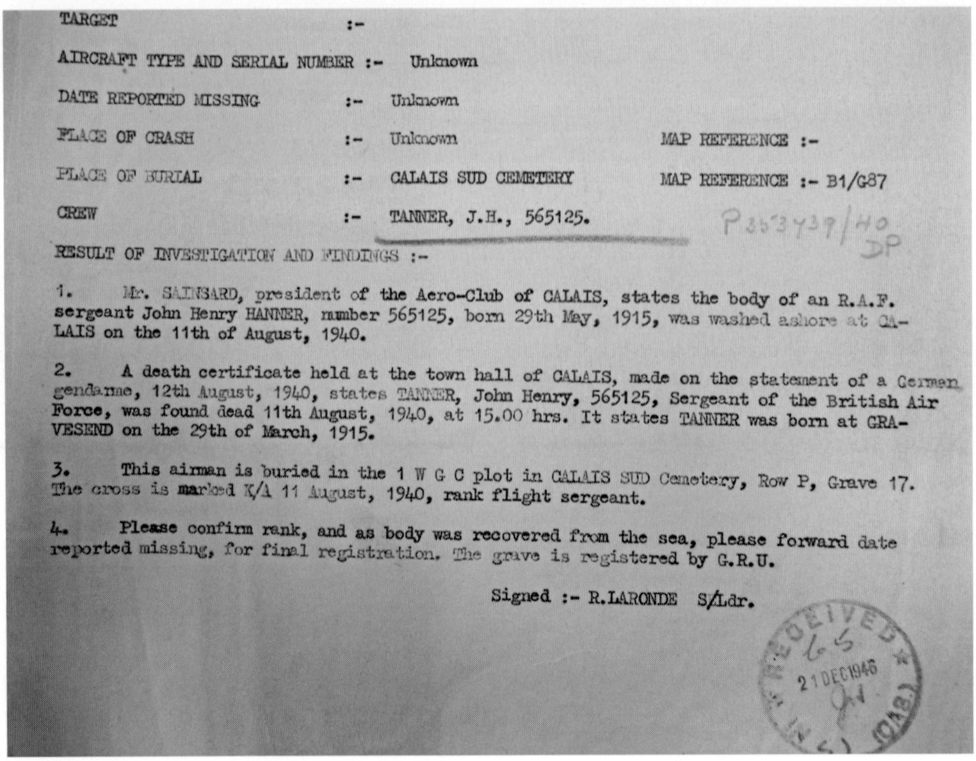

TARGET :-

AIRCRAFT TYPE AND SERIAL NUMBER :- Unknown

DATE REPORTED MISSING :- Unknown

PLACE OF CRASH :- Unknown MAP REFERENCE :-

PLACE OF BURIAL :- CALAIS SUD CEMETERY MAP REFERENCE :- B1/G87

CREW :- TANNER, J.H., 565125.

RESULT OF INVESTIGATION AND FINDINGS :-

1. Mr. SAINSARD, president of the Aero-Club of CALAIS, states the body of an R.A.F. sergeant John Henry HANNER, number 565125, born 29th May, 1915, was washed ashore at CALAIS on the 11th of August, 1940.

2. A death certificate held at the town hall of CALAIS, made on the statement of a German gendarme, 12th August, 1940, states TANNER, John Henry, 565125, Sergeant of the British Air Force, was found dead 11th August, 1940, at 15.00 hrs. It states TANNER was born at GRAVESEND on the 29th of March, 1915.

3. This airman is buried in the 1 W G C plot in CALAIS SUD Cemetery, Row P, Grave 17. The cross is marked K/A 11 August, 1940, rank flight sergeant.

4. Please confirm rank, and as body was recovered from the sea, please forward date reported missing, for final registration. The grave is registered by G.R.U.

Signed :- R.LARONDE S/Ldr.

RECEIVED 21 DEC 1946

The grim details of Tanner's death were finally revealed in a document dated 26 October 1946. It had been a long wait for the pilot's family to discover his fate. (*TNA, AIR 81/1304*)

He had been washed ashore at Calais, so may have baled out of his Spitfire too low, or ditched it, only to drown. Although Tanner was originally buried in the North Cemetery in Calais, his wife received news on 28 July 1943, that his body had been moved to a Military Cemetery, Calais South, Row P, Grave No. 17. The only comfort that his family could take from this distressing news, was that at least they had a grave which they could visit to pay their respects, albeit once peace had returned. Another report, just two weeks later, suggested that this may not have been John Henry Tanner, but a crewman from a Blenheim which had crashed at Calais on the same day. This was ultimately proven to be incorrect, and Tanner was confirmed to be buried in the above grave in Calais Sud Cemetery. However, with echoes of S/Ldr Franks's death, it highlights the difficulties in identifying the war dead.

Sgt William John Neville, aged twenty-six and from Middlesex, had no known grave, having presumably been shot down into the Channel. He is remembered on Panel 17 of the Runnymede Memorial, becoming yet another member of 610 Squadron to be honoured there. Neville's short spell with his squadron was typical of so many pilots who lost their lives during the Battle. The VR pilot had only been with 610 Squadron for sixteen days before he was killed, barely enough time to get to know his comrades. His final patrol was only his second recorded sortie, the first being when he reportedly crash-landed at Wittersham.

He was incredibly inexperienced, having come straight from an OTU, so the odds were stacked against him, as he would have been all too aware. It must have been a hard decision for S/Ldr John Ellis, to send such a novice into battle, but it could not be avoided. He must have felt Neville was

Above left: The final resting place of F/Sgt Tanner. (*Copyright http://www.bbm.org.uk/airmen/Tanner.htm*)

Above right: John Henry Tanner with his pilot's 'Wings'. (*Copyright After the Battle*)

Above left: William John Neville's name inscribed on the Runnymede Memorial. (*Author*)

Above right: Sgt Bill Neville, aged twenty-six, Killed in Action on 11 August 1940. (*Copyright After the Battle*)

competent to fly operationally, otherwise he would have sent him away for further training. Once again luck played its part—if another section had been ordered to intercept the Heinkel 59, both sergeants would probably have lived to fly another day with another patrol under their belts, but their luck had run out, in Neville's case, before it had even really started. His father received a letter six months later, confirming that Sgt William Neville was presumed to have been killed in action, as no further news had been received about him.

On Monday 12 August, the *Luftwaffe* planned to mount a series of raids against the RAF's forward aerodromes of Hawkinge, Manston and Lympne, along with the coastal RDF stations, as a prelude to *Adlertag* on the following day. *Adlertag*, or Eagle Day, was the German code name for launching the main operations to destroy RAF Fighter Command. In the face of this, countless 11 Group squadrons, including 610 Squadron, had been waiting at readiness since dawn. The County of Chester Squadron's men, possibly still at Biggin Hill given the timescales involved in the ensuing action, did not have long to wait. As raids came in, at 0731 hours, the Squadron's dispersal hut received a telephone call from the sector controller for a squadron scramble—'Red, Yellow, Blue & Green sections ordered to intercept enemy raid approaching DUNGENESS' (ORB). Twelve pilots ran to their Spitfires, before taking off, forming up and heading for the deadly skies over England's south-eastern corner. It was the turn of the following pilots to nervously scan the sky in search of black-crossed machines:

DW-W.	R.6993	S/Ldr. J. ELLIS.	Blue 1	42
DW-K.	X.4067	SGT. ARNFIELD, S. J.	Blue 2	44
DW-V.	K.9970*	P/O. H. K. COX.	Blue 3	3
DW-Q.	R.6891**	F/O. F. T. GARDINER.	Green 1	21
DW-M.	K.9947	F/O. D. S. WILSON.	Green 2	6
DW-N.	N.3124***	SGT. GARDNER, G.	Green 3	2
DW-H.	K.9818†	F/LT. E. B. B. SMITH.	Red 1	60
DW-J.	R.6599††	SGT. CHANDLER, H. H.	Red 2	10
DW-S.	K.9975†††	SGT. WILLCOCKS, C.§	Red 3	1

DW-A.	R.6976	F/O. P. G. LAMB.	Yellow 1	40
DW-E.	P.9433	P/O. C. O. J. PEGGE.	Yellow	20
DW-F.	X.4028	P/O. B. V. REES.	Yellow	1

*As ORB, but DW-V was probably P.9330 until after this flight when it was possibly damaged. K.9970 did go on to become DW-V.

**As ORB, but actually DW-Q, P.9545 on this patrol, R.6891 replaced it.

***As ORB, but DW-N was probably R.6806 until after this flight when it was possibly damaged. N.3124 listed in ORB but only believed to have joined 610 on 11 September 1940.[17]

†As ORB, but actually DW-H, L.1044 on this patrol, K.9818 replaced it.

††As ORB, but DW-J was probably N.3284 until it left 610 Squadron around 7 September 1940.[18] Also recorded in Merrick's logbook. It was probably replaced by R.6599.[19]

†††As ORB, but DW-S was probably R.6621 until after this flight when it was possibly damaged.

§As ORB, but Willcocks's initials are 'P. H.'. I have highlighted the error the first time it occurs.

With John Ellis leading the Squadron in Blue Section and some of the other pilots recording their formation positions in combat reports, it is likely that the Squadron was in the above sections, Ellis leading 'B' Flight and Brian Smith leading 'A' Flight. A quarter of those on this patrol were noticeably very inexperienced, Sgt Willcocks and P/O Rees on their first recorded patrols. While this was almost certainly true of Willcocks, who had been with the Squadron for little more than a fortnight and was probably under Flight Commander Smith's watchful eye, Rees had joined the Squadron in mid-June and it is quite possible that some of his patrols simply have not been recorded. With Sgt Gardner and P/O Cox carrying out only their second and third recorded patrols respectively, a large number of the formation were being thrown in at the deep end, where it was hoped they would survive. To increase their odds, each of them was placed in a section with two other experienced pilots, although the likely composition of Green Section meant that F/O Gardiner had two inexperienced wingmen, as F/O Wilson, lacked combat experience.

The *Luftwaffe's* prime target was the advance aerodrome of Lympne. Having climbed to 10,000 feet, Ellis led his formation straight towards Dungeness; within forty-five minutes of being scrambled, enemy aircraft were sighted. As ever, the squadron leader provided a comprehensive combat report:

> I was leading 610 Sqdn. which was detailed to intercept raid approaching Dungeness. Nine enemy bombers were sighted at 16,000 ft. over New Romney in very tight vic formation in sections of three, Sections were also in vic. The presence of the bombers was first noticed after a stick of bombs was seen to fall just out to sea off New Romney. Our height at the time was 10,000ft. We climbed to attack the bombers which were flying towards Rye. When we were 1,000ft below them and about 1000 yds behind, twelve escorting Me 109s came diving down out of the sun on to our tails. We were forced to break off our attack on the bombers and a general dog fight ensued with the enemy fighters. We were told by the controller soon after taking off that we were to deal with enemy bombers and that another Sqdn above us would deal with the escorting fighters.
>
> In the dog fight I chased one solitary Me. 109 flying very fast and diving slightly. He rolled on to his back as I opened fire and I continued firing as he started his vertical dive, I could see my bullets entering the side of his fuselage as I followed him down. I broke off the attack as I was convinced he was diving out of control, he was also drawing away from me rapidly. F/O. Lamb, who was behind me, later reported he saw this e/a continue its dive into the sea and break up.
>
> I climbed up again to 15,000 over Dungeness and spotted another Me 109 climbing up into the sun. I caught him at about 20,000. He started to spin down to the left soon after I opened fire, I fired the remainder of ammunition at very close range as he was spinning, but he presented an extremely difficult target, when I broke off the attack his engine was ticking over slowly and he was still spinning

> violently and he appeared to be out of control. Noticing a scrap going on just above I left the Me 109 and returned to re-arm.
>
> J. Ellis: S/Ldr. (TNA, AIR 50/172/22)

The bombers, (Ellis stated in his report's preamble that they were 'He 111s (not certain)'), were heading from New Romney to Rye, taking them directly away from Lympne. This suggests that the bombers had already hit the airfield before 610 Squadron encountered them, one bomber perhaps suffering a hang up, hence the stick of bombs falling in the sea off New Romney. Ellis was in the worst position to try and engage them, but believing he had another fighter squadron providing top cover for him, he bravely led his men in a hard climb to engage the bombers. At the last minute, 610 faced the nightmare of being bounced from out of the sun by a large number of Me 109s. It is possible to sense the anger in Ellis's report when he stated the controller told him to deal with the bombers, leaving the escort to another squadron—the inaccuracy of this information could prove fatal for some of 'The Chesters'.

However, despite being at such a disadvantage, Ellis rectified the situation and turned the tables on the enemy fighters in another whirling dogfight, claiming one Messerschmitt 109 confirmed thanks to F/O Lamb's observations, and another Me 109 unconfirmed. The first 109 he hit with, 'One burst, 200yds—100 yds, 10 secs' (TNA, AIR 50/172/22), and after this extended burst of fire, it is little wonder the Messerschmitt fell out of the sky. The second 109 he hit with, 'Two bursts. 300 yds & 50 yds. 4 secs each' (TNA, AIR 50/172/22)—the exceptional fighter pilot used up all his ammunition in two lethal attacks, pressed home from close range. What is most telling about Ellis's character here, and typical of the Battle of Britain fighter pilots, is that although out of ammunition and exhausted, he was already preparing himself to go straight back into the fray, having spotted a dogfight going on above him. Here was a real fighter leader in the making.

One of the CO's wingmen following in behind him was the inexperienced P/O Cox. The VR pilot would have faced mixed emotions as he closed in on the enemy formation, finally putting all his training to the test in his first combat, while trying to control the fear which must have gripped him. Cox recalled the encounter thus:

> I was flying as blue III, we were climbing up to attack a formation of bombers (about 8). As we approached the Squadron Leader ordered line astern for the attack, we were then attacked by ME 109 which were above us. I lost my leader in the sun so turned to find a target. I saw a M.E. 109 on a Spitfires tail this I attacked and he turned over and went down apparently out of control. P/O Rees confirms destruction of this E/A. As I turned to watch him another ME 109 appeared in my sights at very close range. I finished off my remaining ammunition in short bursts. He went down over the vertical definitely out of control. (TNA, AIR 50/172/14)

When looking at a series of combat reports about one *mêlée*, it is inevitable that different pilots recall different incidents about the combat and as a result one can piece together an ever-growing picture of events as they happened. Here, Ken Cox supplied the additional fact that Ellis had ordered his Squadron into 'line astern' as the Spitfires approached the bombers. This textbook method of attacking unescorted bombers, which is what they appeared to be, was the favoured tactic of the Squadron. Ellis undoubtedly felt this was the correct order, given that another squadron was supposed to be protecting them from above, but because these friendly fighters did not show, it left some of 610's pilots very vulnerable, particularly in 'A' Flight at the rear of the formation.

Cox shows the confusion of a dogfight when he lost Blue 1 in the sun—one can imagine the fear he must have felt as the desperate order to, 'Break, Break', rang through the headphones of his R/T set, instantly followed by an adrenaline rush as he engaged two aircraft in quick succession. Cox shot a 109 off a friend's tail, and as it was witnessed by P/O Rees, Cox claimed his first confirmed victory, while the second 109 was claimed as unconfirmed destroyed. Cox opened fire at close range, again showing the importance of closing in on enemy aircraft to ensure success, something he stressed in his combat report: '(i) 2 BURSTS 8–10 SECS IN ALL AT 250 YDS. (ii) 4 SHORT BURSTS AT 100 YDS. All rounds fired, P/O Cox' (TNA, AIR 50/172/14). Despite the nerve-wracking moments as the 109s bounced him, the operation would have been a real fillip for Cox, having claimed his first victories so early in his operational life—he had proved himself as a fighter pilot and shown his worth to the Squadron.

'B' Flight's final combat report was filed by Green 3, the inexperienced Sgt Bernard Gardner. He made no mention of the initial engagement or enemy bombers, but he did note that the interception was assisted by AA fire, unlike the other reports. Gardner had a very eventful engagement where, '25 Approx. Me 109s', were sighted at 0810 hours:

> Observed one Me 109 and gave chase. 1st burst 300 yds 2nd 250 yds and 3rd 100 yds. saw smoke and flame pour out of 109 and it crashed off French coast 1 mile to sea.
>
> On way back from 1st engagement saw Spitfire attacking Me 109 and joined in. Got on 109's tail and gave four bursts smoke poured out of 109 and it went into a shallow glide with prop stopped, over towards France.
>
> On way back saw a large ship (5000 tons) with black funnel and green bands, 2 miles from French coast, also saw parachutist descending.
>
> Reaching English coast saw "dog" fight at 10000 ft so went up. Saw Me. 109 over Lympne area and approached from sun on to the tail, gave burst at 20 yds and saw tracers entering cockpit and engine, long plumes of smoke gushed out and he went on to his back and started to spin. Ammunition now exhausted so made for base and saw large plume of smoke come up from ground to my left in vicinity of Hawkinge.
>
> Immediately landed.
>
> Evasive action employed by enemy aircraft in (2) was as follows.
>
> Steep turn to starboard, followed by stall turn. On to back and dive, followed by steep climbing turn then into roll. I gave burst as he came in the sights and after roll evasive action ceased. (TNA, AIR 50/172/29)

Gardner's first engagement came after the Squadron turned its attention to the escort, this 109 apparently high-tailing it for home. He closed range on the Me 109 during a lengthy chase, which made each burst of fire more effective. The final burst from 100 yards was fatal, although with no-one to witness it crash, he could only claim an unconfirmed. His second combat resulted in another unconfirmed destroyed—as the 109's propeller had stopped, its pilot would have had a worrying glide home, although this should perhaps have been a 'shared' with the other Spitfire pilot who had already attacked it. His detailed description of the enemy aircraft's evasive action in this dogfight, shows how interested the intelligence officer was in accumulating the maximum amount of information about the *Luftwaffe's* tactics. That the German's evasive manoeuvres broke off, supports the idea that the aircraft was doomed. Despite the rigours of two combats against the lethal Messerschmitt 109, Gardner did not head for home, but on seeing another dogfight, and with enough ammunition left for one last attack, he showed his bravery and determination by returning to the fray at 10,000 feet over Lympne. He also showed that he had been quick to learn the tricks of the fighter pilot's trade, closing in on a lone 109 to point blank range, before opening fire from 'up sun'. His bullets hit the cockpit and engine, almost certainly proving fatal. Having expended all his ammunition, Gardner landed and filed his claims after a remarkably successful second recorded patrol. They were recorded as three unconfirmed Me 109s by the intelligence officer, who must have been very busy dealing with the numerous claims as the pilots returned.

'A' Flight's men, at the formation's rear as it swung into line astern to attack the bombers, also became embroiled in this large dogfight. Sgt Horatio Chandler recorded:

> The bomber formation was sighted in "vic" approx. 12 in number, heading EAST at 200 m.p.h. I was RED 2 as we turned to "port" to carry out attacks astern. I sighted 40 (?) M.E. 109s 1 mile behind bombers, 2000' above. I warned Leader who discontinued attack and swung to meet fighters head on. I attacked a 109 with a long burst at full deflection. Heavy smoke resulted. I was attacked from rear immediately so took evasive action. The targets were so numerous that I was able to get five other short attacks, but unfortunately without visible results. E/a used mainly tracer ammunition. Standard markings but possibly painted sea-green in place of usual colouring. (TNA, AIR 50/172/11)

Once again, a slightly different slant is given on this patrol, as a fairly accurate picture of events starts to build up from different reports. Chandler put the number of escorting *Luftwaffe* fighters at around forty, being just a mile behind the bombers with additional height advantage—tall odds indeed for the County of Chester's Spitfire pilots. It was evidently Chandler who spotted the escorts at about 0810 hours and '1 mile South of Lympne', and his warning allowed Ellis to lead his men into a head-on attack against the 109s, which suggests they just about avoided being bounced.

Chandler took on a difficult deflection shot against one of the fighters, opening fire at close range, an eight second burst from 200 yards which caused damage, and he was awarded the claim of a damaged Me 109. The sergeant pilot's description, although being very much to the point, manages to convey the chaos of the dogfight, where he had to cut short his first attack due to the unwanted attention of another 109, before getting off five further snap shots, using up 2,000 rounds in total. Perhaps his observation that the enemy were mainly using tracer bullets indicated he saw plenty of it flying past him during the course of the combat. Chandler now had claims of a destroyed, an unconfirmed destroyed, a shared destroyed and a damaged and he was quickly becoming one of the Squadron's more effective pilots.

Chandler's was the only report from Red Section, but Yellow Section, at the formation's rear, provide two more, with P/Os Pegge and Rees both giving further insight into this major battle. There was clearly some confusion as to who held which position in Yellow Section, as both men claim to have been Yellow 3. Here is how Joe Pegge recorded the engagement:

> On the 12.8.'40 I was No.3 of Yellow section of 'A' Flight 610 Sqdn. At about 08.10, after a fight with Me 109s, in which I did not fire, I got detached from the rest of the Squadron so I climbed up to 23,000 feet.
>
> At 08.15 I saw 6 Me 109s going round in a circle about 3000 feet below me. I came down & from a range of about 100 yds I gave one a burst of 1–2 secs. Smoke & flame came from it & it went down slightly inland & I climbed back to 23,000 again.
>
> At 08.25 I again saw 5 Me 109s in a circle below me. I attacked one with a short burst from about 100 yds astern saw bits fly off & it went into a spin just over the sea. (TNA, AIR 50/172/58)

This was Pegge's twentieth recorded patrol and having survived numerous combats and with a 109 already claimed destroyed and a Do 215 damaged, he was able to put what he had learnt to devastating effect on this patrol, despite being alone. In the face of daunting odds, Pegge fearlessly engaged Messerschmitt 109 formations above Hawkinge at 0815 hours at about 20,000 feet and above Dover ten minutes later at about 18,000 feet, claiming two of the small fighters destroyed by diving down and attacking their blind spot. Neither of the German pilots would have known what had hit him. Pegge was clearly a fine marksman, and it was a remarkable success given he was alone.

P/O Rees also provided an illuminating report:

> I was flying No. 3 in yellow section acting as lookout for E/A attacking from behind. We were vectored around and at approx. 8.30 we sighted enemy bombers in formation, we were about to deliver an attack on the bombers, when we were warned of the approach of a large formation of enemy fighters behind.

> The formation broke up and a general dogfight ensued. I got on to several E/A but was forced off before I could open fire. I then got on the tail of a Me 109 and delivered two long bursts from 350 yds down to 100 yds. White and black smoke poured out of E/A cockpit and from behind. I did not see it crash as another E/A was on my tail this was attacked by another Spitfire and shot down. I discovered after landing that my good Samaritan was P/O Cox. (TNA, AIR 50/172/64)

Rees makes it clear that Yellow Section was operating as the lookouts for any attack from the rear, an unenviable position, but an essential one if the Squadron was not going to suffer heavy losses at the hands of the marauding 109s. Thankfully on this occasion, Sgt Chandler had spotted the enemy fighters positioning themselves for an attack, Rees recording that there were up to '50–69 approx, Me 109' (TNA, AIR 50/172/64), which establishes the magnitude of the task faced by the twelve Spitfire pilots. Again, the chaotic nature of the dogfight is apparent. Rees repeatedly closed in on enemy fighters but had to frantically break off to avoid being shot down himself, before finally latching on to a 109 at which he fired all his ammunition, from 250 to 100 yards. As Rees concentrated on his target, he almost fell victim to another Messerschmitt, the vengeful German fighter being shot down off his tail by P/O Cox, referred to as a 'good Samaritan'. The humour of this understatement acknowledges that Rees realised Ken Cox had probably saved his life. Brian Rees, flying his first recorded patrol, would have had mixed emotions once he got his feet back on *terra firma* between 0830–0900 hours; grateful that his luck had held despite the heavy odds; very thankful that Cox had been in the right place at the right time; jubilant at being credited with an unconfirmed Me 109 on his first run-in with the enemy. He had survived, and such hard won experience, even in the space of little more than an hour, would be of more benefit to him than he could imagine.

As Brian Rees added his claim to the list being compiled by the intelligence officer, it became clear how well the Squadron had done in the face of the large enemy formation, which had originally enjoyed the better tactical position. The ORB recorded the following claims:

> 2 M.E.109s, confirmed
> 6 M.E.109s, unconfirmed
> 2 M.E.109s, probable, 1 damaged,

a remarkable achievement. Based on combat reports, they seem to be credited to the following pilots:

> Ellis—one Me 109 confirmed, one unconfirmed,
> Cox—one Me 109 confirmed, one Me 109 unconfirmed,
> Gardner—three Me 109s unconfirmed,
> Chandler—one Me 109 damaged,
> Rees—one Me 109 unconfirmed.

This leaves two Me 109 probables recorded in the ORB, presumably those claimed by Joe Pegge as destroyed, as it appears nobody witnessed his claims. There is inevitably some confusion over the claims, which is compounded by 11 Group's intelligence report having different records again, with two less in total than the ORB, including only one destroyed confirmed, when there certainly appear to have been two. This perhaps reflects the unavoidable problem of over-claiming, mentioned earlier. This intelligence report provides further conflicting evidence, as it states 610 Squadron did not suffer any casualties. Given that a superior number of fighters caught 610 Squadron from above, it was inevitable that this was not a one-sided affair and some of the Spitfire pilots found themselves in trouble, desperately fighting for their lives.

'A' Flight was being led by the veteran F/Lt Brian Smith, on his sixtieth recorded patrol who already had claims for one destroyed, two shared destroyed, two probably destroyed, one unconfirmed

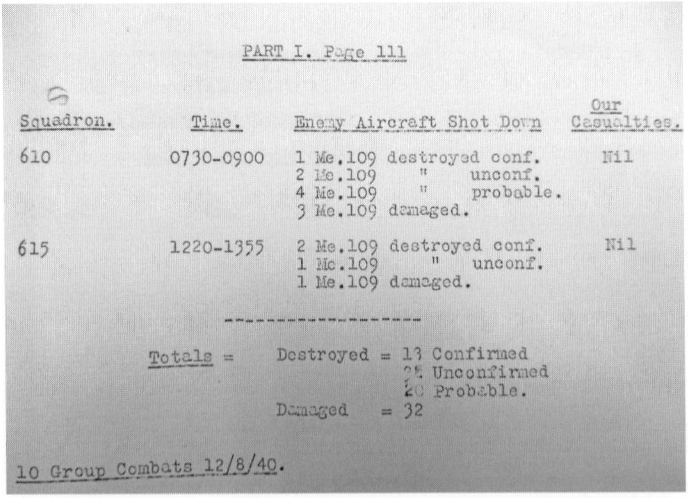

PART I. Page 111

Squadron.	Time.	Enemy Aircraft Shot Down	Our Casualties.
610	0730-0900	1 Me.109 destroyed conf. 2 Me.109 " unconf. 4 Me.109 " probable. 3 Me.109 damaged.	Nil
615	1220-1355	2 Me.109 destroyed conf. 1 Me.109 " unconf. 1 Me.109 damaged.	Nil

----

Totals = Destroyed = 13 Confirmed
[illegible] Unconfirmed
20 Probable.
Damaged = 32

10 Group Combats 12/8/40.

'11 Group Intelligence Bulletin' for 12 August 1940. (*TNA, AIR 25/197*)

destroyed and one damaged and one shared damaged to his name. However, even all this experience was not always enough to keep you safe in the vicious dogfights over the Channel, and the twenty-five-year-old's Spitfire was caught by a 109, receiving '2 cannon shells in the cockpit' (ORB). The explosive power of two cannon shells in such a confined space, so close to the pilot was devastating, and Smith's aircraft, (DW-H, L.1044, not as the ORB reported DW-H, K.9818, which was lost the following month), started to fall out of the sky in flames. Unsurprisingly, Smith still had a vivid memory of that morning. He recalled the events to me as follows:

> We'd met some people coming in, and as happens, quickly done what we could or whatever it was. Then we all went home. Silly bugger, I decided to have a look round. I was doing almost stationary, you know, well of course there was a bloke underneath doing the same thing. All I knew was, I suddenly blew up, never saw anybody! Fire everywhere, I was slightly burnt. Clambered out, parachuted down about 24,000 feet I think. And I remember seeing ... it's the only Spitfire I ever cost them, but it passed me going down. The wind was off the land so I landed in the sea, and happily was spotted by a trawler doing anti-invasion patrol.
>
> So they threw me something and pulled me out and gave me some dry clothes. So, I went up on top to see what's going on, and it was commanded by a naval reserve second lieutenant, or whatever they were, and the old skipper of the old trawler you see. This is the whole point of it, I said, 'You come from the north of Ireland don't you?' and he said, 'Yes'. We were school boys together, at boarding school, Rockport Craigavad. And he survived the war, he's died since. I think most of the people in those days with businesses, a lot of them were linen makers. Just trying to think of his Christian name, but it doesn't come. But Thompson was his name—that really was incredible!
>
> Went into Dover, 'cause there was an air raid on, and they took me off to hospital … But it was entirely my own fault. Instead of packing up and going home with the rest—to be on your own was absolutely stupid, but I was very lucky. I obviously wasn't thinking.

A little later, when I suggested it was perhaps a result of his tiredness, he added, 'My own fault completely! Instead of going home with the crowd, I just was having a look round and just blew up. I never saw anybody because they were just doing the same underneath. You couldn't see underneath, very tricky ...' Being shot down in flames was a fighter pilot's worst nightmare, and Smith, a young, fair-haired, handsome man, in his own self-deprecating words was 'slightly burnt', which coupled with the shell splinters, parachute descent and dunking in the Channel, made for a very traumatic experience, which he was incredibly fortunate to survive.

S/Ldr Ellis wrote a description of events for Biggin Hill's CO, confirming everything Wg Cdr Smith recounted to me about his harrowing experience. Unfortunately, the report was very hard to read on being reproduced, so here is the written version:

> FLYING BATTLE CASUALTY:- F/LT E.B.B.SMITH.
>
> Sir …
>
> Flight Lieutenant Smith was leading "A" Flight, 610 Squadron, when the Squadron became engaged with numerous M.E. 109s. In the general dog fight that ensued, Flight Lieutenant Smith's aircraft received two cannon shells in the vicinity of the cockpit and petrol tanks, his aircraft caught fire, and he himself was slightly burnt, and wounded by shell splinters.
>
> He managed to bale out, however at about 20,000 feet, and fell into the sea eight miles out between Dover and Dungeness.
>
> After 10 minutes in the water he was picked up by a Naval trawler, and brought into Dover.
>
> His aircraft, Spitfire L.1044, crashed into the sea and was destroyed. (TNA, AIR 81/1337)

Brian Smith obviously needed time to recover from his burns and regain his strength after such an ordeal, and he would now be away from the Squadron to recuperate. Losing another senior member was a serious blow for the Squadron, Smith having been with the Squadron since 22 September 1936. At least he would be back once his injuries healed.

John Ellis particularly would have felt the loss of such an experienced pilot and leader, in the midst of what was turning into a titanic struggle. It was sobering for the younger pilots too, who looked up to their flight commanders just as they would to Ellis, as 'old hands' who always came back in one piece. The realisation would have sunk in that nobody was safe—experience helped, but when your luck ran out there was not much to be done.

The Air Ministry informed Smith's parents of the incident the following day and although alarmed, they were naturally relieved to hear that the wounds were not 'serious' (TNA, AIR 81/1337). It had been a whirlwind couple of weeks for Brian Smith; having got married on 3 August and had a brief honeymoon, he had rejoined his Squadron in the thick of the air battles, being shot down and hospitalised on his second recorded combat with the enemy in as many days upon his return. While recovering from his burns, he did receive some very welcome news. His bravery and leadership throughout the Dunkirk evacuation and the opening stages of the Battle of Britain had not gone unnoticed: sixty recorded patrols in total being the second highest number flown of all the Squadron's pilots, up to the end of August. In recognition, Smith was awarded the Squadron's second DFC, as announced on 20 August 1940 in '11 Group Intelligence Bulletin No. 32' (TNA, AIR 25/197). The details of the award were made clear to the public in *The London Gazette* on 30 August 1940:

> Awarded the Distinguished Flying Cross.
>
> Acting Flight Lieutenant Edward Brian Bretherton SMITH (90340), Auxiliary Air Force. This officer has led his flight with great success; twenty-five enemy aircraft have been destroyed since June, 1940. One day in August he led the flight almost to the French coast to attack two enemy aircraft flying over the Channel. Despite strong opposition an enemy seaplane was damaged and, whilst on the return journey, another aircraft was attacked and damaged. Flight Lieutenant Smith was the only member of his section to return from these engagements. The next day, he was involved in an attack by twelve or more Messerschmitt 109s. His aircraft was hit by two shells, damage being inflicted near the cockpit and petrol tanks. His aircraft eventually caught fire and, although he himself was enveloped in flames, he successfully abandoned his aircraft and was rescued about eight miles out to sea. Flight Lieutenant Smith has now destroyed six enemy aircraft. He has displayed great courage and leadership.[20]

This laudatory citation encapsulated Smith's bravery during the heavy fighting in which the Squadron had been involved, particularly focusing on his leadership since taking command of 'A' Flight. The two incidents mentioned at the end of the paragraph, refer to the combats on 11 and 12 August, and it is clear from this that his burns were significantly worse than he subsequently mentioned, given that he 'was enveloped in flames'—such an image does not bear thinking about.

It was a very proud moment for the young flight lieutenant and nothing less than his actions over the past three months deserved. The only other such award the Squadron had received, belonged to S/Ldr Ellis, so it was a clear indication of Smith's standing in the Squadron. His local newspaper back home, *The Chronicle*, included a column on Saturday 31 August 1940 about Smith being decorated, which provides further interesting information:

> CHESHIRE AIRMAN AWARDED D.F.C
>
> FLIGHT-LIEUTENANT E. BRIAN SMITH
>
> Friends in all parts of Cheshire will join "The Chronicle" in congratulating Flight Lieutenant E. Brian B. Smith, younger son of Mr. and Mrs C. Francis Smith of Tattenhall, and grandson of the late Mr. T. Finch Jackson, Tattenhall Hall, on being awarded the Distinguished Flying Cross…
>
> Unofficial news had reached Chester some time ago that he had been awarded this honour, but the official announcement was only made on Tuesday afternoon.
>
> RECENTLY MARRIED
>
> Flight Lieutenant Smith who, earlier this month, married Miss Pamela Ledward Smith, younger daughter of Mrs. and the late Mr. Jerome L. Smith, The Homestead, Upton, was recently wounded and has been spending sick leave with his parents…
>
> Flight Lieutenant Smith has taken part in some of the fiercest air battles…Smith also did conspicuous work in the air during the evacuation of the B.E.F. from Dunkirk.
>
> He was one of the first to join the Auxiliary Air Squadron when it was formed at Hooton four years ago. He devoted all his week-ends to flying and was regarded as a promising pilot before the outbreak of war…
>
> Mrs. Smith was one of the earliest recruits to the Women's Auxiliary Air Force, and was an assistant section leader. Her husband modestly refuses to discuss his successes. Intimate friends, however, know he has shot down a number of enemy 'planes'. An old friend said, "Brian did not let his people know of his award. He hates to 'shoot a line'…"[21]

On 7 September 1940, while Smith was still recovering, his parents acknowledged this tribute with a mixture of thanks for their son's survival, but also a remembrance of all those fellow pilots from the Squadron who had been lost already. Their letter to the Editor in *The Chronicle* read as follows:

> Sir—We do indeed thank you for your beautiful words in reference to our son, Flight Lieutenant E. B. B. Smith, and also all who helped to rescue him on the boat, and all our friends who have so very kindly written to us. We gratefully thank God; and we also very gratefully remember the friends who have gone to the Great Unknown, part of that happy band of brothers at Hooton whose names live for evermore. We are glad to state that our son is progressing—Yours, The Parents C. F. and C. M. C. Smith.[22]

Another pilot who found himself facing an uphill struggle during this dogfight on 12 August, was F/O Gardiner, seemingly flying as Green Section leader. He was on the receiving end of a concerted attack by the Me 109s, which left him, 'wounded slightly in the left leg by a cannon shell, his left aileron, wing & petrol tank being also damaged' (ORB). Having finally shaken off his attacker, Gardiner used all his flying nous to coax his badly damaged Spitfire to Hawkinge. As his fellow pilots and the rest of the station watched him approach in DW-Q, P.9545, they must have been very concerned, S/Ldr Smith's death while

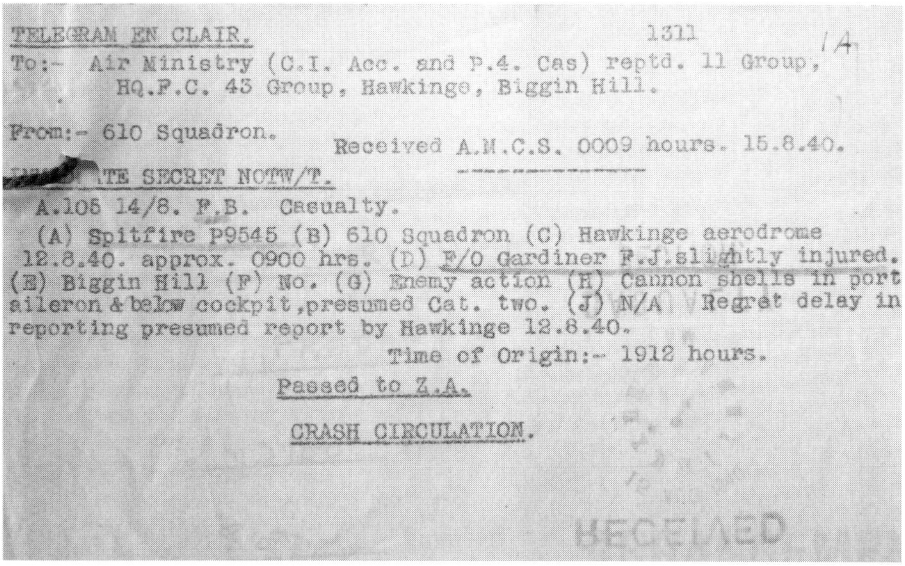

TELEGRAM EN CLAIR. 1311 14

To:- Air Ministry (C.I. Acc. and P.4. Cas) reptd. 11 Group, HQ.F.C. 43 Group, Hawkinge, Biggin Hill.

From:- 610 Squadron. Received A.M.C.S. 0009 hours. 15.8.40.

TE SECRET NOTW/T.

A.105 14/8. F.B. Casualty.

(A) Spitfire P9545 (B) 610 Squadron (C) Hawkinge aerodrome 12.8.40. approx. 0900 hrs. (D) F/O Gardiner F.J. slightly injured. (E) Biggin Hill (F) No. (G) Enemy action (H) Cannon shells in port aileron & below cockpit, presumed Cat. two. (J) N/A Regret delay in reporting presumed report by Hawkinge 12.8.40.

Time of Origin:- 1912 hours.

Passed to Z.A.

CRASH CIRCULATION.

RECEIVED

The information sent from 610 Squadron to the Air Ministry, confirming the basic facts surrounding Gardiner's combat on 12 August. This was sent three days late, but it mentions the pilot was 'slightly injured' and that Spitfire P.9545 was a Category 2. (*TNA, AIR 81/1396*)

nursing back a damaged aircraft fresh in their minds. Their relief would have been unbounded once he landed, and Gardiner was given time to recover from his wounds back at Biggin Hill. It is hard to be sure exactly how long he was off operational flying, as on 21 August the ORB noted, 'F/O. F.T.GARDINER (72100) reposted to this Unit on ceasing to be non-effective sick', but it had already been recorded that he was involved in a patrol on 18 August, which meant he had been off ops for six days.[23]

The ORB stated that one Spitfire was classed as Category 3 and four were Category 2, Smith's DW-H, L.1044 (see photo p. 193) being the Category 3 write-off and Gardiner's, DW-Q, P.9545, one of the four 'Category 2' damaged aircraft. Therefore three other pilots had received battle damage, further proof that the Squadron had been involved in a hectic scrap. As six of the pilots had all filed combat reports, stating that their aircraft had not received damage, it is reasonable to suppose that the three pilots whose Spitfires had been hit were any three from Sgts Arnfield and Willcocks, and F/Os Wilson and Lamb, although it is unlikely we will ever know which three for sure. At least some of this is confirmed by *Then and Now*, which records that the Squadron had lost two aircraft and had two damaged:

> **L1044.** Shot down in flames during combat over New Romney 8.00 a/m. Crashed in sea. Pilot Officer E. B. B. Smith baled out. Rescued from the sea and admitted to Dover Hospital with burns. **DW-H** lost.
>
> **R6806.** Damaged in the port wing, aileron and fuel tank by Bf 109 over New Romney 8.00 a.m. Further damaged in heavy landing at base. Flying Officer F. T. Gardiner slightly wounded in leg. **DW-N** repairable.
>
> **R6621.** Damaged in combat with enemy fighters off Dover 8.00 a.m. Pilot unhurt. Aircraft damaged but repairable.
>
> **P9495.** Severely damaged in action with Bf 109s over Romney 8.05 a.m. Pilot believed unhurt. **DW-K** a write-off.[24]

We now know Gardiner was actually flying DW-Q, P.9545, which would not fly with the Squadron again,[25] not DW-N, R.6806. Perhaps R.6806[26] was actually damaged on this interception, but this could be a myth or mix up, as Sgt Gardner who was flying DW-N, did not report any damage to his Spitfire in his combat report. I have tried to establish the other damaged aircraft mentioned in the ORB, using a variety of sources. Usually with the ORB, the pilot's name is correct, as is the identification letter for the Spitfire involved, but the Spitfire's serial number is sometimes not the relevant one to the identification letter, but a later one. This suggests that at times the ORB for August was completed retrospectively in terms of aircraft used, as mentioned previously by Raymond Ellis. For example, Sgt Willcocks was operating 'DW-S' on this patrol on 12 August, and although the ORB recorded his aircraft as DW-S, K.9975, this machine did not join the Squadron until 14 September 1940,[27] so it was probably the earlier 'DW-S', R.6621, which tallies with *Aeromilitaria*[28] and *Then and Now*. R.6621 had flown with 610 at the end of July and was reportedly damaged on this day.

The same applies to Sgt Arnfield, recorded in the ORB as flying 'DW-K', X.4067; this machine did not join the Squadron until mid-September either,[29] and it was probably P.9495 which was damaged on 12 August.[30] So it is likely that one of the damaged aircraft was Arnfield's DW-K, P.9495, another veteran from the famous photos taken at the end of June (see p. 190). The other possible aircraft is DW-V, P.9330, which was reportedly damaged on 12 August too.[31] Smith's L.1044 was certainly written-off, Gardiner's P.9545 was badly damaged or written-off, while DW-S, R.6621 and DW-K, P.9495 were probably two of the three remaining damaged Spitfires, the third being uncertain.

Such a number of damaged Spitfires would have been met with dismay by the ground crew, who spent so many hours looking after them. Replacements were now required and Raymond Ellis recalled the routine which had to be gone through following the arrival of a new Spitfire:

> On the evening of a day in which we had lost a Spitfire, a replacement would arrive from the M. U. flown by a civilian pilot of the A. T. A. (Air Transport Auxiliary)…
>
> Our first job on the new aircraft was to spray on the light grey letters 'DW' followed by the individual letter of the aircraft on both sides of the fuselage. We had a selection of large stencils that had been cut from Air Ministry linoleum originally intended for the floors of barrack rooms. In order to ensure that the letters were straight, a base line was provided by the flick of a long chalked string held taught against the fuselage.
>
> Of course there were a number of more technical jobs to be done on the engine and airframe of a new aircraft including the installation of radio, IFF, and the eight Browning guns and their ammunition. After the engine had been 'ground-run' and a 'Daily Inspection' had been carried out by all trades and signed up in the Form 700, a pilot would taxi it over to dispersal. On welcoming a new aircraft to the squadron, I had mixed feelings of pleasure and sadness.[32]

Ellis was all too aware that he was preparing a machine which could be taking a pilot to his death.

Researching further into this dogfight, it seems 610 Squadron may have become embroiled with Messerschmitts from several *Jägdgeschwader*, due to the scale of the dogfight, and various sources provide different accounts of them engaging any of JG 52, 26 and 54. Although some of these accounts suggest 610 Squadron had pursued the 109s instead of engaging the enemy bombers, the fact of the matter was that the 109s had clearly attacked the Spitfires as they approached the bomber formation. 610's pilots believed that the escort would be dealt with by other RAF fighters. But if anything, this highlights how confusing the combats could be, even when trying to look at them historically.

JG 54 was certainly heavily involved on 12 August, and Smith or Gardiner may have fallen victim to Max-Hellmuth Ostermann of JG 54, who claimed his third aerial victory on this day, along with three other JG 54 pilots who also made claims against Spitfires in the area. However, the most likely unit 610 Squadron encountered was JG 26, which was escorting *Kampfgeschwader* [KG] 2 and 3 on their attacks against Hawkinge and Lympne airfields. Donald Caldwell states that it was JG 26's First *Gruppe* led by Hptm. Kurt Fischer, providing close escort to the bombers attacking Lympne that 610 encountered.[33] The diary of JG 26 credits two pilots with claims, but they are from the Third *Gruppe*, Uffz. Högel making his first claim, south of Folkestone at 0920, recorded possibly as a 610 Squadron Spitfire confirmed, while

Alf Bridson and Steve Biggs hold down the tail of DW-F for an engine test. (*Copyright 610 Squadron Association*)

Lt. Ruppert claimed his second victim, also south of Folkestone at 0915 hours, possibly a 610 Squadron Spitfire,[34] although no mention is made of the other damaged Spitfires. One JG 26 pilot who did not make it home was Oblt. Freidrich Butterweck, whose 109 exploded over Elham, Kent. Various sources have stated that 610 Squadron shot him down. With the timing of Butterweck's loss also confirmed in *Then and Now*, it seems reasonable to suppose that he had fallen to the guns of 610 Squadron:

> **I/JG26**
>
> **Messerschmitt Bf 109E-1.** Shot down over Ashford by British fighters. Exploded over Standard Hill Farm, Elham 8.30 a.m. Oblt. Butterweck killed. Aircraft a write-off.
>
> *Site investigated by the Brenzett Aeronautical Museum and many small parts recovered.*[35]

Other sources believe that Butterweck was shot down by 54 Squadron, which again goes to show the almost impossible nature of attributing dogfight claims.

Following this early morning patrol on 12 August, 610 did not carry out any further recorded operational activity during the day. Presumably they returned to Biggin Hill, as if they had remained at Hawkinge they would have become embroiled in further dogfights. It is possible that 610 Squadron had been relieved by 32 Squadron, as it flew down from Biggin Hill at 1335 hours, arriving at Hawkinge twenty minutes later. The Hurricane squadron then got involved in a large dogfight between 1650 and 1810 hours, and after topping up with fuel at the forward airfield, 32 Squadron was back at Biggin Hill by 1900 hours. Hawkinge had been hit by two raids one composed of Junkers 88s, which was followed up by a formation of Dorniers. Despite damage to one of the hangars, several buildings and numerous casualties amongst the ground personnel, Hawkinge was operational again the following day.

Monday 12 August also saw the return of some of the pilots who had been sent away by S/Ldr Ellis for conversion to Spitfires a few weeks earlier. They would at least have been familiar with their aircraft now. We know this from P/O Merrick's logbook, as he noted, 'No 610 SQDN BIGGIN HILL 12.8.40', while Kenneth Wynn confirmed that P/O Gray, P/O Aldous, and Sgts Beardsley, Manton and Baker all arrived too, probably as a result of the Squadron's recent casualties; two pilots killed and two wounded in two days. Thanks to Sgt Bamberger's logbook, it is apparent that he completed the course on 16 August 1940. Merrick's logbook makes for interesting reading about the training they had carried out.

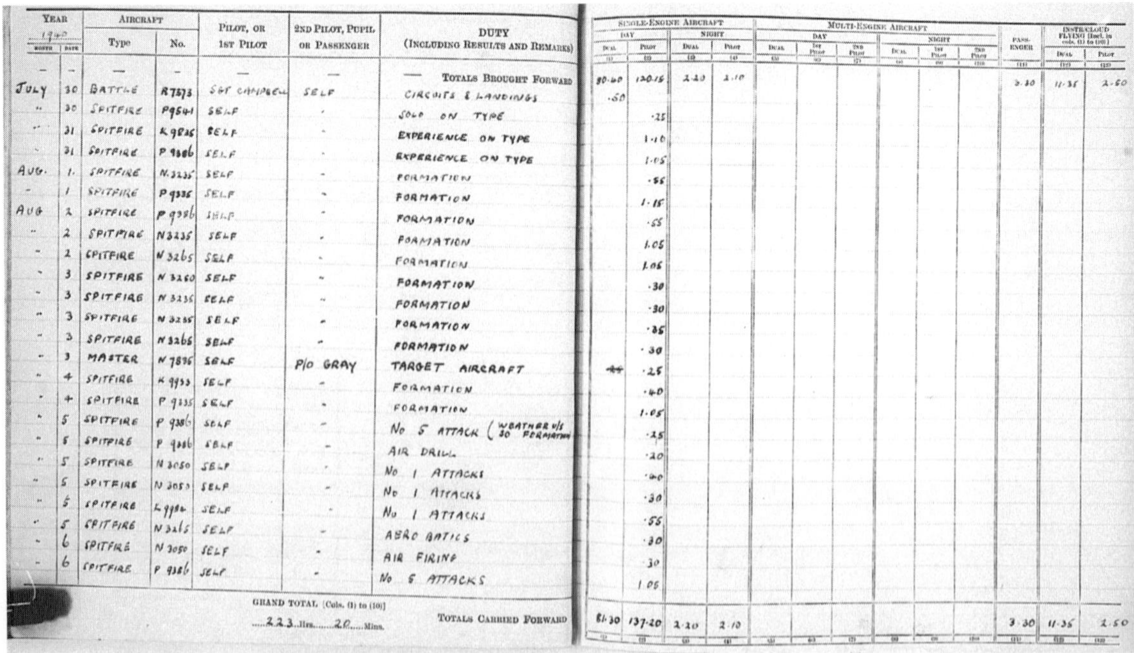

Year 1940 Month	Date	Aircraft Type	Aircraft No.	Pilot, or 1st Pilot	2nd Pilot, Pupil or Passenger	Duty (Including Results and Remarks)	Single-Engine Aircraft Day Dual (1)	Single-Engine Aircraft Day Pilot (2)	Single-Engine Aircraft Night Dual (3)	Single-Engine Aircraft Night Pilot (4)	Multi-Engine Aircraft Day Dual (5)	Multi-Engine Aircraft Day 1st Pilot (6)	Multi-Engine Aircraft Day 2nd Pilot (7)	Multi-Engine Aircraft Night Dual (8)	Multi-Engine Aircraft Night 1st Pilot (9)	Multi-Engine Aircraft Night 2nd Pilot (10)	Passenger (11)	Instr/Cloud Flying (Incl. in cols. (1) to (10)) Dual (12)	Instr/Cloud Flying Pilot (13)
—	—	—	—	—	—	— Totals Brought Forward	80.40	120.15	2.20	2.10							2.30	11.35	2.50
July	30	Battle	R7573	Sgt Campbell	Self	Circuits & Landings	.50												
"	30	Spitfire	P9541	Self	"	Solo on type		.25											
"	31	Spitfire	K9825	Self	"	Experience on type		1.10											
"	31	Spitfire	P9386	Self	"	Experience on type		1.05											
Aug.	1.	Spitfire	N.3235	Self	"	Formation		.55											
"	1	Spitfire	P9335	Self	"	Formation		1.15											
Aug	2	Spitfire	P9386	Self	"	Formation		.55											
"	2	Spitfire	N3235	Self	"	Formation		1.05											
"	2	Spitfire	N3265	Self	"	Formation		1.05											
"	3	Spitfire	N3260	Self	"	Formation		.30											
"	3	Spitfire	N3235	Self	"	Formation		.30											
"	3	Spitfire	N3235	Self	"	Formation		.35											
"	3	Spitfire	N3265	Self	"	Formation		.30											
"	3	Master	N7836	Self	P/O Gray	Target Aircraft	~~44~~	.25											
"	4	Spitfire	K9953	Self	"	Formation		.40											
"	4	Spitfire	P9335	Self	"	Formation		1.05											
"	5	Spitfire	P9386	Self	"	No 5 Attack (Weather u/s 30 Formation)		.25											
"	5	Spitfire	P9386	Self	"	Air Drill		.20											
"	5	Spitfire	N3050	Self	"	No 1 Attacks		.40											
"	5	Spitfire	N3053	Self	"	No 1 Attacks		.30											
"	5	Spitfire	L9980	Self	"	No 1 Attacks		.55											
"	5	Spitfire	N3215	Self	"	Aero batics		.30											
"	6	Spitfire	N3050	Self	"	Air Firing		.30											
"	6	Spitfire	P9386	Self	"	No 5 Attacks		1.05											
					Grand Total (Cols. (1) to (10)) 223 Hrs. 20 Mins.	Totals Carried Forward	81.30	137.20	2.20	2.10							3.30	11.35	2.50

Extract from Merrick's logbook, showing his training routine during his Spitfire Conversion Course at Hawarden. (*Crown Copyright RAF Museum*)

His first flight at Hawarden was on a Fairey Battle, a change from the Harvard in which he had spent most of his flying time on, doing circuits and landings for fifty minutes in preparation for moving on to Spitfires. Later that day, Merrick had his first experience of flying the Supermarine Spitfire, which must have been exhilarating for him, but also quite daunting, as the Spitfire's performance was much more powerful than anything he had flown previously. This solo flight was for twenty-five minutes in Spitfire P.9541.

For the next eight days, Merrick spent his time flying a Spitfire in situations which would soon be a daily feature of his life—formation flying, practising some of Fighter Command's ubiquitous fighter attacks and firing his guns. It is amazing that this appears to be the only opportunity he would have had to fire his eight Browning machine guns before joining his front-line Squadron. This seems to have been the case for each of the pilots, as Mark Bamberger, Sgt Bamberger's son, recalled that his father only fired his guns once, into a sand bank, before he flew in combat. Merrick completed his conversion course on 7 August, just nine days after he had first taken off in this special aircraft. The last part of his training was probably the most important—seventy-five minutes of dogfighting. Again, it is hard to believe that Merrick and his 610 Squadron comrades would have such minimal experience of this vital aspect of their daily role as fighter pilots. Being able to get the best out of the Spitfire in a dogfight, was literally a life or death matter for the young pilots.

Merrick had gained twenty-two hours and ten minutes flying time on the Spitfire, an improvement on the zero hours he had on arriving at 610 Squadron in the first instance. He was in a much better position now, and Ellis had done all the new pilots a big favour in sending them to 7 OTU. But it is very sobering to know that Fighter Command's new recruits had such little flying experience on the machine they would be fighting for their lives in and also the defence of the nation. They did not know the Spitfire's strengths and weaknesses in a combat situation anywhere nearly as well as they should have done. They would have to learn very quickly indeed when they arrived back at 610

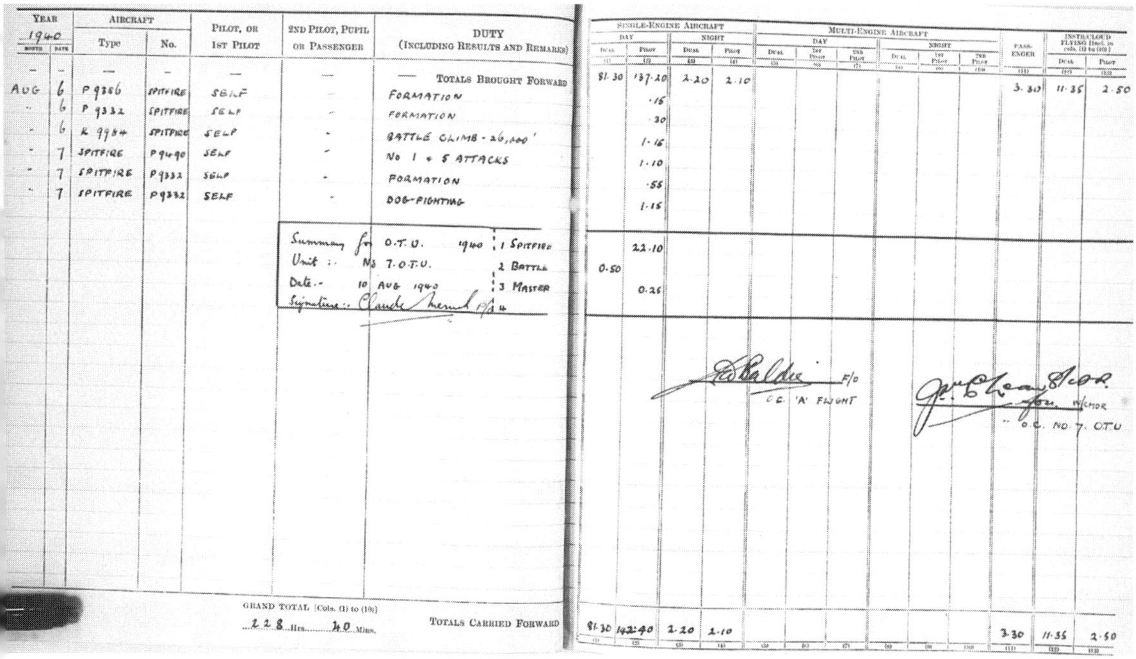

Year 1940 Month	Date	Aircraft Type	No.	Pilot, or 1st Pilot	2nd Pilot, Pupil or Passenger	Duty (Including Results and Remarks)	Single-Engine Day Dual	Single-Engine Day Pilot	Single-Engine Night Dual	Single-Engine Night Pilot	Passenger	Instr. Flying Dual	Instr. Flying Pilot
—	—	—	—	—	—	Totals Brought Forward	81.30	137.20	2.20	2.10	3.30	11.35	2.50
Aug	6	P9386	Spitfire	Self	–	Formation		.15					
"	6	P9332	Spitfire	Self	–	Formation		.30					
"	6	K9984	Spitfire	Self	–	Battle climb - 26,000'		1.16					
"	7	Spitfire	P9440	Self	–	No 1 + 5 attacks		1.10					
"	7	Spitfire	P9332	Self	–	Formation		.55					
"	7	Spitfire	P9332	Self	–	Dog-fighting		1.15					
					Summary for O.T.U. 1940 / Unit: No 7 O.T.U. / Date: 10 Aug 1940 / Signature: Claude Merrick P/O	1 Spitfire		22.10					
						2 Battle	0.50						
						3 Master		0.26					
				Grand Total (Cols. (1) to (10)) 228 Hrs. 40 Mins.		Totals Carried Forward	81.30	142.40	2.20	2.10	3.30	11.35	2.50

F/O O.C. 'A' Flight

W/Cdr O.C. No. 7. O.T.U.

Details of Merrick's final two days at Hawarden. (*Crown Copyright RAF Museum*)

Squadron, if they were to survive in the cauldron of air fighting over south-eastern England, against the *Luftwaffe's* highly experienced aircrew.

For 610 Squadron, Tuesday 13 August was a very quiet day, which is surprising given that it was supposed to herald the arrival of Göring's *Adlertag* and the beginning of the end for Fighter Command. The *Luftwaffe's* bombastic leader had attempted to rouse his airmen by stating that they would soon wipe the RAF from the skies. It sounded ominously simple, but he believed the previous day's raids had been much more successful than they actually had been. While Lympne, Manston and Hawkinge had all been hit hard, some by secondary raids later in the day, Hawkinge for example was still very much operational, as is clear from 32 Squadron's ORB. Twelve of their Hurricanes landed at Hawkinge at 0905 hours after a fruitless interception, with the Squadron carrying out two more morning patrols from the advance airfield, before returning to Biggin Hill at 1320 hours. 32 Squadron returned to Hawkinge at 1735 hours, carrying out one patrol from there, before returning to Biggin Hill by 2100 hours, without encountering the enemy (32 ORB).

It is possible that 610 Squadron had flown to Hawkinge at dawn and been replaced by 32 Squadron, and that 610 had operated from Hawkinge at alternate times to the Hurricane squadron with whom they shared Hawkinge. Either way, it was operational, thanks to the tireless work of a diverse group of people who filled in the bomb craters on the landing ground during the night of 12 August. Although 610 Squadron almost certainly carried out patrols similar to those recorded by 32 Squadron, 'The Chesters' failed to cross paths with the enemy. Thanks to Claude Merrick's logbook, we know that some flying was possible, as he noted three flights from Biggin Hill. The first was a formation flight lasting twenty-five minutes in Spitfire X.4065, then some dogfighting practice in the same aircraft for half an hour, followed by a patrol of his home station for twenty-five minutes (1) at 3,000 feet in X.4070. Whether the latter was on his own to familiarise himself to the area, or as part of a larger formation, is unclear.

Another reason for the lack of 610 Squadron's activity on this infamous day may well have been the weather, which had more than a dampening effect on Göring's great plans, given the importance of *Adlertag* for the *Luftwaffe*. The depth of cloud cover was disastrous for Göring, but the *Luftwaffe* did successfully hit some targets, such as Eastchurch airfield on the Isle of Sheppey, (this was mainly a Coastal Command aerodrome), while in the late afternoon a large raid hit Southampton, causing heavy damage to the port. As the biggest raids yet seen over England had taken place, it was hardly surprising that both sides felt they had achieved success, or at least claimed to have: 'it seemed to the Germans that they had destroyed 84 British fighters. The British reckoned they had knocked down 64 German aircraft. The true figures were closer to 47 German losses against 13 British fighters in the air, 3 of whose pilots were killed. The importance of the day lay in the fact that Goering's *Luftwaffe* had failed to land anything like the sort of heavy blow on which his plan's success depended'.[36] Such over-claiming was understandable given the nature of the dogfights, but it could eventually prove critical if the *Luftwaffe* expected to see fewer Fighter Command aircraft coming up to meet them as the battle went on, only to be disappointed. It would be a severe blow to morale.

One excellent piece of news for the Squadron on Eagle Day, was that S/Ldr John Ellis received his DFC. It recognised his leadership and bravery during the heavy fighting over Dunkirk, not to mention June and July over south-eastern England, the first award the Squadron had received. Ellis's citation was advertised in *The London Gazette* as follows:

> Awarded the Distinguished Flying Cross.
>
> Acting Flight Lieutenant John ELLIS (37850).
>
> This officer was employed on offensive patrols over Dunkirk during the evacuation of the British Expeditionary Force and led his flight with great courage. On two occasions, whilst deputising for his Commanding Officer, he led a patrol of four squadrons, displaying great initiative and leadership. During these patrols Flight Lieutenant Ellis destroyed two enemy aircraft.
>
> Later, whilst engaged on home defence duties, he shot down one enemy bomber. In July, 1940, whilst leading the squadron, he destroyed two enemy aircraft and on the following day he shot down a further three of eight enemy aircraft destroyed by his squadron. Flight Lieutenant Ellis has displayed courage and leadership of a high order.[37]

Ellis's ability as a fighter pilot is highlighted here, particularly when he led two patrols over Dunkirk on 30 May. His exceptional marksmanship skills had also been recognised, notably his feat on 24 and 25 July when he brought down a total of five enemy aircraft. Ellis deserved this recognition and his men would have seen these qualities in him and been glad to have their lives resting in such competent hands. It would have been cause for celebration that evening in one of the local pubs around Biggin Hill, or the mess. Fighter Command's pilots used such opportunities to unwind and forget the terrible situation they found themselves facing on a daily basis. They never knew if it would be their last chance.

14

14–17 August 1940: 'Never in the field of human conflict was so much owed by so many to so few'

As was often the case for 610 Squadron, a day of inactivity proved to be the calm before the storm. Although Wednesday 14 August began quietly enough, this did not last long. At midday, both flights were ordered to take off on a Squadron patrol to intercept large incoming raids, in weather conditions described as: 'Clouds in layers 4/10s from 3,000 feet' (ORB), making an interception more tricky. S/Ldr Ellis was not flying on the patrol and so while Acting F/Lt William Warner led 'B' Flight on his first recorded patrol of August, P/O Stanley Norris led 'A' Flight as a result of his experience and ability to lead under pressure—both pilots were only twenty-one years of age. Warner most likely led the Squadron, as Norris reported he was at the helm of 'A' Flight rather than the Squadron, and the rest of the formation was probably composed as follows:

DW-T.	X.4064	P/O. S. C. NORRIS.	Red 1	47
DW-H.	K.9818	SGT. PARSONS, C. A.	Red 2	17
DW-B.	X.4166	P/O. D. M. GRAY.	Red 3	1
DW-F.	X.4028	SGT. HAMLYN, R. F.	Yellow 1	29
DW-Q.	R.6891	SGT. CHANDLER, H. H.	Yellow	11
DW-J.	R.6599	P/O. C. MERRICK.	Yellow	2
DW-Z.	R.6802	F/O. W. H. C. WARNER.*	Blue 1	55
DW-N.	N.3128**	P/O. B. V. REES.	Blue 2	2
DW-O.	X.4011	SGT. CORFE, D.	Blue 3	3
DW-L.	P.9311***	SGT. ELSE, P.	Green 1	27
DW-M.	K.9947	SGT. GARDNER, F. G.	Green 2	3
DW-P.	P.9451	SGT. RAMSAY, N. H. D.	Green 3	25

*As ORB, but Warner should be listed as a 'F/Lt.' here, and in subsequent lists.
**N.3128 is not listed as a 610 Squadron aircraft in the production lists, and is recorded as having been written-off during a night take-off on 2 August 1940.[1] Have included it in subsequent lists, as recorded in ORB, but possibly a simple typographical error for N.3124.
***As ORB, but most likely DW-L, P.9496. P.9311 probably replaced it after 26 August 1940.

P/Os Merrick and Gray, who had now converted to the Spitfire, found themselves thrust into the fray. Merrick was probably flying as wingman to the experienced Sgt Hamlyn and Gray appears to have operated as Number 3 to P/O Norris—both section leaders would have been keeping an extra careful eye on these new pilots. Merrick's logbook recorded a patrol of Dover at 12,000 feet which lasted one hour and twenty minutes. He inserted an 'A' after it, presumably indicating he was part of 'A' Flight, and given that this was his only flight on 14 August, it must have been this one.

The twelve Spitfires made an impressive sight as they roared off from their home base and gained as much height as possible, receiving vectors from ground control to patrol Manston and then Hawkinge. It is probable from the available reports that the two Flights split up, 'A' Flight reaching about 15,000 feet, while 'B' Flight flew at a lower altitude, and at least one section was scouting for enemy fighters reportedly shooting down the Dover Barrage Balloons. As the pilots scanned the sky, carefully searching for enemy aircraft, their eyes were drawn to a mass of black dots emerging from the direction of the French coast. They quickly grew into a huge formation of *Luftwaffe* bombers and fighters, stacked up from 8,000 feet to around 15,000 feet, with some German fighters flying well above this as top cover. It would have been an impressive yet terrifying sight; the ORB recorded that 'Red, Yellow, Blue and Green sections left BIGGIN HILL, ordered to MANSTON, then HAWKINGE, then engaged E/A over FOLKESTONE at 15,000 feet. E/A were in hundreds J.U.87s, M.E.109s & M.E.110s'.

Suddenly, the twelve Spitfires would not have looked quite as impressive in the face of this aerial armada, especially if they had been split up to deal with differing threats, although three other RAF squadrons were in the vicinity. 610's pilots were undaunted, and those that were able to went straight in to the attack. Stan Norris found himself in just the right position to lead 'A' Flight at a group of *Stuka* dive-bombers. The infamous Junkers 87 had terrorised Allied troops during the *Blitzkrieg* across Europe, culminating in its attacks on Dunkirk, where its precision bombing had also cost the Royal Navy numerous warships, not to mention the little ships which had gathered to rescue the BEF. However, over those beaches the *Stukas'* aircrew soon realised how vulnerable they were to the RAF's fast, modern fighters, something which would become increasingly etched in their minds during their raids on England. This operation on 14 August was no exception. Stanley Norris described the encounter as follows:

> I was RED 1 leading "A" Flt. when 610 Sqdn were ordered to Manston on approaching Manston we were vectored to Hawkinge. A Flt. patrolled at 15000' above cloud between Dover & Folkestone at 12.26 sighted a large formation of E.A. approaching Folkestone at the same height as ourselves.
>
> I manoeuvred the flight to attack, & I noticed there were about fifty or more Ju 87s flying in a large close Vic formation. I attacked the rear Ju 87 and it went down in smoke & flames turning over on its back.
>
> As I broke away I saw the formation start to break up. As we were close to the cloud I found I had broken away into it. On coming out I could not see the rest of my section but saw another formation of ME 110s & Ju 87s over Dover at the same height. I attacked a Ju 87 on the outside of the formation which went down issuing smoke, & burning rapidly. I gave a short burst at another at very close range—I only saw him swerve from the formation erratically I think he was probably damaged.
>
> RED 2 confirmed that the first formation completely broke up after our attack. (TNA, AIR 50/172/53)

Norris estimated that there were approximately 300 enemy aircraft droning towards England's shores, consisting of Junker 87s, Messerschmitt 110s and the ever-present Me 109s, so he had to act swiftly to line up his Flight for the best position to attack this onrushing formation.

Having singled out a large formation of dive-bombers, he felt he had destroyed one of the slow *Stukas*, having opened fire at just 100 yards. Typically with Norris, he followed up this initial attack, despite being on his own, with further attacks against the 87s, again from close range. Having fired 2,100 rounds of ammunition, Stanley Norris claimed two Ju 87s destroyed and a third as damaged upon his safe return, his most successful day so far. He was now one of 610's most effective pilots with four destroyed, one unconfirmed, one damaged and one shared damaged to his name—clearly this was one of the reasons he had been put at the head of 'A' Flight.

Coming straight in behind Stan Norris were his wingmen, Sgt Parsons, and the novice P/O Gray. Parsons was in the thick of the action as follows:

A remarkable close-up shot of the notorious Junkers Ju 87B *Stuka* in France, 1940. Its distinctive 'gull wing' is clearly visible and the dive-bomber seems to ooze power, straining to get airborne. However, it proved to be extremely vulnerable to the RAF's fighters over England during the Battle of Britain. (*Ron Mackay*)

> I was Red 2 flying at 10—12,000 feet South of Folkestone on 14th August, 1940, when on my right I saw about 12—16 JU87s in close formation. The E/A were turning slightly to their right. I received line astern from Red Leader and took up my position immediately. We turned right and placed ourselves on the tails of the [*sic*] two of the E/A. I got in one short burst of fire before being forced to break off sharply by a ME109 who attacked me from the rear. The JU87 turned over and went down vertically skidding badly and apparently out of control.
>
> I then attacked a ME109 who tried to get away from me by doing diving turns and then suddenly climbing. After a dog fight lasting about 1—2 minutes I managed to get in one short burst of about 1½ secs. as he disappeared into a cloud. This E/A was probably considerably damaged. Owing to being separated from my leader and not having used my ammunition all up I joined with Blue Leader and returned to home base, after cruising round until short of petrol. C. A. Parsons. Sgt. (TNA, AIR 50/172/57)

Although Norris did not mention it, he had ordered his men into line astern for the attack, the Squadron's favoured formation, as it allowed the pilots to scan more of the sky than if they were flying in their obsolete tight 'Vics' of three. After encountering three enemy aircraft in quick succession, Parsons had manged to link up with Bill Warner for mutual protection. Upon returning to base, he claimed a Junkers 87 probably destroyed and an Me 109 damaged.

Parsons's report was supported by Sgt Hamlyn's combat report. As Yellow 1, Hamlyn had followed Red Section in to the attack and almost certainly yelled a warning as the 109s attempted to bounce Red Section, a *Schwarm* (tactical section of four aircraft) going after Parsons. Hamlyn's combat report summary was similar to his flight commander's, as it initially referred to the enemy formation as being about 300 strong and composed of Ju 87s, Me 109s and Me 110s which he encountered in the Folkestone—Dover area, at 15,000 feet at 1231 hours:

> I was leader of Yellow Section. I was flying behind Red Section when the enemy were sighted. Red 1 and Red 2 attacked some Junkers 87s, but as they were attacking, four Me.109s dived down, to attack Red 2, so I at once engaged one of them. After about a 1 second burst, I saw a lot of smoke pour out and it went into cloud. Owing to some more Me 109s attacking me, I was unable to confirm the enemy casualty, but it was about 5 - 10 miles West of Dover over the land. I saw one Me 109 going down in flames and crash, but this is not the one I attacked. (TNA, AIR 50/172/34)

The brief nature of this combat is confirmed by Hamlyn's description of his firing as, 'Range—200 yds one burst of about one second, rounds fired—100' (TNA, AIR 50/172/34), while one senses the dogfight's frantic nature from the experienced Sgt Pilot's terse description. He was quick to spot the danger to Red Section and his prompt action almost certainly saved the leading section's pilots, especially his fellow Sgt Claude Parsons, from a lethal attack. It also showed that he was another good marksman, as one snap shot caused the 109 enough damage to force it to break off, smoke pouring from it. Hamlyn believed that although he could not claim it as confirmed, its pilot would have struggled to return to his base, as the combat took place five—ten miles inland from Dover.

Another pilot from Hamlyn's section filed a combat report against an Me 109, although at the much lower altitude of 7,000 feet, two miles south of Folkestone, at 1232 hours, perhaps in the aftermath of Yellow Section's initial counter-attack against the escorts. Sgt Horatio Chandler described how he:

> Attacked e/a which seemed to be alone. Attempted to get on his tail, he immediately turned left to return the attack. We manoeuvred for a long while, during which he fired quite a fair amount. I got two short bursts which had no effect. After about 12-15 minutes he tried to out climb me, I immediately went into fully fine pitch and easily caught up. The instant at which I opened fire, he rolled over and went straight down. I followed him and he started to smoke and eventually went into the sea. I steered 300° and after about 6-8 minutes made a landfall 3 miles West of Dungeness. (TNA, AIR 50/172/11)

The first thing of interest about this dogfight was its duration, as twelve to fifteen minutes in a sustained one-on-one dogfight was very unusual, with the great majority of combats being almost over before they had started—one pilot usually held the upper hand. (S/Ldr Ellis's combat on 25 July had lasted five minutes and seemed long!) One reason for this extended dogfight was that the Messerschmitts had not used up their precious fuel in a prolonged patrol across Kent, but were operating relatively close to home, so could stay in contact with the RAF for longer. While Chandler clearly had the initial advantage, canny flying by the German pilot enabled him to turn the tables slightly, with Chandler coming under considerable fire. Eventually, the Me 109 pilot was forced into a fighting withdrawal, conscious that his fuel would have been guzzled up at the high speeds involved in the dogfight, and it was perhaps with a sense of desperation that he tried to climb away from the Spitfire in a bid to lose his persistent opponent.

It is striking how Chandler easily caught him up by altering his propeller's pitch, and now the sergeant from Bexhill was definitely on target with another short burst of fire. From the remarkable effort put up by the German, it seems the *Luftwaffe* was losing an experienced pilot. Once again the range at which Chandler fired from, 200 yards, was critical, taking just sixty rounds from each gun in, 'three very short bursts,' to down his skilful adversary. Ray Chandler, credited with an Me 109 destroyed, his fifth claim, would have been shattered after such a draining dogfight.

While 'A' Flight's Sections had been operating at the same altitude as the raiders, Blue Section had been slightly lower, as they had to climb to engage the enemy. Nevertheless, they were soon heavily engaged, and although F/Lt Warner did not file any claims, his two wingmen, P/O Rees and Sgt Corfe were both involved in dogfights. Brian Rees, only on his second recorded patrol with the Squadron, quickly singled out one of the many Junkers 87s, as follows:

> I was flying No.2 in Blue Section "B" flight. Ordered to intercept E/A over Hawkinge. We climbed through the low cloud and were about 13,000 feet between two layers of Cumulus clouds. We sighted a large formation of JU87s above us. We climbed into the clouds and broke up. I remained in the cloud until I saw some JU87s diving down about to attack a ground objective. I picked on enemy A/C on the left side of the Vic and delivered a long burst from about 300—200 yards. The E/A turned round (almost like a spin) and disappeared into the low cloud. It seemed definitely out of control. I did not see any smoke of any description. I then returned to base owing to shortage of petrol and ammunition. B. V. Rees. P/O. (TNA, AIR 50/172/64)

Rees's estimation that they were opposing a raid of up to 450 raiders underlines the size of the task facing the RAF's pilots, a terrifying prospect for them to overcome. Rees was forced to operate alone and while this was dangerous for him and the other pilots, it suited him to stalk the enemy dive-bombers until a suitable target arose, on which he expended three quarters of his ammunition in one long burst. On his safe return, he claimed a Ju 87 as a probable, to add to his earlier claim for an Me 109 unconfirmed.

Douglas Corfe's combat report as Blue 3 mirrors Rees's, in that it states how his section was operating beneath the enemy, and it split up on trying to engage them, while the summary at the start of the report echoes the overwhelming odds the Squadron faced: 'E/A—300 approx., JU87. ME110. ME109., 12.31, Dover—Folkestone, 13,000 feet'. The ensuing description of his combat gives an incredibly intense picture of the dogfight:

> I was flying Blue 3 when E/A were sighted behind and above. We were at 10,000 feet. We turned and climbed to attack and I lost sight of Blue Leader and Blue 2. I climbed through cloud and came out about 1,000 yards from 15 ME109s flying in a circle line astern. 3 ME109s detached themselves from the formation and attacked me. I went into a steep right hand turn through 360° and saw one ME109 ahead at same level. I closed to 300 yards and fired 5 1 sec. bursts, closing range. Flames came from his engine and a piece flew off his starboard wing. He rolled on his back and went down flaming. I dived into cloud and came out again. About ½ minute later right on top of another ME109 I fired 3 2 sec. bursts at him. Smoke came intermittently from his exhausts giving the impression that his engine was missing. He then did a shallow dive into the cloud, and as I then saw several ME109s diving on my tail I dived below cloud losing them. I cruised about for a few minutes and then returned to Base on Sapper's[2] instructions without seeing any other E/A. (TNA, AIR 50/172/12)

Once again, a Spitfire pilot turned the tables on enemy fighters that had the advantage of height. The Spitfire's superior turning capabilities allowed Corfe to escape and then bring his guns to bear on another enemy fighter, which he sent down in flames with five short, accurate burst of fire from 300 yards. Corfe was quick to use the cloudy conditions to his advantage, while there was a huge amount of luck involved in his second combat, as he descended out of the cloud straight onto another Me 109, which he opened fire on from just 150 yards. Douglas Corfe had done extremely well to come away unscathed from this combat, as he had numerous run-ins with Me 109s and was operating alone. The twenty-one-year-old pilot from Meols must have been relieved to make it back home, having fired 1,600 rounds of ammunition in claiming one Me 109 destroyed and one damaged, his first claims on what was his third recorded patrol.

Initially, Green Section seems to have been detailed to engage the enemy aircraft attacking Dover's barrage balloons. This was effectively trying to kill two birds with one stone for the *Luftwaffe*, as it cleared a path for their bombers and forced Fighter Command into sending up fighters to try and prevent it, while the *Luftwaffe* fighters held a tactical advantage of being able to spring a trap. Green Section arrived too late to intervene on the initial attack on the balloons, as noted by Sgt Else in his

One of the photographs taken at Hawkinge on 29 July 1940, this is an excellent and atmospheric shot of a fighter pilot in his cockpit. The pilot is Sgt Douglas Corfe, his name visible on the microphone of his oxygen mask and one can sense the cramped conditions which had to be endured in a Spitfire. Note also the vital rear-view mirror which has been added to the top of the canopy, to help the pilot check his tail for enemy aircraft approaching his blind spot. (*Copyright Imperial War Museum, HU 54419*)

combat report. Peter Else had gained a lot of experience during June and July, having carried out twenty-seven recorded patrols primarily as a wingman. This experience had stood him in good stead, and he was probably Green Leader here:

> I was circling just behind Dover at about 8,000 feet trying to spot E/A which were firing at Balloons when a Spitfire came out of the cloud bank pursued by two ME109s.
>
> I fired at the astern 109 which broke away into the cloud. The other then attacked the Spitfire and I in turn attacked him. I fired a long burst at him and saw my explosive rounds flashing as they struck him. The E/A then disappeared into the cloud but just as he entered it a large black cloud of smoke came from him consistent with a petrol type fire.
>
> I estimate that we had by then just crossed the English Coast just off Dover. Else P. Sgt. (TNA, AIR 50/172/23)

Once again, the combat began in a split second, and it was likely that his swift actions saved the unknown Spitfire pilot's life, who was probably from 610 Squadron, as his fire forced the *Rotte* of Me 109s to break off their pursuit. The second Me 109 pilot he engaged would have endured a very nerve-wracking return flight across the Channel, if he made it at all. Else fired for seven seconds from between 200–250 yards, roughly 1,600 rounds, and as he had witnessed his incendiary de Wilde rounds (to aid marksmanship) interspersed with the normal .303 rounds hit home, he was credited with an Me 109 damaged at approximately 1225 hours.

Sgt Bernard Gardner was flying his third recorded patrol in four days. The Hampshire man was in formation with Green Section at the lower altitude of 8,000 feet, trying to intercept the 'balloon busters', when at 1230 hours they ran into what he recalled as twenty enemy aircraft made up of He 113s and Me 109s. His terse combat report read:

> I was Green 2 when our formation broke up to attack enemy bombers at about 8000 feet off Dungeness. I saw an enemy aircraft coming head on and firing, I immediately took evasive action and chased it to the sea where I gave it one long burst, smoke came pouring out from it and I saw it crash into the sea—I believe this e/a was a He 113. The fuselage was black on top and had yellow tips to the wings. It was very fast and seemed to have four machine guns. I then went to attack ten e/a and received a tracer bullet in the left arm. I forced landed in a field at Wye and was taken to Ashford Hospital. (TNA, AIR 50/172/29)

Despite having attempted to engage the bombers, most likely the Ju 87s encountered by Red Section, Gardner was headed off by the escorting fighters, but quickly gained the upper hand against the enemy fighter he believed to be a Heinkel 113, although this must have been another 109. Heinkel had built a prototype single-engined fighter, the Heinkel He 112, but the *Luftwaffe* decided to back Messerschmitt's Bf 109, ahead of Heinkel's fighter. The handful of Heinkels in existence were photographed, promoted as the Heinkel He 113 and the Nazi's excellent propaganda machine convinced the RAF into believing it to be a real threat, hence repeated sightings of He 113s in 1940.

Gardner saw this aircraft crash after his long burst of fire hit it decisively, and he was credited with a confirmed enemy fighter destroyed. Gardner had not finished yet though, and heroically attacked a formation of Dornier Do 215s, despite facing heavy odds, before being wounded by return fire and forced out of the combat. Receiving a tracer bullet in the arm was a serious injury, and as his Spitfire was badly damaged too, Gardner was lucky to make it back alive. The flying battle casualty report written by his squadron leader, states that his arm had been wounded by an 'incendiary' bullet which caused him to faint twice, making his survival all the more remarkable. It also confirms that his aircraft was DW-M, P.9540, not DW-M, K.9947 as erroneously recorded in the ORB and numerous other sources.

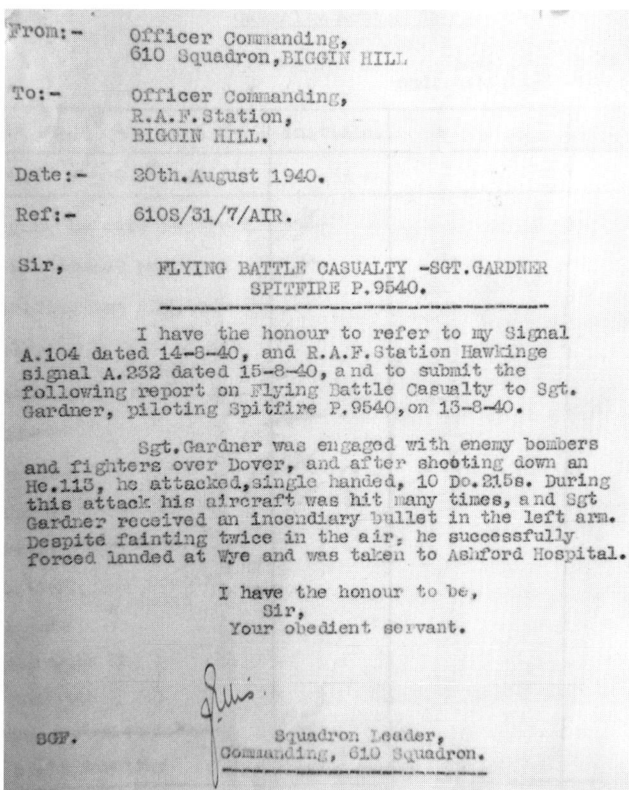

From:- Officer Commanding,
610 Squadron, BIGGIN HILL.

To:- Officer Commanding,
R.A.F. Station,
BIGGIN HILL.

Date:- 20th. August 1940.

Ref:- 610S/31/7/AIR.

Sir, FLYING BATTLE CASUALTY -SGT. GARDNER
SPITFIRE P.9540.

I have the honour to refer to my Signal A.104 dated 14-8-40, and R.A.F. Station Hawkinge signal A.232 dated 15-8-40, and to submit the following report on Flying Battle Casualty to Sgt. Gardner, piloting Spitfire P.9540, on 13-8-40.

Sgt. Gardner was engaged with enemy bombers and fighters over Dover, and after shooting down an He.113, he attacked, single handed, 10 Do.215s. During this attack his aircraft was hit many times, and Sgt Gardner received an incendiary bullet in the left arm. Despite fainting twice in the air, he successfully forced landed at Wye and was taken to Ashford Hospital.

I have the honour to be,
Sir,
Your obedient servant.

SGF. Squadron Leader,
Commanding, 610 Squadron.

S/Ldr Ellis's report concerning Sgt Gardner's forced landing, although the date has been recorded in error as 13 August, a day earlier than it occurred. (*TNA, AIR 81/1394*)

During my research, I met John Morris, who recalled seeing this Spitfire which crashed just outside the picturesque village of Wye when he was a boy, at the end of a long inviting field, the AMCB file calling it Winchcombe Farm. The wounded Gardner would have been desperate to land his badly damaged machine wherever he could, and the field, overlooked by the crown carved into the chalk of the hill to commemorate Edward VII's coronation, must have seemed ideal—assuming there were no anti-invasion obstacles across his path. Gardner took his chance and landed in the field, finally coming to an abrupt stop after dropping down nose first into a narrow lane running from the far end of the field to Wye village itself, called Coldharbour Lane which leads into Scotton Street. John pointed out the gap in the hedge, still just visible, which had been caused by the Spitfire's impact. Bernard Gardner would then have faced great difficulty getting out of the cockpit given the steep angle at which his Spitfire would have settled and his wound, but eventually he was taken to Ashford Hospital. The Spitfire is believed to have been towed away on the back of a lorry, having probably endured a wheels up landing, given P.9540's damage.

This was twenty-four-year-old Gardner's last action in the Battle, as his injury was more serious than he mentioned in his combat report. He had lasted just nineteen days on the front line, having completed three recorded patrols, proving how dangerous life was for the inexperienced pilots. But his skill and incredible bravery are evident for all to see from his combat reports, where no matter the odds, he tried to take the fight to the *Luftwaffe*. This is reflected in his claims for one Me 109 destroyed (the He 113) and three Me 109s unconfirmed in these three patrols.

It is unclear when Gardner officially left 610 Squadron, the ORB failing to mention his return to the unit from Ashford Hospital. However, he was killed just under a year later, on 28 June 1941, albeit in confusing circumstances. Two sources record he was killed, 'as a Flight Sergeant with 75 Signals Wing',[3] 'flying as a passenger in Blenheim MK IV V5755, which was shot down by enemy aircraft',[4] and he was buried in Hollybrook Cemetery, Southampton, aged twenty-four. However, the Battle of Britain website, 'Airmen's Stories', records his death as a result of friendly fire—'His Blenheim IV V5755 was shot down by friendly AA at Lydd, Kent',[5] while 610 Squadron's Association heard from a relative, who claimed Gardner should not even have been on board the Blenheim. Whatever had happened, it was a tragic end to another of the brave pilots of 'The Few'.

Green Section's third pilot was Sgt Ramsay, and this more experienced pilot, on his twenty-fifth recorded patrol, made some interesting observations on Green Section's activities:

> I was Green 3 in a Section patrolling between Dover and Folkestone at about 7000 ft. At 12.29 we sighted a large number of E/A diving, through the clouds.
>
> My leader ordered 'Line Astern'. For some time I waited for No. 2 to get into position and then called him up myself. He then got into position only he was a long way behind the leader. As I was also a long way from the leader I lost him.
>
> I climbed up and found myself below and behind a Me 110, coming up astern of him, I fired a short burst at about 150 yds. He immediately started to climb to the left with smoke coming from his engines. As I was positioning myself for another attack one of the crew jumped out. I fired again and the E/A seemed to drop out of the sky turning on its back and going down with smoke pouring from it. I estimate this last action took place approximately in mid-Channel. I did not follow him down and the last I saw was when he disappeared in the clouds out of control. N. H. D. RAMSAY. (TNA, AIR 50/172/63)

It is evident from the young sergeant's report that the three Spitfires were operating as a separate group from the rest of the Squadron and that on seeing the enemy aircraft, Else ordered his men into the usual line astern combat formation. For some reason, possibly his inexperience, Gardner took his time to carry this out this manoeuvre, which effectively broke up the section, as Ramsay,

A poignant photo of Sgt B. G. D. Gardner, wounded on 14 August 1940. He was later killed on 28 June 1941. (*Approved for use by the Biggin Hill Memorial Museum Trust*)

remarkably patiently given their life and death situation, waited for him to carry out the instruction before repeating the order and getting them into the attack. It is fascinating to see three different reports from three pilots in the same section, about the same combat, as each one saw it differently.

It is easy to see how Gardner came under attack so quickly for example, when he was not as prompt at carrying out the orders as his more experienced comrade, so would have been a tempting target for the Me 109s. However, this also highlights Gardner's bravery in being able to press home his attacks after getting himself out of trouble. Ramsay had attacked a powerful Messerschmitt 110, which was increasingly vulnerable to the RAF's single-seater interceptors, and with three or four bursts of fire, using 1,000 rounds from 200–250 yards, destroyed his target, at least one of its crew having baled out.

This patrol, which lasted about an hour, had been a remarkable success in the face of extremely heavy odds, with claims for six enemy aircraft destroyed, two probable and five damaged, as follows:

Norris—two Ju 87s destroyed, one Ju 87 damaged
Corfe—one Me 109 destroyed, one Me 109 damaged
Parsons—one Ju 87 probable, one Me 109 damaged
Chandler—one Me 109 destroyed
Ramsay—one Me 110 destroyed
Gardner—one Me 109 (the He 113) destroyed
Rees—one Ju 87 probable
Hamlyn—one Me 109 damaged
Else—one Me 109 damaged.[6]

Another plus was that P/Os Merrick and Gray had survived their first combat experience. Remarkably, only three pilots did not make a claim—the two new boys and the most experienced pilot on the patrol, F/Lt Warner. It is fascinating to note at this juncture the number of sergeants flying with the Squadron, more than half the patrol on this occasion. It was a far cry from the Dunkirk operations where virtually every pilot was an officer. The casualties had certainly taken their toll.

The Squadron would now be without the injured Sgt Gardner for the remainder of the Battle. There is also the possibility that another 610 Squadron pilot made a forced landing somewhere in Spitfire L.1009, as recorded in *Then and Now*: '**L1009.** Severely damaged in combat over Folkestone 12.30 p.m. Pilot believed unhurt. **DW-B** damaged but repairable'.[7] Typically, there is no record of L.1009 (see photo p. 193) having flown on this patrol in the ORB. However, L.1009 is reported as being damaged on 14 August in the Spitfire production lists, so this is perhaps another example of an aircraft being annotated retrospectively based on its identifying squadron letter.[8] In this instance it is 'B', which was being flown by P/O Gray, so perhaps his first operational sortie had been more complex than originally thought. The ORB lists 'B' as X.4166, which the production lists state joined the Squadron the following day,[9] presumably as a replacement for L.1009. So it is logical to assume that these sources are correct and DW-B, L.1009, one of 610's original Spitfires, had been damaged and put of action for repairs. Following its repairs, it joined 92 Squadron in October.

In different accounts of the day's fighting it is acknowledged that an enormous dogfight had developed over the south coast, for example, *Jagdwaffe vol. Two* states that the raid:

> began at about noon when some 80 Ju 87s, escorted by all three *Gruppen* of JG 26, headed towards targets at Dover, Folkestone and Hawkinge. Met by no fewer than four squadrons of RAF fighters, an immense dogfight involving some 200 aircraft developed above Dover … During the clash between these units, Ju 87s sank a lightship and some Bf 109s shot down a number of barrage balloons, neither of these activities contributing to the objective of defeating Fighter Command.[10]

These were the 109s shooting down balloons that Green Section had been ordered to intercept. It goes on to record that the escorting fighters lost several aircraft, some of which almost certainly fell to 610's pilots, 'By the end of the day's fighting *Jagdwaffe* (*Luftwaffe's* fighter arm) combat losses amounted to six Bf109E fighters with five pilots killed and one taken prisoner',[11] while the *Stukas* of 10/LG1 had also suffered casualties. After such a draining battle, 610 Squadron's pilots would have been glad not to be called into action again that day, and been proud of their efforts during such a large scale dogfight. However, it must have seemed all too likely that the day's combat was a sign of things to come.

Although Thursday 15 August got off to a poor start on the weather front, by mid-morning it had improved and the first of several attacks was launched against Fighter Command's airfields and the RDF stations, not only on the south coast as usual, but also from Norway and Denmark against north-eastern England. For 610 Squadron, the day's main action did not come until 1840 hours, when the telephone rang at dispersal and eight Spitfires of 'B' Flight were scrambled to intercept an unopposed raid crossing the south coast. *Luftflotte* 2 was attempting to attack Biggin Hill and Kenley, its heavily-escorted bombers given additional support by JG 26's Me 109s, which were using their favoured means of operating, the *Freie Jagd*. Veteran Bill Warner was leading the interception as Blue Leader, with the rest of the battle order as follows:

DW-Z.	R.6802	F/Lt. W. H. C. WARNER.	Blue 1	56
DW-V.	K.9970	P/O. H. K. COX.	Blue 2	4
DW-R.	X.4239	SGT. RAMSAY, N. H. D.	Blue 3	26
DW-S.	K.9975	SGT. ARNFIELD, S. J.	Green 1	45
DW-L.	P.9311	SGT. ELSE, P.	Green 2	28
DW-O.	X.4011	SGT. CORFE, D.	Green 3	4
DW-P.	P.9451	P/O. B. V. REES.		3
DW-T.	X.4064	P/O. S. C. NORRIS.		48

From the combat reports, one can establish who was flying in which role in the formation, apart from Norris and Rees, particularly as Stanley Norris usually flew with 'A' Flight—perhaps they flew as a pair covering the other six Spitfires from a rear attack. Again, the formation was made up of some of the Squadron's most experienced pilots along with some novices, as can be seen from the figures. Sapper control at Biggin Hill calmly ordered F/Lt Warner to get his formation to Angels One Five, with their throttles 'through the gate', in order to block the path of the German formation, which the controller believed was targeting the vital sector stations. Although it was a below-strength force of Spitfires, 32 Squadron's Hurricanes had also been scrambled from Biggin Hill, and 111 Squadron's Hurricanes had taken off from nearby Croydon.

Bill Warner led his men in a hard climb and having done well to reach 15,000 feet within seven minutes of being scrambled, 'about 10 miles to the S.E (of Biggin Hill), they met about 25 D.O.215s escorted by many M.E.109s. The bombers flying at 14,000 ft. and the fighters at 16,000 ft' (ORB). Warner had used all his experience to attain as much height as possible, and also to use the conditions to his advantage, so that his small force was positioned to attack the German bombers from out of the sun. It was imperative to attack the bombers, as they posed the threat to the sector station, but it was touch-and-go whether it would be possible.

A large number of Me 109s once again enjoyed a height advantage, and were watching and waiting for the best opportunity to bounce the Spitfires. The odds were stacked against the RAF pilots, and it was down to the finest of margins as to whether they would get through to the stately procession of Dornier 215s, as was later recalled in the combat reports. P/O Ken Cox, a wingman to 'B' Flight's leader, reported how at 1850 hours, 'I was flying as Blue 2 when about thirty bombers were sighted. We were about to attack from the sun when I saw an ME109 on my Port side, apparently about to make a beam attack' (TNA, AIR 50/172/14). Sgt Douglas Corfe goes into further detail, 'I was flying Green 3 in B Flight. We climbed to 15,000 and sighted about 25 Dornier 215s flying at 14,000 just South of Maidstone. We dived out of the sun at the Dorniers when several ME109s came down on us' (TNA, AIR 50/172/12).

The Messerschmitts, flying at about 17,000 feet according to Corfe, had timed their intervention to perfection, thwarting the Spitfires' attack on the bombers and now 610 Squadron's pilots became involved in another dangerous dogfight with the escorts. The Spitfire pilots' earphones would have been filled with cries of, 'Watch out! 109s! Break, break!' as they were forced to divert their attention to the onrushing fighters. Ken Cox reported that after spotting the 109 on his port side, he:

> turned and engaged, got on his tail and after three short bursts he went into a vertical dive with engine on. I lost sight of him in the ground haze at 6,000 (Crews on Biggin Hill Aerodrome saw a ME109 go vertically into ground not smoking). I had by then lost all sight of the enemy, I called control but received no reply so patrolled around alone for a while then contacted with control and landed. (TNA, AIR 50/172/14)

Cox had spotted the 109s in the nick of time and having warned his comrades, used the Spitfire's better turning capabilities over the Me 109 to escape. Having fired three short bursts from 250 yards range, Cox claimed an Me 109 as probably destroyed, eventually returning to base unscathed.

Douglas Corfe continued his report on the action thus:

> I engaged one ME109 and fired 4 3 sec. bursts at him. My tracer appeared to hit him about the rear of the fuselage and wings. He employed evasive tactics and I then had to break away and attack another ME109 who was on my tail. I fired the remainder of my ammunition off at this ME109 without appreciable effect, and then returned to base to re-arm. (TNA, AIR 50/172/12)

Corfe had also done well to avoid the 109's surprise attack and gain the initiative against his original assailant, damaging the Me 109 with his fire from 250 yards, before the weight in number of escorts took their toll and Corfe had to break off again. That he returned to Biggin Hill to 're-arm', suggests he fully expected to be immediately scrambled again, despite having just been in a vicious dogfight, showing the extreme pressure the young men were under, not to mention the scale of the battle at this point. Douglas Corfe was credited with a 109 damaged to add to the 109 destroyed and 109 damaged from the day before—it was proving a successful couple of days for the twenty-one-year-old sergeant.

The battle-hardened Green Section leader, Sgt Arnfield, also filed a combat report, although he focused on his run-in at 1850 hours with the escorts at 14,000 feet over Maidstone:

> I was leading Green Section while "B" Flight 610 Squadron were on patrol, and we sighted approximately 25 DO215s or 17s escorted by ME109s. I got on the tail of one ME109 and overtook until I was at 250 yards range. He did not observe me as I was coming out of the sun. He was accompanied by a second ME109. I started firing at 250 and sighting my bullets he did a steep turn to the right while I followed him up firing when he was in my sight and closing in on him.
>
> The second ME109 turned to get on my tail but before he could do so my ammunition ran out. Just then my target began to smoke badly and seemed to lurch over to the left and go in a gentle dive. His No.2 was by this time firing at me and being out of ammunition I flew for home, not waiting to see what had happened to my ME109. The second ME109 made not the least attempt to follow me. (TNA, AIR 50/172/5)

Once again, the importance of achieving surprise by coming out of the sun was key. Having closed to 250 yards, and fired all his ammunition, Arnfield would have been disappointed not to have definitely shot the enemy aircraft down, especially as he was playing a dangerous game by taking on two enemy fighters on his own. The *Rotte* was partly designed so that the wingman could easily close on anyone attacking his leader, as seen here—although the German pilots were initially caught napping, the wingman was quickly in a firing position on Arnfield. The sergeant was canny enough to know not to stick around and watch the fate of his target, but accepting it as damaged, concentrated on evading the other 109, before heading back the short distance home. The second German pilot's lack of determination is striking; he was perhaps happy just to try and return home, probably running low on fuel.

The only other pilot to make a claim was William Warner, who wrote the following report about the encounter with twenty—twenty-five enemy aircraft:

> I was leading "B" Flight 610 Squadron and was told that enemy aircraft were approaching Biggin Hill about 10 miles to the South East. The DO215s were escorted by ME109s. The bombers were about 1500 to 2000 feet below the escort. I intercepted an ME109 and gave it three long bursts, after which it did a half roll and I got in another burst. Smoke started coming from the fuselage, and it dived down vertically. I followed it down to six thousand feet and lost it in the haze. When last seen it was still going down vertically at about 350 m.p.h. (TNA, AIR 50/172/77)

Surprisingly, Warner made no mention of positioning his men to attack the bombers first, before being set upon by the escorts. Instead, he concentrated on the dogfight with the 109, which he hit with three long bursts and one short one, before it fell in an apparent terminal dive. Someone, possibly Warner himself, had neatly handwritten on his report that this was claimed as a probable, which meant from the individual combat reports that the Squadron had claimed two probably destroyed 109s and two more damaged. However, the ORB states, 'Enemy casualties:– 1. M.E.109 (destroyed). 1 M.E.109 (probable). 2 M.E.109s (damaged)', casting some confusion as to whether Warner or Cox had successfully shot a 109 down.[12]

When reading the reports of Warner and Cox, it seems possible they had both hit the same 109, as both of them noted that their target was last seen at 6,000 feet going straight down, but was lost to sight in the haze. That ground crews at Biggin Hill saw one Messerschmitt go vertically straight in, meant that at least one 109 had been destroyed. Given that both pilots stated that their respective 109s were 'probables', it seems best to agree with them, and so the claims would be as follows:

Warner—1 Me 109 probably destroyed
Cox—1 Me 109 probably destroyed
Arnfield—1 Me 109 damaged
Corfe—1 Me 109 damaged.

On the positive side, 610's interception had been successful, as the pilots made these claims against the enemy, with all eight Spitfires safely returning to Biggin Hill. This was all the more remarkable given they had been on the receiving end of a dangerous 'bounce'. Several of them had lucky escapes, but it was also due in some cases to their hard fought experience, that they had come through unscathed. On the negative side, they had not managed to intercept the bombers, admittedly by fractions of seconds, but the bombers were able to carry on and drop their bombs, although 32 Squadron had more success against them, shooting down two of them before they too had to take on the escorts. 32 Squadron also got involved with *Erprobungsgruppe* [Erpro.] 210's low-level raid, and claimed to have shot down some of them.

Realistically, 'The Chesters' did remarkably well in confronting the raiders ten miles to the south-east of Biggin Hill, given the short time scales involved from being scrambled to being in combat, which was primarily due to F/Lt Warner's leadership skills. That the Spitfires were able to land back at Biggin Hill at around 1930 hours was more good news for 610 Squadron, as the vital sector station had been left unharmed. The bombers had actually dropped their loads on another airfield, West Malling, which lay some miles south-east of Biggin and was still being built.

The ORB refers to 610 Squadron intercepting the bombers ten miles to the south-east of Biggin Hill, however all four combat reports mention being in the vicinity of Maidstone. As the crow flies, it is about twenty-one miles from Biggin Hill to Maidstone. These miles would have been eaten up very quickly by the approaching *Luftwaffe* formation; P/O Cox even referred to the dogfight being within sight of Biggin. The fact that West Malling is only five miles to the east of Maidstone could suggest that the German bombers panicked and dumped their bombs on the nearest airfield in the face of Biggin Hill's advancing fighters. It could simply have been a genuine case of mistaken identity, the German bomber crews thinking they had found their target, even though they were fifteen miles short. Although Biggin, perched high up on its hill, must have been a distinctive target even from altitude, Cox and Warner both mentioned a ground haze at 6,000 feet which would have made identification much more difficult. Perhaps 610 and 32 Squadrons had thwarted the bombers after all, and the Germans just dumped their payload on the nearest target of opportunity, returning to their French bases as quickly as possible. Although it had been a close-run thing, the primary target of Biggin Hill had not been hit and the vital sector station remained fully operational.

The other key sector station at Kenley also had a lucky escape, with the low-level attack experts of Erpro. 210 mistaking Croydon for Kenley. While Croydon was badly hit, it would prove to be a costly case of mistaken identity, as the aerodrome lay within Greater London, which Hitler himself had decreed should not be bombed. If the RAF carried out reprisal raids on Berlin, then London could become a prime target for the *Luftwaffe*. Over the course of the day which had seen some of the fiercest fighting, in the north and the south, the RAF lost thirty-four aircraft. But the *Luftwaffe's* losses had been severe—losing seventy-five aircraft with a much larger number of aircrew was a heavy blow. Amongst the *Luftwaffe*, 15 August became known as 'Black Thursday'. 610 Squadron had certainly played its part in Fighter Command's success on this momentous day.

After dealing with the last raid of the previous day, 610 Squadron's pilots were probably hoping they were not scrambled too early on the morning of Friday 16 August 1940, despite having been up for dawn readiness. At about 1100 hours, raids started being plotted approaching England, their targets once again being the airfields. West Malling took another pasting, being put out of action for four days. A little later in the afternoon the pin-point accurate *Stukas* targeted Tangmere, one of 11 Group's vital sector stations on the south coast, causing heavy damage. It was becoming another busy day for Fighter Command, and at some point, most likely in the late morning or early afternoon, twelve Spitfires led by S/Ldr Ellis, flew down to Hawkinge. Interestingly, 32 Squadron carried out four patrols from Biggin Hill between 1110 and 1745 hours, proving how frequent the patrols had become. While 32 Squadron operated from Biggin, it is all the more likely that 610 had gone to Hawkinge by midday.

Flying from Hawkinge placed the Squadron right on the front line of the country's defence, and by mid-August, it is possible the move was not met with great enthusiasm by the pilots, as the situation had changed. In July, they had spent many days on the forward airfield to better-protect the convoys, which had been the *Luftwaffe's* primary target. Now, if they were scrambled from Hawkinge to meet an incoming raid, they had less opportunity to gain the vital height advantage, which although never guaranteed, was much more likely when intercepting from Biggin Hill, all those miles inland. Also, when operating from Biggin Hill, the Squadron could be in position to intercept a raid by flying directly towards it; from Hawkinge, they either had to fly inland first while gaining height to intercept, or spiral up from the airfield, leaving themselves vulnerable to prowling packs of Me 109s, which had already found a favourable altitude over France and the Channel. Furthermore, Hawkinge was very vulnerable to bombing raids and sudden strafing attacks from *Luftwaffe* fighters—it was a highly dangerous place to be.

As the afternoon wore on, 610 Squadron remained at readiness, seemingly being held in reserve as the number of raids being plotted grew. Unfortunately the weather became more cloudy, and some of the raiders went unreported, so when 610 Squadron was scrambled to intercept the enemy in the Dungeness area at 1615 hours, it was a more confused situation than usual. As the pilots jumped up from their chairs, or from lounging on the grass, where they had been trying to relax as best they could, they had already taken in the far from ideal conditions overhead, wondering what the patrol held in store for them. But the quick sprint to their respective aircraft, brief take-off drill before taxying out and becoming airborne as quickly as possible, would have pushed such thoughts to the back of their minds. Having missed his Squadron's last two successful patrols, John Ellis would have been glad to be at the head of the formation as they quickly formed up and gained height over Hawkinge, leading the following men:

DW-W.	R.6993	S/Ldr. J. ELLIS.	Red 1	43
DW-A.	R.6976	F/O. P. G. LAMB.		41
DW-D.	L.1037*	P/O. D. M. GRAY.	Red 3	2
DW-T.	X.4064	P/O. S. C. NORRIS.		49
DW-F.	X.4028	SGT. HAMLYN, R. F.		30
DW-H.	K.9818	SGT. PARSONS, C. A.		18
DW-Z.	R.6802	F/O. W. H. C. WARNER.		57
DW-V.	K.9970	P/O. H. K. COX.		5
DW-N.	N.3128	P/O. B. V. REES.		4
DW-X.		SGT. ARNFIELD, S. J.		46
DW-L.	P.9311	SGT. ELSE, P.		29
DW-R.	X.4239	SGT. RAMSAY, N. H. D.		27

*As ORB, and probably coded DW-D, but this was most likely X.4065, see letter in Association archive about it being repaired.

The Squadron had some of its most experienced pilots on this patrol, with F/Lt Warner now on his fifty-seventh recorded operation, P/O Norris on his forty-ninth, Sgt Arnfield on his forty-sixth and the CO on his forty-third. Many of the pilots who had joined the unit in June, Sgts Else, Ramsay, Hamlyn and Parsons, now formed a highly-skilled backbone to the Squadron, their nerve-wracking early flights having become a thing of the past. Those feelings were now being endured by other inexperienced pilots: P/O Gray on his second recorded patrol, probably a wingman to S/Ldr Ellis, while Bill Warner possibly had P/O Cox on his fifth recorded patrol and P/O Rees on his fourth, to watch over.

From the information available, this is one of the patrols where it is hard to work out who was flying in which section, although John Ellis was certainly leading 'A' Flight as Red 1 and F/Lt Warner was leading 'B' Flight as Blue 1 (which was unusual, as Ellis normally led as 'B' Flight's, Blue leader). Norris was probably leading Yellow Section and Arnfield Green Section—he had led Green Section before due to his experience, but technical problems probably hindered this today. What becomes apparent from the three available combat reports, is that it was a tricky interception. The ground controller gave the Squadron several different vectors, before 610 finally contacted the enemy, an exasperating experience for the Spitfire pilots. There were also large numbers of RAF fighters being ordered to intercept the raiders, twelve other squadrons in total (TNA, AIR 25/197).

The ORB stated that 'Red, Blue, Green & Yellow sections took off from HAWKINGE to intercept raid in DUNGENESS, they encountered 50 J.U.88s escorted by 12 M.E.109s at 25,000 ft.', which outlines succinctly the odds faced by 610's men if the other squadrons did not materialise. The ever-reliable John Ellis comes up with the goods in terms of his combat report, describing the Squadron's situation, before concentrating on his own combat. In the preamble, he stated he was in 'A' Flight, encountered thirty Ju 88s at 1700 hours at 25,000 feet over Dungeness, before continuing:

> I was leading 610 Sqdn. which took off from Hawkinge at 16.15 hrs. After much vectoring and changing of height in extremely bad visibility during which the flights got split up 5 a/c of 'A' Flt. intercepted 30 Ju. 88. escorted by 12 Me.109. Red Section carried out a No.3 attack on the rear section of bombers while the 2 a/c in Yellow Section dealt with the fighters. The bombers broke up after being attacked and dived very steeply. After a 4 secs burst at 200 yds the a/c I was attacking was emitting clouds of grey smoke from the vicinity of the engine and wing roots. I had to break off the attack due to overshooting, but on turning round to start a fresh attack I noticed about six Me.109s above and behind me. As they did not attack I continued to chase the Ju.88 which by now was diving extremely steeply and although I was doing 360 mph ASI at 15,000', I was not gaining on the enemy a/c which was fast approaching a layer of cloud. I fired the remainder of my ammunition at the Ju.88 at 600 yds and I last saw this a/c enter the cloud diving very steeply and smoking slightly 20 miles S. of Dungeness. I experienced continuous return fire (M.G) during both attacks. (TNA, AIR 50/172/22)

Ellis was quick to establish the difficulty the Squadron had in finding the enemy formation, in terrible visibility. On the basis of time alone, it took 'The Chesters' forty-five minutes to engage the enemy when on other occasions, with good use of the RDF, better controlling (although that's not to say the controller was at fault), and better weather conditions, the Squadron had engaged the enemy within ten minutes of being scrambled. The other negative for Ellis was that the formation had separated in the confusion of the wild goose chase around the murky skies of Kent, leaving him in command of five Spitfires of 'A' Flight to take on thirty Ju 88s and twelve Me 109s.

Undaunted by the situation, two Spitfires of Yellow Section attempted to stave off the Messerschmitts, while Ellis led Red Section in a fairly despairing No. 3 attack on the bombers, the three fighters simultaneously engaging a section of bombers. Although it successfully broke up the bomber formation, it is a little surprising to see the Squadron still using such obsolete attack methods, especially when enemy fighters were in the vicinity. After a high-speed chase, Ellis claimed the Ju 88 as damaged, having fired an initial burst from 200 yards for four seconds which did the damage, before it escaped into cloud. It is also surprising that Ellis could not catch the Junkers 88 up again, due to the speed it had built up during its rapid descent to 15,000 feet.

Inexperienced P/O Gray also described the enemy formation as, 'approx. 50 Ju 88s & M.E.109s, 1700hrs, Dungeness, 20,000 ft', and he had done well to keep formation during the lengthy search and subsequent attack on the bombers, but his combat report reveals he did not share his leader's luck:

> Flying No. 3 in Red Section, took off to patrol Hawkinge. We then received several vectors and encountered formations of J.U.88s and M.E. 109s, south of Dungeness at 20,000 ft. I followed S/Ldr Ellis in an attack on a formation of J.U. 88s, and delivered a short burst at the extreme range 250 yds, but had to break off the attack to evade one or more 109s which dived on me. I fired a burst at a 109, which turned over and went into a dive, engine smoking. I saw five M.E. 109s diving on me and started a steep climbing turn to the right but received hits with two cannon shells, one of which struck the machine at the root end of the wing at the trailing edge, the other hit near the radio housing wrecking the set and blowing the panel off the other side, and the machine became uncontrollable. I regained control at three thousand feet and found I had no pressure, rendering the guns unusable. I flew north, reached the coast and followed a railway home. Machine appears to be completely U.S. (TNA, AIR 50/172/30)

Gray bravely pressed home his attack against the bombers, knowing he did not have long before the German fighters came swooping down on him. It is interesting that even such an inexperienced pilot described firing from 250 yards as being extreme range. The Squadron's veterans must have impressed upon the new recruits the need to really close the range before opening fire, to make their attack count. Unlike Ellis, Donald Gray had to break off his attack due to the attention of the 109s, which had again timed their intervention well. Gray could claim a probable against one of these, but then his luck ran out. Despite further evasive action, the young pilot officer came to understand the devastating effect of his opponent's firepower, when two cannon shells hit his Spitfire. It must have been a terrifying experience for Gray, as bullets flashed past him before hammering into his aircraft, wrecking his Spitfire, leaving it out of control and falling out of the sky.

Bravely staying with his aircraft, Gray eventually regained control at just 3,000 feet having lost about 15,000 feet, a horrific descent to cope with, wondering if they were to be his final moments. It is testament to Gray's courage and skill as a pilot that he made it back to Biggin Hill, but having battled to get his precious mount back home, it was felt to be beyond repair. Nevertheless, an exhausted Gray would simply have been glad to have returned after such a frightening experience. He and the rest of the pilots were all too aware of the Me 109's superiority in armament. It was a stark contrast to the number of bullets usually required by an RAF pilot to bring an opponent down, but Gray could take heart from the fact that he filed a claim for a probable Me 109, having fired 700 rounds in two bursts.

There is some confusion as to whether Gray was injured, as '11 Group's Intelligence Bulletin No. 29', states that Gray was wounded after this combat (TNA, AIR 25/197). Given that Gray's combat report states that he was uninjured, despite the damage to his Spitfire, and that he would be flying the next day, it is likely that this was an error. *Then and Now* recalls this loss as follows: 'Spitfire. Attacked by Bf 109 over Dungeness 5.20 p.m. Returned to base R/T damaged. P/O D. McI. Gray unhurt. DW-D repairable'.[13]

The identity of Gray's aircraft is something of a mystery, indicated by the lack of a serial number in the above source. The ORB notes it as DW-D, L.1037, but it is likely that this was inaccurate, and a letter in 610 Squadron's archive perhaps identifies his Spitfire as X.4065. The correspondence was sent to John Ellis from the Castle Bromwich Factory, where X.4065, quite possibly DW-D, had been sent as an exhibit to the workers who were building and repairing Spitfires. Given Ellis wrote his original letter on 22 August and the note on the reply refers to similar damage that happened to Gray's aircraft on 16 August, it is highly likely that this was Gray's machine on 16 August. We know

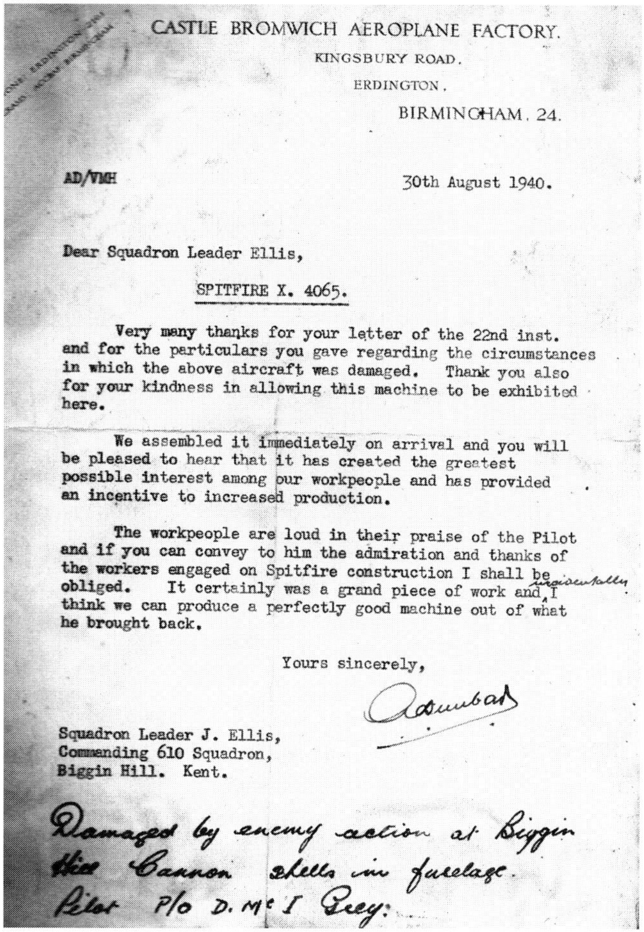

CASTLE BROMWICH AEROPLANE FACTORY.
KINGSBURY ROAD.
ERDINGTON.
BIRMINGHAM. 24.

AD/VMH

30th August 1940.

Dear Squadron Leader Ellis,

SPITFIRE X. 4065.

Very many thanks for your letter of the 22nd inst. and for the particulars you gave regarding the circumstances in which the above aircraft was damaged. Thank you also for your kindness in allowing this machine to be exhibited here.

We assembled it immediately on arrival and you will be pleased to hear that it has created the greatest possible interest among our workpeople and has provided an incentive to increased production.

The workpeople are loud in their praise of the Pilot and if you can convey to him the admiration and thanks of the workers engaged on Spitfire construction I shall be obliged. It certainly was a grand piece of work and I think we can produce a perfectly good machine out of what he brought back.

Yours sincerely,

Squadron Leader J. Ellis,
Commanding 610 Squadron,
Biggin Hill. Kent.

Damaged by enemy action at Biggin Hill Cannon shells in fuselage.
Pilot P/O D. McI Grey:

The letter to S/Ldr Ellis, outlining how seeing the serious damage to X.4065 and the obvious bravery required to fly it home, spurred on the Castle Bromwich workers. (*Copyright 610 Squadron Association*)

X.4065 joined 610 on 12 August and also that P/O Merrick flew it twice on 13 August and earlier on 16 August. The description of the damaged aircraft on display certainly indicates it had been badly damaged, but it seems the effort was worth it. X.4065 did eventually return to operations, but the machine is believed to ultimately have been lost on 11 August 1941.[14]

The other combat report available from this engagement is from the Squadron's veteran Sgt Pilot, Stanley John Arnfield. This was a particularly testing patrol for him, as on taking off he found that his R/T system was not working, making this a very dangerous sortie. He would not hear any instructions on where to go or warnings of enemy attack, but would have to rely on his experience to stay with the formation. The easy option for Arnfield, would have been to signal his problem to another pilot and return home to have the radio investigated. However, he determinedly pressed on, keeping the Squadron at full strength. I have included a photo of his own typewritten account of the action, against about fifty Ju 88 bombers and Me 109 fighters, at 1700 hours (see p. 328).

Arnfield's reference to 'flying in the box of Red Section' simply meant he was in the same formation as Red Section, probably at the rear of the 'Vic', perhaps as a result of his R/T problems. He establishes that the German aircraft were returning to France having completed their raid, while the problem of having a broken R/T also becomes apparent. The weather conditions were far from ideal, the thick haze explaining why, so unexpectedly, he came across the Spitfire being attacked—was it a 'DW' aircraft from his Squadron, with one of his colleagues in dire straits? As he went in pursuit of the

15

I was flying in the box of Red Section 610 Squadron on patrol over Hawkinge. We apparently had several vectors but my R/T was dead and I could hear nothing. Eventually while at 20-25,000 ft flying in land we saw a large bomber formation proceeding out to see some miles to our left. Red leader turned to attack leaving me rather far behind so that eventually I lost him in the sun. I saw more aircraft following. The main formation, and climbed to attack the rear one of these, a straggler from out of the sun. However another Spitfire beat me to it so I chased after the rest which were visible in conditions of very thick haze. Suddenly I saw to my left front two M.E. 109'S attacking a Spitfire which spun down, apparently out of control with the 109's following it down. I dived to attack these one in my sight, but almost as soon as I opened fire I was on top of him. I could see bullets going into his cockpit and mainplanes and had to swerve vioently to avoid a collision, carrying on down to under 8,000 ft before I could pull out. I was not attacked by the second M.E. 109, and did not see the result of my fire on the first, and the fate of the Spitfire. Being short of petrol I made for home striking the coast at Hastings, and landing at Biggin Hill.

Sgt Arnfield's combat report, 16 August 1940. (*TNA, AIR 50/172/5*)

two 109s, his dive was extreme, as it took him from around 20,000 feet to 8,000 feet before he could pull out. Arnfield tried to close with the 109s as quickly as possible, to force them off the unfortunate Spitfire pilot, who was in a parlous situation. The action was over in seconds, and Arnfield could only claim one Me 109 as damaged, 'Over sea off Dungeness' (TNA, AIR 50/172/5), having fired 480 rounds of ammunition in a four—five second burst from 200 yards. That he returned to the English coastline at Hastings, Sussex, around seventeen miles away from Dungeness, was a good example of the distances easily travelled in these dogfights.

The weather, described in the combat summary as, 'Visibility was very hazy 10:10ths cloud at 3,000 ft' (ORB), is reflected in the equally hazy information about this patrol. The various vectors and altitude changes in extremely bad visibility had split up the two flights, but what happened to 'B' Flight's pilots is largely unclear. However, once the Spitfires had trickled home by 1730 hours, it was obvious that despite making claims for one Me 109 probably destroyed (Gray), a 109 (Arnfield) and a Ju 88 (Ellis) both damaged,[15] the Squadron had lost one of its number in the hazardous, hazy skies over Dungeness and the English Channel. The Spitfire which Sgt Arnfield desperately tried to assist, as it spun down out of control while being assailed by two Me 109s, had the Squadron identification letters of 'DW-Z'. This meant the Squadron had lost another of its long-standing members, 'B' Flight's commander, F/Lt William Henry Cromwell Warner.

Yet again, the system for reporting a potential casualty swung into action. While the Air Ministry was informed on the following day, news was sent to the Warner's family home in Oxton, Wirral too, informing them that their son had been reported as 'Missing' (TNA, AIR 81/1480). Sir Lionel Warner seemed to accept very quickly that his son had gone forever, unlike some parents, who maintained a hopeful belief that their son would turn up, even after the War, some five years later. In this case, the next of kin seems to have been made more aware of the fate that had befallen Bill, as S/Ldr Ellis clearly explained what had happened during Warner's final operation. It is likely that this was partly due to Sir Lionel Warner's long-standing connection with the Squadron, as he had been amongst the guests of an officers' mess guest night back in April 1937, when the current situation was still a distant threat.

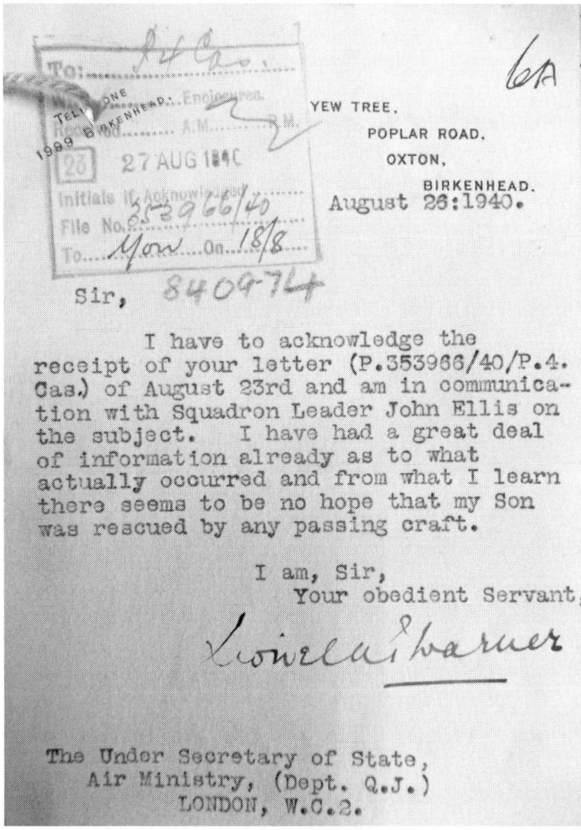

6A

TELEPHONE
1999 BIRKENHEAD.

YEW TREE,
POPLAR ROAD,
OXTON,
BIRKENHEAD.

27 AUG 1940

File No. 353966/40

August 26:1940.

Sir, 8409764

I have to acknowledge the receipt of your letter (P.353966/40/P.4. Cas.) of August 23rd and am in communication with Squadron Leader John Ellis on the subject. I have had a great deal of information already as to what actually occurred and from what I learn there seems to be no hope that my Son was rescued by any passing craft.

I am, Sir,
Your obedient Servant,

Lionel Warner

The Under Secretary of State,
Air Ministry, (Dept. Q.J.)
LONDON, W.C.2.

Sir Lionel Warner's letter, grimly accepting the loss of his younger son, William. (*TNA, AIR 81/1480*)

Ellis's flying battle casualty report for Biggin Hill's station commander on 20 August, included some additional details to what had been apparent in the immediate aftermath of Warner's loss. Ellis confirmed the patrol's chaotic nature, with numerous vectors at greatly varying heights in hazy and cloudy conditions and how Warner became separated from his own wingmen and Ellis's 'A' Flight while climbing through clouds. This must have distracted Warner; having possibly had inexperienced wingmen with him in such difficult circumstances, may explain how he came to be so isolated. Tiredness was probably another factor, as he was involved in his third combat in as many days, not to mention any potential unrecorded patrols and having been in action for so long anyway, with fifty-seven recorded patrols to his name.

The CO's investigation established that it could only have been Spitfire DW-Z, R.6802, and therefore F/Lt Warner, who had been shot down off Dover at 1655 hours. That the two rescue boats only found a small amount of wreckage and no body, reflects what Sir Lionel Warner had said in his letter to the Air Ministry; this was presumably the information John Ellis had passed on to Warner's father. No more news was ever heard of 610 Squadron's young flight commander, and the Air Ministry ultimately sent the dreaded letter to the Warner family on 25 March 1941, stating that he was now considered to have been killed in action on 16 August 1940 (TNA, AIR 81/1480). Although in his letters Sir Lionel Warner had stoically accepted his son's death, this letter has a crushing finality about it, eradicating any glimmer of hope his father secretly may have had, not to mention Warner's mother Nina, and his brother and sister. The sad news that he was listed as 'Missing' was reported on 24 August 1940, in the press which was local to the Squadron's pre-war station of Hooton Park. Three papers reported the loss of the twenty-one-year-old pilot, see one example on p. 331.

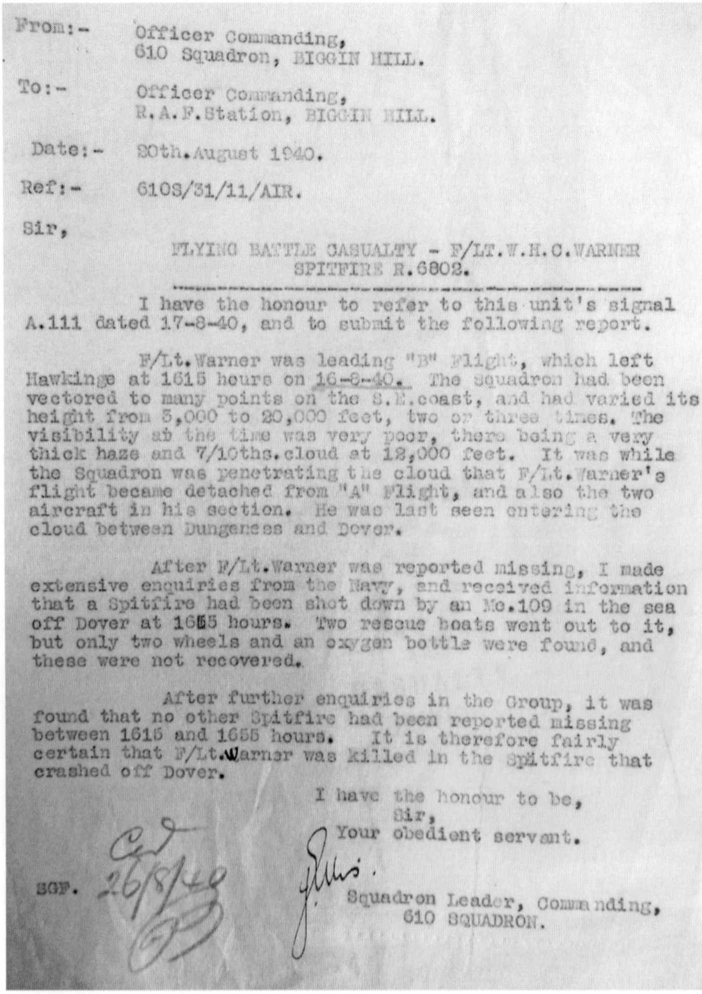

From:- Officer Commanding,
610 Squadron, BIGGIN HILL.

To:- Officer Commanding,
R.A.F.Station, BIGGIN HILL.

Date:- 20th.August 1940.

Ref:- 610S/31/11/AIR.

Sir,

FLYING BATTLE CASUALTY - F/LT.W.H.C.WARNER
SPITFIRE R.6802.

I have the honour to refer to this unit's signal A.111 dated 17-8-40, and to submit the following report.

F/Lt.Warner was leading "B" Flight, which left Hawkinge at 1615 hours on 16-8-40. The squadron had been vectored to many points on the S.E.coast, and had varied its height from 5,000 to 20,000 feet, two or three times. The visibility at the time was very poor, there being a very thick haze and 7/10ths.cloud at 12,000 feet. It was while the Squadron was penetrating the cloud that F/Lt.Warner's flight became detached from "A" Flight, and also the two aircraft in his section. He was last seen entering the cloud between Dungeness and Dover.

After F/Lt.Warner was reported missing, I made extensive enquiries from the Navy, and received information that a Spitfire had been shot down by an Me.109 in the sea off Dover at 1655 hours. Two rescue boats went out to it, but only two wheels and an oxygen bottle were found, and these were not recovered.

After further enquiries in the Group, it was found that no other Spitfire had been reported missing between 1615 and 1655 hours. It is therefore fairly certain that F/Lt.Warner was killed in the Spitfire that crashed off Dover.

I have the honour to be,
Sir,
Your obedient servant.

SGF. 26/8/40

Ellis.

Squadron Leader, Commanding,
610 SQUADRON.

S/Ldr Ellis's report on the loss of Warner, giving the clearest indication of what had happened to his trusted flight commander. (*TNA, AIR 81/1480*)

This was on the newspapers front page, highlighting the position and status of Warner's family on the Wirral and the surrounding area. Tragically for William Warner's parents, family and his friends on the Squadron, news of his safety would never arrive, and they had to accept the awful realisation that they would never see William again.

Bill Warner's loss was another hammer blow to the Squadron, as yet another of the Squadron's most experienced and long-serving pilots had gone. Warner had earned his 'Wings' with the Squadron on 3 November 1938, so was an integral part of the Squadron, having formed strong bonds with the men he had trained with and fought alongside. His death would have been particularly felt by the Squadron's veterans like Ellis and Norris, with whom he had survived so much since the Dunkirk evacuation. John Ellis had promoted Warner to flight commander based on his ability as a leader and pilot, a rank he had done remarkably well to reach at the age of twenty-one. Warner had claims against the *Luftwaffe* of an He 111 shared destroyed, a 109 unconfirmed destroyed, plus a 109 probably destroyed just the day before. It was a real setback for the squadron leader to have lost his second in command. William Warner, Bill or Billy to his friends, is remembered for evermore on the Runnymede Memorial, Panel 5.

Warner had been surprised by a *Rotte* of 109s. From various records, it is possible he fell to the guns of either Hptm. Horst Tietzen or Leutnant [Lt] Hans-Otto Lessing of 5/JG 51, as they both made

Sir Lionel Warner's Son Missing

DURING R.A.F. OPERATIONS.

The younger son of Sir Lionel and Lady Warner, Flight-Lieutenant William Henry Cromwell Warner, of the Auxiliary Air Force, is reported missing following air operations that took place this month. Flight-Lieutenant Warner who lives with his parents at Yew Tree Poplar-road, Birkenhead, is twenty-one years of age.

The younger of the two sons of Sir Lionel Warner, C.B.E., the general manager and secretary of the Mersey Docks and Harbour Board, Flight-Lieut. Warner was educated at Malvern College, where he distinguished himself in the various school activities. While he was still at school he was appointed a pilot officer of the Auxiliary Air Force in the Merseyside area in May of 1937. From the outbreak of the war he has served with the Royal Air Force, and it was during operations this month that he was reported missing.

Flight-Lieut. W. H. C. WARNER.
Photo. by James Bacon and Sons.

(*Birkenhead News, Saturday, 24 August 1940, copyright Mirrorpix/Wirral Archives Service*)

claims against Supermarine Spitfires—one possibly being Warner and the other Gray's damaged aircraft, although this cannot be certain. If it was Tietzen and Lessing, it was an amazing coincidence, as these two possibly shot down 610 aircraft on 25 July, while Tietzen had almost certainly shot down and killed P/O Litchfield just under a month earlier. The same units did frequently and unwittingly engage each other during the Battle of Britain's heavy fighting, and the possibility that Tietzen had cost the lives of three 610 Squadron pilots in three separate engagements is incredible, not to mention Lessing being linked with two 610 Squadron losses. Tietzen was well on his way to becoming one of the *Luftwaffe's* top aces, with this claim being his nineteenth, however, he did not have long left himself.

The make-up of the Auxiliary Squadron had now irrevocably changed, as of the eighteen pilots who had originally been with the Squadron during the Dunkirk evacuation, there were just four left operational. Warner's death meant yet another flight commander needed to be found, the Squadron having lost two squadron leaders and two flight commanders since operations against the *Luftwaffe* began. The loss of these most experienced of men was evidence of the desperate nature of the fighting, with F/Lts Brian Smith and William Warner respectively having been wounded and killed within just five days.

Naturally, Ellis looked to one of his most experienced pilots to fill the void, this time turning to P/O Stanley Norris, aged twenty-one, from Tooting, who had joined the RAF on a short service commission in December 1937, before joining 610 Squadron on 23 October 1939. It is quite unusual for a pilot officer to be promoted to the rank of acting flight lieutenant, but the Squadron's heavy losses over Dunkirk had included four flying officers, and the ensuing casualties in the following months left F/O Lamb and P/O Norris as the battle-hardened officers. Why Norris was chosen ahead of Lamb, one of the last Auxiliary members is unclear, but presumably the CO thought Norris was more experienced, having already led the Squadron on patrols. With claims for four destroyed, one unconfirmed and two damaged, Stanley Norris was an accomplished fighter pilot, and it must have been a proud moment for him to be put forward as a flight commander. Friday 16 August had turned into a bleak day for the Squadron, in losing a well-liked and experienced pilot and leader in Bill Warner, especially as the Squadron could only file claims against a probable and two damaged. As Wg Cdr Smith recalled when I asked him about his friend Warner, he replied thoughtfully 'Billy Warner yes ... Yes, very much, a very nice lad. Awful shame that we lost him ...'

610 had intercepted an enemy formation which was retreating after an attempted raid on Biggin Hill, and by chance, this combat helped to provide the conflict which became known as the Battle of Britain with its most famous description. The young RAF pilots' efforts were being observed from afar, miles inland at 11 Group's HQ at Uxbridge, by a very prestigious and fascinated individual, Prime Minister Winston Churchill. Looking down at the plotting table, Churchill would have realised all too starkly, the fine margins which Dowding and Park had to deal with in the face of the *Luftwaffe's* onslaught. He was understandably stirred by the actions of Fighter Command's brave pilots, who were toiling against heavy odds in Britain's cause, frequently paying the ultimate sacrifice, just like William Warner. It is a fitting epitaph for young F/Lt Warner, that as his Spitfire spiralled down out of control into the English Channel, Churchill, so moved by what he had seen on the plotting table, first formulated the words which came to immortalise the Battle of Britain: 'Never in the field of human conflict was so much owed by so many to so few'.[16]

Claude Merrick's logbook provides some additional information into other flights carried out on 16 August, which the ORB omits to report. Merrick (3) carried out a patrol of Dover at 12,000 feet in X.4065—this does not seem to be the interception led by John Ellis at 1615 hours, but unfortunately Merrick does not record the time the patrol took place, just that it lasted thirty minutes. Because it is probable that P/O Gray brought X.4065 back badly damaged following the late afternoon combat, and Merrick was not listed on the patrol anyway, it is almost certain Merrick's flight was carried out before that patrol. It is likely to have been a second patrol, carried out as part of at least a section or possibly a Flight, but because no enemy aircraft were encountered, it was not entered into the ORB. Merrick (4) also patrolled Biggin Hill at 3,000 feet for fifty minutes, in DW-X, R.6641, although we have no idea when. This may have been carried out on his own, but again could possibly have involved other pilots too. Sadly, we'll never know.

The next day, Saturday 17 August, dawned fine and clear. S/Ldr Ellis and his men must have feared another day of constant readiness and almost inevitably another dogfight, high in the skies over Kent and the English Channel. John Ellis wasted no time in making the necessary arrangements for Stanley Norris to fill the breach as his flight commander, 'P/O. S. C. NORRIS (40361) granted the acting rank of Flight Lieutenant', being duly noted in the ORB. Remarkably, given the perfect weather conditions for the continuation of *Luftwaffe* operations, the Squadron did not meet the enemy, indeed, the ORB does not report any patrols as having taken place, which allowed Stanley Norris to get to grips with his new responsibilities. However, Claude Merrick's logbook once again comes to the rescue, recording that he flew to Hawkinge in X.4166 (most likely DW-B), the usual twenty-minute flight (5), in preparation to operate from the advance airfield. His following entry records, 'TO B. HILL & SQUADRON FORMATION PRACT', surprisingly in a different Spitfire, this time DW-X, R.6641. The flight lasted sixty-five minutes, and shows how S/Ldr Ellis took the opportunity to drill his men in matters which were crucial when it came to aerial combat. Merrick's logbook highlights the fact that flights were being carried out which were not recorded in the ORB, such a pity as we do not know who else was involved. Although this seemingly gives Merrick (along with Bamberger and Else thanks to their logbooks) a greater number of recorded patrols than most of those with a similar level of experience, it does show just how often the pilots were going on patrol. All the pilots were carrying out such numbers of patrols, but in Merrick, Bamberger and Else's case, we have a bit more information to go on.

Some news that the ORB did report, was that intelligence officer Walter Lloyd had been promoted to flying officer with effect from 12 July 1940. Little was recorded about Lloyd, but he was carrying out an essential role for the Squadron, gleaning as much information as possible from the pilots after their combats, to help create a clear picture of the *Luftwaffe's* activity and losses. The day passed without encountering the enemy, and 610 Squadron must have been thankful for a relative rest, while being all too aware that the *Luftwaffe* would not have been wasting its time either. Everybody recognised that their German counterparts also needed to rest, train fresh aircrew and repair aircraft, generally gearing themselves up for further raids in the days to come. It was hard to imagine another day of rest on the following day—much more likely was a 'maximum effort' from the *Luftwaffe*.

15

18 August 1940: The Hardest Day

As it turned out, Sunday 18 August got off to a slow start, with the pilots again attempting the impossible—trying to rest, while faced with the prospect of being scrambled at a moment's notice. Claude Merrick's logbook provides some additional information, as he had a twenty-minute flight (6) to Hawkinge in DW-E, R.6629, indicating that some of the Squadron went to the advance airfield for a spell. Nothing of note happened and he returned to Biggin Hill, probably quite early in the morning (7). It was not until noon that the RDF began picking up an enormous number of enemy aircraft and for the next thirty minutes the enemy formation was plotted and tracked as AVM Park tried to establish what was going to be the target of this latest *Luftwaffe* raid. He had brought all his squadrons to readiness and now decided on a course of action, deploying at least thirteen squadrons (TNA, AIR 25/197).

It was a strong response to a very menacing raid, but the RAF pilots were still outnumbered, as they had to be thinly spread. In fact, the large number of enemy aircraft operating over southern England was causing Fighter Command's plotting system problems and it was just as well for Biggin Hill that the sector station had a highly competent officer in command: 'on his own initiative the station commander, Group Captain Grice, scrambled Nos. 610 and 32 Squadrons. Group orders did not come through until after the raid, due to the mass of plots on the situation map'.[1] 610's home station was indeed top of the *Luftwaffe's* agenda for the day, and a two-pronged attack was heading straight for Biggin Hill in an attempt to put the vital fighter station out of action. First would come a high-level attack by sixty heavily-escorted Heinkel 111s from KG 1, followed by nine low-level Dorniers of KG 76. It was the aerial armada of around 100 high-level enemy aircraft that 610 Squadron was scrambled to take on at 1300 hours.

Impressively, the County of Chester Squadron had fifteen Spitfires available to attack the *Luftwaffe's* formation, thanks to the hard work of the ground crew, who must have worked incessantly to have the Spitfires ready for action—the previous day of non-combat had certainly helped. As Sgt Bamberger was later to recall about this vital work: 'The ground crews worked very long hours and frequently through the night. They'd been up, working on the aircraft before dawn and when we stood down, they had to put the aircraft to bed. They worked longer hours than the pilots'.[2] It appears that twelve Spitfires took off in the first instance while a reserve section was kept on the ground until the German aircraft were in sight of Biggin Hill, being scrambled as a last line of defence. 32 Squadron also scrambled, their ORB, noting, 'Ordered to intercept E Bombing Raid on Aerodrome at Biggin Hill. The Squadron met Approx. 60 bombers escorted by 40 fighters who were attempting to bomb the aerodrome from 15,000' (32 ORB). With thirteen Hurricanes and fifteen Spitfires scrambling from Biggin Hill at virtually the same time, it must have made for an inspiring sight, while also being a little hectic for those involved, given the close proximity of the raiders. 610 Squadron's pilots would have been glad of the previous day's formation flying practice!

S/Ldr Ellis, probably Blue 1 as normal, led the following men in the defence of their home station:

DW-W.	R.6993	S/Ldr. J. ELLIS.	Blue 1	44
DW-A.	R.6976	F/O. P. G. LAMB.		42
DW-D.	L.1037	P/O. D. M. GRAY.		3
DW-T.	X.4064	P/O. S. C. NORRIS.	Red 1	50
DW-F.	X.4028*	SGT. HAMLYN, R. F.		31
DW-H.	K.9818	SGT. PARSONS, C. A.	Red 3	19
DW-V.	K.9970	P/O. H. K. COX.	Blue 3	6
DW-N.	N.3128	P/O. B. V. REES.	Black 1	5
DW-X.		SGT. ARNFIELD, S. J.	Blue 2	47
DW-L.	P.9311	SGT.CHANDLER, H. H.	Black	12
DW-P.**	X.4239	F/O. F. T. GARDINER.	Green	22
DW-S.	K.9975***	P/O. C. O. J. PEGGE.	Red 2	21
DW-Q.	R.6891	SGT. CORFE, D.		5
DW-E.	P.9433	SGT. ELSE, P.	Green 3	30
DW-J.	R.6599	F/O. D. S. WILSON.		7

*Hamlyn was probably not flying this aircraft. DW-F was probably R.6694, flown by Pegge, see explanation later on.

**Probably a clerical error and should be 'R'. Same applies on 22 August.

***Probably a clerical error and should be DW-F, R.6694, see explanation later on.

Ellis was under clear orders to take his formation to high altitude and engage the expected Messerschmitt 109s, hopefully leaving 32 Squadron's Hurricanes relatively unmolested to attack the bombers, Fighter Command's favoured tactic. (This was another patrol where the distribution of the pilots between sections is not very clear.) The pilots would have had to coax every ounce of speed from their Spitfires in an attempt to reach the 109s before they could fall on them from above, and after a climb to 31,000 feet, Ellis led his men into the escorts of JG 54, commanded by Maj. Martin Mettig.[3] Ellis, again leading 'B' Flight, described the encounter as follows:

> I was leading 610 Sqdn. which took off from Biggin Hill at 1300 hrs on 18/8/40. The Sqdn. was detailed to deal with enemy fighters which were intercepted at 31,000'. As the two fighters I attacked were intent only on escaping from combat I gave up the chase on sighting 6 bombers in tight vic. formation in sections astern stepped up. I caught these bombers which turned out to be He.111s near Cranbrook and delivered an astern attack from above out of the sun on the left hand a/c. The cross fire was so severe that I decided to carry out a quarter attack. This attack was successful as the left hand machine of the rear section dropped back and began to ~~wallow a bit in air~~ fly rather erratically. I then carried out a beam attack approaching from ahead, this set the port engine on fire and as I had no more ammunition left I watched the flaming a/c go down in the sea 7 or 8 miles off Dungeness. It broke up on hitting the sea and sank in a few seconds. Confirmed by F/O Lamb. (TNA, AIR 50/172/22)

Once again John Ellis led by example, engaging two Me 109s before turning his attention to the bombers, which he would have been able to pick out due to his great height advantage. He engaged the He 111 formation at 1345 hours, 17,000 feet over Cranbrook, about twenty-six miles from Biggin Hill and the pursuit continued all the way to the Channel. The danger of attacking enemy bomber formations was evident in this combat report. Ellis experienced severe return fire and his Spitfire, DW-W, R.6993 suffered damage during these three attacks, which Ellis pressed home from 300 to 200 yards, firing for five seconds each time. His determination and bravery paid off though, as sickeningly, the Heinkel crashed into the Channel. Throughout this lengthy battle over the Kent countryside, terminating about eight miles off Dungeness, F/O Lamb was probably covering his CO's tail, as it is unlikely that Lamb witnessed the Heinkel's demise by chance, although there is no evidence of Lamb's combat report. If this was the case and Ellis knew he was being protected by one of the Squadron's veterans, it would have allowed him to focus on trying to bring the bomber down, highlighting the importance of such team work. Ellis's mounting list of claims against the *Luftwaffe* was now at nine confirmed destroyed, one unconfirmed, two shared destroyed and one damaged, which stood as testimony to the young CO's ability as a fighter pilot.

Another experienced pilot who had followed his squadron leader into the high altitude dogfight was Sgt Johnny Arnfield, on his forty-seventh recorded patrol since the dark days over Dunkirk. He noted that they had intercepted a formation of about eighty Do 17s and Me 109s, before describing his combats with two of the escort:

> I was ordered off the ground as Blue 2 with 610 Sqdn. to intercept a raid. We contacted the enemy fighters as ordered at about 25,000' and went into attack. I attacked a ME109 and after a short chase to get in range was able to give him a short burst at about 100 yards range. He immediately seemed to pull his nose up a little, wobble and then turn over on his back. Smoke was pouring out and he hung upside down for about a couple of seconds and then went into a steep spiral dive on fire with a long smoke trail behind him. Time approx. 13.15 hrs., height 25,000', place Edenbridge (very approx). The sky appeared very empty though the presence of bombers below indicated that there must still be fighters about. I chased after many I saw but they all turned out to be either Hurricanes or Spitfires. Eventually I saw a ME109 and chased him for about 10 minutes, getting in range towards the coast—he appeared to be making for home as fast as he could, and didn't notice me. I was able to get within 50 yds. of him and gave him a very short burst. He, too, went down immediately, spinning and with dense black smoke and flames issuing from him. After looking in vain for more fighters I heard Control ordering us to land and returned to base. Place of second attack a few miles N. of Dungeness. Ht. about 20,000', time 13.40 hrs. (TNA, AIR 50/172/5)

Arnfield reiterates that 610 had been instructed to engage the escorting fighters, and his experience is clear from the description of a short chase before he fired at just 100 yards range. In another example of the effectiveness of the RAF's air defence system, within fifteen minutes, Arnfield had gone from being scrambled, to engaging enemy aircraft at high altitude and shooting one down. He noted how the sky seemed empty, this being a common occurrence following the initial engagement, especially involving fighter-versus-fighter combat. Arnfield then immediately sought out other German fighters, even though he could see bombers beneath him. He finally engaged a second 109 at about 20,000 feet, moving to within fifty yards, before firing a two second burst which proved decisive. Arnfield, like Ellis, showed real determination to engage the enemy, particularly in following instructions to attack the enemy fighters. He also showed remarkable marksmanship, as he fired just three seconds worth of ammunition, approximately 400 rounds, in dispatching two enemy fighters. The twenty-six-year-old pilot was enjoying a particularly successful August, with claims now for two 109s destroyed and two damaged in the past four days, along with a shared destroyed Heinkel in June.

Another Blue Section pilot intent on engaging the bombers' escort was P/O Cox. Now on his sixth patrol against the *Luftwaffe*, Cox had already proven he had a good fighter pilot's instinct against the dangerous single-engined *Luftwaffe* fighters, with claims against three Me 109s, one destroyed, one unconfirmed and one probable. Cox described his initial engagement, at about 1345 hours against approximately sixty enemy aircraft as follows:

> I was flying as Blue 3, we climbed up and saw a large formation of Bombers DO215s (?). We did not attack as our orders were to engage fighting above. We intercepted ME109s at 31,000 feet. I engaged two, firing short bursts at each. I then got one long burst and one went down in flames. I lost sight of the other. (TNA, AIR 50/172/14)

Once again, it is evident that 610 Squadron did not engage the vulnerable Dornier bombers, but followed the orders to attack the escorting fighters, to keep them at bay from the Hurricanes below. Cox bravely took on two of the Me 109s at high altitude, approximately five miles south of Biggin Hill, sending one down in flames. However, Cox was not finished yet, as his report continued:

> After a short while I saw a ME109 about to attack me from behind. I was overanxious and "Ham" blacked out, stalled and spun. On recovering I found I was immediately underneath the DO215, so I finished off my remaining ammunition in a climbing attack and broke away, as I looked back I saw a large smoke trail but could not see a machine, so I turned for home. Cox. K.H. (TNA, AIR 50/172/14)

Cox had been lucky not to fall foul of the fate he had handed out to an enemy fighter minutes earlier—thankfully he was keeping a sharper lookout and noticed the silhouette of a 109 sharking in on him. The fact that he was caught unawares is apparent from his frantic evasive action, as Cox was still inexperienced, despite his successes. Fortunately for him, his heavy-handed action quite probably saved his life, but also emphasised the pure chance involved in surviving aerial combat, as it lined him up for an attack on a Dornier 215. On his return to Biggin Hill, Ken Cox was able to claim a 'probable' Do 215, along with his Me 109 destroyed.

Red Section was also in the thick of the fighter-versus-fighter combat, as reported by P/O Pegge, who engaged the Me 109s at 1320 hours, although he had not managed to stay with the majority of the formation: 'I was No. 2 of Red section in "A" Flight of 610 Sqdn. & got detached at 25,000 feet. I attacked an Me 109 from behind & above. I opened fire at 200–100 yds & gave it three two second bursts & saw it spin down on fire' (TNA, AIR 50/172/58). It was almost inevitable that some of the Spitfires would become separated in their desperate climb to 31,000 feet, but he still managed to engage the bomber force's escort between 23–25,000 feet, and could now claim his third confirmed Messerschmitt 109 destroyed during August.

Joe Pegge was not out of ammunition yet, and with height on his side, struck another blow against the *Luftwaffe*, at about 1340 hours at 18,000 feet near Dungeness:

> I attacked an He 111 from behind & above from a range of 100 yds closing to 20 yds, giving it a burst of about 8 seconds. Pieces fell away from the fuselage & engines. After breaking away & coming to attack again it had disappeared.
>
> On returning to base I was attacked by an Me 109 which scored several hits on my aircraft. On landing I struck a small bomb crater which caused the aircraft to crash. (TNA, AIR 50/172/58)

Pegge decided to attack the bombers, much as Ellis did, as they had become the best target of opportunity following their initial run-in with the escorts. Pegge closed in to just twenty yards, firing for six to eight seconds, a devastating burst which did heavy damage to the German bomber. One wonders whether this unfortunate Heinkel 111 pilot could have coaxed his aircraft back across the Channel, and from Pegge's point of view, he was unlucky only to be credited with a damaged. While John Ellis had found the 109s he encountered all too eager to head for home, Joe Pegge, drained after forty minutes of combat and chasing enemy aircraft across country, was unfortunate to be accosted by a more determined *Luftwaffe* pilot. It seems Pegge had switched off slightly on his return trip to Biggin Hill and was caught by surprise. The fact that his Spitfire suffered several hits probably indicated heavy damage, given the Messerschmitt 109's firepower, while the incident highlighted the danger of being alone in the combat area. Pegge was also injured as shall be seen, but thankfully survived the encounter with a bomb crater at Biggin Hill, which further damaged his hapless Spitfire. Brian Smith would later recall that Joe Pegge, 'really was a character', and this patrol sums up his spirit. Pegge must have been glad to scramble out of the aircraft and get his feet back on *terra firma* after such an eventful sortie—he would also make sure to keep a sharper lookout on his future return journeys!

The other Red Section pilot to file a successful combat report was Sgt Claude Parsons, who thought they encountered forty—sixty Me 109s and Do 17s south-east of Biggin Hill:

> On Sunday, August 18th, I was No.3 in Red Section of No.610 Squadron. We took off from Biggin Hill at 1300 hours to intercept E/A approaching our base. We climbed to 31,000 feet to engage protecting fighters. We paired off in two's and attacked a ME109. I then got separated from my leader and saw a formation of DO17s at about 15,000 feet. These E/A immediately went into a defensive circle on seeing me approach. I climbed into the sun and waited for the circle to break up. They broke up after about 5 minutes. I attacked a DO17 from the rear, putting the rear gunner out of action immediately. I then carried out a quarter attack on his port side and finished by firing at the port engine, which stopped running. I broke to the right and carried out a further quarter attack on his starboard side during which I ran out of ammunition. I made two further quarter attacks and forced the E/A to descend quickly. At 500 feet I saw the E/A make a forced landing in a field on Romney Marsh near Brookland Station.
>
> During my quarter attacks the E/A tried small turns to the left and right, though these decreased when the port engine stopped running. I noticed that immediately the engine stopped the undercarriage went down. (TNA, AIR 50/172/57)

Parsons had managed to stay with his leader (probably Norris, Red 1) in the tense climb for altitude, one point of interest from this report being that the pilots paired off before engaging the 109s. This suggests that 610 was starting to adopt the *Luftwaffe's* tactics. Bitter experience had taught them that the tight 'Vics' of three they had used since before the War, were obsolete and potentially lethal in the face of the *Luftwaffe's* fighter pilots, who flew in the much more practical *Rotte* and *Schwarm*. While the lead pilot engaged the enemy aircraft, the wingman watched his leader's tail, allowing the leader to concentrate on shooting down the target. Parsons on this occasion had acted as the wingman. However, it was inevitably difficult for the pair to stay together in a high-speed fighter-versus-fighter dogfight, and Claude Parsons lost his leader in the *mêlée*.

When he turned his attention to the German bomber formation, it had adopted the popular circular defensive formation frequently used by the twin-engined Messerschmitt 110s when they were intercepted. Each aircraft could offer crossfire support, making it more hazardous for any approaching RAF fighters. Parsons showed he had benefited from his growing experience, by patiently waiting for the bombers to revert back to their more open formation, before launching a devastating attack. This was another lengthy pursuit, Parsons having travelled from his home base to just short of the south coast, from 31,000 feet to ground level, in order to bring his opponent down forty-five minutes after being scrambled. With the smouldering Dornier, (he was unsure whether it was a 17 or 215), lying on the grass near Brookland Station, Parsons could claim his first confirmed victory, in addition to one shared destroyed, one shared damaged (both Do 215s), a probable Ju 87 and an unconfirmed Me 109.

Green Section's pilots became embroiled in this heavy fighting, one of whom was F/O Gardiner. He seemed to be flying his first patrol since being wounded six days earlier, his second wound during the Battle. However, the ORB recorded that he did not return to 610, 'on ceasing to be non-effective sick', until Wednesday 21 August 1940. This may refer to a subsequent incident between 18–21 August, although it was probably a clerical error during a very busy time in the Squadron's history. Nevertheless, Gardiner was certainly flying on this operation, his twenty-second recorded patrol, as the Squadron attempted to engage the enemy top cover.

Gardiner's combat reports tend to be succinct, without much scene-setting, and this is how he described his combat a few miles to the south-east of Biggin Hill:

> I saw about 15 ME110s at 22,000 feet circling to the right, some of which were about 500 feet higher than the majority. I attacked one E/A but had to break away almost at once to avoid a collision. There was no visible damage to this A/C. I climbed up again and attacked another E/A. As I opened fire, with a slight deflection shot, the E/A decreased the rate of turn and I then gave it a continuous burst of about 8—10 secs., and then broke away. The port engine was smoking very heavily and a large part of the a/c (about 10 feet × 6 feet approx) was seen to fall off. The A/C was not seen to crash but appeared to be on fire. F. T. Gardiner. (TNA, AIR 50/172/28)

Whether Gardiner stayed with the Squadron in the initial pursuit of the high-flying Me 109s is unclear, as he stated his particular combat took place at 1345 hours at 22,000 feet. The other combat reports at this time largely relate to a second combat (Ellis, Arnfield, Pegge, Parsons), following on from some sort of initial contact with the Me 109s. Perhaps he had been unsuccessful in engaging the Me 109s and then picked on a target of opportunity, especially given the altitude at which his combat took place. It appears Gardiner was on his own when he took on the Me 110s, which made it an amazing effort given the odds stacked against him. But the knowledge that this formation was supporting bombers that were attacking his home base, would have spurred him on. Gardiner's second attack hit the *Zerstörer* hard, and upon his safe landing, Fred Gardiner was credited with an Me 110 destroyed to add to the Me 109 unconfirmed already to his name. Following his close escapes from death, it was a real indication of Gardiner's courage that he could engage such an enemy formation on his own, having been wounded twice already. It was this type of spirit, evident throughout Fighter Command's squadrons, which would be needed to survive the *Luftwaffe's* onslaught.

The other pilot from Green Section whose combat reports exist are those of Sgt Else, now on his thirtieth recorded patrol. Peter Else described his first interception of the day as follows:

> I was acting as Green 3 when we sighted approximately 20 DO215s below us circling above Biggin Hill and peeling off to bomb it. I followed Green 1 into the attack but could not fire as he got in my way. I broke off, climbed and attacked again on my own. I saw pieces fly off the E/A I was firing at and then had to break off to avoid hitting same. I then found myself in the middle of the E/A and had to climb out of the circle. Fortunately my aircraft was not hit. I stopped the fire from the rear gunner of the E/A I attacked. I found best way to attack was to get astern of last E/A in circle as one broke off away to dive to bomb—thus leaving a large space in the circle. (TNA, AIR 50/172/24)

It is worth noting that neither Gardiner nor Else, both of Green Section, mention engaging the top cover 109s. Gardiner did not engage any aircraft until 1345 hours, whereas Else's first engagement against these Dorniers took place at 1315 hours, and as Green 3 he followed Green 1 into the attack on the bombers. While this suggests that Gardiner was therefore Green 2 and had become separated from the rest of his section, it seems Else was ordered by his section leader, or possibly the squadron leader, to engage the bombers, rather than continue in pursuit of the top cover. The sight of unengaged enemy aircraft bombing their home base was clearly ample reason for this section at least to engage the bombers.

Else followed his leader down to 12–15,000 feet in order to take on the Dorniers, which were operating a similar defensive circle to those Claude Parsons engaged a little later. Else damaged his target with a 2–4 second burst of fire, closing to 150 yards, miraculously escaping without damage to his Spitfire, to continue his patrol. At about 1330–1335 hours he encountered another formation of Dorniers at 12,000 feet, to the south-east of Biggin Hill:

> I observed eight E/A making for home in a very ragged box formation. I attacked the rearmost one from astern below, and saw pieces fly off and smoke pour from one engine. I was then experiencing

> considerable cross fire from the other E/A who were using a considerable amount of tracer bullets. Only one bullet hit me in the wing I found on landing.
>
> I broke off the attack and was going in for another when I observed a Hurricane on my tail. This pilot after a bit recognised I was a Spitfire and went off, but by then the E/A had disappeared. I followed in their direction but could not find them.
>
> The first three E/A kept good vic formation and were much higher than the rear machines and were firing at me over the rear ones until I was protected from their fire by my target when the flank machines had a go.
>
> I saw one DO215 spin in after this, S.E. of West Malling following an attack from a Hurricane. (TNA, AIR 50/172/24)

Else sensibly chose to try and pick off the rearmost Dornier, once again bravely pressing his attack home to 250 yards and causing damage to the retreating bomber with a continuous burst of six seconds. He was again fortunate to avoid being hit by more than just a single bullet by the Dorniers' gunners. If the lone Hurricane had not forced Else to break off his attack, he might have brought the Dornier down, which now had smoke billowing from one engine. But Peter Else could be pleased with his work in having engaged the enemy formations and been credited with two Dorniers damaged. Having been one of the most successful pilots during July with claims of one destroyed, one shared destroyed, one unconfirmed and a damaged, Else had added three more damaged enemy aircraft to his tally during the course of four recorded patrols in August.

While 610 Squadron's ORB noted that, '15 aircraft took off from BIGGIN HILL to engage about 50 E/bombers & 50 E/fighters approaching the aerodrome from the south', we know that S/Ldr Ellis led twelve Spitfires of Red, Yellow, Blue and Green Sections up in an anxious climb for high altitude. The three remaining Spitfires stayed on the ground as a reserve section at cockpit readiness, to intercept at the last possible moment any raiders who broke through the defences. This was Black Section, left under P/O Brian Victor Rees's command, flying just his fifth patrol; it seems John Ellis felt he had acquitted himself well enough to be given this responsibility. Rees was faced with the unenviable proposition of scrambling with enemy aircraft directly overhead, which left Black Section very vulnerable to escorting fighters and their own AA guns.

Rees describes the action as follows:

> I was leading Reserve Section 610 Squadron, we waited until the enemy were in sight of the aerodrome to N.W. We took off and immediately split up as we were amongst the enemy. I chased a Dornier which was separated from the rest and delivered two long bursts, his port engine went on fire, smoking very badly, also there were bits flying off. It lost height rapidly, I was following it down when I was attacked from behind, I could not see my attacker but I could see the tracer from it passing me. I put my propeller in fine pitch and throttled back. My attacker shot passed [past] me and I gave it a very long burst at very short range. At about 150 yds. It suddenly turned over and crashed into a wood about 10 miles from the aerodrome. This was an ME109. (TNA, AIR 50/172/64)

In the brief résumé before the actual combat report, Rees states that the enemy aircraft numbered between forty and fifty, and were engaged to the south-east of his airfield at 1330 hours between 3–5,000 feet, with AA fire 'all around' (TNA, AIR 50/172/64). It must have been terrifying. As Black Section had engaged the enemy at the last minute, there was no time to plan an attack. They just relied on instinctive flying and luck to stay alive in such a last-ditch situation. Having caused a terminal engine fire on a Dornier 215, with two bursts of machine gun fire, Rees made the potentially fatal mistake of following his victim down, a decision which compounded his original problem of lack of altitude. Sure enough, grey tendrils of smoke hurtled above and either side of his cockpit, from an unseen assailant sitting on his tail. However, instead of panicking, he made a critical instinctive decision. By switching his Spitfire's propeller to fine pitch and throttling back, the enemy fighter suddenly found itself accelerating past Rees's fighter, giving the RAF pilot a point-blank shot. The 109 had gone in a split second from the hunter to the hunted, and under a hail of .303 machine gun fire, it crashed ten miles from Biggin Hill. The *Luftwaffe* pilot would barely have had chance to realise how quickly the tables had been turned on him before he was downed; it vividly shows how ruthless these dogfights were.

It is likely that this tactic had been passed on to Rees by the Squadron's senior pilots, and such advice had ultimately saved his life. Rees had been in the air only moments before shooting down two enemy aircraft and almost being killed himself—his state of mind upon landing can hardly be imagined. One emotion that Brian Rees should have felt later that day was pride, as he had survived a fraught situation through his own skill, having put into practice what he had been taught. Rees was another 610 pilot who was coming to the fore in August as a result of the heavy fighting, with claims for two destroyed, one unconfirmed and a probable, a remarkable effort for one of the least experienced pilots.

Ray Chandler was Black Section's other pilot to file a combat report, but this is much more terse and concise, focusing purely on his encounter with a smaller enemy formation of Dornier 215s out of an overall total of thirty—forty, at 1345 hours at 2,500 feet:

> I sighted five D.O215s not in formation over Croydon. Attacked one on beam coming round to astern of e/a. One long burst. Both motors caught fire. E/a crashed five miles S.Croydon with tremendous explosion. Also attacked another from astern until ammunition was finished. This aircraft was later destroyed by a Hurricane. (TNA, AIR 50/172/12)

Once again, a lot happened in a very short space of time after being scrambled. Chandler immediately found himself in the thick of the enemy, along with furious fire from the airfield's ground defences. The five German bombers were not in formation so they were not mutually covered by their gunners, leaving them more vulnerable to the RAF fighters, with devastating consequences. At least two of the five went down in quick succession. Chandler's tactic was to get in close enough and slow enough to deliver one continuous burst of fire, which he recorded as being ten seconds from 200–100 yards. This had a murderous impact on the first Dornier, and with both engines on fire its demise was inevitable. Ray Chandler used up the remainder of his ammunition on a second Dornier, which also did not make it home thanks to the efforts of a Hurricane pilot, who finished off what Chandler had started.

The efforts of Black Section's pilots were remarkable given their lack of altitude, while probably struggling for a decent combat speed. However, these problems were almost an advantage in this situation, as they were immediately in amongst the attacking low-level bombers, and at a better speed to engage their slower targets. That they claimed three destroyed and one damaged, which was then shot down, is proof of the reserve section's effectiveness. It is likely that Black Section had benefited from a mix up in the German raiders' timetable, as instead of coming in after the high-level raid, with Biggin Hill a scene of chaos, the low-level Dorniers arrived beforehand, with the defenders waiting for them.

It had been a very successful day for the Squadron in terms of the claims-versus-losses ratio, the ORB perhaps most concisely summarising it thus:

> Enemy Cas: - 5 M.E.109s, 3 D.O.215s, 1 H.E.111, 1 M.E.110, destroyed.
> 3 D.O.215s, 1 H.E. 111 damaged.
> Our Cas. NIL.

Ten enemy aircraft claimed destroyed and four damaged, without losing a pilot, was a real achievement for the unit in the face of seemingly insurmountable odds. It does great credit to the leadership of the experienced pilots and the bravery and skill of each and every one of them. 610 Squadron's final claims from the combat reports are listed below:

Arnfield—2 Me 109s destroyed
Rees—1 Me 109 destroyed, 1 Do 215 destroyed
Cox—1 Me 109 destroyed, 1 Do 215 probable
Chandler—1 Do 215 destroyed, 1 Do 215 damaged
Pegge—1 Me 109 destroyed, 1 He 111 damaged
Ellis—1 He 111 destroyed
Gardiner—1 Me 110 destroyed
Parsons—1 Do 17 destroyed
Else—2 Do 215s damaged.

From these figures it seems that P/O Cox's claim for a probable Do 215 had been recorded as a damaged in the ORB, where there was also no mention of Chandler's second combat, when he damaged a Do 215. So the final figures should read ten destroyed, one probable and four damaged, fifteen claims in total, not the fourteen in the ORB.[4] In terms of these statistics alone, it had been a huge battle, although six of the pilots did not file a claim, including Peter Lamb and Stanley Norris. Perhaps even these veterans were too busy keeping enemy aircraft off their own tails, to press home an attack with any certainty.

Ellis's and Pegge's Spitfires were in fact damaged as noted in *Then and Now*:

> **R6694.** Hit by Bf 109 during return to base and further damaged hitting a bomb crater on landing 1.50 p.m. P/O C. O. J. Pegge unhurt. **DW-F** damaged but repairable.
>
> **R6993.** Returned to base damaged by cross-fire from He 111s engaged over Dungeness. 2.00 p.m. F/Lt J. Ellis unhurt. **DW-W** repairable.[5]

On balance, it is most likely that Pegge was flying DW-F, R.6694, which had joined the Squadron on 7 June 1940, as it is recorded thus in the *Aeromilitaria* Spitfire production details.[6] The ORB is probably in error stating that Pegge was flying DW-S, K.9975, as K.9975 is thought to have joined the Squadron on 14 September; the ORB notation may have been added retrospectively. (This would mean that Hamlyn was not flying DW-F, as listed in the ORB.) *Aeromilitaria* states that DW-Q, R.6891 crashed in soft ground (not a bomb crater!) on this day at Biggin Hill,[7] but it probably was not the machine being flown by Pegge, as the ORB listed Sgt Corfe as flying R.6891. This crash probably occurred on a later patrol. The ORB seems accurate in recording Ellis as flying DW-W, R.6993, which had joined the Squadron on 26 July.[8]

As is evident, there are some anomalies with 610's ORB for 18 August, when cross-referencing it with other documents. P/O Merrick recorded two patrols of Biggin Hill in his logbook (8 & 9), after his return journey to Hawkinge, although various sources state fifteen of 610 Squadron's Spitfires took part in the patrol, and none of them was flown by Merrick. It means neither of these patrols were the same as the one described above, or if they were, that he was acting alone. He indicated that the first took place at 25,000 feet and lasted an hour, and he was flying DW-J, N.3284. However, according to the ORB, F/O Wilson was flying DW-J coded R.6599 on the Squadron patrol. It is unlikely that this is the correct code, as this aircraft did not join the Squadron until 11 September 1940,[9] so Wilson was probably flying Spitfire DW-J, N.3284, meaning Merrick's patrol was at a different time.[10] Merrick's second patrol lasted forty minutes in DW-E, R.6629, at 16,000 feet, causing similar confusion. In the

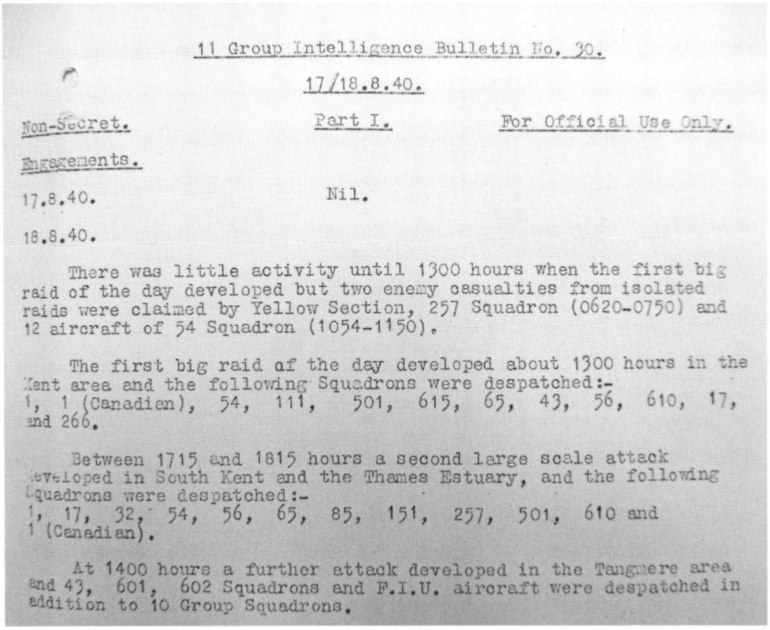

11 Group Intelligence Bulletin No. 30.

17/18.8.40.

Non-Secret. Part I. For Official Use Only.

Engagements.

17.8.40. Nil.

18.8.40.

There was little activity until 1300 hours when the first big raid of the day developed but two enemy casualties from isolated raids were claimed by Yellow Section, 257 Squadron (0620-0750) and 12 aircraft of 54 Squadron (1054-1150).

The first big raid of the day developed about 1300 hours in the Kent area and the following Squadrons were despatched:- 1, 1 (Canadian), 54, 111, 501, 615, 65, 43, 56, 610, 17, and 266.

Between 1715 and 1815 hours a second large scale attack developed in South Kent and the Thames Estuary, and the following Squadrons were despatched:- 1, 17, 32, 54, 56, 65, 85, 151, 257, 501, 610 and 1 (Canadian).

At 1400 hours a further attack developed in the Tangmere area and 43, 601, 602 Squadrons and F.I.U. aircraft were despatched in addition to 10 Group Squadrons.

Extract from '11 Group Intelligence Bulletin No. 30'. (*TNA, AIR 25/197*)

ORB, Sgt Else was flying DW-E, P.9433 in the main Squadron patrol. According to production records, DW-E, P.9433 was operational with 610 between some point in August and 20 October 1940 and DW-E, R.6629 was operational with 610 from 31 May to 31 August 1940, one of which is probably incorrect.[11] (It seems likely that the operational DW-E on this day at least, was R.6629.)

Frustratingly, we'll never know what time Merrick's patrols took place, but it does seem possible that 610 actually had more than fifteen Spitfires in the air defending the home base, even if it was to prevent Spitfires being destroyed by bombing. Merrick seems to indicate patrols he carried out as part of a larger formation with a letter 'A' next to them, presumably for 'A' Flight in which he always operated. This is not the case here, so perhaps he was operating alone on these instances—it is impossible to say. The Squadron did carry out a second patrol in the early evening of 18 August, although no contact was made with the enemy, as mentioned in 11 Group's ORB Appendices, see photo above. For some reason, this second operation between 1715 and 1815 hours was not recorded in the Squadron's ORB, but perhaps it tallies with one of Merrick's flights recorded in his logbook, meaning it was probably a patrol of Biggin Hill. This could well have been when R.6891 crashed in soft ground, as previously mentioned.

One reason for the particularly successful operation on 18 August, was perhaps that for the first time the *Luftwaffe's* bombers had got through to 610's home at Biggin Hill and were trying to knock it out of action. Whether they were defending convoys or intercepting enemy aircraft randomly across the English countryside, 610's pilots pressed home their attacks with great bravery and courage on each and every occasion. However, the fact that the bombers were trying to hit their very own home, where so many friends and loved ones were living, reliant on them to stop the *Luftwaffe's* attack, certainly gave the pilots that extra spur to bring down enemy aircraft. As Claude Parsons noted when describing the later raids on London, where his girlfriend lived:

> As we intercepted the raiders I would be thinking of a girl friend who was probably at that moment hurrying to a shelter from the office in which she is employed. I catch a glimpse of a few crafty sods breaking up, turning for home, and then a few seconds later about turning and on again towards London. It was my ambition to fire at one of these types and explode his bombs for him.[12]

There is real animosity in these words and as the attacks became more personal, such feelings would have been echoed in each of 610 Squadron's pilots, as they witnessed bombs falling on Biggin Hill for the first time. 32 Squadron had been equally determined in the defence of their home aerodrome, having 'shot down or damaged 15 enemy aircraft' (32 ORB).

Although the German bomber formation had succeeded in forcing its way through, the bombs which fell did little structural damage, the biggest problem being the cratering of the landing ground. Claude Parsons recalled the problem:

> On my way back I could hear the Controller telling all A/C to be extremely careful when landing. When I got to the base and saw the condition of the flying field, I thought the Controller a perfect optimist, for I couldn't see a place at first in which to land, there were so many bomb craters. However, I studied the position and decided to land on one runway with a large crater about two-thirds of the way down it. I juggled the aircraft in safely, feeling greatly relieved. I had hardly enough petrol to go farther.[13]

P/O Pegge was less fortunate, coming unstuck in a small bomb crater, although this may have been as much due to his injury and battle-damaged Spitfire as the craters. Parsons recorded:

> To my amazement there was a Spitfire in the crater on the runway. It was our Jitterbug fan, Mr. "Pegleg". His windscreen had stopped a direct hit, it had also shattered some of the Perspex screen and cut his face. He couldn't see where he was going after landing, so finished in the crater.[14]

In typical fashion, Joe Pegge made no reference to this windscreen damage in his combat report, probably caused when the 109 attacked him on his way home.

Pegge had been unlucky to come a cropper in a bomb crater, but it was the courage and initiative of a WAAF Sergeant at Biggin Hill, which prevented more of the returning pilots from suffering a similar prang, or worse. Sgt Mortimer had bravely remained at her post at the switchboard in the armoury throughout the raid, passing on important messages around the aerodrome. However, once the bombs had finished falling, she then fearlessly went out onto the aerodrome to mark the unexploded bombs with red flags, to alert the returning pilots. One bomb went off while she was close by, but having picked herself up, she continued with her vital work. Sgt Elizabeth Mortimer was awarded the Military Medal for her valiant efforts.

Raymond Ellis vividly recalled the events of that day thus:

> The 18th was a Sunday, and Stan and I happened to have the day off duty. It promised to be a lovely day so we set off to walk to Sevenoaks, accepting a lift in a bus for the last couple of miles. On leaving a café, we heard the roar of an aircraft. It was an Me 109 fighter streaking low over the rooftops; a second later it was followed by one of our Spitfires. I had never before experienced such a thrill …
>
> We turned and started back for Camp by train and bus, wondering how our boys had fared in the air and on the ground.
>
> That raid had caused some casualties. Harry Peters, a fitter of 'Six Ten', was badly wounded. An AA gun had been hit; one of its crew had been killed and the others wounded. A number of the bombs had a delayed action and made neat round holes in the ground. The Station Commander, Group Captain Grice, spoke on the Tannoy PA to tell us that we could expect these to go off during the night. One bomb was alongside the Officers' Mess; this went off killing the Armament Officer who was attempting to disarm it.[15]

This injury to one of 610's own ground crew, would have hammered home that they were now in the front line, as much as the pilots. Harry Peters was a twenty-six year old whose parents lived in Winnington, Cheshire. The file detailing his wound was amongst those recently-released at Kew in June 2017.

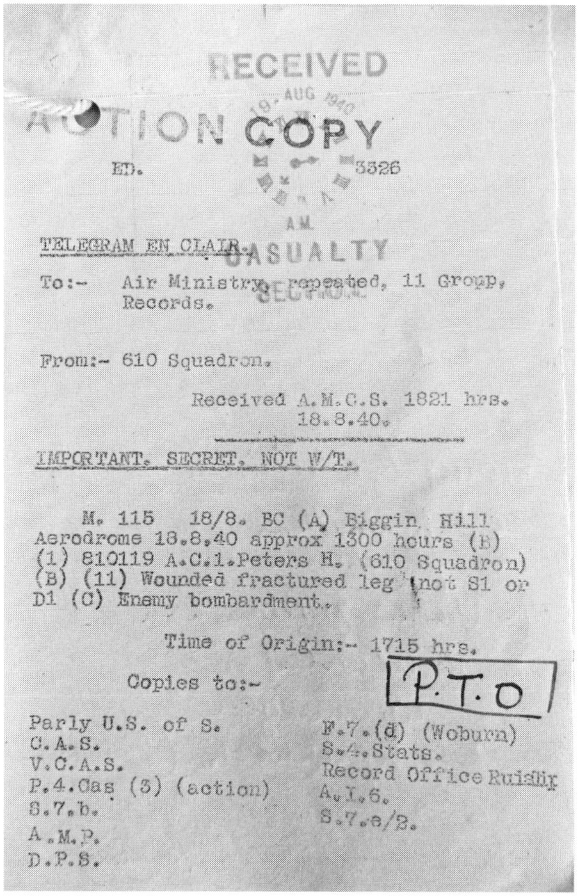

RECEIVED
19 AUG 1940
ACTION COPY
ED. 3326
A.M.
CASUALTY SECTION

TELEGRAM EN CLAIR.

To:- Air Ministry, repeated, 11 Group, Records.

From:- 610 Squadron.

Received A.M.C.S. 1821 hrs. 18.8.40.

IMPORTANT. SECRET. NOT W/T.

M. 115 18/8. BC (A) Biggin Hill Aerodrome 18.8.40 approx 1300 hours (B) (1) 810119 A.C.1.Peters H. (610 Squadron) (B) (11) Wounded fractured leg (not S1 or D1 (C) Enemy bombardment.

Time of Origin:- 1715 hrs.

Copies to:- P.T.O

Parly U.S. of S.
C.A.S.
V.C.A.S.
P.4.Cas (3) (action)
S.7.b.
A.M.P.
D.P.S.
F.7.(d) (Woburn)
S.4.Stats.
Record Office Ruislip
A.I.6.
S.7.e/2.

Telegram *en clair* from 610 Squadron, informing the Air Ministry that Harry Peters had been badly injured during the bombing. (*TNA, AIR 81/2629*)

Given the raid's scale, it is interesting to note that some historians over the years have commented on 610 Squadron's apparent failure to get through to the bomber formation and break it up. However, such statements ignore the simple fact that 610 was specifically ordered to intercept the fighter escorts, not the bomber formation at all. The Spitfire pilots of 610 were not prevented from attacking the bombers by the escorts, but had deliberately taken on the 109s, to enable 32 Squadron's Hurricanes to concentrate on the bombers with less fear of being bounced. Also, some of 610's pilots did engage the bombers first, like the pilots of Black Section, while even Ellis reverted to attacking and destroying a He 111 once the escorting fighters refused combat; the Squadron's pilots filed claims against the bomber formations of four destroyed, one probably destroyed and four damaged!

The odds facing 610 were inevitably a serious problem, but in a real team effort alongside 32 Squadron and the ground defences, they had helped prevent much more serious damage. Indeed, it is remarkable that despite the bombers' large escort, the enemy fighters did not succeed in shooting down a single Spitfire out of the fifteen which went up against them, with only Joe Pegge receiving damage from an enemy fighter. On the evidence available, 610 Squadron had put up a valiant defence of its home base and key sector station, as had the other squadrons in the area, and 11 Group's hierarchy were delighted with their efforts in repelling a large and determined attack against such an important target.

However, the fact that the *Luftwaffe* had got through to Biggin Hill, along with other vital stations such as Kenley, Hornchurch and North Weald, would have given the commanders and all personnel based at these aerodromes, the knowledge and fear that they may come again, and next time they might not escape so lightly. Sunday 18 August also confirmed a fear of Dowding and Park, as it marked a change in *Luftwaffe* tactics, moving from attacks on the coastal convoys, RDF sites and forward aerodromes in July and the first half of August, to hitting Fighter Command's key sector stations. This would force RAF fighters up *en masse* to defend the bases which they relied on, providing the bombers with the chance to knock Fighter Command out on the ground, while the escorting fighters would have many targets to choose from. Even a small number of bombs on the airfield caused additional worries for the pilots, as Joe Pegge had found to his cost. But the biggest problem here was the increased take off time. The Spitfires could not have their mass scrambles in flight or squadron strength, but would have to jockey their way into a smaller strip, free of bomb craters, and start to form up in the air, depriving them of valuable seconds in their climb for altitude. The ground personnel also had to work through the night to get the landing strip as free of craters and UXBs as possible for the following morning.

That evening though, such thoughts would have been pushed gradually to the back of the minds of 610 Squadron's fighter pilots, as they celebrated their successes in the mess and local pubs, such as the 'White Hart' in nearby Brasted, alongside 32 Squadron's equally successful pilots. Having had some torrid times during the past couple of months, the pilots of 610 more than deserved some respite in the evening after another testing day of combat, particularly as they had all played an important part in, and survived, what became known as 'The Hardest Day', for reasons made clear by Bungay:

> In the air fighting, the Luftwaffe lost sixty-nine aircraft destroyed and thirty-one damaged, to Fighter Command's thirty-four destroyed and thirty-nine damaged. The RAF lost another twenty-nine destroyed and twenty-three damaged on the ground. The total aircraft were about equal, but Fighter Command achieved a kill ratio of 2:1 in the air. Adding together all the material losses, both sides suffered more damage than on any other day.[16]

The significance of 18 August 1940 was highlighted in the Seventy-fifth Anniversary Commemoration of the day in 2015, when flights of Spitfires and Hurricanes were assembled at Biggin Hill for a mass 'scramble', before they flew across various symbolic routes across the south-east of England, a truly magnificent and memorable sight. The heavy losses suffered by the *Luftwaffe* that day, included Hptm. Horst Tietzen and Lt Hans-Otto Lessing of JG 51, both of whom it will be remembered, had cost 610 Squadron dear, particularly Tietzen, one of the *Luftwaffe's* leading Aces. As the fighting became ever-heavier, nobody was safe, on either side.

16

19–24 August 1940: Weather's Respite and Sergeant's Success

Given the *Luftwaffe's* heavy losses, it is possible that Monday 19 August would have been a relatively quiet day anyway. Nevertheless, bad weather during the course of the next five days meant the *Luftwaffe*, and therefore the RAF, could rest and recuperate after the intensive fighting of recent days. This respite would have been more than welcomed by 610 Squadron, and the enforced rest is reflected in the ORB, which provides scant information as to the unit's activity from 19–21 August. Thankfully, Claude Merrick's logbook gives some insight to the Squadron's operations, recording that he flew down to Hawkinge and carried out a short patrol (10) of the aerodrome in DW-X, R.6641 for forty minutes, and then probably repeated the patrol on the return flight (11), given it was another forty-minute flight. This sortie was probably at least in Flight strength, if not the whole Squadron, and it appears no enemy aircraft were encountered. Sgt Else's logbook,[1] records a fifty-minute return flight in DW-L, P.9496 to Hawkinge (31 and 32), presumably a different patrol from Merrick's.

There was reduced *Luftwaffe* activity again on 20 August, and the Squadron ORB made no mention of any patrols being carried out. However, Merrick, Else and Bamberger's logbooks record the following flights, even if they do not exactly corroborate! Else noted that he flew down to Hawkinge, then carried out a one hour and forty-minute patrol and return flight to Biggin Hill, before flying down to Hawkinge again, most likely a return trip given that it lasted fifty-five minutes, all in his favoured DW-L, P.9496 (33–35). Merrick, (no mention of his aircraft code provided from now on), carried out a lengthy patrol (12) of the Thames Estuary at 6,000 feet from Biggin Hill, presumably as part of 'A' Flight, without encountering the *Luftwaffe*, before flying to their forward base for a stint at 'Readiness' (13). Only the return flight to the sector station is referenced after that (14), indicating that no patrols were carried out from Hawkinge, most likely due to the weather. It is probable that the Squadron was operating on a Flight basis, as the weather had reduced the chance of encountering the enemy, and that Merrick and Else were operating in 'A' and 'B' Flights respectively. 'Bam' Bamberger also carried out his first operational patrol on 20 August, as evidenced in his letter to Peter Blythe, who carried out research into Sgt Manton. This was probably his 'Station Defence' patrol which lasted fifteen minutes in DW-P (no serial number). He also flew to Hawkinge in DW-N, which took twenty-five minutes, and then did a patrol of Dover and return flight to Biggin Hill lasting one hour and twenty minutes (3). This was probably the same one as Else's first patrol of the day.

It is worth noting 32 Squadron's activity during this period, as it quite possibly mirrored that of 610 Squadron. On 19 August they flew down to Hawkinge, landing there at 0850 hours, returning to Biggin Hill at 1335 hours, returned to Hawkinge at 1710 hours, and then back again to their home aerodrome at 2030 hours for the night. It is likely that 610 Squadron was based at Biggin when 32 Squadron was at Hawkinge and vice versa, although this is purely guesswork. If this was true, then the time spent at Hawkinge by Merrick and Else on 19 August was most likely in the afternoon, between 1335 hours and 1700 hours. On 20 August, 32 Squadron flew to Hawkinge at dawn, returning to

Biggin by 0935 hours for the remainder of the day, carrying out an interception of a Do 215 during the afternoon. If 610's stint at Hawkinge was the opposite of 32 Squadron's, it would seem likely that the County of Chester Squadron's Spitfires were at readiness at Hawkinge in the late morning/afternoon, given that they had already carried out a patrol of the Thames Estuary. However, the two Squadrons could both have been operating out of Hawkinge at the same time if required.

While carrying out similar defensive duties to 32 Squadron between Biggin Hill and Hawkinge, 610 would also have been preparing itself for the next spate of raids, which were nervously awaited when the weather improved. The Squadron's ground crew would have concentrated on getting as many aircraft serviceable as possible, while the novice pilots tried to get in some flying hours on Spitfires, under the watchful eyes of their flight commander and the other veterans. The old hands would have been keen to catch up on some much needed rest, away from the nerve-wracking ring of the dispersal telephone, while some lucky pilots, would have gone on some well-earned leave to visit family and friends.

On Wednesday 21 August, the bad weather continued, and for 610 Squadron's pilots, it was a fairly quiet day, with no mention in the ORB of them being called to action for a third day in succession. However, Claude Merrick, Cyril Bamberger and Peter Else's logbooks gave the lie to it. Merrick (15 and 16) recorded a twenty-five-minute flight to Hawkinge and back, while Else (36 and 37) was slightly busier, flying X.4011: a thirty-minute flight to Hawkinge; a patrol and return to Biggin Hill lasting one hour and ten minutes; a ten-minute flight to Gravesend, with the return journey classed as night flying.[2] 'Bam' Bamberger (4 & 5) carried out the same patrols as Else, suggesting they were in the same flight. The two flights were probably operating alternately from Hawkinge, although it is possible that the whole Squadron flew to Hawkinge, and Else's 'B' Flight carried out a patrol before returning to Biggin Hill, while Merrick's 'A' Flight just carried out the return flight. At least we know they were operating on these dates, filling in some of the ORB's blanks. It is impossible to know how many times individual pilots were flying, as, if Merrick did fly to Hawkinge and back with some of his Squadron, we have no record of the other pilots involved.

The only note in the ORB for 21 August was a slightly confusing one, 'F/O. F. T. GARDINER (72100) reposted to this Unit on ceasing to be non-effective sick. P/O. D. Mc.I.GRAY posted to R.A.F. Station Biggin Hill, non-effective sick'. For Gardiner, this presumably relates to the injuries he suffered on 12 August, although the fact that he had already flown on 18 August when he shot down an Me 110, suggests that this entry should have been recorded earlier. The entry for Gray is equally confusing, as although his Spitfire had been badly damaged on 16 August, he was said to be unhurt in his own combat report and had also flown on 18 August—perhaps the entry had also been misplaced, it is impossible to say. While this break from the intensive operations of recent days came as a real boon to the pilots throughout Fighter Command, the down side was that the *Luftwaffe* was able to prepare for the next stage of attacks on England. And just as with the previous lull, one thing was certain; it would not last for long. On Thursday 22 August, 610 Squadron would once again find themselves back in the fray.

The day dawned with similar conditions to recent days, and sailors on Convoy Totem, passing through the Channel, probably hoped to escape unscathed, but suddenly found themselves under attack from a seemingly invisible enemy. The convoy was being escorted by five Hurricanes of 32 Squadron, which had taken off at 0825 hours. On landing at 0940 hours, they reported that the convoy had been shelled by German heavy coastal batteries (32 ORB). As the convoy plodded slowly on, hugging the famous white cliffs, the pilots of 610 Squadron were wondering if another day without combat would pass; as lunchtime came and went it seemed increasingly likely.

Unfortunately, the ineffectual shelling of Convoy Totem meant that a *Luftwaffe* raid was ordered, intending to use the cloud cover to thwart any intervention from the RAF. The *Luftwaffe* unit which was best suited to such an attack was Erpro. 210, and as they went through their final preparations before take-off, the orders came through for 610 Squadron to patrol the Folkestone area at 1300 hours, presumably to offer Convoy Totem protection. Red, Blue, Green and Yellow Sections were all ordered up with S/Ldr Ellis leading the following pilots:

DW-W.	R.6993*	S/Ldr. J. ELLIS.	Blue	45
DW-Q.	R.6891	SGT. RAMSAY, N. H. D.		28
DW-P.	X.4239**	SGT. CORFE, D.		6
DW-O.	X.4011	F/O. F. T. GARDINER.	Green	23
DW-N.	N.3128	P/O. B. V. REES.		6
DW-V.	K.9970	P/O. J. ALDOUS.***		1
DW-T.	X.4064	P/O. S. C. NORRIS.	Red	51
DW-H.	K.9818	P/O. C. O. J. PEGGE.		22
DW-D.	L.1037	SGT. WILLCOCKS, W.		2
DW-A.	R.6976	F/O. P. G. LAMB.	Yellow	43
DW-K.	X.4067†	P/O. D. M. GRAY.		4
DW-F.	X.4028	SGT. HAMLYN, R. F.		32

*Ellis's Spitfire R.6993 had been damaged on 18 August and possibly was not yet ready, so this may be inaccurate—this applies to subsequent references to R.6993.

**Corfe was almost certainly flying a different Spitfire, see later explanation.

***As ORB, but Aldous's initials were 'E. S.'. I have highlighted the error the first time it occurs.

†X.4067 should probably be X.4102, lost on 24 August—subsequent references to it on 24 August are probably inaccurate.[3]

It seems most likely that the sections were led as follows: Ellis leading 'B' Flight in Blue Section, with Gardiner leading Green Section and Norris leading 'A' Flight and Red Section, with Lamb leading Yellow Section. While the number of patrols these experienced pilots had flown was steadily mounting, fresh pilots were still being drafted in for operational flying. Perhaps following some intensive training over the previous few days, P/O Eric Stanley Aldous was thrust into the action, probably as a wingman to Fred Gardiner. Less than a month after leaving 9 FTS, the twenty-two year old from Sanderstead, Surrey, was climbing through murky clouds to face the enemy for the first time. The other novice pilots were sprinkled through the sections as usual, with Sgt Willcocks and P/O Gray on their second and fourth recorded patrols respectively, while P/O Rees and Sgt Corfe, were both on their sixth recorded patrols. They would have felt more sure of themselves after surviving thus far and having shot down three enemy aircraft between them, along with others claimed as probable and damaged.

S/Ldr Ellis received orders to take his men to 15,000 feet and patrol the Folkestone area, watching for enemy aircraft approaching the convoy, but as expected, the conditions made this difficult. Despite the bright sunshine at that altitude, there was plenty of cloud cover, which meant no chance of spotting the enemy at a distance. For Ellis, it was a case of hoping to catch a glimpse of the enemy and directing his men towards them, while trying to ensure his formation was not surprised by any high-flying Messerschmitts using the clouds or sun in which to hide. As 610 Squadron patrolled, the pilots scanning the sky for a tell-tale shadow or flash of Perspex canopy, the Me 110s of Erpro. 210 escorted by 109s, went on the attack. The coastal air raid sirens started up their mournful wail, recorded by Mary Smith in her diary, 'Raid warning 1–2.50 p.m.—nothing but a few distant bangs and buzzing'.[4] What she did not realise was that this noise represented 610 Squadron's pilots, alongside 54 Squadron, once again becoming embroiled in a desperate dogfight, as the 110s attacked the convoy.

Due to a lack of combat reports, it is necessary to rely solely on the Squadron's ORB for information about the engagement. Whether Ellis was about to attack the enemy fighter-bombers is unclear, but the Squadron had failed to spot a formation of 109s lurking above them, and suddenly the County of Chester Squadron found itself in the worst possible position:

> Red, Blue, Green & Yellow sections were patrolling FOLKESTONE area at 15,000 ft., when they were attacked from above out of the sun by about 20 M.E.109s. E/A made one attack & continued their dive into cloud. Squadron were unable to engage with the exception of Sgt. Hamlyn & F/O. Gardiner who fired short bursts with no visible effect. (ORB)

It must have been a terrifying experience to have such a large formation of enemy fighters diving down, guns blazing as they swept through the unsuspecting Spitfire pilots, who would frantically have broken formation in all directions, trying to escape. The nature of the attack meant that the Spitfire pilots could not catch the 109s, who must have built up considerable speed in their power dive. During the bounce, Sgt Corfe's Spitfire was, 'hit by cannon fire & crashed near HAWKINGE aerodrome—aircraft burnt out—pilot uninjured' (ORB). Although some historians have stated that Corfe baled out, in reality it seems he managed to coax his mortally damaged Spitfire down to earth as indicated in the ORB, a belief also held by expert on the period, Dave Brocklehurst. Dave, who first started digging the sites of crashed aircraft aged just ten, runs *The Kent Battle of Britain Museum*, situated on the site of the former airfield at Hawkinge, where his vast knowledge of the Battle of Britain is so well brought to life. Ultimately, luck was with Corfe as he escaped unhurt, although more than a little shaken by his experience.

Then and Now records the loss of Corfe's Spitfire thus, '**R6695.** Shot down in flames during combat with Bf 109s over Folkestone 2.15 p.m. Crashed and burned out at Hawkinge. Sgt. D. F. Corfe unhurt. **DW-P** a write-off',[5] again confirming Corfe had crash-landed, at the more specific time of 1415 hours. Despite the ORB recording him as flying DW-P, X.4239, this was incorrect as X.4239 was flying with the Squadron much later in the year, and this identity had probably been added retrospectively. Research suggested that it was probably Spitfire DW-P, R.6695 which had been destroyed, having been with the Squadron since 7 June 1940.[6] However, recent information from The National Archives has contradicted this possibility, as R.6695 was lost on 29 August with a different pilot. So until the AMCB file for Corfe is released, there is no definitive answer to the identity of his Spitfire, although he was probably flying DW-P.

The ORB concluded its report with the usual flippant style of a sports report when discussing potential matters of life and death: 'Enemy Cas. Nil. Our Cas. 1 A/C Cat .3. 3 A/C unserviceable', which made for particularly bleak reading. It is unclear who was flying the three damaged Spitfires, as they came in to land at 1430 hours, however, there is one possible clue to the identity of one of these other pilots. While Sgt Corfe had endured quite an ordeal and he was uninjured, his next recorded patrol did not come until seven days later. So perhaps Ellis ordered him to have a break, or the medical officer had seen that a rest would do him good to get over his lucky escape. This seems reasonable to assume, when the other pilots involved in this patrol were back in action the next time the Squadron went up, except P/O Brian Rees. If Corfe was given a rest, so too perhaps was Rees, as he did not fly another operation from 11 Group with 610 Squadron. Maybe Brian Rees had been injured on landing a shot-up aircraft and it was not recorded in the ORB. This would explain why he did not participate in another patrol, especially when he had flown six patrols in eleven days, with claims of two destroyed, one probable and a damaged. It is strange that both men were left out of the coming operations unless they had been injured slightly or needed some recovery time. There are no clues as to the identity of the other two pilots, who had returned in unserviceable Spitfires, unless some evidence surfaces with time.

The belief that P/O Rees had been injured during this patrol has been given more credibility when studying Cyril 'Bam' Bamberger's logbook. On 22 August, 'Bam' carried out an hour's air firing practice in DW-N (no serial number). Interestingly, his next flight was in a two-seat Miles Magister, taking P/O Webster to Hawkinge, the flight lasting forty-five minutes. His return flight (sixty minutes) brought P/O Rees back to Biggin Hill. This would seem to indicate that Webster was replacing Rees for any subsequent patrols that day from Hawkinge, and quite possibly explains why there are no more recorded flights by Rees. Later, Bamberger carried out an eighty-minute patrol (6) in DW-U (no serial number) of 'Red Queen', the code name for Deal. This patrol was not recorded in the ORB, so it is unclear who he was operating with.

It had been a bad day for the Squadron, with four of their precious Spitfires out of action to varying degrees, and no claims made against the enemy. Although S/Ldr Ellis and his men must have been disappointed, they would have taken comfort from the fact that, given the number of enemy fighters which had bounced them, the outcome had not been much worse; 610's three unserviceable aircraft could all have been sent flaming earthwards, with their pilots helpless at the controls. This could have been due to good fortune, or poor marksmanship by the *Luftwaffe* pilots. Equally, it could have been down to the split-second decisions of some of the veteran pilots, whose reactions in such a situation did just enough to save them from disaster.

The other major positive point to be taken from the day was that Convoy Totem was undamaged. 54 Squadron had also been on patrol in response to the *Luftwaffe's* activity, and they claimed two destroyed and a probable for the loss of one pilot (54 ORB). 610's lengthy patrol, which saw some of the pilots in the air for ninety minutes, at first appears to be the only time the Squadron was called on that day, as the ground crew set to work on repairing the damaged Spitfires. However, 32 Squadron had a busy day flying back and forth to Hawkinge, from where it operated, first sortie being at 0820 hours. The Squadron returned to Biggin at 1935 hours, having carried out four convoy patrols and one escort of an Anson, which led to an interception in the early evening. Given that 32 Squadron was so busy, it is possible 610 Squadron carried out further patrols in the afternoon, which went unrecorded as they did not make contact with the enemy. The logbooks of Merrick and Else are of no assistance, as they did not operate on 22 August. Again, this highlights the difficulty of interpreting 610 Squadron's ORB and why this is the first detailed study of the Squadron's history.

Thanks to the weather, the *Luftwaffe* mounted only a few small raids on Friday 23 August, and the Squadron ORB had no entry whatsoever for the day. Even 32 Squadron's more reliable ORB showed a lack of activity; the Hurricanes flew to Hawkinge at 0540 hours for two early morning patrols and had returned to Biggin by 0940 hours. One other two-aircraft patrol of Biggin Hill was carried out from 0900 hours for forty-five minutes. Reading Claude Merrick and Cyril Bamberger's logbooks (Else seems to have been given a break for three days after the 21 August, most likely some leave), we know that 610 Squadron did actually carry out a few patrols. Merrick flew to Hawkinge to carry out two patrols (17 & 18) of Hawkinge itself, one at 10,000 feet lasting thirty-five minutes, the other at 2,000 feet for ten minutes, before returning to Biggin Hill, the flights to and from Hawkinge involving a further fifty minutes of flying (19 and 20). Bamberger flew in DW-U all day as follows; to Hawkinge (7) (twenty-five minutes); patrol of Hawkinge (8) (thirty-five minutes); return to Biggin Hill (9) (twenty-five minutes); back to Hawkinge (10) (thirty-five minutes); and finally a return to Biggin Hill (11) (twenty-five minutes). This was an exhausting schedule, as even the flights to and from Hawkinge, would have been nerve-wracking experiences, as enemy machines could appear at any moment in the skies over Kent.

Meanwhile, the ground crew would have toiled away trying to get a full complement of Spitfires ready for the following day, Biggin Hill reverberating at irregular intervals to memorable sounds, such as the Merlin engines being tested. Despite the lull, the constant threat of danger was always present, whether in the air for the pilots, or while working on the airfield for the ground crew and Squadron personnel. Such periods of comparative inactivity and the dreaded waiting, were terribly trying in their own way. With the approach of dusk, as Biggin Hill was put to bed for the night, the meteorological reports would have been studied for the next day, foretelling fine summer weather. In other words, everyone would have feared that they were in for a 'Blitzy' day.

Saturday 24 August 1940 began as expected. 610 Squadron's pilots rising at dawn at Biggin Hill, would have nervously glanced up at the clear blue skies as the sun gradually started its ascent, knowing

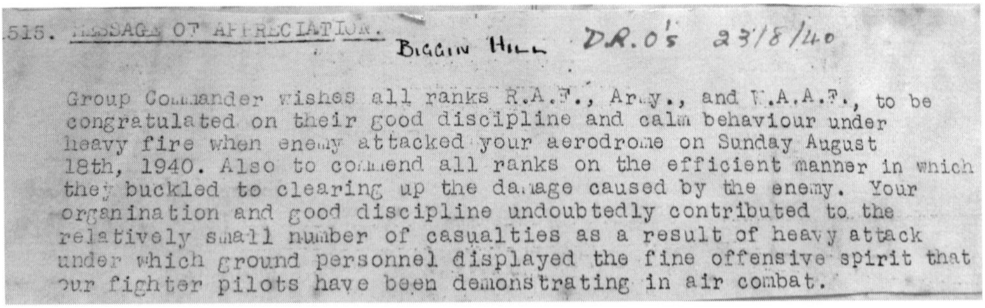

515. MESSAGE OF APPRECIATION. Biggin Hill D.R.O's 23/8/40

Group Commander wishes all ranks R.A.F., Army., and W.A.A.F., to be congratulated on their good discipline and calm behaviour under heavy fire when enemy attacked your aerodrome on Sunday August 18th, 1940. Also to commend all ranks on the efficient manner in which they buckled to clearing up the damage caused by the enemy. Your organination and good discipline undoubtedly contributed to the relatively small number of casualties as a result of heavy attack under which ground personnel displayed the fine offensive spirit that our fighter pilots have been demonstrating in air combat.

Commendatory message from AVM Park to everyone at Biggin Hill on 23 August 1940, for their efforts in the face of the heavy attack on 18 August 1940. (*Copyright 610 Squadron Association*)

in their hearts that, as expected, it was going to be a busy day. This scene would have been repeated throughout Fighter Command's aerodromes across the south of England. The pilots prepared themselves for combat, each one secretly wondering if this would be the last time they sat together at dispersal, having an early cup of tea, grabbing a bite to eat for breakfast, and carrying out rituals to which they had become accustomed in the nervous moments awaiting the scramble. At least 610's pilots may have had a party to look forward to that night, as Douglas Corfe, fortunate to survive the last action, was celebrating his twenty-second birthday. For Corfe, it was to be a day off operations, but for the pilots at dispersal, it was the beginning of a very long day.

Claude Parsons described a typical scene he experienced on many such an occasion, just like the morning of 24 August:

> Readiness would be at 4 o'clock in the morning. Some of the pilots had slept at Dispersal and others would roll up in the brake looking tired, for hours were long in those days, usually from daybreak to dusk. The kit would be put in our respective aeroplanes by the crew, who had already revved the engine to full power and checked everything and reported to the flight-sergeant.[7]

With their aircraft inspected and section positions in the battle order allotted to them, the pilots then had to wait for the call to scramble, an order to fly to their forward base or, eventually, to be stood down. Every call of the dispersal telephone jerked them wide awake. Although the ORB does not make it clear, it seems from Claude Merrick's logbook, that the Squadron flew down to Hawkinge early on the morning of 24 August, in anticipation of action, where Merrick also carried out a patrol of the aerodrome for half an hour (21 & 22). Cyril Bamberger also recorded a flight to Hawkinge and a patrol (12) lasting seventy-five minutes in DW-U (no serial number). Fighter Command's pilots would not have long to wait for the first of six major attacks launched during the course of the day.

This signalled the start of an even more determined assault by the *Luftwaffe* against the key fighter airfields, in a bid to destroy Fighter Command both on the ground and in the air. Such information is only available with hindsight though, so when the telephone rang at 0758 hours with the order of "'Dog Rose' Squadron, Scramble!", and the pilots ran to their aircraft, they would have looked on this as any other scramble, not a key turning point in the Battle. The Squadron battle order would have been chalked up on a blackboard as follows:

DW-M.	K.9947	F/O. D. S. WILSON.	Blue 1	8
DW-X.		P/O. J. ALDOUS.		2
DW-O.	X.4011*	SGT. BAMBERGER, C.		13
DW-Z.		F/O. F. T. GARDINER.		24

DW-S.	K.9975	SGT. ARNFIELD, S. J.		48
DW-N.	N.3128	SGT. RAMSAY, N. H. D.		29
DW-Y.		P/O. S. C. NORRIS.	Red 1	52
DW-K.	X.4067	P/O. D. M. GRAY.		5
DW-E.	P.9433	SGT. BAKER, C.		1
DW-A.	R.6976	F/O. P. G. LAMB.	Yellow 1	44
DW-Q.	R.6891	SGT. HAMLYN, R. F.	Yellow 2	33
DW-B.	X.4166	P/O. C. MERRICK.		23

*As ORB, but Bamberger's logbook records him flying in DW-U on 24 August 1940.

This definitely represented a less experienced unit than the one that had been in action on 22 August. It would seem that Stan Norris was leading the formation, presumably as Red Leader of 'A' Flight, with S/Ldr Ellis having been replaced at the head of Blue Section by F/O Douglas Wilson, on just his eighth recorded operation, while it would be logical that either F/O Gardiner or Sgt Arnfield were leading Green Section and Peter Lamb was leading Yellow Section. However, Sgt Cyril Baker, a pre-war member of the Squadron's ground crew, was being given his baptism of fire in the air, having completed his Spitfire conversion course. When P/Os Aldous and Gray and Sgt Bamberger were added to this, more than a quarter of the pilots being scrambled that morning had very little combat experience.

This shows in the microcosm of a squadron, the problem that Fighter Command as a whole was facing: the gaps in long-serving, battle-experienced units like 610 Squadron were being filled, but with very inexperienced replacement pilots, who were unlikely to survive for long. This increased the pressure on the old hands, as they had less experienced pilots looking out for them, and would have felt compelled to pay greater attention to the inexperienced pilots in the formation. In this context, it is easy to see why Ellis had sent Bamberger amongst others, to gain some experience on Spitfires before being thrown into combat, to give the novice pilots a better chance of survival. At last, the hours of training would be put to the test and fittingly, Sgt Bamberger later recalled a typical scramble:

> When you were scrambled, you ran to the aircraft. The commanding officer's aircraft was the closest and mine was about 100 yards away so I had to run as fast as I could to make certain I was ready on time. The ground crew handed you your straps and your helmet and shut the cockpit door for you. From the moment you scrambled, you weren't scared because you had so much to think about; getting into the aircraft, strapping yourself in, turning the oxygen on, hoping that the engine would fire properly, taking off in formation, listening to the controller … I always flew with a silk scarf round my neck so that I had the freedom to turn my neck through 360°.[8]

As the pilots jumped into their Spitfires, and in time started bumping across the grass at Hawkinge, the controller's instructions began to come through, ordering them to intercept an incoming raid off the south-east coast. Despite the favourable condition, 'No cloud—visibility 20 miles' (ORB), the Squadron received numerous vectors from control over the course of about thirty minutes and split up. Again, 'Bam' provides some insight into this:

> When you got airborne, the first communication was the squadron leader using the squadron call sign, communicating with control, asking, "Have you any information for me?" The controller might say, "We have 20 bandits coming in at such and such a height and such and such a course. Vector 180°". Everyone was listening to this and you all knew what was going on … The average pilot wouldn't say a word on the radio from take-off to touchdown unless he had engine problems or he saw enemy aircraft. You couldn't allow chatter.[9]

At about 0825 hours, Sgt Hamlyn, flying in 'A' Flight, was the only Squadron pilot to see any enemy aircraft. They were '10 miles south east of Ramsgate' (ORB), probably heading for Manston, at a height of 12,000–15,000 feet, his attention brought to the bomber force by AA fire. Hamlyn described the interception as follows:

> I was Yellow 2.
>
> I saw three waves of bombers approaching the S. Coast. I attacked one of these waves in which there were about 15–18 Junkers 88 at about 300–350 yds. I received a large amount of cross fire but I didn't open fire until 250 yds. I gave a two second burst and saw one JU.88 dive away from the rest and I watched it crash into the sea. I did not break away but throttling back an ME109 overshot me and pulled up right in front at about 150 yds. I opened fire and saw it starting to smoke. I followed it down and saw it also hit the sea.
>
> METHOD OF ATTACK. JU.88 ASTERN AND ABOVE ATTACK AIMING AT PORT ENGINE. ME.109. ASTERN AIMING AT CENTRE OF FUSELAGE. (TNA, AIR 50/172/34)

Hamlyn's report is very concise in describing the demise of a *Luftwaffe* bomber and fighter. On his own, Hamlyn faced an incredibly daunting task, with countless gunners on the Junkers 88s targeting him with their 7.9 mm MG15 machine guns which opened up at a considerable distance, trying to ward him off. However, he pressed home his attack with great bravery, and in closing to 250 yards before firing for just two seconds, he devastated the bomber's port engine, causing it to crash into the sea.

Whether Hamlyn had seen the escorting 109s diving on him from behind is unclear, but the frequently used tactic amongst 610's pilots of throttling back, forced the unfortunate German fighter pilot to hurtle past Hamlyn's Spitfire, presenting the twenty-six-year-old sergeant with a prime target from 150 yards. The Yorkshireman fired another devastating two second burst, which sent the 109 in

An interesting photo of a *Luftwaffe* ground crew straining to load-up a Junkers Ju 88 with its payload. In the background, another Ju 88 sits ready for its next operation. This was the type of bomber which Sgt Hamlyn shot down on 24 August 1940. (*Ron Mackay*)

a terminal dive into the English Channel. This was reported as being at about 0830 hours, so in five minutes Hamlyn claimed two enemy aircraft destroyed using 500 rounds of ammunition, without suffering any damage himself. It was a remarkable outcome given that he was vulnerably flying on his own, and another example of what could be achieved by opening fire at the enemy from close range. The text in capitals seems to have been added as a note for the intelligence officer to possibly pass on to the other pilots or to HQ, emphasising the use of astern attacks. It is possible Hamlyn had shot down a fighter belonging to JG 26, as the unit lost one Third *Gruppe* Messerschmitt around this time.[10]

Despite Ronnie Hamlyn's success, 'Remainder of Squadron ... did not engage or see any E/A' (ORB), which was surprising given the clear conditions. During the evident confusion that arose from the various vectors the Squadron received, some Messerschmitt 109s were able to attack 610 Squadron, picking off one of the most experienced pilots, Sgt Johnny Arnfield, who was on his forty-eighth recorded patrol. Surprisingly few details surrounding this incident had been available, apart from the ORB noting that the Squadron lost, '1 A/C—Sgt. Arnfield baled out & fractured his ankle on landing. He was taken to Victoria Hospital DEAL.' The summary of events confirmed this, adding 'injuries received due to enemy action.' However, on 30 June 2017, The National Archives released a fresh batch of AMCB files, which included several of 610 Squadron's casualties from late August 1940. One of these was Arnfield's, so it is now much clearer what happened to him, thanks to his squadron leader's flying battle casualty report. The time mentioned would suggest that Arnfield was shot down prior to Hamlyn's encounter with the *Luftwaffe*.

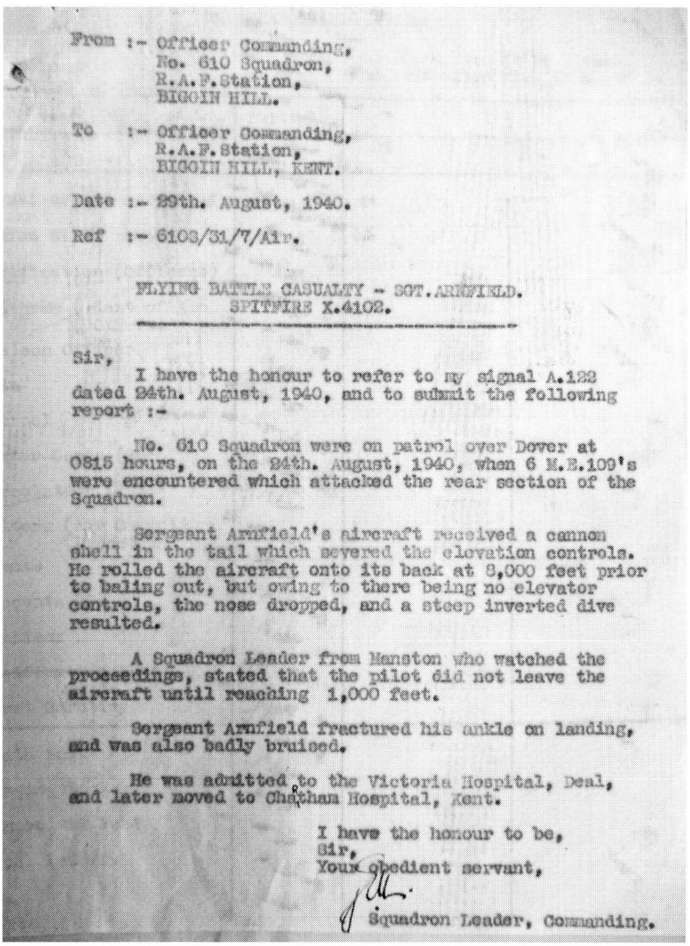

From :- Officer Commanding,
No. 610 Squadron,
R.A.F. Station,
BIGGIN HILL.

To :- Officer Commanding,
R.A.F. Station,
BIGGIN HILL, KENT.

Date :- 29th. August, 1940.

Ref :- 610S/31/7/Air.

FLYING BATTLE CASUALTY - SGT. ARNFIELD.
SPITFIRE X.4102.

Sir,

I have the honour to refer to my signal A.122 dated 24th. August, 1940, and to submit the following report :-

No. 610 Squadron were on patrol over Dover at 0815 hours, on the 24th. August, 1940, when 6 M.E.109's were encountered which attacked the rear section of the Squadron.

Sergeant Arnfield's aircraft received a cannon shell in the tail which severed the elevation controls. He rolled the aircraft onto its back at 8,000 feet prior to baling out, but owing to there being no elevator controls, the nose dropped, and a steep inverted dive resulted.

A Squadron Leader from Manston who watched the proceedings, stated that the pilot did not leave the aircraft until reaching 1,000 feet.

Sergeant Arnfield fractured his ankle on landing, and was also badly bruised.

He was admitted to the Victoria Hospital, Deal, and later moved to Chatham Hospital, Kent.

I have the honour to be,
Sir,
Your obedient servant,

Squadron Leader, Commanding.

S/Ldr Ellis's report on 610 Squadron's veteran NCO, Sgt Arnfield, being shot down. (*TNA, AIR 81/2741*)

Arnfield was probably in his usual Green Section when it was bounced, either flying as Green Leader or a wingman to F/O Gardiner, and he was lucky to survive a very traumatic experience, having only managed to get out of his doomed Spitfire at 1,000 feet. Arnfield must have realised how fortunate he was to be alive and it was miraculous that his injuries were not a lot worse. Again, the incident highlighted that no matter how experienced the pilots were, anyone could fall prey to the escorting fighters, as they so often had the most advantageous position. Wynn reports that Arnfield was shot down off Ramsgate by an Me 109, while, 'His stricken aircraft crashed in flames at Hammill, near Eastry'.[11] Arnfield's Spitfire had been hit catastrophically by the enemy fighter, which was probably flown by a JG 51 pilot, as this unit was operating at this time in the area on an escort mission. It is believed that Hptm. Josef Föző, an up and coming *Luftwaffe* pilot of 4/JG 51, possibly shot down Arnfield. Over the years there has been the usual intrigue over the Spitfire involved, as the ORB recorded Arnfield's as DW-S, K.9975, while most other records reported the aircraft as DW-S, R.6686 (which it could not have been, as R.6686 was still operational between September and November 1940). However, the AMCB file now confirms definitively that Arnfield's Spitfire, which was destroyed, was X.4102, probably coded DW-K.[12]

Arnfield's broken ankle side-lined him for some time, and it was a sad end to his efforts in the Battle, being one of the few pilots left from the Squadron's first patrols over Dunkirk. Arnfield had been with the unit since 24 September 1939 and had gone on to prove himself an accomplished fighter pilot, with two Me 109s destroyed, one Heinkel shared destroyed and two Me 109s damaged during the forty-eight recorded patrols he undertook. As such long-standing, experienced members were now few and far between, it was a blow to the Squadron both in the air and also on the ground. As the veteran NCO, he would have been a key figure in the sergeants' mess, particularly with the number of inexperienced sergeants now with the unit. Brian Smith recalled: 'Arnfield yes! Now wait a minute, Arnfield, I was just trying to remember what happened to him. Did we lose him somewhere? Oh yes, well you see we'd go on and we wouldn't know what happened behind … oh I remember Arnfield, a very nice bloke'. Johnny Arnfield evidently spent some time recovering from his injury, as he stayed in two hospitals, and the ORB does not mention him returning to 610 Squadron. Arnfield's war was far from over though. He went on to serve as an instructor in Canada, before being commissioned, becoming a Lancaster bomber pilot and being awarded a long-overdue DFC. He died relatively young of a heart attack on 24 September 1954,[13] exactly fifteen years after he had joined 610 Squadron.

There would have been the usual mixed reaction to the patrol's outcome as the Spitfire pilots returned (seemingly to Biggin Hill), and reports filtered through regarding Sgt Arnfield's injury, whose fate for a short time was uncertain. The pilots would have been frustrated at the numerous vectors relayed to them by the controller, which had caused confusion and meant so many of them failed to make contact with the large enemy formation. In fact, the third entry in P/O Merrick's logbook, 'AUG 24 PATROL DUNGENESS (A) 1.45', probably relates to this patrol. The fact that it lasted one hour and forty-five minutes, Merrick's longest flight in a Spitfire, and it was recorded as being over Dungeness, when Hamlyn reported engaging the enemy ten miles south-east of Ramsgate, corroborates the length and range of the patrol.

Hamlyn's claims for two destroyed would have alleviated this mood of frustration, as would the inevitable phone call informing the Squadron that Arnfield was alive, albeit with a broken ankle. It was certainly a blow, but it could so easily have been much worse. The CO would have decided swiftly about which pilot to bring 'on state' for the next potential patrol, as the men were debriefed. The Spitfires were hurriedly turned round in case of the need to scramble, which given the perfect weather for the *Luftwaffe* and the early first raid, seemed inevitable. With most of the pilots having returned by 0900 hours, they were just about back on readiness, their Spitfires rearmed and refuelled, when the next raid was seen to be building up. As part of Fighter Command's response, 610 Squadron received an order to scramble at 1035 hours, around one hour and thirty-five minutes after returning from the previous patrol, from which nerves would have been stretched by the nature of the interception. It was going to be another busy day for 'The Chesters'.

This unusual photograph shows some of 610 Squadron's ground crew with an Albion Tanker, a vital piece of equipment for refuelling the Squadron's Spitfires between sorties. AC Alf Bridson is sitting in the petrol bowser's cab, whilst AC Osbourne Jennings is wearing the tin hat. (*Copyright 610 Squadron Association*)

One of the other key roles the ground crew carried out was rearming the Squadron's Spitfires between sorties. Here, 610's AC2 Goff can be seen filling the ammunition boxes at Hawkinge during the Battle of Britain. (*Copyright 610 Squadron Association*)

The squadron leader returned to lead his men on this patrol, effectively replacing the loss of Arnfield's experience, while P/O Pegge was flying instead of Sgt Ramsay, and the third change was Sgt Baker being left at home having experienced his first patrol, to be replaced by P/O Webster, who was about to undertake his own first recorded operational patrol. Frank Webster, the VR pilot from the Isle of Wight, had been on the Spitfire conversion course, and Ellis felt he was ready to be tested in a combat environment. As is often the case, it is hard to establish each pilot's position in the formation, but the battle order in the ORB lists the usual mixture of veterans and inexperienced pilots:

DW-W.	R.6993	S/Ldr. J. ELLIS.	Blue 1	46
DW-M.	K.9947	F/O. D. S. WILSON.		9
DW-X.		P/O. J. ALDOUS.	Green 3	3
DW-O.	X.4011*	SGT. BAMBERGER, C.		14
DW-Z.		F/O. F. T. GARDINER.	Green 1	25
DW-T.	X.4064	P/O. F. K. WEBSTER.		1
DW-Y.		P/O. S. C. NORRIS.	Red 1	53
DW-E.	P.9433	P/O. C. O. J. PEGGE.		23
DW-K.	X.4067	P/O. D. M. GRAY.		6
DW-A.	R.6976	F/O. P. G. LAMB.	Yellow 1	45
DW-Q.	R.6891	SGT. HAMLYN, R. F.	Yellow 2	34
DW-B.	X.4166	P/O. C. MERRICK.		24

*As ORB, but Bamberger's logbook records him flying in DW-U on 24 August 1940.

S/Ldr Ellis would have been leading the patrol as Blue Section leader at the head of 'B' Flight, with F/O Gardiner probably leading Green Section, with the very inexperienced triumvirate of Webster, Aldous and Bamberger all in their flight. Meanwhile, Stan Norris would have been leading 'A' Flight as Red Leader, accompanied by Pegge and Gray, and Peter Lamb as Yellow Leader, with Hamlyn and Merrick as his wingmen. In Merrick's logbook, the next patrol is described as, 'AUG 24 PATROL BIGGIN HILL (A) 1.00'. As the ORB referred to how the Squadron 'patrolled base', it seems the Squadron had returned to Biggin Hill after the earlier engagement as suggested, and was now operating from the sector station.

As the twelve Spitfires roared off from the aerodrome, the pilots would have been hoping for less confusion in trying to locate the enemy formation than earlier that morning, so would have been glad to be patrolling their base. While this ensured that the sector station was protected from any possible repeat of the raid on 18 August, it allowed the Squadron to spiral up to an advantageous altitude over their home base with a reduced threat of being bounced by any high-flying *Luftwaffe* fighters. In the meantime, the controllers could judge what they thought was the likely target of the raid, as around 100 fighters and bombers began to approach Dover. In light of this, S/Ldr Ellis was ordered to take his formation to 'GRAVESEND, then DOVER where an engagement took place against 6 enemy fighters … No cloud—visibility 15 miles' (ORB). Once again, the Squadron was vectored around in an attempt to intercept the enemy formation, and from surviving combat reports, it is difficult to establish the order of events, but each report confirms that the encounter with the Messerschmitt 109s took place at 1135 hours. Sgt Hamlyn, found himself in the thick of things once more, against six Me 109s at 18,000 feet:

> I was Yellow 2.
>
> I was attacked while in formation over Dover. After a short dog fight I got on to the Me.109's tail and he at once flew for France. I followed and while I was chasing him I saw another dog fight between two Spitfires and one Me109. The ME109 went down smoking badly but carried on flying eventually going into the sea off Cape Grez-Nez [Cap Gris-Nez]. By this time I had got into range of the ME109 I was chasing but did not open fire until I had crossed over the coast into France, after about three

more bursts I saw it go out of control with smoke pouring out and watched it crash in a field. I did not experience any A.A. fire while over France. The ME109 that I saw crash into the sea was the one destroyed by F/O Lamb—Yellow Leader.

METHOD OF ATTACK. ASTERN AND UNDERNEATH AIMING AT CENTRE OF FUSELAGE. (TNA, AIR 50/172/35)

So at least some of 610 Squadron's pilots were bounced by a numerically inferior force of Me 109s, which carried out a lightning attack on the more unwieldy formation of Spitfires. Hamlyn was able to use his skill to turn the tables on the attacking 109s, although the sergeant's decision to chase the 109 all the way to the French coast was not recommended by Fighter Command's hierarchy. Just six days earlier, it had ordered against such tactics, to prevent the needless loss of pilots in the Channel, which had steadily mounted during the Battle of Britain. However, Hamlyn knew he had the upper hand in this dogfight, and was determined to bring his assailant down. With his Spitfire pushed to its limits to close the range quickly, the urge to open fire at extreme range must have been hard to resist. But knowing how effective his fire had been earlier in the morning from close range, he did not open fire until he was within 250 yards. He fired approximately six bursts of three seconds, all his ammunition, his last bursts being fired at 150 yards. Once again, the tactic had the desired result as he witnessed the Messerschmitt go down. Having completed the worrying return flight across the Channel and reached Biggin Hill, Hamlyn was able to claim a third enemy aircraft destroyed in the space of a morning, his operation having lasted one hour and thirty-five minutes. It is possible that 610 Squadron had run into the Messerschmitts of JG 26, and that Hamlyn had brought down 9 *Staffel's* Fw. Artur Beese: '9/JG26 Messerschmitt Bf 109. Crash-landed at St Inglevert following combat over the Channel. Fw. Beese unhurt. Aircraft 11+1 a write-off'.[14]

During his chase across the Channel, Ronnie Hamlyn had a bird's-eye view of the demise of another Messerschmitt which 610 had tangled with, as Peter Lamb pursued a 109 which crashed into the sea off Cap Gris-Nez. Lamb described his encounter, which also took place at 1135 hours, as follows:

I was Yellow leader while patrolling Dover area at 22,000 ft. The Squadron was told that Manston was being bombed. The Leader set course for Manston when I sighted 2 Me 109s above and to the starboard diving towards the French Coast. I was flying in the Box of Blue Section so I broke away and chased them. One dived steeply towards [illegible place] The other started turning to the right. I followed him and a mild dog fight ensued. He eventually made off for home. I fired several short bursts and noticed smoke issuing from either side of the fuselage. I broke off the attack and made for Manston to attempt to rejoin the Squadron.

Yellow 2 (Sgt Hamlyn) who also pursued a 109 across the Channel saw the machine I attacked crash into the sea.

Peter G Lamb F/O

P.S. The ME 109 had yellow wing tips and yellow roundels on the fuselage. (TNA, AIR 50/172/45)

It is apparent that Yellow and Blue Sections were in the same formation, and it is also interesting that the Squadron received a final vector, to Manston, before they met the 109s. Lamb, unlike Hamlyn, was not attacked by the 109s but saw them as they were diving away from the formation. Perhaps they were two of the original six spotted by Hamlyn, which did not directly engage the Spitfire formation. As with Hamlyn, Lamb gained the initiative forcing the Messerschmitt pilot to break for home. Peter Lamb seemed to have little difficulty in keeping up with the 109, both aircraft presumably going flat out, as he opened fire at just, '100 yards closing to 50 yds 3 bursts of 1. sec each' (TNA, AIR 50/172/45). Lamb followed the instruction of not straying too far from the English coast and left the apparently damaged 109 to its fate. It was only thanks to Hamlyn, that Lamb could claim an Me 109 destroyed.

Sgt Hamlyn mentioned two Spitfires attacking Lamb's target and from his apparent grandstand view of events, there is no reason to doubt it. Lamb makes no mention of another Spitfire. He may not have been aware of it, or it could have been his other wingman, Claude Merrick, covering his tail, while he delivered the fatal blows; we shall never know.

The other surviving combat report was from twenty-two-year-old P/O Aldous, on just his third recorded patrol. He suddenly found himself fighting for his life at 17,000 feet east of Dover as a pair of 109s singled him out for attention, again possibly two of the six that Hamlyn originally identified attacking their formation. He described his first combat as follows:

> I was Green 3. I sighted 2 Me.109s, one of whom attacked me almost head on. I turned round and found one E/A in front and above—I climbed and attacked him giving him one 3 sec burst, after which he dived away and I followed him down and gave him 2 more 3 secs bursts. I saw him smoking heavily, emitting black & blue-ish smoke at about 3,000' over the sea. I broke away and returned to base. He employed no evasive tactics, except to dive steeply. (TNA, AIR 50/172/4)

It must have been a frightening experience for this novice pilot to see an Me 109 coming for him head-on, the cannon and machine gun muzzles flashing as the German pilot tried to pick him off. It is likely that as the shells came whizzing past him some struck his Spitfire, the thud and clang of bullets adding to Aldous's fear as the Messerschmitt hurtled by. Having survived this initial attack, the training which had been drilled into him came into play as he put his Spitfire into a sharp turn which brought him behind a Messerschmitt, possibly the one by which he had just been attacked, enabling him to turn the tables, much as Hamlyn and Lamb had done.

It is interesting that the less experienced Aldous opened fire from, '300 yds–250 yds, 3 bursts of 3 secs. each' (TNA, AIR 50/172/4), a considerably greater distance than the more seasoned pilots. As a result, the Browning machine guns were not as effective, although the aircraft was seen to dive away smoking heavily. Sensibly, given that he seems to have been alone and in a damaged aircraft, Aldous resisted the urge to follow his adversary down and managed to return to Biggin Hill, where he would have been elated to be awarded a claim for a probable. The ORB states that Aldous was flying 'DW-X' without a serial number, and although various sources state he was flying R.6641, this is impossible, as recently-released information from The National Archives has shown that R.6641 was being flown by another pilot, so the serial number of Aldous's Spitfire remains a mystery.

Inevitably, 'The Chesters' had not had things all their own way, and given that at least some of the Squadron had been bounced by enemy fighters, it was unsurprising that the ORB concluded, 'Our Cas. P/O. Gray wounded—A/C crashed'. P/O Donald Gray was carrying out his sixth recorded patrol, making it a very eventful ten days for the young man. During this time, he had a very close shave with an Me 109 on his second patrol, when he also claimed an Me 109 as a probable, while there was the confusion over his injury and being reported non-effective sick on 21 August, despite no mention of it elsewhere. This is probably just a mix up over the dates, and should perhaps refer to 24 August, following this patrol. The AMCB file for Gray was released on 30 June 2017 and has cast some confusion as to when he was shot down.

The 610 ORB, 11 Group ORB and the updated information from 610 Squadron to the Air Ministry in the file, state that Gray was shot down on this second patrol of the day, at approximately 1215 hours at Eythorne. However, the first message from 610 Squadron to the Air Ministry and S/Ldr Ellis's Flying Battle Casualty Report, state that it happened at 0815–0830 hours at Shepherd's Wells, (probably Shepherdswell), which would have been the first patrol. Given the weight of information supporting the fact that it took place on the second patrol, I have included it here, particularly as the updated information from 610 to the Air Ministry states that it was 1215 hours. Ellis wrote his report five days after the event, probably at the same time as he wrote the report on Arnfield being shot down on the early patrol. It seems he may have mixed the two patrols up, possibly having used the first report from 610 to the Air Ministry, which stated 0815–0830 hours. However, it is possible that the first report is correct and that Gray was shot down at Shepherdswell (which is where it is believed he crash-landed) at 0815–0830 hours, and was then taken to the first aid post at Eythorne, which is where he was at 1215 hours.

On whichever patrol Gray was shot down, his Spitfire had evidently been hit hard by the 109's firepower, with damage to the rudder controls, glycol radiator, engine, airscrew and starboard plane, and Gray did well to perform a wheels-up landing. For all this damage, the aircraft was repairable. The serial number of Gray's Spitfire raised the usual questions, as the ORB reported him in DW-K, X.4067, while various sources believed he was flying DW-K, X.4102. However, thanks to the AMCB information, we know for certain that Gray was actually flying Spitfire R.6641, the aircraft which Aldous was thought to have flown. At first, Gray was reported to have been seriously wounded, suffering multiple shrapnel wounds to his legs, arms, hands and face. Although the messages from 610 to the Air Ministry later referred to them as superficial wounds, the emergency medical services forms in the file, the last such one dated 14 September, still referred to multiple bullet wounds in the legs and arms as being 'Serious' (TNA, AIR 81/2768). Gray seems to have been tended to at a first aid post at Eythorne first, near to Shepherdswell, where he landed, before being taken to Waldershare Hospital to have his wounds investigated. Once again, it seems likely that there is a mix up in the ORB regarding dates, as this is dated 25 August, when he would almost certainly have gone to Waldershare Hospital immediately after his crash-landing.

Gray's participation in the Battle was over, and as a result of the 'injuries received due to enemy action, (*was*) transferred to Royal Masonic Hospital on 28.8.40' (ORB), which was perhaps better suited to deal with his shrapnel wounds. Donald Gray's father, John, of Palmers Green, London, was immediately notified of the serious nature of his son's injuries, although the AMCB file does include a note that Donald had written to his father on 27 August, to update him on his condition and alleviate some of his concerns.

Thankfully, Gray had survived his ordeal, but 610 Squadron was now missing another pilot, meaning an even less experienced pilot had to be called on to fill the gap. Gray had been with the Squadron for twenty-nine days, only ten of which seem to have been as operational, before being wounded. The future would not have looked bright for the other novice pilots who had joined with him in late July. Donald Gray spent some time convalescing, much of which would have been at the Royal Masonic Hospital, in central London. If he was still there when the big *Luftwaffe* raids hit London, he must have cursed his luck at being on the receiving end of the aerial bombardment, when he could have been protecting the capital. Gray also spent time at Biggin Hill in a role at the sector station, perhaps in the operations room as some of his colleagues had done, until he was fit again for flying duties.

The Squadron had more than held its own in the dangerous dogfighting which was taking place across the south-east of England, the day's tally now being four destroyed and one probable for the loss of two wounded pilots and at least two aircraft. After two dogfights, the Squadron would have hoped for a quiet afternoon, following their return to base around midday. There was unfortunately no chance of this, as every squadron was in the same boat. As one of the most experienced Spitfire units, flying from such a key aerodrome, it was inevitable that with the afternoon ahead of them on such a lovely summer's day, they would be back in action.

At 1545 hours, after three-and-a-quarter hours of anxious waiting, a call came through from operations for Biggin Hill to scramble nine Spitfires and intercept raiders north of the Thames. During the afternoon, S/Ldr Ellis had seen fit to bring in some fresh men, so of the nine pilots who took off, three flew their first patrol of the day. The experienced Sgt Parsons was back on patrol, not having been on an operation since destroying a Dornier six days earlier, while the other two were novices, desperate to learn and try and survive at the same time. Sgt Beardsley was the latest to be given his first taste of combat, while Sgt Willcocks was to face the *Luftwaffe* for the third reported time, John Ellis probably keeping them close by as his wingmen. Ellis, Joe Pegge and Eric Aldous were all flying their second interceptions of the day while the remaining three pilots, Stan Norris, Ronnie Hamlyn

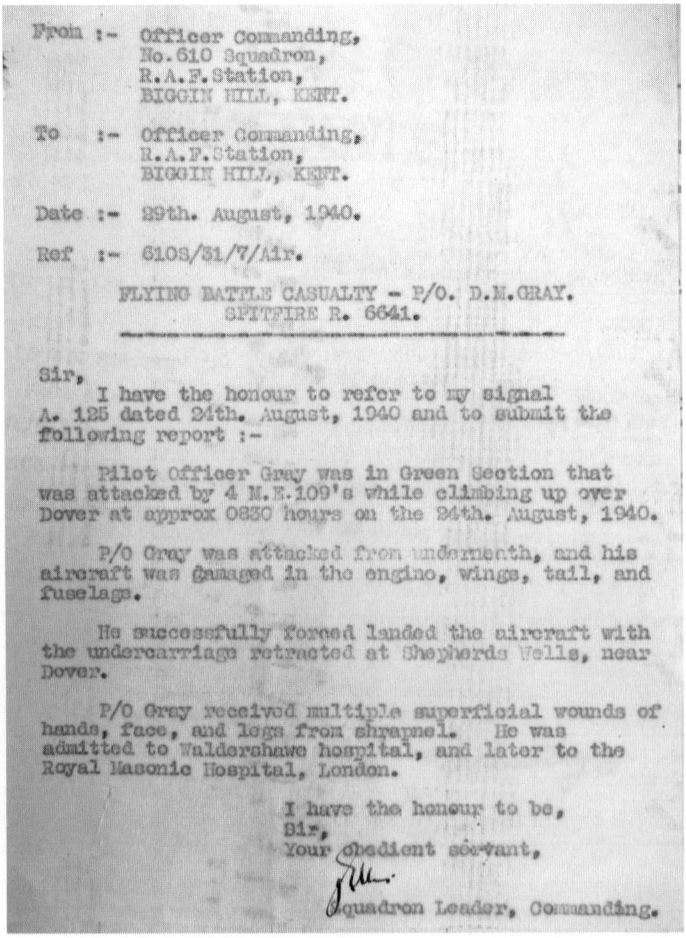

From :- Officer Commanding,
No.610 Squadron,
R.A.F.Station,
BIGGIN HILL, KENT.

To :- Officer Commanding,
R.A.F.Station,
BIGGIN HILL, KENT.

Date :- 29th. August, 1940.

Ref :- 610S/31/7/Air.

FLYING BATTLE CASUALTY - P/O. D.M.GRAY.
SPITFIRE R. 6641.

Sir,

I have the honour to refer to my signal A. 125 dated 24th. August, 1940 and to submit the following report :-

Pilot Officer Gray was in Green Section that was attacked by 4 M.E-109's while climbing up over Dover at approx 0830 hours on the 24th. August, 1940.

P/O Gray was attacked from underneath, and his aircraft was damaged in the engine, wings, tail, and fuselage.

He successfully forced landed the aircraft with the undercarriage retracted at Shepherds Wells, near Dover.

P/O Gray received multiple superficial wounds of hands, face, and legs from shrapnel. He was admitted to Waldershawe hospital, and later to the Royal Masonic Hospital, London.

I have the honour to be,
Sir,
Your obedient servant,

Squadron Leader, Commanding.

S/Ldr Ellis's report on the circumstances surrounding P/O Gray being shot down. Note the time is given as 0830 hours, although various other sources indicate he was shot down during the second patrol of the day. (*TNA, AIR 81/2768*)

and Claude Merrick would have been feeling the strain as they each notched up their third recorded operation of the day. The pilots were assigned to the sections as follows, with F/Lt Norris leading 'A' Flight as Red 1, Sgt Hamlyn leading Yellow Section, and 'B' Flight's Blue Section being led by the CO:

DW-T.	X.4064	F/Lt. S. C. NORRIS.	Red 1	54
DW-E.	P.9433	P/O. C. O. J. PEGGE.	Red 2	24
DW-A.	R.6976	SGT. PARSONS, C. A.	Red 3	20
DW-Q.	R.6891	SGT. HAMLYN, R. F.	Yellow 1	35
DW-D.	L.1037	P/O. C. MERRICK.	Yellow 2	25
DW-J.	R.6599	SGT. BAKER, C.	Yellow 3	2
DW-W.	R.6993	S/Ldr. J. ELLIS.	Blue 1	47
DW-O.	X.4011	SGT. BEARDSLEY, W.*	Blue	1
DW-K.	X.4067	SGT. WILLCOCKS, W.	Blue	3

*As ORB, but Beardsley's initials were 'R. A.'. I have highlighted the error the first time it occurs.

F/Lt Norris's report of the battle which took place at about 1600 hours, was as follows:

> I was leading "A" Flt. when we were ordered to intercept E.A. over Gravesend. After taking off and climbing to about 5000' I sighted the enemy almost immediately about 3 miles ahead and about 10000' above. We gave chase and after some minutes caught them up. When first sighted they were on a westerly course but turned North before we reached them. We came up astern to carry out an attack on the enemy bombers of which there were about twenty, when we were attacked by about twenty ME 109s diving down from above us and in front.
>
> In the ensuing battle I saw one ME 109 breaking away apparently running away. I gave chase & fired a short burst just before we entered a thin layer of cloud. The E.A was still in front of me when we came out smoking faintly. I gave another 2 sec burst & clouds of black smoke enveloped the aircraft. I overshot him at a height of 1000'. He was diving vertically by this time & could not have had time to pull out. I did not see him hit the ground. I circled round but could not find the E.A. (TNA, AIR 50/172/54)

610 had been at a distinct height disadvantage when Norris spotted the enemy, apparently with the assistance of AA fire. The flight lieutenant would have told his CO, who would have given the 'Tally Ho!' to the controller, and ordered his men to push their throttles, 'through the gate', to close on the enemy formation of twenty Junkers 88s, a fast aircraft for a medium bomber. Having caught up with the enemy formation within fifteen minutes of being scrambled, and positioned his formation for an astern attack at 15,000 feet, Ellis's plans were thwarted by a formation of Messerschmitt 109s.

The escorts counter-attack was well timed, yet again, and the larger formation forced the Spitfires to break off their attack on the bombers and become embroiled in another twisting, fighter-versus-fighter dogfight. According to the combat reports, the dogfight took place around the Thames Estuary, on the north side of the river, roughly operating twenty miles north of the Isle of Sheppey, a long trip for the *Luftwaffe* fighters. Although they had done their duty well, the *Jägdflieger* now found themselves between a rock and a hard place. They had instigated the dogfight, but having made the initial pass, they could not get involved in a sustained dogfight due to fuel limitations. A high-speed combat would guzzle the 109s fuel supply, so they soon found themselves having to operate a fighting withdrawal, or in the case of the 109 Norris latched on to, simply attempting to reach home by outpacing the RAF fighters. This was a mistake against a veteran like Stan Norris, who only used 400 rounds to bring down his foe having closed to a short range, and 'Dog Rose' Red Leader was able to claim his fifth confirmed victory. Norris was now an 'Ace'.

Norris was fortunate in probably having two of the Squadron's more experienced pilots as his wingmen, Claude Parsons and Joe Pegge, the latter having also filed a combat report:

> On 24.8.40 I was No 2 of Red section of 610 Sqdn.
>
> In a dogfight which ensued while chasing Ju 88s I got behind an ME 109 which half rolled & started to dive out—I gave it a short burst & saw pieces come off around the cockpit. The Me 109 then went into a slow spiral & I climbed away as there were other 109s above & behind me. (TNA, AIR 50/172/58)

Pegge's description is much more succinct than Norris's, although he does note in the preamble the assistance provided by AA fire in sighting the bombers and that the combat took place at 11,000 feet against twenty Me 109s, north of Gravesend on the north side of the Thames Estuary, at 1600 hours. Pegge had been able to get in a telling burst of 240 rounds from 150–200 yards, but he could only claim a probable as he did not follow the 109 down, perhaps having learnt his lesson from 18 August. Seeing that 'Snappers' (enemy fighters) were above and behind him, he decided that discretion was the better part of valour, and returned to Biggin Hill safely.

While Red Section had recovered well from being attacked by the escorts, Yellow Section followed in next, as recorded by their section leader Ronnie Hamlyn. He noted that at 1555 hours they ran into twenty Junkers 88s and thirty Me 109s halfway between Southend and Hornchurch at 15,000 feet, before detailing the following report (see photo p. 364).

I was Yellow Leader, on taking off we started to fly towards Gravesend but on reaching 5,000 feet we saw A.A. Fire over N.E. London, so we changed course. At about 12,000 feet I first sighted about 20 Junkers, 88 heading in a Westerly direction. I lead my section towards them but I saw a bunch of Me 109s just above me so I pulled up and attacked one, after two bursts some smoke started pouring out and he fell away out of control. I was just about to break away when I saw tracer bullets passing me. I at once turned sharply and saw my number three being attacked by a Me 109. So I attacked it a d it started to pull up, I gave another butst and it started smoking after another burst it caught fire and went down with pieces falling off it. The last I saw of the Spitfire My No 3 was that he was still diving and he looked out of control.

(Signed) R.F. Hamlyn Sgt

METHOD OF ATTACK.

(i) ME.109. QUARTER ATTACK ON E/A STARBOARD SIDE FOLLOWED BY ASTERN ATTACK AIMING AT CENTRE OF FUSELAGE.

(ii) ME.109 ASTERN FROM UNDERNEATH AIMING AT CENTRE OF FUSELAGE.

(TNA, AIR 50/172/35)

AA fire had evidently proven vital in assisting this interception, the Spitfires heading directly for the raiders from some distance, on seeing the ground fire the bombers had attracted. Hamlyn was aware of the escorting fighters above the bomber formation, and he climbed directly up into the escorts. Hamlyn was instantly in the thick of another dogfight, quickly shooting down a 109, before having to evade an attack himself. In attempting to assist his Number 3, Hamlyn's marksmanship is apparent, as this enemy aircraft finally went down in flames. Hamlyn used up all his ammunition with two bursts of three seconds to dispatch the first 109 and three bursts of three seconds fire to destroy the second enemy fighter—his patrol lasted forty-five minutes. It had been a remarkable day for the twenty-six year old from Harrogate, as by the time he landed and had his claims verified, he could claim five enemy aircraft destroyed in a day, four of which were the fearsome Messerschmitt 109. However, despite his understandable elation, Hamlyn knew he might not have been in time to save his Number 3.

Fortunately, Yellow 3, Sgt Baker, was holding his own in the dogfight at 12,000 feet over the River Thames, to the west of the Isle of Sheppey. Baker also noted that AA fire had assisted in the interception, before stating:

> I was Yellow 3 and saw an ME 109 being attacked by 2 Spitfires and closed up. As I arrived the 2. Spitfires had broken away on either side after what appeared to be an individual attack. White smoke was coming from the 109 and it was in a slight dive. I closed to 250 yds range, approaching from the rear port quarter and fired a 2 second burst. As I broke away I saw flames and black smoke issuing from the M.E.109 which continued in its dive and disappeared into the clouds. (TNA, AIR 50/172/6)

It seems certain that the Messerschmitt which Baker happened upon had already been damaged by the other Spitfires. The German pilot had his work cut out trying to make it back home, when Baker came in on his tail to close range and opened fire for two seconds, using just 240 rounds. On returning to Biggin Hill, Baker was able to claim this Messerschmitt as destroyed, although it seems likely that it should have been shared destroyed. Whether or not the other two Spitfires were from 610 Squadron is unclear, but it is easy to see from this example, how over-claiming could occur. What is clear, is that the Spitfire which Ronnie Hamlyn saw diving away out of control was not his Number 3, Sgt Baker, as he escaped unscathed.

As the Spitfires returned to Biggin Hill at about 1645 hours, it became evident that a Spitfire had failed to return and that it belonged to Hamlyn's other wingman, Yellow 2, P/O Merrick. As it transpired, Claude Merrick, having been hit by fire from the 109 which Hamlyn had shot down from off his tail, had managed to crash-land his Spitfire in a field of stubble on Lampitt Farm, Fyfield, Essex (TNA, AIR 81/2780). Merrick's recently-released AMCB file does not have a flying battle casualty report by S/Ldr Ellis, but it still has some interesting snippets of information.

Merrick had been slightly wounded by 'multiple gunshot wounds (metal splinters from small shells)' (TNA, AIR 81/2780) and he was taken to War Memorial Hospital at Ongar, Essex, for treatment. Fyfield is a picturesque village some distance inland from where the engagement started, and it is possible Merrick was heading for RAF North Weald, given that its proximity to where he crash-landed was less than five miles. The Squadron would have been delighted to hear that Merrick had survived, although his wounds were serious enough to mean he had had flown his last operation during the Battle of Britain. Merrick's father, living in Bognor Regis, Sussex, was duly informed of his hospitalisation, stressing that his wounds were not serious.

It must have been incredibly exhausting for an inexperienced pilot to have flown five times during the day, including three combat patrols, and fatigue may have taken its toll on his reaction to the attacking 109. The ORB mentioned one aircraft being unserviceable, logically Merrick's, but the aircraft loss could be endured, it was the injury of yet another pilot which both the Squadron and Fighter Command could not cope with indefinitely. Merrick did not note down in his logbook which aircraft he was flying, and while the ORB stated he was flying DW-D, L.1037, this was unlikely to have been the case, as L.1037 was operational until late September. We now know for certain he was actually flying R.6696 (TNA, AIR 81/2780).

The last point at which Merrick's logbook is of any help to this work, is when he recorded his crash-landing; he must have been shot down at about 1610 hours, as his flight time was twenty-five minutes and they took off at 1545 hours. (The AMCB file stated it was slightly earlier, at 1600 hours.) Also, by the time he had been shot down, he had flown for four hours and five minutes that day, underlining a fighter pilot's gruelling existence, with the pressures they were under every time they took to the sky.

Merrick only survived eleven days before being wounded, again highlighting the dangers and hardship of being a novice pilot in such a lethal situation. By the time he was shot down, Merrick had gained another seventeen hours and twenty minutes on the Spitfire with 610, in addition to his twenty-two hours and ten minutes at the OTU, but this was very little time to be able to effectively operate a high-powered machine in a war zone. It was combat experience which really counted, and he could only learn that by being thrown into the fray, where the odds were stacked heavily against him.

From Merrick's logbook, it appears he rejoined 610 Squadron on 24 October, although it is hard to decipher and there is no mention of returning to 610 in the ORB. He then joined Station HQ at Biggin Hill until 10 November 1941, presumably in a non-flying role. He required a new logbook, as his original one was destroyed in the bombing of Biggin Hill on 1 September 1940. Merrick later went on to convert to twin and four-engined aircraft, flying Blenheims, Albemarles and Stirlings, serving with 296 and 295 Squadrons between September 1942 and September 1944. While he was with 295

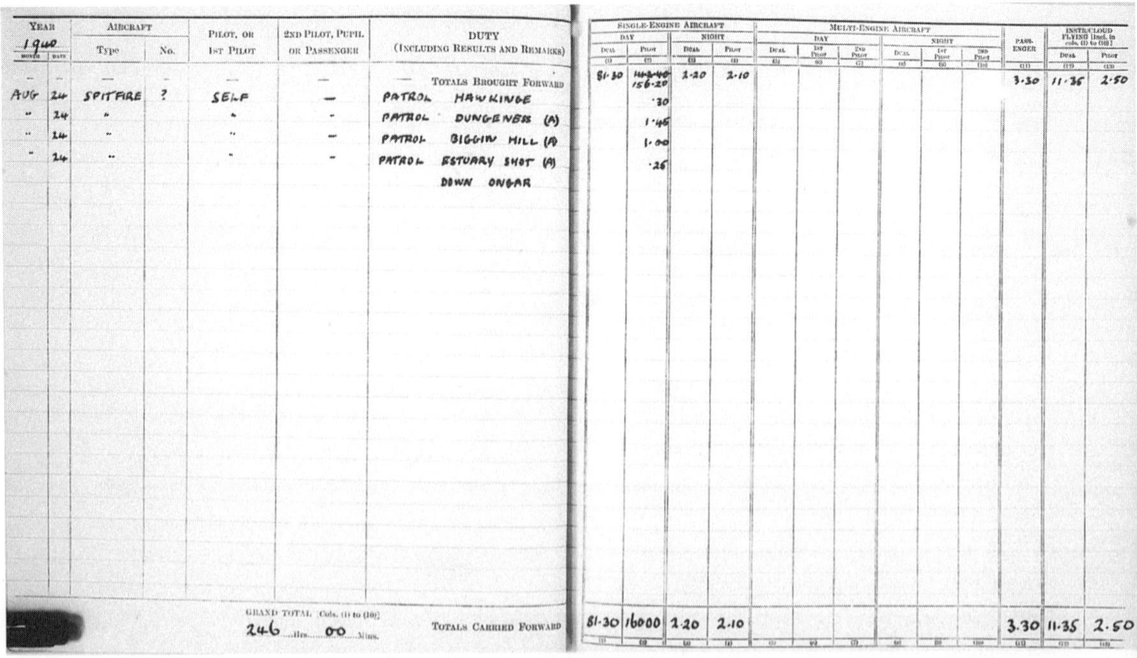

Year 1940 Month	Date	Aircraft Type	No.	Pilot, or 1st Pilot	2nd Pilot, Pupil, or Passenger	Duty (Including Results and Remarks)	Single-Engine Day Dual	Single-Engine Day Pilot	Single-Engine Night Dual	Single-Engine Night Pilot	Passenger	Instr/Cloud Flying Dual	Instr/Cloud Flying Pilot
—	—	—	—	—	—	Totals Brought Forward	81-30	143-40 156-20	2-20	2-10	3-30	11-35	2-50
AUG	24	SPITFIRE	?	SELF	—	PATROL HAWKINGE		·30					
"	24	"		"	-	PATROL DUNGENESS (A)		1·45					
"	24	"		"	—	PATROL BIGGIN HILL (A)		1·00					
"	24	"		"	-	PATROL ESTUARY SHOT (A) DOWN ONGAR		·25					
					Grand Total (Cols. (1) to (10)) 246 Hrs. 00 Mins.	Totals Carried Forward	81-30	160-00	2-20	2-10	3.30	11-35	2-50

Details of Merrick's last flight with 610 Squadron, being shot down and hospitalised on 24 August. (*Crown Copyright RAF Museum*)

Squadron, he won a DFC for his actions during the Normandy landings. Merrick was the pilot of an Albemarle which dropped ten paratroopers led by Lieutenant Bobbie Midwood at 0017½ hours on Drop Zone 'K' on 6 June, to the north-west of Caen. He dramatically described this key event in 'Operation Overlord' in his logbook as, 'opening the Western Front'. Merrick went on to reach the rank of wing commander before he left the RAF. He died in 1984.[15]

It had been a successful patrol for the Squadron, as although their attack on the Junkers 88s had been thwarted, they had battled effectively against the escorting fighters, which held the advantage at the start of the dogfight. The RAF pilots managed to turn the tables on their *Luftwaffe* counterparts in the face of odds of 4–1, claiming four destroyed and a probable. One of these 109s could well have belonged to JG 3: '9/JG3 Me 109 Messerschmitt Bf 109E-4. Crashed in sea off Herne Bay 4.10 p.m. during combat with RAF fighters. Lt. Achleitner baled out and rescued from sea by Herne Bay life-boat. Aircraft 8+1 lost'.[16]

What happened to Blue Section during this patrol is unclear, as none of the pilots filed a combat report, unusual given that the section was led by John Ellis. He was possibly being more cautious, having two inexperienced wingmen, but Sgts Beardsley and Willcocks had certainly gained valuable flying time in combat. S/Ldr Ellis had used eighteen different pilots during the course of the three patrols, proof that he was doing his best to prevent tiredness from creeping into his men, just three of his pilots having flown all three sorties.

An interesting addendum to the day's action, is that the intelligence officer, F/O Walter Lloyd's, report 'Form F', to HQ Fighter Command from 11 Group's HQ on 24 August 1940, has survived the years (recorded as 24.9.40, instead of 24.8.40), seemingly the only such report to have done so in relation to 610 Squadron. It read as follows:

INTELLIGENCE PATROL REPORT. 610 Squadron 24.9.40.

9 Spitfires 610 Squadron left Biggin Hill at 1545 hours to intercept e/a over Gravesend. They saw about 20 Ju.88s in tight formations escorted by 20 Me.109s at 15,000 feet. An engagement took place about 15 to 30 miles North of the Isle of Sheppey.

Sgt. Hamlyn destroyed 2 Me.109s making his total five e/a destroyed in three different engagements to-day. P/O Merrick crashed at Fyfield and was taken to hospital at Ongar slightly wounded.

7 a/c landed at Biggin Hill from 1615 to 1645 hours. 1 a/c landed at Biggin Hill at 1715 hours.

8 a/c serviceable.

ENEMY CASUALTIES. Destroyed 4 Me.109s
Probable 1 Me. 109

OUR CASUALTIES. 1 Pilot wounded—P/O Merrick.
1 a/c unserviceable. (TNA, AIR 50/172/82)

The report provides extracts from the successful combat reports of Hamlyn (two destroyed), Norris (one destroyed), Baker (one destroyed) and Pegge (one probable). Although little additional information is gained from the above, it is interesting to see that this was the process—the pilots reported to their intelligence officer, he filed a report to 11 Group HQ, which was then sent to Fighter Command's HQ as a summary of the key events. Given that the Squadron had fought in three engagements, and only one is referenced here, it is unclear whether one was carried out by each squadron's intelligence officer per engagement, or per day; either way it was a lot of information to cypher through. We do learn from the above that the pilots did scramble from Biggin Hill on this operation, and one of them was airborne for a good half hour longer than the rest, although who this was and why is impossible to tell.

This seems to have been 610's final patrol of the day and so, although the Squadron had not lost any pilots killed, which was remarkable given such a hectic day of fighting, the unit had lost three to their wounds/injuries, none of whom could take any further action in the Battle, and at least four Spitfires were now unserviceable. On 1 August 1940, the Squadron had a complement of thirty pilots, eight of whom were on a Spitfire conversion course and would shortly return. However, by the end of 24 August, just three and a half weeks later, three pilots had been killed and five wounded and out of action, leaving a total of twenty-two pilots. This was still a high number of operational pilots for a unit to have during the Battle of Britain, and they were giving an excellent account of themselves. On 24 August alone, despite the losses, 610 was able to claim eight destroyed and two probables, all bar one of these being against the menacing single-engined Me 109. In overall terms, since the start of August, for the effective loss of eight pilots, the unit had claimed twenty-eight destroyed, six unconfirmed, eight probables and fifteen damaged, so despite the tragic losses, 610 Squadron was playing a vital role in the defence of the country.

It had been a particularly successful day for Sgt Hamlyn flying DW-Q, R.6891, whose feat attracted the attention of the Press—it even led to a radio interview describing his actions that day. The RAF was keen to highlight the efforts and success of its fighter pilots, and to date there had been few endeavours as noteworthy as that of Hamlyn having destroyed four Me 109s and a Ju 88 in a day. As Sgt Jimmy Corbin recalled when talking about joining 610 Squadron, 'One sergeant had got five Jerries in one day'.[17] Hamlyn had more than gained the respect of his peers as a fighter pilot, while he had earned the nickname of the 'Pied Piper of Harrogate' amongst the ground crew, following his numerous claims against the enemy. It also led to his award of the DFM, which had a humorous side to it, as Hamlyn remembered 24 August as much for, 'the official admonishment he also chalked up on that day, having landed a Spitfire wheels-up two months earlier. His conversation with a group captain on the subject of damaging the King's property had to be fitted in between scrambles'.[18] This crash seems to have dated back to his accident on 5 June, at the end of his time with 72 Squadron.

After a heavy day of fighting, the weary pilots would almost certainly have roused themselves for some drinks to celebrate Hamlyn's remarkable feat and also Douglas Corfe's twenty-second birthday—after his recent experiences he must have felt a lot older. Nevertheless, the celebrations would have been tempered by the knowledge that they would have to do it all over again the following day, as the *Luftwaffe* evidently was now targeting Fighter Command's aerodromes. Despite the need to celebrate their successes when the opportunity arose, the pilots had to be sure that they were as alert as possible the next day, given what was at stake—both their own lives and the future of the nation.

During the night of 24 August, an event occurred which had untold consequences not just for the Battle of Britain, but the way aerial warfare came to be waged later in the War. As the *Luftwaffe* continued its attack on England by night, bombs mistakenly fell on several districts of London, with nine people killed and fifty-eight injured. Göring was livid when he found out what had happened, as this was not part of Hitler's plans. This simple error by the *Luftwaffe's* crews, when Greater London had already been accidentally bombed on 15 August, unwittingly set in train the RAF's retaliatory raids on Berlin and other German cities. This in turn soon led to another change in tactics by the *Luftwaffe's* hierarchy in further retaliation; when the *Luftwaffe* switched its primary target from the RAF's aerodromes to London in early September, it crucially relieved the dangerous pressure on Fighter Command's bases and infrastructure. But, this vicious cycle of raid and counter-raid, would ultimately lead to nightly attacks on cities across Britain in the *Blitz* and the massive night time raids launched by Bomber Command, that devastated many German cities later in the war.

Ronald Hamlyn in the cockpit of a Spitfire, as an officer later in the war. (*Copyright 610 Squadron Association*)

17

25–31 August 1940: Relentless Scrambles for 'Dog Rose' Squadron

After 610 Squadron's exertions on the previous day, the pilots must have craved for a less frenetic day's flying on 25 August. The ground crew had worked miracles on the Spitfires overnight and by dawn on this Sunday morning, they were back up to an operational full strength. As was sometimes the case during these crucial summer days, the *Luftwaffe* obligingly got off to a slow start, also being in need of a brief respite from the strain of continuous operations. However, at 1700 hours, any fanciful thoughts that there might not be any raids to intercept were swept aside, as Ventnor RDF station, high on the cliffs of the Isle of Wight at St Boniface, plotted a massive formation of over 300 aircraft approaching between Swanage and Portland.

While Fighter Command's squadrons on the south coast were scrambled to deal with this raid, 610 Squadron's pilots waited anxiously at readiness for another call to action, much like their friends in 32 Squadron. Thanks to Sgt Else's logbook, we know that he was back flying with the Squadron, possibly after a brief period of leave, and that a twenty-five-minute patrol (38) to Hawkinge for a stint on readiness was carried out. His logbook noted that he was in his favoured aircraft, DW-L, P.9496, the return journey lasting the same time (39). As usual, 32 Squadron's ORB is much more detailed in terms of sorties carried out by its pilots, hinting at the possible activity of 610 Squadron; nine Hurricanes went to Hawkinge at 0825 hours, from where they carried out a patrol before returning to Biggin. This was repeated just before 1700 hours, this time by eight pilots—the Squadron's long spell in the front line was beginning to tell on pilots and aircraft serviceability alike.

Thanks to Else's logbook, we know 610 Squadron carried out a similar routine, both units ready at a moment's notice to go back into the fray. The waiting was interminable though, as Cyril 'Bam' Bamberger recalled:

> The most stressful thing in the Battle of Britain was sitting at readiness waiting for the scramble telephone bell to ring. I couldn't relax. You tried to read a book or you tried to play draughts or you pretended to doze. The phone would ring and immediately you jumped up but it was probably to say that the NAAFI van was coming with tea. Then you flopped back and tried to relax again.[1]

Even the hot summer days could make the waiting worse, as 'Bam' recollected: 'Every day seemed to be a nice sunny day during the Battle of Britain and people would lug these chairs out and sit outside. The sun didn't agree with me so I used to stay inside'.[2] Although it was getting late in the day for the *Luftwaffe* to start further operations, the long summer nights meant that there was still plenty of daylight left and sure enough, at about 1830 hours, another raid was forming over the French coast, before heading across towards Dover and Dungeness.

32 Squadron's eight Hurricanes had already taken off from Hawkinge between 1820 and 1830 hours, to patrol Dover. Else's logbook informs us that it is likely that 'The Chesters' were at Biggin Hill, but they

may well have been aware that their sister squadron had just been sent up, the twelve pilots on readiness wondering if their turn to scramble would come. As the raid droned relentlessly towards the coast, and its full extent was realised, the dreaded call came through to 'Dog Rose' Squadron's dispersal area, at 1852 hours. Yet again, the twelve Merlin engines were fired up; the pilots sprinted to their Spitfires, settled in their cockpits, before streaking off across the aerodrome and gaining altitude as quickly as possible. S/Ldr Ellis was at the head of his men, a formation composed of more battle-hardened pilots, just three of them, Sgts Beardsley, Bamberger and Willcocks, being novices. The Squadron battle order was composed as follows, with John Ellis as Blue 1, F/O Gardiner probably Green 1, leading 'B' Flight's two sections, F/Lt Norris as Red 1 leading 'A' Flight and F/O Lamb as Yellow Section's leader:

DW-W.	R.6993	S/Ldr. J. ELLIS.	Blue 1	48
DW-M.	K.9947	F/O. D. S. WILSON.		10
DW-N.	N.3124	SGT. RAMSAY, N. H. D.		30
DW-P.	P.9451*	F/O. F. T. GARDINER.	Green 1	26
DW-L.	P.9311	SGT. ELSE, P.		40
DW-O.	X.4011	SGT. BAMBERGER, C.**		15
DW-T.	X.4064	F/Lt. S. C. NORRIS.	Red 1	55
DW-Y.		SGT. PARSONS, C. A.		21
DW-E.	P.9433	SGT. WILLCOCKS, W.		4
DW-A.	R.6976	F/O. P. G. LAMB.	Yellow 1	46
DW-Q.	R.6891	SGT. HAMLYN, R. F.		36
DW-J.	R.6599	SGT. BEARDSLEY, R. B.	Yellow 3	2

*As ORB, but this was DW-R, K.9931.

**As ORB, but Bamberger's logbook records him flying in DW-O to forward base and back to Biggin Hill, fifty minutes in total (patrols 15 & 16). So he might not have been on this patrol.

As the pilots set course for the familiar skies above Dover, 32 Squadron was probably already engaging part of the 100-strong *Luftwaffe* formation. 32 Squadron intercepted twelve Do 215s and thirty-six Me 109s, shooting down one bomber and two fighters, while one Hurricane pilot survived uninjured having baled out, and one was listed as 'Missing' (32 ORB). It is likely that 610 had been ordered up slightly later in order to intercept any *Luftwaffe* fighters that planned to cover the withdrawing bombers, and their escorts running low on fuel. The Spitfires would also have been helping to protect RAF units like 32 Squadron, which were now pulling out of the combat, at their most vulnerable, low on ammunition, fuel and possibly damaged or with wounded pilots.

610's ORB recalled that in clear skies, with visibility at twenty miles, 'Red, Yellow, Blue and Green sections encountered 8 to 12 M.E.109s 5,000 ft. above them while flying at 22,000 ft. over Dover'. Although this was a dangerous situation to be in, aggressively, Ellis ordered his men to climb towards the enemy at full throttle, and shortly afterwards the two formations clashed. Else records a flight in his logbook, again in DW-L, P.9496, which is likely to have been this patrol, taking off from Biggin Hill, as his earlier entry showed that they had returned to the sector station. The only available combat report belongs to Sgt Beardsley, who thought they engaged about twenty Me 109s between Dover and Dungeness:

> I engaged one ME109 at approximately 20,000 ft. and at about 300 yds firing a short burst of between 10–15 rounds from each gun at the cockpit. The enemy A/C flicked on to its back and went into a vertical dive. The attack made was a beam attack. I saw the aircraft disappear into the clouds at about 7,000 ft. F/O LAMB confirms seeing this E/A crash. I was Yellow No.3 and F/O. LAMB was my leader. (TNA, AIR 50/172/10)

Here, Beardsley purely focused on his attack on the Me 109, but he had not had everything his own way, and he states in the report's opening section that his aircraft was damaged by an enemy fighter. Thankfully he was physically unhurt, and made it back in one piece. Upon landing, he filed his report with the intelligence officer, while the riggers, fitters and armourers swarmed over his Spitfire to assess the damage. It was noted that he had only fired approximately eighty rounds of ammunition, which made his sharp-shooting all the more impressive. Because Lamb had witnessed the German fighter crash, the twenty-year-old sergeant could claim the 109 as destroyed on his second recorded patrol.

As the pilots filtered back to Biggin Hill, it became clear that Beardsley's claim was the only one. However, during the course of the dogfight, the likely leader of Green Section, F/O Gardiner, who had already been wounded twice during the previous month and a half, found himself in trouble with some enemy fighters. As his Spitfire took hits, (K.9931, not P.9451 as listed in the ORB), he was forced to break off the combat and, 'crashed near SANDWICH & was taken to Waldershore [Waldershare] Hospital wounded' (ORB). Although the ORB makes no reference to it, Gardiner had actually been forced to bale out: '**K9931.** Shot down in combat with Bf 109s over Dover 7.20 p.m. Crashed and burned out on Stoneheap Farm near Northbourne. F/O F. T. Gardiner baled out slightly wounded admitted to Waldershare Hospital'.[3] Records released at The National Archives and in *Aeromilitaria* also agree that he was flying K.9931 (TNA, AIR 81/2794),[4] which had earlier been recorded as DW-R.

The AMCB file for this incident does not include a squadron leader's report, so there are still some gaps in what actually happened. However, there are two emergency medical services forms in the file, the first dated 25 August. This one states that he had been brought from Elvington, Dover, presumably to the Royal Victoria Hospital, Waldershare, suffering from burns to his right hand, second degree burns to his eyelid and a small shrapnel wound in right foot, and that, 'plane shot down in flames by enemy' (TNA, AIR 81/2794). The second form, dated 29 August, states that he had originally been sent from Eythorne, and was suffering 'Multiple wounds face chest limbs' (TNA, AIR 81/2794), which were now classed as serious. It is likely he would have been reunited with P/O Gray in Waldershare Hospital.

Gardiner had been transferred on 28 August, although it is unclear where he went. 610's ORB noted, '25th August, 1940, F/O. F.T.GARDINER (72100) posted to R.A.F. Station, Biggin Hill, on admission to Waldershaw [Waldershare] Hospital' (ORB), without mentioning another hospital. It is likely he had an extended spell in hospital due to his burns. Gardiner had certainly earned a rest from operational flying, being wounded three times during the course of twenty-six recorded operations, having claimed an Me 110 destroyed and an Me 109 as unconfirmed, (possibly another damaged on 20 July). The Squadron had again lost one of its more senior pilots in Fred Gardiner, who had flown his last patrol of the Battle of Britain.

It seems 610 Squadron, supported by the Spitfires of 616 Squadron, had engaged JG 26 led by the legendary Maj. Adolf Galland. The 109s claimed four Spitfires shot down, one by Galland himself, and it is likely that Gardiner was one of their victims, the other successful German pilots being Fw. Muller twice and Fw. Carl.[5] Once Gardiner had recovered, the young Irish flying officer went on to perform some light duties at Biggin Hill, and his experience would have been put to good use in a non-operational role, before returning to 610 Squadron before the year's end.

The last pilot to return from this operation was almost certainly Sgt Claude Parsons, who 'sighted a green streak in the water about 5 miles off DOVER at 1954 hours, he circled round until the pilot was picked up by a motor boat' (ORB). Given the coloured dye, this was probably a *Luftwaffe* airman, as German aircrew were fortunate to have this simple but effective device to aid their rescue. Parsons's keen eyesight had helped to save an unknown enemy airman from drowning in a true example of selflessness. Parsons had made himself a tempting target for any roving enemy fighters, but by circling the stranded man, he ensured his rescue.

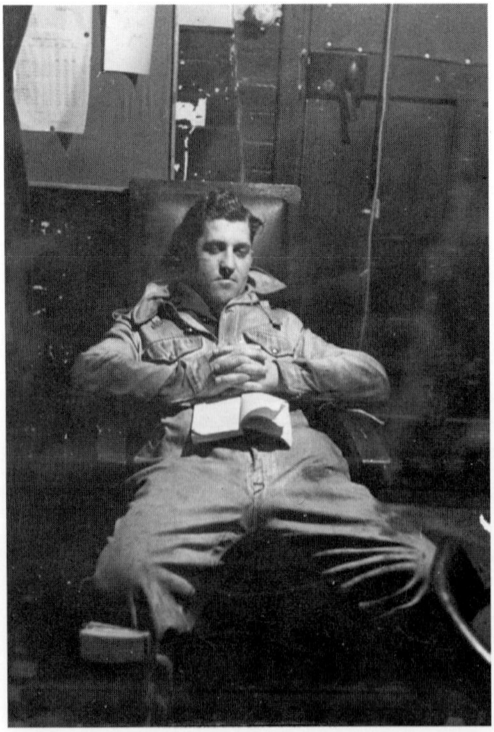

Although taken during the calm of 610's time at RAF Wittering, this photo depicts perfectly how the now S/Ldr John Ellis must have felt during the last few days of August, following such an extensive period in the front line. (*Copyright 610 Squadron Association*)

For 610 Squadron, honours had been even, with another combat-experienced pilot in Gardiner out of action, in exchange for the 109 claimed by Beardsley. With the loss of another pilot, John Ellis must have worried about his key pilots becoming too tired and combat-fatigued, which he would have felt himself after being in near constant action since late May. It was essential that such experienced men as Ellis, Stan Norris and Peter Lamb kept flying though, to provide leadership to the new pilots filling the gaps, and to ensure that German formations were intercepted by the most experienced pilots. There was a reason that these three were the only survivors from the original group of Dunkirk pilots—they were very good fighter pilots, and they simply had to try to keep on going.

The same applied to those who had joined in June, such as P/O Pegge and Sgts Hamlyn, Else and Parsons, who had all survived numerous operations in incredibly dangerous situations. As for the new recruits like Sgts Bamberger, Beardsley and P/O Webster, they would have to trust in their training, the advice passed on from the senior pilots and also hope that luck was on their side. The pilots knew that the dog-days of August would probably bring perfect weather to assist the *Luftwaffe's* mass raids, and so it was a matter of staying in the fight for as long as possible, without sustaining grievous losses. The Squadron had received no new recruits since 28 July, and as the casualties increased, now ten in August alone, so did the pressure on the remaining pilots. The margin between survival and success not just for 610 Squadron, but for each squadron in Fighter Command, was becoming increasingly narrow. A prime example was 32 Squadron, alongside which 610 had operated in the firing line for so long. On this patrol on 25 August, they were down to just eight Hurricanes and with their latest losses, the Squadron was struggling to put a flight in the air—something would have to give.

As dawn broke on 26 August, 610 Squadron's pilots would once again have been taken down to their dispersal areas, ready to endure the anxious wait for the call to scramble, but given the cloudy conditions, no mass raids of bombers and fighters were reported. Instead, a series of reconnaissance flights were seen approaching the coast, which the Observer Corp tried to track and report back to the nearest sector station once they came inland. Sgt Peter Else's logbook indicates that at some stage 610 Squadron was sent to Hawkinge, a twenty-five-minute flight with Else again in DW-L, P.9496, in readiness for the *Luftwaffe's* expected attacks. Else's logbook records a twenty-five-minute patrol from Hawkinge (41 & 42), although enemy aircraft were not encountered.

The CO again had a very experienced group of pilots ready for the day, with only Sgt Willcocks and P/O Webster having less than ten recorded patrols to their name. They would soon be in action, as over 150 *Luftwaffe* aircraft approached the Kent coast in the late morning. As this attack developed, nine RAF squadrons were ordered to intercept (TNA, AIR 25/197). One of them was 610 Squadron, the call coming through to their dispersal at Hawkinge at 1142 hours, with instructions to patrol the airfield and hopefully intercept a formation of Me 109s reportedly in the area.

The Spitfire pilots scurried to their machines as the dreaded routine was set in motion, Merlin engines sparking into life. With a flurry of activity involving ground crew and pilots alike, the Spitfires, which moments earlier were stock still, noses pointed towards the sky, quickly taxied over the bumpy ground of the patched-up airfield, before slipping off the turf, starting to form up and climb for altitude, their wheels clunking into the wells as they turned inland. On 25 August, AVM Park had officially noted to his controllers that Biggin Hill's squadrons were to climb inland first when operating out of Hawkinge, to avoid climbing out to sea under the enemy formations, thereby reducing the likelihood of being at a dangerous tactical disadvantage.

Ellis was leading the following men as Blue Leader:

DW-W.	R.6993	S/Ldr. J. ELLIS.	Blue 1	49
DW-N.	N.3124	SGT. RAMSAY, N. H. D.	Green 2	31
DW-X.		F/O. D. S. WILSON.	Blue 2	11
DW-M	K.9947*	SGT. ELSE, P.	Green 1	43
DW-O.	X.4011**	P/O. WEBSTER. H. K.***	Green 3	2
DW-T.	X.4064	F/Lt. S. C. NORRIS.	Red 1	56
DW-B.	X.4166	P/O. C. O. J. PEGGE.		25
DW-F.	X.4028	SGT. PARSONS, C. A.	Red 2	22
DW-A.	R.6976	F/O. P. G. LAMB.	Yellow 1	47
DW-Q.	R.6891	SGT. HAMLYN, R. F.	Yellow 2	37
DW-Y.		SGT. WILLCOCKS, W.		5

*As ORB, but was actually DW-L, P.9496.
**As ORB, but was actually DW-O, R.6595.
***As ORB, but Webster's initials were 'F. K.'.

The actual composition of the Squadron is difficult to decipher from the information available, as there is a lot of contradictory evidence. Normally, Ellis led 'B' Flight composed of Blue and Green Sections, while Stanley Norris led 'A' Flight as Red Leader, accompanied by Yellow Section. However, on this occasion Yellow Section seems to have been in formation with Blue Section, which had been mentioned on a couple of earlier patrols, while Ellis noted the sections operated in groups of four.[6]

Ellis was again possibly trying a new formation for the Squadron, more like the *Schwarm* used so successfully by their *Luftwaffe* counterparts, as it is noticeable that on this patrol several pilots worked in pairs. The ORB noted that Red, Yellow, Blue and Green Sections took part in the operation, adding to the confusion, as how did the four sections become three groups of four unless they were already in that formation? Another anomaly is that Ellis referred to twelve Spitfires yet there are only eleven logged on the ORB. The twelfth man may well have been Sgt Bamberger, as his logbook records three patrols (17–19) on 26 August, all in DW-U (no serial number), the first of which was a patrol of Dover for an hour, which would fit in.[7] So Ellis and Wilson were Blue 1 and 2, with Lamb and Hamlyn as Yellow 1 and 2. Norris was almost certainly Red 1 with Parsons as Red 2 and we also know Ramsay was Green 2. Else was probably Green 1 with Webster perhaps Green 3, Pegge as Red 3 and Willcocks Yellow 3, although these last three names do not tally with operating in pairs, and Pegge and Willcocks perhaps operated as another pair. This would only account for eleven pilots.

As the formation reached 'Angels 15' above Hawkinge, Ellis was ordered to intercept enemy fighters said to be operating at 22,000 feet over Dover. This immediately left Ellis and his men at a disadvantage and they would have been better advised to attain that altitude before getting so close to the enemy. However, 'Red, Yellow, Blue & Green sections engaged about 8 M.E.109s which were bombing FOLKESTONE at 5,000 ft' (ORB). There was, 'Cloud 10/10ths. at 6,000 ft—no cloud over Channel' (ORB). Ellis takes up the story in his usual style:

> I was leading 610 Sqdn. who were ordered to intercept enemy fighters at 22,000' over Dover. The Sqdn. climbed to 15,000' when enemy fighters were spotted both above us and below us. I ordered two sections of 4 a/c to deal with the fighters above while I took my section of 4 to attack the a/c bombing Folkestone from 5,000'. It looked to me as though the Me.109s were bombing as I saw no enemy bombers.
>
> I and my No2 attacked a pair of Me 109 from astern and above taking them both by surprise. Immediately after I had opened fire a large piece of exhaust manifold flew off the Me 109 and hit my wing. As I broke away I saw the e/a burst into flames and plunge into the sea 400 yds off the beach at Folkestone. This is confirmed by F/O D. S. Wilson. (TNA, AIR 50/172/22)

Although this report is dated 27 August, perhaps having been written up a day late, it definitely refers to this interception on 26 August, and once again shows Ellis's skill as a pilot and ability as a leader.

With his formation in the predicament of having enemy fighters both above and below him, he sensibly split up his force, sending eight aircraft to deal with the more dangerous top cover, before he led the remainder of his formation down on the six Messerschmitts below, which were taken by surprise. Having maintained formation with his wingman Wilson, John Ellis opened fire at close range, a single five second burst from 200 yards to just twenty yards, which devastated the unsuspecting German pilot's machine. Wilson had witnessed the 109's demise, so Ellis could make a 'conclusive' claim for his ten and a half confirmed victory of the conflict, eight of which had been against the much vaunted Messerschmitt 109, plus one shared destroyed, one unconfirmed and one damaged. Ellis was fortunate that the debris from the doomed *Luftwaffe* fighter did not do his Spitfire any lasting damage. The remarkable aspect of this combat is how quickly 610 Squadron engaged the enemy. The Squadron took off at 1142 hours and just thirteen minutes later Ellis was in the process of shooting down an Me 109. It was another example of how expert ground controlling, working in tandem with an excellent squadron leader commanding experienced pilots, could lead to a successful interception, even if they were in a dicey situation. Part of the strain the pilots underwent was that one minute they could be lounging on deckchairs in the sun outside their dispersal, but literally fifteen minutes later they could be at 15,000 feet and fighting for their lives.

Ellis had been followed into the attack over Folkestone by his faithful Number 2, F/O Wilson:

> As Blue 2 in the leading flight of 610 Squadron we were ordered at [blank] hours to patrol Hawkinge at 15,000 feet. When at about 12,000 feet the leader's attention was drawn to aircraft over Folkestone at about 6/7000 feet.
>
> He led his Section down giving them line astern. The leader chose one ME109 and saw it disintegrate and burst into flames. I followed on to another but first weaved to ensure that I wasn't being followed. The 109 took an evasive stall turn, and I gave it a deflection burst which appeared to hit. The 109 then went into a steep dive towards France and I gave a second burst and the aircraft started smoking and went right in. I saw no wreckage or pilot, merely the splash and rings.

> I then returned to Hawkinge and circled until recalled to home base. (TNA, AIR 50/172/74)

The thirty-four-year-old Wilson noted in his report's preamble, that he also believed these Messerschmitts had been bombing the coastal town. Ellis had ordered his section into the usual line astern, and it proved to be successful, with the RAF fighters enjoying complete surprise over the *Luftwaffe* formation.

Wilson had covered Ellis's tail while simultaneously lining up his own target, but it is interesting to note that he carried out a weave to check he was not about to be bounced; despite the risk of losing his target, the message of always checking your tail had been drilled home to the pilots. With two short bursts of ammunition of four and then three seconds in length, he brought the enemy aircraft down. There is a horribly bleak feeling to the sentence, 'I saw no wreckage or pilot, merely the splash and rings'—for how many aircrew had this been the epitaph already during the conflict? Wilson, the tall Scot, who had been with the Squadron since its early days, was able to claim his second Me 109 destroyed of the Battle.

It is unclear whether any other pilots made up Blue Section as they dived to attack the Messerschmitts, but Yellow Section, despite being part of 'A' Flight, seems to have been part of the force Ellis ordered to follow him down. The experienced F/O Lamb reported:

> I was yellow 1 flying in the Box of Blue Section.
>
> The Squadron Leader saw 6 109s below and to seaward as we were patrolling Hawkinge. We dived down to attack. As we were doing so I noted another bunch of 109s coming in behind us. I detached myself and attacked them head on. In the meleé that followed I noticed a parachute descending into the sea. I stayed with it until the pilot was picked up. I then noted balloons being shot down over Dover. I went over to investigate and happened to notice a Dornier flying home out to sea off Deal. It was coming in the opposite direction to me and some 1,000 ft below. I half rolled and came into astern position to deliver No. 1 attack. After a burst of about 8 secs the std [starboard] engine began smoking and rear gun fire ceased. The machine was losing height when last seen. The pilot of this was picked up 12 miles South of Dover. (TNA, AIR 50/172/45)

For Peter Lamb, the wisdom of always checking his six o'clock position had paid off, as the veteran spotted the enemy top cover coming down on them from behind. By attacking them head-on, he enabled Blue Section to successfully continue their attack. Just like Claude Parsons in the previous patrol, Lamb broke off from the dogfight to ensure the safety of an unknown pilot vulnerably descending into the sea, presumably none the wiser as to his nationality. Rumours abounded of pilots being machine-gunned as they floated helplessly earthwards, and in leaving himself open to attack in the midst of a raging dogfight, it suggests that Lamb felt such rumours were true, while highlighting Lamb's gallantry.

Following the mystery pilot's rescue, at about 1230 hours Lamb's keen eyes picked out the lone Dornier against the bluey-green of the English Channel, and he immediately engaged it using a tactic which had been drilled into him before the war. The No. 1 attack was carried out in textbook fashion, as Lamb fired an eight second hail of ammunition into it from 200 to just seventy-five yards. Despite the often inadequate power of the eight Browning .303 machine guns against German bombers, Lamb's aim proved fatal. While he broke off the engagement uncertain of the outcome, the fate of the German aircraft was confirmed by its fortunate pilot being rescued twelve miles off Dover. It had been Lamb's fourth recorded operation in three days, during which he had shot down two German aircraft to add to two previously shared destroyed. The experience he had gained since the first engagements over Dunkirk was paying off, and as one of the senior pilots, he was becoming increasingly vital to the Squadron's efforts.

Sgt Ronnie Hamlyn, another lynchpin of the Squadron, was Lamb's Number 2. Hamlyn must still have been flushed from his success two days previously, and proceeded to carry on from where he had left off:

> I was Yellow 2. We were flying at 12,000 to 15,000 feet when the leader turned and dived towards Folkestone. I followed and at about 9,000 feet I saw an ME109, I attacked it with two long bursts and saw it start to smoke and turn downwards. Just then I noticed another ME109 to the left of me just coming out of a dive at about 3,000 feet. I turned and came up astern and underneath it. The first burst I did not notice any results, but the second a very long one set the cockpit on fire, and before I broke away I noticed the whole of the fuselage was in flames. It went straight down into the sea about a mile off Folkestone. Sgt. Parsons, Red 2, saw and confirms this. (TNA, AIR 50/172/35)

In this dogfight which took place at 1155 hours, Hamlyn claimed his fifth confirmed Me 109 as it had been witnessed by Sgt Parsons, while his first target was declared a probable. He had used up all his ammunition, firing long bursts from 250 yards with lethal results.

The group of Messerschmitts at lower altitude had been dealt with fairly roughly by the Squadron's Spitfires, with three, possibly four of the six being shot down, but this was the formation over which the Spitfires had the advantage of height, speed and surprise. The same could not be said for the eight Spitfire pilots who had been detailed to engage the Messerschmitts flying above them as top cover, presumably led by Stanley Norris as Red 1. They faced a much tougher proposition in defending both themselves and their colleagues below from the dreaded bounce. The only surviving combat report from these pilots belonged to Sgt Norman Ramsay, now a battle-hardened veteran on his thirty-first recorded patrol. Ramsay, flying in Green Section as part of 'B' Flight, described what happened at 1155 hours:

> I was Green 2, and we were flying at 12,000 feet when the leading section dived to attack some E/A over Folkestone. My leader saw aircraft above and did not follow down. He ordered 'line astern' and started turning in a circle. I saw the E/A coming down at different angles, one came down astern with me. I turned very steeply to the left, and eventually got on to his tail, he started turning left and right and I fired three short bursts. On the last burst he emitted a cloud of black smoke and started spiralling down very fast. As he went down the smoke ceased and he vanished into the cloud looking very much out of control. I did not go through the cloud immediately because I wanted to see if there were any more E/A near me. There were some above, but I decided they were too high so I went through the clouds and saw an E/A blazing on the ground West of Folkestone. (TNA, AIR 50/172/63)

In the combat report's preamble, Ramsay stated that they were faced with twenty Me 109s, which explains why S/Ldr Ellis split his force as he did. It is of interest that Ramsay's section leader, probably Sgt Else, ordered his section to adopt line astern before starting to turn in a circle. This was a *Luftwaffe* tactic the pilots frequently encountered, particularly resorted to by Messerschmitt 110s when they found themselves at a disadvantage and were trying to withdraw for home. Green Section certainly found themselves in an unenviable situation here, being at a real tactical handicap. Provided the aircraft could maintain their formation, each aircraft could cover the tail of that in front of him in a follow-my-leader circle—in theory at least. It would suggest that once again the Squadron was adopting different tactics, mimicking those the pilots found to be effective for the enemy, to increase their own chances of survival.

One can imagine the Me 109s coming down on the circling Spitfires, twenty-one-year-old Ramsay drenched with sweat as he fought for his life. It was a terrifying position to be in, but he had to rely on his training and experience to stay alive. The multiple attacks from above by the swarm of 109s forced Ramsay to tighten his turn, to keep his tail clear and then engage one of the enemy fighters to prevent the Spitfires beneath him being attacked. However, this broke up the defensive circle and left both him and his colleagues who were engaging the enemy top cover vulnerable. Ramsay successfully stayed with the 109, despite the German pilot's best efforts and in firing off two seconds worth of ammunition from 250 yards, he hit the 109 with an effective burst. Ramsay exhibited wise caution, checking for enemy aircraft before trying to ascertain the fate of his target. As a result, Norman Ramsay could only claim a probable Me 109, but at least he had survived to fight another day.

However, as aircraft started to fall from the sky, sadly amongst those plunging earthwards were Spitfires with the distinctive DW code adjacent to the super-sized roundels, signifying aircraft of the County of Chester Squadron. Once the surviving pilots had returned to base at around 1240 hours, it became apparent that two of their number had failed to return, the evidence indicating they had been part of the formation detailed to engage the Me 109s above them.

Sgt Else was, as usual, in Green Section and given the other pilots on patrol, it is logical that he was flying as Green 1 (Norris, Parsons and Pegge were all usually 'A' Flight, so probably Red Section, while Webster and Willcocks were too inexperienced to lead a section). If so, Else, possibly following Norris's lead with Red Section, ordered his section into line astern and to circle in an attempt to protect themselves and the four Spitfires below. As Sgt Ramsay observed, once they came under increased attack from different angles, the defensive circle broke as the Spitfire pilots tightened their turns and tried to engage the onrushing enemy aircraft. Just as Ramsay had latched onto an Me 109, so it seems did Peter Else, but the action did not go anywhere nearly as well for Else. Thanks to Dave Brocklehurst's help, it has been possible to work out in some detail what happened to Sgt Else, in the pilot's own words. The twenty-three-year-old VR's final entry for August 1940 in his logbook, provides the basic grim details as follows: 'ATTACKED ENEMY A/C. SHOT DOWN FROM BEHIND. IN FLAMES. ABANDONED A/C BY PARACHUTE RECEIVING WOUNDS CAUSING SUBSEQUENT AMPUTATION OF LEFT ARM ALSO BURNS. STOPPED FLYING.'[8]

These terse sentences completely understate the terror and horror of this dogfight for Else, which ultimately left him maimed and burnt for life. His AMCB file, released on 30 June 2017, described him as 'dangerously ill', from shock, lacerations and burns (TNA, AIR 81/2784), and his wife must have been urgently informed of the devastating news. It is impossible to imagine what Peter Else must have felt in the immediate aftermath of his wounds. In a newspaper article published as part of the 50th Anniversary of the Battle, Else recalled what happened in further detail:

> The morning of 'that day'—August 26, 1940—dawned bright and sunny. Sergeant Pilot Peter Else and his Squadron of Spitfires were scrambled from Hawkinge airfield on the Kent coast, to intercept yet another raid by German bombers and fighters.
>
> 'We were soon mixing it with the Luftwaffe, and I was on the tail of a Messerschmitt 109, pumping a burst of machine gun fire into him,' Mr Else recalls.
>
> He was sure he had struck his target—but then came a shout in his earphones from one of the other Spitfire pilots, telling him there was a German fighter on his tail.
>
> 'I suddenly felt a thump in the Spitfire just behind the cockpit, and the whole instrument panel disappeared in a sea of flame.'
>
> When he tried to get the cockpit hood open, it jammed. He managed to get his left arm out, but then came another burst of gunfire, and the arm fell, useless, to his side.
>
> 'I knew I must get out, and to this day I do not know how I did it. I found myself at 25,000 feet above the Channel somersaulting over and over. My left arm was just hanging in my flying jacket and my right hand was caught under the parachute straps, so I could not pull the cord to open it. Then I was not sure if the parachute had been burned away. So I prayed for help—and it worked. The parachute opened.'

> Mr Else had good reason to fear that his troubles were still only beginning. He saw an aircraft approaching, and at first thought it was the German pilot returning to finish him off. But it was another Spitfire, which circled round for a while, protecting him.[9] Even so, Mr Else was certain he would drift into the sea—wearing a jacket which, though designed to keep him afloat, was full of holes where it was burned away.
>
> **Hope**
>
> 'So I said another prayer, and hoped it would be heard.'
>
> Mr Else is sure it was—because his parachute drifted towards Folkestone, and miraculously, he saw Hawkinge airfield in the distance.
>
> 'I drifted down over the airfield and actually landed less than 200 yards away from where I had taken off a few minutes before,' he said.[10]

Else was taken to the Kent and County Hospital in Canterbury, for treatment of the burns to his hands and face. His left arm was also amputated above the elbow.

It is clear that Else had attacked the top cover he had been ordered to engage by Ellis, but in concentrating on his target had failed to spot another 109 closing in, before suffering from its lethal armament at close range. It was a miracle Else baled out and survived given both the traumatic shock he suffered from his injury and his loss of blood—it was often almost impossible to bale out uninjured, never mind having been so badly maimed. Else was a sitting duck when the second burst of fire hit him as he was about to bale out, his aircraft already doomed. The German fighter pilot was clearly making sure that this Spitfire and its pilot would not take to the skies again, indicating the brutal nature of the combat above 'Hellfire Corner'. It really was a 'kill or be killed' environment. In taking that second burst of fire, the Messerschmitt pilot was unnecessarily leaving himself at risk of being attacked, again indicating what a determined attack Else had to endure. There is a tendency to view aerial combat as a chivalrous, almost 'clean' form of combat, unsullied by the horrors of ground warfare, the combat being machine-versus-machine. Time and again, the pilots themselves referred to how they felt they were bringing down enemy aircraft and not the crew inside. But the armament aboard both fighters and bombers was designed to bring down machines, so the impact it had on the aircrew did not bear thinking about, as borne out by Sgt Else's ghastly, life-changing wounds.

Thanks to Else's logbook, there is no confusion over which aircraft he was flying, which was DW-L, P.9496, (the ORB inaccurately recorded him as flying DW-M, K.9947). This is also confirmed in his AMCB file, which states that P.9496 was 'destroyed by impact and fire' at Cole Farm, Paddlesworth, at approximately 1210 hours (TNA, AIR 81/2784). However, it transpired that P.9496's crash site had caused some confusion, primarily because Sgt Else was convinced he saw it go down into the English Channel. In around 1979–80, Dave Brocklehurst and two others did a hand dig of the crash site of a Spitfire which turned out to be that of Sgt Else. As Peter Else slowly descended under his parachute, it is likely the aircraft he saw going into the Channel was a different one from his own, as it was now possible to irrefutably prove that the aircraft at the crash site they had dug, was indeed Sgt Else's, much to the pilot's amazement.

So 610 Squadron had lost another pilot to his wounds, as the ORB recorded in its usual blunt style: '741332 SGT./PILOT ELSE,P. admitted to Kent & Canterbury Hospital—injuries received due to enemy action, & posted to R.A.F. Station, Biggin Hill, non-effective sick'. Else faced a long period of recuperation, as if the amputation was not enough to cope with, he had been badly burnt. This is evident in the newspaper article where Else records his recovery and subsequent departure from the RAF:

> Months of agonising treatment followed for his serious burns. Surgeons removed the rest of his left arm. Then came his discharge from the RAF.
>
> 'They gave me a suit, a ration book and thirty shillings (£1.50) without a word of thanks, and I was back in Civvy Street,' said Mr Else.

Above: Else standing next to Spitfire, DW-L, P.9496, his regular mount in which he was shot down on 26 August 1940. (*Cambridge Evening News*, 6 July 1990)

Right: Sgt Peter Else. (*Copyright Cambridge Evening News, 6 July 1990*)

> But he was not unemployed for long—Marshall's offered him back his old job as an engineer, repairing war damaged aircraft. Soon afterwards he was back in the cockpits of those planes—flying them with the aid of a special left 'arm' designed and made by his colleagues. And he remained in a top engineering job with Marshall's until his retirement … at the age of 70.[11]

It is testament to Else's bravery and determination that he went on to recover from his injury and burns, even to fly again. Peter Else died of a heart attack in Addenbrooke's Hospital in 1991.[12]

He had become an experienced fighter pilot when he was shot down on his forty-third recorded patrol with 610, having flown with the unit throughout the opening stages of the Battle in July, and the increasingly heavy fighting of August, with 136 hours and forty-five minutes on Spitfires, many more hours than the newer recruits like Claude Merrick. Else had claimed one destroyed and one shared destroyed, one unconfirmed and four damaged. But for all his experience, it showed again that anyone could be caught out—a split second too long chasing an enemy aircraft without checking your own tail, could cost you so very dear. But it also came down to luck. The eight covering Spitfires were heavily outnumbered given Ramsay's description of facing twenty Me 109s, and it was as much luck as Ramsay's skill that he survived unscathed, while Peter Else's life was irrevocably changed. Unhappily, Sgt Else was not the only loss, and while experienced pilots such as Else could be shot down, it was indisputable that inexperienced pilots on their first few operations were the most vulnerable, this patrol being a case in point.

Despite the difficulty in working out who was flying in which section on this patrol, P/O Frank Webster, on just his second recorded patrol, was definitely in Green Section, probably as Green 3. He had been with the Squadron for twenty-nine days and flown his first recorded patrol in combat two days earlier, when he survived a sharp engagement with a formation of Me 109s. Novice fighter pilots naturally found their first few combats a blur of whirling aeroplanes, as they desperately tried to stay with their leader and simply stay alive. Webster would have gone into line astern behind Else and Ramsay and started to circle, trying to keep an eye on the enemy fighters above. Once the 109s dived down to attack and the circle split, it became every man for himself and the twenty-six year old would have been vulnerable as he tried to identify the aircraft around him. Just as 610 Squadron's veterans were quick to pick out stragglers in *Luftwaffe* formations, the same applied to the experienced *Luftwaffe* pilots, and as the Messerschmitts dived down, it is probable that one of them singled out Webster's Spitfire, DW-O, R.6595, assuming he was shot down. Whatever happened high in the skies over Folkestone, the ORB stated that 'P/O. Webster's A/C caught fire on crashing at HAWKINGE, the pilot being killed'. This short sentence suggests that he may have been trying to coax his badly damaged Spitfire back to his airfield, replicating the situation which had cost S/Ldr Tom Smith his life a month earlier. This has certainly been the picture built up by various publications, however, Dave Brocklehurst, chairman of the Kent Battle of Britain Museum, knew that this image was far from the truth.

Brocklehurst helped dig the crash site of Webster's Spitfire in the mid-1980s, the site having originally been excavated in about 1974. The fact that there was a major crash, some twelve feet into the ground, and the Spitfire had been crushed by the impact, meant that the aircraft had fallen from a great height, straight into the earth; Webster had not been attempting to land his damaged aircraft. The remains of Webster's Spitfire, DW-O, R.6595, along with some personal affects found in the cockpit, are on display in the Kent Battle of Britain Museum, to commemorate his tragically short life. They serve as a poignant reminder of the pilot, who died in defence of his country. DW-O, R.6595,[13] which had been depicted in the famous series of photographs (see p. 381) and had survived so much of the air fighting over south-eastern England, was finally lost on 26 August 1940.

P/O Webster's AMCB file was one of those released shortly before the publication of this book, and it has provided some extra additional information. S/Ldr Ellis's report was written a month later on 29 September, and some of the details seem to have been confused. In his combat report, Ellis clearly ordered two sections of four to stay as top cover, while his section of four engaged the low-flying enemy, which is corroborated in other combat reports. This flying battle casualty report states the opposite (see p. 381). However, it does confirm that Webster was in Green Section and that his Spitfire dived vertically down straight into the ground from around 16,000 feet, as believed by Dave Brocklehurst. Although Ellis notes that Webster was shot down during the engagement with the enemy fighters, the final statement, 'His aircraft appeared to be undamaged before the crash', seems a little strange, although probably meant that Webster was not suffering from any obvious technical issues. It seems most likely that Webster had been killed at the controls of his Spitfire, before crashing into the Kent countryside.

The file also contains the various telegrams *en clair* from 610 Squadron to the Air Ministry about Webster's death. The first, sent at 1330 hours on 26 August, states the Spitfire was lost at 1210 hours, the identity of the pilot and machine being unknown. A second telegram, sent at 1850 hours, had identified the Spitfire as R.6595, while P/O Webster was listed as 'Missing', the crash taking place at approximately 1200 hours. Telegrams were sent to Frank Webster's wife and mother on the morning of 27 August, informing them that he was 'Missing' as a result of air operations on 26 August. A third telegram from 610 Squadron, received at 1315 hours by the Air Ministry on 27 August, confirmed that Webster had been killed. This in turn meant that Webster's wife in London and mother on the Isle of Wight, were again contacted with the dreadful news on the afternoon of 29 August.

Another of the famous photos taken of 610 Squadron on patrol at the end of June 1940, the leading Spitfire, DW-O, R.6595, being flown by John Ellis. It is hard to imagine that this is the very same aircraft in which P/O Frank Webster was killed two months later. (*Copyright Imperial War Museum, CH 740*)

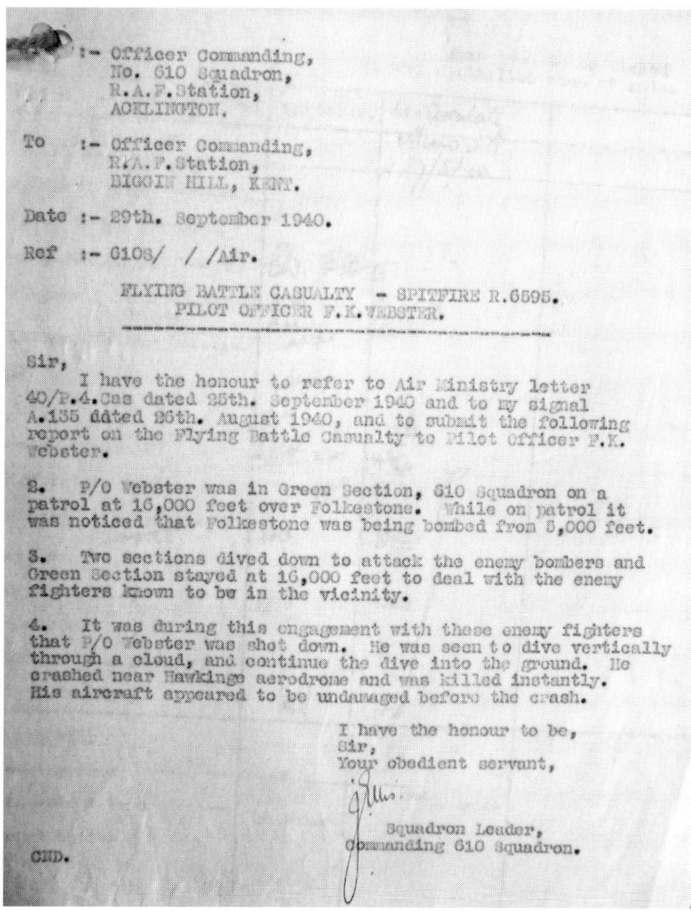

:- Officer Commanding,
No. 610 Squadron,
R.A.F.Station,
ACKLINGTON.

To :- Officer Commanding,
R.A.F.Station,
BIGGIN HILL, KENT.

Date :- 29th. September 1940.

Ref :- 610S/ / /Air.

FLYING BATTLE CASUALTY - SPITFIRE R.6595.
PILOT OFFICER F.K.WEBSTER.

Sir,

I have the honour to refer to Air Ministry letter 40/P.4.Cas dated 25th. September 1940 and to my signal A.135 dated 26th. August 1940, and to submit the following report on the Flying Battle Casualty to Pilot Officer F.K. Webster.

2. P/O Webster was in Green Section, 610 Squadron on a patrol at 16,000 feet over Folkestone. While on patrol it was noticed that Folkestone was being bombed from 8,000 feet.

3. Two sections dived down to attack the enemy bombers and Green Section stayed at 16,000 feet to deal with the enemy fighters known to be in the vicinity.

4. It was during this engagement with these enemy fighters that P/O Webster was shot down. He was seen to dive vertically through a cloud, and continue the dive into the ground. He crashed near Hawkinge aerodrome and was killed instantly. His aircraft appeared to be undamaged before the crash.

I have the honour to be,
Sir,
Your obedient servant,

J Ellis

Squadron Leader,
Commanding 610 Squadron.

CHD.

S/Ldr Ellis's report on the death of P/O Webster, a month after he was killed. (*TNA, AIR 81, 2814*)

Frank Webster, right, photographed at Hove, before he had gained his 'Wings'. (*Copyright After the Battle*)

Webster was buried on the Isle of Wight, in Sandown Cemetery, Lake. I visited his grave on a damp summer's day, and it was refreshing to see that children from the local Broadlee primary school tend to the grave, which was covered in flowers. It was a reminder of the importance of making sure even the very young of today are aware of the sacrifices made for their future, by so many during the Second World War. Frank Webster was buried in the same grave as his father, Captain Webster. The simple word 'Sunset' on the headstone is a moving epitaph for the pilot whose sad end was typical of so many inexperienced RAF pilots that summer, who paid the ultimate sacrifice for their country and beliefs.

A very poignant letter from Frank Webster's mother to his former headmaster survives in Bedford Modern School's archives, see page 383.

It must have been particularly sad news for Mr Liddle, who had exchanged letters with Frank about the state of Nazi Germany in the late 1930s, following his business trips to Germany with Messrs. Bourne and Hollingsworth and about Frank's wish to join the RAFVR. Liddle could never have imagined what fate had in store for his old pupil within nineteen months. Despite Webster's mother's grief, one can sense her pride in her son bravely defending the nation 'with no regrets'. Five days later, a death notice appeared in *The Isle of Wight County Press* (see photo p. 383), providing an interesting obituary to the young pilot officer's tragically short life.

From the Squadron's point of view, they had lost another experienced pilot to serious wounds and another killed in action, devastating news once it filtered back to Biggin Hill, despite the unit's success, having claimed four destroyed and two probable; but by now the men had become accustomed to such bad news. There is also mention in some sources of another Spitfire having come down on Castle Hill: '**R6970.** Shot down in combat with Bf 109s over Folkestone 12.40 p.m. Crashed and burned out at Castle Hill, Hawkinge. Pilot believed unhurt. **DW-M** a write-off'.[14] This is supported in the *Aeromilitaria* series, which records that R.6970 joined 610 on 19 August and was damaged on 26 August, before being sent to Heston Aircraft on 13 September 1940 for repairs.[15]

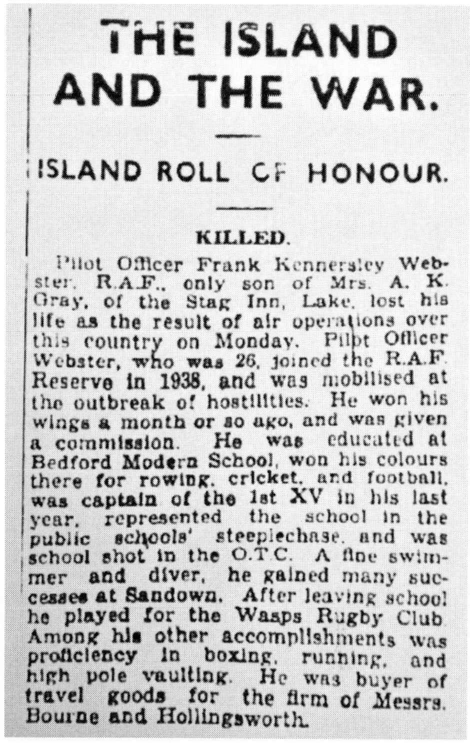

THE ISLAND AND THE WAR.

ISLAND ROLL OF HONOUR.

KILLED.

Pilot Officer Frank Kennersley Webster, R.A.F., only son of Mrs. A. K. Gray, of the Stag Inn, Lake, lost his life as the result of air operations over this country on Monday. Pilot Officer Webster, who was 26, joined the R.A.F. Reserve in 1938, and was mobilised at the outbreak of hostilities. He won his wings a month or so ago, and was given a commission. He was educated at Bedford Modern School, won his colours there for rowing, cricket, and football, was captain of the 1st XV in his last year, represented the school in the public schools' steeplechase, and was school shot in the O.T.C. A fine swimmer and diver, he gained many successes at Sandown. After leaving school he played for the Wasps Rugby Club. Among his other accomplishments was proficiency in boxing, running, and high pole vaulting. He was buyer of travel goods for the firm of Messrs. Bourne and Hollingsworth.

Above left: P/O Frank Kinnersley Webster's final resting place, aged twenty-six, at Sandown Cemetery. (*Author*)

Above right: Article from 31 August 1940, p. 3. (*Copyright The Isle of Wight County Press Archive*)

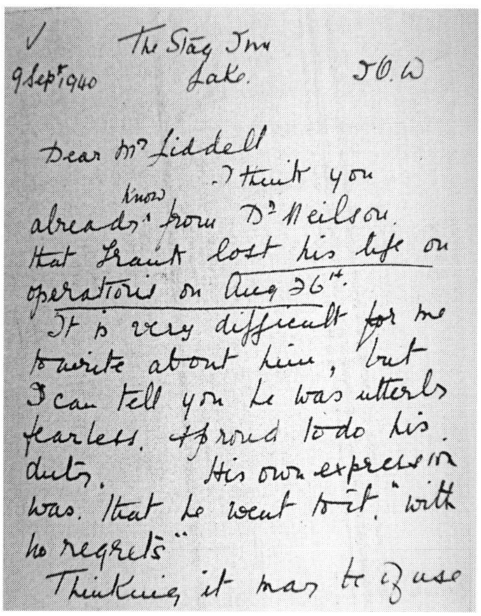

✓ The Stag Inn
9 Sept 1940 Lake. I.O.W

Dear Mr Liddell
I think you know already from Dr Neilson that Frank lost his life on operations on Aug 26th.
It is very difficult for me to write about him, but I can tell you he was utterly fearless & proud to do his duty. His own expression was, that he went to it "with no regrets"
Thinking it may be of use

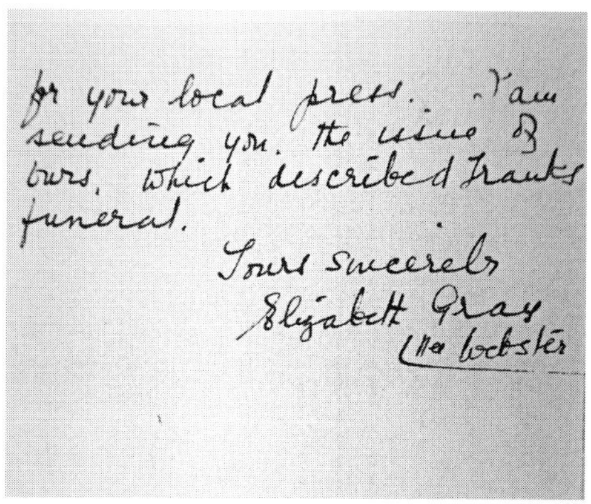

for your local press. I am sending you the issue of ours, which described Frank's funeral.
Yours sincerely
Elizabeth Gray
(Mrs Webster

Above and left: Letter written by Webster's mother. (*Reproduced with permission of Bedford Modern School Archive*)

However, R6970 is not listed in the ORB as being part of the patrol. Given that K.9947 had been operating as DW-M, it seems likely that R.6970 was damaged in September, hence the time of it being sent to Heston. While some believe the pilot of this aircraft may have been F/O Lamb, it seems unlikely as there is no mention of it in his detailed combat report. A crash-landing would almost certainly have been mentioned, as more often than not the pilots reported any damage to their aircraft. The ORB only lists eleven Spitfires as having taken part, and does not include R.6970, however Ellis states there were three sections of four Spitfires. Perhaps the one which crash-landed at Castle Hill was the twelfth, and was forgotten about when the ORB was being written up, it is unlikely we will ever know.

Given their predicament with enemy fighters above and below them, 610's pilots had yet again acquitted themselves well and could be proud of their efforts. This one combat encapsulates the importance of height in a dogfight, with the Spitfires which dived down on the lower group of Me 109s having real success, while the Squadron's losses were suffered by the pilots who in turn found themselves being attacked from above by enemy fighters. This is confirmed when none of Red Section's pilots, presumably part of 610's top cover alongside Green Section, could file a claim against the *Luftwaffe* fighters, despite probably involving Stanley Norris, Joe Pegge and Claude Parsons, all experienced men. It is likely that one of the Me 109s which had been shot down belonged to, '**3/JG52** Messerschmitt Bf 109E-1. Shot down by No. 610 Squadron fighters during action over the Channel off Dover 11.55 a.m. Crashed in sea. Fw. Ziegler rescued by shore boat and captured. Aircraft lost.'[16]

The second big raid of the day in the North Foreland—Thames Estuary Area was met by 11 Squadrons, including 610 Squadron, as indicated in '11 Group's Intelligence Bulletin No. 37, Part 1' (TNA, AIR 25/197). Although the Squadron's ORB does not mention the second patrol, 'The Chesters' carried out a patrol between 1500 and 1615 hours, but did not make contact with the *Luftwaffe*. (This was almost certainly one of the other two patrols which Bamberger carried out.) The day's third major raid was in the Southampton—Portsmouth area, which did not involve 610 Squadron, and as late afternoon merged into dusk, the pilots realised they were not going back up. Gradually they would have started to relax, tried to wind down, and once released from readiness returned to their respective messes, before some perhaps headed off to The White Hart in Brasted, to try and forget the war for a few hours.

The following morning, Tuesday 27 August, the weather had taken a turn for the worse, much to the relief of 610 Squadron's pilots and Fighter Command as a whole, particularly Park and Dowding, who took the opportunity to rotate some of the more battle-weary squadrons from the front line. One of these was 32 Squadron which had shared Biggin Hill with 610 Squadron for so long, a bond having developed between the two squadrons, Brian Smith recalling how 'they were very good to us' and 'excellent people'. Following 32 Squadron's last patrol on 26 August, the surviving pilots were to head north on 27 August for rest, recuperation and to train new pilots, passing on the knowledge they had gained in the hope of giving the replacements a fighting chance.

They were classed as a Category 'C' Squadron in Dowding's new plan to rotate squadrons and pilots in and out of the heaviest fighting in 11 Group. There were three of these categories: 'A' Squadrons were based in 11 Group, along with those in 10 and 12 Groups which would be the first to provide support to 11 Group when required—these squadrons would be kept at full strength with more experienced pilots; Category 'B' Squadrons were kept in reserve in 10 and 12 Groups, but with a number of fully trained, experienced pilots; Category 'C' Squadrons, as mentioned above, were removed to 13 Group in the north, well away from the front line, to rest and also train replacement pilots for the Category 'A' Squadrons. They would maintain a handful of experienced pilots to train the replacements in air combat, and once the majority of veteran pilots had recuperated, they too could be sent back to 11 Group.

32 Squadron was to be replaced by 79 Squadron, also operating Hurricanes, as can be seen from the two units' record books. On 27 August, 32 Squadron was, 'Under orders to proceed by air to Acklington

on arrival of No. 79 Squadron from Acklington' (32 ORB). However, the bad weather which had prevented the *Luftwaffe* from continuing its raids, even played havoc with Fighter Command's attempt to rotate its Squadrons, 79 Squadron's ORB stating, '79 Squadron Ordered to move to Biggin Hill. Aircraft and 32 men only. 12.15 15 Hurricanes took off for Biggin Hill landed at Hucknal [Hucknall] on the way, due to weather' (79 ORB). So 32 Squadron's weary pilots had to endure another day in the front line, although they would not carry out another patrol.

The day also throws up a couple of anomalies for 610 Squadron, particularly the fact that the death of P/O Webster is recorded as having happened on this day, 'as a result of a flying accident. Due to enemy action' (ORB). This can only be put down to a clerical error during the trying times all personnel at Biggin Hill endured, as Webster evidently died on 26 August 1940. Another discrepancy which appears in a couple of history books, is that S/Ldr Ellis claimed an He 111 destroyed near Cranbrook at 1245 hours. With no combat report to support the claim, it is likely this Heinkel has become confused with the one he shot down over Cranbrook on 18 August, and should be ignored, especially as the ORB does not record a patrol or encounter with the *Luftwaffe* on 27 August.[17] Even more confusing is that Ellis had a combat report noted as 27 August, but that seems to have been another clerical error, as this was actually the combat which took place the day before, against the Me 109s. All very confusing!

Following this unexpected day of relative rest, Fighter Command must have expected a flurry of activity on Wednesday 28 August. Although there were clouds over the Channel, the weather was fairly good for the *Luftwaffe* to go back on the offensive, an opportunity which was quickly taken. The usual early morning reconnaissance missions were carried out by lone German aircraft, followed up by a raid between 0830 and 1145 hours, which 610 Squadron was not required to intercept. Following 79 Squadron's enforced overnight stop at Hucknall airfield, just north of Nottingham, S/Ldr Heyworth would have been keen to get his men down to Biggin Hill as early as possible, before any *Luftwaffe* incursions took place. The fifteen Hurricanes must have swept in to Biggin Hill very early, as by 0825 hours they were on their first interception since returning to 11 Group, making claims of four probably destroyed, with one Hurricane being damaged (79 ORB). Now 32 Squadron could finally leave the sector; all their aircraft took off at 1300 hours on 28 August, 'On relief by No. 79 Squadron from Acklington. Arrived Acklington 1440 hours' (32 ORB). 32 Squadron, still under S/Ldr Crossley's command, had more than earned their rotation from the front line, having been in the midst of the action since Dunkirk. The remaining pilots must have been completely exhausted, with nothing more to give. 79 Squadron, which had flown from Biggin Hill pre-war, would now share operational duties from Biggin Hill with 610 Squadron.

The main raids of the day were composed chiefly of Me 109s and Me 110s, some of which flew at the speed of bombers, to try and lure the RAF up into a mass fighter-versus-fighter combat, when the Germans felt they had the advantage. Some of 79 Squadron were soon back in action, 'At 11.00 hours Flight took off from Hawkinge to intercept 2 He.59 Floatplanes, escorted by 3 Me.110s. 1 He. 59 was shot down by F/Lt. Clerke. **11.30** 4 aircraft of B Flight were ordered to patrol base and 1 He.59 was probably destroyed' (79 ORB). This was part of the second raid of the day, from between 1129 and 1345 hours, but 610 Squadron still had not been ordered off by the early afternoon, or at least had not encountered the enemy. 'Bam' Bamberger's logbook records four sorties on 28 August, and it seems likely that the first two of these took place in the morning/early afternoon. He was flying DW-U (no serial number), for a patrol to Dover (thirty minutes) and a patrol to Hawkinge (forty-five minutes) (22 & 23). The pilots again must have wondered if they were going to be lucky enough to have a second day without combat. However, a day of heavy fighting meant that few, if any squadrons could be spared and 28 August was no exception.

The third large raid started to build up over France and head towards England in the middle of the afternoon, involving mainly fighter sweeps across Kent at high altitude. Park responded by sending six squadrons to try and intercept. One of these units was the County of Chester Squadron, the order to scramble coming through at 1530 hours, and twelve Spitfires led by S/Ldr Ellis roared off from Biggin to meet the German formation. Once again, the tactic of some fighters flying at the speed of bombers, made it difficult for the ground controllers to know whether or not it was a 'genuine' raid, with the *Luftwaffe's Jägdflieger* hoping to make the most of their height advantage and element of surprise. As luck would have it, Churchill was visiting 'Hellfire Corner', and he may have glimpsed signs of the combat high in the sky above Dover Castle.

610 Squadron again desperately climbed for height as they headed south-east towards the approaching raiders. The formation was composed of a mixed bag of experience and inexperience, with the three veterans Ellis, Norris and Lamb all present, alongside the relatively inexperienced Ken Cox on his seventh recorded operational flight and Sgt Edward Manton on his first recorded patrol. There is some confusion here regarding the Squadron's formation, as there are discrepancies, but we do know that the following pilots were involved:

DW-W.	R.6993	S/Ldr. J. ELLIS.	Blue 1	50
DW-N.	N.3124	SGT. RAMSAY, N. H. D.		32
DW-X.		F/O. D. S. WILSON.		12
DW-T.	X.4064	F/Lt. S. C. NORRIS.		57
DW-M.	K.9974*	SGT. CHANDLER, H. H.		13
DW-Q.	R.6891	SGT. HAMLYN, R. F.	Yellow 1	38
DW-Y.		SGT. PARSONS, C. A.		23
DW-E.	P.9433	SGT. MANTON, E.	Yellow 4	1
DW-O.	X.4011**	SGT. BAMBERGER, C.	Green 3	24
	P.9511	P/O. H. K. COX.		7
DW-H.	K.9818	P/O. C. O. J. PEGGE.	Red 2	26
DW-A.	R.6976	F/O. P. G. LAMB.		48

*Should be K.9947, ORB error.

**Bamberger's logbook records him as flying DW-U (no serial number).

The ORB refers to 'Red, Yellow, Blue & Green sections', taking part in the twelve-aircraft patrol, which leads us to believe that the Squadron was operating in four sections of three. But in the combat reports, Sgt Manton is referred to as Sgt Hamlyn's 'number 4', meaning Yellow Section was composed of four Spitfires. Perhaps there were two sections of four and two sections of two, which would be possible given that Ellis (nearly always Blue 1), Lamb and Norris all usually led sections, along with Hamlyn as Yellow 1. However, this is conjecture, and one cannot say with any certainty how the formation operated.

The ORB reports that the four sections 'were ordered to engage E/A approaching the coast. They encountered about 20 M.E.109s near DOVER—DEAL at 18,000 ft, an engagement took place, the "AA" fire giving the position of the enemy'. The Squadron had been airborne around forty-five minutes before the engagement happened, the enemy aircraft being spotted between 1610 and 1615 hours. P/O Pegge explained how:

> I was Red 2 in A Flight of 610 Sqdn. patrolling just beneath a thin layer of cloud at 18,000 feet. A.A bursts indicated the position of about 15 Me109s. I climbed into the cloud & through it & saw more Me109s above. I dived through the cloud & saw three 109s with yellow cowlings & wing tips below me. I selected the near one which was about 50 yds away & gave it a short burst seeing tracer enter fuselage upon which it caught fire & went down being confirmed by Sgt. Parsons of 610 Sqdn.
>
> Attack was made from above, rear & slightly from the starboard side. (TNA, AIR 50/172/58)

Encountering such a large formation of 109s must have been daunting, the Messerschmitts' distinctive yellow markings making them all the more visible to their opponents, against the blue sky and white/grey clouds. Pegge's adversaries seemed oblivious to the Spitfire on their tails, and he picked off the rearmost from just fifty yards, in a textbook attack using only 400 rounds of ammunition. As Claude Parsons had witnessed the 109 crash, Pegge could add to his growing list of claims, this being the fifth Me 109 which he had claimed destroyed, which meant he was now an 'Ace', the fourth of 610 Squadron's pilots to achieve this feat.

Another 'A' Flight pilot who found himself embroiled in the dogfight at 18,000 feet was fellow Ace, Ronnie Hamlyn. He described the number of enemy aircraft as between fifteen—twenty Me 109s, and he also recorded in his preamble that the AA fire was 'Very good' in having aided the interception. His report reads as follows:

> I was Yellow Leader.
>
> We first sighted the enemy below thin cloud just above us at 18,000 ft., travelling in the opposite direction. The A.A. gave us their position.
>
> I picked one M.E.109 out and made my attack from astern, slightly above. After a few bursts he fell out of the sky, straight down. I followed him until he disappeared. This I claimed as a probable, as there was no smoke or fire coming from him and I was too high to see him crash. But my number 4 (Sgt. Manton) confirms that this crashed inland after catching fire about 200 ft.
>
> The M.E. 109 engaged all had their engine cowlings painted a bright yellow and were very easy to see from above. They also had yellow on their wings. (TNA, AIR 50/172/35)

From these two reports, it is clear they had caught the enemy aircraft largely by surprise, as Hamlyn was initially beneath the 109s, but was able to climb above them to deliver his attack from above and behind the unwitting German fighter pilot. He only fired for two seconds from 250 yards, using 200 rounds, which was enough to send the 109 down, and he could claim his seventh confirmed solo victory, as Sgt Manton saw it crash. It was a good day all round for Hamlyn, as at some stage on 28 August, news would have filtered through that he had been awarded the DFM for his brave actions in the last two months (TNA, AIR 25/197), but especially for having shot down five of the raiders in one day.

While Hamlyn would have been pleased with another successful engagement, Manton must simply have been relieved to survive his first skirmish unscathed, especially as it was against a large formation of Messerschmitt 109s. Hamlyn, like Pegge, noted the relatively new yellow markings being employed by this group of fighters, something Sgt Chandler had observed too. Although Chandler's combat report is not in evidence, the ORB recorded, 'Sgt. Chandler fired without visible effect at a twin engine A/C larger than a fighter which also had a yellow nose'. These sightings coincided with a *Luftwaffe* decision for the *Jägdgeschwader* to paint their engine cowlings, wingtips and rudders with bright yellow paint, to aid identification in what were now very crowded skies. While the German intention was to reduce the likelihood of 'friendly-fire' incidents, the RAF's pilots mistook these flamboyant markings for being the sign of the *Luftwaffe's* elite units. Fighter Command's pilots could be excused this belief, as such distinctive markings also suggested a certain amount of arrogance on the *Luftwaffe's* behalf, seemingly scorning the camouflage which was fastidiously employed by the RAF. However, 610's pilots may well have realised that it was to reduce the risk of firing on their own aircraft, given that their own Spitfires famously had a very large yellow band on the roundel on the fuselage, much more distinctive than many RAF squadrons, along with outsized squadron letters to aid identification in the air.

With the enemy fighters so visible on this patrol, it is perhaps questionable whether S/Ldr Ellis should have simply led his men away from such a battle, given Park and Dowding's orders that *Luftwaffe* fighters should only be engaged if they were escorting bombers. Ellis clearly positioned his men in an advantageous position to attack, despite the 109s' original height advantage. If Ellis had decided discretion was the better part of valour and avoided combat, his formation may well have been bounced by the numerically superior enemy formation, so he seems to have taken the logical decision.

It is likely that most of 610 Squadron attempted to engage the enemy fighters, as one of 'B' Flight's pilots filed a combat report, indicating that this flight also engaged the enemy. The inexperienced Sgt Bamberger referred to fifteen–twenty enemy aircraft at 18,000 feet between Deal and Dover, their presence being indicated by AA fire. His logbook records a patrol of 'Red King' and 'Red Queen' (Deal) which lasted eighty minutes, which was probably this patrol. Bamberger's report is much more concise, concentrating on the immediate details of the dogfight:

> I was Green 3.
>
> We first sighted enemy above & in front travelling directly towards us. I made an astern attack on an ME109 opening fire at about 250 yds gradually closing the range. After my third burst the ME 109 turned over on its back & black smoke came from the engine. I did not see enemy A/C crash as I was engaged by another enemy A/C. (TNA, AIR 50/172/8)

The details of Bamberger's attack are very similar to those of Sgt Hamlyn. 'Bam' went on to fire three bursts of two seconds from 250 yards, using 800 rounds of ammunition, but could only claim a probable as nobody witnessed its fate, including Bamberger himself, who had been set upon by one of his target's comrades bent on revenge. As was typical of these dogfights, the advantageous position was lost in a millisecond, as hunter became hunted, then hunter again, with a tightened turn or increased dive. Bamberger returned to Biggin Hill to file his first claim. Although no mention of it is made in the ORB, Bamberger's logbook records another patrol (25) on 28 August, which lasted fifty-five minutes, flying in his usual Spitfire, DW-U (no serial number). It is probable that no enemy aircraft were encountered, which is why it was not recorded in the ORB.

It is important to remember here, that Bamberger's tally of patrols has increased much more quickly than all the other pilots, as I have had access to his logbook, thanks to the Bamberger family. It highlights the fact that 610 Squadron's ORB was not completed each time 610 Squadron carried out a patrol, but during the hectic days of the Battle of Britain, the adjutant or clerk only completed the ORB when the Squadron encountered the *Luftwaffe*. So Bamberger's number of patrols reflects the number of patrols all the Squadron's pilots would have been carrying out—the Squadron was much busier than the ORB suggests. However, the tally of patrols for each pilot is an indication of their experience in comparison with each other; one needs to remember that Bamberger was still one of the least experienced pilots at this time, with a similar number of recorded patrols as Sgt Beardsley, who had completed just two recorded patrols at this point.

Unfortunately, as was too often the case in these run-ins with the high-performance Me 109, not everyone had been so lucky to make it back to Biggin Hill alive. This time the missing man was P/O Kenneth Cox, who had last flown a recorded sortie ten days earlier, during the large-scale attack on Biggin. It is unclear why he had not been on operations since then, when the Squadron was so active. He may have been on leave, or picked up an unrecorded wound or illness, but the undoubted fact was that the twenty-four year old from Birmingham, flying his seventh recorded combat patrol on 28 August 1940, had shown real potential as a fighter pilot. Not only had he survived his first handful of patrols, but he had also given an excellent account of himself, claiming two Me 109s destroyed, one 109 unconfirmed, one probable and a Dornier 215 probable. He was certainly an accurate shot, the one skill which often marked out good *fighter* pilots from good pilots. Cox's position in the formation during this patrol is impossible to prove, but previously he had flown in 'B' Flight, primarily as Blue 2 or Blue 3, so it is safe to assume he was flying as a wingman in Blue, or possibly Green Section. Unfortunately, his AMCB file has not been released yet, so it is impossible to definitively say what happened to him, until it is finally made available to the public.

Whether or not Cox pressed home a successful attack against the 109s is unclear, however, it is almost certain that at some point he came under attack from the Messerschmitts which his own formation had engaged. Cox's aircraft was evidently badly hit, and it fell away from the dogfight over Deal and Dover, going into a terminal descent. Tragically, Cox did not get out of his aircraft, P.9511 as agreed on by all sources including the ORB, and it is likely that much like P/O Webster two days earlier, Cox was mortally wounded by enemy fire during the combat. Having discussed the incident with Dave Brocklehurst, it seems Cox's Spitfire fell straight out of the sky, as P.9511 (there seems to be no record of its DW identification letter, possibly as it had only joined 610 on 25 August[18]) was involved in a major crash when it hurtled into a house in Stelling Minnis, a small village about six miles inland from Hawkinge. The ORB reports this casualty as being the, 'result of a flying accident due to enemy action', but the phrase 'flying accident' does not truly reflect the likely circumstances in which Cox had lost his life. This was not a pilot trying vainly to crash-land his badly damaged aircraft, but a severe impact, the Spitfire having come straight down from altitude. A wheel from Cox's Spitfire is on display in the Kent Battle of Britain Museum, a poignant reminder of the loss of the young pilot.

The death of Cox in such uncertain circumstances is typical of so many RAF fighter pilots during the Battle, although the gradual release of AMCB files is starting to answer some of the mysteries. In Stelling Minnis, distinguished by a windmill situated just outside the small Kentish village, there is no sign of what happened there in 1940, when another promising life was snuffed out. Also typical of so many pilots who gave their lives during that long, hot summer, was that Cox had been with his unit for just thirty-two days from joining 610 until his death. Having survived his first few sorties, it seemed that he had got through the worst period. In reality, while even the most experienced pilot could be shot down and killed, as has been so apparent, those with less experience simply had much less chance of surviving. And nothing could be done about 'luck'—if your number was up, then that was it.

Cox's parents, Henry and Beatrice of King's Heath, Birmingham, would have been duly informed of their loss, and he was cremated at Birmingham Municipal Crematorium, where his name is remembered at the back of the chapel. In another indication of the Volunteer Reservist's passion for flying, his ashes were scattered at the Old Castle Bromwich aerodrome.

Above left: P/O Kenneth Henry Cox, Killed in Action on 28 August 1940. (*Approved for use by the Biggin Hill Memorial Museum Trust*)

Above right: P/O Cox's name recorded at the Birmingham municipal crematorium chapel. (*Author*)

Once again, 610 Squadron's pilots had more than held their own in a dogfight with the *Luftwaffe's* feared fighter, claiming two destroyed and one probably destroyed. Nevertheless, P/O Cox's death would have been felt keenly by the whole Squadron, pilots and ground staff alike. Raymond Ellis of the ground crew, had this sad memory of losing Kenneth Cox:

> On the morning of 28th August a smart black Austin saloon was driven into the Belfast hangar. W/O Bentall emerged from the driver's door and called me over. He told me that the new Station Standing Orders required all vehicles on the camp to be camouflaged and that I was to do the ghastly deed. The car belonged to P/O Cox who would collect the car on his return from operations with the squadron. As I was covering up the windows with greased newspapers I noticed a broken wine glass on the back shelf. Inside the hangar the camouflaged car was more conspicuous than before I had started. With its windows cleaned the car stood waiting for P/O Cox, but he never returned to collect it. I thought what a cruel memento I had created for the young man's family.[19]

Despite 610 Squadron's fine record against the *Luftwaffe*, the steady drain of losses must have taken its toll on the pilots, both through the death or injury of another friend, and the constant threat to themselves of being killed or maimed. During August alone, Cox was the fifth pilot to be killed, while another seven had been put out of action wounded. The first week of August had seen no combat flying for 610, so these losses had come in only twenty days, 28 August representing the twelfth day of combat for the Squadron. Such figures show that despite the early lull in activity, the fighting became very intense, particularly as the month reached its climax. In those same twelve days of combat, the squadron claimed to have shot down thirty-five enemy aircraft, plus seventeen probably destroyed or unconfirmed and a further fifteen damaged, evidence of their success as a fighting unit, despite the inevitable over-claiming. The Squadron's losses were inescapable, particularly when facing such heavy numerical odds on each sortie. But it was the Squadron's ability to keep knocking down significant numbers of these formations which kept them going, despite their exhaustion, some of them having been in the front line since the Dunkirk operations. Somehow, the eighteen surviving pilots, at least one of whom was not fit for flying, had to find it in themselves to keep going up into the deadly skies, as the *Luftwaffe* had now built up a head of steam which would be hard to quell.

Dawn on Thursday 29 August brought mixed weather, which meant there was little aerial activity, although the most likely reason for this was that the *Luftwaffe* had been busy bombing British towns during the night. The city which had been hardest hit, by about 160 bombers on the night of 28 August and the small hours of 29 August, was Liverpool. The importance of the city cannot be stressed enough, as its extensive docks along the River Mersey brought a steady stream of merchant shipping to help sustain the island fortress of Great Britain. When the vital dockyards at Cammell Laird's in Birkenhead on the Wirral Peninsula were added to this, it was easy to see why the *Luftwaffe* focused so many attacks on such inviting targets on both banks of the Mersey, second only to London. As news of these raids eventually filtered through the chains of command, it would have been met with particular dismay and anger by the County of Chester Squadron. Many of the pilots and ground crew hailed from Wirral, Chester and Liverpool and their former home station of Hooton Park was on Wirral's bank of the Mersey. They must have been terribly worried for their families, living in areas all too prone to a misplaced payload of bombs aimed at the Mersey's dockyards.

As the *Luftwaffe* rested on the morning of 29 August, Fighter Command's pilots once more faced the intolerably anxious wait at dispersal for the telephone to ring, to send them into battle. It is probable that 610 Squadron was sent to Hawkinge in the morning, as Sgt Bamberger's logbook records a twenty-minute flight to the advance airfield, followed by a twenty-five-minute return flight to Biggin Hill (26 and 27). In the middle of the afternoon large formations of Me 109s and Me 110s escorting a small number of bombers formed up over France, before starting to cross the Channel.

With such a massive raid approaching England, AVM Park had to respond in force. However, as the raid developed he spotted the trap and only four of the thirteen squadrons engaged the enemy, thwarting the *Luftwaffe's* plan of engaging in a mainly fighter-versus-fighter battle (TNA, AIR 25/197).

It was against this backdrop that at 1530 hours, 610 Squadron's pilots were jolted from their nervous reveries, conversations and chess playing, by the jangle of the telephone. Seconds later, they were once more scrambling for their Spitfires. Thanks to the number of *Luftwaffe* fighters involved in this raid, the formation of bombers had made good progress, 610 Squadron's ORB implying that the target was Biggin Hill again. This fear was supported by the 'maximum effort' put up by the Squadron: '14 aircraft took off from BIGGIN HILL to engage about 60 DO.215s, M.E. Jaguars, & M.E.110s approaching from the south. The enemy bombers were engaged at varying [heights] from 18,000ft. to 20,000ft. over MAYFIELD', with 'Cloud 10/10ths at 10,000 ft' (ORB).

Given the incessant action in which the Squadron had been involved for so long, it was a remarkable achievement by the ground crew to get so many fighters airborne. The increased production of new fighter aircraft in the factories, which could be flown in to the squadrons when replacements were required, was a critical factor in this too. The sight of such a strong formation of Spitfires forming up behind John Ellis and climbing towards the south-east must have filled him with immense pride, and once again the formation was composed of men with the whole spectrum of combat experience, from F/Lt Norris embarking on his fifty-eighth recorded patrol, to the least experienced pilot Sgt Manton on just his second recorded patrol. Although undoubtedly fearful of what lay ahead, the twenty-five-year-old pilot from Bebington must have been as thrilled as his squadron leader, as he glanced around at the other Spitfires while juggling the controls to try and keep formation; not so long ago he had been cycling through Wirral villages, delivering post, and working in a sorting office, now he was defending his country, in the midst of a powerful force of modern fighter aircraft.

Given the size of 610's formation, it is difficult to decipher who flew in which section, although the ORB recorded the following pilots on the battle order:

DW-W.	R.6993	S/Ldr. J. ELLIS.	Blue 1	51
DW-N.	N.3124	SGT. RAMSAY, N. H. D.		33
DW-X.		F/O. D. S. WILSON.		13
DW-Q.	R.6891	SGT. HAMLYN, R. F.	Green 1	39
DW-F.	X.4028	SGT. CORFE, D.		7
DW-E.	P.9433	SGT. MANTON, E.		2
DW-T.	X.4064	F/Lt. S. C. NORRIS.	Red 1	58
DW-H.	K.9818	P/O. C. O. J. PEGGE.	Red 2	27
DW-M.	K.9974*	SGT. CHANDLER, H. H.	Red Section	14
DW-A.	R.6976	F/O. P. G. LAMB.	Yellow 1	49
DW-Y.		SGT. PARSONS. C. A.		24
DW-O.	X.4011	SGT. BAKER, C.	Yellow 3	3
RESERVE		SGT. BEARDSLEY, R. A.	Yellow Section	3
RESERVE**		SGT. BAMBERGER, C.		28
?		P/O. E. S. ALDOUS.***	Green 2	4

*Should be K.9947, ORB error.

**Bamberger's logbook records him as flying DW-U (no serial number) all day.

***Aldous not included in ORB.

It is possible to ascertain where certain pilots were in the formation from their combat reports, as noted above, and it is safe to assume S/Ldr Ellis was Blue 1 as usual and the experienced Sgt Hamlyn was probably leading Green Section, but it is not possible to say with some of the pilots. That Sgts

Beardsley and Bamberger were flying aircraft recorded as 'RESERVE', indicates that it was an all-out effort by the Squadron to defend against a perceived large raid on their home base.

The ORB mentions fourteen aircraft being involved, but omitted P/O Aldous from the list—we know he was flying, so either there were actually fifteen Spitfires in the formation or one of the pilots without a combat report is listed in error. About thirty minutes after being scrambled, the pilots were vectored onto their targets, unsurprisingly being at a height disadvantage. F/Lt Norris provided a typically detailed account of proceedings:

> I was Red Leader when the Sqdn was ordered to intercept 50 E.A. approaching home base at 20000'. E.A. were sighted flying in the opposite direction about 5000' above us—we being at 15000'.
>
> The Sqdn gave chase but the E.A. were drawing away into the sun while we were climbing to their height.
>
> On reaching 18000' I suddenly sighted 12 Do 215s flying on a westerly course in echelon formation about 2000' below us. I gave the order to attack. Half way through we were attacked ourselves by about 50 ME 110s & ME Jaguars. I attacked one ME Jaguar and after two or three bursts his starboard engine began to smoke badly—he went into a very steep spiral to the left & disappeared into the clouds. I did not see the machine again. S. C. Norris F/LT. 610 Sqdn. (TNA, AIR 50/172/54)

The experienced flight commander stated that this engagement took place at 1600 hours, fifteen miles south of Tunbridge, which fits in with the general description of it taking place over Mayfield. Once again, the fearlessness of the account is striking, as Norris was leading his men into much larger enemy formations, with the odds heavily stacked against the RAF fighter pilots. Norris felt the raid was being directed against Biggin Hill, so the pilots' determination to intercept it was all the more understandable, chasing the main formation despite being at a height and positional disadvantage.

Norris was quick to change target though when the twelve Dorniers presented themselves, but unfortunately the Messerschmitt 110s entered the fray in the nick of time to head off Red Leader's men. The *Zerstörer* pilots must have feared the worst when they had to dive down to protect the bombers, having learnt that the Spitfire was superior to their own aircraft. However, if they could get in an effective burst of fire with their heavy armament against the Spitfire pilots, who were busy concentrating on the bombers, then they might just succeed. 610 had plenty of old hands though and Norris used his combat experience to turn the tables on a 'Jaguar', before opening fire at 150 yards for two seconds, leaving it with a smoking engine and a long, fractious return flight for its pilot. Given the length of the return journey and the aircraft's state as it spiralled downwards, Norris was awarded a 'probable' when he returned home. With claims of five destroyed, one unconfirmed, one damaged and one shared damaged, this ninth claim confirmed his status as one of the Squadron's crack pilots and a courageous leader.

P/O Pegge also reported seeing twelve Do 215s with thirty—forty Jaguars and Me 110s at 1615 hours over Mayfield. In his terse account, it is apparent he had attacked the bombers knowing full well that they had a large escort. They had flung self-preservation and caution to the wind in attacking them, realising they had seconds to act before the escorts intervened:

> I was Red 2 of A Flight of 610 Sqdn at 18000 when we sighted 12 Do215s in Echelon Starboard at 12000 feet with Jaguars & Me110s at varying heights above & below us.
>
> I attacked the last Do215 giving it a short burst from above & behind & saw pieces come off the fuselage but with no other effect. I then broke off the attack as I was harassed by Me110s. (TNA, AIR 50/172/58)

Like his flight commander, Pegge escaped and returned to Biggin Hill unscathed, despite the best efforts of countless Messerschmitt 110s. Pegge was credited with one Dornier 215 damaged to add to his growing tally of victories, firing one short burst of one—two seconds fire before he had to save himself. Joe Pegge had used his experience effectively, firing from 100 yards to maximise the impact of the short burst of machine gun fire on the German machine. It is again questionable whether the Do 215 would have made it back home, given this damage.

Sgt Ray Chandler was also in Red Section, probably Red 3, and he only mentioned the twelve Dornier 215s which he engaged at 1550 hours, ten miles North of Dungeness (the discrepancies in timing and place being understandable given the nature of aerial combat). The main difference for Chandler was that he stated he initially delivered a head-on attack:

> … in which I failed to make any results. Having over-shot the formation I returned to deliver astern attack but bombers were attempting to form a defensive circle. I singled out a straggler which I attacked from a-beam, with four long bursts which definitely damaged him. I broke away but did not resume attack. E/a did not go down, though he must have been severely hit. I saw no escort fighters at all. (TNA, AIR 50/172/12)

Although Chandler's brave head-on attack did not achieve any visible results, it would have unnerved the German pilots. Indeed, Ray Chandler noted how the bombers had been forced into a defensive circle, before picking on a straggler, hitting it with four long bursts of 1,000 rounds from 400–100 yards. This hail of lead damaged the enemy aircraft, and another German crew faced a nerve-wracking return flight over the menacing English Channel, a journey which was loathed by the *Luftwaffe's* aircrew. Sgt Chandler returned to base and was credited with a Do 215 as damaged to complete a successful operation for Red Section. It is interesting that while Norris and Pegge were both uncomfortably aware of Me 110 fighters trying to shoot them down, Chandler did not spot a single one. Perhaps he had just been fortunate to avoid the attention of the *Zerstörers*, but it indicates how varied a dogfight could be in the skies over southern England.

The remainder of 'A' Flight in Yellow Section, led by F/O Lamb, followed his order to engage the 110s, possibly having seen them trying to attack Red Section. Lamb stated that the action took place at about 1615 hours between Tunbridge Wells and Rye:

> I was Yellow 1 while flying at about 22.000 ft on Easterly course. We sighted a number of Dorniers and Jaguars flying towards the west. Red Section dived to attack Dorniers. I led my section into the Jaguars who were flying in Echelon std. When we approached from astern 7 turned left one to right. This machine kept in the turn until almost coming head on to me, at this point I opened fire (about 800 yds). He continued in the turn and I held my fire as long as possible seeing my bullets hitting him underneath.
>
> My number 3 who was some distance behind saw this machine go down issuing smoke and crash. (Sgt Baker). (TNA, AIR 50/172/45)

Lamb was quick to engage the Me 110 which broke formation alone, possibly an inexperienced pilot making a fatal error. Despite its predicament, the firepower of a Messerschmitt 110 in a head-on attack was fearsome and Lamb would have been all too aware of the danger facing him as the enemy aircraft approached, its two 20-mm MG FF cannon and four 7.9-mm MG17 machine guns winking and flashing defiance as the two aircraft closed. On this occasion, the fact that Lamb opened fire at the extreme range of 800 yards was testimony to his experience, as the tremendously high closing speed of the two fighters meant that he had split seconds to sight his fire and attempt to shoot down his opponent. Peter Lamb's four second burst of fire proved lethally accurate, with Sgt Baker observing the German aircraft crash, enabling Lamb to claim his third victory in his last five patrols.

Cyril Baker was flying just his third recorded operation, and his synopsis of the interception was that it took place at 1550 hours against a mixture of approximately forty Me 110s and Do 215s at between 18–20,000 feet over Mayfield, before providing a detailed description of the ensuing battle:

> I was Yellow 3 and kept in formation until my leader attacked and destroyed a ME 110 Jaguar. I was then split up from the formation and attacked a ME 110 Jaguar from the rear, slightly to the port quarter and from underneath. I closed to approximately 200 yards and gave a 3 second burst which caused white smoke to issue, apparently from the engine, and then the aircraft heeled over into a dive which I did not follow. I then attacked a Do 215 from about the same position as before and gave 2 bursts of about 3 seconds each which caused the aircraft to go into an over the vertical dive, which I did not follow. On breaking away from the engagement I found my Glycol temperature excessively high and, therefore had to force-land at Gatwick aerodrome. The machine is safe but will require repair. (TNA, AIR 50/172/6)

The first thing of interest here is that the inexperienced sergeant had done very well to stay in formation with Lamb. Although Baker was not perhaps as close to Lamb as he might have been, from what Lamb had noted, he was still offering his leader some protection, as was expected. However, they eventually became separated and while fending for himself, he was able to claim a probably destroyed Me 110 and Dornier 215. During the dogfighting, Baker's Spitfire had been damaged presumably by return fire from one of his targets, and he made a forced landing at Gatwick which was much nearer to the combat area of Mayfield than Biggin Hill, no mean feat for an inexperienced pilot.

Cyril Baker was having a very eventful start to his life as a front-line fighter pilot, but fortune was favouring him at the moment and he now had claims for one destroyed and two probably destroyed in his first three patrols. The ORB recorded that Baker's Spitfire was DW-O, X.4011, and for once most sources seem to agree, the Spitfire needing repairs before it continued to serve with 610 Squadron for another few months.[20]

The other pilot in Yellow Section was the equally inexperienced twenty-year-old Sgt Beardsley. Although Peter Lamb had ordered his section to engage the escort and Beardsley noted that at 1555 hours they engaged approximately forty Me 110s and Do 215s at 19,000–20,000 feet, the opportunity arose for Beardsley to engage the bombers:

> I delivered a stern attack on a Do. 215 on the port side of an enemy formation over Mayfield, Kent. I fired bursts of about 100 rounds each at a range of between 250 and 150 yards. After the first two bursts no fire was met with from the 215. I presume that all gunners were silenced. The aircraft was badly damaged by my fire and pieces flew off and holes appeared all over the enemy. He went down in series of short jerky dives and seemed definitely out of control. After using all my ammunition on the aircraft I followed it to the base of the clouds to about 5000–6000 ft where I lost him in the haze. When last seen he was still going down. (TNA, AIR 50/172/10)

Opening fire from close range as had become customary, Beardsley's aim was accurate, but the old problem that the Squadron's pilots faced in the early Channel convoy battles arose again; the inability of the eight .303 machine guns to bring bombers down, even though numerous hits were being achieved. Despite appearing to be out of control and riddled with holes, Beardsley could only claim a probable. This was a problem faced throughout Fighter Command, a problem which probably cost numerous lives, as pilots like Robert Beardsley followed damaged enemy aircraft down to try and establish if they had crashed. Without ammunition and losing altitude, not to mention his attention being focused on the struggling bomber, Beardsley was a sitting duck for any roving escort fighters, of which there were clearly plenty about. He was lucky indeed that he was not picked off, but having survived another encounter with the enemy and with a second claim to his name in just three patrols, his self-belief would understandably have been growing.

Overall, 'A' Flight's pilots could be well pleased with their efforts, claims of one destroyed, four probably destroyed and two damaged, with only Baker's Spitfire suffering damage, indicates the large scale of the engagement. 'B' Flight does not appear to have enjoyed as much success as there is only one combat report available from Blue and Green Sections, from another inexperienced pilot. Twenty-two-year-old Eric Aldous, on his fourth recorded sortie, noted he engaged about fifty Jaguars, Me 110s and Dornier 215s at 1555 hours near Mayfield. He ultimately tackled a bomber at the much lower altitude of 10,000 feet, along with the rest of his section:

> I was Green 2.
>
> When on patrol near Mayfield, my Squadron sighted three formations of Me.110s, DO.215s & Jaguars. My section attacked a formation of DO.215s which broke up. I followed one down to near the top of the clouds and fired a long burst from abeam when the E/A was turning. He dived steeply into the clouds and I did not see him again. (TNA, AIR 50/172/4)

This was a fairly fleeting encounter, and although Aldous fired 200 rounds per gun from 250–300 yards, the results were inconclusive. The Dornier found safety in the welcoming cloud blanket at 10,000 feet, which may explain why there are no other combat reports from 'B' Flight, while also explaining the numerous unconfirmed claims by 'A' Flight. Aldous returned to base without injury to himself or his Spitfire, and was able to add a Do 215 as damaged to the Squadron's tally.

As the majority of pilots returned to Biggin Hill by 1700 hours, others such as Sgt Baker reported his crash-landing at Gatwick, and Sgt Parsons made contact from Hawkinge to say he had landed there; it became apparent that there was no sign of Sgt Manton. He was only on his second recorded patrol, the least experienced pilot in the formation, seemingly flying in Blue or Green Sections. There were no sightings of him by his comrades, so he was reported as 'Missing'. It would seem that reports of a crashed Spitfire on the Great Wigsell Estate in Hurst Green, Sussex, filtered through and it was confirmed that Sgt Edward 'Ted' Manton had indeed been shot down and killed during the combat near Mayfield at about 1600 hours. Manton had joined the Squadron in its earliest days of 1936 as an AC, before training as an airman under training pilot in the AAF. So his loss would have been badly felt throughout the unit, but particularly amongst the other inexperienced pilots, Sgts Bamberger, Beardsley and Baker who had all been to 9 FTS with Manton and who had been on his final patrol. Edward Manton was buried in Hawkhurst Cemetery, Kent; Plot A, Grave J.62, on 4 September 1940. His nieces Joyce and Frances informed me that he was buried in the field that he crashed in, and that Lady Milner, the owner of the Great Wigsell estate, had the ground consecrated, which led to the creation of Hawkhurst Cemetery, set in very peaceful surroundings in rolling countryside, a stone's throw from Bodiam Castle.

There is some confusion over Manton's date of death, the headstone recording that it was **28** August 1940, while 610 Squadron's ORB clearly refers to it as **29** August. Both *Men of the Battle of Britain* and *Then and Now* record his loss as taking place on 29 August, the latter noting, 'Official Casualty Records state that this airman was killed in action on August 28, 1940 contrary to the details shown in the Form 540, No. 610 Squadron Operations Record Book. The burial register of Hawkhurst Cemetery also shows the date of death of 'Sergeant (Pilot) Edward Manton 810081 RAF (Aux) 610 Squadron 28 August 1940'.[21] However, all the evidence points to there being an error and that the former postman from Bebington was actually killed in action near Mayfield on 29 August 1940, probably by an escorting Me 110 or possibly a gunner on one of the Do 215s had got in a lucky burst.

In the final stages of my research, Leonard Woodgate contacted the 610 Squadron Association, in relation to Manton's death, as he had witnessed the tragic event as a schoolboy standing near an air raid warden's post, during his summer holiday. When I contacted him, he recalled how there was a dogfight just to the north-east of Robertsbridge, when, 'Suddenly there appeared a fighter, (which later was confirmed as Sgt Edward Manton's), doing a Falling Leaf descent; I cannot remember any signs of fire, or the pilot attempting to bale out. The plane, and the pilot, crashed into a field at Great Wigsell Farm, between Hurst Green and Hawkhurst'. Leonard originally thought the aircraft was a

The final resting place of Edward Manton in Hawkhurst cemetery; note the date, which has caused so much confusion. (*Author*)

German one, but was corrected by the local shopkeeper, who also witnessed the terrible moment. Leonard believed the crash occurred on Thursday 29 August.

Thanks to an article in the journal of The Second World War's Experience Centre, *Everyone's War*, there is a fascinating account of Lady Milner's recollections of the events surrounding Manton's death. Lady Violet Milner had lived in the Jacobean manor house of Great Wigsell for over thirty years and Manton's death brought back some painful memories of her own from the First World War. Her son George had been killed in action in 1914, while serving with the Grenadier Guards, while her daughter Helen's son, also George, was now of military age. She recorded her observations of the period in her diary, noting that on:

> 29 August, the air once again was 'full of bullets and zooming planes'. A stricken Spitfire crashed in flames near the house, the pilot was dead. 'The flames burnt for nearly an hour', wrote Violet. She picked some flowers to lay on the young man's remains: 'As I waited with my flowers for the van carrying the body to come down the lane, I saw in my mind's eye, the figures of the boys, my own George, who so often walked that way, and who lived here, and of Helen's George … I thought of them and of this boy—the unknown boy—who was now coming along the same path'.
>
> August and September were always a bad time of year for Violet, when her lost boy was uppermost in her thoughts, 'This day I think even more of him, of the bitter loss'. She went to the funeral of the dead pilot, Sergeant Manton, and talked to his parents and fiancée, Miss Barclay.[22]

Lady Milner's poignant recollections clearly provide further first-hand evidence that Sgt Manton was killed on 29 August.

Sgt Manton's AMCB file was released by The National Archives on 30 June 2017, just in time to help with this publication. In most cases, the files clarify the situation surrounding the death of a pilot, but although this file does provide much interesting and very sad information, it certainly highlights the

The caption to this grainy, but very rare photo in *Everyone's War*, of Sgt Manton's wrecked Spitfire was as follows: '29 August 1940: The crashed Spitfire Mk 1 of Sgt E. Manton, with Great Wigsell in the background. (By courtesy of Mrs R. Q. Edmonds)'. Great Wigsell is just visible in the clearing on the right. The Spitfire's engine can clearly be seen, as can the leading edges of the wings. (*Copyright Everyone's War and Mrs R. Q. Edmonds*)

confusion over Sgt Manton's death. It seems that Manton's body was brought into Hawkhurst Cottage Hospital on 29 August, and that at 1800 hours on 31 August, the matron managed to contact a Wg Cdr Burgess at the Air Ministry, for advice on how to proceed and the need for a funeral to be arranged. Due to the bombing which had taken place at Biggin Hill, 610 Squadron was hard to contact, and so the matron, Miss G. E. Hazleton, proceeded to help arrange Manton's funeral for 4 September. In a later letter from the matron regarding some of Manton's belongings, she wrote, 'He crashed in his plane in this locality on August 29th, 1940' (TNA, AIR 81/2936), while the burial return form also states his death took place on **29** August. The funeral went ahead with military honours and his family was present, much of which was thanks to the local hospital's caring matron.

However, on 31 August, 610 Squadron had sent a telegram to the Air Ministry stating that Manton was 'Missing' at approximately 1730 hours on **28** August, clearly before news had been received that his body had been found. Further confusion was added by S/Ldr Ellis's report on the fatality, only written up on 10 October 1940, a delay which could understandably have caused an error to creep in (see photo p. 398).

This report referred to Manton being shot down on **27** August, with R.6970 described as the Spitfire involved, when it was originally listed as R.6695 (the identity of the Spitfire will be looked at again). The contradictory dates were finally picked up on in the following missive (see photo p. 398) from the Air Ministry to 610 Squadron in January 1941, demanding for the issue to be resolved. It is very sad that such an important fact as the date of someone's death could become so confused, although there were factors affecting both 610 Squadron and Biggin Hill, which brought about the situation.

Although Ellis's report gives the **27** August as the date in question, 11 Group's ORB states that there was very little flying on this day, none of it involving 610 Squadron (TNA, AIR 25/197). F/O le Fleming, the Squadron's adjutant, responding on behalf of 610 Squadron, confirmed the date of Manton's death as **28** August 1940. This was probably as a result of the initial telegram from 610 Squadron to the Air Ministry on 31 August, which stated he was 'Missing' on 28 August, and this original telegram was probably responsible for the date on his headstone. As a result, the Air Ministry issued the statement on 4 February 1941, that Manton had been killed on **28** August 1940.

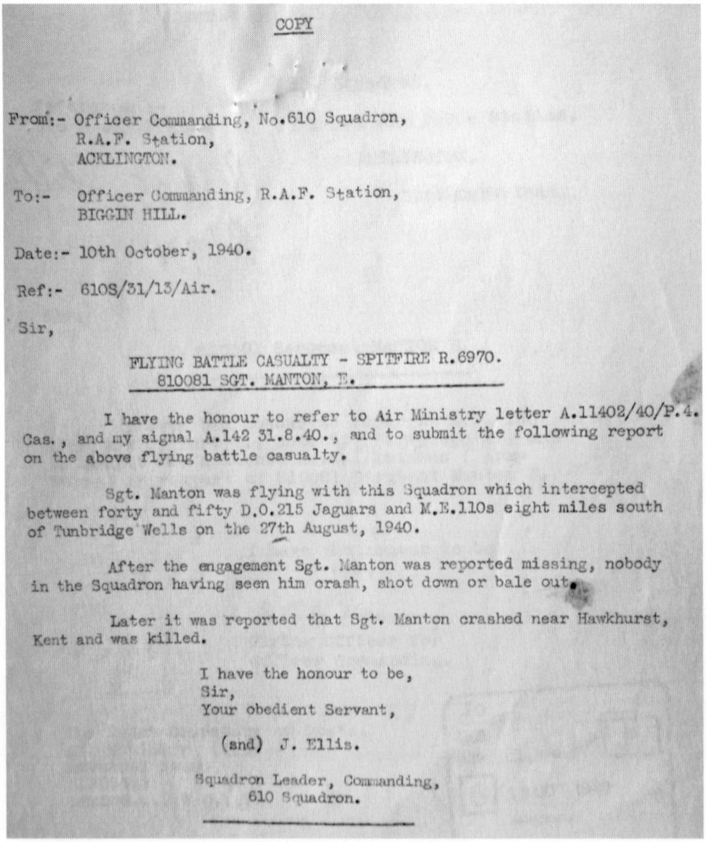

COPY

From:- Officer Commanding, No.610 Squadron,
R.A.F. Station,
ACKLINGTON.

To:- Officer Commanding, R.A.F. Station,
BIGGIN HILL.

Date:- 10th October, 1940.

Ref:- 610S/31/13/Air.

Sir,

FLYING BATTLE CASUALTY - SPITFIRE R.6970.
810081 SGT. MANTON, E.

I have the honour to refer to Air Ministry letter A.11402/40/P.4. Cas., and my signal A.142 31.8.40., and to submit the following report on the above flying battle casualty.

Sgt. Manton was flying with this Squadron which intercepted between forty and fifty D.O.215 Jaguars and M.E.110s eight miles south of Tunbridge Wells on the 27th August, 1940.

After the engagement Sgt. Manton was reported missing, nobody in the Squadron having seen him crash, shot down or bale out.

Later it was reported that Sgt. Manton crashed near Hawkhurst, Kent and was killed.

I have the honour to be,
Sir,
Your obedient Servant,

(snd) J. Ellis.

Squadron Leader, Commanding,
610 Squadron.

S/Ldr Ellis's report, which refers to the original aircraft Manton was believed to have been flying, along with the incorrect date of his death. (*TNA, AIR 81/2936*)

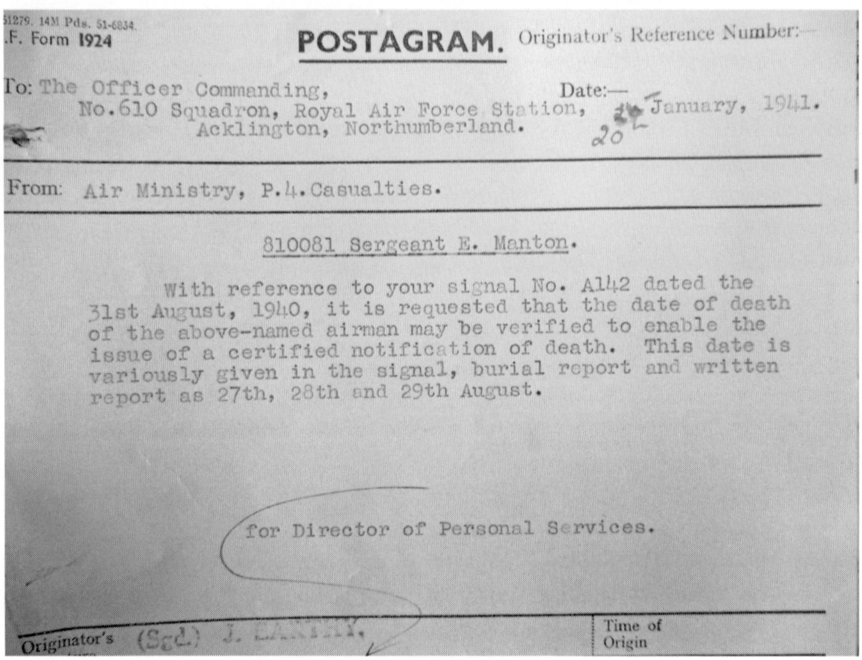

51279. 14M Pds. 51-6834.
.F. Form 1924

POSTAGRAM. Originator's Reference Number:—

To: The Officer Commanding, No.610 Squadron, Royal Air Force Station, Acklington, Northumberland.

Date:— 20 January, 1941.

From: Air Ministry, P.4.Casualties.

810081 Sergeant E. Manton.

With reference to your signal No. A142 dated the 31st August, 1940, it is requested that the date of death of the above-named airman may be verified to enable the issue of a certified notification of death. This date is variously given in the signal, burial report and written report as 27th, 28th and 29th August.

for Director of Personal Services.

Originator's (Sgd.) J. [illegible]

Time of Origin

The Air Ministry request for the date of Sgt Manton's death to be confirmed. (*TNA, AIR 81/2936*)

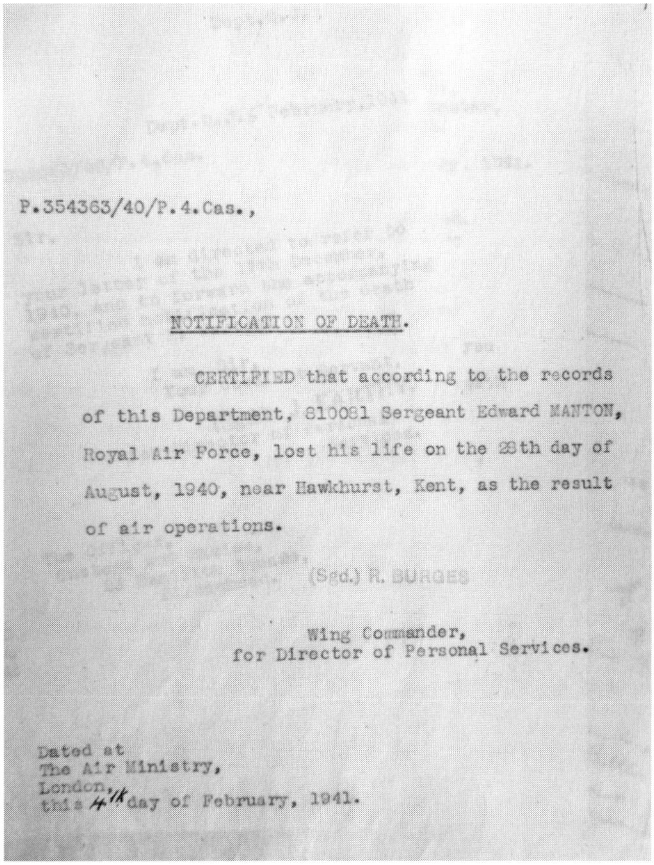

P.354363/40/P.4.Cas.,

NOTIFICATION OF DEATH.

CERTIFIED that according to the records of this Department, 810081 Sergeant Edward MANTON, Royal Air Force, lost his life on the 28th day of August, 1940, near Hawkhurst, Kent, as the result of air operations.

(Sgd.) R. BURGES

Wing Commander,
for Director of Personal Services.

Dated at
The Air Ministry,
London,
this 4th day of February, 1941.

The official confirmation that Manton lost his life on 28 August 1940. (*TNA, AIR 81/2936*)

However, to my mind, le Fleming seems to have missed some vital evidence which indicates, to me at least, that the young sergeant from Bebington lost his life on **29** August. In summary, Manton is recorded as having witnessed the demise of the 109 Sgt Hamlyn claimed on the patrol on 28 August, a patrol which Manton must have survived. This is the only recorded patrol for 610 on 28 August, which took place between 1530-1645 hours over Dover and Deal. Therefore, unless another patrol took place later that day, which has not been recorded, and mirrored the raid intercepted by 610 Squadron on the next day, Manton could not have been killed on **28** August.

The details in Ellis's account of the raid in which Manton was lost, do accurately portray the raid intercepted by 610 Squadron on **29** August, albeit with the wrong date. The Squadron's ORB unambiguously states that Manton was lost during the interception over Mayfield on **29** August, not far from where Manton crashed at Hawkhurst, as does the 11 Group ORB. The matron of the local hospital states that Manton died on **29** August, as does the burial form. The witnesses Leonard Woodgate and Lady Wigsell also corroborate this date. It seems that the time lapse involved between Manton being fatally shot down and 610 Squadron contacting the Air Ministry, during a period of incredible turbulence for 610 Squadron, led to a simple administrative error causing so much confusion. Therefore, it appears that Sgt Manton's death should have been recorded as **29 August 1940**.

There is also some debate about the identity of his Spitfire, the ORB recording him as flying DW-E, P.9433, although this seems impossible as DW-E, P.9433 had a long service history after this date, and Manton's Spitfire had been destroyed.[23] Until the AMCB file had been released, it was popularly believed that it was actually: 'R6629. Shot down in combat over Mayfield area 4.00 p.m. Crashed at Great Wigsell

Sgt Edward Manton, with his fiancée Doris Barclay, who was in the WAAF. (*Copyright Manton family*)

Estate, Hurst Green. Sgt. E. Manton killed. DW-E a write-off'.[24] This aircraft also had a long service history after Manton's death, which made this impossible.[25] Thankfully, information released at The National Archives in June 2017 has confirmed that Manton was flying DW-P, R.6695, which had previously been thought to be the Spitfire Sgt Corfe was flying when he was shot down on 22 August. R.6970 is briefly mentioned in the AMCB files, as having been Manton's machine, but it seems to have been corrected to R.6695. Spitfire R.6970 had possibly been damaged on 26 August. It was believed that the remains of Manton's Spitfire were excavated from a crater, suggesting the Spitfire fell from altitude at high speed in a major crash, much like Cox and Webster, the other recent fatalities. But very little is known about the circumstances of the crash, as shown by S/Ldr Ellis's report. The excavation was led by, '*the Robertsbridge Museum which excavated complete surviving remains and all major components. Some fragments in the Kent Battle of Britain Museum*'.[26] However, the fact that we now know the airman's body was brought to Hawkhurst Cottage Hospital seemingly without a full excavation by the RAF, plus the photographic evidence, and the testimonies of Lady Milner and Leonard Woodgate, perhaps indicate a less severe impact.

Manton's parents, Edward and Sarah, of 64 Acres Road, Bebington, Wirral, ensured they left a fitting personal tribute from a hymn on his headstone, 'The strife is o'er, The battle done; Now is the victor's triumph won', where he lies so far from his home village, like so many other brave Fighter Command pilots that summer. Ted's niece Frances recalled that it was a very tough time for the family back on the Wirral; Manton's mother died of a heart attack six weeks later, while his sister had a baby in September, the baby girl touchingly being called Doris, after Ted's fiancée. His nieces' mother found it terribly hard to come to terms with his loss, and could never face visiting his grave, which highlights how traumatic the tragic events were for each family who lost a loved one.

Recently a Close in Manton's home village of Bebington was named after him, as was an apartment block, Manton Court, in nearby Prenton, which serve as fitting reminders of his sacrifice and show that Edward Manton's loss is still remembered with gratitude after all these years. This was thanks to Peter Blythe, whose research raised interest in the Battle of Britain pilot in 2005, and along with the efforts of Wirral councillor Jerry Williams and Manton's nieces, Frances and Joyce, helped bring about the naming of Manton Court on the Wirral.

Returning to the raid on 29 August, the enemy formation was, 'broken up & were last seen returning to the French coast' (ORB), and the pilots could again take great pride in their efforts despite having

The road sign in Bebington, Wirral, in memory of Sgt Edward 'Ted' Manton. (*Author*)

suffered a further casualty. The County of Chester Squadron had thwarted another raid against their own vital home aerodrome, regardless of the heavy odds stacked against them, with claims of one destroyed, four probably destroyed and three damaged, to stand testimony to their endeavour, as follows:

Lamb—Me 110 destroyed
Norris—Me 110 probably destroyed
Baker—Me 110 probably destroyed
Baker—Do 215 probably destroyed
Beardsley—Do 215 probably destroyed
Aldous—Do 215 damaged
Pegge—Do 215 damaged
Chandler—Do 215 damaged.

The successful outcome of this patrol, despite being heavily outnumbered, encapsulates the Battle of Britain as a whole, along with the death of a young RAF pilot with so much of his life ahead of him, for a cause he felt was so worthwhile. Unfortunately, there was no time for the pilots to rest and recuperate from the dogfight, or reflect on their missing comrade, as the *Luftwaffe* had other ideas.

As the day wore on, the *Luftwaffe's* fighter pilots continued to try and lure RAF squadrons into combat, and once 'Dog Rose' Squadron had refuelled and rearmed, the pilots would have been back at Biggin Hill, waiting at readiness for another scramble. Sure enough, just an hour after landing, the order to go up again and patrol Hawkinge came through at 1800 hours. Such was the short turnaround time between these operations, the pilots would not have known the fate of Sgt Manton, although remarkably, Sgt Baker had returned from Gatwick, to scramble in Red Section, and Sgt Parsons had managed to get back from Hawkinge in time to participate in this patrol. Apart from Manton, the other pilots who did not take part who had been in the earlier engagement were S/Ldr Ellis, F/O Wilson and P/O Aldous. In the ORB list, a P/O Aldridge seems to have been brought in for his first patrol, to bring the Squadron up to full strength. There is some confusion over Aldridge's participation on this patrol, as according to the ORB and other sources, he did not join the Squadron until 3 September 1940, so why he is recorded here is a mystery. One possibility is that this patrol was written up at a later date, and Aldridge was written down instead of Aldous, which would make it a simple typographical error.

Stanley Norris was leading the Squadron as Red 1 and the following men took to the skies behind him:

DW-T.	X.4164*	F/LT. S. C. NORRIS.	Red 1	59
DW-H.	K.9818	SGT. BAKER, C.	Red 2	4
DW-E.	P.9433	SGT. CHANDLER, H. H.		15
DW-A.	R.6976	F/O. P. G. LAMB.	Yellow 1	50
DW-F.	X.4028	SGT. PARSONS, C. A.		25
DW-Y.		SGT. BEARDSLEY, R. A.	Yellow 3	4
DW-Q.	R.6891	SGT. HAMLYN, R. F.		40
DW-L.	P.9311	SGT. CORFE, D.		8
DW-R.	X.4239	SGT. RAMSAY, N. H. D.		34
DW-B.	X.4166	P/O. PEGGE, C. O. J.		28
DW-X.		P/O. J. ALDRIDGE**		1
DW-N.	N.3124***	SGT. BAMBERGER, C.		29

*This was probably a simple typographical error, and should read X.4064, as X.4164 did not serve with 610.[27]

**As ORB, but Aldridge's initials were 'F. J.'. I have highlighted the error the first time it occurs.

***Bamberger's logbook states that he was flying DW-U (no serial number) all day.

Experienced pilots would have been leading the other sections with Lamb probably leading Yellow Section, and Hamlyn and Pegge leading one of Green or Blue Sections. It is remarkable that there were eight sergeants on this patrol, indicative of how the Auxiliary Squadron's composition had changed once hostilities with Germany had begun, but also the number of casualties suffered by 610. Being a pilot in the AAF was definitely no longer the domain of officers.

Norris led his men towards Hawkinge, the scene of several hectic dogfights over recent weeks, climbing hard for altitude in a routine the old hands could do in their sleep. The controller anticipated that the enemy aircraft would be fighters, sending the Spitfires to an altitude of over 26,000 feet, a luxury seldom enjoyed by the defenders. On reaching their patrol height, the Squadron set about searching for the enemy, each pilot's head swivelling as he methodically scanned the sky for the tell-tale vapour trails of high flying 'snappers'. Around forty-five minutes after being scrambled, one of the eagle-eyed pilots spotted their quarry beneath them, and Norris ordered his men into a dive to engage them. However, despite, 'No cloud, visibility good ...' (ORB), only two pilots engaged the enemy fighters, both of whom had lost the rest of the Squadron during the dive. Cyril Baker was flying as wingman to Stanley Norris on this occasion, and Baker described how at about 1845 hours:

> I was Red 2 and, after climbing in formation, I lost my leader in a dive onto the enemy. I saw a ME109 on the tail of one of our fighters and dived onto it from the rear. I got in a 2 seconds burst which caused it to turn away to the left and, following it round I got in another burst of 2 seconds from the rear and slightly underneath. This caused black smoke to issue from the aircraft which went into a steep dive towards the sea. I did not follow it down. (TNA, AIR 50/172/6)

Baker rapidly lost 10,000 feet in this engagement, two short bursts of fire sending the Messerschmitt into a smoke-filled dive, but he sensibly stopped short of following the 109 all the way down. Somebody else presumably witnessed it crash, as he was able to add another destroyed enemy aircraft to his claims of one destroyed and two probably destroyed. That Baker had also saved one of his colleagues from being bounced, suggests that following the initial dive onto the enemy formation, a dogfight had broken out.

During his engagement, Baker had spotted three enemy fighters, but the only other pilot whose combat report survives was Sgt Beardsley who had the misfortune of being engaged by six fighters, an unimaginably frightening situation, especially when he was alone. He described the dogfight, which also occurred at 1845 hours, as follows:

> I was Yellow 3.
>
> On being sperated [separated] from my flight when the squadron dived I found myself engaged with six M.E. 109s. I engaged two of them at approximately 25,000—26,000 ft. I delivered a beam attack on one of them which was at approximately 250—300 ft range. The aircraft went down in a steep turning dive. I was then attacked by other M.E.109s and broke off the engagement. He was last seen at approximately 15,000 ft in a dive. I fired about 20—30 rounds from each gun. (TNA, AIR 50/172/10)

From Beardsley's report, it is evident that the Squadron had attained a good altitude from which to bounce any enemy formations, as his engagement was initially at 25–26,000 feet between Hawkinge and Dungeness. Beardsley only had time to fire 200 rounds from close range, before the other 109s forced him to break away and fight for his life. Bob Beardsley managed to extricate himself from this dangerous predicament and on his return to base was credited with an Me 109 as damaged, his second claim of the day.

Given the near ideal conditions for 610's pilots, with height advantage and clear blue skies, it is surprising that more of the pilots did not file claims, but, 'The rest of the Squadron did not engage' (ORB). However, as the pilots returned to Biggin Hill in the dusk, (three landed at Hawkinge first to refuel, one staying overnight (ORB), and it was clear that everyone had survived in exchange for claims of a 109 destroyed and a 109 damaged, the Squadron would have been happy with the outcome. The ground crew would also have been delighted to know that all aircraft were serviceable, from that patrol at least (ORB). It is possible that 610 had encountered JG 26, as they suffered two losses that evening in the vicinity in which 610 was patrolling, although this cannot be certain.

After such a long day at readiness, including two eventful patrols, once the pilots had been debriefed by the intelligence officer and filled in their combat reports, 610 Squadron's men certainly deserved a relaxing drink in The White Hart. However, some of them would have been ready to return to their billets, exhausted, knowing that another day of equally intense action awaited them early the next morning. All the pilots would have mourned Sgt Edward Manton's death, their sixth colleague to be killed in August, before reflecting on their success during the two patrols, which amounted to two enemy aircraft destroyed, four probably destroyed and four damaged. Yet again 610 Squadron had given a very good account of itself, and in routing the enemy bomber formation in the afternoon raid, had prevented another attack on Biggin Hill. Such daunting odds would have been lurking at the back of each of the remaining pilots' minds as they tried to drift off to an uneasy sleep, making any real rest impossible.

During the night, the *Luftwaffe*, 'delivered its second attack on Liverpool and over 130 bombers reached the target',[28] scattering bombs across the city. As the sleepy pilots roused themselves on the morning of 30 August 1940, such news would have steeled their resolve to add to the month's mounting tally of enemy aircraft claimed. The pilots probably wondered whether there was to be a repeat of the previous day, with a quiet morning and then afternoon raids in the wake of the *Luftwaffe's* nocturnal activity. As the sun gradually rose in the morning sky, the tense atmosphere would have increased at 'A' and 'B' Flight dispersals at Biggin Hill.

The ORB had stated the previous day that all aircraft were serviceable after the second patrol, so it seems odd that the Squadron only had ten pilots at readiness, especially as there were several pilots presumably available to bring the squadron up to full strength for a patrol. F/O Wilson and Sgts Ramsay and Bamberger had flown on 28 August and both patrols on 29 August, while Sgt Corfe had also flown both patrols on the previous day. Bamberger was certainly on operations on 30 August, as his logbook records three flights. Perhaps these four were lucky enough to be rested for this patrol, although several of the pilots down at the 'flights' had been flying almost continuously for the past week, so it is unlikely. Of the remaining three pilots, P/O Rees had not flown since 22 August and it is likely that he may have been wounded or ill without it being reported, Sgt Willcocks had not flown since 26 August, while the third pilot was P/O Iain Hunter Stewart, yet to fly operationally and seemingly suffering from ill health.

That left the ten pilots on readiness and the strain on them must have been immense, especially for the 'old hands', Stanley Norris, Peter Lamb and John Ellis, on whom the greatest responsibility fell—quite how they managed to keep on going was a testimony to their willpower and dedication to duty. For the best part of three and a half months they had been based in 11 Group, constantly facing the threat of combat and death. If they were sent up on 30 August as seemed likely, Norris would be flying his sixtieth recorded combat patrol, while Ellis would be flying his fifty-second and Lamb his fifty-first. They must have longed for a break from the constant pressure of life at Biggin Hill, despite knowing that they were carrying out their vital role so well.

The pilots did not have as long to wait as the previous day, as at 1045 hours the call came through to the dispersal areas and S/Ldr Ellis would have shouted over to his men on picking up the receiver, "'Dog Rose' Squadron, Scramble", instigating yet another dash for their waiting Spitfires. Ellis's Spitfire, apparently his usual mount DW-W, R.6993, would have been positioned at one of the more convenient dispersal points, to ensure he was one of the first airborne. Despite the number of occasions on which he had found himself sprinting for his aircraft during a scramble, these must have been amongst the most perturbing moments, before being strapped into his Spitfire and the routine of his cockpit drill settled the nerves. As Ellis taxied out, it must have sent a thrill of exhilaration through him as he glanced around at the other Spitfires all with engines firing up and edging forward, to know that he had helped form them into one of the finest squadrons in Fighter Command, resident of Biggin Hill for two and a half months since the conflict began. He must also have wondered how long both he and his men could keep on going.

The pilots following Ellis were listed as follows:

DW-W.	R.6993	S/Ldr. J. ELLIS.	Blue 1	52
DW-V.	K.9970	P/O. E. ALDOUS.	Blue 2	5
DW-Q.	R.6891	SGT. HAMLYN, R. F.	Green 1	41
DW-O.	X.4011	SGT. BAKER, C.		5
DW-T.	X.4064	F/Lt. S. C. NORRIS.	Red 1	60
DW-B.	X.4166	P/O. C. O. J. PEGGE.	Red 2	29
DW-G.		SGT. BEARDSLEY, R. A.	Yellow Section	5
DW-A.	R.6976	F/O. P. G. LAMB.	Yellow 1	51
DW-F.	X.4028	SGT. PARSONS, C. A.		26
DW-E.	P.9433	SGT. CHANDLER, H. H.	Yellow Section	16

As Ellis took off with his wingman P/O Aldous, the other section leaders would have waved their wingmen forward, engines snarling with the power necessary to get them airborne as quickly as possible. It is likely that Sgt Hamlyn led a two-man Green Section, Sgt Baker forming up on him, while F/Lt Norris, nearly always Red 1, gained altitude accompanied by the accomplished P/O Pegge, and probably Sgt Parsons. From the surviving combat reports and ORB, it seems that F/O Lamb was leading Yellow Section involving at least three aircraft, including Sgts Chandler and Beardsley; Parsons may have been a fourth pilot and the section was working in pairs—it is impossible to say with certainty. What is clear is that the *Luftwaffe's* High Command was plotting a day of continuously heavy raids in order to force up Fighter Command's aircraft, aiming to overrun the RAF's aerial defence system. This was the chaotic scene into which John Ellis was leading his men, the surviving combat reports ranging from 1110–1150 hours. 610 was joined by several other squadrons that AVM Park had ordered up, some of the combat reports mentioning the presence of other RAF fighters.

79 Squadron's ORB noted, '8 aircraft took off from Biggin Hill at about 11.30', which suggests they ran into the German formation somewhat later than 610 Squadron, although some historians state the two Biggin Hill squadrons attacked the German formation together. Whether 610 was joined by 79 Squadron is slightly immaterial, as other RAF fighters were in the area, but the odds were still heavily stacked against 610: '10 aircraft were ordered to engage about 50 bombers & about 50 fighters made up of H.E.111s, D.O.215s, M.E.109s & M.E.110s' (ORB)—terrifying odds to say the least. As 610 gained altitude, the information was fed through to Ellis from the ground controller, placing them on a collision course with the massive German force. The wait before they hove into sight must have been tense, knowing that such a numerically superior force was approaching, while also being aware that high-flying 109s would be positioning themselves to bounce them from above. An increasing number of black specks in the sky signalled the arrival of the *Luftwaffe en masse*, 'The bombers were in vic formation the fighters circling above' (ORB), and having reached his patrol area, S/Ldr Ellis was able to position his formation for an effective, yet highly dangerous, head-on attack, aiming to stop the *Luftwaffe* raid dead in its tracks.

Although Ellis's combat report has not survived, the ORB does mention that the CO carried out his plan successfully: 'S/Ldr. Ellis made a head on attack at the leader of a section of 3 H.E.111s, he broke up the E/A formation but could not observe the result of his attack'. The nature of a head-on attack made it nigh on impossible for Ellis to see the result of his fire, but given his marksmanship, it is likely that he damaged at least one of the Heinkels. It was almost inevitable that the bombers broke formation, given the vulnerability of the Heinkel's cockpit to the Spitfire's eight Browning machine guns. Bomber pilots must have dreaded having to face a Spitfire or Hurricane hurtling towards them from dead ahead, as they sat helplessly in their cockpits. Once any of the bombers had fallen out of formation, they became much more vulnerable, and the original attack by Ellis almost certainly helped the rest of his squadron to pick off stragglers or isolated aircraft, as becomes apparent. It had been noted in a Fighter Command 'Intelligence Bulletin' on 25 August, that 'Head on and deflection shooting should be increasingly employed as opportunity offers' (TNA, AIR 25/197), particularly against the *Luftwaffe's* bombers, due to their lack of armour on the cockpit and engines. S/Ldr Ellis would have been aware of this instruction, and his determination to carry it out underlined his bravery in the face of heavy odds.

Ellis was followed by his wingman P/O Aldous, who described his encounter against about 100 He 111s and Me 110s at 15,000 feet as follows:

> I was Blue 2.
>
> My Squadron sighted a formation of He 111s escorted by Me. 110s when on patrol N. of Ashford. I attacked a He 111 which was separated from the rest of the formation. Attacking from almost abeam I fired three bursts of about 4 secs each. As I broke away, his starboard engine was on fire and he was losing height rapidly. Shortly afterwards I fired a short burst (the remainder of my ammunition) at a Me. 110 without any visible effect. (TNA, AIR 50/172/4)

It is unclear whether or not Aldous had managed to carry out a frontal attack behind Ellis, while he reported that the engagement took place at 1150 hours, which meant the Squadron had been in the air for over an hour. The timings of these combat reports will be investigated later on. It is possible that the bomber Aldous attacked with a devastating twelve second burst of fire from 250 yards abeam, was one of the Heinkels that Ellis had forced out of formation. With its starboard engine in flames and losing altitude, the Heinkel 111 was doomed and Aldous left it to its fate, possibly due to the intervention of the escort. After firing all of his ammunition, Aldous was now very vulnerable himself, and disengaged as quickly as possible from the Messerschmitts, before returning to Biggin Hill. He was credited with his first enemy aircraft destroyed on this his fifth recorded patrol, in addition to his earlier claims of a 109 probable and a Do 215 damaged.

F/O Peter Lamb at the head of 'A' Flight's Yellow Section, provides the best description of events as a whole, as he tried to lead his section against the massed ranks of Heinkels and Me 110s, numbering 100 at 15,000 feet North of Ashford:

> I was Yellow 1.
>
> My Squadron had been somewhat strung out owing to a number of friendly aircraft coming to identify us which meant taking a certain amount of evasive action. We then sighted several formations of HE.111 escorted by ME. 110s flying North over Ashford about 2000 ft above us. The Squadron Leader was some distance in front of me and he manoeuvred to deliver a head on attack. I was following him when I noticed a HE 111 diving away from the formation towards me. I climbed towards him and opened fire at about 800 yds. The weather conditions were such that the Bullets were leaving smoke trails giving a wonderful tracer effect. I saw my bullets going into the under side of the E/A. I held my fire until in the vertical position when I passed just under his tail. I could also notice the De Wilde ammunition exploding. After this attack I was completely stalled and got into a spin. I did not see E/A again. Sgt Beardsley and Sgt Chandler who were behind me saw this and confirm destruction of this E/A. (TNA, AIR 50/172/45)

Two Me 109s from JG 54 collided near Biggin Hill on 30 August, both pilots successfully baling out. Some of 610's men went to inspect the remains of the aircraft. On the left is Brian Rees who had not flown since 22 August. Next to him, holding a piece of a 109 is Peter Lamb, who shot down a Heinkel 111 that day. On the right is John Ellis, complete with polka dot silk scarf and the DFC ribbon below his 'Wings'. (*Copyright 610 Squadron Association*)

The first point of interest is that 610 had become strung out after avoiding RAF fighters, which must have mistaken them for a formation of Me 109s; thankfully, their evasive action had prevented any friendly-fire incidents. They probably belonged to some of 43, 79 and 603 Squadrons. It is clear that John Ellis deliberately manoeuvred himself into a position to carry out the lethal head-on attack, Lamb trying to get his section to follow suit. The impact of Ellis's attack is apparent, as Lamb engaged a Heinkel which had probably been forced out of formation by his squadron leader. At a height disadvantage, Lamb engaged this bomber at the extreme range of 800 yards, but in concentrating his fire on the Heinkel 111 by using his tracer bullets, the bomber must have taken some fearful punishment as they closed to point blank range. Lamb expended 1,120 rounds during his determined attack, and Yellow Section had evidently stayed fairly compact throughout the various manoeuvrings of the unit as both his wingmen, Sgts Beardsley and Chandler, were able to confirm the Heinkel's demise. Having recovered from his spin, the experienced pilot returned to Biggin Hill to refuel and rearm, having claimed his fourth enemy aircraft destroyed in the last six days.

Both Bob Beardsley and Horatio Chandler filed their own combat reports on the huge battle which had developed over Ashford and the surrounding Kent countryside, the time and place referred to becoming increasingly varied. While Lamb had engaged the Heinkels north of Ashford at 1150 hours, Beardsley described his engagement as taking place at approximately 1110 hours, five miles north-west of Hawkinge. With their aircraft flying at maximum speed such distances could be covered very quickly, but the timings involved are still puzzling. Beardsley, another pilot who was growing in experience, reported:

> I attacked a Heinkel 111k at approximately 14,500 ft. after it had become detached from its formation. I delivered short bursts at 200 yards range from astern. By the time we had reached 10,000 ft it appeared badly damaged with one (starboard) engine smoking and the undercarriage down. He headed towards France but after more bursts of fire from my guns, he turned and flew towards the coast between Dungeness and Folkestone. I had then expended all my ammunition, but did two or three mock dives to keep him going down. On the last of these he released 4 red verey [Very] lights. This aircraft crashed into the sea approximately between Dymchurch and Folkestone. The crew were rescued by naval launch. (TNA, AIR 50/172/10)

Bob Beardsley, thrown into the fiercest of combats with no experience, had managed to return home unscathed again. This victory represented his second destroyed enemy aircraft along with a probable and one damaged, all in the space of his first five patrols, proving the intense nature of the fighting. The bomber Beardsley engaged is thought to have been:

> **10/KG1** Heinkel He 111H-2 (5125). Became separated from formation and attacked by Spitfires over the English coast. Forced to land on the sea off Folkestone harassed by Sgt. Beardsley of No. 610 Squadron. Uffz. Burger, Gefr. Hildebrand, Gefr. Feierabend, Gefr. Roggemann and Gefr. Klapphplz all rescued from the sea and landed at Dover. Aircraft V4+MV lost.[29]

Given the scale of the raid, and the odds stacked against them, 610's pilots had continued to give a very good account of themselves and the battle-hardened Sgt Chandler also made a claim. He reported encountering twelve Me 110s at 1140 hours at an altitude of 13,000 feet over Lympne, again suggesting the battle was spreading across Kent towards the coast. He only ran into these *Zerstörers* once he had carried out a head-on attack against some Dorniers:

> Fifteen Dorniers at 13,000 heading 340° \T/over Lympne. We manoeuvred to carry out head on attack. For my pass this failed and I carried on to attack ME110s who were 2000' above and behind bombers.

> This was at first unsuccessful so I fired a burst at random. One broke away and I further attacked from rear and fired another burst at Star. [starboard] engine, which started to smoke heavily and later to burn. E/a dived for cloud and headed for France. I was unable to again engage e/a. I received single machine gun return fire from e/a. (TNA, AIR 50/172/12)

Chandler's description is proof of the inherent difficulty of the head-on attack, as despite having the opportunity to position himself to carry out the attack, his pass was unsuccessful. This was probably down to the simple fact that the two formations had closed at speeds of over 500 mph. With no shortage of secondary targets, Chandler went on to set an Me 110's starboard engine on fire with some accurate machine gun fire, firing 1,600 rounds in one short and one long burst. He lost it in the clouds which the ORB reported as 7/10ths at 7,000 feet, but this 110, with a burning engine trailing a plume of smoke, may well have been shot down by other RAF fighter pilots in the vicinity. Horatio Chandler was able to claim the Me 110 as probably destroyed having successfully completed his sixteenth recorded operational sortie.

Another 'A' Flight pilot who made a claim during this engagement was P/O Pegge. He stated that they engaged the enemy nearer the south coast than the other pilots, recording in the preamble that they intercepted 100 plus Heinkel 111s, Me 110s and Me 109s at 1115 hours over Dungeness:

> I was Red 2 of A Flight in 610 Sqdn. Large numbers of enemy aircraft were seen approaching from the Channel. I attacked the leader of a large Vic formation of He 111s at about 12000 feet from in front & below from a range of 200 closing to 50 yds. The He111 stopped leading & went straight down. Sgt Farnes saw the enemy aircraft crash into the sea.
>
> I finished up right through the formation of He111s & almost reached some Me 110s which were above & behind. I then broke away sharply downwards. (TNA, AIR 50/172/58)

Joe Pegge was also at a height disadvantage to the massive enemy formation which was rolling in from France, which made engaging them all the more daunting. Just how strung out the Spitfires had become is impossible to say, but Pegge also employed the head-on attack, which indicates they could still function as a unit. The pilots coming in behind S/Ldr Ellis would actually have had fractionally more time to line themselves up on a target. This was the case with Pegge, who unleashed a two–three second burst of fire from 200 yards on a Heinkel which was leading a formation, causing maximum disruption to the enemy. It would have been demoralising for the other German crews to see their leader fall out of formation and go straight down. The demise of Pegge's Heinkel was witnessed by 501 Squadron's Sgt Farnes, proving how close to the coast they were. The time of 1115 hours is hard to corroborate with the other accounts of fighting near Ashford. It is possible that Pegge's original attack took place inland and that Farnes saw the Heinkel fall into the sea after it had turned tail while attempting to get home, Dungeness being the place where the Heinkel crashed as opposed to where the engagement took place. Joe Pegge returned safely to Biggin Hill, and was eventually credited with a Heinkel 111 destroyed, having expended just 500 rounds of ammunition, proof of the effectiveness of the head-on attack.

The destruction of this bomber represented Pegge's fifth confirmed victory in August alone, along with claims for one probable and two damaged. It was a sign of his growing prowess as a fighter pilot, and that he was one of the unit's most accomplished pilots. This interception was Pegge's eleventh recorded operation since 11 August, so he had been involved in virtually all of August's heavy fighting. Having survived five recorded patrols in June and thirteen more during July, these had stood him in good stead for August's dogfights, which had dwarfed even the largest raids of the previous month. The proof of this is evident in that he only claimed one probable in July, although he was much less experienced in July. In some sources, Pegge has been credited with the destruction of a Heinkel 111 at Blackboys, Sussex, although this does not match Sgt Farnes's description, so it is possibly the wrong aircraft to link to P/O Pegge.

Another key pilot in the Squadron with a similar amount of combat experience to Pegge was Sgt Pilot Hamlyn who was leading Green Section (reportedly in 'A' Flight), on his forty-first recorded patrol, fourteen of which had been carried out since 11 August. Hamlyn had also been incredibly successful during August, having claimed seven destroyed, one probable and a damaged, all of them bar one being against the *Luftwaffe's* dreaded Me 109, to which could be added a Dornier 17 shared destroyed and a Dornier 215 shared damaged in July. This tally currently placed him as the Squadron's second most successful pilot, second only to John Ellis, proof of his ability as one of Dowding's fighter boys.

Given the nature of this dogfight, it is unsurprising that the 'Pied Piper of Harrogate' had engaged the large formations of *Luftwaffe* aircraft—he also reported approximately 100 Heinkel 111s, Me 109s and Me 110s:

> I was Green Leader.
>
> I first sighted enemy aircraft over Ashford and started to attack them but a number of M.E. 110s attacked me before I could open fire. So I eventually fired at one of the M.E.s. He fell away from the rest, but I could not possibly see any results owing to the other enemy aircraft.
>
> On returning home at 10,000 ft I noticed more aircraft bombing Biggin Hill. I at once climbed up to about 20,000 ft and was attacked by 5 M.E. 109s which were circling. Owing to my slow speed I was easily able to get on the tail of the last 109. I fired a burst of about 2 seconds from astern with slight deflection. He fell away from the others smoking badly. I followed him and gave him the rest of my rounds in one burst. He went straight in the ground. I came down to the place I thought I had seen him hit and there was a large fire burning in the wood round West Malling aerodrome. (TNA, AIR 50/172/35)

It is likely that Hamlyn originally attacked the Heinkel 111s which 610's other pilots had already engaged, but while these pilots had carried out their attack before the 110s could intervene, Green Section was coming in behind the other sections, so the *Zerstörers* could prevent Green Section from getting to their charges. In Hamlyn's case at least, this was achieved, and the Yorkshireman eventually became embroiled with five of his old foes, the Me 109. Maintaining his composure, he used his lack of speed to his advantage by latching on to the last 109, and after damaging it with his first two second burst, he claimed the demise of his seventh confirmed 109 with a long burst from 250 yards using all his ammunition. This took place at 1150 hours, over an hour after he had taken off, and he must have been exhausted physically when he landed. Some sources have speculated that Hamlyn brought down Oblt. Harbauer of JG 2, however Harbauer was shot down at about 1655 hours,[30] so it must have been a different 109.

Despite the size of the raid on Biggin Hill, thankfully the German bombers failed to do serious damage to the aerodrome. Nevertheless, for those on the airfield who endured the attack, it was a terrifying experience as the bombs started to fall. Thanks to the testimony of Raymond Ellis of 610 Squadron's ground crew, we can see first-hand what it was like to be on the receiving end of this attack:

> Friday 30th August 1940—Morning
>
> This would be the day that none of us would be likely to forget. It was a warm and sunny summer's day, but that was not why we remember it! ...
>
> When the warning came over the Tannoy, I was in the Belfast hangar working with others renewing the stern of one of our Spitfires that had suffered a heavy landing loosening rivets around the stern frame. We grabbed our 'tin' hats and ran out across the wide apron to the air-raid shelter that had been allocated to Servicing Flight. It was good to be together.

> This shelter was a trench approximately six feet deep, six feet wide and possibly twenty feet long. Along each side there was a wooden seat. The earth floor between the wooden seats was covered by duck-boards. Overhead we were 'protected' by an arch of corrugated steel that was covered by a mound of earth that had grassed over. There was access at each end down steep steps at right angles to the line of the trench.
>
> The entrances to the shelter were screened by sandbags. Whilst we sat there in the semi-darkness, Bert Alkins preferred to stand on the entrance step.
>
> It was my first experience of sitting in the middle of a bombing target. There was some timely banter that helped us to relax whilst waiting for the first explosion. We did not have long to wait…
>
> The smaller bombs of 100 kg or so seemed to be in 'sticks' of six. Presumably, the six bombs were released in rapid succession from their particular bomb-bay. It was possible to identify the stick that was most relevant to our situation by the increasing loudness of the 'crumps' ...
>
> Bert called out that they had gone … We emerged and were surprised to find everything as we had left it, except for the craters that had appeared on the airfield, but none were quite as close as we had imagined …
>
> Whilst others were detailed to fill in craters, we returned to the hangar. There was our solitary Spitfire just as we had left her.[31]

As personnel came out of their shelters to survey the damage, Biggin Hill's squadrons began to return, Ronnie Hamlyn being one of the last of 610's men back at around midday. By the time he had got back to his dispersal hut, it is likely the last of the unit's pilots to make a claim, Sgt Baker, was already discussing his part in the engagement, as follows:

> I was in A Flight and sighted about 30 Do 215 and HE 111K. I was separated from my section and proceeded to attack a Do 215 which was circling with the other E/A. I attacked from the rear and gave a 2 second burst at 200 yards which caused it to separate from the other E/A and go into a gentle dive. I closed and gave another 2 second burst from the port quarter at 200 yards, which caused black smoke to issue from the port engine, and the E/A increased its dive. I was unable to follow it down as I proceeded to attack the other E/A without any apparent effect. (TNA, AIR 50/172/6)

Baker had probably been operating as a wingman to Hamlyn, when at 1130 hours he encountered the enemy aircraft over Ashford at about 13,000 feet. Becoming separated from his section in the build-up to the attack, Baker pressed home his own attacks determinedly against the bomber formations, forcing one bomber into a descent with a smoking engine. It is likely the bomber joined the increasing number of *Luftwaffe* aircraft which would not return to their home bases that afternoon, and he claimed the Dornier 215 as a probable. Despite his inexperience, Baker had been a quick learner and an adept fighter pilot, claiming two destroyed and three probably destroyed in a short space of time, again highlighting the increased intensity of the air fighting by the end of August.

Given the size of the raid 610 Squadron had intercepted, it is remarkable that all ten pilots returned safely, especially as they had become split up and been engaged for a sustained period of time, from between 1110 hours to midday. In doing so, they had thwarted the bulk of the German bombers from getting through to Biggin Hill, and claimed five destroyed and two probable, a highly successful engagement by any standards. It is interesting that neither John Ellis nor Stanley Norris, the two most experienced pilots, made a claim for this raid, but their presence certainly helped the less experienced men like Baker and Aldous in attacking the raiders.

Ellis should take much credit for his interception of the raid, as he had positioned his men extremely well to carry out the initial devastating attack. But 610 Squadron's fighter pilots had little time to reflect on the outcome of the interception, and as their Spitfires were frantically turned round by the ever-reliable ground crew, they would have filed their reports on the action, before trying to snatch a bite to eat at dispersal, and returning to readiness. Raymond Ellis, still working on 'his' Spitfire which had been under repair, sheds some light on the type of activity that was going on:

> Despite the absence of engine cowlings, and being up on trestles, she looked more like an aeroplane than she had the previous day. The new stern was complete with fin, rudder, tail planes, elevators and tail wheel. We still had to finish connecting the control cables, making sure that those to the three trimming tabs were routed correctly, and that all turnbuckles were properly tensioned and securely locked.
>
> The electrician had connected up the tail lamp. The wireless mechanic had fitted the radio and I. F. F. sets, and connected up the aerial. Steve, our instrument 'basher', had been and gone. The armourers were loading the ammunition boxes. The engine fitters were still working on the engine.[32]

As 30 August wore on, the *Luftwaffe* raids showed no sign of abating, and Fighter Command found itself stretched to its limits. At 1300 hours, 79 Squadron was, 'ordered to move to forward base at Hawkinge, 10 aircraft to readiness there' (79 ORB), which almost certainly meant that 610 Squadron was on immediate readiness at Biggin Hill. At 1500 hours, 79 Squadron's Hurricanes took off from Hawkinge to return to their home base, but as the raids continued to flow in from France, and with a gaping hole in the RDF defences, the sector controller at Biggin Hill thought it advisable to send up a defensive force for Biggin Hill. At 1520 hours, 'A' Flight was ordered to patrol the airfield, possibly to ensure 79 Squadron's safe arrival, as the Hurricanes would have been very vulnerable on their circuit to land, given that there were roaming groups of 109s about. The six pilots who carried out this patrol were led by F/Lt Norris (61) as Red Leader (DW-T, X.4064), with Sgts Parsons (27) (DW-Q, R.5891, clerical error, should be R.6891) and Beardsley (6) (DW-G, no serial) as his wingmen, and Yellow Section led by P/O Pegge (30) (DW-B, X.4166), with Sgts Chandler (17) (DW-E, P.9433) Yellow 2 and Baker (6) (DW-H, K.9818) Yellow 3 following him, all of whom had been on the previous sortie.

As Stan Norris led his men up in a spiralling climb above Biggin Hill, the pilots would have been scanning the sky in a spread out formation, more reliant on their eyes than ever, due to the number of RDF stations which were down from the previous raids. On reaching 'Angels 18', they patrolled their home base, when at 1540 hours, twenty minutes into their patrol, two Messerschmitt 109s suddenly came out of nowhere, flashing through their formation in an audacious bid to shoot down one of the unsuspecting Spitfires. Luckily, Sgt Horatio Chandler was alert to the danger: 'One flight on patrol over aerodrome. I was Yellow two. Leader was suddenly attacked from astern. I got a lucky short burst at close range. E/a dived straight down and pilot was seen to bail [*sic*] out by a sergeant gunner on this aerodrome' (TNA, AIR 50/172/12).

This very short combat report encapsulates the dangerous life of a fighter pilot in the summer of 1940. One moment the pilots were calmly climbing in formation to their patrol altitude, everything under control, everyone alert to the potential danger, and yet within seconds a much smaller force surprised them from behind and probably out of the sun, turning an outwardly serene patrol into a maelstrom of tracer and swirling machines, as the unsuspecting pilots suddenly had to fight for their lives. As was often the way, the hunter became the hunted and the attacking Me 109 pilots found themselves in trouble. In trying to pick off a section leader, the German had left himself vulnerable to attack. The fact that Chandler got in a lucky burst at just fifty yards, suggests that it was Yellow 1, P/O Pegge, who was the 109's target and who had the fortunate escape. The 109s would have approached at high speed, so it was an excellent piece of shooting by Chandler to have brought the Me 109 down, having fired just sixty-five rounds per gun. The fatally-struck *Luftwaffe* fighter continued straight down about four miles east of Bromley, clearly within sight of 'A' Flight's home, the pilot being seen to bale out. Chandler modestly referred to this victory as being lucky, but it was clearly more due to his ability as a fighter pilot, this being his fourth confirmed victory along with claims for one unconfirmed, one probable, three damaged and a shared damaged, making him the unit's fifth most successful pilot.

Nobody else was able to engage the second Me 109; given his fellow countryman's demise, its pilot probably wished he had not bothered attacking the tempting target of six Spitfires. 610's formation reformed, thankful that none of them had been hit, before continuing their eventful thirty-five-minute patrol, returning to land at 1555 hours. P/O Pegge would have thanked his Number 2 for shooting his assailant down, and it showed yet again that even the most experienced pilots could still be surprised, miles inland over their home base. No one was ever safe, no matter where they were operating in the south-east of England. But the County of Chester Squadron's personnel must have been pleased to have survived a patrol unscathed again, having claimed another enemy aircraft destroyed in the process. Stan Norris had carried out his sixty-first recorded patrol, ten more than his squadron commander John Ellis, a remarkable feat given the incessant nature of their patrols and the constant threat from the enemy. The strain on these experienced pilots must have been becoming unbearable.

According to the ORB, this was the last patrol 610 Squadron's pilots carried out while in 11 Group during the Battle of Britain period, understandable given their continuous presence on the front line during July and August. However, it is surprising that there is not at least one more patrol recorded as having taken place on 30 August. As 'A' Flight's pilots were debriefed, yet more massive raids were building up, once again targeting 11 Group's sector stations and aircraft factories. 610 Squadron was possibly alternating standing patrols of Biggin Hill with 79 Squadron, as at 1635 hours five Hurricanes, 'of A Flight took off and saw a lot of Me.109s but as they were 2,000 feet higher the C. O. did not order attack ... All landed 17.35' (79 ORB). Interestingly, Sgt Bamberger's logbook lists three flights (30–32) that day; a twenty-five-minute flight to Hawkinge, a seventy-minute patrol of 'Red Queen' (Deal), followed by a fifty-minute patrol and return to Biggin Hill. The actual time when he was operating

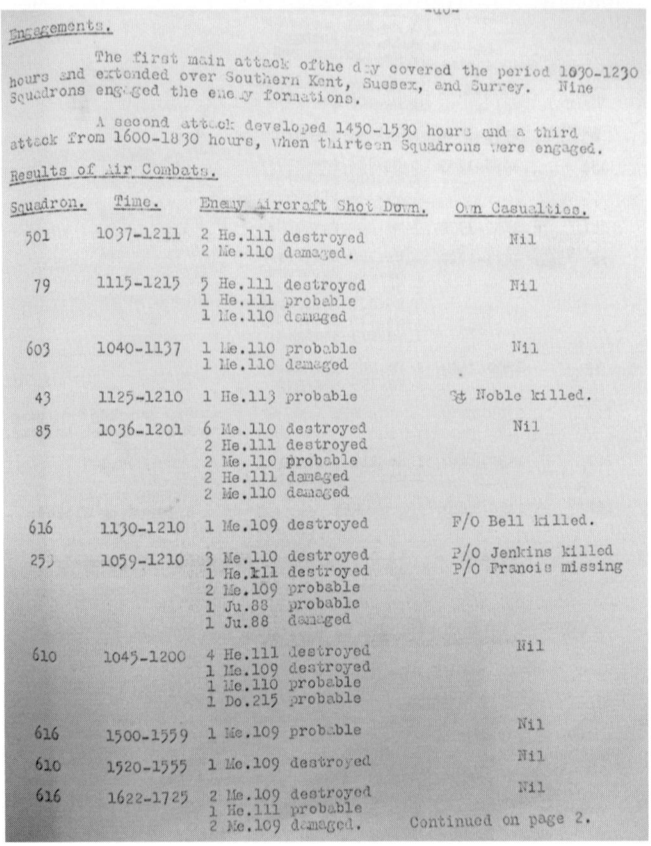

Engagements.

The first main attack ofthe day covered the period 1030-1230 hours and extended over Southern Kent, Sussex, and Surrey. Nine Squadrons engaged the enemy formations.

A second attack developed 1450-1530 hours and a third attack from 1600-1830 hours, when thirteen Squadrons were engaged.

Results of Air Combats.

Squadron.	Time.	Enemy Aircraft Shot Down.	Own Casualties.
501	1037-1211	2 He.111 destroyed 2 Me.110 damaged.	Nil
79	1115-1215	5 He.111 destroyed 1 He.111 probable 1 Me.110 damaged	Nil
603	1040-1137	1 Me.110 probable 1 Me.110 damaged	Nil
43	1125-1210	1 He.113 probable	Sgt Noble killed.
85	1036-1201	6 Me.110 destroyed 2 He.111 destroyed 2 Me.110 probable 2 He.111 damaged 2 Me.110 damaged	Nil
616	1130-1210	1 Me.109 destroyed	F/O Bell killed.
253	1059-1210	3 Me.110 destroyed 1 He.111 destroyed 2 Me.109 probable 1 Ju.88 probable 1 Ju.88 damaged	P/O Jenkins killed P/O Francis missing
610	1045-1200	4 He.111 destroyed 1 Me.109 destroyed 1 Me.110 probable 1 Do.215 probable	Nil
616	1500-1559	1 Me.109 probable	Nil
610	1520-1555	1 Me.109 destroyed	Nil
616	1622-1725	2 Me.109 destroyed 1 He.111 probable 2 Me.109 damaged.	Nil

Continued on page 2.

This photo from '11 Group Intelligence Bulletin No. 40', shows how heavy the fighting was during the first two raids on 30 August 1940. (*TNA, AIR 25/197*)

from Hawkinge is unclear, and it is also unclear who Bamberger was operating with. But this perhaps explains where the Squadron was in the late afternoon of 30 August.

At 1805 hours, 79 Squadron reported another patrol of the sector station presumably by 'B' Flight, but they were in for a surprise: 'Six aircraft took off and they saw aerodrome bombed while they were doing first circuit after the take off. Apparently 15 to 20 J.U.88, 30 Me.109 and 30 Me.110s or Jaguars. F/Lt. Haysom got one probable Me 109. Sgt. Bolton thinks he got a Me.109 also. All landed by 18.30 …' (79 ORB). The fact that the Hurricanes were still forming up in a circuit suggests that this was a patrol, more than a scramble to engage an immediate threat to Biggin Hill. Finally the aerodromes defences had been breached, with disastrous consequences, and it is surprising that the whereabouts of 610 Squadron is not better known, although Bamberger's logbook entries possibly hold the key.

Once again, Raymond Ellis provides vivid recollections of the raid and its aftermath:

> At about half past five, Stan (Harold Stanley—engine fitter) called me to join him for early tea. We left the fitters working on the engine—Cpl. Reg Lewis and probably Tom Walker, face usually streaked with oil. My fellow airframe fitter, Arthur Rushton, carried on inside the fuselage whilst I went off. Harold Lunt and another armourer were getting the eight Browning guns ready…
>
> On our way to the cookhouse (Airmen's Mess), I remember passing about six new arrivals in best blues in front of the Guard Room … We sat down with our spam and mugs of tea at a table directly below an open sash window. It was a hot day, and the lower sash was up as high as it would go. Before we had time to even taste our tea, the Tannoy called out: 'Air Raid! Take cover immediately!'
>
> Never had we responded to an order more promptly! Grabbing our mugs, 'irons', gas masks and 'tin hats', we were on the table and through the window in a flash and sprinting the hundred yards or so to our trench shelter. On our way, we passed a superior concrete shelter into which men were diving. As we arrived at our shelter, someone said, 'Look at those Blenheims!' We looked and saw a couple of twin-engine planes approaching low over South Camp hangars directly towards us. Three seconds later, from inside the shelter, we heard the first heavy crump followed by what sounded like the end of the world …
>
> The eruptions continued. Some were VERY close. Unlike the earlier raid, the bombs were not in sticks of six. Each of the nine bombers carried two 500 kg. bombs. Two of the bombs failed to explode or remained in their bomb-bays—16 didn't! ...
>
> The identity of the bombers is disputed. Those of us who thought they looked like Blenheims believed them to have been Junkers 88s. However, Alf Bridson [see photo p. 235] and others out on 610's dispersal were sure that the bombers had twin tails which suggested that they were Dorniers. Their first thought was that they were Hampdens. Being farther from South Camp than we were, the boys on the dispersal area had about two seconds longer to view them before taking cover…
>
> It seems that the formation that attacked us that evening had flown up the Thames Estuary before sharply changing course. This cunning tactic gave Group HQ little time to plot its track and predict its likely target. As a result, the warning was less than a minute in advance of the first bomb…
>
> At the time of the raid, 610 Squadron's Spitfires were far away on another interception. 79 Squadron managed to get six of their Hurricanes into the air, but they were too late to catch the enemy bombers…
>
> In silence we emerged from our humble shelter. There had been no 'All clear'. It was very quiet. All around us there were large chunks of clay earth. About 30 yards away towards the Cookhouse, I was vaguely aware of a large mound of earth upon which were strewn the bright red and blue remains of airmen. Still slightly stunned, we returned to the hangar… As we entered the open doorway of the first bay, we followed the upward gaze of the others. There, held by the web of roof trusses, was the Station Commander's big Humber estate car upside down. Directly above the car the blue sky was visible through a hole in the roof that mirrored the shape of the car and provided evidence of its flight path…

> Facing the closed doors of the middle bay was our precious Spitfire still up on trestles. All was well with her apart from a covering of dust and debris from the hole made by the intruder which was almost directly above her new stern … Now, it was our job to remove our Spitfire away from the hovering Humber, and out onto the comparative safety of the airfield where we could complete our tasks.
>
> During the evening the bad news filtered through. Three of our Squadron had been killed—LAC 'Jacko' Jackson (Airframe Fitter of Servicing Flight), AC Burton (ACH-GD), and Pte. J. Tarrant (Royal Corps of Signals, attached to our Wireless Section).
>
> The concrete shelter near to our trench had received a direct hit. The bodies that we had seen were those of the new arrivals. Volunteers worked long and hard to open up the smashed shelter, but the chunks of broken concrete were difficult to move without causing a further collapse. The task seemed impossible and there was little hope that any could have survived. Late that evening a team of miners was brought in from the Kent coalfields. It was believed that amongst those in the shelter was one of our engine fitters—Jack Moore. His chum, Gordon Hughes, worked with the rescuers until eventually his loyalty was rewarded. Jack was brought out alive, and he survived the ordeal. All the others were dead…
>
> 610 Squadron's dispersal was at right angles to the bombers' path and escaped damage. Without the Spitfires, it was not such a conspicuous target. Some of the men would have gone to North Camp for tea, whilst the rest waited for the Squadron's return.[33]

The heavy casualties suffered on the ground at Biggin Hill, thirty-nine killed and twenty-six wounded, made this a particularly bad day for the RAF, as the station was critical to 11 Group's operations. Many buildings had been destroyed, including workshops, a hangar, the sergeants' mess and WAAF quarters. On a more personal level, it was a black day for 610 Squadron in suffering the loss of three of its ground staff. John Joseph Jackson was an Auxiliary, aged twenty-three, and was a fitter when the Squadron moved to Wittering back in October 1939, so would have been well-known by everyone. He was married to Hilda, of Wellington, Shropshire and she inscribed his headstone with the heartfelt, 'In remembrance Of my dear husband At rest'. Jackson was listed as 'Missing' following the attack on Biggin Hill, at approximately 1810 hours on 30 August, although one of the forms mistakenly mentioned his death as being on 31 August 1940. He was ultimately identified by his identity discs, according to the burial return (TNA, AIR 81/2912). Jackson was buried near Biggin Hill on 5 September 1940, at St Mary Cray Cemetery, Kent, in Plot E, Division 3, Grave 139B. Sadly, his wife could not attend the funeral, as she was in a nursing home (TNA, AIR 81/2912).

Joseph Henry Thomas Tarrant, aged twenty-eight, was a Private in the Royal Army Ordinance Corps and had been attached to 610 Squadron as part of the wireless section. He was married to Miriam

Raymond Ellis's view from his shelter in the aftermath of the evening raid on 30 August, taken by LAC Tom Woodfine. The guard room is in the background, the badly damaged airmen's mess on the right and the destroyed concrete shelter and other damaged shelters are in the foreground. (*Copyright Diane Reid née Woodfine*)

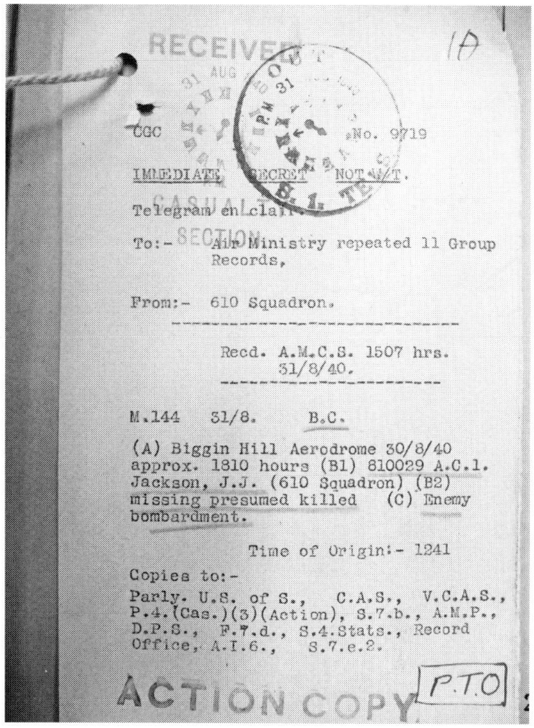

RECEIVED 31 AUG

CGC No. 9719

IMMEDIATE SECRET NOT W/T.

Telegram en clair.

CASUALTY SECTION

To:- Air Ministry repeated 11 Group Records,

From:- 610 Squadron.

Recd. A.M.C.S. 1507 hrs. 31/8/40.

M.144 31/8. B.C.

(A) Biggin Hill Aerodrome 30/8/40 approx. 1810 hours (B1) 810029 A.C.1. Jackson, J.J. (610 Squadron) (B2) missing presumed killed (C) Enemy bombardment.

Time of Origin:- 1241

Copies to:-

Parly. U.S. of S., C.A.S., V.C.A.S., P.4.(Cas.)(3)(Action), S.7.b., A.M.P., D.P.S., F.7.d., S.4.Stats., Record Office, A.I.6., S.7.e.2.

ACTION COPY P.T.O

610 Squadron's communication to the Air Ministry that John Joseph Jackson was missing presumed killed. (*TNA, AIR 81/2912*)

Violet and his parents were Thomas James and Annie Elizabeth Tarrant, of Monewden, Suffolk, where he is buried in St Mary's Churchyard. It appears he died as a result of his wounds, as the date attributed to his death is actually 6 September 1940.[34] A 'J. H. Tarrant' is listed as having been taken to Farnborough Hospital with facial injuries and suffering from shock after the raid, although he was listed as an AC 2, not a private (TNA, AIR 81/2944). It would seem to be too much of a coincidence not to be the Tarrant in question.

Archibald Charles George Burton, aged twenty-six, born in London to Archibald William and Rose Lilly Burton, had joined the VR, and was married to Elizabeth, with whom he had lived in Dagenham, Essex. His grave, 455 in Square E, in Eastbrookend (Dagenham) Cemetery (known as Becontree Cemetery), Essex, is fittingly inscribed with an abbreviated version of Churchill's famous words, 'Never was so much owed By so many to so few'. Details of Burton's death were found in an AMCB file for multiple casualties at Biggin Hill, due to the bombing on 30 August 1940. This also mentioned an LAC J. Moore, who was admitted to Farnborough Hospital with a cut scalp and bruising, probably the 'Jack Moore' mentioned by Ellis, who had survived the direct hit on the shelter.

As is evident, different raiders have been given credit for this daring attack, but it is now recognised as having been carried out by Me 110s of low-level experts Erpro. 210, thanks to historian John Vasco's research. Raymond Ellis's belief that 610 was patrolling too far away to intervene is also supported by *The Bump*, which states that, '610 was already engaged on a distant sortie',[35] but no record of this operation is mentioned in the ORB. We will probably never know for certain where the Squadron had been sent to when they were so badly needed at Biggin Hill, but it does seem possible that 610 had been operating out of Hawkinge when the bombers struck. The chaos caused by the raiders extended to the notation of the Squadron's ORB, with everybody focusing on the priority of getting the station operational as soon as possible, rather than recording the details of 610's patrol, which would also explain why the records from the end of July had been mixed up with those of the end of August.

Archibald Burton, from 610 Squadron's ground crew, tragically killed during the air raid on Biggin Hill on 30 August. (*Approved for use by the Biggin Hill Memorial Museum Trust*)

When the County of Chester Squadron's pilots returned to Biggin Hill, alarmed by the lack of R/T communication with Biggin Hill, which had suddenly failed as a result of the bombing (79 ORB), they would have been devastated to see the death and destruction that had been caused in their absence, particularly as three of the Squadron's own airmen had lost their lives. The human cost caused by the raid had been heavy indeed, and it would have rammed home to those left helplessly in the path of the bombs, that nowhere was safe in the face of the *Luftwaffe's* aerial onslaught. While the loss of life was tragic, the *Luftwaffe's* tactic of launching a steady stream of continuous raids on Fighter Command's most vital stations was clearly working. Hornchurch, another 11 Group sector station, took over Biggin Hill's Sector, while a huge effort began to get Biggin operational again.

The importance of such repair work should not go unmentioned, with RAF ground staff combining with civilians and even miners, to keep Biggin Hill in the fight. Personnel of the General Post Office who worked tirelessly to repair the broken lines of communication, both here and at all the bomb-damaged aerodromes, were particularly unsung heroes. But if such raids continued to get through and were repeated at the other sector stations, the structure of Fighter Command's 11 Group would slowly but surely disintegrate. The defensive capabilities of fighter squadrons would be severely curtailed when it came to protecting key targets in the south-east and London areas. It was something of which Dowding and Park were all too aware during late August and early September.

As night fell on 30 August, and rescue and repair work was carried out at Biggin Hill, the pilots of 610 Squadron would have reflected on a very mixed day. On the one hand, they had carried out two successful patrols, with claims for six destroyed and two probably destroyed enemy aircraft, for no loss of their own pilots. But any elation gained from these patrols would have immediately dissipated, following the deaths and damage at Biggin Hill during 610's final, unrecorded patrol. Unfortunately, the Squadron would have gone where the ground controller directed it, so there was nothing it could have done to prevent the raid which had crept through the gaps in the RDF defences. Indeed, it had only been a matter of time before the station was badly hit, and in the coming days more and more raids would get through to Biggin Hill.

It is testament to 610 Squadron, along with 32 and latterly 79 Squadrons, that Biggin Hill had escaped largely unscathed for so long. As noted in *The Bump*, 610 Squadron had been in constant action during August, 'against seemingly overwhelming odds, and perhaps its finest hour came on the 18th—the hardest day—when it intercepted a massive formation of German bombers and prevented what would probably have been the heaviest raid ever on Biggin Hill'.[36] Nevertheless, such courageous actions came at a cost. The early starts, long periods of readiness, followed by violent dogfights and sudden deaths, combined with the general strain of serving for three and a half months in the front line at 11 Group airfields, had left the County of Chester Squadron's pilots physically exhausted. Even the least experienced pilots would have been incredibly drained. For 610 Squadron, which had valiantly given so much, it was time for a long-overdue rest.

It is unclear when 610 Squadron's orders were received precisely, but it is likely it was at quite short notice, probably on the evening of 30 August. 72 Squadron, the unit replacing 610, was warned at 2230 hours on 30 August (TNA, AIR 25/241), that they would be moving south the next day to replace 610, so it is possible 610's personnel only found out at a similar time in the evening. They would leave the eye of the storm at Biggin Hill on 31 August, for quieter skies in the north-east of England—RAF Acklington was to be their new home, where they would become a Category 'C' Squadron.

For some of the ground crew, the news was not quite so good, as Raymond Ellis recalled in his reminiscences about 30 August:

> Word came that the Squadron was to fly to Acklington in Northumberland early the next morning for a well-earned break from the front line. There they would join our Hurricane friends of 32 Squadron. 610 Squadron was to be relieved by the Spitfires of 72 Squadron from Acklington ... The intention was that 610's Servicing Flight and the ground crews of 'A' and 'B' Flights would remain at Biggin Hill to look after 72 Squadron's Spitfires for an unspecified period—presumably until 72 Squadron's own ground staff had got themselves organised. This assumed that 72 Squadron would be able to operate from Biggin Hill.[37]

So Raymond Ellis and his friends would have to wait a while longer for a rest. For the bulk of 610 Squadron, following in the footsteps of 32 Squadron was a double-edged sword—yes, they got their rest, but at what price to the unit as a whole on becoming a Category 'C' Squadron? Each squadron prided itself on its own unique identity. Having a group of squadrons which primarily trained new men for other units could obviously have a negative impact on morale, something of which Dowding was very conscious. Also, although relieved to be out of the firing line, experienced men like Ellis, Norris and Lamb, who had survived for so long in such danger, possibly felt they should see the battle out. But the Squadron could not go on forever in the front line, and it was time for it to be rotated away. Those who could not see this had perhaps already been pushed too hard.

On 1 August 1940, the Squadron could boast a complement of thirty pilots, having received thirteen replacement pilots at the end of July, eight being on a Spitfire conversion course, while others were not yet operational. That just thirty days later, seven of these new recruits, more than half, had been killed or wounded tells its own story. However, that a further six of the Squadron's more experienced pilots had also been killed or wounded shows how savage the fighting had become. The only remedy for this came when the order for rotation arrived, and 30 August brought that news for 610 Squadron. As the pilots trooped off to bed that night, they could look forward to leaving an increasingly dangerous Biggin Hill and swap it for Acklington and Northumbria's safer skies. It is worth bearing in mind here, that it was during these chaotic events at Biggin Hill at the end of August, that Sgt Manton's death was being looked into, as earlier discussed. Given the upheaval at the Squadron's home station due to the bombing raids and then 610 Squadron's imminent departure for the north-east, it becomes more understandable how the confusion over the date of his death arose.

It would have been a bitter pill for 610 Squadron's personnel to spend their last night surrounded by smouldering ruins, but the Squadron's achievements while serving in 11 Group cannot be underestimated and it is interesting to look at them on a monthly basis. In May, when 610 (County of Chester) Squadron's untried fighter pilots were first sent into the fray over the BEF's evacuation from Dunkirk, they lost seven pilots killed and one wounded in just four encounters with numerically superior *Luftwaffe* forces. These were horrific losses of virtually 50 per cent. In return, the Squadron filed claims for ten destroyed, three unconfirmed and one damaged, a good account of itself given the difficult circumstances and the RAF's outmoded tactics in the face of such a formidable enemy. During the course of June, one pilot was lost on a training exercise and the Squadron claimed one enemy aircraft destroyed. In July, things started to hot up again over the Channel convoys and the Squadron claimed fourteen enemy aircraft destroyed, a further ten unconfirmed destroyed or probable and four damaged, for the loss of three pilots killed in action, one while training, plus two wounded in action, one of whom would return to action. Again, the Squadron had put up an excellent effort in the defence of Britain.

610 Squadron was able to take this hard fought experience into the heavier fighting of August, as the *Luftwaffe* really ramped up its offensive. As a result, during August the Squadron claimed forty-three enemy aircraft destroyed, with another seventeen probable and six unconfirmed, plus nineteen damaged—an impressive tally of eighty-five claims of varying sorts. Such figures alone show how the severity of fighting had increased in August, especially as 610 Squadron's first reported run-in with the enemy came a full week into the month. The vast increase in claims inevitably led to an increase in losses, particularly those suffering bad wounds, and the stark figures of six pilots killed and ten wounded (two pilots possibly being wounded twice) show just how great a sacrifice the Squadron paid. By the time the Squadron had fought its last battle operating from 11 Group in August 1940, it had lost eighteen pilots killed (sixteen killed or missing in action, two in accidents) and twelve or thirteen wounded, having claimed sixty-eight destroyed, nineteen probable, seventeen unconfirmed and twenty-four damaged; claims against 128 aircraft in total. Although the losses were heavy indeed, and the cream of the pre-war Squadron had gone even before the Battle of Britain had begun, the effort of 610 Squadron in such a desperate situation during that long summer of 1940, is one of which everyone associated with the Squadron can be very proud.

Perhaps the most sobering fact is that of the original eighteen pilots who were with 610 Squadron just before the Dunkirk evacuation in late May 1940, only three of them were still operational just three months later, eleven having been killed and three wounded, the eighteenth having left the Squadron. The three originals, John Ellis, Stanley Norris and Peter Lamb, had more than inflicted heavy losses of their own, doubtless driven by the deaths of so many of their close friends, shooting down a combined total of nineteen and a half destroyed, two shared destroyed, two unconfirmed, one probable, two damaged and one shared damaged. They had made sure the loss of their colleagues had not been in vain.

The survival of the veterans, with their hard-won experience, meant that those joining the unit during the summer of 1940 had a vital source of knowledge from which to learn: men like Ronnie Hamlyn, Joe Pegge and Horatio Chandler who had all quickly progressed to become very effective fighter pilots, with numerous claims. But just as important were pilots such as Norman Ramsay and Claude Parsons, who had achieved fewer victories but had survived and gained vital experience; they had all helped to form a very successful Spitfire squadron. Some of these more experienced pilots would now be used to train the new pilots coming straight from OTUs, desperate for any tips and advice which could be passed on to them, before they were posted to one of the units left in 11 Group, to face the *Luftwaffe* for the first time. The full list of pilots' claims for August 1940 was as follows:

Hamlyn:
109 damaged 14/8
109 destroyed 24/8
109 destroyed 24/8
109 destroyed 24/8
109 destroyed 24/8
88 destroyed 24/8
109 destroyed 26/8
109 probable 26/8
109 destroyed 28/8
109 destroyed 30/8

Pegge:
109 destroyed 12/8
109 destroyed 12/8
109 destroyed 18/8
111 damaged 18/8
109 probable 24/8
109 destroyed 28/8
215 damaged 29/8
111 destroyed 30/8

Lamb:
109 destroyed 24/8
215 destroyed 26/8
110 destroyed 29/8
111 destroyed 30/8

Chandler:
109 damaged 12/8
109 confirmed 14/8
215 destroyed 18/8
215 damaged 18/8
215 damaged 29/8
110 probable 30/8
109 destroyed 30/8

Norris:
87 confirmed 14/8
87 confirmed 14/8
87 damaged 14/8
109 destroyed 24/8
110 probable 29/8

Ellis:
109 confirmed 12/8
109 unconfirmed 12/8
88 damaged 16/8
111 destroyed 18/8
109 destroyed 26/8

Baker:
109 destroyed 24/8
110 probable 29/8
215 probable 29/8
109 destroyed 29/8
215 probable 30/8

Cox:
109 confirmed 12/8
109 unconfirmed 12/8
109 probable 15/8
109 destroyed 18/8
215 probable 18/8

Rees:
109 unconfirmed 12/8
87 probable 14/8
109 destroyed 18/8
215 destroyed 18/8

Beardsley:
109 destroyed 25/8
215 probable 29/8
109 damaged 29/8
111 destroyed 30/8

Arnfield:
109 damaged 15/8
109 damaged 16/8
109 destroyed 18/8
109 destroyed 18/8

Gardner:
109 unconfirmed 12/8
109 unconfirmed 12/8
109 unconfirmed 12/8
113 (109) confirmed 14/8

Parsons:
87 probable 14/8
109 damaged 14/8
17 destroyed 18/8

Aldous:
109 probable 24/8
215 damaged 29/8
111 destroyed 30/8

Ramsay:
110 confirmed 14/8
109 probable 26/8

Corfe:
109 confirmed 14/8
109 damaged 14/8
109 damaged 15/8

Gardiner:
110 destroyed 18/8

Wilson:
109 destroyed 26/8

Warner:
109 probable 15/8

Bamberger:
109 probable 28/8

Gray:
109 probable 16/8

Else:
109 damaged 14/8
215 damaged 18/8
215 damaged 18/8

E. B. B. Smith:
He 59 damaged 11/8

August claims

	Destroyed	Probable	Unconfirmed	Damaged	Total Claims
Me 109	28	8	6	9	51
Me 110	3	3	N/A	N/A	6
He 111	5	N/A	N/A	1	6
Do 17	1	N/A	N/A	N/A	1
Do 215	3	4	N/A	6	13
He 59	N/A	N/A	N/A	1	1
Ju 87	2	2	N/A	1	5
Ju 88	1	N/A	N/A	1	2
Total	43	17	6	19	85

610 (County of Chester) Squadron had done all that had been asked of it and so much more during its lengthy time in the front-line defence of the nation. Like all the Auxiliary units, it had proven that, 'by 1940 the weekend flyers were as effective in the air as any regular squadron'.[38] Too many of its brave pilots paid the ultimate sacrifice, to whom we in the modern world owe so much; they should never be forgotten. Now it was time for the survivors to get their deserved rest, try to restore their shattered nerves and pass on their knowledge to the fresh recruits.

When dawn broke on 31 August, for the first time in many weeks, 610's pilots knew that by the end of the day they would be out of 11 Group, and the Squadron would have been busy readying itself for the move, the ORB stating, 'Biggin Hill 31st August, 1940 ... Pilots and crews move to R.A.F. Station, Acklington'. Raymond Ellis recalled how, 'It was to be another warm and sunny day that should have reminded us of happy holidays past, but it was not the time for dreaming. However, there was a sort of relaxed atmosphere out in 610's dispersal. It was our pilots' turn for a well-earned break from the front line'.[39] Nevertheless, the *Luftwaffe* was not intending to ease up on the attacks, with round the clock raids now being the norm. The night-time attacks continued to keep the defending forces on their toes and once again, Liverpool had been the hardest hit during the night. The momentum which had built up during the course of these raids continued on 31 August, and as 610's pilots readied themselves to fly out, the *Luftwaffe* mounted raids against several key Fighter Command aerodromes. North Weald, Debden and Duxford all found themselves under attack from raids which came in around 0800 hours, but another heavily-escorted formation of bombers was directed at Biggin Hill.

79 Squadron was now responsible for Biggin Hill's defence:

> **08.40** Squadron Available at Dawn. At 08.40 hours Twelve aircraft ordered off to patrol base. F/Lt.Haysom got one Me.109 destroyed. S/Ldr. J.H. Heyworth One Ju.88 Probable. P/O. Nelson-Edwards forced landed and injured his eye. The remainder were ordered to land at Croydon at approximately 10.00 hours. (79 ORB)

Once again the *Luftwaffe's* bombers had got through, and it is possible 'The Chesters' had been released from operations, as they did not engage this raid, as they prepared to move out. However, from Bob Beardsley's account of 31 August to Geoffrey Simpson, it seems at least some of the Squadron had attempted to intercept the raid:

> 'On the 31st we had been directed to Croydon (which was bombed after we landed) and on our return to Biggin I was obliged to hop over the bomb craters as I landed. I overshot the perimeter track and ran over some coils of barbed wire'. Beardsley and his Spitfire finished up in the entrance to a bell tent, 'causing shock/horror to the squaddies who were enjoying a tea break'.[40]

Raymond Ellis had vivid memories of being on the receiving end of another *Luftwaffe* attack:

All that now remained to be done by Servicing Flight on this lone Spitfire was the pre-flight Daily Inspection by one of each trade who would then be required to initial the appropriate column of the Form 700. Warrant Officer Bentall gave me the job of inspecting the airframe …

The aircraft had been thoughtfully parked on the grass about thirty yards from our trench shelter. Its tail was up on a trestle in order to keep the load off the tail wheel and thence off the stern bulkhead. This was so I could check the tightness of each of the four longeron studs and the fifty two 2 BA bolts around the bulkhead flanges that secured the whole tail unit to the fuselage. To enable me to do this, I was lying full length on my back inside the fuselage surrounded by control cables and by structural members that made their presence felt. The familiar sounds of normality were suddenly joined by a distant bugle call being repeated and getting louder. Someone outside shouted, 'Air Raid!' and 'It's those b… Jerries again' or something to the same effect …

Cursing the interruption, I wriggled my way feet first and one hip at a time through that so-called inspection hole in the starboard side, and dropped down onto my toolbox. The others had a few seconds' lead, but I was close behind as we dived into our shelter. It was about midday.

The crumps were not as loud as those made by the big ones on the previous evening. There were a lot more in number, and they were in sticks of six. Some were uncomfortably close. When we emerged, there was no sight of our 'look-out' Bert Alkins. Our precious Spitfire was off its trestle and on fire.

Sometime later I learned that the bugler had been blown off his bicycle by a bomb. Bert Alkins had spotted this from the steps of our shelter, and, whilst bombs were still falling, had carried the injured bugler to the casualty station. For this gallant action, Bert was mentioned in despatches … Although I was frequently with Alkins during the next fortnight, I never heard him mention anything about the bugler incident …

The airfield was plastered with craters so that the returning Hurricanes of 79 Squadron had to land at Croydon … Biggin Hill was non-operational until its airfield had been made suitable for the Hurricanes of 79 Squadron to return.

We were now without a single aircraft to work on. Warrant Officer Bentall called the members of Servicing Flight together near the burnt out remains of our Spitfire. He said that he had a 48 Hours Pass for one of us. Our names were duly dropped into a forage cap, stirred and shaken up. A name was drawn—it read 'ELLIS' …

Back in our barrack block I attempted a dry shave, changed into my 'best blue', clean boots and found my best forage cap to replace the one that had been burnt in our bombed Spitfire. Grabbing my haversack, steel helmet and gas mask, I hastened towards the Guard Room. As I was passing a low sand-bagged building, an RAF ambulance pulled up.

The driver jumped out and called me to give him a hand. As I took one end of a stretcher, I looked down on the dead, ashen grey, face of George Wright, one of Six-Ten's metal workers.

Later I learned that George Wright and Tommy Topping had been working in the wrecked workshops when the raid started. They had dived into the open pipe trench mentioned earlier. Unfortunately, George had been hit by a piece of shrapnel from an exploding bomb. The building into which I helped to carry poor George was the Camp's Mortuary.[41]

The loss of another member of 610's ground crew was recorded in the ORB, '810068 A.C.I. WRIGHT, W. killed as a result of enemy action', Ellis forgetting his name was actually William, not George, unless the latter was how he was known. An AC 1 Wright had moved with the Squadron to Wittering back in October 1939, and like the ground crew losses of the previous day, it would have been felt heavily amongst men who had been under so much strain for so long, pilots and ground staff alike. This was probably even more so when the end seemed to be in sight in terms of their spell in the front line.

The details surrounding Wright's death were amongst those released by The National Archives in June 2017. He was born in Birkenhead on 26 September 1917 and his parents, William and Margaret Ann Wright, lived at 45 Mersey Bank Road, New Ferry, Birkenhead. William Wright was an Auxiliary, and was buried privately by his family on 7 September 1940, in Bebington Cemetery, Wirral, in Section

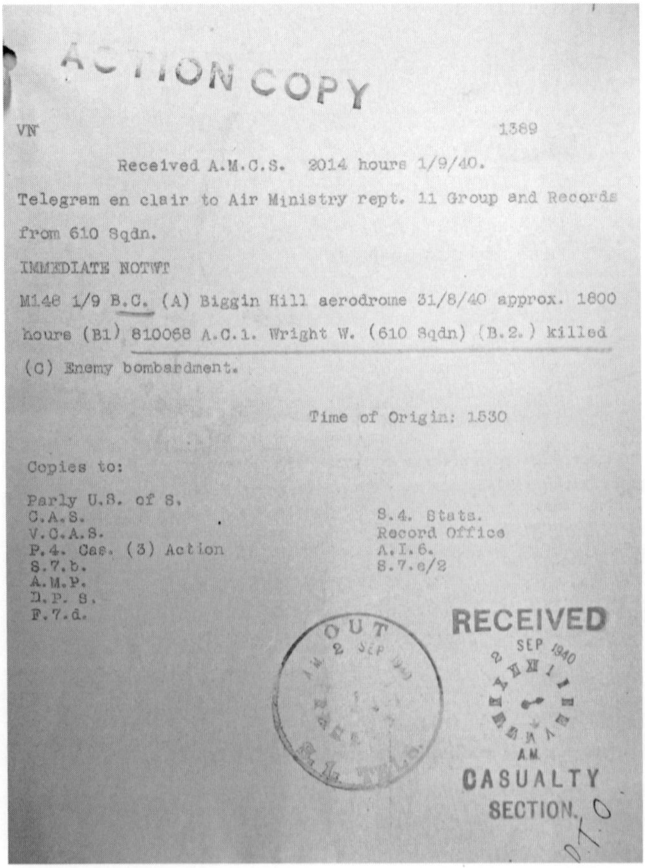

ACTION COPY

VN 1389

Received A.M.C.S. 2014 hours 1/9/40.

Telegram en clair to Air Ministry rept. 11 Group and Records from 610 Sqdn.

IMMEDIATE NOTWT

M148 1/9 B.C. (A) Biggin Hill aerodrome 31/8/40 approx. 1800 hours (B1) 810068 A.C.1. Wright W. (610 Sqdn) (B.2.) killed (C) Enemy bombardment.

Time of Origin: 1530

Copies to:

Parly U.S. of S.
C.A.S.
V.C.A.S.
P.4. Cas. (3) Action
S.7.b.
A.M.P.
D.P.S.
F.7.d.

S.4. Stats.
Record Office
A.I.6.
S.7.e/2

OUT 2 SEP 1940

RECEIVED SEP 1940 A.M. CASUALTY SECTION.

610 Squadron's notification to the Air Ministry about the death of young William Wright. (*TNA, AIR 81/2977*)

C of the Church of England section, Grave 825 (TNA, AIR 81/2977). His headstone's inscription highlights his selfless sacrifice: 'At rest. He gave his life that others might live'. It movingly sums up the sacrifice of so many during the Second World War, for the greater good of the country.

Meanwhile, 72 Squadron would have been preparing to replace 610 Squadron, as they had received further news of their move that morning: '**Acklington 31.8.40 0715** Group Headquarters instructed 72 Squadron to move to Biggin Hill with 32 riggers and fitters. **1230** Squadron airborne for Biggin Hill. **Biggin Hill 1520** Squadron arrived at Biggin Hill' (72 ORB). 72 Squadron's inexperienced pilots could not possibly have been prepared for the scenes which met their arrival at Biggin Hill on 31 August, as recalled by one of their number, Sgt William Rolls:

> … owing to the state of the airfield and the fact that there could be no formation landings, I had plenty of time to get a good look at the bombed-out aerodrome below. I was shocked to see the number of bomb craters which had been hastily filled in and which littered the grass field. I could clearly see the hangars which had been blown up the day before.
>
> Very little except the walls was left standing and several buildings were just a pile of rubble. My immediate thoughts went out to those poor buggers who had been in the thick of it for the past month whilst my pals and I had been enjoying ourselves at Acklington …
>
> Whether it was the smell of burning, cordite, the sight of the bombed-out hangers and buildings, or just plain anticipation of the danger to come, I did not know, but I did know one thing—we were now in the war with a capital W …

William Wright's grave in Bebington cemetery, Wirral. (*Author*)

> I walked down the corridor towards the staircase and saw some luggage which had been piled up by the door. As I approached my room, I thought I saw an airman coming out of it, carrying some suitcases and I asked him if we were moving. 'No, sarge,' he replied, 'these belong to the sergeants who were killed recently'.
>
> I could not reply … In those few seconds I saw the ugly truth; these few precious belongings of the pilots killed would be all that their families would see of their loved ones. I thought of my wife at home with the baby. I said a silent prayer, 'Dear God, please don't let my wife have to go through that …'.[42]

These belongings could quite easily have been Sgt Manton's, who had so recently been killed in action.

Having studied various squadron, station and Group ORBs, it seems that 610 left Biggin Hill in two groups. One section of three went straight to Acklington as an advance party, while nine other pilots left Biggin Hill for RAF Digby, where they spent the night as the guests of their former CO, Wg Cdr I. R. Parker, the station's CO. It will be recalled that Parker had also offered to do this when 610 Squadron withdrew from the Dunkirk operations, although Parker would now have known noticeably fewer survivors from his time with 'The Chesters', namely Ellis, Lamb and Norris. Given their arrival times at these two destinations, it seems 610 awaited the arrival of 72 Squadron, swapping at least some of their aircraft for 610's battle-ready Spitfires, before finally leaving Biggin Hill. We know that some of 610's former aircraft were given to 72 Squadron, as some of 72 Squadron's earliest casualties involved 610's old Spitfires.

The departure of 610 Squadron from Biggin Hill must have been a terribly poignant moment for S/Ldr Ellis and his men, as they said farewell to the many friends they had made at the fighter station over the course of such a long time. The pilots would undoubtedly have had mixed memories of friends lost and rowdy nights of celebration in the nearby pubs, possibly some feeling remorse

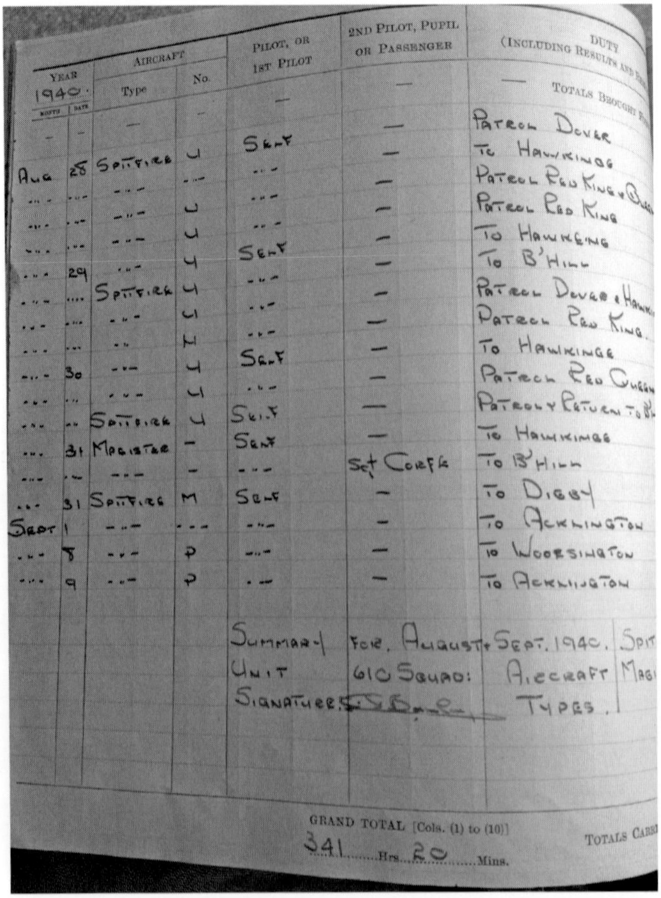

A fascinating photo from Sgt Bamberger's logbook, showing his final patrols from Biggin Hill with 610 Squadron in August 1940. Interestingly, he flew to Hawkinge to bring his friend Sgt Doug Corfe back to Biggin Hill, before 610 Squadron headed to RAF Digby and finally RAF Acklington. (*Copyright Bamberger family*)

at being removed from the front line when the battle was reaching a critical phase. But all of them were filled with relief at the prospect of an end to the ever-present strain of scrambles in the face of overwhelming odds, and the chance to restore themselves mentally and physically. They had more than done their bit, now it was time for someone else to take the strain. The waiting ground personnel who were also able to leave, must have been envious of the pilots, who did not face the lengthy road and rail journeys to their new aerodrome in the north-east.

The arrival of the County of Chester Squadron's first aircraft at Acklington is recorded in the Station's ORB as follows: '31/8/40 No. 610 Squadron machines and pilots arrived from Biggin Hill. (3)'. Thanks to 13 Group's ORB Appendices, we know that this advance party landed at its new home at 1950 hours, while it also noted that, '12 Group advise 9 aircraft of 610 Squadron landed at Digby' at 2100 hours. One of these was Sgt Bamberger, who noted in his logbook that he was flying DW-M (so probably K.9947), for the eighty-minute flight. Finally, the pilots could start to relax, as the trials of life in 11 Group were over. 610 could now look forward to a relative rest, apart from the over-worked Servicing Flight left behind. The ordeal was not over for this group of ground crew, who remained at the 11 Group sector station, to help 72 Squadron's ground crew become accustomed to servicing their aircraft in the front line. As Raymond Ellis recalled: 'surrounded by ruins, the situation looked grim. Although we did not know about the Nazi's 'Operation Sea Lion' planned for 15th September, we felt sure that the invasion was likely to start any day. Each of us already had a rifle and a fabric bandolier holding about 35 rounds of ball ammunition in clips…'.[43] They were worrying times indeed.

18

September 1940: Out of the Firing Line at Acklington

RAF Acklington's ORB notes that on 1 September 1940, 'The remainder of No. 610 Squadron machines and pilots arrived from Biggin Hill', which we now know were actually from RAF Digby, Lincolnshire. Geoffrey Simpson kindly passed on an interesting anecdote, told to him by Sgt Ronnie Hamlyn, which indicated that 610 had visited Digby *en route* to Acklington. Having been entertained by Wg Cdr Parker, S/Ldr Ellis led his nine Spitfires from Digby to complete their journey to Acklington, Northumberland. However, Hamlyn recalled that as they took off, the controller asked John Ellis to lead his formation to investigate a reported 'X'-raid. Much to the relief of his exhausted pilots, Ellis refused to do so, stating that they had been stood down from operations. This would have taken some nerve from 610's CO, and is a good example of his character. It also shows his concern for his men, which was why Ellis was such a popular leader. According to Sgt Bamberger's logbook, the flight to Acklington lasted one hour, the nine Spitfires arriving without mishap.

Details of the Squadron's activities are much harder to accurately follow during the remainder of 1940, as the days of Squadron scrambles and daily dogfights against the *Luftwaffe* were in the past. Now, the Squadron's role was to train new recruits from the OTUs in order to get them ready to join a Spitfire squadron based in the front line in 11 Group, while also allowing the veterans some respite from being at constant readiness and the strain of aerial combat. Indeed, the ORB's first note for September reflects this change in their status, as the main event on 1 September, aside from stating that the unit was now based at Acklington, was that, 'All airmen of 610 Squadron authorised to draw "War Pay" at the rate of 6*d*. per diem'. This was quite a change from the daily reports of enemy raids engaged, losses inflicted on the *Luftwaffe* and those sustained by 610 Squadron.

It is reasonable to suppose that after such a continuous stint in front-line conditions, many of the surviving pilots would have been granted a few days leave with family and friends, to recover from the rigours of combat. Although leave was available to the pilots and ground crew while in 11 Group, now was the time for a slightly longer spell away from the unit, as it acclimatised to its new role. At first, the time away from the chaos of 11 Group seems to have been spent on getting the Squadron's 'household' in order, and on 3 September some long-awaited promotions came through. John Ellis, who had been acting as squadron leader since mid-July, was still officially holding the rank of flying officer, and he was promoted to flight lieutenant, although he was the squadron leader, while F/O Douglas Wilson, one of the few remaining pre-war Auxiliaries, was promoted to flight lieutenant.

The other two promotions involved P/Os Pegge and Rees becoming flying officers, both of whom had joined the Squadron on 16 June. Since then, Brian Rees had flown six recorded patrols, claiming two enemy aircraft destroyed, one probable and one damaged in the process, which clearly underlined his ability as a fighter pilot. However, it remains unclear why he did not fly another recorded patrol after 22 August. Joe Pegge's efforts throughout June, July and August made him the Squadron's third most successful pilot, which had clearly not gone unnoticed; it had just been a matter of time until his

This unusual photograph is believed to show Spitfire DW-K, X.4241, which suffered a 'Category 3' accident on 2 September 1940, which would almost certainly place it at Acklington. Surprisingly, no record of the collision with the Bristol Blenheim is made in the Squadron's ORB and it is unclear which pilot was involved. It is likely that the guilty party was the Blenheim's pilot, given its buckled propellers. (*Copyright Sandra Hemsworth née Blackburne*)

promotion. Doubtlessly, this raft of promotions would have been suitably celebrated! The arrival of the first intake of new recruits also came on 3 September, with several officers joining the Squadron from 7 OTU Hawarden, all keen to gain as much experience as possible before being sent to the main battle area. They were all volunteers for Fighter Command from Army co-operation squadrons, which highlights the shortage of pilots from which Fighter Command was suffering.

One of the new recruits was the pre-war 610 Auxiliary, P/O P. J. Davies-Cooke, who had gained his 'Wings' on 16 December 1938, but left 610 Squadron three months later, having been granted a permanent commission in the RAF as a university entrant. Whether or not his earlier association with the County of Chester Squadron had led to him being reunited with the unit sixteen months later is unclear, but the now F/O Paul Davies-Cooke had since then, 'completed his training and probably went to 10 B&GS, as a staff pilot. On January 8 1940 Davies-Cooke joined 613 Squadron at Odiham from Annan, which was a satellite landing ground for 10 B&GS. In August 1940 Davies-Cooke volunteered for Fighter Command. He arrived at 7 OTU, Hawarden, on August 22',[1] and after converting to Spitfires he rejoined 610 Squadron. Davies-Cooke must have been shocked at the changes in personnel that had taken place, and saddened to hear that men like William Warner, John Kerr Wilson and Tom Smith, with whom he had spent so many weekends learning to fly, had been killed. Indeed, the only two pilots he would have recognised from those early days were Peter Lamb and Douglas Wilson, a sobering fact for any new recruit.

The other new flying officer was Ian Lewis McGregor Hallam, an experienced RAF pilot who probably recognised that his experience was most needed by Fighter Command at this moment in time. Kenneth Wynn describes his earlier life as follows:

> Hallam, the son of a doctor, was born in Edinburgh on November 2 1918 and was educated at Repton School. He joined the RAF on a short service commission and began his ab initio course on March 15 1937, as a pupil pilot. He went on to No 1 RAF Depot, Uxbridge on May 18, for a short induction course.

Paul Davies-Cooke enjoying a relaxing drink in better times before the war. (*Copyright Medcalf family*)

> He was posted to 2 FTS, Digby on June 5 and with intermediate and advanced training completed, he joined 2 (Army Co-operation) Squadron at Hawkinge in January 1938.
>
> The squadron went to France on September 6 1939 and was withdrawn to England on May 19 1940. Hallam was sent to the PRU [Photographic Reconnaissance Unit] at Heston on July 6 1940, for training, following which he joined 225 (AC) [Army Co-operation] Squadron at Tilshead.
>
> In August he volunteered for Fighter Command and arrived at 7 OTU, Hawarden on the 22nd.[2]

He then joined 610 Squadron following his conversion to Spitfires. It is evident how quickly the new pilots were being hurried through this conversion on to single engine fighters, just twelve days being spent at Hawarden before Hallam was sent to 610, where his training would be completed. However, it was still better that these men could gain vital knowledge and experience under the watchful eye of John Ellis and his pilots in the relatively quiet northern skies, than being flung untried into the maelstrom above south-eastern England.

Four pilot officers, Draper, Aldridge, Davies and Mileham, were also part of the intake from 7 OTU. Gilbert Graham Fairley Draper was born on 7 December 1920 (TNA, AIR 81/4029), and attended:

> Uppingham School from 1934 to 1937. He joined the RAF on a short service commission in August 1939 and began his elementary flying at 19 E&RFTS, Gatwick on August 8 and finished it at 18 E&RFTS, Fair Oaks.
>
> On October 23 1939 Draper was posted to 3 FTS, South Cerney for No 30 Course, which ran until April 27 1940. Draper then went to No 1 School of Army Co-operation at Old Sarum and on May 28 he joined 2 (Army Co-operation) Squadron at Bekesbourne.
>
> He was detached from the squadron back to Old Sarum for an Artillery Reconnaissance Course on July 14 1940. Draper volunteered for Fighter Command in August and was posted to 7 OTU, Hawarden on the 22nd,[3]

where he converted to Spitfires prior to joining 610 Squadron.

Denys Edgar Mileham was, 'one of 3 brothers and 3 sisters, the children of Edgar and Irene Mileham. He was born in December 1919 and grew up in Boxmoor at Old Fishery House … His father worked as a solicitor in London'.[4] Mileham:

Above left: A striking photo of Hallam, standing under the propeller of a County of Chester Spitfire in September 1940. (*Copyright 610 Squadron Association*)

Above right: P/O Draper. (*Copyright 610 Squadron Association*)

> joined the RAFVR about July 1938, as an Airman u/t Pilot (741902). Called up on September 1 1939, he completed his training, was commissioned on February 1 1940 and then went to No 1 School of Army Co-operation, Old Sarum. By May 17 1940 Mileham was with 26 Squadron at Authie in France, flying Lysanders on army co-operation duties.
>
> Mileham later volunteered for Fighter Command and was posted to 7 OTU, Hawarden on August 21,[5]

for Spitfire training and then joined 610 Squadron.

Alfred Eric Davies, known as Eric, belonged to the AAF before the war, with 604 (County of Middlesex) Squadron, and he was, 'commissioned in June 1939. He was called to full-time service on August 24. With his flying training completed, he joined the staff of No 1 School of Army Co-operation, Old Sarum. From there he joined 26 (Army Co-operation) Squadron at West Malling on June 7 1940',[6] before following the now familiar route to 610 Squadron.

P/O Frederick Joseph Aldridge was born in Dublin, and:

> joined the RAF in 1939, as a candidate for a short service commission. He began his elementary flying training, as a pupil pilot, on June 12 1939 at 22 E&RFTS, Cambridge. Having successfully completed the course, he went to No 1 RAF Depot, Uxbridge on August 5 for a short induction course.
>
> He was posted to 2 FTS, Brize Norton on the 21st for intermediate and advanced training, on No 40 Course, which he completed on February 17 1940. It is almost certain that he did an Army Co-operation course before joining 4 (AC) Squadron in France on May 12 1940.
>
> Aldridge volunteered for Fighter Command and was posted to 7 OTU, Hawarden on August 22,[7]

Above left: P/O 'Den' Mileham in September 1940. (*Copyright 610 Squadron Association*)

Above right: P/O Davies. (*Copyright 610 Squadron Association*)

before joining 610. Although the ORB actually lists a 'P/O. J. Aldridge' as taking part on a patrol on 29 August 1940, it is most likely that this was a clerical error, perhaps mistaking Aldridge for Aldous, as Aldridge is clearly listed in the ORB as joining the Squadron on 3 September.

Another pilot to join was Ivor Henry Cosby, who had just turned twenty-one when he left 13 Squadron, as an experienced Army co-operation pilot:

> Cosby was born in London on August 19 1919 and educated at Bournemouth School. He learned to fly in 1938 at Air Service Training Ltd at Hamble and joined the RAFVR as an Airman u/t Pilot.
>
> He went into the RAF on a short service commission in May 1939. With flying training completed, he joined 13 (Army Co-operation) Squadron in France in April 1940.
>
> After the heavy fighting from May 10, the depleted squadron withdrew by road in late May to Cherbourg, to England by sea, then to Hooton Park to reform. In August 1940 Cosby volunteered for Fighter Command,[8]

ultimately joining 610 Squadron. It is possible Cosby joined the Squadron earlier, as he recalled in Geoffrey Simpson's 'The flight of The Few' article, that he joined 610 at Biggin Hill in August 1940, while, 'his conversion course consisted of about 20 hours on Spitfires over six days at Hawarden. After 610 went to Acklington he continued in the front line at Biggin Hill with 72 Basutoland Squadron.'[9] (The 610 Squadron ORB made no record of him leaving, although he is mentioned carrying out patrols as late as 23 September 1940.)

Although the Squadron ORB does not mention it, two other pilots joined the Squadron on 3 September, as listed in *Men of the Battle*. One was Bernard Walter Brown, a New Zealander:

Above left: P/O Cosby. (*Copyright Wynn, Men of the Battle, p. 106*)

Above right: The New Zealander, P/O Brown. (*Copyright 610 Squadron Association*)

Born at Stratford, New Zealand on December 6 1917, Brown was educated at Stratford Technical High School and subsequently worked for the Post Office. He applied for a short service commission in February 1938, was accepted and left for England on September 22 in the RMS *Rangitane*.

Brown began his training at 5 E&RFTS, Hanworth on October 31 1938, as a pupil pilot. In late January 1939 he was posted to 5 FTS, Sealand. At the end of August, with training completed, he went to No 1 School of Army Co-operation at Old Sarum, for a course on Lysanders, and then joined 613 Squadron at Odiham on October 6 1939.

In May 1940 the squadron was made operational and moved to Hawkinge. On the 26th Brown was flying one of six Hectors detailed to dive-bomb gun emplacements near Calais. En route, he test-fired his forward gun but the omission of a split pin caused the muzzle attachment to fly off, penetrate the fuselage and hole the main fuel tank. Brown jettisoned his two bombs and turned back, making a forced landing on Herne Bay golf course.

He volunteered for Fighter Command in August 1940 and went to 7 OTU, Hawarden on the 22nd.[10]

Then he joined 'The Chesters'.

The other pilot was also from 613 Squadron, P/O John Gage Lecky, who:

was born in Yokohama, Japan. His father was Language Officer at the British Embassy. He was educated at Highfield Preparatory School, Liphook and Wrekin College, Shropshire.

Lecky entered RAF College, Cranwell in April 1939, as a Flight Cadet. After the outbreak of war, Cranwell cadets, who had not completed their courses, were enlisted in the regular RAF on September 7 1939 as Airmen u/t Pilots and each one was given an Airman number.

Lecky (581726) graduated on March 3 1940 and was granted a Permanent Commission.

P/O Lecky in mid-September 1940. (*Copyright 610 Squadron Association*)

His first posting was to No 2 School of Army Co-operation at Andover. From there he joined 613 Squadron at Odiham on May 7 1940. Lecky volunteered for Fighter Command and on August 22 he was posted to 7 OTU, Hawarden.[11]

Having successfully converted to Spitfires, he also joined 610.

These nine men represented the first pilots who would pass through 610 Squadron in its role as a 'Category C' training unit. Although they were all experienced pilots, they were not used to flying such high-performance aircraft as the Spitfire I, which would take some getting used to in an operational capacity. A pilot called David Denchfield, who later joined 610 Squadron after his own spell at 7 OTU, recalled the following of his introduction to the Spitfire at Hawarden, which all the new men experienced:

> After a solo in a Master, I followed the…normal procedure of visiting the extra-large hut in which sat a Spitfire on trestles connected to an external battery, hydraulics and compressed air. I sat in to receive a more than adequate briefing on operating the Spit from a ground staff Sgt, and spent almost an hour operating flaps, landing gear, landing lights, radiator control, seat, harness lock, fuel cocks and throttle over-ride etc. different boost and rpm settings for different regimes were explained and noted in my diary…At the end of the session the radio control was explained …
>
> The morning after my session in the 'trainer', in fact 25th September 1940 I strapped a Spit to my back for the first time and took off. What a thrill, it was the dream of many youngsters of my age, and the trials and tribulations in attaining the dream were just not in the memory bank any longer. She took me up to 25,000 feet from whence Wales was an island, and her steep turns and slow rolls showed her to be the thoroughbred others had claimed …
>
> The next 10 days passed relatively quickly, flying both Spit and Master and attending lectures given, and organised by that stuttering little Welsh ace from WWI, 'Taffy' Ira Jones who had flown in 74 Squadron with the great 'Mick Mannock' …

> The rain frustrated efforts on several days but … we grafted reasonably to good effect … There was no doubt the system had produced in us well-trained, competent and experienced pilots; but we lacked the knowledge of tactical flying.[12]

Following this rudimentary introduction to the Spitfire, 610's senior pilots would act as tutors, to provide advice and practice flying time, including tactical flying, to prepare the new recruits to face their ultimate challenge in 11 Group.

While these new pilots were finding their feet at Acklington, the Squadron ORB returned to matters in 11 Group on 5 September 1940, stating that the Servicing Flight had been, 'attached to R.A.F. Station Croydon', where the ground crew were putting their great experience to good use, by helping to keep the hard-pressed 72 Squadron's Spitfires operational. The men of Servicing Flight had been left to camp around the perimeter of Biggin Hill. Thanks once again to Raymond Ellis's fascinating memoirs, it is possible to use his own testimony about this vital, yet highly dangerous work:

> … Friday 6th September when Stan and I, bored with nothing to do, sought and obtained passes for the day…We returned to Biggin Hill in the evening to find that our Flight had 'flown'. They had gone to Croydon, and had taken our kit and rifles with them. There was no transport available as most of the MT Section's vehicles had been knocked out. So off we set on 'shank's pony' for a mile or so to find a bus. By devious routes we reached the town of Croydon in the dark.
>
> We did not know where the boys were billeted so we spent an uncomfortable night lying on benches in the deep end of the Public Baths which had been drained to serve as a Public Air Raid Shelter … As soon as it became light we set off for RAF Croydon … It was Saturday the 7th September 1940 …
>
> As far as Stan and I were concerned, the situation was simple—we were reunited with Six-Ten's Servicing Flight at Croydon to sort out an accumulation of unserviceable Spitfires belonging to No. 72 Squadron. Presumably, their own ground staff were still looking after our Spitfires at Acklington. It is likely that the ground crews of No. 111 Squadron had attended to the refuelling and rearming of 72 Squadron's Spitfires since their arrival at Croydon, but no maintenance or repair work had been carried out.
>
> After work and supper, we went with the others to our billet. No. 132 Forester's Drive was a semi-detached house facing north and overlooking the southern boundary of the airfield …
>
> There were about thirty of us in a house meant for a family of four. There was no furniture to clutter up floor space, but that space was limited by the presence of walls. Of course (and quite right too!) Warrant Officer Bentall (our Engineer Officer) and F/Sgt Beaton occupied the front bedroom, which also served as an office. The remainder, all Auxiliaries from Hooton Park, were distributed around the house excluding the bathroom and tiny kitchen. As we were the last to arrive, Stan and I were left with a patch on the floor inside the doorway of the back 'living' room. There must have been at least ten of us in that room. A note in my diary confirms that it was a "H ... of a crush" …
>
> Our first full day at Croydon, the 7th September, witnessed the German High Command's change of plan … It was the beginning of the Blitz on London by day and night …
>
> At Croydon's airfield there was much activity by its two squadrons. No. 111 Squadron had held the fort for at least two months, and was battle seasoned. Its Hurricanes were identified by the letters 'JU'. No. 72 Squadron's Spitfires, identified by the letters 'RN', had been there barely a week, but despite a shortage of serviceable aircraft, were already in action.
>
> The southern 'outback' of the old aerodrome, where we did some of our work, was slightly elevated so that when we faced north we looked over the operational area of the grass field with the old airport buildings to our right. I do not remember any concrete runways, just a large grass field …
>
> London's dockland was about eleven miles to the north, and after sunset on our first day at Croydon, we could see the bright red glow of the fires reaching above the horizon. It was a terrible sight, and it must have been like Hell for those in its midst …

> Meanwhile we were there to do a job. Most of the engine and prop maintenance, and minor airframe tasks, such as replacing control surfaces, were carried out on the Squadron's dispersal. All our work was made more difficult because it had to be done in the open air and on rough ground. We did miss our old Belfast hangar where we had a clean, smooth and level floor to support trestles and ladders, where we could put down tools and parts without losing them, and could use shaded lights after dark.
>
> There was one major airframe job that I remember being done in that southern corner of the airfield close to Forrester's Drive. It was the replacement of a port mainplane. The tail of the Spitfire must have been supported by something, but we lacked adjustable trestles for the mainplanes. I recall this clearly because I was one of the unfortunates who substituted for the missing trestles on the port side. Removing the damaged wing was not too bad—it was comparatively swift. Fitting the new wing was a more protracted and painful procedure. Because of the low height, those of us below the thick root end had to support the wing on our bent backs—I was directly under the main spar. We expected our knees to give way as we gently mated the main spars together and lined up the holes for Corporal Hodges to slide home the fitting bolts …
>
> The two booms of the main spar were each made of multiple concentric square tubes. There were three bolts securing the top boom and four bolts for the bottom boom; a single bolt attached the auxiliary spar towards the trailing edge. Of course there was much else to be done on that wing before the plane was fit to be returned to 72 Squadron …[13]

Bert Lunt had similar memoires of this period: 'After a few days Servicing Flight, with WO Bentall in charge, was ordered to Croydon to restore the serviceability of 72 Squadron which was without a maintenance team. They certainly were in a mess, but we did the job as Servicing Flight always had done.'[14] There is a real sense of the camaraderie enjoyed by 610's Servicing Flight while they helped out another squadron, despite their earlier long stint in 11 Group. The cramped living conditions, constant threat of danger and demanding workload must have taken their toll, not to mention the sight of London burning after the first major raid on the capital in 1940. The men must have yearned to rejoin 610 Squadron in the north.

Meanwhile, at Acklington, it was time for some of the long-standing 610 Squadron members to leave, although in P/O Iain Hunter Stewart's case he was forced to leave on grounds of ill health on 7 September, having his short service commission terminated. Stewart must have been thoroughly disappointed that his role in the RAF had come to such a premature end. He joined the Squadron three months earlier, on the same day as Sgt Norman Ramsay, who became a stalwart of the Squadron during the summer of 1940. Both had come from 92 Squadron and it is remarkable how their paths followed such different routes while with 'The Chesters'.

610 Squadron's Servicing Flight wearing vital 'tin hats', in the back garden of 132 Forester's Drive. Raymond Ellis is crouching down on the end of the front row, to the right. (*Copyright 610 Squadron Association*)

Saturday 7 September also saw *The Isle of Wight County Press* report on the funeral of P/O Frank Webster, who had been buried the previous week. It gives a detailed and moving account of his burial, as follows:

> The funeral took place on Saturday, with Royal Air Force honours, of Pilot Officer Frank Kennersley [Kinnersley] Webster, R.A.F., only son of Mrs A. K. Gray, of the Stag Inn, Lake. As recorded in our last issue, Pilot Officer Webster, aged 26, lost his life in air operations on the previous Monday.
>
> A contingent of the R.A.F, including three officers, supplied an escort, which headed the cortege to the Lake Church, where the service was held, and to Lake Cemetery, where the interment took place in the same grave as that in which rest the remains of Pilot Officer Webster's father, Capt. J. K. Webster. Members of the Lake A.R.P services provided a guard of honour. The coffin, which was draped with the Union Jack, was borne by six sergeants of the R.A.F., and after the committal a trumpeter of the R.A.F. sounded the Last Post and the Reveillé ... The Rev. D. Williams quoted the tribute of the Prime Minister to the deeds of the R.A.F., that 'Never in the field of human conflict was so much owed by so many to so few'. Mr Williams said that they had come to honour one of the few who had given his life for freedom and to save us from horrors unspeakable ... The mourners were Mrs F. K. Webster (widow), Mrs Gray and Mr A. K. Gray (mother and step-father) ...[15]

Webster's death was all the more tragic, as he was leaving behind a young widow. It is interesting to note how quickly Churchill's reference to 'The Few' had been picked up in the contemporary society, fittingly being used by the vicar. He also established the need to focus on Frank's sacrifice for the greater good, which was so deserving of everyone's gratitude.

At this stage, 9 September, 610 Squadron, along with 32 and 43 Squadrons, were only maintaining three operational sections each according to 13 Group's ORB Appendices. Training new pilots was the priority, along with providing some well-deserved respite for the more experienced pilots, before they returned to 11 Group. The first postings of some of the Squadron's pilots back to 11 Group came on Tuesday 10 September. Sgts Corfe, Parsons and Willcocks returned to the front line, to 66 Squadron at Kenley, although the Biggin Hill ORB noted that 66 Squadron had moved to Gravesend on 10 September. After nine days out of the 'firing-line', having enjoyed some rest and doubtless a good send off from 610 beforehand, the three sergeants found themselves back at the focal point of the RAF's defence of Great Britain. 610 Squadron was already fulfilling its role as a 'Category C' Squadron, by rotating experienced pilots back into 11 Group's 'Category A' Squadrons. 66 Squadron certainly fitted the bill in this regard.

The twenty-two-year-old Douglas Corfe, from Meols, Wirral, had been with 'The Chesters' as ground crew back in 1936 before applying for pilot training in October 1939, and rejoining 610 on 25 July 1940 as a pilot. He had carried out two recorded patrols in July and six in August, with claims of an Me 109 destroyed and two Me 109s damaged. He was seen as a suitable early replacement for 66 Squadron, as he had enough experience of combat, including being shot down on 22 August, while he was not as battle-weary as some of the most experienced pilots.

The fighting in the south-east was now as intense as at any point during the Battle, very similar to the savage dogfights 610's pilots had found themselves in during the latter stages of August. Despite his combat experience, Corfe was again shot down by 109s just eight days after joining 66 Squadron, this time near Canterbury, at 1030 hours on 18 September. He baled out wounded and was taken to Chartham Hospital, bringing an end to his participation in the Battle, while his Spitfire R.6603 crashed into Denge Wood, Petham, from where in later years it was excavated.[16] Corfe was posted to Biggin Hill as non-effective sick, a familiar role for fighter pilots recovering from wounds and injuries in the Battle of Britain. In April 1941, Corfe was part of 229 Squadron flying Hurricanes from HMS *Furious* destined for Malta, but they eventually ended up in the desert, where Corfe became an instructor. A year later, Corfe, now a warrant officer, had days to live:

On April 19 1942 Corfe flew one of six Hurricane IICs from Gambut the 720 miles across the sea to Malta, to join the nineteen other Hurricanes of 229, which had arrived in two groups, on March 27 and April 6. On April 25 1942 Corfe, with five other Hurricanes, was sent to intercept Ju 88s, Ju 87s and Bf 109s over St Paul's Bay. He became separated from the other Hurricanes and was attacked by four Bf 109s. Corfe broke away and raced for cover between some hills. He was then hit by local ground fire, losing part of his wing. The Hurricane, BE 708, crashed into rocks and exploded on impact, killing Corfe.[17]

Douglas Corfe was buried in a collective grave in Capuccini Naval War Cemetery. Despite the belief that Corfe had been shot down by friendly fire, it has become apparent that he was probably shot down by one of the Me 109s which had chased him. It is believed that Doug was probably shot down by Hptm. Wolf-Dietrich Wilcke of III/JG 53, an extremely experienced *Luftwaffe* pilot. Eyewitness accounts saw a Hurricane crash around the time in question at Ras-il-Qammieh, where wreckage of a Hurricane's tailplane has been found, although it has not been confirmed whose aircraft it was. Wilcke survived almost another two years, but was shot down on 23 March 1944, by which time the German pilot had claimed 162 Allied aircraft shot down. For all the supposition as to how WO Corfe was killed, Doug's parents, Frederick and Charlotte, had to endure and mourn the loss of a beloved son. The following article in a local paper, perfectly encapsulates how the family remembered their son.

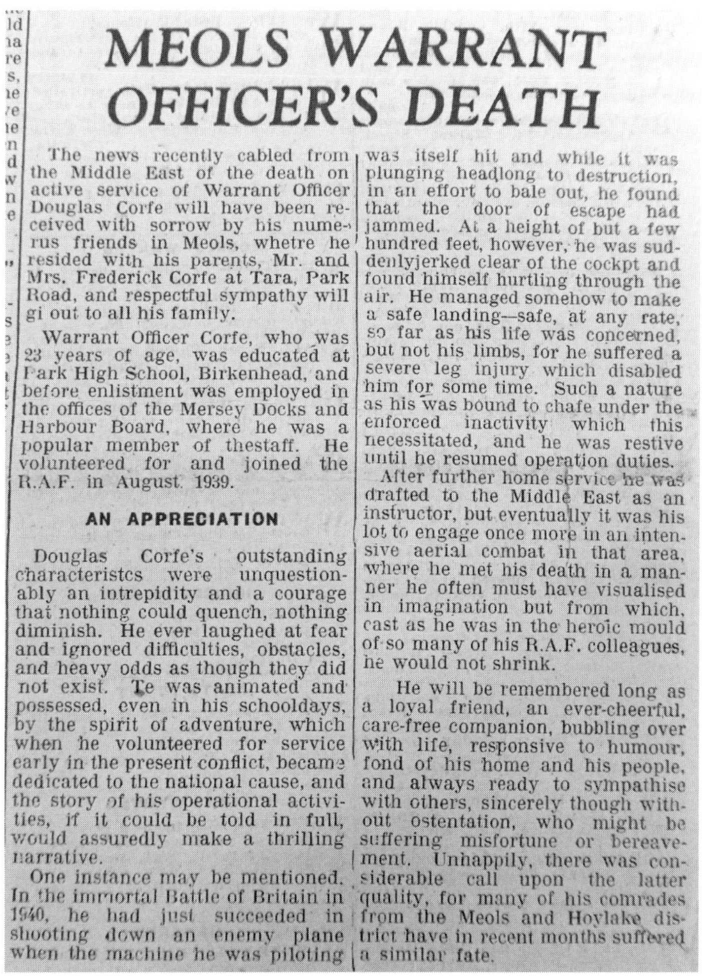

MEOLS WARRANT OFFICER'S DEATH

The news recently cabled from the Middle East of the death on active service of Warrant Officer Douglas Corfe will have been received with sorrow by his numerus friends in Meols, whetre he resided with his parents, Mr. and Mrs. Frederick Corfe at Tara, Park Road, and respectful sympathy will gi out to all his family.

Warrant Officer Corfe, who was 23 years of age, was educated at Park High School, Birkenhead, and before enlistment was employed in the offices of the Mersey Docks and Harbour Board, where he was a popular member of thestaff. He volunteered for and joined the R.A.F. in August 1939.

AN APPRECIATION

Douglas Corfe's outstanding characteristcs were unquestionably an intrepidity and a courage that nothing could quench, nothing diminish. He ever laughed at fear and ignored difficulties, obstacles, and heavy odds as though they did not exist. Te was animated and possessed, even in his schooldays, by the spirit of adventure, which when he volunteered for service early in the present conflict, became dedicated to the national cause, and the story of his operational activities, if it could be told in full, would assuredly make a thrilling narrative.

One instance may be mentioned. In the immortal Battle of Britain in 1940, he had just succeeded in shooting down an enemy plane when the machine he was piloting was itself hit and while it was plunging headlong to destruction, in an effort to bale out, he found that the door of escape had jammed. At a height of but a few hundred feet, however, he was suddenlyjerked clear of the cockpt and found himself hurtling through the air. He managed somehow to make a safe landing—safe, at any rate, so far as his life was concerned, but not his limbs, for he suffered a severe leg injury which disabled him for some time. Such a nature as his was bound to chafe under the enforced inactivity which this necessitated, and he was restive until he resumed operation duties.

After further home service he was drafted to the Middle East as an instructor, but eventually it was his lot to engage once more in an intensive aerial combat in that area, where he met his death in a manner he often must have visualised in imagination but from which, cast as he was in the heroic mould of so many of his R.A.F. colleagues, he would not shrink.

He will be remembered long as a loyal friend, an ever-cheerful, care-free companion, bubbling over with life, responsive to humour, fond of his home and his people, and always ready to sympathise with others, sincerely though without ostentation, who might be suffering misfortune or bereavement. Unhappily, there was considerable call upon the latter quality, for many of his comrades from the Meols and Hoylake district have in recent months suffered a similar fate.

A fitting appreciation of Warrant Officer Corfe's life, which had been cruelly cut short whilst serving his country. (*Hoylake and West Kirby Advertiser, Friday 22 May 1942, copyright Mirrorpix/Wirral Archives Service*)

In June 2009, I visited Douglas Corfe's grave in the Capuccini Naval War Cemetery, Kalkara, Malta. Collective burials were made as the graves had to be cut into the rock, due to the shallow nature of the earth on Malta. F/Sgt Brooks was shot down on the same day as Corfe and their losses are sometimes confused, as they both flew Hurricanes. It is believed Corfe was born on 24 August 1918, in which case he would have been twenty-three when he died, as reported in the local newspaper. (*Author*)

Peter Hamilton Willcocks had joined 610 on 27 July 1940 and had just enough experience under his belt to be considered suitable to be sent back south after a short rest period, as he had flown five recorded patrols during August. His posting to 66 Squadron possibly came too soon, as he had joined 610 straight from 5 OTU, and was lacking Corfe's additional experience. But the decision had been made and he soon found himself caught up once again in the swirling dogfights over Kent. Just four days later, his Spitfire's engine failed and he made a forced landing at 0720 hours one mile south-east of Gravesend, which wrote off N.3029, although he escaped unscathed.[18] During the remainder of the Battle of Britain he shared in the probable destruction of an He 111 and shared in damaging a Ju 88,[19] but he was wounded during a dogfight on 29 September.[20] On 11 October at 1000 hours he, 'Crashed near Newhook on approach to Eastchurch aerodrome in bad visibility' and was unhurt, while Spitfire N.3121 was damaged but repairable.[21] Peter Willcocks's luck finally ran out on 28 November 1940. During a patrol, 'he collided with P/O H. R. Allen over Edenbridge and crashed at Skinners Farm, in Spitfire P 7491',[22] and the twenty-year-old pilot from South Croydon was killed. Sgt Willcocks was, 'cremated at the South London Crematorium, Mitcham',[23] where his name is remembered to honour his sacrifice.

The most experienced of the three departing sergeants was Claude Parsons, who had benefited from joining the Squadron in mid-June as a replacement for the Squadron's Dunkirk losses. He had carried out sixteen recorded patrols in July and eleven in August, during the course of which he had claimed one Dornier 17 destroyed, a Dornier 215 shared destroyed, a 109 unconfirmed, a Ju 87 probable, a 109 damaged and another 215 as shared damaged. After this prolonged spell in action, it is surprising that Parsons was chosen to go in the first draft of replacement pilots. However, it was probably as a result of his experience, that he was posted with two colleagues who were less experienced to varying degrees. Parsons went on to prove that it had been a wise decision, as five days later, on what became known as Battle of Britain Day, 15 September 1940, 'He destroyed a He 111 and damaged a Do 17… and destroyed a Ju 88 and damaged a Bf 110 on the 27th'.[24] His time at 610 had clearly stood him in good stead.

Claude Parsons noted down some of his experiences during the Battle in *Ten Fighter Boys* while with 66 Squadron. However, many of his written accounts relate to his time with 'The Chesters'. Parsons survived the Battle, but, following a dogfight with Me 109s in Spitfire P.7670 on 15 February 1941, still with 66 Squadron, he was badly wounded and hospitalised (TNA, AIR 81/5146). After recovering, Claude returned to operations, and was promoted to F/Sgt, but was reported as missing in action following a sweep over Holland on 8 November 1941.[25]

Jimmy Corbin, another pilot who flew with 610 and 66 Squadrons, was also one of the authors of *Ten Fighter Boys*. He recalled the events surrounding Claude's death in his own book, *Last of the Ten Fighter Boys*:

> I had been detailed to fly another escort for a group of Blenheims on a bombing raid to Holland …
>
> I was all set to go, when the Skipper called me over and told me that he was going to stand me down for that particular mission … "I've decided to send Claude Parsons up in your place". Forbes informed me.
>
> The Squadron took off. I loafed around the base until they returned. The pilots filtered back to the aerodrome on a high … "The bombers did a superb job, scored a direct hit on the steelworks at Ijmuiden in Holland. The factory was completely destroyed," said Bobby Oxspring … "Where's Claude?" I asked. The pilots looked around them as if they expected him to be present. "He's probably landed somewhere else. I saw someone bale out as we crossed the Channel. Maybe that was Claude, I don't know", offered Pickles. "Don't worry, Jimmy, if anyone knows how to get their kite back, it's Claude", said Dizzy Allen.
>
> It turned out that the pilot who baled out was a chap called Durrant … Flight Sergeant Claude Parsons, the squadron's leading expert on Spitfires and all-round good sort, never made it back. He had been with the squadron since the Battle of Britain days. Poor old Parsons—that wonderful source of Spitfire knowledge—was gone. He had already survived being hit by anti-aircraft fire. Dear Claude, who had taken my place in the line-up that day at the very last minute without a second thought, had been shot down and killed.[26]

These moving words from a fellow pilot, show how highly thought of Claude Parsons was and how much he would be missed. While the loss of Parsons was felt heavily amongst his current squadron, the news would have been met with equal sorrow by any of the survivors of 610 Squadron who had fought side-by-side with him through the dark days of June, July and August 1940. He was twenty-seven and his name is remembered on Panel 37 of the Runnymede Memorial.

Along with these departures, 10 September saw the most welcome return of one of 610's senior pilots, Brian Smith. He had recovered enough from his wounds and burns suffered on 12 August, to be re-attached to his old unit from Biggin Hill. While Smith was the ideal pilot to rejoin the Squadron's ranks, with a vast amount of experience to pass on, it also represented a good opportunity for him to return to flying in a safe environment, after being out of action for a month. On 3 September, Smith had received the news that he had been promoted to the full rank of flight lieutenant.

The constant stream of new arrivals followed by departures of familiar faces continued, and 12 September was no exception. 66 Squadron now sent Sgts Clarke, Carter and Corbin to join 610 Squadron at Acklington, for further training away from the front line. Harry Clarke, from Northern Ireland, was educated at Dale Holme Private School, Belfast, and joined the RAFVR in July 1939, aged twenty-two. In 1939, Clarke:

> … made his first solo at 24 E&RFTS in July. Called up on September 1, he went to 3 ITW, Hastings on October 1, moving on to 4 EFTS, Brough on December 18.
>
> Clarke was posted to 14 FTS, Kinloss on April 10 1940. With his training completed, he went to 7 OTU, Hawarden on August 10th, converted to Spitfires and joined 74 Squadron at Kirton-in-Lindsey on the 26th. He moved on to 66 Squadron at Coltishall on the 28th,[27]

before joining 610 Squadron. This yo-yoing between squadrons had become the norm, as pilots who had been rushed through the training system were found to be under-trained by the front-line fighter squadrons and a risk to themselves and their new commander, like 'Bam' Bamberger had been when he first returned to 610 Squadron in August.

This is evident in Wynn's review of Leslie Raymond Carter's early RAF life:

> Carter, from Hertfordshire, joined the RAFVR in June 1939 as an Airman u/t Pilot. Called up on September 1, he completed his training at 14 FTS, Cranfield, on No 7 Course, which ran from April 28 to August 3 1940. He went to 7 OTU, Hawarden on August 10 1940 and after converting to Spitfires, he joined 74 Squadron at Kirton-in-Lindsey on the 26th. Three days later he joined 66 Squadron at Coltishall. When the squadron moved to Kenley that day, Carter remained behind for further training. He rejoined 66 at Kenley on September 7.[28]

However, Carter still was not ready to face the heavy fighting in 11 Group, and with the arrival of more experienced pilots from 610 Squadron, it became possible to send him north to 610 Squadron, until he was adequately prepared to face the *Luftwaffe*. The third sergeant, William 'Jimmy' Corbin, born on 5 August 1920, (who recalled the loss of Sgt Parsons earlier), was from Maidstone, Kent, where he had been educated at Michael's School.

> He joined the RAFVR in April 1939 as an Airman u/t Pilot (754013) and did his weekend flying at 23 E&RFTS, Rochester. Called up on September 1, he completed his elementary training and then moved to 14 FTS, Kinloss, for No 7 Course which ran from April 28 to August 3 1940. On the 10th Corbin arrived at 7 OTU, Hawarden for conversion to Spitfires.[29]

Like Clarke and Carter, Corbin now had brief spells with 74 and 66 Squadrons before joining 'The Chesters'. It is worth noting what his CO, S/Ldr Allen, DFC, who edited *Ten Fighter Boys*, along with Wg Cdr Forbes, DFC, made of him in their introduction to the chapter on Corbin:

> Jimmy always has a moan but, of course, we all know that it just doesn't mean a thing. He was invariably "brassed off," and was forever telling every one just how "brassed off" he was, but in spite of that he always had a cheerful grin. He's short, well-built, dark-haired with an oval face and high cheekbones, and reminds one of a certain well-known comedian of North Country origin [George Formby, author], and is liable to throw something at you if you call him George. He has a great sense of humour, and in his fairly quiet way he often comes out with some gems of remarks, usually in R.A.F. slang.[30]

For all Corbin's attributes, his leaders needed experienced pilots and when he was sent north for further training with 610 Squadron, it is interesting how he described his own emotions:

> We were disappointed when, after about a week's stay at "K," [Kenley, author] on September 10th we were posted to a squadron in N.E. England. This squadron had done remarkably well during the early blitz, and practically all the pilots that were left had the D.F.C. or D.F.M … We were very depressed about this posting, for there was no action up north, although we had a jolly good time with this squadron. We trained and trained with this squadron, formation and more formation, although we were made operational after about three hours' flying. Readiness consisted of standing by, with occasional abortive flaps…Protective patrols over the shipyards were frequent—same boring jobs, never any joy, just round and round.[31]

Corbin gives a vivid picture of life in a 'Category C' Squadron, where the endless training and patrolling with little chance of contact with the enemy, was frustrating for men who wanted to do their bit. This

The three new Sergeants from left to right, Harry Clarke, Leslie Carter and Jimmy Corbin. (*All copyright 610 Squadron Association*)

passage does stress the good reputation that 610 Squadron enjoyed, having fought so courageously during their time in 11 Group, reflected in the number of pilots with medals for bravery and good service. These men, Ellis, Smith, Hamlyn and company, would all have been greatly respected by the new arrivals, and Dowding's plan of training the raw recruits with these experienced hands, out of harm's way, was a sensible measure which clearly worked.

As the three sergeants settled in, they may have briefly met P/O Eric Aldous who was the next of 610's men to return to the front line, another pilot who had notched up some experience at the end of August, having taken part in at least five combat patrols. Aldous had claims for a Heinkel 111 destroyed, an Me 109 probably destroyed and a Dornier 215 damaged, and having survived being thrust in at the deep end, his CO clearly felt no compunction in sending him back to continue the fight. The twenty-two year old from Surrey joined 41 Squadron, which had been based at Hornchurch, Essex, since 3 September. By the time Aldous joined the squadron, it had suffered the loss of three pilots killed including the commanding officer and a flight commander, with three more wounded; Aldous's arrival would have been warmly received by 41 Squadron. He damaged an Me 109 on 18 September, but ten days later, Aldous's Spitfire, X.4345 was damaged by 109s over Kent, and he was wounded when he crash-landed in Pluckley.[32] After surviving the rest of the Battle of Britain, 'He was posted away from 41 on December 7 to 55 OTU, to instruct. On August 7 1941 Aldous joined 615 Squadron at Prestwick'.[33] On 16 October, while operating from Manston, Kent, on a sweep, he was killed near Flushing, Netherlands, aged twenty-three. The 615 Squadron ORB recorded the following details, along with a moving tribute:

The formation encountered intense Flak [AA fire] off Flushing and it is presumed that it was here, that Flg.Off. Aldous, who did not return, was hit. Eric Aldous joined the squadron a few weeks before we left Valley and during that time in his quiet unobtrusive way he had become extremely popular. His keenness was an example and an inspiration to all. Both the squadron and the Service can ill-afford to lose him. (TNA, AIR 27/2123/43-44)

Aldous was buried in Vlissingen Northern Cemetery, Flushing, Netherlands, the headstone listing him as a flight lieutenant, while, 'He is remembered on a memorial plaque at Dulwich College, unveiled on March 14 2002'.[34]

Stanley Norris's highly-deserved promotion to flying officer was announced on 13 September. Norris had still been a pilot officer while serving as acting flight lieutenant in command of 'A' Flight.

Eric Aldous, who at the time of his death had been promoted to flight lieutenant. (*Copyright 610 Squadron Association*)

Norris's promotion to flight commander had been on the basis of his proven ability and experience as a fighter pilot and leader, after previous incumbents had been wounded or killed. He kept this role, but became 'B' Flight commander. Between 10 May and 31 August, he had flown the highest number of recorded patrols, sixty-one in total. He is frequently referred to as 'F/Lt' in the ORB at this time and although both Smith and Wilson also held the rank of flight lieutenant, it is likely that Joe Pegge would soon be the one to take command of 'A' Flight. Also, Sgt Ronnie Hamlyn received his DFM, making it a very memorable day for the twenty-six year old from Harrogate.

The other main point of interest mentioned in the ORB on 13 September, was: 'Personnel of Squadron moves to R.A.F. Station Acklington'. This refers to the return of the Servicing Flight from 11 Group. The move probably arose as, '72 Squadron moved from Croydon to Biggin Hill' (Biggin Hill ORB), while the remainder of 72 Squadron's personnel had left Acklington on 11 September, so would have settled in by this time (Acklington ORB). Once again, there is no-one better than the inimitable Raymond Ellis, to describe the long-awaited departure of 610 Squadron's brave ground crew from 11 Group:

> We must have looked a scruffy bunch of ruffians. Our Drill Sergeant from Hooton Park days would have had a fit had he been able to see us. We wore the same clothes, day and night, for a fortnight so that our tunics were black and stiff with oil, grease and sweat, and our brass buttons were green, but not a word was said about our appearance. We rarely saw a commissioned officer as they were all occupied with flying and associated duties, when a pilot collected a 'plane that we had been working on, he had many things on his mind other than our appearance! Despite the apparent relaxation of discipline, there was the silent bond of loyalty and discipline.
>
> Our own Engineer Officer, W/O Bentall, usually left us to get on with our jobs whilst he arranged the flow of work, and, with the help of Cpl. Alex Turner, urged the supply of the new parts that we needed. F/Sgt Beaton was a quiet, self-effacing fellow who seemed to be engrossed in paperwork—someone had to do it. We had no sergeants to oversee our various trades. However, we had three excellent corporals—all Auxiliaries. Work on engines and propellers was the responsibility of Cpl Reg Lewis (810033) and Cpl Bert Lunt (810093). Work on airframes was the concern of Cpl Allan Hodges (810091).

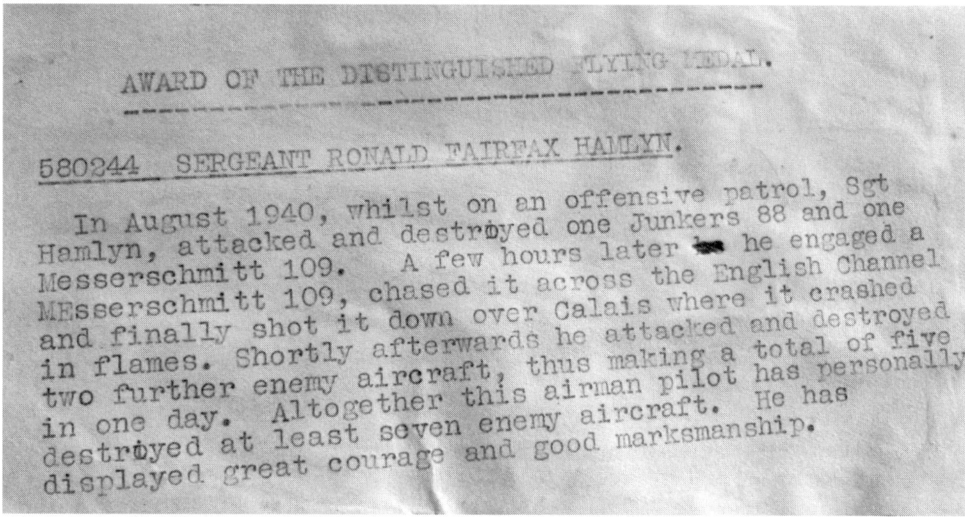

AWARD OF THE DISTINGUISHED FLYING MEDAL.

580244 SERGEANT RONALD FAIRFAX HAMLYN.

In August 1940, whilst on an offensive patrol, Sgt Hamlyn, attacked and destroyed one Junkers 88 and one Messerschmitt 109. A few hours later he engaged a Messerschmitt 109, chased it across the English Channel and finally shot it down over Calais where it crashed in flames. Shortly afterwards he attacked and destroyed two further enemy aircraft, thus making a total of five in one day. Altogether this airman pilot has personally destroyed at least seven enemy aircraft. He has displayed great courage and good marksmanship.

Sgt Hamlyn's citation for the DFM praised his remarkable feat on 24 August 1940. (*Copyright 610 Squadron Association*)

At the end of the week, W/O Bentall told us that we were to rejoin our own squadron at Acklington. I cannot truthfully say we were disappointed by this news. Of course we expected that 610 would soon be returning south to 11 Group but NOT to Forrester's Drive.

Meanwhile, the rejuvenated 72 Squadron would fly off to Biggin Hill to be looked after by its own 'erks' down from Acklington.

And so on Friday the 13th September, without regret, but with a mixture of pride and relief, we left Forrester's Drive forever. The so-called 'personnel carriers' that carted us off were Bedford three-ton lorries covered by a canvas tilt and furnished with crude benches for minimum comfort, but there were no complaints ... as our small convoy proceeded to Kings Cross Station.[35]

Ellis also highlighted the recognition that 610's Servicing Flight received in the following Postscript:

1. Our C.O. S/Ldr. John Ellis received a signal from H.Q. 11 Group commending Servicing Flight of No. 610 Squadron on their help in restoring the serviceability of No. 72 Squadron at Croydon.
2. Warrant Officer W. Bentall was recommended for the Military O.B.E., and he was sent away to be commissioned as an Engineer.
3. LAC Albert Alkins was Mentioned in Despatches for his bravery during bombing of Biggin Hill...
4. Corporal C. H. Lunt and Corporal R. E. Lewis were both Mentioned in Despatches for exceptional service.
5. On rejoining 610 at Acklington, several LAC airmen were promoted to the NCO rank of Corporal and posted to other units. They continued to wear the 'A' badge on their sleeves.[36]

Raymond Ellis survived the war, becoming a squadron engineer at RAF Montrose, Scotland. In later life, he was involved in the research, development and production of polythene at the Brunner Mond Division of ICI in Northwich, Cheshire. He died in 2013.[37]

It had been a tremendous effort and the ground crew were itching for a rest from the trials of life in 11 Group. Given that they worked under the constant fear of being attacked by the *Luftwaffe*, they must have been just as tired as the pilots who had been withdrawn earlier. As the trains headed north with the jubilant ground crew on the following day, the last thing they expected to happen was for

Raymond Ellis later in the war, after his time with 610 Squadron. (*Copyright 610 Squadron Association*)

another of their number to be killed, particularly as it was not the result of enemy action, as recalled by Corporal C. H. (Bert) Lunt:

> The following day was Friday the 13th September. Members of 610 Squadron at Biggin Hill and those still at Croydon all converged on Kings Cross station where we paraded early in the afternoon. We were told to look after ourselves until 10pm when we were to parade for a roll call prior to boarding the train …
>
> After the roll call we boarded the train whilst the air raid continued. With half a bottle of whisky in my pocket to ease the journey, I settled into a corner seat. At about twenty minutes after midnight the train began to move slowly out of the station and then gathering speed we were on our way and I soon dropped into a deep sleep.
>
> I was awakened by the train stopping with a jolt as the emergency brakes were applied. We were in Durham station. Poking my head out of the window, I saw a porter running towards me and shouting, 'Help! Help! A man has been shot'.
>
> In the compartment next but one to ours, a rifle had been accidentally discharged. The bullet had gone through the partition into the next compartment where it had killed David Evans, an Auxiliary who had been married a few weeks earlier.
>
> It seems that, with the coming of the dawn, the men decided to unload their magazines as they were now far from the front line. The bolt mechanism of one rifle was not working correctly. A corporal took charge of the weapon and managed to get the bolt to withdraw and eject the rounds. Failing to check if there was a round still 'up the spout', he pulled the trigger to release the firing pin. Of course, he should have pointed the rifle upwards, but there was little headroom. It was a tragedy for all concerned.[38]

The ORB recorded the following about this fatal accident on 14 September 1940: '810182 A.C.2 EVANS, D. died as a result of bullet wound accidently received whilst travelling by rail from Biggin Hill to Acklington' (ORB). David Evans, an Auxiliary aged twenty-six, was husband to Eva, and his parents were Mr and Mrs W. Evans, for whom it must have been a devastating shock. He is buried in Ellesmere Port Overpool Cemetery, Cheshire, in Section M, Grave 124. Fittingly, his final resting place was very close to 610 Squadron's old home, Hooton Park.

David Evans's headstone in Overpool cemetery. (*Author*)

The Squadron's ORB began recording Squadron patrols again on 14 September. Whether or not this is extensive in detail is unclear, but at least we have some idea of what the Squadron was now doing in terms of operations. Red Section of 'B' Flight took off from Acklington at 1100 hours with orders to orbit the Farne Islands at 13,000 feet. The pilots involved were as follows, the latter two gaining their first recorded operational patrols with the Squadron, a particularly long-awaited event for Paul Davies-Cooke:

DW-R.	X.4239	F/O. P. G. LAMB.	52
DW-F.	X.4028	F/O. P. J. DAVIES-COOKE.	1
DW-H.	X.4615	P/O. G. G. F. DRAPER.	1

However, the patrol was summed up with, 'Nothing seen' (ORB), and the Spitfires landed at 1200 hours.

The next day, 15 September 1940, has ever since been remembered as Battle of Britain Day, the climax of the Battle. Göring launched two huge raids at London, aiming to devastate the capital, while simultaneously drawing up the remaining RAF fighters which the *Luftwaffe* supposed were left to defend Britain. Their destruction would clear the path for an invasion force. Fighter Command clearly had not read its lines, and although still hard-pressed, Dowding and Park sent all their 11 Group fighters, backed up by the likes of Douglas Bader's 'Big Wing' from Duxford in 12 Group, a phalanx of aircraft in itself. In the heavy fighting which followed, large numbers of raiders were shot down—originally claimed to be 175, it was actually fifty-six, while the RAF lost twenty-six aircraft shot down and thirteen pilots killed. This still represented a heavy blow for the *Luftwaffe*, especially as their crews had been led to believe that Fighter Command was all but spent as a cohesive fighting force.

By the end of the day, the *Luftwaffe's* severe losses in terms of aircrew killed or taken prisoner were particularly telling, especially when the *Luftwaffe* had been in constant combat since May, and suffered draining losses during the *Blitzkrieg* on Europe and over Dunkirk. The *Luftwaffe's* veterans were becoming exhausted, as they had no rotation out of the front line, a tactic which Dowding wisely employed to keep his men fresh. The RAF fighter pilots, and indeed the country's leaders and people were unaware of it at the time, but despite further big raids during the dog-days of September and into October, with more costly losses on both sides, the *Luftwaffe's* spirit had been effectively broken on Sunday 15 September. For all the best efforts of the most powerful contemporary air force in the world, which had pushed the RAF to the brink, Fighter Command's brave pilots had kept the

Luftwaffe at bay. They had been supported just as importantly by the ground crew and a network of other groups from AA gunners and the Observer Corps, those operating the RDF sites, sector stations, and the crews of Bomber Command, right through to the people of Britain who defied the *Luftwaffe's* raids; they had all remained firm. There would be no 'Operation Sea Lion', thanks in the first instance at least, to Dowding's 'fighter boys'.

For Sgt Ramsay, 15 September was the day he was posted from 610 Squadron to 222 Squadron in 11 Group, Hornchurch. The twenty-one year old had carried out thirty-four recorded patrols between the end of June to August, and his posting was another blow to 'The Chesters'. Despite having so many patrols under his belt, Ramsay had comparatively few claims to show for his efforts, one Me 110 destroyed, a Dornier 17 shared destroyed and a probable Me 109—perhaps his role had been more as a trusted wingman, guarding his section leader's tail. The fact that he had made these claims and was still alive after over two months in the front line, was proof positive of his ability as a Spitfire pilot. It was an aircraft he loved more than most, having worked as an apprentice at Vickers Supermarine in Southampton before the war, much like Claude Parsons. 222 Squadron's historian, Ernie Burton, recorded that Ramsay was: '… a badly needed replacement pilot. He flew a total of 33 sorties during the Battle of Britain [with 222 Squadron, author] although he did not gain any victories. After the Battle of Britain … Ramsay stayed with 222 Squadron as they moved North to Coltishall to reform and regroup'.[39] Kenneth Wynn recorded the rest of his successful RAF career as follows:

> Commissioned in March 1941, Ramsay shared in the probable destruction of a Ju 88 on April 4. He was posted away to 61 OTU, Rednal on October 22, as an instructor. He went to West Kirby for overseas on December 17 1942 and on January 11 1943 he joined 1435 Squadron at Luqa, Malta. Ramsay was posted back to the UK on July 29 1943 and awarded the DFC (28.9.43).
>
> He held a series of staff appointments until August 20 1946, when he was posted to 61 OTU for a refresher course before joining No 1 Squadron at Tangmere on September 11. Ramsay retired from the RAF on July 29 1962, as a Flight Lieutenant. He later went to live in New Zealand and died there in 2002.[40]

Monday 16 September saw the arrival of five more new pilots to the Squadron, all fresh from 7 OTU, Hawarden, Flintshire, in the shape of P/Os Bacon and Douglas and Sgts Horner, Murray and Ward-Smith. Charles Bacon was twenty-one, having been born in Manchester on 15 January 1919 (TNA, AIR 81/3546):

> A Demi (Half Fellow) of Magdalen College, Oxford … He joined the Oxford University Air Squadron and transferred to the RAFVR in June 1939, as an Airman u/t Pilot (754287). He was called up on September 1. Commissioned on September 26 1939, Bacon was on No 6 Course at RAF College FTS, Cranwell from November 6 1939 to May 9 1940.
>
> Bacon arrived at 10 B&GS, Warmwell with the Advanced Training Squadron from Cranwell FTS on April 26. With the course completed, he joined 98 Squadron in France in early May 1940, flying Battles. It was withdrawn to England in early June. It re-assembled at Gatwick on the 15th and in July it was preparing for a move to Iceland for coastal patrol duties. When 98 departed on July 27, Bacon stayed at RAF Gatwick, as a supernumerary. He joined 4 (C) Ferry Pilot Pool on August 1.
>
> Along with other pilots with Merlin engine experience, he went to 7 OTU, Hawarden on September 3,[41]

before converting to Spitfires, and joining 610 Squadron at Acklington.

His fellow officer, nineteen-year-old William Douglas, from Edinburgh, had followed a very different route to the Squadron, having joined his local AAF unit, 603 (City of Edinburgh) Squadron:

A rare photo of some of 610 Squadron's heroes from the summer of 1940. From left to right, Sgt Hamlyn, Sgt Corfe, F/O Pegge, middle, Sgt Ramsay and Sgt Baker. Given that Hamlyn has been awarded his DFM, this photograph would have been taken between the end of August and early September 1940, as Corfe had left 610 on 10 September 1940. (*Copyright Bamberger family*)

Above left: P/O Charles Harvey Bacon photographed shortly after joining 610 Squadron. (*Copyright 610 Squadron Association*)

Above right: P/O William Anderson Douglas. (*Copyright 610 Squadron Association*)

> on April 23 1939 and was commissioned in June. He had done some flying training before being called up on August 24 1939. Douglas was posted to 7 FTS, Peterborough on October 7 and after completing his training, he rejoined 603 Squadron at Montrose on March 17 1940. He was posted away to 3 BGS, Aldergrove as a staff pilot on May 7, moved to 8 BGS, Evanton on July 3 and on September 5 he went to 7 OTU, Hawarden,[42]

where he converted to Spitfires before his posting to 610 Squadron.

Frank Horner, unsurprisingly known as 'Jackie', joined the VR in, 'July 1939, as an Airman u/t Pilot (754738). Called up on September 1, he completed his training and arrived at 7 OTU, Hawarden, on September 2 1940',[43] before following the now familiar path to 'The Chesters'.

Peter Ward-Smith, aged twenty-three and from Epping, Essex, had been:

> educated at Brighton College and before the war was an Insurance Broker at Lloyds. On July 22 1938 Ward-Smith joined the RAFVR, as an Airman u/t Pilot (741823) and carried out his flying training at 20 E&RFTS, Gravesend and later 13 E&RFTS, White Waltham. He was called to full-time service on September 1 1939 and after completing his training, he arrived at 7 OTU, Hawarden on September 2 1940,[44]

before moving on to 610 Squadron.

James Murray, 'joined the RAF in March 1935 as an Aircrafthand. He later applied for pilot training and was selected. With training completed, he arrived at 7 OTU, Hawarden on September 2 1940',[45] then joined the ranks of 610 Squadron, to finalise his transition into a fighter pilot.

If the new recruits had arrived first thing, they would have witnessed the Squadron's DW-coded Spitfires roar off into the sky at 1045 hours, to patrol Acklington at 10,000 feet. The following pilots were involved, Norris leading two more novices on their first recorded patrols with the Squadron:

DW-T.	X.4064	F/Lt. S. C. NORRIS.	62
DW-P.	P.9451	P/O. I. H. COSBY.	1
DW-V.	K.9970	SGT. CORBIN W. J.	1

Blue Section returned to Acklington at 1115 hours without incident. However, a little later in the morning, in an unrecorded patrol in the ORB, Corbin carried out an unusual interception, as mentioned in his chapter of *Ten Fighter Boys*:

Sgt Frank Horner before he got his 'Wings'. Sgts James Murray and Peter Ward-Smith in a Squadron photo, taken shortly after they joined 610 Squadron. (*All copyright 610 Squadron Association*)

> My first operational trip was early one morning; dawn was just breaking. We climbed to 15,000 feet to intercept the supposed enemy. I must admit I had a curious feeling in my stomach. The cause of this flap appeared two hours later, when we were ordered off to prevent a Heinkel seaplane from taking-off again after he had "forced-lobbed" with engine trouble off the Farne Islands. He was attempting to take off when we arrived but, unfortunately for the Heinkel, there was difficulty in the form of three Spits ... This was a very encouraging start, but the only other interception we had were two Hudsons and a Battle, which were of little use to us.[46]

It is very surprising that the ORB does not record this event, as it must have caused quite a stir. The unfortunate Heinkel seaplane was almost certainly a Heinkel 115C, of 3/506, as recorded in *Then and Now*:

> **Monday September 16th 1940**
>
> **3/506**
>
> Heinkel He 115C (3261) Suffered engine failure during operational sortie and ditched in North Sea off Berwick 1.00 a.m. Capsized aircraft brought into Eyemouth harbour. Hptmn. Kriependorf, Oblt. Lucas, Hptmn. Bergmann (Staffel Kapitan) and Fw. Kalinowski rescued from dinghy by fishing boat and captured. Aircraft S4+CL a write-off.[47]

The crew, probably from Stavanger, Norway, were experienced men and it was quite a coup to capture a '*Staffel Kapitan*', although the Germans had been unlucky in having 610's Spitfires arrive when they did.

With the arrival of the new pilots to swell the Squadron's ranks, 610 saw the departure of another two pilots to 41 Squadron at Hornchurch. Sgt Bamberger left on 17 September and Beardsley on 18 September, although it was not mentioned in the ORB, where they were reunited with P/O Aldous. In that time, 41 Squadron had lost another commanding officer to wounds and another pilot killed, while several others had survived being shot down, so the arrival of Bamberger and Beardsley would have been a great relief. 'Bam' had thirty-two recorded patrols under his belt against the enemy, plus a claim for a probable Me 109, and with the extra flying time gained on Spitfires while at Acklington, was now more than ready to return to the fray. Ten days later on 27 September, 'Bam' filed the Squadron's only claim during the afternoon patrol for an Me 109 damaged.[48] On 5 October, the twenty-one year old from Port Sunlight, Wirral, claimed his first confirmed victory, when he shot down a Messerschmitt 109.[49]

'Bam' went on to have a very eventful War. Having volunteered to go to Malta, he had a lucky escape, during his journey on the aircraft carrier HMS *Argus*. Bamberger was not part of the original group of twelve Hurricanes which took off for Malta on 17 November 1940, guided by two naval Skuas. Only four fighters completed the 450 mile journey, the others having run out of fuel. When Bamberger finally arrived in Malta in December, it was in the midst of the heavy attacks on the island. 'Bam' joined 261 Squadron and shot down two Junkers 87 dive-bombers over Grand Harbour in January 1941. He returned to Britain in June 1941, and provided gunnery training for American pilots, before again returning to Malta in 1943, when he shot down further enemy aircraft during the Sicilian and Italian campaigns, receiving his DFC on 28 September 1943. He returned to Britain as a gunnery instructor in July 1944, being awarded a Bar to his DFC on 14 November 1944, but was demobilised after the War.

S/Ldr Bamberger was recalled to the RAF for the Korean War, working as an intelligence officer at the Air Ministry. His career with 610 Squadron was completed when he became the Squadron's CO from 1950–52, when it was stationed back at Hooton Park, overseeing the introduction of Meteor jet fighters. He finally retired from the RAF in 1959, when he had also been awarded the Air Efficiency Award and Bar. He later became managing director of a packaging company and ran an antiques business, while he was an important figure at the Bentley Priory Battle of Britain Trust, being the vice-chairman. He and his wife, Heather, had four children and seven grandchildren. He died on

Cyril Stanley 'Bam' Bamberger, fittingly shown in a Spitfire's cockpit. (*Copyright 610 Squadron Association*)

3 February 2008, aged eighty-eight.[50] I had the pleasure of hearing 'Bam' talk extremely vividly of his experiences of the Battle of Britain at an event in Chester, organised by 610 Squadron's Association on 16 December 2005, which acted as another spur to my research into 610 Squadron. In 2011, a plaque was unveiled at his former school, St John Plessington Catholic College, Bebington, Wirral.

Sgt Beardsley had much the same experience as Bamberger, the pair having joined 610 Squadron on 27 July 1940. Bob Beardsley had also completed six recorded combat patrols at the end of August, and he had made several claims against the *Luftwaffe*. 41 Squadron was constantly in combat throughout his time on the squadron, and he had a couple of narrow escapes, along with further victories. In *RAF Fighter Squadrons in the Battle of Britain*, Robinson credits Beardsley with claims of two Me 109s damaged on 18 September,[51] a memorable first day with 41 Squadron. On the last day of September, the twenty-year-old Londoner claimed a Dornier 17Z and an Me 109 both probably destroyed, before he, 'then had to evade attacks from six Bf 109s and his Spitfire was badly damaged by their fire. His engine caught fire and flames and glycol fumes reached the cockpit, but Beardsley … was then able to bring off an extremely skilful forced-landing at RAF Hawkinge',[52] at 1420 hours, his aircraft P.9394, being repairable.[53] He made further claims on 25 October, when he was flying a Mark II, P.7371,[54] Steve Brew describing how: 'Sergeant Pilot Bob Beardsley initially damaged an Me109, but subsequently attacked a second, which he claimed destroyed'.[55]

Beardsley survived the rest of the Battle of Britain and the remainder of the War, thanks in no small way due to his initial time spent with 610 Squadron. He was commissioned in June 1941 while still with 41 Squadron and awarded the DFC on 17 October 1941, having claimed a further 109 probably destroyed and one damaged. Following a period as an instructor he joined 93 Squadron for the invasion of North Africa, during which he probably destroyed a Focke-Wulf Fw 190. After another spell as an instructor, he joined 222 Squadron at Tangmere after the Normandy landings, before a staff job in Cairo and being released on 20 December 1945. He rejoined the RAF as a flight lieutenant in April 1949, and finally retired from the RAF in July 1970. He died on 17 October 2003, aged eighty-three.[56]

A flurry of activity at Acklington came on 19 September, with Red and Yellow Sections being ordered to patrol fifty miles out to sea. The first patrol took off at 1315 hours, the sections being led by the veterans Lamb and Hamlyn:

This photograph was taken at Acklington between 17-19 September 1940, given the arrival and departure date of each pilot. John Ellis proudly sits on top of the engine, with back row from the left: Lecky, Clarke, Carter, Bacon, Draper, Brown, Baker, Corbin, Douglas and Horner. Front row: Davies, Lamb, Hamlyn, Pegge, Mileham, Hallam, Davies-Cooke, Norris, Smith, Murray, Ward-Smith and Wilson. (*Copyright Smith family*)

DW-R.	X.4239	F/O. P. G. LAMB.	53
DW-F.	X.4028	F/O. P. J. DAVIES-COOKE.	2
DW-H.	X.4615	P/O. G. G. F. DRAPER.	2
DW-Q.	X.4679	SGT. HAMLYN, R. F.	42
DW-L.	P.9311	P/O. A.* BROWN.	1
DW-M.	X.4245	SGT. CLARKE, H. R.	1

*This should be 'B' for Bernard, ORB error, repeated in next battle order too.

With nothing to report, the Spitfires returned to base after forty-five minutes. Following a quick refuel, and a change in some personnel and aircraft, the same sections repeated the exercise at 1430 hours, Lamb still presumably leading Red Section, while Davies-Cooke, perhaps as a result of his rank and greater experience, led Yellow Section:

DW-R.	X.4239	F/O. P. G. LAMB.	54
DW-F.	X.4028	P/O. J. G. LECKY.	1
DW-L.	P.9311	SGT. CLARKE, H. R.	2
DW-B.	K.9892	F/O. P. J. DAVIES-COOKE.	3
DW-P.	P.9451	P/O. A. BROWN.	2
DW-U.	R.6686	P/O. W. A. DOUGLAS.	1

Once again no aircraft were sighted, and the sections returned to Acklington at 1505 hours. As frustrating as these patrols were, they were good experience for the novice pilots.

By mid-September, as the movement of aircrew in and out of the Squadron continued, the number of experienced pilots in need of a rest with 610 had reduced, so now the most adept replacement pilots would be moved south to the main combat area. Therefore, on 20 September, F/O Davies-Cooke and P/O Brown were posted back to the ever-dangerous 11 Group and 610's former home at Biggin Hill, where they joined 72 Squadron. Davies-Cooke's second spell with 610 Squadron had lasted just seventeen days and although he had gained flying time on Spitfires, it is proof of the strain that 11 Group's squadrons were under, that he was called into action so soon.

Sadly, Paul Davies-Cooke was to last a week in the front line, before he was shot down and killed by a Messerschmitt 109, over Sevenoaks, Kent, at 0925 hours on 27 September. His AMCB file was released at The National Archives just before the printing of this book. His Spitfire was seen spinning down from a great height, but at about 1,000 feet, it pulled into a steep dive and Davies-Cooke was observed to leave the aircraft. While it is unclear from the witnesses whether he attempted to bale out or fell from his Spitfire, it was later proven that his parachute had failed to open (TNA, AIR 81/3448). Tragically, he fell to his death near Hayes Station, while his Spitfire N.3068, crashed into Numbers 70 and 72 Queensway, West Wickham, leaving a scene of total devastation, although the occupants survived.[57] It was evident from the wreckage, that his Spitfire's windscreen had received a direct hit from a cannon shell (TNA, AIR 81/3448), and this terrible story is proof if any were needed of just how horrific aerial combat was in 1940. It took incredible bravery from the pilots to keep going up, knowing what they could face at any moment.

There is a remarkable photograph of Davies-Cooke's pilotless Spitfire, moments before it hit the ground in West Wickham (see photo p. 451). The unfortunate twenty-three-year-old was buried on 4 October 1940 in St John's churchyard, Rhydymwyn, Cilcain, Flintshire (TNA, AIR 81/3448). It was crushing news for the young pilot's family, Paul's parent's losing their youngest son in particularly unpleasant circumstances. Davies-Cooke's strong links with 610 Squadron meant there were many still with 'The Chesters' who knew him very well, like Brian Smith and Peter Lamb, better than the men in 72 Squadron with whom he went into battle that fatal day.

Twenty-two-year-old Bernard Walter Brown lasted even less time than Davies-Cooke, before being put out of action. Despite his flying experience with Army co-operation units, Brown was not an experienced fighter pilot and all his training could not compare to the lethal form of flying which was raging over south-eastern England. Just three days later, a 109 shot him down over Gravesend, and he, 'baled out and landed on marshy ground near Eastchurch, wounded in one leg and an elbow by cannon shell splinters. He was admitted to Minster Hospital and later transferred to Maidstone. Brown was posted from 72 to RAF Biggin Hill, as non-effective sick'.[58] Brown went on to become an instructor in the then Rhodesia, before becoming a ferry pilot between Britain and the Middle East. He joined the Royal New Zealand Air Force in 1944, and after the war became an airline pilot.[59] When he died on 23 January 2017, aged ninety-nine, he was believed to be the last surviving member of 610 Squadron from the Battle of Britain and the last New Zealander to have fought in the Battle too.

Although the ORB fails to mention it, a third pilot, Ivor Cosby, also left 610 for 72 Squadron. Some sources believe he had already joined 72 Squadron by this time, while the 610 ORB records him flying a patrol with 610 on 23 September. However, it is likely that:

> On the 20th Cosby moved to 72 Squadron, also at Biggin Hill. On the 23rd he shared in destroying a Bf 109. In October, when 72 went to Leconfield to reform, Cosby was posted to 222 Squadron at Hornchurch on November 4 1940. When the squadron went to Coltishall on November 11, he joined 602 Squadron at Westhampnett.[60]

Last seconds of a Spitfire. This ghostly photo shows Davies-Cooke's pilotless Spitfire, N.3068, moments before crashing into the houses on Queensway, West Wickham. (*Copyright After the Battle*)

F/O Davies-Cooke, probably photographed less than ten days before his death. (*Copyright 610 Squadron Association*)

Cosby survived the War, with several nocturnal claims made against the *Luftwaffe*. He died in September 1994, with the rank of wing commander.[61]

It is interesting to note here that of the ten pilots 610 had sent back to 11 Group in the first twenty days of September, after either training or a rest, only five survived the Battle unscathed—the more experienced Parsons, Ramsay, Beardsley and Bamberger, plus the relatively inexperienced Ivor Cosby. Sgt Willcocks survived the Battle with minor wounds, but had three crashes, while of the remaining four, one was killed and three others put out of the Battle with wounds. Such simple statistics give a true indication of how heavy the fighting was, and the inherent danger for inexperienced pilots, despite the wisdom passed on to them at Acklington. Two of those with no previous fighter aircraft experience had lasted a combined total of just ten days in the front line, a grim fact for any of 610's recent recruits, who would be heading south soon.

There was also a two-aircraft, thirty minute patrol on 20 September, which took off at 1145 hours. Red Section had been ordered to patrol Blyth, south of Acklington on the coast, at 9,000 feet. Red Leader was Peter Lamb (55), in DW-R, X.4239, while he was accompanied by P/O Bacon (1) in DW-F, X.4028, on his first recorded patrol, just four days after joining 610 Squadron. Nothing was seen.

The next noteworthy event came on 22 September with the arrival of yet more officers from 7 OTU, Hawarden; F/O Kirkwood and P/Os Drever and Ross. Mark Tyzack Kirkwood was born on 18 May 1915 (TNA, AIR 81/4154) and he:

> Joined the RAF on a short service commission and began his ab initio course on October 12 1936, as a pupil pilot. Kirkwood was posted to 10 FTS, Ternhill on January 16 1937, completed his training and then joined the staff at 3 Armament Training Station at Sutton Bridge on May 4 1938. He was with 4 Ferry Pilot Pool, when he went to 7 OTU, Hawarden on September 6 1940,[62]

where he converted to Spitfires, before joining 610 Squadron. Kirkwood had been in the RAF much longer than the other two pilots with whom he was joining the Squadron.

Nigel George Drever, was born in Edinburgh, on 19 January 1920.

> He was the second of four children of Walter and Mabel Drever who had moved to the mainland from the Orkneys. The family settled in Dundee where Nigel was educated at the Harris Academy. He was sixteen when he left school, securing his commission in the RAF with the help of the enthusiastic backing of his headmaster.[63]

Drever, 'joined the RAF on a short service commission in May 1939 and he began his *ab initio* course on June 12, as a pupil pilot',[64] gaining his 'Wings' on the day war was declared, 3 September 1939, aged nineteen. He completed his training and joined 98 Squadron flying Fairey Battle light bombers, which was held in reserve in France in 1940, near Nantes. After the Dunkirk evacuation, Drever was part of 98 Squadron's party instructed to leave France on board the ill-fated Cunard liner RMS *Lancastria*, on 17 June 1940. The great ship was attacked and sunk by the *Luftwaffe* off Saint-Nazaire, being the worst maritime disaster in British history. It was terrible for Drever, and he later recalled:

> … the agonisingly slow progress as he and his fellow servicemen climbed up to the deck. In the event, up to 90 members of his Squadron died in the disaster. "There were explosions and we were told to make our way aloft … It was so slow climbing up the spiral, it seemed to last for ever with the boat lurching … we all waited patiently for the chap in front. Oh dear, they took so long, but somehow I found I arrived on deck."… Drever had become a strong swimmer during childhood holidays in the Orkneys and he calmly took off his uniform, walked off the edge of the ship and swam away as fast as he could to avoid being sucked under as it sank. He reached a lifeboat but was told not to try to

Above left: Mark Tyzack Kirkwood. (*Copyright http://www.bbm.org.uk/airmen/Kirkwood.htm*)

Above right: Nigel Drever whilst with 610 Squadron. (*Copyright 610 Squadron Association*)

> get aboard. When he tried again with a second lifeboat he was threatened with an oar. Eventually he spotted ships farther out to sea and reached one after a lengthy swim … In a letter to a nephew many years later, Drever recalled that dreadful experience. "Nothing can possibly describe the horror of watching about 5,000 men die singing 'There'll always be an England', as they went down", he wrote.[65]

After a period of recuperation, 'Drever was posted to 4 Ferry Pilot Pool on July 22 1940 and then to 7 OTU on September 3',[66] for conversion to Spitfires.

Alexander 'Sandy' Richard Ross, from Surbiton, was the least experienced of the new pilots, having been:

> educated at Haileybury College and then at Imperial College, where he studied Engineering. He was a member of the London University Air Squadron in 1938. He transferred to the RAFVR on June 30 1939, as an Airman u/t Pilot (754232). Called up on September 1, he completed his training at FTS on August 30, was commissioned next day and went to 7 OTU, Hawarden,[67]

before arriving at his new Squadron. As these pilots started to settle in, although the ORB did not record it, a patrol of Seaham Harbour was carried out by Red Section at 1854 hours (13 Group ORB Appendices).

On the following day, 23 September, three more pilots reported for duty, from 7 OTU; Sgts Sutcliffe, Payne and York (the ORB had it as 'Yorke', but 'York' is correct). William Alfred Sutcliffe:

> from Middlesex, was educated at Spring Grove Central School. He joined the RAF in January 1931, as an Aircraft Apprentice and passed out in December 1933, as a Metal Rigger. He later served in the Middle East. Sutcliffe later applied for pilot training and was selected. With training completed, he arrived at 7 OTU, Hawarden on September 2 1940,[68]

Above left: 'Sandy' Ross, enjoying life as a more experienced pilot with 610 Squadron. (*Copyright 610 Squadron Association*)

Above right: William Sutcliffe, a new recruit for 610 Squadron. (*Copyright http://www.bbm.org.uk/airmen/Sutcliffe.htm*)

for his customary conversion to Spitfires before heading to Acklington.

Alec Dawson Payne was another southerner joining the County of Chester Squadron:

> Born in Croydon, Payne joined the RAFVR in May 1939. He began his flying training at 19 E&RFTS, Gatwick on July 9 1939 and soloed on the 18th.
>
> Called up on September 6, Payne went to No 1 ITW, Cambridge in November. He continued to fly Tiger Moths at 22 EFTS, moving later to a further flying course at RAF Yatesbury.
>
> Payne was posted to 8 FTS, Montrose, for No 20 Course, which ran from June 10 to August 31 1940. He moved on to 7 OTU, Hawarden on September 2,[69]

before ultimately joining 610 Squadron.

Making up the triumvirate of new sergeants was Ronald Lewis York, who came from Weston Favell in Northamptonshire. He, 'joined the RAFVR about July 1939, as an Airman u/t Pilot. Called up on September 1, he completed his training and arrived at 7 OTU, Hawarden on September 2 1940',[70] before eventually joining 'The Chesters' as a Spitfire pilot.

Against this backdrop of receiving new recruits, another section patrol was carried out. It was led by Stanley Norris, still being recorded as a flight lieutenant, while two of the newer recruits made up Blue Section:

DW-T.	X.4064	F/Lt. S. C. NORRIS.	63
DW-O.	X.4648	P/O. I. H. COSBY.*	2
DW-V.	K.9970	SGT. CORBIN W. J.	3

*Cosby is recorded in some sources as already having left 610 Squadron by this date.

Above left: A boyish looking Alec Dawson Payne. (*Copyright Wynn, Men of the Battle, p. 408*)

Above right: Sgt Ronald Lewis York. (*Copyright Wynn, Men of the Battle, p. 579*)

The patrol took off at 0938 hours, with orders to orbit the Farne Islands at 12,000 feet—nothing was seen and they returned to Acklington at 1012 hours.

On 24 September, Norris was acknowledged as having been awarded the DFC, although the original announcement of this award was made in '11 Group Intelligence Bulletin 42' on 1 September 1940 (TNA, AIR 25/197). The citation read:

> Acting Flight Lieutenant Stanley Charles NORRIS (40561).
>
> In August, 1940, this officer was leading his flight on an offensive patrol when twenty Junkers 88s were sighted. Flight Lieutenant Norris ordered his flight to attack them, but were themselves attacked in turn by twenty Messerschmitt 109s. It became necessary to abandon the attack on the enemy bombers, and to engage the enemy fighters. During the combat Flight Lieutenant Norris destroyed one Messerschmitt 109. This officer has personally destroyed six enemy aircraft and damaged a further two. He has displayed outstanding determination and skill as a leader.[71]

The incident highlighted occurred on 24 August. By this stage, Norris was established as one of the Squadron's cornerstones, his experience gained through months of constant action having propelled him to flight commander. It was testament to his flying ability that he had survived so long in such a dangerous environment, and his fellow pilots would have been quick to celebrate his award with him, feeling lucky to have Norris in their midst. Other news was that Corporal S. G. Forster had been posted to 13 Group's HQ, although nothing more is known of what he was going to do (ORB).

Four days later, another of 610's pilots was posted to 11 Group: Alfred Eric Davies was sent to Hornchurch, to join Sgt Ramsay with 222 Squadron. The twenty-three-year-old pilot officer lasted thirty-two days with his new Squadron before being killed on 30 October 1940, when his wing was shot off in combat with Me 109s. Davies's Spitfire, N.3119, crashed and burned out at Upper Wilting

Farm, Crowhurst, and he was buried on 6 November 1940 (TNA, AIR 81/4031), by his wife and family in St Mary Magdalene churchyard extension, Tanworth-in-Arden, Warwickshire.[72] Another of the men who had spent weeks getting their final training and tips from 610's veterans, had paid the ultimate sacrifice in the skies over south-eastern England. Davies was no longer a novice by the time of his death, having survived for a month in the thick of the action, with a claim for an Me 109 probably destroyed on 25 October.[73] He was one of the last men of Fighter Command to die in the 'official' period of the Battle of Britain, commonly referred to in Britain as having finished at the end of 31 October 1940.

On the following day, 29 September, three more pilots headed off to Hornchurch, this time to join 41 Squadron. Sgt Cyril Baker, who had enjoyed a month out of the front line, would have been hoping to be reunited with P/O Aldous and Sgts Beardsley and Bamberger. In fact, Baker may well have been replacing Aldous, who had been wounded the previous day. Cyril Baker was probably particularly glad to be back in Bamberger's company, whom he had known from pre-war days as ground staff with 610 Squadron. The pair had also attended flying training together. Baker was an accomplished fighter pilot already, having made several claims against the *Luftwaffe* in his six combats. While 610 would have been sad to see him go, 41 Squadron would have welcomed him with open arms. Having survived his time with 41 Squadron, Baker was, 'Commissioned in April 1941… later went to the Middle East and joined 112 Squadron in the Western Desert in February 1942. On June 6 Baker destroyed a Bf 109 and on July 19 he damaged a Ju 88. On completing his operational tour, he was awarded the DFC (4.12.42). Baker was released from the RAF in 1946 as a Flight Lieutenant'.[74] He died in 1978.

The other two pilots being posted to Essex were P/Os Draper and Mileham. Gilbert Draper, aged nineteen, survived unscathed for just over a month with his new Squadron, until on 30 October, 'During a combat over Ashford … [he] was shot down in Spitfire P 7282. He crashed at New Barn Farm, Postling, slightly injured, and went to Willesborough Hospital'.[75] It was the same day that Alfred Davies was killed with 222 Squadron. Having recovered from these wounds, Draper went back on operations: 'On August 7 1941 Draper was shot down over Fruge, near Lille, and captured. At some time he was held in Stalag Luft 3 at Sagan and Belaria (PoW No 3669). Freed in early May 1945, he went on to the RAFO on September 1 1945. Draper died in 1997'.[76]

A cheerful Sgt Baker, shortly before he was posted to 41 Squadron. (*Copyright 610 Squadron Association*)

Denys Mileham's training at Acklington was put to immediate use, as within a week of joining 41 Squadron he claimed a 109 destroyed on 5 October. He survived the remainder of the Battle of Britain, and destroyed another 109 on 17 November, but, 'He was killed on April 15 1942, as a Flight Lieutenant with 234 Squadron, aged 22. Mileham is remembered on the Runnymede Memorial, Panel 66'.[77]

As the three pilots left for Hornchurch, replacements were expected immediately with P/O Fenwick and Sgts Page and Miller due to arrive from Hawarden. However, in what seems to have been an administrative howler made on the order of the 6, 1 and 0, the three men were sent to 601 Squadron, which operated Hurricanes and was based at the opposite end of the country, in Exeter! The ORB states that they had been, 'Attached to No.601 Squadron Exeter from 30.9.40 to 17.10.40', suggesting a deliberate ploy rather than an administrative error, but on looking at their actual arrival at 610 Squadron, it does seem to have been a mistake.

Two patrols took place during the afternoon, the first at 1410 hours involved Red Section, but was not recorded in 610's ORB (13 Group ORB Appendices). Then, the last recorded operation of the month took place, with 'B' Flight's Red Section being ordered off at 1719 hours led by F/O Pegge. Instructed to orbit Usworth, they encountered a Fairey Battle and returned to Acklington at 1810 hours. The pilots and aircraft were:

DW-B.	K.9892	F/O. C. O. J. PEGGE.	31
DW-T.	X.4064	SGT. CORBIN W. J.	4
DW-V.	K.9970	SGT. CARTER, E. F.*	1

*Carter's initials were 'L. R.', so ORB error.

Another posting took place on Monday 30 September, with F/O Ian McGregor Hallam being sent to 222 Squadron, where he was reunited with Eric Davies. The pair had trained together at Hawarden—having a familiar face on a new unit must have been a great help in fitting in, and seems to have been a feature of the posting of pilots from 'Category C' units. The twenty-one year old from Edinburgh was another pilot who profited from his time with 610's veterans, as, 'During the Battle of Britain, Hallam is believed to have claimed one Bf 109 destroyed, another probably destroyed and four damaged'.[78] Hallam served with several other squadrons before ending up a PoW in Germany on 24 August 1942. He survived the War, but was killed on 10 May 1952 during a training flight, while he was commanding officer of the Aberdeen UAS.[79] It was a tragic end for such an experienced man, whose work with the UAS was important in bringing on the pilots of the future.

The month ended on a very sorrowful note for 610 Squadron, with the loss of a pilot, the first Squadron aircrew casualty since Sgt Manton's death on 29 August. Charles Bacon, recently promoted to flying officer, took off from Acklington on 30 September in Spitfire DW-H, K.9818, with Irishman Harry Clarke in DW-D, L.1037, as recalled by Jimmy Corbin, who was part of Clarke's section:

> One particularly unremarkable day, the CO came in to address us all.
>
> "Right lads, in the absence of the real thing, I have decided you can spend the day doing combat practice. Right Blue Section, we will have you and Red Section go up first. Keep your distance from each other".
>
> I was Blue Section along with Nick [Sgt Carter, author] and Clarke. We climbed into our Spits and took off. When we reached 30,000 feet, we took up our positions for the staged dogfight. The idea was that we would dive down after each other and then climb back up again. We would then swoop past each other and turn to repeat the performance just to give ourselves a mild taste of what a real dogfight was all about.
>
> We engaged in our pretend battle. I dived down after Nick and followed him as he banked and swooped upwards to gain height on me. We then turned away from each other before turning back to face each other. We flew towards each other before peeling off in plenty of time to avoid a collision. It was controlled, measured and planned and, in fact, nothing like the real thing.

> Next it was Clarke's turn. He repeated a similar manoeuvre with a pilot from the other section. All was proceeding well with the planes chasing each other across the skies as Nick and I flew around them and watched from a safe distance.
>
> Then quite suddenly one of the planes misjudged its distance from the other and instead of careering past each other in style, they collided in mid-air. There was a loud bang followed by a bright yellow flash. Debris shot out from the core of the explosion.
>
> From my cockpit, I watched with total horror as both planes dropped like stones, trailing black smoke before smashing into the ground near the airfield. I knew both pilots must have been killed instantly.[80]

Either Charles Bacon or Harry Clarke had made a tiny misjudgement and the two Spitfires collided at about 14,000 feet. Derek Walton, a Northumbrian aviation historian, noted the following: 'One wing of Spitfire Mk.I *K9818* was severed in the collision, causing the aircraft to spin into the beach near Alnmouth, the wing fell onto a nearby cricket field'.[81] Spitfire K.9818 had joined the Squadron at some stage in August, the ORB mentioning it carrying out patrols from 14 August, as it had probably replaced the machine Brian Smith was shot down in on 12 August, DW-H, L.1044. It is believed to have been officially struck off charge on 7 October 1940, following this collision.[82] The AMCB files for this incident were released just prior to publication, and in Bacon's file, S/Ldr Ellis noted that 'Pilot Officer Bacon appears to have delayed his break away until too late. He must either have been stunned in the collision or been unable to bale out as he crashed with his aircraft and was killed' (TNA, AIR 81/3546). Bacon had only joined 610 Squadron a fortnight earlier on 16 September, but with 196.15 hours solo flying time in total, including 40.25 hours on Spitfires, he was more experienced than many of his colleagues (TNA, AIR 81/3546). The ORB's blunt statement, 'Pilot Officer C. H. BACON (74324) killed as a result of a flying accident on Alnmouth beach', makes no reference to the collision, or the terror Bacon must have endured following the impact.

The twenty-one-year-old was buried on 3 October 1940 in the Bacon family grave, in the extension of St Mary's churchyard, Windermere, now simply known as Windermere Cemetery, leaving behind his distraught parents William Charles and Charlotte. As a result of his recent promotion, his old rank of pilot officer still appears on his headstone, although he was actually a flying officer, his promotion having come through just four days earlier. Bacon flew at least one recorded patrol during the Battle of Britain period with 610 Squadron, so he is remembered as one of 'The Few'.

Corbin continued his description of these traumatic events, as when he had landed, it emerged that Clarke had managed to bale out:

> Then the CO appeared. "They have found Clarke. He's a bit mashed up, but they think he's going to be all right. They're taking him to hospital now."
>
> Later that evening Nick and I paid Clarke a visit. He was a mass of bandages, but he managed a smile as he saw us approaching …
>
> Nick and I sat by his bedside and listened enthralled to Clarke's heavily-accented account of the accident.
>
> "There was a huge bang and I seemed to be sailing through the air. I must have passed out because the next thing I came round just above the cloud. I looked down and was amazed to see my parachute just below me.
>
> I also realised I was hanging by one strap with the other one wrapped around my leg. I pulled myself up and held on to the remainder of the harness, and that's the last thing I remember. I must have passed out just before I hit the deck."
>
> The following day Nick and I examined his parachute. Two white silk panels had been completely ripped out. The pack was ripped to threads and the quick release box was missing altogether. Clarke swore he did not pull the parachute's rip cord and so when he collided with the other plane, the force

Bacon's grave in the peaceful cemetery at Windermere. (*Author*)

> of the impact must have thrown him out of the cockpit. His chute pack must have caught on some part of the aeroplane, ripping it open. By rights, looking at the shreds of material that had once been a parachute, he shouldn't have survived.
>
> It was a remarkable escape. His only injuries were several minor bruises and a deep cut on his chin which was probably caused when his helmet was wrenched off as he was thrown from the cockpit. He was, of course, in shock.
>
> Flying accidents during training were not widely publicised by the RAF despite their frequency. It was unbelievable to think that more pilots were killed in training than they were in combat.[83]

Clarke's AMCB file records that his Spitfire crashed two miles west of Alnmouth, at Bilton Farm, Bilton, Northumberland. The cause of the collision becomes apparent in Clarke's own report written for the subsequent investigation, as follows:

> Pilot Officer Bacon and I commenced dog-fighting practice at 10,000 feet with a head on attack. Previous arrangements had been made for the aircraft to break starboard after the attack.
>
> The aircraft approached each other slightly to starboard, making starboard breakaway difficult. I hesitated momentarily to see which way P/O Bacon would break. I then turned hard to port but starbo [starboard] wings of both aircraft collided. I baled out. (TNA, AIR 81/3543)

Clarke had 148.20 hours solo flying time, including 43.20 hours on Spitfires, and his CO John Ellis obviously thought highly of him despite the collision, according to his report on the incident: 'Sergeant Clarke is well above the average of pilots posted to this unit from O.T.U's [*sic*], but in this case he failed to appreciate that to hesitate before breaking away in a head on attack is inviting danger' (TNA, AIR 81/3543). This tragically highlights the incredibly small margins over life and death in an RAF squadron, even when training.

Clarke's escape from death was extraordinary, and if the collision was not enough, the parachute descent would have put many off flying for good. But after recovering from this incident, Clarke continued to fly operationally. He left 610 Squadron on 16 December 1940, for 602 Squadron at

Prestwick. He went on to be a test pilot, and was released from the RAF on 2 May 1947. He died on 26 July 2010, at the age of ninety-two.[84] The remains of Clarke's Spitfire were excavated by Derek Walton on 4 June 1995 and are on display in Bamburgh Castle's Aviation Museum. The display forms a poignant memorial to this fatal collision, which cost F/O Bacon his life, but also acts as a testament to Clarke's life, which must always have been haunted by the fateful events of 30 September 1940. Clarke's Spitfire, DW-D, L.1037, possibly joined the Squadron during August, when it was recorded as flying patrols, but this could be inaccurate.[85]

Given that the Squadron had received twenty-six pilots with minimal experience on the powerful Spitfire, which they suddenly found themselves flying day-in-day-out, it was remarkable that there had not been a lot more accidents during this first month. Much credit should go to the 'old hands', who were bringing the new boys on as fighter pilots, which they would continue to do in October.

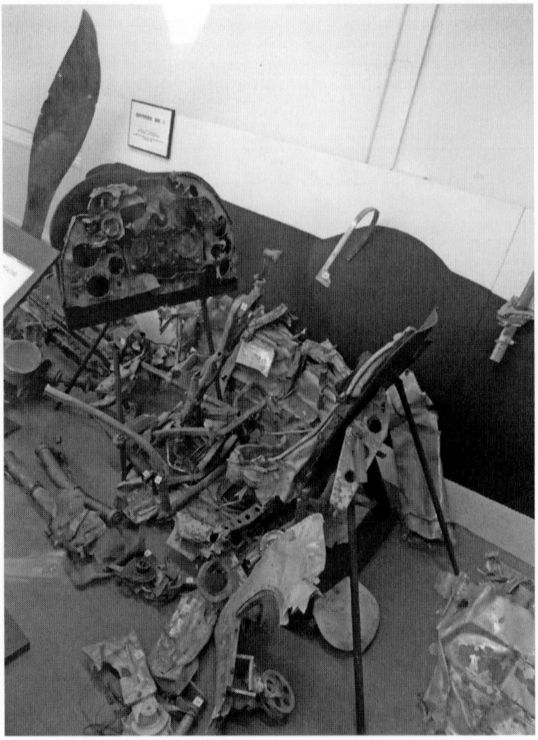

The tangled remains of Clarke's Spitfire, DW-D, L.1037. The pilot's seat, instrument panel, engine parts and propeller are prominent. (*Author's photo, copyright Bamburgh Castle Aviation Museum*)

19

October 1940: Closing Stages of The Battle of Britain

Despite the arrival of a new month, there was no change in procedure for 610 Squadron. As a 'Category C' Squadron, the carousel of pilots coming in for training and leaving to fill up gaps in other hard-pressed Squadrons continued unabated. On the morning of 1 October 1940, the Nominal Roll for the Squadron would have looked something like this:

1 S/Ldr. J. Ellis
2 F/Lt. E. B. B. Smith
3 F/Lt. D. S. Wilson
4 F/Lt. S. C. Norris
5 F/O. C. O. J. Pegge
6 F/O. P. G. Lamb
7 F/O. B. V. Rees[1]
8 Sgt. H. H. Chandler
9 Sgt. R. F. Hamlyn
10 P/O. F. J. Aldridge
11 Sgt. H. R. Clarke
12 Sgt. L. R. Carter
13 Sgt. W. J. Corbin
14 P/O. W. A. Douglas
15 Sgt. F. C. Horner
16 Sgt. J. Murray
17 Sgt. P. Ward-Smith
18 F/O. M. T. Kirkwood
19 P/O. N. G. Drever
20 P/O. A. R. Ross
21 Sgt. W. A. Sutcliffe
22 Sgt. A. D. Payne
23 Sgt. R. L. York
24 P/O. J. G. Lecky.

However, by the end of the day, Sgt Carter and P/Os Aldridge and Lecky had been posted to 11 Group, joining 41 Squadron at Hornchurch. Carter was to experience a similarly petrifying experience to Harry Clarke a little over a week later. On 11 October, 41 Squadron was scrambled to intercept some 109s, when Carter collided mid-air with F/O O'Neill. Both pilots managed to bale out, but O'Neill's parachute did not open and he was killed. Leslie Raymond Carter must have been badly traumatised by this tragic accident, but continued operational flying and survived the Battle of Britain. He was reported 'missing' on 6 July 1941 while with 74 Squadron,[2] and is remembered on Panel 35 at the Runnymede Memorial.

Life with 41 Squadron got off to a good start for the nineteen-year-old P/O Lecky, as he claimed a 109 as damaged on 5 October and shot down a Dornier 17 the following day.[3] The ever-changing fortunes of war were never clearer than in Lecky's short combat life though, as on 11 October, during the same patrol that Carter had his collision, John Lecky was shot down by 109s and killed, despite having baled out.[4] His Spitfire P.9447 is believed to have crashed at Preston Hall in Maidstone, although there is some debate about it. Lecky was buried in the All Saints' churchyard in Tilford, Surrey—his parents were Lieutenant-Colonel John Gage Lecky and Marion Dorothy Hume Lecky, of Lower Bourne.[5]

October was proving to be just as dangerous for 11 Group's pilots as the previous months had been, the different tactics required to take on the *Luftwaffe's* nuisance raids and high-flying fighter-bombers having to be learnt as they went along. P/O Aldridge seemed to have more luck with this than the other two pilots, progressing to be a very capable fighter pilot, clearly benefiting from his time with 610 Squadron. During October, he claimed two Me 109s destroyed and in November a 109 destroyed and one damaged.[6] Aldridge survived the War, serving with 238 Squadron in the Western Desert in 1941; on 6 December he destroyed an Me 109 and damaged a second. In 1942 he joined 274 Squadron and damaged a Ju 88 near El Adem, near Tobruk.[7] In April 1945, as a squadron leader at an FTS in Alberta, Canada, he was commended for valuable services in the air. Aldridge was released from the RAF in 1947.[8]

The lives of the three pilots who left 610 on 1 October, seem to sum up the fates of many of the new recruits being posted south from 'Category C' Squadrons, one killed within ten days, one very fortunate to be alive after the same period, while Aldridge managed to survive and put into practice what he had trained to do. There could be no fathoming the fortunes of war.

Meanwhile at Acklington, patrols were still being carried out and 610 had a busy morning and early afternoon. On 1 October 1940, Red Section was ordered off first at 1025 hours to investigate an 'X' raid over the Farne Islands at 20,000 feet. The following pilots were involved. Note, the ORB no longer uses the pilots' initials, and it only uses the identifying letter of the Spitfire, not its serial code, which I have replicated:

DW-E.	Sgt. Hamlyn.	43
DW-R.	P/O. Drever.	1
DW-F.	Sgt. Payne.	1

They landed safely at 1125 hours. Yellow Section, operating as a pair, was ordered up five minutes after Red Section had taken off, to patrol Seaham Harbour and Blythe at 10,000 feet, situated to the south and north of Newcastle, but the following pilots did not encounter anything either and landed at 1110 hours:

DW-T.	F/Lt. Pegge.	32
DW-N.	Sgt. Yorke. [York]	1

At least Sgt Ronald York had got his first recorded operational patrol under his belt. It is interesting to note that Joe Pegge is referred to as flight lieutenant, although no official mention of it was made in the ORB. It is apparent he had become the 'A' Flight commander, a resounding endorsement of his ability as a leader and length of service with the Squadron, as he had only recently been promoted to flying officer. Stan Norris was 'B' Flight's commander.

At 1225 hours, Red Section was again sent to investigate an 'X' raid over the Farne Islands at 24,000 feet:

DW-A.	P/O. Lamb.*	56
DW-R.	P/O. Drever.	2
DW-F.	Sgt. Payne.	2

*Throughout October, the ORB lists Lamb as a pilot officer in the 'Detail of work carried out'. This is an error, as he should be recorded as 'F/O'. I have left it as the original.

The pilots returned at 1255 hours without seeing anything. On 2 October, the Squadron had to carry out a couple of late afternoon to early evening patrols, the first of which took off at 1600 hours to investigate another 'X-raid' raid over the Coquet Islands at 20,000 feet. The pilots were:

DW-A.	P/O. Lamb.	57
DW-R.	P/O. Drever.	3
DW-F.	Sgt. Ward-Smith.	1

They returned safely an hour later. As the evening approached at Acklington, the Squadron was ordered to put up a section for dusk patrol, and S/Ldr Ellis (53) in DW-W, along with P/O Douglas in DW-P (2), took off at 1845 hours, returning at 1930 hours without anything to report.

On 3 October, 610 Squadron had a fairly busy morning, with three patrols completed by 1040 hours. Red Section was ordered up at 0640 hours to patrol the Coquet Islands at 20,000 feet:

DW-A.	P/O. Lamb.	58
DW-R.	P/O. Drever.	4
DW-F.	Sgt. Ward-Smith.	2

They returned at 0735 hours, but five minutes into Red Section's patrol, P/O Douglas (3) was ordered off at 0645 hours in DW-P, for the ubiquitous 'Dawn patrol'. It was inevitably uneventful and he was back on the ground twenty minutes later. After a brief lull, Red Section was ordered up again, at 0950 hours, involving three different pilots:

DW-W.	F/Lt. Norris.	64
DW-T.	P/O. Ross.	1
DW-O.	Sgt. Murray.	1

Norris was instructed to patrol Seaham harbour at 25,000 feet, but it was a fruitless trip, and they landed back at Acklington at 1040 hours. This was the first recorded operational patrol of both Ross and Murray, who had arrived only recently and they could not have had a more experienced leader for the patrol.

On 5 October, P/O Keighley, one of the Squadron's stalwarts, received instruction to return to the fold. He had remained on attachment at Biggin Hill, classed as 'non-effective sick' since being shot down and wounded on 20 July. His welcome return to the Squadron seems to have actually occurred on 7 October, and he would have been warmly received by his old friends still serving with the Squadron. Another arrival on 5 October was Sgt Pilot Raine, straight from 7 OTU. He was now ready for Squadron duties away from the front line. Woodrow Raine, nicknamed 'Billy', hailed from Cumberland and had, 'joined the RAFVR about February 1939 as an Airman u/t Pilot. He was called up on 1st September and completed his training at 22 EFTS and 5 FTS. While converting to Spitfires at 7 OTU Hawarden he survived a forced landing in Spitfire N3269 on 18th September',[9] before joining 610 Squadron.

On the same day, 610 Squadron carried out a couple of patrols, the first involving F/O Lamb (59) in DW-W, leading Sgt 'Jackie' Horner in DW-U on his first recorded operational sortie. Blue Section took off at 0755 hours and patrolled the Farne Islands at 15,000 feet, but nothing was encountered and they were back on *terra firma* at 0850 hours. The second patrol is not recorded in the Squadron's ORB, but 13 Group's ORB Appendices noted a dusk patrol was carried out by one 610 Squadron aircraft at 1859 hours, to patrol Seaham to Blyth. Nothing of note occurred.

A much bigger influx of pilots arrived on 6 October, when eight sergeants joined: 'Sergeants: Cranwell (741969), Denchfield H. D. (748168), Doley A. S. (754184), Ballard J. E. W. (745731), Warden N. P (748342), Cooper R. N. (758092), Cooper J. E. (745777) and Greig J. N. (742423) posted to this Unit from No. 7 O.T.U. HARWARDEN [Hawarden]' (ORB). Edward William Cranwell, known as Ted, was born in London on 25 September 1915. He: 'joined the RAFVR in August 1938 (741969) and did his weekend flying at 21 E&RFTS, Stapleford Abbots. He was called up in late 1939, went to 3 ITW,

Sgt Woodrow Raine in Spitfire '*Venture I*'. (*Copyright Nigel Denchfield*)

Hastings and then to 11 EFTS, Perth. On June 15 1940, Cranwell went to 15 FTS, Brize Norton on No 10 Course, which moved in August to Chipping Norton.'[10] On 10 September, he had a lucky escape when he landed at Chipping Norton without lowering his undercarriage, leaving Harvard P.5783 badly damaged (TNA, AIR 81/3199). Thankfully, Cranwell was not seriously injured and he finally moved to Hawarden to convert to Spitfires, before joining 'The Chesters'.

David Denchfield was, 'born on November 2 1919 at Eckington, near Staveley, Derbyshire. He finished his education at Hemel Hempstead Grammar School and after leaving, he worked as a clerk.'[11] Denchfield later recalled his time in the RAF and 610 Squadron, including a memorable account of joining the RAFVR and his time as a novice pilot:

> It would be in about December 1938 that I received all the bumph regarding the RAFVR and began explaining to mum and dad it was safer than the RAF for we flew in little aircraft, and yes if war came the RAF would mobilise me, but then I would be called up in any case from civvy street—and that might be into the Army! It was a long haul which went on until just after the New Year before dad saw sense and signed the forms for me and I sent them off in about early February 1939. In April I received an answer from the RAF telling me to report to the Town Centre of the No: 29 E & RFTS, RAFVR in Bute Street, Luton on 18th May 1939, for medical & suitability checks. At about 5.30 pm a lad named Browne and myself were the last ones to be ruled fit and proper to join the RAFVR and were duly attested and sworn in to serve King and Country—as Sgt/pilot u/t.
>
> On Sunday 21st May 1939 I had my very first flight—in a Miles Magister at Luton airport … That flight was stupendous, and the start of a 3-month period in which I flew most weekends although some flights were of short duration. We had to attend the Luton Town Centre on two particular evenings a week for ground lectures in military aviation subjects …
>
> We flew on Sundays and as sometimes I only got 40 min flights things tended to drag. Still I finally went solo on 16th July at which time the international situation looked to be well on to crisis point.

Sgt 'Ted' Cranwell is in the flying jacket, in the middle of the back row. Next to him in the middle with his 'Wings', is Sgt Joe Doley. The other men are not known, but were possibly ground crew. (*Copyright Nigel Denchfield*)

Not for the last time did I think the pace of training could have been greatly accelerated—we did seem to spend lots of time needlessly doing nought.

So we drifted uneasily along until that fateful Friday, 1st September 1939, when around midday we heard a rumour—soon confirmed—that Poland was invaded! ...

On 2 November I was 20 years old ... In the first week of November all VRs not yet posted (95% of us!) were called to a meeting in the Town Centre to be told that as the RAF had had few casualties all training schools were choc-a-bloc and there was no likelihood of postings for some long time and those who wanted to return to their civilian jobs for a time could do so ... A week later I drove Ollie Cooper and two others to Luton and we dropped in at the Town Centre. Holding pints we idly crossed to the notice board and I still hear Ollie's shout of pure joy, "Dave we're posted to Bexhill!" and so we were along with 48 other fortunates on 29th November.

On arrival at Bexhill, staying in the Metropole Hotel he continued:

We were given a reasonable meal, and a "bull" session in which we were told we were No 3 Squadron of 4 ITW ... Then there began a rigid unchanging routine up at 6 am and out for PT at 6.15 am on the sea front (however cold and vile the weather!); back at 7 am for a clean-up and breakfast at 7.30 am ... for the main parade at 9 am. From this we dispersed into lectures, drills, and sport (much as at Luton but now with a far greater sense of continuity and urgency in the knowledge that failure meant no flying course ...).

The extreme weather that winter combined with an overloaded training system delayed things, but eventually in April 1940 a crowd of us were posted to 15 EFTS at Redhill where we flew Magisters. After a few days I went solo, although I was beaten to this by Ollie, who won the first of several 2/6 bets between us. In June we had to move up to Carlisle as Redhill was clearly going to be in the front line. On the 15th June we were posted to 15 SFTS at Brize Norton where we found mainly Oxfords and a few Harvards ... At the end of our time at Brize we took our "Wings" exams (successfully!) and

> in August were posted to 15 AFTS [Advanced Flying Training School] at Chipping Norton. This is where flying became much more akin to operational flying as well as teaching us much more advanced control. Then in September we went to 57 OTU at Hawarden (Chester) where we were to fly Masters before graduating to Spitfires …
>
> In October Ollie, Bill Ballard and myself were chuffed when we were posted along with Ted Cranwell and Joe Doley to 610 (County of Chester) Squadron at Acklington north of Newcastle … I think the original pilots were all gone, one-way or the other, but all the ground staff, as usual with Auxiliary squadrons, remained. They could not be posted to another unit against their wishes; hence most spent the war with their original squadron. A great spirit resulted.
>
> Bill Ballard and myself were allocated a small room at the end of a communal block holding some 30 airmen; it was small indeed but warm and cosy … We started flying the following day in between rain showers, the visibility was atrocious, but I think the six remaining pilots of 610 were anxious to see how we would all shape. Even at this late stage we found a pressure to succeed. After Hawarden the Mess was sheer luxury, solid brick-built with a billiard room, large ante-room filled with leather arm-chairs, and a large, quiet dining room in which we were served by white-coated mess waiters. The food was good, and, perhaps best of all, there was no 'atmosphere' between pilots and ground staff. Bill, myself and Cranwell were in 'A' Flight with F/Lt Pegge, whilst Ollie, Joe Doley and another newcomer, Billy Raine (proper Christian name—Woodrow!) were in 'B' Flight with F/Lt Norris. The other two originals were F/O Douglas [should probably be Lamb, author] and Sgt Hamlyn (whose a/c bore a Walt Disney Pied Piper and 15 rats—each with a swastika collar). The squadron was commanded by Sqdn Ldr Ellis.[12]

The distinctive markings on Hamlyn's aircraft clearly reflected his nickname of the 'Pied Piper of Harrogate'.

John Enerton Cooper, Denchfield's best friend 'Ollie', was from Luton, and he and David followed exactly the same path to 610 Squadron. Unfortunately little has been recorded of Anthony S. Doley and James Eric William Ballard, although both are referred to by Denchfield and trained with him at Hawarden. 'Joe', as Doley was known (see photo p. 465), does not seem to have flown an operational patrol with 610 Squadron before the end of October, so failed to qualify as one of 'The Few'. The same applied to 'Bill' Ballard, who came from Tooting, Surrey.

Little is also recorded of Noel Proctor Warden, who originated from Andover, Hampshire, his parents being Norman Charles and Eva.[13] However, he joined the VR in, 'May 1939, as an Airman u/t Pilot (748342). Called up on September 1, he completed his training and arrived at 7 OTU, Hawarden on September 23 1940',[14] before converting to Spitfires and joining 610 Squadron, where he would fly operationally in the Battle of Britain.

Ray Norman Cooper was from Paulsgrove, Portsmouth, his parents being George Albert and Lily May Victoria, while Ray married Dorothy, of Hilsea, Portsmouth.[15] He 'joined the RAFVR in July 1939 as an Airman u/t Pilot (758092). Called up on September 1, he completed his flying training and arrived at 7 OTU, Hawarden on September 23 1940',[16] before arriving at Acklington. Unfortunately, even less is known about Sgt J. N. Greig and as he was not recognised as a Battle of Britain pilot, he could not have become operational until at least November 1940.

While these new men arrived, the never-ending patrols continued. On 6 October, this time taking off from Acklington at 1125 hours to investigate another 'X' raid over Newcastle, Red Section was composed of the following sergeants:

DW-Q.	Sgt. Hamlyn.	44
DW-E.	Sgt. Sutcliffe.	1
DW-F.	Sgt. Horner.	2

Above left: David Denchfield, not long before the Squadron returned to the south. (*Copyright 610 Squadron Association*)

Above right: Sgt Bill Ballard. (*Copyright 610 Squadron Association*)

Above left: John Enerton Cooper, known as Ollie. (*Copyright Wynn, Men of the Battle, p.102*)

Above right: Sgt Noel Proctor Warden. (*Copyright 610 Squadron Association*)

Photograph of Sgt Ray Norman Cooper with 91 Squadron, at Hawkinge, 21 October 1941. Cooper is third from the left. (*Copyright 610 Squadron Association*)

They reached 25,000 feet before carrying out a patrol, but once again did not encounter anything and were back on the ground by 1150 hours. On 7 October, the only recorded sortie was a dusk patrol carried out by Peter Lamb (60) in DW-W, taking off at 1825 hours and returning at 1940 hours.

F/O Lamb (61) was on duty again in the same aircraft the following morning at 0630 hours. Operating as Blue 1, he patrolled Whitley Bay at 15,000 feet, returning to Acklington at 0705 hours, without incident. Just after midday, Red Section was ordered to investigate an 'X' raid at the cloud base of 4,000 feet over their aerodrome, as follows:

DW-Q.	Sgt. Hamlyn.	45
DW-E.	Sgt. Horner.	3

They took off at 1215 hours and returned fifteen minutes later.

On 11 October, Sgt R. N. Cooper received orders to join 65 Squadron based even further north at Turnhouse, Scotland, meaning he had spent just five days with 610 Squadron. However, he was recognised as one of their Battle of Britain pilots, so is presumably thought to have been the 'Cooper' who flew with S/Ldr Ellis that morning. Little is recorded of Ray Cooper, but having survived the War, he met an unusual fate, being, 'killed on October 28 1945, as a flying officer with the Anti-Locust Flight. He was 29 and is buried in the European Cemetery, Jinja Road, Kampala, Uganda.'[17]

Friday 11 October also heralded the return of another of the Squadron's wounded pilots, P/O Donald McIntosh Gray. Like Keighley, Gray seems to have been on ground staff duties at Biggin Hill, while he recovered from his wounds suffered on 24 August. Gray had carried out six recorded patrols in

August, claiming an Me 109 probably destroyed, before being shot down and wounded. He probably welcomed time to reacquaint himself with the Spitfire, out of the main combat area. There was quite a bit of flying activity during the day too, with three patrols and an 'X' raid being investigated by the following pilots, although Sgt. Payne is listed twice:

Red Section.

DW-W.	S/Ldr. Ellis. Patrol.	0625–0735	54
DW-N.	Sgt. Payne.		3

Green Section.

DW-A.	P/O. Lamb.		62
DW-C.	Sgt. Horner.		4
DW-N.	Sgt. Payne.		

Red and Green Sections ordered to patrol Tyne Area at 10,000 feet. No E/A sighted.

DW-B.	F/O. Pegge. Patrol.	0800–0920	33
DW-U.	Sgt. Yorke. [York]		2
DW-T.	Sgt. Corbin.		5

Blue Section ordered to patrol from Woolsington to Acklington at 10,000 feet. No E/A sighted.

DW-W.	S/Ldr. Ellis. Patrol.	1025–1110	55
DW-M.	Sgt. Cooper.*		1

*Probably R. N. Cooper.

Green Section ordered to patrol base at 10,000 feet. No E.A sighted.

DW-Q.	P/O. Lamb. Investigate "X" Raid.	1055–1110	63
DW-F.	Sgt. Cranwell.		1
DW-E.	Sgt. Denchfield.		1

Red Section ordered to investigate 'X' raid over Coquet Islands at 20,000 feet. No E/A sighted.

It was unusual for a flight of aircraft to be used on such a patrol as the first one, so perhaps a more tangible threat was felt to be in the offing, but ultimately it only proved to be good formation flying practice. At least by the day's end, Cooper, Cranwell and Denchfield all had their first recorded sorties under their belts. David Denchfield's recollection of preparing for such a patrol with 610 makes for interesting reading:

> Most days we had one flight on training flights with the other on readiness in case anything hostile came over. Those on readiness sat in the pilot's hut reading, chatting, listening to the radio, or more usually the gramophone, or just plain dozing. Helmets were in the a/c draped over the gun sight (against all authority), with the wireless lead plugged into the socket just in front of the seat and the oxygen tube plugged in up on the right hand side of the cockpit. Parachutes sat, with straps hanging, on the port wingtip (as mine was) or on the tail plane. If a flap came, once out at the a/c it was a mere 10 seconds to duck under the two shoulder straps, and holding them pull the 'brolly' off the wing to bring the waist half-belt and locking box round on to the stomach. Then clip the shoulder straps into the box, bend down and bring the two leg straps through the crutch loop and into the box. A quick leap onto the wing, and then right-footed into the cockpit wriggling the brolly pack into the seat well.
>
> Then it was a mess of arms and legs, mine and those of the rigger and fitter on the wing roots. Mine would be grabbing the four harness straps from the rigger on the right hand side and assembling them

> onto the pillar fitted to the left hand shoulder strap and finally poking the quick release clip through the hole in the pillar. The fitter on the left meanwhile would be setting throttle and pitch levers, pulling up the two central fuel levers, turn the priming cock on, unscrewing the Ki-gas, priming then screwing it up again and finally putting the ignition switches up before pressing the starter button to bring the Merlin coughing into life.
>
> By this time I would have just about managed to drag my helmet on, sometimes even to fasten both it and the oxygen mask, but usually this was completed during the taxy out. As the two helpers dropped off the wing to grab the chock ropes and the erk on the trolly-acc pulled the power lead out of the a/c socket and hauled it clear out of harm's way, I used to be able to put my left hand out to grab the top of the bottom-hinged cockpit door and pull it to the landing/take-off shut position; this locked the door about ½ inch open to prevent the open hood sliding shut during a crash landing and so baulking easy egress. Once airborne the door was completely shut and the hood closed.
>
> A raised hand to the section leader some 50 yards away signalled the erks to drag the wheel chocks away clear, and then with one of them dragging back on one wingtip to help the turn it was throttle up to follow after the leader, and 3—sometimes 6, and more rarely 12—Spits would lurch one behind the other to the take-off spot selected by No. 1 (leader) whilst each pilot frantically finished his cockpit checks and settings. At the take-off spot, Nos 2 and 3 swung into tight 'Vic' to right and left respectively of No 1 whilst facing across wind, and then all turned in Vic into wind and opened up to rush as one in the take-off run. Nos 2 and 3 maintained, by juggling throttles, their a/c in a constant position to No 1 with wingtips about 3 ft behind and 4 ft out from his, and as his wheels left the ground so they allowed their own a/c to lift off. There are few things more satisfying than a well-held close formation take-off![18]

On 12 October, 610 had another active day, with Red and Yellow Sections both on duty:

DW-B.	F/O. Pegge. Patrol.	0910–1010	34
DW-T.	F/O. Kirkwood.		1
DW-M.	P/O. Ross.		2

Red Section ordered to patrol Tyne Area at 20,000 feet. No E/A sighted.

DW-L.	Sgt. Hamlyn. Patrol.	1315–1430	46
DW-C.	Sgt. Warden.		1
DW-E.	Sgt. Sutcliffe.		2

Red Section ordered to patrol Tyne Area at 15,000 feet. No E/A sighted.

DW-M.	F/O. Pegge. Patrol.	1405–1530	35
DW-U.	Sgt. Corbin.		6

Yellow Section ordered to patrol Farne Islands at 25,000 feet. No E/A sighted.

DW-C.	P/O. Lamb. Patrol.	1515–1650	64
DW-E.	Sgt. Horner.		5
DW-L.	Sgt. Payne.		4

Red Section ordered to patrol Tyne Area at 15,000 feet. No E/A sighted.

DW-T.	P/O. Ross. Patrol.	1630–1745	3
DW-U.	F/O. Kirkwood.		2
DW-M.	Sgt. Yorke. [York]		3

Yellow Section ordered to patrol Coquet Islands at 15,000 feet. Nothing seen.

Yet again, no enemy aircraft were encountered, but these patrols were as much about giving experience to the novice pilots, getting them used to formation flying and the Spitfire in operational conditions. Warden had his first recorded patrol, while Kirkwood managed his first two recorded patrols. Such men who were on a very steep learning curve, would have been only too glad of this flying time, where there was still the chance of encountering an opportunistic German bomber.

Although no mention of it is made in 610 Squadron's ORB, thanks to 13 Group's ORB, it is evident that the pilots carrying out a training exercise had a much more eventful day of it, as it was reported at 1325 hours that, '4 a/c written off on landing at Acklington of 610 Squadron, leaving 6 a/c serviceable. These aircraft were on training when bad weather came on very suddenly. Nobody hurt' (13 Group ORB Appendices). It is very strange that the Squadron's ORB makes no mention of such a major event. It is also surprising that the bad weather must have disappeared as quickly as it arrived, as 610 Squadron had continued operational patrols during and after the incident, as seen earlier. However, 13 Group's ORB notes that the patrol involving Yellow Section (Ross/Kirkwood/York) was recalled at 1720 hours due to the fog. Remarkably, it seems certain that the events surrounding this incident were recalled by David Denchfield, as follows:

> I was up at about 20,000 feet over Berwick aerobatting when ops sent out a general recall to base …
>
> It was a sea mist, which up there used to come and go with great suddenness, and although this one was thin enough to see through vertically with some success, the forward vision was of a blinding white opaqueness. I missed the field on the first attempt and turned back when the Newcastle balloons appeared! ... I dropped to about 1,000 feet, and succeeded in orbiting the perimeter, watching for trees, huts etc. After the second orbit, I decided on my east/west approach, and was on a dummy run … when ops called up and said all a/c were to land north to south, and whilst positioning myself heard Cranwell call to ask ops to get a starter truck to him as he'd stopped his engine in the middle of the field. So consigning him to the Devil for his lack of public spirit, I then flew two dummy runs … and then in for real … She touched down just about 100 yards inside the boundary, ran up the slope and rolled down the other side. She was almost stopped, when she did! Very abruptly too. The prop stopped very violently amid a veritable Devil's chorus of sound! Looking around the right hand side of the windshield I was horrified to see my starboard wing embedded in a Spit rudder, and one blade of my prop stuck firmly down into the Spit fuselage just behind the armour plate and at the front of a trail of rear fuselage damage. Unstrapping, I leapt out, walked to the front, kicked my tyre, called the other a/c a naughty and revolting word, and then stood in horrified wonderment as the other, apparently unoccupied, cockpit suddenly spawned a very white and frightened face. Yes it was Cranwell still in his a/c …
>
> He later said he was waiting for his starter trolley acc. (starting batteries on wheels), which came along 2 mins later with a crowd from dispersal … when he heard a gentle 'pop-pop-pop', and turned to watch the inexorable arrival of my a/c. My prop had hit the rear of his armour plate knocking it, the seat and him forward about 6 ins …
>
> Two days later I was called from the Sgts mess to the admin block … to face the O/C (Officer Commanding) Acklington, charged with having damaged two of His Majesty's a/c. He wanted to know why I had refused the ops room order to divert to Usworth, this had come through while I was orbiting the airfield. I said that I had already identified my orbit when ops intervened, and wasn't at all happy at the thought of dropping down into bad visibility—even if it were better than that at base—and being unable to see balloon cables if I strayed at all. He seemed satisfied and let me off with an 'admonishment', which meant 'bad luck, don't do it again' … Poor Cranwell wasn't so lucky as he was put permanently on to watch officer duties for a spell. They ruled he had shown poor airmanship in remaining in his a/c in such poor visibility whilst other a/c movements were taking place …

The damage to Cranwell's Spitfire is clearly visible, showing how fortunate the pilot had been. (*Copyright Nigel Denchfield*)

> At the same time … a Spit that had been endlessly orbiting finally came in to land … From the a/c identification we saw it was Joe Doley who went off only 5 minutes before the recall, and so with plenty of fuel to spare was able to orbit, if needs be for 90 minutes …[19]

Following his tenth attempt to land, Doley came in too fast, and being in danger of hitting the ground staff hut:

> Joe slanted left, then immediately back right, missing the hut, took his a/c at about 4 mph clean as a whistle into Sqdn Ldr Ellis' dispersal bay, in which sat his a/c secure behind its sandbagged blast walls … Joe entered the gap and was immediately blanketed from view by an eruption of dust, steam … and general corruption. The C/O who had been admiring my accident watched Joe attempt a dual effort with his own beloved a/c and, with a string of the most foul language we'd heard so far, went haring over to what looked like a bomb blast; while the rest of us followed at a more sedate pace. One old sweat was shaking his head and saying 'You don't want to go over there—he'll have had it—I've seen it all before'.
>
> But, as we drew near the mess we could hear two angry voices and one was clearly Joe's—'Don't you shout at me—I've just had an accident and don't feel like being shouted at!'
>
> When the dust and tempers had settled, we could see that Joe's a/c was pointing back the way it had come—both wings were torn off, the fuselage was on its side with the tail assembly twisted through 90 degrees. One u/c leg was torn off and the other barely attached. Smoke and steam drifted gaily away and lots of little tinkling noises came from an extremely hot engine. Miraculously, the C/O's a/c had just one penny-sized dent in the very front of the propeller spinner.[20]

Given the Squadron's training role, accidents were inevitable, as seen with F/O Bacon's death. Although the damage to so many Spitfires was costly in this incident, the main thing was that none of the pilots had been wounded or killed, which could so easily have happened.

The mangled mess of Joe Doley's aircraft. (*Copyright Nigel Denchfield*)

On 14 October, three more new recruits joined 610 Squadron from the usual feeder unit, 7 OTU, Hawarden. P/Os Ogilvy and Grey and Sgt Richardson were ready to complete their training with an operational Spitfire squadron. Little is recorded of James Eric Ida Grey, (Jimmie), possibly because he did not manage to fly an operational patrol in the Battle of Britain.

The same may have applied to Charles Alexander Ogilvy, but for his daughter Susan's determination to have him recognised as a Battle of Britain pilot. I had the pleasure of meeting Susan Ogilvy in 2016, and Susan kindly allowed me to use his logbooks to help with my research. Ogilvy, known as Alastair, was born in Kelso on 30 November 1915, the eldest of five sons, and educated at Edinburgh Academy. After leaving school, he moved to London and worked for the Northern Assurance Company. He played rugby for the London Scottish Rugby Football Club and joined the RAFVR in 1939, training as a pilot at 8 E&RFTS Woodley (Reading) from 18 April to 29 November 1939.

His first flight occurred on 6 May, in a Magister. He attended 4 ITW, Bexhill, from 29 November 1939 to 13 May 1940, having also married in 1939. He then went to 6 EFTS, Sywell, Northamptonshire, until 1 July 1940, before a week at 9 EFTS, based at RAF Ansty, Coventry. From 6 July he was at Sealand with 5 FTS, where he was rated 'Above average' as a pilot on 28 September 1940, before progressing to nearby Hawarden and 7 OTU. Ogilvy's first flight in a Spitfire came on 30 September, but the day was not quite as auspicious as he might have hoped, as he had an 'Error of Judgment—faulty cockpit drill', causing his Spitfire to be damaged. Remarkably, by the time Ogilvy left 7 OTU thirteen days later, he had only amassed eleven hours and five minutes on Spitfires. 610's veterans would have had to quickly make him feel more at home with the thoroughbred fighter, before he was classed as operational.

Sgt Roland Richardson, aged twenty, had followed exactly the same training path as Ogilvy, joining the VR, 'in May 1939, as an Airman u/t Pilot (748340)',[21] before being posted to 610 Squadron.

Another patrol was carried out by Yellow Section on 15 October, taking off at 1525 hours to cover the Tyne area at 20,000 feet. The formation was:

Above left: P/O Jimmie Grey. (*Copyright 610 Squadron Association*)

Above right: P/O Ogilvy with his wife and eldest daughter, probably taken in 1940. (*Copyright Susan Ogilvy*)

Roland Wharrier Richardson. (*Copyright 610 Squadron Association*)

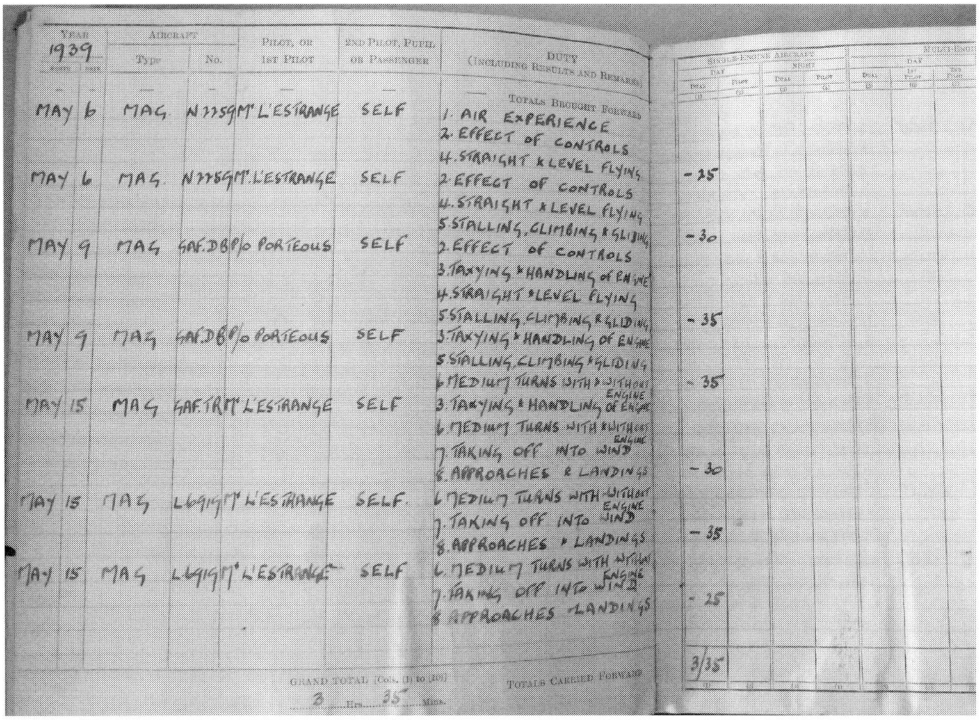

Ogilvy's logbook, detailing his first few flights in a Magister in May 1939. (*Copyright Susan Ogilvy*)

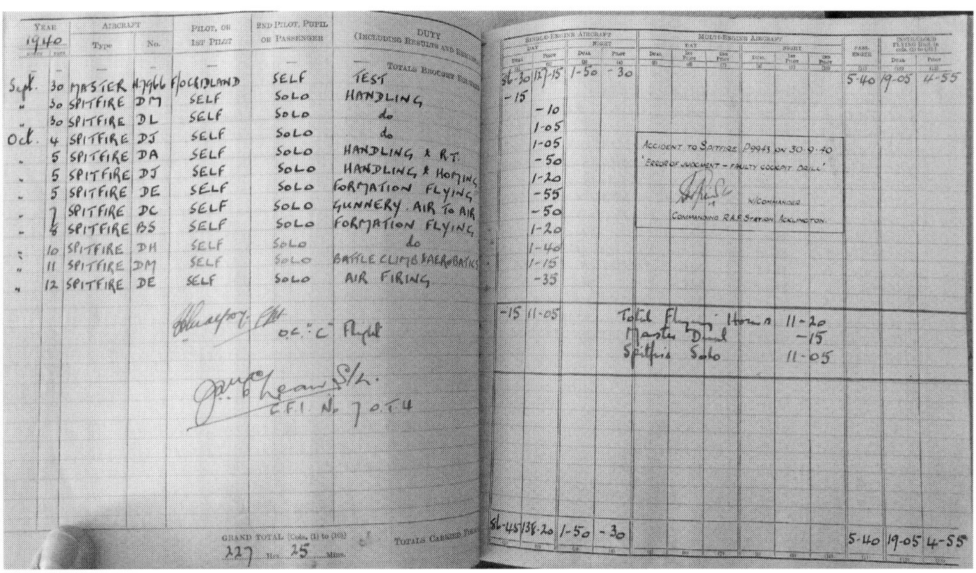

Ogilvy's flying time concisely recorded whilst at Sealand. At this point, Ogilvy had 227 hours and twenty-five minutes flying experience. (*Copyright Susan Ogilvy*)

DW-M.	F/O. Pegge.	36
DW-P.	Sgt. Murray.	2
DW-O.	P/O. Ross.	4

They returned at 1650 hours following an uneventful sortie. The day also saw 13 Group's ORB appendices note, 'B Flight, 610 now operational'. This probably indicated that 610 was now fully operational, having previously only had three operational sections at Acklington, although this is not confirmed by the Squadron ORB. Unfortunately, the vagaries of the Squadron's ORB return once again and there are no recorded patrols between 16–23 October. They were probably misplaced, as from Ogilvy's logbook, it is evident that flying was taking place.

The belated arrival of P/O Fenwick and Sgts Miller and Page, who had been sent to 601 Squadron at the end of September, came on 18 October. Charles Raymond 'Charlie' Fenwick was born on 3 November 1920, so was only nineteen and prior to joining 610 Squadron, he had:

> joined the RAFVR in May 1939 as an Airman u/t Pilot (748345). Called up on September 1, he first went to 18 EFTS Fair Oaks and completed his training at 5 FTS, Sealand on No 49 Course, which ran from June 16 to September 7 1940. He was commissioned and sent to 7 OTU, Hawarden. Fenwick converted to Spitfires and he was posted to 610 Squadron at Acklington on the 29th.
>
> An administrative error sent him instead to a Hurricane squadron 601 at Exeter. Fenwick flew some operational sorties before it was discovered that he was overdue at 610. He arrived at Acklington on October 17 and was taken on to the strength of 610 Squadron the next day.[22]

The confusion over his posting would have been shared with the two sergeants. Ian Malcolm Keith Miller, another VR, was born on 4 January 1915 in Alton, Hampshire, the only son of Alfred Edward, a pharmacist, and Elizabeth, who during the Second World War lived in Thame, Oxfordshire. Prior to this,

Above left: Charles Fenwick at Acklington, 1940. (*Copyright 610 Squadron Association*)

Above right: Vernon Douglas Page. (*Copyright 610 Squadron Association*)

the Millers lived in Ramsgate and Ian attended St George's Church of England School in Ramsgate, followed by Chatham House School, also in Ramsgate, the latter from 16 September 1926 to 26 July 1933. He was a very talented pupil, and in his final year was in the football, cricket and rugby first teams, while he was also Victor Ludorum. Miller was a senior prefect and won the Leslie Award for his academic achievements, clearly a real all-rounder. After leaving school, Miller had joined Broadstairs's town council as a surveyor.[23]

Vernon Douglas Page, aged twenty-six and called 'Doug', had been born in Oldcroft in the Forest of Dean on 14 December 1913:

> He grew up in Blakeney and went to the village school there, where his father was a teacher. He won a scholarship to Rencomb College, near Cirencester and matriculated from there in 1931. He did an apprenticeship with the English Electric Co at Stafford and became a transformer designer. In November 1938 he joined the RAFVR, as an Airman u/t Pilot (742443) and he had completed 50 hours on Magisters at 28 E&RFTS, Meir at the outbreak of war.
>
> Called up on September 1, Page was posted to 3 ITW, Hastings, completed his elementary flying training at 18 EFTS, Fair Oaks and then went on to Harvards at 6 FTS, Little Rissington. At the end of the course, Page went to CFS, Upavon for an instructor's course, but in September 1940 he went to 7 OTU, Hawarden to convert to Spitfires.
>
> An administrative error sent him on September 30 to a Hurricane Squadron, 601 at Exeter, where he carried out three operational sorties …,[24]

before he finally joined 610 Squadron.

For Alex Ogilvy, 18 October was a very important day, as he had a ten-minute flight with F/Lt Brian Smith in a Master, his first flight with the Squadron, before going on two Spitfire flights. These were both sector reconnaissance, the first for forty-five minutes in DW-E, the second for thirty-five minutes in DW-A. They were to give him more time on his new aircraft, but also to familiarise him with the area and landmarks over which he would be operating. It would not be long before he was classed as operational.

Shortly after this, two of the Squadron's veterans received recognition, with the award of the DFC to F/O Joe Pegge, now acting as a flight lieutenant, and the DFM to Sgt Ray Chandler, both of which were long overdue by 22 October 1940. The awards reflected their bravery and service throughout the Battle of Britain. Joe Pegge had carried out thirty recorded patrols between June and August in 11 Group, his claims making him the third most 'successful' pilot on the Squadron. The incident singled out for particular commendation in the citation was on 18 August 1940, when he had shot down an Me 109, before landing his badly damaged Spitfire on a bomb-cratered Biggin Hill, despite being wounded. This remarkable feat summed up Joe Pegge's ability.

Ray Chandler received the Squadron's second DFM, being the Squadron's fourth highest scoring pilot with claims of four destroyed, one probably destroyed, one unconfirmed, three damaged and one shared damaged. The commendation seems to indicate that his claims of probably destroyed and unconfirmed had been officially attributed as destroyed. That Chandler's award made front page news on the local paper where he had worked before the war, *The Birkenhead News and Wirral General Advertiser*, reflects the pride and interest felt by those who knew Chandler—the knowledge of such an award would have been a real boost to those on the Wirral. These two awards would undoubtedly have been met with a party in Acklington or perhaps a trip to Newcastle, Joe Pegge being a keen party-goer.

The likelihood of such a 'do' is all the more credible given that the following day the Squadron would be saying farewell to another stalwart, P/O 'Peter' Keighley. He was attached to RAF Usworth the following day, 23 October. It seems likely that after his recuperation from wounds, Keighley had spent some time working in a non-flying role at Biggin Hill, possibly in the operations room, and the attachment to Usworth was building on this experience. On 4 December 1940, his attachment became a permanent move at Usworth, 'for squadron leaders post Operations Room Duties' (ORB).

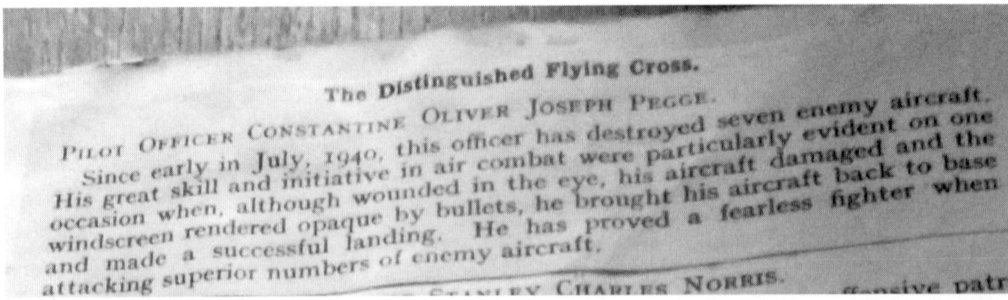

The Distinguished Flying Cross.

PILOT OFFICER CONSTANTINE OLIVER JOSEPH PEGGE.

Since early in July, 1940, this officer has destroyed seven enemy aircraft. His great skill and initiative in air combat were particularly evident on one occasion when, although wounded in the eye, his aircraft damaged and the windscreen rendered opaque by bullets, he brought his aircraft back to base and made a successful landing. He has proved a fearless fighter when attacking superior numbers of enemy aircraft.

The citation used for Pegge's DFC. (*Copyright 610 Squadron Association*)

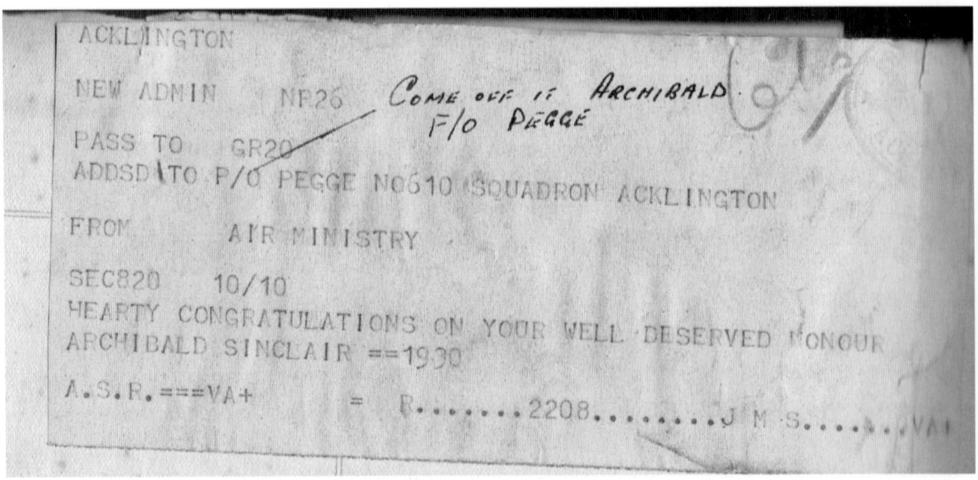

ACKLINGTON

NEW ADMIN NR26 COME OFF IT ARCHIBALD F/O PEGGE

PASS TO GR20

ADDSD TO P/O PEGGE NO610 SQUADRON ACKLINGTON

FROM AIR MINISTRY

SEC820 10/10

HEARTY CONGRATULATIONS ON YOUR WELL DESERVED HONOUR

ARCHIBALD SINCLAIR ==1930

A.S.R.===VA+ = R.......2208........J M S.......VA+

Recognition received at Acklington congratulating Pegge on his award, with a caustic correction to Pegge's rank, possibly by the man himself, for the benefit of Archibald Sinclair, the then Secretary of State for Air. (*Copyright 610 Squadron Association*)

Joe Pegge was a cheerful man, full of mischief from different accounts of him, yet fearlessly brave at the controls of his Spitfire. (*Copyright 610 Squadron Association*)

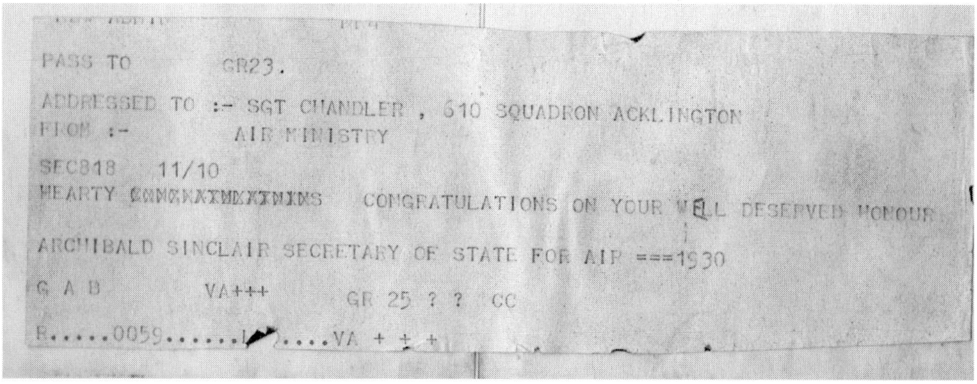
PASS TO GR23.
ADDRESSED TO :- SGT CHANDLER , 610 SQUADRON ACKLINGTON
FROM :- AIR MINISTRY
SEC818 11/10
HEARTY CONGRATULATIONS ON YOUR WELL DESERVED HONOUR
ARCHIBALD SINCLAIR SECRETARY OF STATE FOR AIR ===1930
G A B VA+++ GR 25 ? ? CC
R.....0059.......1.....VA + + +

The Secretary of State for Air also sent congratulations to Chandler. (*Copyright 610 Squadron Association*)

Jo Keighley informed me that his father soon got involved with ground-to-air radar, becoming the senior RAF liaison officer with the US Air Force on ground-to-air radar, eventually being promoted to wing commander. Keighley's US counterpart told Jo how, 'he and my father had climbed up the Eiffel Tower (doing the last bit externally while roped together) and were the first people to examine the German ground-to-air radar at the top of the tower when Paris fell to the Allies', a quite amazing escapade, showing 'Peter' Keighley's great bravery. Ultimately, he received an OBE, which probably related to his work on radar and he remained great friends with Pete Lamb after the war.

Keighley was married three times and had one child with each wife. He worked in the City after leaving the RAF in 1946. Tragically, he died at the very young age of fifty-two from a duodenal ulcer: the operation went wrong and he died of peritonitis. Jo Keighley seemed to inherit a love of flying from his father, and Jo has subsequently learnt to fly a Spitfire himself at the Boultbee Flight Academy. Jo informed me that he had recently been presented with the RPM gauge from his father's Spitfire, N.3201 which had crashed in Wootton on 20 July 1940, in another amazing turn of events.

The next day, 24 October, saw a return to the recording notation of operational flying, this time a forty-minute patrol of the Farne Islands at 20,000 feet. This duty fell to Blue Section, including Sgt Raine, who gained his first recorded sortie, but unsurprisingly it was fruitless. The following men took off at 1320 hours and landed at 1400 hours:

DW-T.	F/Lt. Norris.	65
DW-P.	P/O. Ross.	5
DW-N.	Sgt. Raine.	1

On 25 October, Sgt Jimmy Corbin received his posting back to 66 Squadron at Gravesend. Although he had evidently enjoyed his time with 610 Squadron, after being disappointed to be posted to the north-east, he was happy to return to 11 Group, and Corbin went on to become a very experienced fighter pilot. During his first tour of operations Corbin had claims of a Heinkel 111 probably destroyed and a Messerschmitt 109 destroyed,[25] before leaving 66 Squadron on 21 September 1941 to become an instructor. He joined 72 Squadron a year later as a pilot officer, and was posted to North Africa. He made numerous claims: an Me 109 shared destroyed, a 109 probable, two Me 109s and an Fw 190 damaged, plus several vehicles damaged and an MTB type sunk,[26] which led to his award of a DFC on 27 July 1943.

Corbin arrived back in the UK in July 1943 and went on to the gunnery flight at 57 OTU, Eshott, Northumberland. In April 1944 he was sent to 11 Armament Practice Camp at Fairwood Common near Swansea, where he finished the war instructing pilots who were resting after the invasion of

P/O Geoffrey 'Peter' Keighley (*Copyright Keighley family*)

Europe. He was released from the RAF in December 1945 as a flight lieutenant, going on to become a teacher, while rejoining the VR until 1952. Corbin lived in Maidstone, had a business park named after him in 2007 and died on 8 December 2012.[27]

During the early hours of 25 October, Peter Lamb had carried out a nocturnal patrol of Acklington, taking off at 0030 hours in DW-A (65). He managed to locate a 'Bandit' and chased it to the west, but does not appear to have filed a claim. He landed safely at 0130 hours. Blue Section was on Readiness later in the day, as the following pilots were ordered off at 1030 hours to patrol the Farne Islands at 'Angels 20':

DW-W.	F/Lt. Norris.	66
DW-U.	Sgt. Cooper.*	1
DW-V.	Sgt. Raine.	2

*This must have been James Enerton Cooper.

No enemy aircraft were encountered and they returned safely at 1110 hours. In the early afternoon, Blue Section was again called upon, this time to patrol the Coquet Islands at 25,000 feet, at 1255 hours. Peter Lamb (66) was leading in DW-X, while P/O Fenwick in DW-N mounted his first recorded operational patrol. Nothing of interest was reported and the section returned at 1335 hours.

Perhaps it was one of these Spitfires which had been on patrol, which 13 Group's ORB appendices reported had crashed on landing, having overshot. The aircraft belonging to 610 was described as a Hurricane, but must have been a Spitfire—thankfully the pilot was unhurt. This was an important day for Lamb, as he was promoted to flight lieutenant. The news was thoroughly deserved following his long service, bravery and leadership in 610 Squadron, since the days of the Dunkirk evacuation, which must have seemed a lifetime ago.

It was also an important day for P/O Ogilvy. Although the ORB does not make a record of it, thanks to his own logbook, we know he flew his first two operational patrols with 610 Squadron on 25 October, in DW-B, against 'X-Raids'. The first lasted twenty minutes and the second was for an hour; these patrols ensured he should be recognised as one of 'The Few'. Remarkably, over the passage of time, Ogilvy's

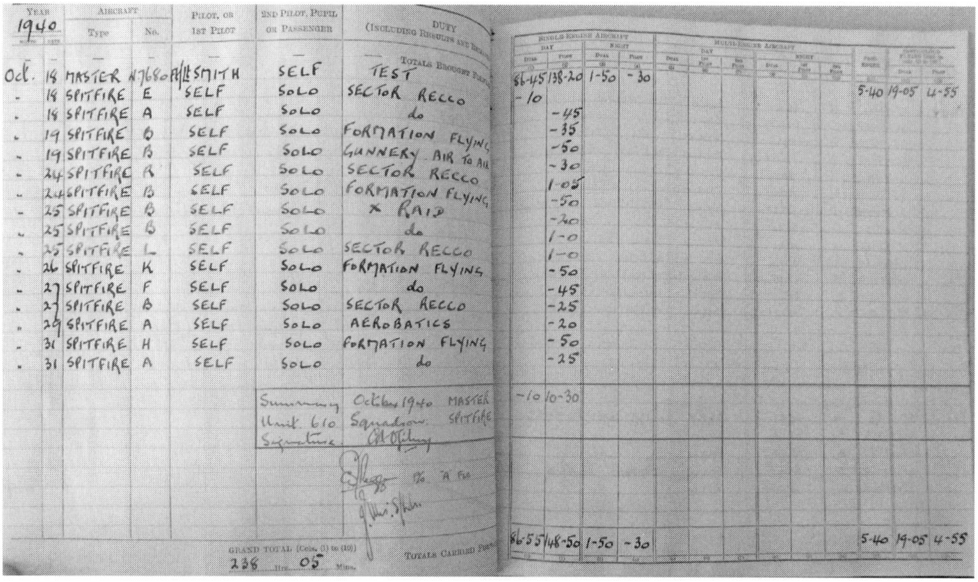

Ogilvy's two operational sorties can be seen on 25 October 1940. (*Copyright Susan Ogilvy*)

participation in the Battle of Britain became overlooked, and he was omitted from the official records as a Battle of Britain pilot. It was only when his daughter, Susan, discovered his Battle of Britain Clasp, following the death of her mother, that she realised his bravery in 1940 had been overlooked.

Ogilvy's name did not appear on the Battle of Britain monument at Victoria Embankment, London, or the Battle of Britain memorial wall at Capel-le-Ferne, Folkestone and other memorials and books to 'The Few'. It is unclear how this happened when he had originally been acknowledged as such by the award of his Battle of Britain Clasp, which demanded the pilot had flown at least one operational patrol in Fighter Command between 10 July and 31 October 1940. 610 Squadron's ORB did not help matters, but thanks to research subsequently carried out by Susan, and the evidence of his logbooks, his name was eventually added to the different memorials. A service was carried out on 26 July 2010 to mark his name being added to the monument, situated on the bank of the River Thames, opposite the London Eye.

On 26 October, F/Lt Norris (67) was on night patrol duty in DW-W, taking off on his fourth recorded patrol of the month at 0135 hours. With no sign of any enemy aircraft, he returned to Acklington at 0205 hours. The following day, 27 October, passed uneventfully until late afternoon. Although some of the information in the ORB is difficult to decipher, (mainly the aircraft identification letters, which are best guesses from the records), the following took place: at 1745 hours, Blue and Red Sections were ordered to patrol Saltburn at 20,000 feet, in a rare patrol above section strength. The pilots were:

Blue Section		
DW-X.	Sgt. Cooper. [J. E.]	2
DW-P.	P/O. Fenwick.	2
DW-N.	P/O. Gray.	7
Red Section		
DW-O.	P/O. Douglas.	4
DW-U.	P/O. Ross.	6
DW-L.	F/Lt. Norris.	68

A dramatic section of sculpture on the London Battle of Britain Monument and P/O Ogilvy's name added to it after Susan Ogilvy's efforts on her brave father's behalf. (*Author*)

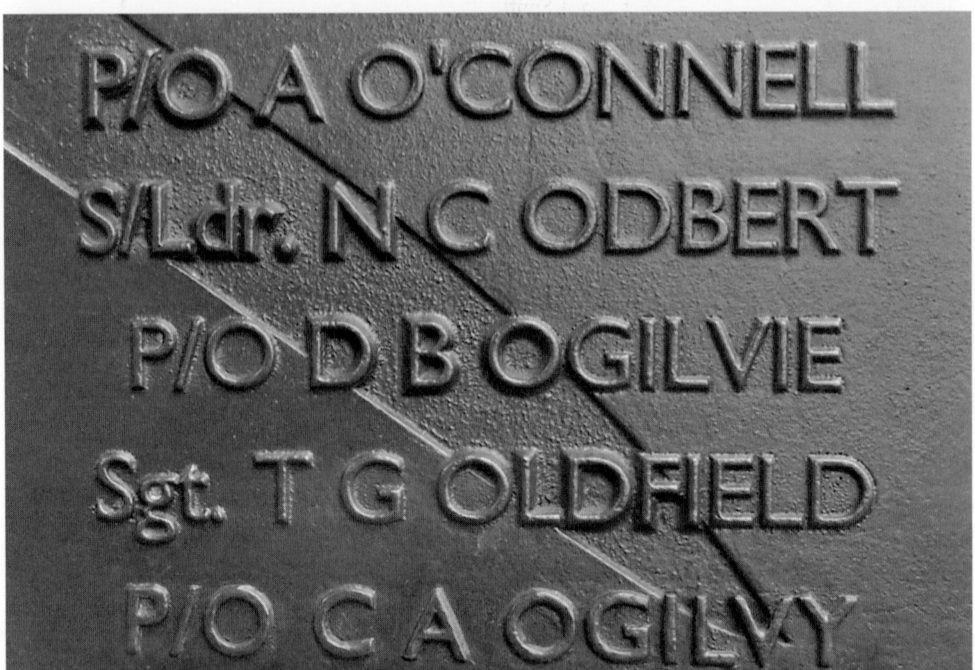

The patrol did not encounter any aircraft and Norris, on his sixty-eighth recorded patrol since 10 May, led his men back home, landing at 1835 hours.

However, disaster befell one of the pilots, as the 13 Group ORB appendices reported the following: 'at approximately 19.00 hours a Spitfire of 610 crashed and Sgt. Pilot Cooper baled out, unhurt. He became separated from his section and with failing light and bad conditions, came down low to get bearings, got out of R/T touch, climbed, and went into a spin' (TNA, AIR 25/241). Although 610's ORB fails to mention the event, it is believed that he was flying Spitfire N.3264. While Cooper survived the parachute descent unscathed, his aircraft probably crashed near Langley Park, County Durham. Different records have N.3264 as having been lost with 610 Squadron at Manston, which is probably an error or typographical error, as it had crashed there earlier with 41 Squadron, so Langley Park appears to be the most likely place. N.3264 had only joined 610 Squadron on 13 October from 9 MU, after being repaired from battle damage in the Battle of Britain. It is believed to have been struck off charge on 29 October 1940,[28] which fits in with a crash two days earlier.

In the meantime, another flight of Spitfires had left Acklington at 1805 hours, to carry out night flying duties from RAF Woolsington (which is now Newcastle International Airport). There is some confusion as to the sections involved in these two patrols, as Blue Section is listed twice, presumably in error and the same applies to some of the aircraft involved, which could not have been in two places at once. Either way, the second flight went to Woolsington, 'for night flying patrol of Saltburn and night flying patrol of a convoy. No E/A sighted' (ORB). They returned to Acklington at 1350 hours the following afternoon. The pilots involved on this unusual exercise were as follows, (the first pilot's name was illegible in the ORB):

Green Section		
DW-Q.	[Illegible officer]	
DW-X.	Sgt. Ward-Smith.	3
DW-P.	Sgt. Horner.	6
Blue Section		
DW-A.	P/O. Drever.	5
DW-F.	Sgt. Warden.	2
DW-C.	Sgt. Page.	1

As October drew to a close, the unit continued unabated in its training role, with two fresh recruits arriving from Hawarden on 28 October, Sgt Pilot A. Smith and P/O G. H. Hadland. Although little is recorded of Hadland, Alan Smith would go on to have a distinguished career in the RAF. Smith was born in South Shields, Tyne and Wear on 14 March 1917. He attended Bede College, Sunderland, until 1931, when he helped his mother run an ironmonger's shop, following the death of his father. Smith joined the RAFVR in 1939 and following the usual training regime, was sent to 7 OTU, before his posting to 'The Chesters'.

Meanwhile, Sgt Pilot Murray received orders for his posting to 610's old home at Biggin Hill, where he joined the famous 74 'Tiger' Squadron, having completed a month and a half of additional flying with 610 in the north-east. Information on James Murray is fairly scant, but he, 'destroyed a Bf 109 and shared another on December 5 1940. Murray was killed in the Middle East on April 3 1943, serving as a warrant officer with the Aden Communications Flight. With no known grave, Murray is remembered on the Alamein Memorial, column 269'.[29]

Another of the Squadron's veterans also left on 28 October. It was finally time for Peter Lamb, who had been with the Squadron throughout the darkest days of Dunkirk and the heaviest fighting in July and August of the Battle of Britain, to move on to pastures new. F/Lt Peter Gilbert Lamb was one of the few pre-war Auxiliaries still with the Squadron, the first mention of him in the ORB being, 'Mr. P. G.

Sgt Alan Smith posing in a Spitfire which probably belonged to 610 Squadron. (*Copyright 610 Squadron Association*)

Lamb gazetted 25/4/38'. His flying record was more than backed up by his ability as a fighter pilot, having destroyed four enemy aircraft in August, along with two others claimed as shared destroyed. By the time of his last flight from Acklington, Lamb had amassed sixty-six recorded patrols since 10 May, although in reality it was almost certainly a lot more.

Lamb's skill as a pilot was recognised by his superiors, as he was posted for staff pilot duties at 10 FTS, Tern Hill. This may have been the complete break from squadron life that Lamb needed after such a long stint with 610 Squadron and the constant menace of danger. Also, the number of men he had seen killed, recorded 'missing' or wounded, including many old pre-war friends, would have taken their toll on his spirits. So with one final celebratory party to send him on his way, Peter Lamb left Acklington probably feeling slightly the worse for wear.

After his spell at Tern Hill, Lamb seems to have been posted to Canada as a flying instructor, and his devotion to this role led to him being awarded an AFC. The award was recorded in *The London Gazette* on 22 October 1943, when Lamb was reported to be an acting wing commander.[30] Wynn noted that, 'He was released from the RAF in 1945, as a Squadron Leader. In June 1946 he began to reform 610 Squadron at Hooton Park, it having been disbanded on March 3 1945. Lamb commanded the squadron from July 31 1946 to March 1950'.[31] He died of tuberculosis in the early 1950s.[32]

On 31 October 1940, 610 Squadron carried out its final patrol of the month, when Red Section was ordered to patrol the Tyne area at 'Angels 20'. The following pilots took off at 1005 hours:

DW-N.	Sgt. Warden.	3
DW-T.	F/Lt. Norris.	69
DW-U.	P/O. Gray.	8

They returned to Acklington at 1110 hours, without making contact with the enemy. Stan Norris had notched up his sixty-ninth recorded patrol since 10 May 1940, while at the other end of the spectrum Noel Warden was carrying out only his third recorded patrol.

Peter Lamb, photographed with 610 Squadron at Acklington, mid-September 1940. (*Copyright 610 Squadron Association*)

Thursday 31 October 1940 came to mark the end of the Battle of Britain, from a British point of view at least. It was a somewhat arbitrary date set by Dowding when he looked back at the battle much like the opening date which he decreed was 10 July 1940. By the end of October and into November, the large heavily-escorted bomber raids had all but stopped, the main threat now being lone bombers, or groups of fighter-bombers which hoped to draw up RAF fighters, before scattering their bombs and taking on the defenders. While the nightly raids would intensify, the *Luftwaffe* had failed in its aim of destroying Fighter Command, to pave the way for an invasion force to attempt to cross the Channel. As highlighted on 15 September 1940, the RAF's steady flow of fighters into the skies of southern England which had continued throughout October came as an unpleasant shock to the *Luftwaffe*. Fighter Command had inflicted the first major defeat on Hitler's forces since they had gone on the offensive in Poland, on 1 September 1939. Britain, and particularly the RAF and units like 610 (County of Chester) Squadron, had stood firm against the might of the *Luftwaffe*; it really was their finest hour.

During October, 610 Squadron had carried out thirty-one recorded operational patrols, involving at least seventy-one hours and thirty minutes flying time, the very minimum the unit had carried out. The vagaries of the ORB meant it was probably quite a bit higher. For example, this does not include the patrols we know that P/O Ogilvy carried out on 25 October, to qualify for his Battle of Britain Clasp. The Squadron had trained seventeen inexperienced Spitfire pilots during the month, with one being posted to serve with an 11 Group Squadron, while five others who had joined earlier also went to 11 Group Squadrons. Thankfully, although there had been at least six Spitfires damaged or written off in crashes, with one pilot baling out, which was understandable given the Squadron's training role on such a high-powered aircraft, there had been no fatalities during October. This stood testament to the training provided by the veterans. That forty inexperienced fighter pilots had joined or passed through 610 Squadron since their withdrawal to Acklington and F/O Bacon was its only casualty during this time, was quite remarkable. Nevertheless, following this 'rest' period, by the end of October, 610 Squadron's personnel were much changed from when they had withdrawn from 11 Group at the end of August, with just seven or eight pilots left, six of whom had been decorated.

However, the Squadron was now not just training pilots as a 'Category C' Squadron, ready to join other 11 Group Squadrons, but was also starting to forge its own identity again. By keeping some of these new pilots to build a fresh nucleus for 610 Squadron, the unit could then once again return to a front-line position.

A lovely photograph of DW-W in its revetment at Acklington. This is almost certainly S/Ldr Ellis's Spitfire, as a Squadron Leader's pennant is visible underneath the front of the cockpit. (*Copyright Sandra Hemsworth née Blackburne*)

20

November–December 1940: 'Who falls for love of God, shall rise a star'

On 1 November 1940, the Squadron's Nominal Roll of pilots, looked something like this:

1 S/Ldr. J. Ellis
2 F/Lt. E. B. B. Smith
3 F/Lt. D. S. Wilson
4 F/Lt. S. C. Norris
5 F/O. C. O. J. Pegge
6 F/O. B. V. Rees
7 Sgt. H. H. Chandler
8 Sgt. R. F. Hamlyn
9 P/O. D. McI. Gray
10 Sgt. H. R. Clarke
11 P/O. W. A. Douglas
12 Sgt. F. C. Horner
13 Sgt. P. Ward-Smith
14 F/O. M. T. Kirkwood
15 P/O. N. G. Drever
16 P/O. A. R. Ross
17 Sgt. W. A. Sutcliffe
18 Sgt. A. D. Payne
19 Sgt. R. L. York
20 Sgt. W. Raine
21 Sgt. E. W. Cranwell
22 Sgt. H. D. Denchfield
23 Sgt. A. S. Doley
24 Sgt. J. E. W. Ballard
25 Sgt. N. P. Warden
26 Sgt. J. E. Cooper
27 Sgt. J. N. Greig
28 P/O. C. A. Ogilvy
29 P/O. J. E. I. Grey
30 Sgt. R. W. Richardson
31 Sgt. I. M. K. Miller
32 Sgt. V. D. Page
33 P/O. C. R. Fenwick
34 Sgt. A. Smith
35 P/O. G. H. Hadland.

Unfortunately, the ORB did not provide a list of pilots at this stage and a couple of the thirty-five men listed above may have already left. For example, F/O Rees had probably moved on to another squadron or role, as earlier commented.

Throughout November, the Squadron continued to train new pilots, five joining on Monday 4 November. P/Os T. A. Stevens and J. R. Scott, and Sgts H. B. McGregor, P. McDougall-Black and G. Mains, all came from 7 OTU, although sadly little is known about them. 610 only carried out nine recorded patrols in November, all of which were uneventful and involved the following pilots: Norris, Pegge, Ward-Smith, York, Horner and Hamlyn each flew three patrols, while Page, Payne, Cooper, Ellis, Raine and Stevens notched up one patrol.[1] The very changeable weather regularly curtailed operations, as is evident in 13 Group's ORB appendices, with only the experienced pilots being allowed to go on patrol at times.

Despite the lack of operational activity, the Squadron suffered two tragic deaths on consecutive days in early November, which hit 'The Chesters' hard. On 4 November, Sgt Ian Malcolm Keith Miller was carrying out a practice flight in the morning, possibly performing aerobatics, when he lost control of

Spitfire L.1094 and crashed into boggy ground near Eglingham, Northumberland. News of the tragedy was reported in 13 Group's ORB appendices at 1232 hours, where the following was noted: 'place of crash Tillington, went into a spin at 5,000 and crashed with an explosion'. Miller had survived just over a fortnight with 610 Squadron. His death would have been a brutal reminder for the five new recruits, of the dangers which lay in wait for them. Although the crash site was investigated at the time of the incident, it was not until the 1950s that the pilot's remains were recovered, at the request of Miller's parents, Alfred and Elizabeth, who later moved to Ramsgate, Kent. The VR pilot, aged twenty-five, was buried at Thame (St Mary's) churchyard, Oxfordshire.[2] L.1094 had first served with 65 Squadron but been damaged on 8 August and again on 22 August. Following repairs, it arrived at 610 Squadron on 27 October 1940, but was written off just eight days later during this crash at Craigs House Farm, Eglingham.[3]

The investigations into Sgt Miller's death would barely have begun, when disaster befell the County of Chester Squadron again, this time early in the morning of Tuesday 5 November. Night flying had become an increasingly important task for 610 Squadron in recent weeks, with nocturnal sorties becoming more frequent. It was a vital role given the number of nightly *Luftwaffe* raiders, but the Supermarine Spitfire was much better suited to its intended role as a daytime interceptor. Despite being a battle-experienced pilot, Donald McIntosh Gray would probably have been a little anxious as he prepared for a non-operational flight in Spitfire DW-O, X.4011 just after midnight. This was probably his first nocturnal flight in a Spitfire. 13 Group's ORB appendices noted at 0017 hours on 5 November, 'reports Spitfire on fire when taking off from Acklington'. At 0130, it continued, 'Usworth report that P/O Dray [Gray] was killed in the Spitfire and the machine was burnt out. It is thought that he hit a gun post in taking off'. Tragically for Gray, who had rejoined his squadron just under a month earlier, things unravelled for him in seconds, as described by Chris R. Davies:

> He was instructed to use the south to north runway to commence his patrol. As the aircraft took off, he reported that he was having difficulties. To the right of the north end of the runway is a white house. P/O Gray pulled the struggling aircraft to the right to avoid the building and touched down in a grass field to the north side of the aerodrome. The left wing caught a gun post and was torn off; the aircraft then carried on for a further 250 yards and crashed into the raised hedge at the end of the Triangle Field, 300 yards to the west of Acklington Village, on the south side of the Broomhill to Acklington highway, bursting into flames. The engine detached and crossed the road, settling in the paddock next to Inglenook. P/O Gray was thrown from the wreckage onto the highway and was killed.[4]

Just prior to this book being printed, the AMCB file concerning this fatal incident was released at The National Archives, providing the official answers into the cause of the crash. In the investigation, F/O Jackson, the technical officer, believed that the crash was 'consistent with an attempt to take off with airscrew in coarse pitch, although no direct evidence available' (TNA, AIR 81/4085). S/Ldr Ellis was more certain when he wrote the following report:

> Pilot Officer Gray a fairly experienced Spitfire pilot. It was a perfect night at the time with a good horizon. As stated above [by Jackson], P/O Gray took off in coarse pitch but left the ground about 100 yards from the aerodrome boundary. He was airborne for at least 300 yards. He then hit this pill-box which is on a slight rise 200 yards from the aerodrome boundary. (TNA, AIR 81/4085)

The file notes that Gray had 46.15 hours on Spitfires, several of which had been in combat earlier in the year, whilst overall he appears to have had 231.10 hours flying time, so he clearly was quite experienced. However, it seems he only had 2.45 hours flying at night, and it was probably this lack of night flying experience which had proved fatal.

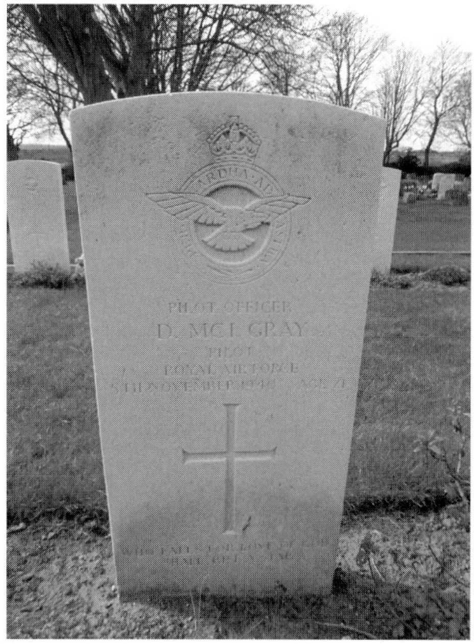

P/O Gray was buried in Chevington cemetery, Northumberland. His headstone has the moving inscription, 'Who falls for love of God, shall rise a star', a quote from Ben Johnson. (*Author*)

The unlucky Donald Gray, son of John and Mary Jane from Palmers Green, Middlesex, was buried on 9 November 1940 in Chevington Cemetery, Northumberland, Section H, Grave 285 and is also remembered on the memorial to twenty-nine aircrew in St John the Divine church, Red Row, near the site of the former airfield. In the early hours of Bonfire Night 1940, the twenty-one-year-old pilot from Middlesex had become one of the first of 'The Few' to fall after the official period of the Battle itself. His final, abrupt and saddening mention in the ORB was, '**5.11.40.** P/O. D. Mc. I. Gray killed as a result of a flying accident at Acklington'.

Another accident occurred on 13 November, listed in 13 Group's ORB appendices at 1533 hours: '610 Red 1 a/c crashed on landing at Usworth'. Fortunately, the pilot survived, although another note was added at 1600 hours, 'Usworth report a/c which crashed on landing, overshot runway. Workman injured and taken to hospital. A/c damaged undercarriage and airscrew'. This may well have been Sgt Horner, who reportedly crash-landed X.4240 'wheels-up' on this day, although this was listed as taking place at Acklington. The Spitfire had only joined 610 Squadron on 7 October 1940.[5]

Thanks to the AMCB files which were released just before this book went to press, it has come to light that an accident also occurred on 15 November 1940. Sgt Peter Ward-Smith was injured flying Spitfire R.6976, when he undershot and hit the boundary hedge when landing at Woolsington at 1710 hours (TNA, AIR 81/4234). *Aeromilitaria* confirms the damage to R.6976, although it refers to it being caused by air combat which is incorrect.[6] R.6976, a Squadron veteran from 24 July 1940 and for the remainder of the Battle of Britain, probably as DW-A, would not return to 610 after being repaired, but survived the War, being struck of charge on 25 May 1945. Mercifully, Ward-Smith was only slightly injured, and he was flying again ten days later.

Four days later, on Tuesday 19 November, two more incidents occurred. With the assistance of P/O Ogilvy's logbook, we have a little more idea of what happened with one of them, although not as much as one might expect; Alex Ogilvy very much played down the incident. Once again, it appears that 'Dog fighting practice' was the cause of the accident. Remarkably, Ogilvy made no reference to this traumatic event in his logbook, but continued with his minimalistic style, the only clue being that it was an unusually short flight for a dogfighting practice. This suggests something had happened, as only his first flight in

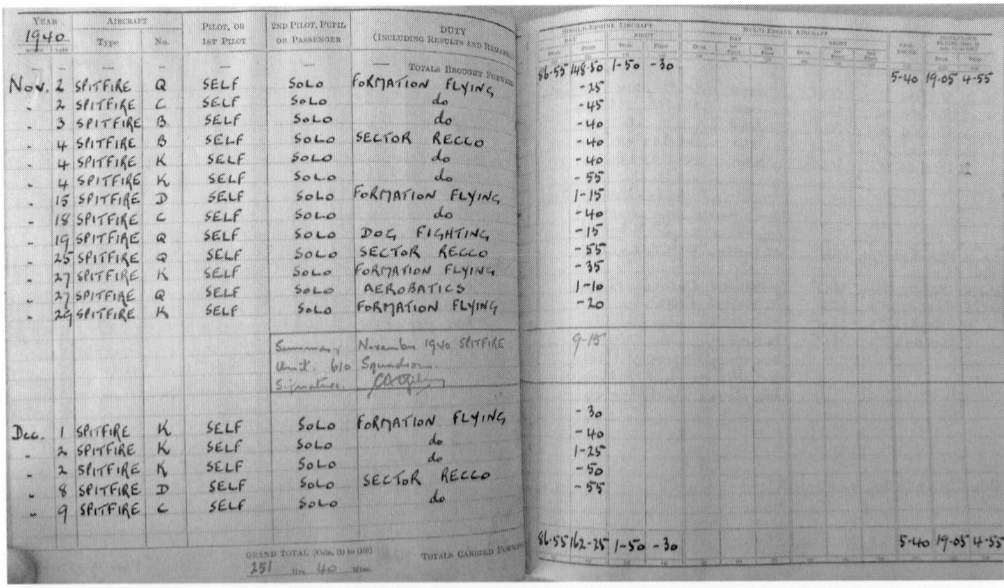

Year 1940	Aircraft Type	No.	Pilot, or 1st Pilot	2nd Pilot, Pupil or Passenger	Duty (Including Results and Remarks)	Single-Engine Aircraft Day
—	—	—	—	—	Totals Brought Forward	86-55 148-50 1-50 -30
Nov. 2	SPITFIRE	Q	SELF	SOLO	FORMATION FLYING	-25
2	SPITFIRE	C	SELF	SOLO	do	-45
3	SPITFIRE	B	SELF	SOLO	do	-40
4	SPITFIRE	B	SELF	SOLO	SECTOR RECCO	-40
4	SPITFIRE	K	SELF	SOLO	do	-40
4	SPITFIRE	K	SELF	SOLO	do	-55
15	SPITFIRE	D	SELF	SOLO	FORMATION FLYING	1-15
18	SPITFIRE	C	SELF	SOLO	do	-40
19	SPITFIRE	Q	SELF	SOLO	DOG FIGHTING	-15
25	SPITFIRE	Q	SELF	SOLO	SECTOR RECCO	-55
27	SPITFIRE	K	SELF	SOLO	FORMATION FLYING	-35
27	SPITFIRE	Q	SELF	SOLO	AEROBATICS	1-10
29	SPITFIRE	K	SELF	SOLO	FORMATION FLYING	-20
				Summary November 1940 SPITFIRE Unit: 610 Squadron Signature: [signature]		9-15
Dec. 1	SPITFIRE	K	SELF	SOLO	FORMATION FLYING	-30
2	SPITFIRE	K	SELF	SOLO	do	-40
2	SPITFIRE	K	SELF	SOLO	do	1-25
8	SPITFIRE	D	SELF	SOLO	SECTOR RECCO	-50
9	SPITFIRE	C	SELF	SOLO	do	-55
				Grand Total 251 Hrs. 40 Mins.	Totals Carried Forward	86-55 162-25 1-50 -30

Instrument flying totals: 5-40 19-05 4-55 (brought forward); 5-40 19-05 4-55 (carried forward)

P/O Ogilvy's logbook, showing his very short flight on 19 November 1940. (*Copyright Susan Ogilvy*)

a Spitfire was shorter than this one. *Aeromilitaria* confirms for Spitfire R.6891: 'Control lost; abandoned and crashed in flames, Black Lough, 2m NE of Edlingham, Northumberland, 19.11.40'.[7] Author Chris Davies informed me it was 150 m SE of Stirkhill Plantation. DW-Q, R.6891, had joined 610 on 13 August 1940 and suffered minor damage on two occasions, while if the ORB was correct, this was the Spitfire in which Hamlyn had managed to shoot down five *Luftwaffe* aircraft on 24 August 1940.

Ogilvy survived this emergency thanks to his parachute, and he was back flying another 'DW-Q' just six days later. By cross-referencing with 13 Group's ORB, this event was recorded as having happened at 1139 hours. As a result of baling out, he received a Caterpillar Club Badge, which his daughter, Susan, proudly showed me—the caterpillar's red eyes are believed to indicate that his Spitfire crashed as a result of engine fire. Without this badge and its accompanying letter from the Irvine Parachute Company, it is very unlikely that anyone would have known of Ogilvy's lucky escape, as 610's ORB does not mention it.

Thankfully, Ogilvy survived the frightening incident, but another accident occurred on the same day, involving Sgt Woodrow Raine. He was reportedly flying DW-U, R.6686, when on coming in to land a tyre burst, the undercarriage leg collapsed and the aircraft ended up on its nose.[8] Raine survived this alarming event, which was fortunately the last of the recorded accidents in November. However, two deaths, one pilot injured, another baling out and at least two other lucky escapes in one month, prove how dangerous life was in an RAF squadron, even in the relative peace and quiet of Northumberland.

On 18 November, an example of the awful weather conditions which were hampering operational flying in the north-east is evident in a note made in 13 Group's ORB Appendices at 1515 hours. It reads: '610 Squadron now report 3 aircraft bogged and 1 aircraft now buried at Acklington. Aerodrome u/s for training flying on Spitfires. Can operate with skilled pilots only, using runway only. 610 have 12 operational pilots'. By 20 November, 610 was only willing to operate single aircraft, due to the state of the aerodrome, while Usworth was not operational at all. These were clearly difficult and dangerous conditions for experienced pilots, so must have hampered the progress of the novice pilots.

On 22 November, F/O F. T. Gardiner was finally reunited with the Squadron, three months after being wounded. He was, 'posted to this Unit from R.A.F Station Biggin Hill' (ORB), where he had been performing light duties. Having witnessed the climax of the Battle from this key airfield, his return to the Squadron was short-lived. Just five days later, his association with 'The Chesters' ended, when he received the following orders: '**27.11.40.** 'F/O. F. T. Gardiner (72100) posted to Central Landing Establishment [CLE] Ringway' (ORB), where his hard-earned experience could be passed on to the newest recruits. Over the course of the next couple of years, Gardiner made good use of his pre-war experience as a glider pilot:

> On January 17 1941 Gardiner was attached to AFDU [Air Fighting Development Unit], Northolt from RAF Detachment, Thame, an off-shoot of the CLE, to develop the glider for military use and to set up trials of fighter versus glider. He returned to Thame on February 10 1941.
>
> During 1941/42 Gardiner instructed Army glider pilots and in 1943 he returned to operational flying, when he joined 254 Squadron at North Coates, flying Beaufighters. In early 1944 Gardiner was commanding 254 Squadron and was awarded the DFC (10.3.44).
>
> It is believed that he later served in the Middle East until the end of the war. He was released from the RAF in 1946, as a Squadron Leader. He married in 1947 and the family emigrated to Victoria, Vancouver Island, Canada.
>
> Gardiner started work as a deckhand on a fishing boat for several seasons and then established an engineering business, which he operated until the mid-1970s. He developed a great love for yachting and cruising, beginning in 1953 and carrying on until he was in his eighties. He died in Victoria on November 2 2003.[9]

Only two other pilots left the Squadron during November 1940 according to the ORB, the first being twenty-five-year-old F/O Mark Tyzack Kirkwood on 4 November. He had been with the Squadron since 22 September and had gained plenty of experience on Spitfires, his patrols with 610 Squadron during October qualifying him for a Battle of Britain Clasp. He was posted to 603 Squadron at Hornchurch, where he only survived for four days: 'On the 7th Kirkwood shared in the destruction of a Bf 110. He was reported 'Missing' on November 8, when he failed to return from a combat with Ju 87s and Bf 109s E of Deal, in Spitfire P 7285. Kirkwood is remembered on the Runnymede Memorial, Panel 4'.[10]

The other departure came on 22 November, when long-standing member F/Lt Douglas Wilson was attached to Woolsington, a satellite of Acklington. He had first joined 610 in October 1936 and destroyed two Me 109s during the Battle of Britain. Aged thirty-four, Wilson was old to be flying operationally, particularly on fighters, and although little is known of his war exploits, he did become a controller at Usworth on 16 January 1941 (ORB). Wilson survived the War, but was released from the RAF on 5 October 1945, as medically unfit, having attained the rank of wing commander. He died on 31 July 1985.

As 1940 came to a close and the dark winter nights of December swept in, operations became even more limited, with the ORB recording just five days in the first fortnight when operations took place. Weather conditions regularly limited the operational capabilities of aerodromes such as Acklington and Usworth in 13 Group, as had been the case during November. The following pilots carried out patrols: Hamlyn, Stevens, Warden, McDougall-Black and Page all three patrols; Horner, Norris, Cooper, Richardson, Denchfield, Ross and Ballard all two patrols; Douglas, Fenwick, Pegge and Drever one patrol each. On 1 December, three pilots were posted to 74 Squadron at Biggin Hill, Sgts Sutcliffe, York and Payne ending their association with the Squadron with which they had become members of 'The Few'.

William Sutcliffe did not stay long with 74 Squadron, moving to the CFS, Upavon, on 15 December, for an instructor's course. Sutcliffe's life there was tragically short, being killed in, 'a flying accident at Upavon, on December 17 1940, flying in an Airspeed Oxford of the CFS, as a Flight Sergeant. The aircraft crashed at Rowde, near Cleeve, Wiltshire, as a result of icing. He was twenty-five and is buried in St Wyllow's churchyard, Lanteglos-by-Fowey, Cornwall'.[11]

Ronald Lewis York did not survive the war either, being killed in particularly freakish circumstances. On 28 March 1942, as a flight sergeant, he was flying as an instructor on a spinning test in a new

Douglas Strachan Wilson at Acklington, September 1940. (*Copyright 610 Squadron Association*)

Master, at Hawarden. Suddenly, the main spar snapped at 8,000 feet and the aircraft went straight down, killing York, aged twenty-two and his pupil. He is buried in the churchyard of St Peter and St Paul, Abington, Northampton.[12] Ronald's younger brother, Stanley, was killed in action while flying with 144 Squadron, almost exactly three years later, on 24 March 1945, aged twenty-one. He is buried in Norway: what unimaginable losses for their parents, George and Edith.[13]

With regard to Alec Dawson Payne, he shot down an Me 109 over France on 2 February 1941, but crashed on a night patrol on 23 May, suffering severe injuries. He went on to flying control duties and then non-operational flying, serving in North Africa and Lagos, before leaving the RAF as a warrant officer in 1946. He died on 16 December 2010.[14]

These postings were compensated for by the arrival of Sgt Arthur Oliver Sharples from 54 Squadron on 2 December and P/O M. C. McQueen from 57 OTU Hawarden on 3 December. Another pilot to arrive at Acklington the following day, was P/O G. H. Francis, who followed in Sharples's footsteps from 54 Squadron; little has been recorded of these men. In the midst of these comings and goings, another accident occurred, on Tuesday 3 December, which saw the demise of Spitfire X.4678, which had only joined the Squadron on 23 November. It crashed and overturned on landing, while trying to avoid obstructions at RAF Woolsington, the pilot being unknown.[15]

On 8 December, Sgt Peter Ward-Smith celebrated his twenty-fourth birthday, while 9 December saw another accident occur for one of the novice pilots, when Sgt McDougall-Black belly-landed at Acklington in DW-L, P.9311. McDougall-Black was safe, but the Spitfire was damaged. P.9311 had joined 610 Squadron in mid-August and following repairs carried out at Acklington after this incident, went on to serve with 602 Squadron.[16]

Monday 9 December was also a memorable day for F/Lt Brian Smith, DFC, as he was posted from 610 Squadron for the last time, to join 2 CFS, Cranwell. Since 10 May, he had flown at least sixty recorded sorties against the *Luftwaffe* and successfully claimed one destroyed, two shared destroyed, two probably destroyed, one unconfirmed, one damaged and one shared damaged. Such an experienced pilot would have been badly missed by John Ellis and his men, particularly as he was the last of the original pre-war Auxiliary Officers—how the Squadron had changed since then! Over the course of the next couple of years, it was time for Smith to pass on this hard-won experience as an instructor, frequently training future bomber pilots, spending time at Ayr, Scotland and Sealand, Flintshire, where he instructed on night flying. Brian Smith was then posted overseas, as he recalled 'I didn't know where the hell I was going! I actually turned up in North Africa at Algiers, and then Algiers to Tunis, Tunis to Malta, Malta to Sicily, and was then involved with the invasion of Italy'. He had commanded the Advanced Flying Unit in Setif, Algeria and a parachute school in Sicily, where he trained troops and agents for parachuting into Italy and the Balkans. Smith regularly carried out jumps, along with his dog, Sally, who had her own parachute. He went on to serve with the HQ of the Balkan Air Force. Smith left the RAF in February 1946, having also received the Air Efficiency Award.

He was now ready to return home after three long years of service abroad, despite having enjoyed his time in the Air Force. Brian was offered a job working for Shell in Venezuela, which obviously did not fit in with his plan of returning home. So he joined J. Bibby and Sons in Liverpool, an animal feed producer, later working around the country for the company, before settling in the village of Cropthorne, Worcestershire, with his wife Pamela and three sons. I had the great honour of meeting Wing Commander Smith on 5 August 2011. He could not have been more welcoming, entertaining, or helpful in providing me with information on his time with 610 Squadron, and his memories of old friends whom he held close to his heart. Smith's encouragement to continue my research into his old squadron, which had not received the recognition he felt it deserved over the years, has been a great source of inspiration in writing this book. It was a meeting I will always remember fondly and with great pleasure. Wing Commander Smith died aged 98 in 2013, fittingly on 15 September, Battle of Britain Day.

610 Squadron was struck by another fatal flying accident on 11 December, when Sgt Hugh Biggans McGregor was killed near Eglingham, the same village where poor Sgt Miller lost his life just over a month earlier. Acklington's record book provides some additional information, noting, '2 Spitfires of 610 Squadron stationed here collided west of Alnwick. P/O Ross baled out uninjured, Pilot Sergeant McGregor was killed'. 13 Group's ORB Appendices adds that at first, at 1109 hours, one of the crashed aircraft was believed to be a Hurricane, but by 1132 hours it was understood to have been two Spitfires which had, 'collided at Pittington Hall about 5 miles due W. of Alnwick'. It also states that Ross had been found by 1159 hours.

Brian Smith resplendent with his DFC under his 'Wings', and 'A' for an Auxiliary on his lapels. (*Copyright Smith family*)

The AMCB file concerning McGregor was released just before the printing of this book, which has resolved some queries over the collision and ensuing events, although Ross's file has unfortunately not been released yet. P/O 'Sandy' Ross, the more experienced pilot, was originally believed to be flying Spitfire X.4649, and while the AMCB file reports it as K.4647, it would seem the former is actually more likely. Sgt McGregor was in P.9451, forming Blue Section with Ross, McGregor having 31 hours and 15 minutes experience on Spitfires, out of a total flying time of 118 hours and five minutes. S/Ldr Ellis made the following report into the collision:

> Sergeant McGregor was No.2 in the formation led by P.O. Ross carrying out No. 5 attacks at 4,000, he did not follow his leader down in the break away, but did a shallow dive and was presumably waiting for his leader to climb up again when the two aircraft collided. (TNA, AIR 81/4529)

Ross's Spitfire crashed to destruction at Titlington Burn, three kilometres SSW of Craigs House Farm, according to aviation historian Chris Davies. 13 Group's ORB appendices goes on to record at 1525 hours: 'Spitfire in which Sgt. McGregor crashed has been found. Dived straight in to ground and is buried about 6 ft. A hole has been made and is full of water. Have not yet found pilot but believe he is in aircraft'. It had crashed in boggy ground near Kimmer Lough, amazingly just 700 metres south of Craigs House Farm,[17] uncannily close to Sgt Miller's crash site.

Hugh Biggans McGregor, a VR pilot, aged twenty-four and from Larkhall, Lanarkshire was buried on 17 December 1940, in the local Larkhall Cemetery, Division 3, Section K, Grave 2, Dalserf, Lanarkshire.[18] In a distressing turn of events, another excavation of the crash site on 30 July 1952 discovered further human remains, which was probably due to the crash site being flooded in the winter of 1940 and the site being inaccessible. As a result, in 1952 the McGregor family had to endure the traumatic interment of these remains in the existing grave, of their brave relative who had been killed twelve years earlier. Finally, Hugh McGregor had been laid to rest by his parents Robert Clark and Elizabeth Harkness McGregor (TNA, AIR 81/4529).

Sgt McGregor's grave. (*Copyright David McNay*)

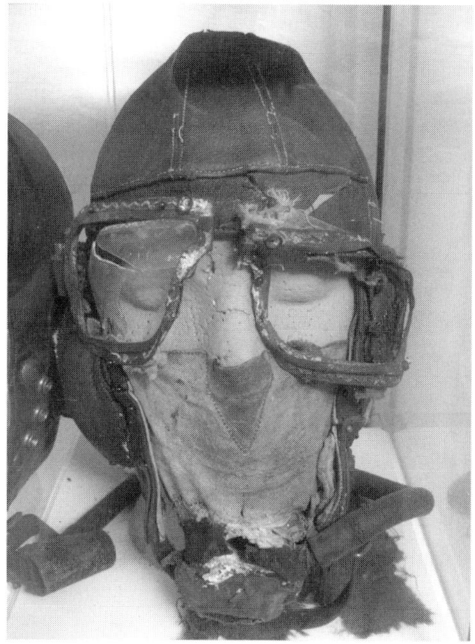

Above left: The remains of P.9451's cockpit. This Spitfire had fought over the Dunkirk evacuation and throughout the Battle of Britain. (*Author, thanks to the Hooton Park Trust*)

Above right: The patched up remains of McGregor's flying helmet, goggles and oxygen mask, make a grim reminder of the pilot's sacrifice. (*Author, thanks to the Hooton Park Trust*)

Supermarine Spitfire P.9451 had been John Ellis's favourite aircraft from May until early July, in which he made several claims, when it was DW-M. When it crashed, it was probably coded DW-P. The remains of the Spitfire were excavated again in July 2000 by the North-West Aviation Heritage Museum, including the complete Rolls-Royce Merlin III engine, the propeller with one blade missing and the pilot's instrument panel and gunsight. Fittingly, the Spitfire's excavated cockpit can be seen at the site of 610's pre-war aerodrome, Hooton Park, where it is displayed by The Hooton Park Trust in tribute to Sgt McGregor, along with the remains of his flying helmet, goggles and oxygen mask. The engine and propeller are due to be added to the remarkable display.

In the three and a half months spent out of 11 Group, the Squadron had seen four pilots killed and another four pilots had lucky escapes by parachute as a result of accidents. At least another eleven Spitfires had been involved in incidents, so a minimum of nineteen Spitfires had been damaged or written off. This indicated just how dangerous flying a Spitfire could be for inexperienced and experienced pilots alike. P/O Gray's death proved that it was not just the novice pilots who were at risk. The loss of Sgts Haines and Ireland earlier in the summer brought the total number of deaths as a result of accidents to six, a heavy price to pay indeed. It is important to remember their sacrifice just as much as the men who were killed in action.

Saturday 14 December 1940 brought news of a big change for the County of Chester Squadron, recorded in the ORB as follows: 'ORDERS RECEIVED FROM 11 GROUP FOR SQUADRON TO MOVE FROM ACKLINGTON TO WESTHAMPNETT'. 610's period of rest, recuperation and training had finally come to an end and it was sent back to 11 Group and the front line, where fresh squadrons were badly needed. 610 Squadron was now deemed ready for a return to the fray. The move to Westhampnett, a satellite airfield of the famous Tangmere aerodrome, near Chichester, was as David Denchfield recorded, '… the news we'd been waiting for, and the whole squadron was as pleased as punch'.[19] However, all concerned would have been starkly aware of the heightened dangers facing them from a base on the south coast, regardless of the amount of training they had carried out, none more so than the remaining veterans.

The story of 610 Squadron after its spell at Acklington is for another book, as the Squadron's role changed. From Westhampnett, they joined the RAF's offensive against the *Luftwaffe* over France, in what would become a very costly campaign. The Squadron's imminent move brought about a flurry of activity in terms of personnel who would remain with the Squadron and those who would be posted elsewhere. This book concludes having detailed the fates of all the current pilots in late 1940. Denchfield noted that 602 Squadron was flying its Spitfires up from Westhampnett, for 610 to take back down to Westhampnett, while 602 Squadron took 'The Chesters' aircraft on to Prestwick.[20]

The advance party heading to Westhampnett, including Engineering Officer Bentall, took the train for the south coast on 14 December, a lengthy journey in wartime conditions. Bentall, who had been promoted from warrant officer to flying officer after his heroic efforts with 610 and 72 Squadrons, remained with the Squadron until 9 June 1941, when he was posted back to Acklington (ORB). Also on 14 December, eight of the Squadron's pilots were posted to 602 Squadron, which would be based at Prestwick; P/Os McQueen, Francis and Stevens and Sgts Sharples and McDougall-Black about whom unfortunately little has been recorded, and Sgts Clarke, Cooper and Smith. Following his remarkable escape from death when he collided with F/O Bacon, Sgt Harry Clarke went on to survive the War, serving with 266 and 255 Squadrons. He later became a test pilot until he left the RAF in 1947. Clarke died on 26 July 2010.[21]

Sgt James Enerton Cooper ended up moving to 91 Squadron after 602 Squadron, and it was with 91 Squadron that he lost his life in the autumn of 1941. 'Ollie' Cooper was killed on 9 September, when his 'Spitfire dived into the sea off Dungeness while escorting a Walrus on an ASR [air sea rescue] exercise'.[22] This close friend of David Denchfield and one of 'The Few', was buried in Luton Church Burial Ground, Grave 1807B.[23]

Sgt Alan Smith on the other hand, survived the War. Smith would not have spent long with 602 Squadron, as he joined 616 (South Yorkshire) Squadron at Tangmere in December 1940, barely a month before Douglas Bader arrived. 610 Squadron would be operating alongside 616 Squadron in Bader's Tangmere Wing. Smith gained particular recognition for being chosen by Bader to be his regular wingman. 'Johnnie' Johnson, another pilot in Bader's section, who would go on to claim the most enemy aircraft shot down by an RAF fighter pilot in the Second World War, and who also became a CO of 610 Squadron later in the War, said that Alan Smith was the perfect wingman. On the day that Bader failed to return and was made a PoW, Smith was not flying due to illness. Alan Smith later won a DFC and bar and made several claims against the enemy. He also served with 93 Squadron in North Africa and went on to various postings as an instructor, including America. After the War, Smith had a very successful career in Scotland in the textile industry and was knighted.[24] Sir Alan Smith died aged ninety-five, on 1 March 2013.

In addition to these postings, the following six pilots were attached to Acklington on 14 December and would not be making the journey south with 'The Chesters'; P/Os Ogilvy and Hadland, along with Sgts Chandler, Greig, Doley and Cranwell. While there is little recorded of Sgt Greig, twenty-five-year-old 'Ted' Cranwell recovered from a crash in early 1941, before volunteering for Bomber Command and completing a tour in 1943, being awarded a DFC. He went on to perform fighter affiliation and general transport duties, before his release from the RAF in 1945. He died in 1993.[25]

P/O Ogilvy also survived the War, in an RAF career which ultimately saw a big change from operating single-engined Spitfires. By the time his flying with 610 Squadron was over, he had gained thirty-five hours and fifty minutes on Spitfires. He remained with the station flight at Acklington until 12 January 1941 and then for the next few years, Ogilvy concentrated on training new pilots.

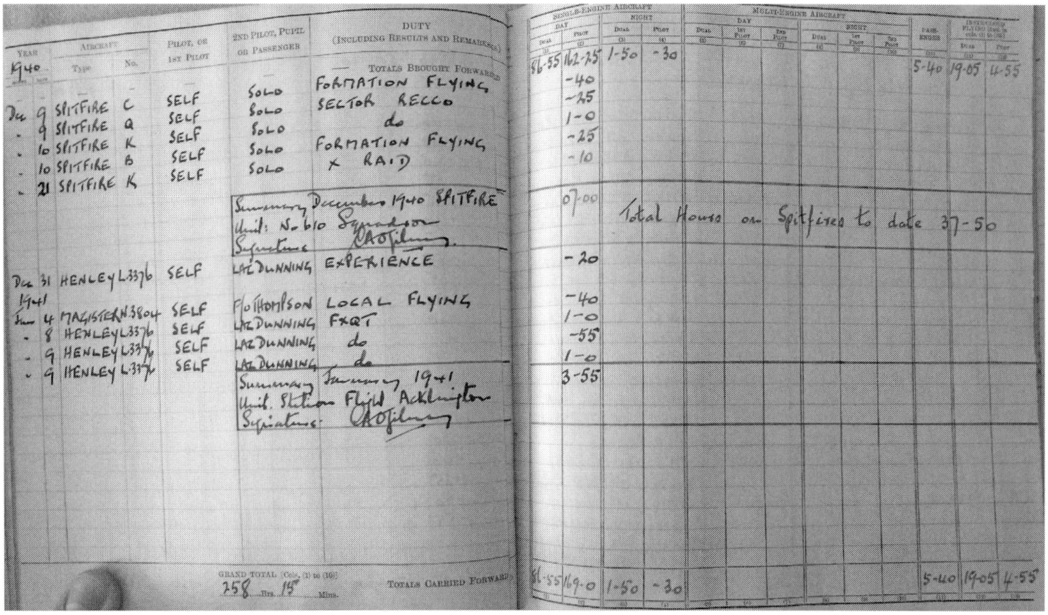

P/O Ogilvy's logbook recording his last few flights with 610 Squadron. (*Copyright Susan Ogilvy*)

He was posted to 2 CFS Cranwell until 29 March 1941, when he was classed as 'above the average' as an instructor. He went to 24 EFTS, Luton, until 8 February 1942, when he was posted to Sealand to continue working as an instructor. Here, he was reunited with Wg Cdr Brian Smith, who was 'B' Flight's commander according to Ogilvy's logbook. Alastair Ogilvy remained at Sealand until 24 March 1944, during which time he trained more than 120 pilots in over 1,000 flights.

Then Ogilvy converted to flying heavy bombers and was posted to 622 Squadron at RAF Mildenhall, where he would fly the Avro Lancaster on sixteen bombing raids between February and May 1945. He went on to carry out food supply drops to The Hague for the starving Dutch, in 'Operation Manna', repatriation of PoWs from Juvincourt, northern France and also the Mediterranean in 'Operation Dodge', when he flew to Bari, Italy, all very rewarding tasks. Ogilvy attained the rank of squadron leader and had two daughters. After the War, he continued to play rugby union for the London Scottish, and became a leading figure in Insurance, before his death on 23 February 1995, aged seventy-nine. As we have seen, it is thanks to his daughter Susan that his service record came to light, particularly in his being established as one of 'The Few'.

In one fell swoop, 610's complement of pilots had dropped by fourteen, and within a few days it would have been adjusted to about twenty-three pilots, more appropriate for an operational squadron. On 15 December 1940, the intelligence officer, Acting flying officer (AFO) Walter Lloyd, drove from Acklington to the Squadron's new home, while F/O Joe Pegge, DFC, now one of the Squadron's flight commanders, travelled by train. Walter Lloyd survived the War, but had to relinquish his commission in the RAF on medical grounds on 3 February 1945 as a (temporary) flight lieutenant.[26]

Pegge officially became an acting flight lieutenant on 16 January 1941, and had the Squadron's first encounter with the *Luftwaffe* on returning to 11 Group on 30 December, but the German aircraft escaped in cloud, Pegge having fired 400 rounds (ORB). Pegge was one of 610's last remaining veterans from the desperate dogfights over the Kentish countryside in the summer of 1940 and his subsequent RAF career, including a brief spell as CO of the County of Chester Squadron, is described in great detail by *The Battle of Britain London Memorial* website:

In January 1941 Pegge was presented with a silver tray by Welwyn Garden City. The reason for this is not recorded but the family understand that it was for shooting down a Heinkel 111 which was attacking Welwyn.

On 18th May 1941 he left 610 to take up an instructor post at 57 OTU Hawarden as flying instructor.[27] Promotion to Flight Lieutenant followed on 3rd September 1941 along with a move to 56 OTU Sutton Bridge. He commanded 610 Squadron from December 1941 until February 1942, when he was posted overseas.

On 9th June Pegge was given command of 127 Squadron in the Western Desert. He destroyed a Me109 on 8th July and two Ju87s on 2nd September. He left the squadron in April 1943 and returned to the UK.

In September 1944 Pegge went to 126 Squadron at Bradwell Bay as a supernumerary Squadron Leader. He took command of 131 Squadron at Friston in October and led it until June 1945. He was then posted to command 607 Squadron in Burma, which he did until its disbandment at Mingaladon on 19th August 1945. Pegge was awarded a Bar to the DFC (gazetted 29th January 1946).

Staying on in the RAF post-war, Pegge was granted substantive promotion to Squadron Leader with effect from August 1947 and he was granted a permanent commission on 22nd June 1948. On 11th January 1949 he was one of the surviving Battle veterans that attended the unveiling of the Battle of Britain memorial window at the Rolls-Royce Works Derby.

Pegge was killed on 9th May 1950 whilst flying in Meteor F4 VT234 of the Central Fighter Establishment, West Raynham. The aircraft flew into the Wash when descending in mist and fog whilst Pegge was flying as No.2 to a course pilot.

He was buried in East Raynham Churchyard on 16th June 1950.[28]

According to 610 Squadron's ORB, the plan was for the squadron to head south to Westhampnett in two groups to replace 602 Squadron. The first group comprised the sergeant pilots, under Sgt Hamlyn's command, the second group being led by S/Ldr Ellis. Hamlyn's group of nine is clearly listed as departing on 16 December, however, the weather which had caused so many problems of late in Acklington's sector, was wreaking as much havoc down on the south coast, from where 602 Squadron

Joe Pegge pictured at Acklington, September 1940. (*Copyright 610 Squadron Association*)

was coming. In a logistical merry-go-round, 610 and 32 Squadrons were heading back south, while 602 and 603 Squadrons were heading out of 11 Group to RAF Prestwick and RAF Drem respectively. Thanks to 13 Group's ORB appendices, it becomes clear just how the best laid plans went awry.

In short, while 32 Squadron successfully departed Acklington in their Hurricanes at 1154 hours, neither 602 from Westhampnett nor 603 from Southend had been able to leave by 1010 hours, due to the weather. At 1218 hours, 602 finally took off, but at 1240 hours, news was received that '602 have had to turn back on account of weather'. As 610 and 602 were going to be swapping aircraft, this prevented 610's departure, and stopped the plan for the sergeants to leave first. The note in the ORB had probably already been written, and then was not subsequently updated.

On 17 December, both 602 and 603 managed to start their journeys north, 602 setting off in fifteen Spitfires at 1045 hours, with one more to follow on. At 1225 hours, they were reported to be refuelling at RAF Catterick, and by 1407 hours they had started out for Acklington. 603 had also refuelled at Catterick, and arrived at Drem at 1545 hours, but suffered two crashes on landing, onc pilot being seriously hurt—tragedy was never far away on an RAF Squadron. 602 Squadron's pilots must have had a quick change around and taken 610's former mounts, as they landed safely at Prestwick at 1709 hours. It had been a remarkable feat of logistics, as other squadrons and their movements had been taken into account as the various comings and goings of different units took place.

It now seems that 610 Squadron was scheduled to head south on 18 December, although the Squadron ORB does not mention it. But yet again, the inclement weather struck! 13 Group's ORB appendices reported that fourteen of 610 had taken off at 1210 hours on 18 December, but eight minutes later, four of them landed again and by 1228 hours, all of the Squadron had returned to Acklington. In explanation, the 13 Group ORB appendices states: '610 had no weather test because machine was bogged, remainder circled aerodrome and section leader decided weather was bad so landed'.

Finally, three days later than at least half the Squadron had expected, 610's men made their farewells to Acklington and at 1025 hours on 19 December: '14 aircraft of 610 airborne—Acklington to West Hampnett [Westhampnett]. One aircraft unable to take off due to engine trouble' (13 Group ORB appendices). The other Spitfire followed on at 1110 hours. Acklington's ORB confirms that fifteen Spitfires of 610 had departed for Westhampnett under the command of S/Ldr Ellis, DFC. It was the start of a new chapter for 610 Squadron, as this group of pilots took the fight to the *Luftwaffe* over Occupied Europe.

As the Squadron's ORB divided the pilots heading to Westhampnett into two groups of sergeants and officers, I have followed suit in my account of what became of the men. Although only fifteen Spitfires headed to Westhampnett, 610's ORB lists nine sergeants and eight officers, so perhaps the two extra pilots went in an unrecorded aircraft such as a Tiger Moth, which may have still belonged to the Squadron, or perhaps they drove or took the train, like Joe Pegge. The list of sergeants was as follows: Hamlyn, Warden, Page, Richardson, Ward-Smith, Denchfield, Raine, Ballard and Horner.

Sgt Hamlyn, one of the few remaining veterans from the summer, would certainly have been looked up to by his less experienced colleagues, and survived the War. Ronald Fairfax Hamlyn was deservedly commissioned on 8 February 1941, before being posted to 242 Squadron at North Weald on 11 June 1941 (ORB). Wynne reports that:

> On a Blenheim escort to Bethune on July 4 he destroyed a Bf 109 and on the 27th he shot one down into the sea. He was made a Flight Commander in late July and remained with the squadron until October 15 1941, when his tour was completed.
>
> He was posted to form and command 275 (ASR) Squadron at Valley, with Lysanders and Walruses. Hamlyn was later given command of 276 (ASR) Squadron at Harrowbeer. He was awarded the AFC (1.1.43) for his work on-air-sea rescue, and he went to the staff of Bomber Command, as ASR Officer. In 1944 he was Tactics Liaison Officer with the 9th Air Force, USAAF in Normandy and later he was posted to Air Ministry, on Air Staff Policy.

An excellent portrait of Hamlyn as an officer, taken after his time with 610 Squadron. (*Copyright 610 Squadron Association*)

In February 1945 Hamlyn was appointed CGI at 41 and later 58 OTUs and in September he became Station Commander RAF Maiduguri, West Africa. He retired from the RAF on October 19 1957, as a Squadron Leader. Hamlyn died in April 1991.[29]

Hamlyn once recorded his firm belief in the resilience of Fighter Command during the Battle of Britain, in simple terms: 'I knew we weren't going to lose, though I didn't know how we were going to win'.[30]

Noel Proctor Warden had probably destroyed a 109 on 13 March near Calais, damaged a Ju 88 over the Channel on 14 March (ORB), damaged another Ju 88 over Guildford during the night of 11 May 1941 and was commissioned on 12 June 1941. Warden was posted to 91 Squadron at Hawkinge on 26 June 1941 (ORB), but was killed on 1 October 1941, 'being shot down off Calais during an ASR escort sortie. He is remembered on the Runnymede Memorial, Panel 35'.[31]

Doug Page, who had turned twenty-seven on 14 December, also enjoyed success against the *Luftwaffe* once the Squadron had settled into life at Westhampnett. He shot down an Me 109 on 5 March 1941, before being commissioned as a pilot officer in June and being posted to 54 Squadron on 12 June 1941 (ORB). He later served with 127 Squadron during the Battle of Alamein and in India with 11 Squadron during the Imphal siege, being awarded the DFC in May 1944 and a Bar in April 1945. He left the RAF in 1945, going on to become chief designer for English Electric in Australia. Page died in 2002 and a plaque was unveiled in his memory at his old school, Rendcomb College, in 2011.[32]

Another of the pilots to head south in mid-December was Sgt Roland Wharrier Richardson, who also survived the War. While with 610 Squadron, he destroyed a Ju 88 on 15 April 1941 with P/O Ross, and he also had a lucky escape from a crash-landing following an operational sweep. He stayed with 'The Chesters' until 21 December 1941, having been commissioned on 3 December,[33] before he served in the Western Desert with 80 Squadron. He later fought with 92 and 93 Squadrons in Tunisia and Sicily respectively. He retired from the RAF as a squadron leader in May 1963 and died on 18 November 1988.[34]

Sgt Frank 'Jackie' Horner also enjoyed early success following this posting to Westhampnett, claiming a probable Me 109 on 26 February, a 109 destroyed on 5 March, a 109 probably destroyed on 13 March, a 109 destroyed on 22 June over Hazebrouck, his final victim being another 109 near Le Touquet on 25 June 1941. While he had been commissioned on 12 June, his fortune ran out on 8 July, when he was shot down in DW-F by Me 109s, while providing escort to Stirling bombers on Circus 40 (ORB). 'He was later reported to be a PoW and at some stage was held in Stalag Luft 3 at Sagan and Belaria (PoW No. 3761). Horner was released from the RAF in 1947, as a Flight Lieutenant'.[35] A member of his ground crew kept his flying gloves and maps safe after he was shot down, indicative of the care they took over looking after 'their' pilot. The gloves and maps are now in the care of 610 Squadron's Association.[36]

Peter Ward-Smith did not manage to file the claims of Horner, and although he was commissioned on 19 June 1941 (ORB), he was shot down while on Circus 42 a couple of days after Horner, on 10 July 1941, being led by Douglas Bader escorting Stirlings to Chocques. Ward-Smith was captured, having successfully baled out of DW-R, P.8523;[37] it had been a bad day for the Squadron as two other pilots were lost. Following his eventual liberation in May 1945, he returned to Britain and was released from the RAF in 1946. Peter Ward-Smith died in 2004.[38]

Woodrow Raine was another pilot who enjoyed some success while operating over France; he damaged a 109 on 13 March 1941, destroyed an Me 109 in the Merville-Béthune area on 22 June 1941, swiftly followed by another probable 109 near St Omer and one damaged on the ground three days later. On 19 July, as part of Circus 51, he probably destroyed an Me 109 over Dunkirk and on 23 July he claimed another shared destroyed with none other than Wg Cdr Bader (ORB). Alas, Raine had little more than a month to live; on 21 August 1941 his Spitfire Vb, DW-P, P.8721 failed to return from Circus 91, on another bad day for 610, when three other pilots failed to return. Raine was listed as 'missing'. Aged twenty-two, the son of James Henry and Annie Raine of Greenhead, Cumberland, was buried in Longuenesse Souvenir Cemetery, St Omer, Plot 9, Row A, Grave 13—one more of 610's 'Few' had fallen.

Sgt Raine's headstone in Longuenesse Souvenir Cemetery, St Omer. Fittingly, the 610 Squadron motto has been engraved underneath the cross. (*Copyright http://www.bbm.org.uk/airmen/Raine.htm*)

Sgt Ballard was lost just a few days later, on 27 August 1941 (ORB). James Ballard, known as Bill, had destroyed a Ju 88 with F/Lt Norris on 3 April 1941, but failed to return in his Spitfire Vb, DW-Q, from a Circus operation. The son of Harold Edward and Elizabeth Beatrice Ballard, of Tooting, Surrey, he is remembered on Panel 39 of the Runnymede Memorial, Surrey.[39] He was particularly unlucky, as it was 610 Squadron's last Circus operation over Europe, before being withdrawn to RAF Leconfield, Yorkshire, a few days later.

The last of the nine sergeants was David Denchfield, and he survived the shortest time of any of them. He was the first pilot to be shot down on their return to 11 Group, becoming a PoW less than two months after moving south, while escorting Blenheims on a raid to St Omer on 5 February 1941. He later recalled the event:

> Just after crossing the French coast I reported some contrails up to port and slightly to our rear, but they extinguished almost immediately, so whatever it was had moved either above or below the contrail level. I had no idea where we were—there was no time to look at the map which was left folded in my left boot—but we must have been near to the target (the airfield of St. Omer), when I caught sight of a flash way up behind as I was about to start the steep turn back towards the centre once more. I held off the turn to have a good check, and then turned back, only to see the squadron a good 800 yards or so away in front of me as my extended run had taken us apart. As speed in regaining position seemed to be vital, it was not clever to be on one's own in enemy skies, I did a quick left and right steep turn during which I had a good shufti behind, and then slung the coal on and went fast to get back with the rest.
>
> I was about halfway back and about to have another look behind, when there was a sudden staccato vibration and sparks seemed to erupt out of my port wingtip. My 'bloody hell' and steep left hand turn initiation only just beat a violent clang from up front, at which the rudder pedals suddenly lost all feel and became seemingly disconnected from the rudder. As the nose fell away the cockpit filled with a white mist accompanied by a foul smell of glycol and 100-octane fuel.[40]

Unfortunately, Denchfield's Spitfire, N.3249 (TNA, AIR 81/5029), was doomed and he took to his parachute at 5,000 feet. On landing, he was captured by the Germans and photographed.

> Denchfield (PoW 426) went first to Dulag Luft at Frankfurt and was subsequently in Stalag Luft I at Barth, Stalag 8B at Lamsdorf, Stalag Luft 3 at Sagan, Stalag Luft 6 at Heydekrug, Stalag 355 at Thorn in Poland and finally Stalag 357 at Fallingbostel, near Hanover.
>
> Released on May 1 1945, Denchfield was flown back to the UK a few days later in a Lancaster of 617 Squadron. He was released from the RAF on December 12 1945, as a Warrant Officer ... He died in December 2012.[41]

The grievous losses suffered by this group of sergeants, show just how dangerous the new tactics of taking the offensive to the Germans were. Out of the nine who left Acklington in Hamlyn's party, just over eight months later, two were killed and three had become PoWs serving with 610, plus another killed with a different squadron.

On 17 December, three new recruits joined the Squadron from 602 Squadron, probably a straight swap for some more experienced pilots, now 610 would be back in the front line. They were Sgt Eade, and P/Os Gage and Fisher. Arthur William Eade had originally flown Battles in France,[42] before converting to Spitfires and joining 266 Squadron during the Battle of Britain, followed by 602 Squadron, and then 610 Squadron. He was shot down on 19 March 1941 by an Me 109, being injured and crash-landed at Hailsham. After recovering from this incident, he went on to become an instructor at 58 OTU on 13 April 1941 (ORB). He survived the War, being released from the RAF in 1947, but died in 1971.[43]

Above: Denchfield just after he had been captured on 5 February 1941. (*Copyright Nigel Denchfield*)

Right: A series of portraits by Olive Snell of 610's pilots: a mixture of the veterans and the newer recruits, each helpfully named. Sgt Eade is middle left and P/O Scott is middle right. (*From RAF Quarterly, copyright 610 Squadron Association*)

P/O Douglas Hugh Gage, an architect before the War, had served with 616 and 602 Squadrons during the Battle of Britain. He was forced to bale out twice on consecutive days with 602 Squadron, before joining 'The Chesters'.[44] Later, he joined 91 Squadron on 4 February 1941 (ORB). He was with this unit when he was killed in action by an Me 109 during an ASR operation, on 6 June 1941, aged twenty-three. He is remembered on the Runnymede Memorial.[45]

Gerald Fisher was one of the Army co-operation pilots who volunteered for Fighter Command at the height of the Battle of Britain. He converted to Spitfires, before joining 602 Squadron in September, claiming three victories before the end of October. Fisher served with 610 Squadron until 4 February 1941, when he joined 91 Squadron, along with Gage, destroying one Me 109 and damaging another. He survived the war and died in 1973.[46]

The officers listed in John Ellis's group, were as follows: Acting F/Lt Norris, DFC, and P/Os Douglas, Ross, Drever, Fenwick, Grey and Scott. Since S/Ldr I. R. Parker had formed 610 Squadron in 1936, nobody else had such an impact on the unit as S/Ldr Ellis, DFC, who had been instrumental in the Squadron's success during the Battle of Britain. Ellis was the Squadron's stand-out pilot, having made claims against the *Luftwaffe* of 10.5 destroyed, one shared destroyed, one unconfirmed and one damaged. He led his newly transformed unit back to 11 Group and claimed a Heinkel 111 shot down on the night of 10 March 1941, a particularly difficult feat in a Spitfire, plus a Ju 88 shared on 14 March. He was finally posted away as an instructor to 55 OTU at Usworth, Northumberland, on 13 April 1941 (ORB). He was awarded a bar to his DFC on 2 May 1941, the citation reading, 'This officer has commanded the squadron since July, 1940, and his personal example and tremendous

Left: Douglas Gage. (*Copyright http://www.bbm.org.uk/airmen/Gage.htm*)

Below: Ellis received the following welcome news on 20 April 1941. (*Copyright 610 Squadron Association*)

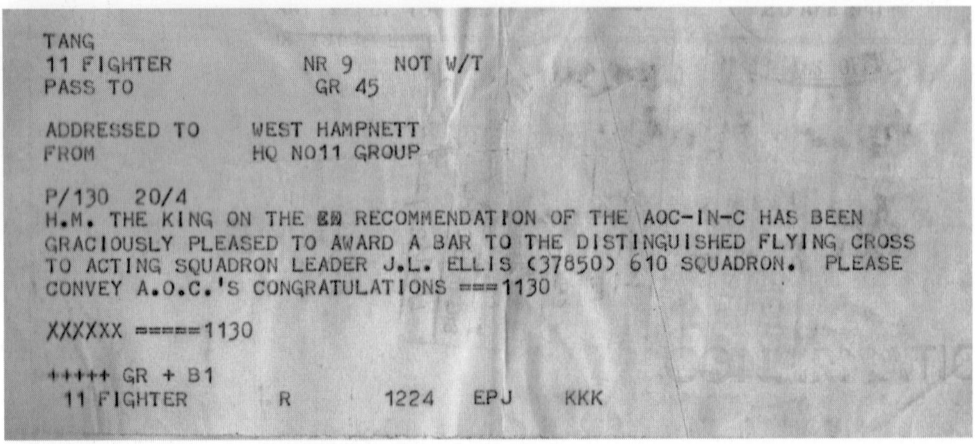

TANG
11 FIGHTER NR 9 NOT W/T
PASS TO GR 45

ADDRESSED TO WEST HAMPNETT
FROM HQ NO11 GROUP

P/130 20/4
H.M. THE KING ON THE [illegible] RECOMMENDATION OF THE AOC-IN-C HAS BEEN GRACIOUSLY PLEASED TO AWARD A BAR TO THE DISTINGUISHED FLYING CROSS TO ACTING SQUADRON LEADER J.L. ELLIS (37850) 610 SQUADRON. PLEASE CONVEY A.O.C.'S CONGRATULATIONS ===1130

XXXXXX =====1130

+++++ GR + B1
11 FIGHTER R 1224 EPJ KKK

energy have been mainly responsible for the high state of operational efficiency. The squadron has destroyed at least 89 hostile aircraft, 11 of which have been shot down by Squadron Leader Ellis'.[47]

John Ellis could certainly look back with real pride on what he had achieved with 610 Squadron. He continued being an instructor in early 1942, when:

> he was posted to another training unit in Khartoum, and later joined the Desert Air Force in North Africa before being posted to Malta as leader of the Krendi Wing. This was involved in providing air superiority over the central Mediterranean in preparation for the Anglo-American landings in Sicily. In June 1943 the engine of his Spitfire failed over the Sicilian coast and after a period of anxious waiting for his wife-to-be Jeannie, a WAAF officer, he was reported to be a prisoner of war. He was eventually sent by the Germans to Stalag Luft III at Sagan in Silesia (now Zagan, Poland). There he spent the remainder of the war, acting as No 2 to Roger Bushell, the leader of the camp's escape committee. He was released and repatriated in time to take part in the Battle of Britain flypast in September 1945.
>
> Converting to jets after the war, Ellis served in one of the first Meteor units. Among his subsequent appointments were staff officer policy and plans Middle East Air Force, based at Nicosia in Cyprus,

and station commander at RAF Bridgenorth in Shropshire. He was appointed OBE in 1956 and advanced to CBE in 1960.

Retiring in 1967, he created a glorious garden at his West Sussex home. He is survived by his wife Jeannie, whom he married in 1946, and by three daughters.

Group Captain John Ellis, CBE, DFC and Bar; fighter ace, was born on February 28 1917. He died on November 19, 2001, aged 86.[48]

In 2006, an apartment block on Borough Road, Birkenhead, Wirral, was named Ellis Court, as a lasting tribute to his service with the local squadron.

Acting F/Lt Norris, DFC, was the Squadron's other most experienced pilot, and Ellis would have been delighted to have such a trusted man still with him, a partnership which eventually ended when they went their separate ways as instructors. While with 610, Norris had claimed five destroyed, one unconfirmed, one probably destroyed, one damaged and one shared damaged, and he added to this when sharing in the destruction of a Ju 88 on 3 April with Sgt Ballard, between 0645 and 0715 hours. Norris finally left 'The Chesters' on 14 April 1941, to become an instructor at 52 OTU, which had recently formed at Debden.

In August 1941 Norris joined 485 Squadron at Redhill, as a Flight Commander. He destroyed a Bf 109 on the 29th. In mid-December 1941 he went to Malta, to command 126 Squadron at Ta Kali.

Norris destroyed a Ju 88 on the 19th and damaged others on January 9 1942 and March 10. Norris was posted to Abadan, Persia on April 4 1942, for a staff job concerned with building up the defences in the oilfields. In October he was made Squadron Leader Flying 243 Wing but took command of 33 Squadron in the Western Desert on November 20.

Norris was rested in February 1943 and went to West Africa, returning to the Middle East in June. He was posted to India in August and in September took command of 11 Squadron.

It had just returned to the fighter role, exchanging its Blenheim bombers for Hurricane IIcs. The squadron became operational in December 1943 and took part in operations at Imphal. In March

S/Ldr John Ellis. (*Copyright 610 Squadron Association*)

Stanley Norris, photographed at Acklington, September 1940. (*Copyright 610 Squadron Association*)

1944 Norris was promoted to Wing Commander Flying of a Fighter Wing there. He was awarded a Bar to the DFC (23.5.44) and returned to the UK in early 1945.

In May Norris took command of RAF Aston Down. He was released from the RAF in September 1947 as a Wing Commander. He became a King's, and later a Queen's, Messenger, serving as such until 1976. He died in 1991.[49]

P/O William Anderson Douglas remained with 610 Squadron until 26 February 1941, when he returned to 603 Squadron, his pre-war unit. He became a fighter ace, enjoying particular success over Malta in 1942, still with 603 Squadron, which he went on to command. He then served as an instructor, was awarded a DFC, later commanded 611 Squadron and finished the war as a wing commander. Douglas was released from the RAF in December 1947 and died in January 1977.[50]

P/O Alexander Richard Ross, 'Sandy', from Surbiton, claimed a Ju 88 shared destroyed with Sgt Richardson between 1730 and 1835 hours on 15 April 1941, while operating as Green 1. However, he reported to the controller that he had been hit by return fire, adding, 'I think I shall have to inflate' (ORB). These were the last words he was heard to say and he was reported 'missing' in Spitfire DW-S, P.7684. 'Sandy' Ross's luck had finally run out after his mid-air collision in October, and he drowned. His body was recovered from the sea on 21 April 1941 and was subsequently buried in Surbiton Cemetery, in the Commonwealth War Dead Section 9, Grave 2675. He was twenty-two and the son of William and Helen Robertson Ross.[51]

Nigel Drever recalled that of all the aircraft he had flown, the Spitfire was the one he loved the most as, 'You immediately became part of it'.[52] On 5 March 1941:

> Drever was flying over the French coast escorting Allied bombers when he was engaged by two German fighters. He believed that he hit one of them and had escaped the second only to see his own engine catch fire. He rolled his aircraft and baled out, but was too low for his parachute to deploy properly. According to Drever, only an oak tree saved him as he crashed into its upper branches. He was briefly

'Sandy' Ross's headstone, which is particularly poignant given the three brothers had died between 1936-47. (*Copyright http://www.bbm.org.uk/airmen/RossAR.htm*)

held up in the canopy before his ripping chute deposited him on the ground. He was immediately captured and taken to a nearby airfield.

The German officer who interrogated him was so delighted with his prize that he threw a champagne supper to celebrate—with Drever as his guest of honour. It was to be his last decent meal of the war.[53]

For the next four years he was held in captivity, including at Stalag Luft III at Sagan in Germany, 100 miles southeast of Berlin. The camp was the scene of the "Great Escape", in which 76 Allied air force officers broke out of the camp in March 1944. Fifty were shot by the Gestapo after being recaptured.

Drever was not selected for the Great Escape … but he was involved in helping to dig the tunnels that made it possible. On one occasion he said he had to be pulled out by his boots after the earth collapsed around him. One of the other skills he learnt as a prisoner-of-war was playing bridge, which became a lifelong passion.

In January 1945 Drever was among thousands of Allied servicemen who were forced at gunpoint in freezing temperatures to walk westwards farther into Germany as the Russians advanced in the east. Hundreds of prisoners died along the way.

Drever survived what became known as "the Long March" by scrounging or scavenging for food, which included a leg of ham which he guarded with his life. He was eventually flown home by Bomber Command and left the RAF in 1946 with the rank of Flight Lieutenant …

He later settled in Burnham-on-Crouch in Essex …

For much of his life he rarely talked of the war or his own exploits, but as he grew older Drever took increasing pleasure in his role as one of the last survivors of "The Few" ... **Flight Lieutenant Nigel Drever, fighter pilot, was born on January 19, 1920. He died on July 16, 2016, aged 96.**[54]

P/O Charles Fenwick survived this dangerous period of operations over Occupied Europe, being wounded while operating as a 'weaver' on 5 February 1941 in Spitfire R.6601, the same day Denchfield was shot down (TNA, AIR 81/5026). However, he went on to an even more high-risk role, joining the Merchant Ship Fighter Unit (MSFU), based at Speke, Liverpool, on 6 June 1941. (ORB)

About thirty-five merchant ships, known as Catapult Aircraft Merchant (CAM) ships, had been fitted with a catapult to enable a Hurricane to be launched in defence of a convoy. This was such a dangerous job for the pilot, because there was no way of landing back on board. If land was not within range, the pilot either had to bale out or ditch in the sea; it was far from certain that a ship would be able to stop and pick up the stranded pilot. Fenwick, 'joined the *Empire Franklyn* on July 3 1941 and was reserve pilot on the *Empire Tide* in the ill-fated convoy PQ 17, which sailed for Russia in late June 1942. The *Empire Tide* was one of only eleven ships that survived German attacks to reach Archangel on July 24, its Hurricane still on the catapult. Fenwick was released from the RAF in 1946 as a Squadron Leader'.[55] Fenwick died in York, in March 1999.[56]

P/O Jimmie Grey was slightly wounded on 26 February 1941 in Spitfire P.7691, during combat between Rye and Rye Harbour (TNA, AIR 81/5273). He damaged an Me 109 over north-east France on 11 July 1941 on Circus 43, and probably destroyed another on 23 July 1941. (ORB) He was posted to 55 OTU for instructor duties on 9 February 1942,[57] and survived the War.[58]

P/O John 'Ronnie' Scott was less fortunate, although he did also claim Me 109s destroyed on 21 June 1941 over Le Touquet and on 25 June about fifteen miles inland from Gravelines, between 1200 to 1300 hours. However, later that day he went 'missing' between 1545 and 1740 hours during Circus 23, in Spitfire II, DW-O, P.8399 (ORB). It was eventually discovered he had become a PoW, spending time in the infamous Stalag Luft III at Sagan.[59]

One pilot who is not mentioned at this point by the ORB, was F/Sgt George S. Mains, who had joined 610 on 4 November from 7 OTU. He remained with the Squadron until he was attached to Acklington from 31 January until 14 February 1941, when he rejoined 610. While operating from Westhampnett later in the year, he destroyed an Me 109 and another probably destroyed on 8 May, while on a patrol in Wg Cdr Bader's section. He then destroyed a 109 over Northern France on 2 July on Circus 29, adding another 109 to his growing tally on 5 July over Lille on Circus 33, between 1215-1350 hours. Mains was posted from 610 Squadron to Tangmere on 11 July 1941 (ORB).

Above left: F/Sgt George Mains. (*Copyright 610 Squadron Association*)

Above right: Horatio 'Ray' Herbert Chandler. (*Via N. Franks*)

Meanwhile, the adjutant, AFO R. C. W. le Fleming,[60] also 'proceeded to R.A.F. Station Westhampnett from R.A.F. Station Acklington on date stated', 19 December. (ORB) On 21 December, 610 Squadron's complement was increased to twenty-three when Sgt Samuel Hamer joined the Squadron from 72 Squadron. Sam Hamer, aged twenty-two and from Bury, was lost on 5 March 1941, when his Spitfire, DW-O, P.7501, stalled and crashed at Wilmington aerodrome near Eastbourne, after a dogfight with 109s (TNA, AIR 81/5365 and ORB). Hamer is buried in Thornton-le-Fylde (Christ Church) Churchyard, Plot F. L. 2, Grave 213. Of the eight pilots who had left for Westhampnett with Ellis, one was killed in action, another wounded and two made PoWs while with 610. This highlights the highly dangerous work Fighter Command was undertaking during 1941, with the incursions over enemy occupied territory. When added to the two killed in action and three made PoW in Hamlyn's group of nine, it was a very heavy price to pay.

The Squadron's ORB for 1940 finished off the year with news of the last few postings in and out, which did not affect the Squadron's front-line operational pilots. On 20 December, a new medical officer, F/O D. W. Higson, was posted to the Squadron from RAF Ford, while on 23 December news was received that Sgt Arthur Samuel Doley's attachment to Acklington had finished and he was posted to 55 OTU, at Aston Down, Gloucestershire. He was posted back to 610 on 13 May 1941 (ORB), but little has been recorded of 'Joe' Doley. He was promoted from warrant officer to pilot officer on 23 June 1943.[61] He survived the war and died in 1996.[62]

Finally, on 30 December, with 610 Squadron's personnel looking towards the New Year and what it might bring, P/O Hadland and the veteran Sgt Horatio Herbert Chandler, followed in F/Lt Brian Smith's footsteps, being posted to 2 CFS. Hadland was still relatively inexperienced, having only joined the Squadron from 7 OTU on 28 October, but Ray Chandler had a wealth of combat experience which he would be able to pass on to some of the new recruits at Cranwell, along with other instructors whom he might train. Chandler had claims of four destroyed, one probable, one unconfirmed, three damaged and one shared damaged. He was, 'Commissioned in June 1941, he later served with 65 and 615 Squadrons. Chandler was awarded the AFC (2.4.43)',[63] in recognition of his excellent work as an instructor. 'He was released from the RAF in 1946, as a Flight Lieutenant, and recommissioned as a pilot officer in the RAFVR Training Branch in June 1946'.[64] After the War, Ray Chandler returned to the family printing business in Bexhill. He died on 18 July 2000.[65]

In conclusion

The Squadron had come a long way from when S/Ldr I. R. Parker started to form it in early 1936, as a bomber squadron, flying obsolete Hawker Harts and Hinds. He could never have imagined how it would have evolved in little more than four years, to be one of the most successful Spitfire squadrons in the RAF. It is hard to believe just how much the Squadron's identity had changed between 1936 and the end of 1940. The weekend flying programme at Hooton Park had been replaced with wartime discipline and deadly dogfights, all of the original Auxiliary officers having either been killed or posted away, and replaced primarily by VR pilots. The only pre-war pilots left were S/Ldr Ellis and F/Lt Norris, while with the departure of Sgt Chandler, just Sgt Hamlyn and F/O Pegge remained from the pilots who had fought so bravely during the summer of 1940. It is ironic that Chandler's departure from the Squadron was the last record in the ORB for 1940, signing off a tumultuous year in the Squadron's history. Ray Chandler was one of the original ground crew before the war, had then applied for pilot training, before returning to become an important member of aircrew as a sergeant. That this former newspaper compositor had now gone full circle and completed a tour of operations as a fighter pilot, reflects in one man's journey, the incredible change of rules and roles the AAF had undergone, between 1936 and 1940.

In terms of facts and figures in 1940, 610 Squadron had lost twenty-two pilots killed or 'missing', fourteen or fifteen wounded and five ground crew killed and at least two wounded, in the eight months since Germany unleashed its *Blitzkrieg* on 10 May 1940. They were terrible casualties indeed. The Squadron had made claims for sixty-eight destroyed, seventeen unconfirmed, nineteen probably destroyed, and twenty-four damaged *Luftwaffe* aircraft, 128 claims in total. These statistics are evidence of the heroic effort made by the Squadron in defence of the Army and Navy at Dunkirk, and then the nation as a whole during the Battle of Britain.

However, there is so much more to the history of 610 Squadron than such stark figures, and hopefully this book has given a greater insight into the lives, and all too frequent deaths, of the people who made up 'The Chesters'. In Britain's greatest hour of need, the pilots and ground crew were willing to pay the ultimate sacrifice in order to maintain our freedom against the tyranny of Nazi Germany. The valiant and courageous actions of 610 (County of Chester) Auxiliary Air Force Squadron's personnel, should never be forgotten.

610 (County of Chester) Squadron's pilots who flew south from Acklington to Westhampnett in mid-December 1940. Back left to right: Richardson, Grey, Warden, Fenwick, Douglas, Ross. Front left to right: Page, Drever, Raine, Horner, Hamlyn, Ellis, Norris, Ballard, Denchfield, Ward-Smith. Pegge is absent. (*Copyright Nigel Denchfield*)

Postscript

On 29 May 2015, the 610 (County of Chester) Squadron Association carried out a commemoration service, in memory of the eight pilots who died while operating from RAF Gravesend in Kent in 1940. During my research into 610 Squadron, I realised that there was not a memorial at Gravesend to 610's pilots, while there was a memorial to the pilots of 66 Squadron and 501 Squadron who had been killed while flying from the airfield during 1940. The 610 Squadron Association arranged for an appropriate plaque to be made, which would be added to the memorial in Cascades Leisure Centre, on the site of the former airfield. A memorial dedication service was arranged with the help of John Tate of Gravesend Airport Heritage Project and Ben Cloke the leisure centre's manager. The service was organised to take place on 29 May 2015, which was seventy-five years to the day that four of the Squadron's pilots were killed over Dunkirk. Relatives of F/Os Medcalf and Kerr and Sgt Medway were present, along with local dignitaries. The well-attended, moving ceremony culminated with the sounding of the Last Post by an RAF bugler and a minute's silence. It was a fitting tribute to the sacrifice of the eight brave men from 610 Squadron.

The 610 Squadron pilots who were killed while operating from Biggin Hill and its satellite airfields, are amongst those remembered on the oak-panelled reredos at St George's RAF Chapel of Remembrance, Biggin Hill. 610 Squadron has a panel listing the sixteen pilots who were killed on operations during 1940 while operating from Biggin Hill, Gravesend and Hawkinge. It does not mention the two pilots who were killed during training. 610 Squadron is one of the seven units honoured with a stained glass window, depicting the Squadron badge, in recognition of 'The Chesters' being stationed at Biggin Hill during the Battle of Britain. The chapel provides the perfect place to reflect in a peaceful and tranquil atmosphere, on the heroism of the 453 who made the ultimate sacrifice, while operating from the Biggin Hill Sector during the Second World War, including the men of 610 (County of Chester) Squadron.

610 Squadron Association's memorial plaque to those who were killed whilst operating from RAF Gravesend. (*Copyright 610 Squadron Association*)

610 Squadron's pilots who were killed whilst operating from the Biggin Hill Sector in 1940. (*Approved for use by the Biggin Hill Memorial Museum Trust*)

Endnotes

Chapter 1

1 Copyright Royal Aero Club Trust.
2 Wynn, *Men of The Battle of Britain* (2015), p. 401.
3 Hough and Richards, *The Battle of Britain* (1990), p. 22.
4 *Flight,* 27 February 1936, p. 228.
5 *Flight*, 3 September 1936, p. 256.
6 *Flight*, 30 July 1936, p. 138.
7 Ellis, *The Rigger's Tale, Appendix 'A1'* (2009), p. 1.
8 *Ibid.*, p. 2.
9 Wynn, p. 313.
10 School information—Catherine Smith, Charterhouse School archivist.
11 Pembroke College information—John Kerr Wilson's nephew, Richard.
12 610 Squadron Association.
13 Stephen Forge—Oundle School archivist.
14 Copyright Royal Aero Club Trust.
15 610 Squadron Association.
16 *The London Gazette*, issue 34343, 24 November 1936.
17 610 Squadron Association.
18 Wilkinson, 'The Auxiliary Air Force', The School of Historical Studies Postgraduate Forum E-Journal (2007/8), p. 8.
19 Copyright Royal Aero Club Trust.
20 *Gazette*, issue 34353, 25 December 1936.
21 *Gazette*, issue 34553, 20 September 1938.

Chapter 2

1 610 Squadron Association.
2 Wilkinson, 'Auxiliary Air Force', footnote 69.
3 *Birkenhead News and Wirral General Advertiser*, 24 August 1940, Mirrorpix/Wirral Archives Service.
4 *Ibid.*
5 Ian Quickfall, Malvern College archivist; the school educated eleven Battle of Britain pilots.
6 For further information on Leathart, see Wynn, pp. 313-314.
7 Wynn, p. 124.
8 School information—David Pritchard, Leeds Grammar School archivist.
9 Christopher Kerr, Malcolm's nephew, for background information on his university, work life and logbook records.
10 *Gazette*, issue 33858, 26 August 1932.
11 *Gazette*, issue 34052, 22 May 1934.
12 *Gazette*, issue 34421, 27 July 1937.
13 610 Squadron Association.

Chapter 3

1 *The London Gazette*, supplement 35819, 8 December 1942.
2 *Gazette*, supplement 36033, 28 May 1943.
3 *Gazette*, supplement 41183, 20 September 1957.
4 *Flight*, 1 July, 1937, p. 30.
5 Foreman, *RAF Fighter Command Victory Claims of World War II Part One 1939–1940* (2003), p. 81.
6 Bungay, *The Most Dangerous Enemy* (Aurum Press 2001), p. 85.
7 *Forgotten Voices of the Blitz and the Battle of Britain* by *Joshua Levine*, published by *Ebury*, reprinted by permission of The Random House Group Limited © 2006, pp. 101-103.

Chapter 4

1 Hough and Richards, p. 22.
2 Lang survived the War, being mentioned in despatches on 24 September 1941 as a wing commander, *Gazette*, supplement 35284, 23 September 1941. He was promoted in substantive rank to group captain on 1 July 1947, *Gazette*, supplement 38020, 18 July 1947.
3 Wynn, p. 556.
4 *Ibid.*
5 Westmacott's Logbook, Crown Copyright RAF Museum. Subsequent references to Westmacott's flying instruction of pupils refer to this source.
6 Levine, pp. 101-103.
7 Wynn, p. 124.
8 School information—John Davies, Leeds Grammar School archivist.
9 Copyright Royal Aero Club Trust.
10 *Hoylake and West Kirby Advertiser*, Friday 22 May 1942, Mirrorpix/Wirral Archives Service.
11 Wynn, pp. 104-105.
12 School information—Louize Brewer, Yardley Court archivist.
13 Copyright Nicholson family.
14 *Ibid.*
15 Lambert Chambers's promotion to flying officer reported in *Gazette*, issue 34591, 20 January 1939, dating back to 1 September 1938.
16 http://www.bexhillobserver.net/news/fighter-ace-remembered-ahead-of-battle-of-britain-wreath-laying-1-1402963
17 Wynn, p. 84.
18 *Birkenhead News and Wirral General Advertiser*, Saturday, 12 October 1940, Mirrorpix/Wirral Archives Service.
19 Ellis, *Appendix 'A1'*, p. 3.
20. Bickers, *The Battle of Britain* (1990), p. 53.
21 *Ibid.*
22 There was a collision on the ground when Hind K.5476 taxied into Hind L.7190 on 11 August, although nobody was hurt, see: www.adf-serials.com.au/nz-serials/nzhind.htm
23 On 9 September 1941, Paul received news of his promotion to wing commander (temporary) *Gazette*, issue 35270, 9 September 1941; he survived the War.
24 Levine, p. 105.
25 Ellis, *Appendix 'A1'*, p.3.
26 For further information on Westmacott, see Wynn, p. 556.
27 Ellis, *Appendix 'A1'*, p. 3.
28 Bungay, p. 71.
29 *Ibid.*, p. 72.
30 *Ibid.*, p. 74.
31 Hough and Richards, p. 37.
32 Copyright Royal Aero Club Trust.
33 Wynn, p. 353.
34 Prichard (90347) probably resigned his commission, retaining his rank as a wing commander of the AAF on 31 December 1942, *Gazette*, supplement 35858, 8 January 1943.
35 Copyright *The Times*, 17 December 2001.
36 Wynn, p. 156.

37 Copyright *The Times*, 17 December 2001.

38 F/Lt J. H. Bowring (41521) later relinquished his commission due to ill health on 4 August 1944, *Gazette*, Supplement 36674, 29 August 1944.

39 http://www.bbm.org.uk/airmen/Arnfield.htm

40 Text by Tony Holmes from *Spitfire vs Bf 109 Battle of Britain*, © Osprey Publishing part of Bloomsbury, p. 9.

41 Bungay, p. 76.

42 *Ibid.*, p. 78.

43 Holmes, *Spitfire vs Bf 109*, p. 9.

44 Levine, pp. 126-127.

45 Ellis, *Appendix 'C'*, p. 1.

46 Ellis, *Appendices Aircraft Held by 610 Squadron 1936–1939*, no page.

47 Ellis, *Appendix 'C'*, p. 1.

48 Information compiled from ORB, Operational patrol notes, and *Aeromilitaria*, volume 32/issue 125/spring 2006.

49 For L.1003 and L.1015 see *Aeromilitaria*, volume 32/issue 125/spring 2006, p. 31, and for L.1076, p. 33. All subsequent references to this series will use the shortened title *Aeromilitaria*.

50 *Ibid.*, p. 32.

Chapter 5

1 Wynn, p. 285.

2 *Ibid.*, p. 287.

3 *Ibid.*, p. 387.

4 *Ibid.*, p. 337.

5 Michael George Pascalis, an Auxiliary, was killed in a mid-air collision on 9 January 1942 as a flying instructor. He was a flight lieutenant and is commemorated at Golders Green Crematorium. Copyright Commonwealth War Graves Commission (CWGC) website.

6 The Squadron had to leave behind both men and machines at Hooton Park, as noted by Raymond Ellis in August 1988: 'The Tiger Moth was retained by the Squadron and followed the Spitfires to Wittering (& beyond). The Hinds, Battles and Tutors remained at Hooton Park with many of the Regular airmen', copyright 610 Squadron Association.

7 This was an RAF camp situated in south-east Lincolnshire, where live ammunition gunnery practice was carried out over the marshland of The Wash.

8 Levine, p. 186.

9 Maurice Francis Mills died aged twenty-six on 16 August 1941. He crashed in a Hurricane and is buried in Sutton Bridge, St Matthew churchyard, Section R, Grave 43. Copyright CWGC website.

10 Copyright Clive Arnold.

11 This is the only mention of Hughman in the ORB. It is likely he had not been with 610 Squadron for long. His commission in the VR had only been confirmed in *Flight*, 5 October 1939, p. 289, the date of his confirmation as a pilot officer on probation being 19 September 1939. 610 Squadron was presumably his first, brief posting.

12 Albrecht left the AAF with the rank of squadron leader, as of 10 February 1954, *Gazette*, supplement 40163, 30 April 1954.

13 Acknowledgements to *The Battle of Britain* and Patrick Bishop: © Patrick Bishop 2009, Reproduced by permission of Quercus Editions Limited, p. 60.

14 *Ibid.*, p. 61.

15 Wynn, p. 322.

16 *Gazette*, issue 34767, 5 January 1940.

17 For further information on Marples, see Wynn, p. 354 and http://www.bbm.org.uk/airmen/Marples.htm

18 L.1074 would rejoin 610 in May; L.1008 would not rejoin the Squadron, *Aeromilitaria*, volume 32/issue 125/spring 2006, p. 31.

19 Copyright *The Times*, 1 February 1941.

20 Franks, *Air Battle for Dunkirk 26 May–3 June 1940* (Grub Street, 2017), p. 17.

21 For further information on Parker, see Wynn, p. 401.

22 Wynn, p. 442.

Chapter 6

1 A vector was a direction in which the pilot steered a course.
2 Wynn, p. 158.
3 For further information on Ensor, see Wynn, p. 158.
4 For further information on Kennard, see Wynn, p. 287.
5 Little is known about Victor Wood. On the last two patrols he was recorded as a flying officer instead of pilot officer. It seems his rank should be flying officer with effect from 10 December 1939, following the promotion reported in *Gazette*, issue 34752, 12 December 1939.
6 This aircraft is not mentioned again in the ORB until 14 May 1940.
7 http://www.bbm.org.uk/airmen/CottamHW.htm
8 Copyright Royal Aero Club Trust.
9 Wynn, p. 158.
10 This Spitfire had already had one landing incident, having taxied through a hole in the ground on 29 February. It now faced a long period of repair, not being mentioned again in the ORB until 6 June 1940.
11 *Aeromilitaria*, volume 32/issue 125/spring 2006, p. 31.
12 For further information on Riley, see Wynn, p. 442.
13 For further information on McGowan, see Wynn, p. 337.
14 Further research revealed that he had become a temporary warrant officer, dating back to 21 February 1942 (*Gazette*, issue 35508, 31 March 1942).
15 Milson's promotion was reported in *Flight* on 18 April 1940.
16 For further information on English, see Wynn, p. 158.
17 For further information on Cottam, see http://www.bbm.org.uk/airmen/CottamHW.htm

Chapter 7

1 Holmes, *Spitfire vs Bf 109*, p. 23.
2 Ellis, *Appendix 'C'*, p. 3.
3 L.1074 had not been mentioned with 610 Squadron since the collision on 16 December 1939.
4 Code word for 'Return to base and land'.
5 Ellis, pp. 2-4.
6 House of Commons *Hansard*, Parliamentary Archives: HC Deb, 13 May 1940, vol. 360 cc1502. Contains Parliamentary information licensed under the Open Parliament Licence v3.0.
7 Holland, *The Battle of Britain* (2010), p. 113.
8 The number after each pilot's name is the author's record of the number of patrols each pilot had flown since 10 May 1940, as listed in the ORB or other sources. This provides a rough guide to each pilot's level of experience as the book progresses.
9 It is possible they operated straight from Biggin Hill (although unlikely), or they remained at Hawkinge (or another advance airfield) overnight to ease this predicament.
10 These patrols probably took place from an advance airfield, either Hawkinge or Manston, but there is no report of this.
11 Extract from *Voices from the Battle of Britain*, Henry Buckton, published by David & Charles 2010, p. 70.
12 Warner, *The Bristol Blenheim: A Complete History* (2005), p. 226.
13 The following day, a different Spitfire unit shot down a Blenheim, this time from 59 Squadron; the three crewmen were killed, Warner, p. 226.
14 *Gazette*, issue 34838, 26 April 1940. This date was later amended to 3 December 1939, *Gazette*, issue 35076, 14 February 1941.
15 Franks, p. 33.
16 Ellis, *Appendix 'C'*, p. 4.
17 Recorded in both the Squadron's and Biggin Hill's record books.

Chapter 8

1 Ramsay, *The Battle of Britain Then and Now* (2006), p. 137. All subsequent references to this book will be shortened to *Then and Now*.
2 Franks, p. 42.
3 Osborne (ed.), *Hellfire Corner* (2010), pp. 10-11.
4 RAF Camera Gun footage: IWM, Combat film No. 39, from 27 May 1940. ARY211-1.

5 *Aeromilitaria*, volume 32/issue 125/spring 2006, p. 31.
6 Osborne, p. 12.
7 *Aeromilitaria*, volume 32/issue 125/spring 2006, p. 32.
8 Franks, p. 73.
9 Levine, pp. 21-22.
10 This time is presumably inaccurate—by 1755 hours the Squadron was embroiled in a dogfight.
11 Caldwell, *The JG 26 War Diary Volume One 1939–1942* (Grub Street, 1996), p. 32.
12 *Aeromilitaria*, volume 32/issue 125/spring 2006, p. 31.
13 Franks, p. 83.
14 *Ibid.*, p. 87.
15 In the ORB, Franks's aircraft is listed as DW-T, P.9452. However, thanks to the Flying Battle Casualty Report, we now know it was N.3177 (TNA, AIR 81/671). This aircraft was probably coded DW-T, having joined the Squadron on 28 March 1940, see *Aeromilitaria*, volume 32/issue 126/summer 2006, p. 71. All references to DW-T, P.9452 in the ORB up to 29 May, should probably be DW-T, N.3177, the information possibly having been updated retrospectively based on the letter identifier 'T'.
16 Franks, p. 17.
17 *Ibid.*, pp. 86-87.
18 Bizarrely, the ORB notes the enemy aircraft as Dornier 215s, despite all three Blue Section pilots calling them Messerschmitt 110s.
19 Some newspaper reports stated that Keighley was shot down by return fire from a Dornier 215. The evidence from the Squadron's contemporary records suggests both Keighley and Lambert Chambers were shot down from behind by Me 109s.
20 Membership to this exclusive club was only open to someone who had successfully baled out of a damaged aircraft and descended by parachute. They received a lapel pin in the shape of a caterpillar.

Chapter 9

1 *Aeromilitaria*, volume 32/issue 125/spring 2006, p. 32.
2 Copyright Nicholson family.
3 Ellis, *Appendix 'C'*, p. 3.
4 Franks, p. 160.
5 House of Commons *Hansard*, Parliamentary Archives: HC Deb, 4 June 1940, vol. 361 cc791-792. Contains Parliamentary information licensed under the Open Parliament Licence v3.0.
6 Wynn, p. 218.
7 *Ibid.*, p. 157.
8 *Ibid.*, p. 434.
9 *Gazette*, issue 34849, 14 May 1940.
10 Copyright Halton Records, www.oldhaltonians.co.uk
11 Wynn, p. 513.
12 *Ibid.*, p. 404.
13 *Ten Fighter Boys*, reprinted by permission of HarperCollins Publishers Ltd, © 1942, Athol Forbes & Hubert Allen, p. 193.
14 *Ibid.*, p. 195.
15 *Gazette*, issue 34881, 25 June 1940.
16 Wynn, p. 437.
17 *Ibid.*, pp. 182-183.
18 *Ibid.*, p. 411.
19 Ellis, *Appendix 'B'*, p. 1.
20 Holmes, *Sky Spy—From Six Miles High to Hitler's Bunker* (1989), p. 25.
21 *Ibid.*, p. 41.
22 *Ibid.*, p. 54.
23 Wynn, p. 543.
24 Ellis, *Appendix 'C'*, p. 4.
25 This Spitfire joined the Squadron on 7 June 1940, *Aeromilitaria*, volume 33/issue 129/spring 2007, p. 26.
26 *Ibid.*, p. 26 and *Aeromilitaria*, volume 32/issue 125/spring 2006, p. 30.

27 One of these photographs was chosen for a First Class stamp and another for the Royal Mail's First Day Cover, for the Seventy-fifth Anniversary of the Battle of Britain. They were actually taken in June 1940.
28 *Ellis, Appendix 'L'*, no page.
29 *Aeromilitaria*, volume 33/issue 129/spring 2007, p. 25 for 'K', p. 26 for 'Q', and volume 33/issue 131/autumn 2007, p. 121 for 'O'.
30 *Aeromilitaria*, volume 33/issue 131/autumn, 2007, p. 122.
31 *Aeromilitaria*, volume 33/issue 129/spring 2007, p. 27.
32 *Ellis*, p. 3.
33 Extract from Corporal Lunt's memoires in *Swift*, No. 3 (summer 2000), p. 11. Copyright NAHM.
34 Ellis, *Appendix 'B'*, pp. 2-4.
35 *Aeromilitaria*, volume 33/issue 129/spring 2007, p. 26.
36 Wynn, p. 84.

Chapter 10

1 For further information on Wallace, see Wynn, p. 543.
2 Ellis, *Appendix 'C'*, pp. 4-5.
3 *Aeromilitaria*, volume 33/issue 129/spring 2007, p. 24.
4 *Ibid.*, p. 27.
5 *Aeromilitaria*, volume 33/issue 131/autumn 2007, p. 127.
6 *Aeromilitaria*, volume 33/issue 132/winter 2007, p. 178.
7 Ellis, *Appendix 'C'*, pp. 5-6.
8 Copyright Nicholson family.
9 Mombeek, with Wadman and Creek, *Jagdwaffe Volume Two, Section One, Battle of Britain Phase One* (2001), p. 11.
10 Forbes and Allen, pp. 197-199.
11 *Aeromilitaria*, volume 33/issue 129/spring 2007, p. 26.
12 Titsey Park now seems to be called Titsey Place.
13 Ellis, *Appendix 'B'*, pp. 2-4.
14 *Aeromilitaria*, volume 33/issue 129/spring 2007, p. 26.
15 Ramsay, p. 322.
16 *Aeromilitaria*, volume 33/issue 129/spring 2007, p. 27.
17 www.doverwarmemorialproject.org.uk/Information/DaybyDay/Mobile%20Exhibition/2010/70%20panel%203.pdf
18 School information—Colonel (Retd) Philip Barry, Dover College.
19 *Aeromilitaria*, volume 33/issue 131/autumn 2007, p. 129.

Chapter 11

1 *Aeromilitaria*, volume 33/issue 131/autumn 2007, p. 123.
2 Forbes and Allen, pp. 203-204.
3 Copyright BBC: http://www.bbc.co.uk/archive/battleofbritain/11431.shtml.
4 *Ibid.*
5 Bungay, p. 144.
6 Ramsay, p. 541.
7 Knight, *Harvest of Messerschmitts* (1981), p. 72.
8 Ellis, *Appendix 'C'*, p. 7.
9 Knight, p. 76.
10 Ramsay, p. 554.
11 Knight, p. 74.
12 Forbes and Allen, pp. 204-206.
13 Wynn, p. 84.
14 Cull, with Lander, *Blue on Blue Volume One, 1939–1940* (2011), p. 82.
15 Parry, *Battle of Britain Combat Archive, Volume Two* (2016), p. 140.
16 Sturtivant, *Fleet Air Arm Aircraft 1939 to 1945* (1995).
17 *Swift*, No. 3, p. 6.
18 Cull, p. 28.
19 Knight, p. 77.

20 Holland, pp. 412-414.
21 Text by John Weal from *Bf 109D/E Aces, 1939–1940*, © Osprey Publishing part of Bloomsbury, p. 69.
22 Ramsay, p. 546.
23 Parry, *Volume Two*, p. 141
24 Mombeek, *Section One*, p. 15.
25 64 Squadron claimed two enemy aircraft shot down, but reported one pilot 'Missing', with two more Spitfires damaged. They returned to base by 1600 hours (64 ORB).
26 *Aeromilitaria*, volume 33/issue 131/autumn 2007, p. 121.
27 *Ibid.*, p. 125.
28 *The Chronicle*, Saturday, 3 August 1940, Mirrorpix/Cheshire Record Office.
29 Ramsay, p. 547.
30 Parry, *Volume Two*, p. 161.
31 Holland, p. 418.
32 Ramsay, pp. 547-548.
33 In 11 Group's ORB appendices 'Results of Air Combats', these claims were listed as one confirmed destroyed, five unconfirmed destroyed and five probably destroyed (TNA, AIR 25/197).
34 Wynn, pp. 104-105.

Chapter 12

1 Ellis, *Appendix 'C'*, p. 6.
2 An error in the ORB—this should be 'K. H. Cox'.
3 Copyright http://www.unithistories.com/officers/RAFVR_officers_A01.html
4 Wynn, p. 6.
5 *Gazette*, issue 34927, 20 August 1940.
6 Wynn, p. 22.
7 *Ibid.*, p. 352.
8 *Ibid.*, p. 36.
9 *Ibid.*, p. 109.
10 *Ibid.*, p. 183.
11 *Ibid.*, p. 565.
12 *Ibid.*, p. 383.
13 *Gazette*, issue 34937, 3 September 1940.
14 All subsequent references to Merrick's logbook are to The RAF Museum, Hendon, Crown Copyright RAF Museum.
15 610's ORB records Merrick's posting as being on 27 July, so perhaps it was a couple of days before he arrived.
16 Wynn, p. 204.
17 Levine, pp. 105-106.
18 Bedford Modern School website.
19 Reproduced with permission of Bedford Modern School archive.
20 *Ibid.*
21 *Ibid.*
22 *Ibid.*
23 Wynn, p. 552.
24 *Ibid.*
25 *Aeromilitaria*, volume 33/issue 129/spring 2007, p. 26. This source does not mention any damage to P.9503 on 29 July 1940.
26 Ramsay, p. 335.
27 Foreman, p. 114.
28 Ramsay, p. 550.

Chapter 13

1 Ramsay, p. 344.
2 Wynn, p. 383.
3 For R.6765 see, *Aeromilitaria*, volume 33/issue 131/autumn 2007, p. 127, and for L.1045, *Aeromilitaria*, volume 32/issue 125/spring, 2006, p. 32.

4 Parry, *volume Two*, p. 255.
5 Saunders, *Convoy Peewit* (2010), p. 138.
6 Forbes and Allen, pp. 199-202.
7 *Aeromilitaria*, volume 32/issue 125/spring 2006, p. 31.
8 *Aeromilitaria*, volume 34/issue 135/autumn 2008, p. 123.
9 *Aeromilitaria*, volume 32/issue 125/spring 2006, p. 28.
10 For P.9453, *Aeromilitaria*, volume 33/issue 129/spring 2007, p. 24; for P.9433 *Aeromilitaria*, volume 32/issue 128/winter 2006, p. 178; for R.6629 *Aeromilitaria*, volume 33/issue 131/autumn 2007, p. 123.
11 For R.6694 see *Aeromilitaria*, volume 33/issue 131/autumn 2007, p. 125, for X.4028 see *Aeromilitaria*, volume 34/issue 134/summer 2008, p. 77.
12 For R.6918, *Aeromilitaria*, volume 33/issue 132/winter 2007, p. 176; for R.6630 *Aeromilitaria*, volume 33/issue 131/autumn 2007, p. 123.
13 Goss, *Luftwaffe Fighters and Bombers, The Battle of Britain* (2011), p. 70.
14 http://www.cieldegloire.com/jg_052.php#pertes1940
15 Parry, *Battle of Britain Combat Archive, Volume Three* (2016), p. 268.
16 Ramsay, p. 557.
17 *Aeromilitaria*, volume 32/issue 126/summer 2006, p. 70.
18 *Ibid*, p. 74.
19 *Aeromilitaria*, volume 33/issue 131/autumn 2007, p. 122.
20 *Gazette*, issue 34935, 30 August 1940.
21 *The Chronicle*, Saturday 31 August 1940, Mirrorpix/Cheshire Record Office.
22 *The Chronicle*, Saturday 7 September 1940, Mirrorpix/Cheshire Record Office.
23 The Squadron's adjutant/clerk probably had more pressing needs during this hectic period and only noted it down on 21 August, or perhaps Gardiner flew earlier than he was instructed to.
24 Ramsay, p. 353.
25 *Aeromilitaria*, volume 33/issue 129/spring 2007, p. 27.
26 *Aeromilitaria*, volume 33/issue 131/spring 2007, p. 129. Reported to have joined 610 on 13 February 1940, although no mention of it in ORB until early July, when it was regularly recorded as DW-N.
27 *Aeromilitaria*, volume 32/issue 125/spring 2006, p. 30.
28 *Aeromilitaria*, volume 33/issue 131/autumn 2007, p. 123.
29 *Aeromilitaria*, volume 34/issue 134/summer 2008, p. 79.
30 *Aeromilitaria*, volume 33/issue 129/spring 2007, p. 25. This is actually recorded as 'Category 3' here, so it had been written-off, which seems debatable.
31 *Aeromilitaria*, volume 32/issue 128/winter 2006, p. 174.
32 Ellis, *Appendix 'C'*, pp. 6-7.
33 Caldwell, p. 52.
34 *Ibid.*, p. 53.
35 Ramsay, p. 561.
36 Bishop, pp. 178-179.
37 *Gazette*, issue 34920, 13 August 1940.

Chapter 14

1 *Aeromilitaria*, volume 32/issue 126/summer 2006, p. 70.
2 Code name for Biggin Hill's Ground Controller.
3 Wynn, p. 183.
4 Approved for use by Biggin Hill Memorial Museum Trust.
5 http://www.bbm.org.uk/airmen/GardnerBGD.htm
6 The '11 Group Intelligence Bulletin' gives slightly better figures of six destroyed, four probably destroyed and three damaged (TNA, AIR 25/197).
7 Ramsay, p. 357.
8 *Aeromilitaria*, volume 32/issue 125/spring 2006, p. 31.
9 *Aeromilitaria*, volume 34/issue 135/autumn 2008, p. 123.
10 Mombeek, with Wadman & Pegg, *Jagdwaffe Volume Two, Section Two, Battle of Britain Phase Two* (2001), p. 103.
11 *Ibid.*

12 The '11 Group Intelligence Bulletin' for 15 August lists three Me 109s as probables, further confusing the issue (TNA, AIR 25/197).
13 Ramsay, p. 362.
14 *Aeromilitaria*, volume 34/issue 134/summer 2008, p. 79.
15 *11 Group Intelligence Report* lists both 109s as probably destroyed (TNA, AIR 25/197).
16 House of Commons *Hansard*, Parliamentary Archives: HC Deb, 20 August 1940, vol. 364 cc1167. Contains Parliamentary information licensed under the Open Parliament Licence v3.0.

Chapter 15

1 Wood, with Dempster, *The Narrow Margin* (1990), pp. 214-215.
2 Levine, p. 238.
3 Mombeek, *Volume Two, Section Two*, p. 125.
4 The '11 Group Intelligence Bulletin' also credited 610 with fifteen claims, as follows: eleven destroyed, one probable and three damaged (TNA, AIR 25/197).
5 Ramsay, p. 372.
6 *Aeromilitaria*, volume 33/issue 131/autumn 2007, p. 125.
7 *Aeromilitaria*, volume 33/issue 132/winter 2007, p. 174.
8 *Ibid.*, p. 179.
9 *Aeromilitaria*, volume 33/issue 131/autumn 2007, p. 122.
10 *Aeromilitaria*, volume 32/issue 126/summer 2006, p. 74. N.3284 left the Squadron around 7 September 1940, so R.6599 almost certainly acted as the replacement DW-J.
11 *Aeromilitaria*, volume 32/issue 128/winter 2006, p. 178 for P.9433 and *Aeromilitaria*, volume 33/issue 131/autumn 2007, p. 123 for R.6629.
12 Forbes and Allen, p. 209.
13 *Ibid.*, p. 207.
14 *Ibid.*
15 Ellis, p. 1.
16 Bungay, p. 231.

Chapter 16

1 This invaluable source was supplied by Dave Brocklehurst from the Kent Battle of Britain Museum, Hawkinge.
2 Else's logbook information, Copyright Kent Battle of Britain Museum.
3 *Aeromilitaria*, volume 34/issue 134/summer 2008, p. 80.
4 Knight p. 101.
5 Ramsay, p. 374.
6 *Aeromilitaria*, volume 33/issue 131/autumn 2007, p. 125.
7 Forbes and Allen, p. 203.
8 Levine, p. 173.
9 *Ibid.*, p. 175.
10 Caldwell, p. 62.
11 Wynn, p. 14.
12 *Aeromilitaria*, volume 34/issue 134/summer 2008, p. 80. This source lists the pilot incorrectly—see latest information at The National Archives.
13 For further information on Arnfield, see http://www.bbm.org.uk/airmen/Arnfield.htm and Wynn, p. 14.
14 Ramsay, p. 594.
15 For further information on Merrick, see Wynn, p. 362.
16 Ramsay, p. 594.
17 Forbes and Allen, p. 68.
18 Hamlyn interviewed by Geoffrey Simpson for 'The Flight of the Few', *Cheshire Life* (September 1990), p. 132.

Chapter 17

1 Levine, p. 169.
2 *Ibid.*, p. 171.
3 Ramsay, p. 382.

4 Also, *Aeromilitaria*, volume 32/issue 125/spring 2006, p. 28.
5 Caldwell, p. 63.
6 From the ensuing combat reports, the pilots of Blue and Green Sections stated they were still 'B' Flight, while Yellow Section was in 'A' Flight.
7 The other two flights he carried out were to Hawkinge and a patrol (forty-five minutes), then a patrol and return flight to Biggin Hill (sixty-five minutes).
8 Copyright Kent Battle of Britain Museum.
9 It is unlikely that this was Peter Lamb. He stated that the pilot he protected descending by parachute, landed in the sea.
10 Copyright *Cambridge Evening News* (Special Supplement—Battle of Britain), 6 July 1990.
11 *Ibid.*
12 Copyright *Cambridge Evening News*, 1 May 1991.
13 An interesting note on this aircraft was found in the *Aeromilitaria* series: 'Note the undersize fin flash with reverse colour sequence (blue at the front) typical of this batch of early R-serialled Mk. Is. In this batch of Spitfires, the 'B' camouflage layout was applied to aircraft with odd numbers', volume 33/issue 131/autumn 2007, p. 121. See cover photograph.
14 Ramsay, p. 384.
15 *Aeromilitaria*, volume 33/issue 132/winter 2007, p. 177.
16 Ramsay, p. 599.
17 The only reference to any operational activity on 27 August 1940 I have found is in Sgt Bamberger's logbook. This records a flight to Hawkinge (twenty minutes) and a return flight to Biggin Hill (twenty-five minutes) (20 & 21). It indicates that at least part of the Squadron was based at the forward airfield.
18 *Aeromilitaria*, volume 33/issue 129/spring 2007, p. 27.
19 Ellis, *Appendix 'C'*, p. 7.
20 *Aeromilitaria*, volume 34/issue 134/summer 2008, p. 76.
21 Ramsay, p. 391.
22 *Everyone's War*, No. 6 (autumn/winter 2002), pp. 54-55.
23 P.9433, *Aeromilitaria*, volume 32/issue 128/winter 2006, p. 178.
24 Ramsay, p. 391.
25 *Aeromilitaria*, volume 33/issue 131/autumn 2007, p. 123.
26 Ramsay, p. 391.
27 *Aeromilitaria*, volume 34/issue 135/autumn 2008, p. 122.
28 Wood, pp. 238-239.
29 Ramsay, p. 608.
30 *Ibid.*, p. 607.
31 Ellis, pp. 4-5.
32 *Ibid.*, p. 5.
33 *Ibid.*, pp. 6-9.
34 Tarrant's information, copyright CWGC website.
35 Wright, *The Bump* (1980), p. 25.
36 *Ibid.*, pp. 65-66.
37 Ellis, pp. 5-6.
38 Bungay, p. 85.
39 Ellis, p. 12.
40 Beardsley interviewed by Geoffrey Simpson for 'The Flight of the Few', p. 133.
41 Ellis, pp. 12-14.
42 Buckton, pp. 152-157.
43 Ellis, pp. 16-19.

Chapter 18

1 Wynn, p. 124.
2 *Ibid.*, p. 215.
3 *Ibid.*, p. 141.
4 http://www.hemelatwar.org/MilehamDShort.html Professor Richard Grayson from 'Hemel at War' granted permission to use this information. The source was an interview with Denys Mileham's nephew, Philip Mileham, published on the 'Hemel at War' website.

5 Wynn, p. 364.
6 *Ibid.*, p. 123.
7 *Ibid.*, p. 6.
8 *Ibid.*, p. 106.
9 Cosby interviewed by Geoffrey Simpson for 'The Flight of the Few', p. 133.
10 Wynn, p. 61.
11 *Ibid.*, p. 314.
12 Nigel Denchfield granted permission to use his father's reminiscences; copyright Denchfield family.
13 Ellis, pp. 16-19.
14 *Swift*, No. 3, p. 12
15 *The Isle of Wight County Press*, 7 September 1940, p. 6.
16 Ramsay, p. 460.
17 Wynn, pp. 104-105.
18 Ramsay, p. 447.
19 Wynn, p. 565.
20 Ramsay, p. 484.
21 *Ibid.*, p. 503.
22 Wynn, p. 565.
23 *Ibid.*
24 *Ibid.*, p. 404.
25 *Ibid.*
26 Corbin, *Last of the Ten Fighter Boys* (2007), pp. 140-141.
27 Wynn, pp. 91-92.
28 *Ibid.*, p. 80.
29 *Ibid.*, p. 104.
30 Forbes and Allen, p. 61.
31 *Ibid.*, pp. 68-69.
32 Ramsay, p. 480.
33 Wynn, p. 6.
34 *Ibid.*
35 Ellis, pp. 20-22.
36 *Ibid.*, p. 23.
37 610 Squadron Association.
38 *Swift*, No. 3, p. 13.
39 Burton, *Go Straight Ahead* (1996), p. 149.
40 Wynn, p. 434.
41 *Ibid.*, p. 19.
42 *Ibid.*, p. 139.
43 *Ibid.*, p. 250.
44 *Ibid.*, p. 546.
45 *Ibid.*, p. 379.
46 Forbes and Allen, p. 69.
47 Ramsay, p. 648.
48 Robinson, *RAF Fighter Squadrons in The Battle of Britain* (1999), p. 92.
49 610 Squadron Association.
50 *Ibid.*
51 Robinson, p. 92.
52 *Ibid.*, p. 94.
53 Ramsay, p. 486.
54 *Ibid.*, p. 522.
55 Brew, with Bradbury, *A Ruddy Awful Waste: Eric Lock D. S. O, D. F. C & Bar* (2016), p. 119.
56 For further information on Beardsley, see Wynn, p. 36.
57 Ramsay, p. 470.
58 Wynn, p. 61.

59 For further information on Brown, see Wynn, p. 61.
60 Wynn, p. 106.
61 For further information on Cosby, see Wynn, p. 106.
62 Wynn, p. 294.
63 Copyright *The Times*, 2 August 2016.
64 Wynn, p. 142.
65 Copyright *The Times*, 2 August 2016.
66 Wynn, p. 142.
67 *Ibid.*, p. 452.
68 *Ibid.*, p. 507.
69 *Ibid.*, p. 408.
70 *Ibid.*, p. 579.
71 *Gazette*, issue 34951, 24 September 1940.
72 Wynn, p. 123. In 1979, Davies's Spitfire's crash site was investigated by the Wealden Aviation Group. Various engine components, manufacturers' labels and cockpit relics were recovered, see Barnes, p. 100.
73 For further information on Davies, see Wynn, p. 123.
74 For further information on Baker, see Wynn, p. 22.
75 Wynn, p. 141.
76 For further information on Draper, see Wynn, p. 141.
77 For further information on Mileham, see Wynn, p. 364.
78 Wynn, p. 215.
79 For further information on Hallam, see Wynn, p. 215.
80 Corbin, pp. 99-100.
81 Walton, *Northumberland Aviation Diary* (1999), p. 54.
82 *Aeromilitaria*, volume 32/issue 125/spring 2006, p. 25.
83 Corbin, pp. 100-101.
84 For further information on Clarke, see Wynn, pp. 91-92.
85 *Aeromilitaria*, volume 32/issue 125/spring 2006, p. 32. This does not mention the collision, but that it was shot down during combat with an He 59 on 11 August—probably confused with Tanner/Neville's aircraft.

Chapter 19

1 Rees was possibly no longer with 610—the ORB does not mention when he left the Squadron.
2 Wynn, p. 80.
3 *Ibid.*, p. 314.
4 For further information on Lecky, see Wynn, p. 314.
5 Copyright CWGC website.
6 Robinson, pp. 97-98.
7 For further information on Aldridge, see Wynn, p. 6.
8 Copyright 610 Squadron Association.
9 www.bbm.org.uk/airmen/Raine.htm
10 Wynn, p. 110.
11 *Ibid.*, p. 131.
12 Copyright Denchfield family.
13 Copyright CWGC.
14 Wynn, p. 546.
15 Copyright CWGC.
16 Wynn, p. 102.
17 *Ibid.*
18 Copyright Denchfield family.
19 *Ibid.*
20 *Ibid.*
21 Wynn, p. 440.
22 *Ibid.*, p. 165.
23 School information—Chris Freeman, Chatham House School.

24 Wynn, p. 399.
25 Corbin, p. 236.
26 *Ibid.*, pp. 236-237.
27 For further information on Corbin's life, read *Last of the Ten Fighter Boys* and *Ten Fighter Boys*.
28 *Aeromilitaria*, volume 32/issue 126/summer 2006, p. 73.
29 Wynn, p. 379.
30 *Gazette*, supplement 36223, 22 October 1943.
31 Wynn, p. 306.
32 610 Squadron Association.

Chapter 20

1 13 Group's ORB Appendices records some additional patrols by 610, but does not mention the pilots involved.
2 Copyright CWGC website.
3 *Aeromilitaria*, volume 32/issue 125/summer 2006, p. 33.
4 Chris R. Davies granted permission to use this extract from *Almost Forgotten: The search for aviation accidents in Northumberland* (2012), p. 188.
5 *Aeromilitaria*, volume 34/issue 135/autumn 2008, p. 125.
6 *Aeromilitaria*, volume 33/issue 132/winter 2007, p. 178.
7 *Ibid.*, p. 174. The place of the crash was actually Eglingham.
8 *Aeromilitaria*, volume 33/issue 131/autumn 2007, p. 124.
9 Wynn, pp. 182-3.
10 *Ibid.*, p. 294.
11 *Ibid.*, p. 507.
12 610 Squadron Association. For further information on York, see Wynn, p. 579.
13 Copyright CWGC website.
14 For further information on Payne, see Wynn, p. 408.
15 http://www.airhistory.org.uk/spitfire/home.html
16 *Aeromilitaria*, volume 32/issue 128/winter 2006, p. 173.
17 Copyright Chris Davies for this information.
18 Copyright CWGC website.
19 Copyright Denchfield family.
20 *Ibid.*
21 For further information on Clarke, see Wynn, pp. 91-92.
22 For further information on Cooper, see Wynn, p. 102.
23 Copyright CWGC website.
24 610 Squadron Association website.
25 For further information on Cranwell, see Wynn, p. 110.
26 *Gazette*, supplement 36945, 16 February 1945.
27 He also claimed an He 111 damaged at night, on 11 May 1941 (ORB).
28 http://www.bbm.org.uk/airmen/Pegge.htm
29 Wynn, p. 218.
30 Hamlyn interviewed by Geoffrey Simpson for 'The Flight of the Few', p. 132.
31 For further information on Warden, see Wynn, p. 546.
32 610 Squadron Association.
33 *Ibid.*
34 For further information on Richardson, see Wynn, p. 440.
35 Wynn, p. 250.
36 610 Squadron Association.
37 *Ibid.*
38 For further information on Ward-Smith, see Wynn p. 546.
39 610 Squadron Association.
40 Copyright Denchfield family.
41 For further information on Denchfield, see Wynn, p. 131.
42 McRoberts, *Lions Rampant* (1985), p. 87.

43 For further information on Eade, see Wynn, p. 149.
44 McRoberts, p. 108.
45 For further information on Gage, see Wynn, p. 181.
46 For further information on Fisher, see Wynn, p. 168.
47 *Gazette*, issue 35151, 2 May 1941.
48 Copyright *The Times*, 17 December 2001.
49 Wynn, p. 387.
50 For further information on Douglas, see Wynn, p. 139.
51 610 Squadron Association website.
52 Copyright *The Times*, 2 August 2016.
53 Drever was reported a PoW on 17 March 1941 (ORB).
54 Copyright *The Times*, 2 August 2016.
55 For further information on Fenwick, see Wynn, p. 165.
56 610 Squadron website.
57 *Ibid.*
58 *Gazette*, supplement 39163, 2 March 1951.
59 610 Squadron website.
60 Fleming's promotion to flying officer was confirmed on 7 March 1941 (ORB).
61 *Gazette*, supplement 36267, 26 November 1943.
62 610 Squadron Association.
63 Wynn, p. 84.
64 For further information on Chandler, see Wynn, p. 84.
65 http://www.bexhillobserver.net/news/fighter-ace-remembered-ahead-of-battle-of-britain-wreath-laying-1-1402963

Glossary and abbreviations

AA	Anti-Aircraft
AACU	Anti-Aircraft Co-operation Unit
AAF/RAuxAF	Auxiliary Air Force
A/c	Aircraft
AC	Aircraftman
(AC) Squadron	Army Co-operation Squadron
ACM	Air Chief Marshal
Adj.	Adjutant
AFDU	Air Fighting Development Unit
AFO	Acting Flying Officer
AFTS	Advanced Flying Training School
Air Cdre	Air Commodore
ALG	Advance Landing Ground
AM	Air Marshal
AMCB	Air Ministry Casualty Branch
Angels	Altitude
AOC	Air Officer Commanding
AOC-in-C	Air Officer Commanding-in-Chief
APO	Acting Pilot Officer
ASR	Air Sea Rescue
Ass. Adj.	Assistant Adjutant
ATA	Air Transport Auxiliary
AVM	Air Vice-Marshal
B&GS/BGS	Bombing and Gunnery School
Bandit	Enemy aircraft
Brig. Gen.	Brigadier General
CAM	Catapult Aircraft Merchant ship
CFS	Central Flying School
CHL	Chain Home Low stations
C-in-C	Commander-in-Chief
CLE	Central Landing Establishment
CO, C/O	Commanding Officer
Cpl	Corporal
CSU	Constant Speed Unit
DFC	Distinguished Flying Cross
DFM	Distinguished Flying Medal
Do	Dornier
DSO	Distinguished Service Order
E/a, e.a.	Enemy aircraft

E&RFTS	Elementary & Reserve Flying Training School
EFTS	Elementary Flying Training School
Erprobungsgruppe/Erpro.	Experimental testing group
FAA	Fleet Air Arm
Feldwebel/Fw.	*Luftwaffe* equivalent of a Flight Sergeant
Flak	Anti-Aircraft fire
F/Lt	Flight Lieutenant
F/O	Flying Officer
Freie Jagd	Free hunt, fighter sweep
F/Sgt	Flight Sergeant
FTS	Flying Training School
Fw	Focke-Wulf
Gefreiter/Gefr.	*Luftwaffe* equivalent of a Leading Aircraftsman
Grp Capt.	Group Captain
Gruppe	Roughly equivalent to an RAF Wing
Hauptmann/Hptm.	*Luftwaffe* equivalent of a Flight Lieutenant
He	Heinkel
IFF	Identification Friend or Foe
ITW	Initial Training Wing
Jägdgeschwader/JG	Equivalent of three RAF Fighter Wings
Jagdwaffe	*Luftwaffe's* fighter arm
Ju	Junkers
Kampfgeschwader/KG	Rough equivalent of three RAF Bomber Wings
LAC	Leading Aircraftman
Lehrgeschwader/LG	Training Wing, which still flew operational patrols
Leutnant/Lt/Ltn.	*Luftwaffe* equivalent of a Pilot Officer
Lt	Lieutenant
Lt-Col.	Lieutenant-Colonel
Maj.	Major
Maj.	*Luftwaffe* equivalent of a Squadron Leader
Me	Messerschmitt
MSFU	Merchant Ship Fighter Unit
MTB	Motor Torpedo Boats
MU	Maintenance Unit
NCO	Non-commissioned officer
Oberfeldwebel/Obfw.	*Luftwaffe* equivalent of a Warrant Officer
Oberleutnant/Oblt.	*Luftwaffe* equivalent of a Flying Officer
O/C	Officer Commanding
ORB	Operations Record Book
OTU	Operational Training Unit
PDC	Personnel Despatch Centre
P/O	pilot officer
PoW	Prisoner of War
PRU	Photographic Reconnaissance Unit
RAFO	Reserve of Air Force Officers
RAFVR/VR	Royal Air Force Volunteer Reserve
RDF	Radio Direction Finding
RFC	Royal Flying Corps
Rotte	Tactical section of two aircraft, two of which composed a *Schwarm*
R/T	Radio Telephony
Schwarm	Tactical section of four aircraft
SFTS	Service Flying Training School
S/Ldr	Squadron Leader
'Snappers'	Enemy fighters

Staffel	*Luftwaffe* equivalent of an RAF Squadron
Staffelkapitäne/Staffelführer	Commanding Officer of a Staffel
Stuka	Dive-bomber
'Through the gate'	Apply maximum engine power
TNA	The National Archives
UAS	University Air Squadron
Unteroffizier/Uffz.	*Luftwaffe* equivalent of a Sergeant
'Vic'	A three-aircraft formation in the shape of a 'V', the leader being the point of the 'V' with his two wingmen flying behind him on either wingtip. It was an obsolete formation, proving lethal for RAF pilots in the early aerial combat of the Second World War.
WAAF	Women's Auxiliary Air Force
Weaver	Pilot(s) covering the rest of the Squadron at the rear of the formation.
Wettererkundungsstaffel	Weather reconnaissance unit
Wg Cdr	Wing Commander
WO	Warrant Officer
Zerstörer	Destroyer—Messerschmitt 110 heavy fighter

Bibliography

Books

Bickers R. T., *The Battle of Britain* (London: Salamander Books Ltd, 1990)

Bishop, P., *Fighter Boys* (London: Harper Perennial, 2004)

Bishop, P., *Battle of Britain* (London: Quercus Publishing Plc, 2009)

Brew, S., with Bradbury, M., *A Ruddy Awful Waste: Eric Lock DSO, DFC & Bar* (Hitchin: Fighting High Ltd, 2016)

Buckton, H., *Voices from the Battle of Britain: Surviving Veterans Tell Their Story* (David Charles Limited, 2010)

Bungay, S., *The Most Dangerous Enemy* (London: Aurum Press Ltd, 2001)

Burton, E., *Go Straight Ahead* (Evesham: Square One Publications, 1996)

Caldwell, D., *The JG 26 War Diary Volume One 1939–1942* (London: Grub Street, 1996)

Corbin, J., *Last of the Ten Fighter Boys* (Stroud: Sutton Publishing, 2007)

Cull, B., with Lander, B., *Blue on Blue Volume 1, 1939–1940* (London: Tally Ho Publishing Limited, 2011)

Crook, D. M., *Spitfire Pilot* (London: Faber and Faber Limited, 1942)

Davies, C. R., *Almost Forgotten* (Stroud: Amberley Publishing, 2012)

Forbes, A., and Allen, H., *Ten Fighter Boys* (London: Collins, 2008)

Foreman, J., *RAF Fighter Command Victory Claims of World War II Part One 1939–1940* (Walton-on-Thames: Red Kite, 2003)

Foster, Wg Cdr R., with Franks, N., *Tally Ho! From the Battle of Britain to the Defence of Darwin* (London: Grub Street, 2008)

Franks, N., *Air Battle For Dunkirk 26 May–3 June 1940* (London: Grub Street, 2017)

Franks, N., *Dowding's Eagles* (Barnsley: Pen & Sword Aviation, 2015)

Goss, C., *Brothers in Arms* (Manchester: Crécy Books Ltd, 1994)

Goss, C., *Luftwaffe Fighters and Bombers, The Battle of Britain* (Mechanicsburg, Pennsylvania: Stackpole Books, 2011)

Holland, J., *The Battle of Britain* (London: Bantam Press, 2010)

Holmes, R., *Sky Spy—From Six Miles High to Hitler's Bunker* (Shrewsbury: Airlife Publishing Ltd, 1989)

Holmes, T., *Spitfire vs Bf 109 Battle of Britain* (Oxford: Osprey Publishing Ltd, 2007)

Hough, R., and Richards, D., *The Battle of Britain* (London: Guild Publishing, 1990)

Isby, D., *The Decisive Duel Spitfire vs 109* (London: Little, Brown, 2012)

Johnstone, S., CB, DFC, *Enemy in the sky* (London: William Kimber & Co Ltd, 1976)

Knight, D., *Harvest of Messerschmitts* (London: Frederick Warne Publishers Ltd, 1981)

Levine, J., *Forgotten Voices of the Blitz and the Battle of Britain* (London: Ebury Press, 2007)

McRoberts, D., *Lions Rampant* (London: William Kimber & Co. Limited, 1985)

Middleton, D., *The Sky Suspended* (London: Secker & Warburg, 1960)

Mombeek, E., with Wadman, D., & Creek, E. J., *Jagdwaffe Volume Two, Section One, Battle of Britain Phase One* (Crowborough: Classic Publications Limited, 2001)

Mombeek, E., with Wadman, D., & Pegg, M., *Jagdwaffe Volume Two, Section Two, Battle of Britain Phase Two* (Crowborough: Classic Publications Limited, 2001)

Mombeek, E., with Wadman, D., & Pegg, M., *Jagdwaffe Volume Two, Section Four, Battle of Britain Phase Four* (Crowborough: Classic Publications Limited, 2002)

Neil, T., *Scramble!* (Stroud: Amberley Publishing, 2015)

Ogley, B., *Biggin On The Bump* (Westerham: Froglets Publications Limited, 1990)

Osborne, K, ed., *Hellfire Corner* (English Heritage, 2010)
Parry, S., *Battle of Britain Combat Archive, Volume One* (Walton-on-Thames: Red Kite, 2015)
Parry, S., *Battle of Britain Combat Archive, Volume Two* (Walton-on-Thames: Red Kite, 2016)
Parry, S., *Battle of Britain Combat Archive, Volume Three* (Walton-on-Thames: Red Kite, 2016)
Price, A., *Spitfire Mark I/II Aces 1939-41* (Oxford: Osprey Publishing, 1996)
Price, A., *The Hardest Day* (St Albans: Granada Publishing Limited, 1980)
Ramsay, W. G., Editor-in-Chief, *The Battle of Britain Then and Now* (Old Harlow: Battle of Britain International Ltd., 2006)
Robinson, A., *RAF Fighter Squadrons in The Battle of Britain* (London: Brockhampton Press, 1999)
Saunders, A., *Convoy Peewit* (London: Grub Street, 2010)
Sturtivant, R., *Fleet Air Arm Aircraft 1939 to 1945*, I.S.O., with Mick Burrow. (An Air-Britain Publication, Air Britain (Historians) Ltd, 1995)
Vasco, J. J., & Cornwell, P. D., *Zerstörer: The Messerschmitt 110 and its Units in 1940* (Norwich: J. A. C. Publications, 1995)
Wallace, G., *R. A. F. Biggin Hill* (London: Putnam, 1957)
Walton, D., *Northumberland Aviation Diary* (Seahouses: Norav Publications, 1999)
Warner, G., *The Bristol Blenheim: A Complete History*, 2nd Edition (Manchester: Crécy Publishing Limited, 2005)
Weal, J., *Bf 109D/E Aces 1939-41* (Oxford: Osprey Publishing, 2004)
Wood, D., with Dempster, D., *The Narrow Margin* (London: Tri-Service Press Ltd, 1990)
Wright, N., *The Bump* (Biggin Hill: RAF Biggin Hill, 1980)
Wynn, K. G., *Men of The Battle of Britain* (Barnsley: Frontline Books, an imprint of Pen & Sword Books Ltd, 2015)
Ziegler, F. H., *The Story of 609 Squadron: Under The White Rose* (Manchester: Crécy Books Ltd, 1993)

Unpublished memoir

Ellis, E. R., *The Rigger's Tale* (2009, thanks to 610 Squadron Association)

Articles/Journals/Magazines

Air-Britain Aeromilitaria, volume 32/issue 125/spring 2006
Air-Britain Aeromilitaria, volume 32/issue 126/summer 2006
Air-Britain Aeromilitaria, volume 32/issue 128/winter 2006
Air-Britain Aeromilitaria, volume 33/issue 129/spring 2007
Air-Britain Aeromilitaria, volume 33/issue 131/autumn 2007
Air-Britain Aeromilitaria, volume 33/issue 132/winter 2007
Air-Britain Aeromilitaria, volume 34/issue 133/spring 2008
Air-Britain Aeromilitaria, volume 34/issue 134/summer 2008
Air-Britain Aeromilitaria, volume 34/issue 135/autumn 2008
Everyone's War, No. 6 autumn/winter 2002
Flight, via https://www.flightglobal.com/pdfarchive/index.html accessed on 17/1/18
Flight, 27 February 1936, p. 228 to *Flight* on 18 April 1940
Louise Wilkinson, 'The Auxiliary Air Force—How typical were the two elite London squadrons in relation to the wider organisation?', *The School of Historical Studies Postgraduate Forum E-Journal Edition* 6, 2007/08, pp. 1-17
Swift, North-west Aviation Heritage Museum No. 3, summer 2000
Swift, North-west Aviation Heritage Museum No. 4, March 2001
'The Flight of the Few' by Geoffrey Simpson, *Cheshire Life*, September 1990, p. 132-133

The National Archives Files

TNA, AIR 27/2106/1-45: All 610 Squadron ORB information
TNA, AIR 50/172: All 610 Squadron combat reports information
TNA, AIR 81: All AMCB files
TNA, AIR 27/360/21-24: 32 Squadron ORB July and August 1940
TNA, AIR 27/511/22-25: 54 Squadron ORB July and August 1940
TNA, AIR 27/589/15-16: 64 Squadron ORB May 1940
TNA, AIR 27/589/19-20: 64 Squadron ORB July 1940
TNA, AIR 50/24: 64 Squadron combat reports
TNA, AIR 27/592/4-5: 65 Squadron ORB July and August 1940
TNA, AIR 27/624/20-24: 72 Squadron ORB August 1940

TNA, AIR 27/629/18-19: 73 Squadron ORB June and July 1940
TNA, AIR 27/664/17: 79 Squadron ORB May–November 1940
TNA, AIR 27/743/1-4: 92 Squadron ORB May and June 1940
TNA, AIR 27/1547/1: 263 Squadron ORB 1 October 1939–30 November 1940
TNA, AIR 27/2123/43-44: 615 Squadron ORB October 1941
TNA, AIR 25/197: ORB No. 11 Group Appendices, 1 September 1939–30 September 1940
TNA, AIR 25/224: ORB No. 12 Group Appendices, 1 September 1939–31 December 1941
TNA, AIR 25/219: ORB No. 12 Group, 1 April 1937–31 December 1941
TNA, AIR 25/232: ORB No. 13 (Fighter) Group, 1 July 1939–31 December 1940
TNA, AIR 25/241: ORB No. 13 (Fighter) Group Appendices, 1 August–31 December 1940
TNA, AIR 28/17: RAF Acklington ORB, 1 August 1939–31 December 1945
TNA, AIR 28/64: RAF Biggin Hill ORB, October 1932–December 1945
TNA, AIR 28/201: RAF Digby ORB, July 1937–July 1945
TNA, AIR 28/345: RAF Hawkinge ORB, 1 July 1935–30 November 1945
TNA, AIR 28/950: RAF Wittering ORB, 1938–1945

Newspapers

Birkenhead News and Wirral General Advertiser, 24 August to 12 October 1940, Mirrorpix/Wirral Archives Service
Cambridge Evening News, 1 May 1991
Cambridge Evening News (Special Supplement—Battle of Britain) 6 July 1990
Hoylake and West Kirby Advertiser, Friday, May 22, 1942, Mirrorpix/Wirral Archives Service
The Chronicle, 4 April 1936 to 7 September 1940, Mirrorpix/Cheshire Record Office
The Isle of Wight County Press Archive, via http://archive.iwcp.co.uk/ accessed 17/1/18
The Isle of Wight County Press, 31 August, p. 3 to 7 September 1940, p. 6
The London Gazette, via https://www.thegazette.co.uk/ accessed on 17/1/18
The London Gazette, issue 33858, 26 August 1932 to issue 35508, 31 March 1942.
The London Gazette, supplement 35284, 23 September 1941 to supplement 41183, 20 September 1957
The Times, 1 February 1941 to 2 August 2016

Websites

http://www.adf-serials.com.au/nz-serials/nzhind.htm accessed 17/1/18
http://www.airhistory.org.uk/spitfire/home.html accessed 17/1/18
http://archive.iwcp.co.uk/ accessed 17/1/18
http://www.bbc.co.uk/archive/battleofbritain/11431.shtml accessed 16/01/18
http://www.bbm.org.uk accessed 17/1/18
http://www.bexhillobserver.net/news/fighter-ace-remembered-ahead-of-battle-of-britain-wreath-laying-1-1402963 accessed 16/01/18
http://www.cieldegloire.com/jg_052.php#pertes1940 accessed 16/01/18
https://www.cwgc.org/ accessed 17/1/18
http://www.doverwarmemorialproject.org.uk/Information/DaybyDay/Mobile%20Exhibition/2010/70%20panel%203.pdf accessed 17/1/18
https://hansard.parliament.uk/ accessed 17/1/18
http://www.hemelatwar.org/MilehamDShort.html accessed 17/1/18
http://www.oldhaltonians.co.uk accessed 04/02/18
http://www.unithistories.com/officers/RAFVR_officers_A01.html accessed 17/1/18
http://www.610squadron.com/ accessed 16/01/18

Index

In cases, ranks are recorded as the person's final rank while serving with 610 Squadron up to the end of 1940. Page numbers in bold indicate a photograph on that particular page.

~ *Celebrity Influencers* ~

LEONARDO DICAPRIO

MARY HERTZ SCARBROUGH

Rourke Educational Media
A Division of Carson Dellosa Education
rourkeeducationalmedia.com

ROURKE'S
SCHOOL to HOME
CONNECTIONS

BEFORE AND DURING READING ACTIVITIES

Before Reading: *Building Background Knowledge and Vocabulary*

Building background knowledge can help children process new information and build upon what they already know. Before reading a book, it is important to tap into what children already know about the topic. This will help them develop their vocabulary and increase their reading comprehension.

Think about it...

1. Why do people enjoy paying attention to celebrities?
2. What is this celebrity famous for?
3. What are some of the qualities about celebrities that make them stand out?
4. What are the similarities and differences between a celebrity and a hero/heroine?
5. How does a person's professional career connect them to personal experiences?
6. How does what we know about the world shape the way we view ourselves?
7. How do our personal experiences shape our view of others?
8. How does the media shape our view of the world and ourselves?

Vocabulary: *Vocabulary Is Key to Reading Comprehension*

Use the following directions to prompt a conversation about each word.

- Read the vocabulary words.
- What comes to mind when you see each word?
- What do you think each word means?

Vocabulary Words:

- *activists*
- *conservation*
- *documentary*
- *endangered*
- *grants*
- *indigenous*

During Reading: *Reading for Meaning and Understanding*

To achieve deep comprehension of a book, children are encouraged to use close reading strategies. During reading, it is important to have children stop and make connections. These connections result in deeper analysis and understanding of a book.

Close Reading a Text

During reading, have children stop and talk about the following:

- Any confusing parts
- Any unknown words
- Text to text, text to self, text to world connections
- The main idea in each chapter or heading

Encourage children to use context clues to determine the meaning of any unknown words. These strategies will help children learn to analyze the text more thoroughly as they read.

When you are finished reading this book, turn to the next-to-last page for **After Reading Questions** and an **Activity**.